Contemporary Psychology
and
Effective Behavior

James C. Coleman
Constance L. Hammen

The University
of California
at Los Angeles

Logan J. Fox
Consulting Author

El Camino College

Scott, Foresman
and Company

Glenview, Illinois
Brighton, England

Library of Congress Catalog Card Number: 73-90898
ISBN: 0-673-07892-2

Preface

It seems only a short time since the second edition of this book was published. But during this period the world has undergone major crises and changes. We have seen wars, famines, and many other tragic events; we have seen the problem of pollution and the energy crisis reach staggering proportions; and we have seen the consequences of "future shock" and the other costs exacted by the ever accelerating rate of technological and social change.

At the same time we have seen marked advances in science, including the field of psychology. While we still have much to learn about the complexities of human nature and behavior, we have seen great improvements in our understanding of personality development and adjustment; we have seen important steps toward the better understanding of group behavior and its impact on the individual; we have seen an increasing tendency to expand the focus of scientific endeavor to include the study of our existential problems—such as courage, faith, love, hope, and despair; and we have seen an increasing capacity for—as well as concern with—building a "good future world" for humanity.

In this new edition, we have attempted to incorporate these new findings and trends, to indicate where they may be leading us, and to show their implications for the achievement of more effective personal behavior and a more fulfilling life.

Toward this end, *Contemporary Psychology and Effective Behavior* has been organized into four parts. Part One deals with the basic nature of human beings, with the problems that confront us today, and with our quest for answers. Part Two deals with the personal context of behavior, including the forces that shape us, the significance of self, our basic needs and strivings, and the problems we face in living and how we go about trying to solve them. Part Three deals with the social context of behavior, with the nature and importance of our interpersonal relationships, with changing premarital and marital patterns, with the world of work, including the special problems faced by women in the work force, and with the mutual interaction between the individual and the group and its impact on both. And Part Four attempts to extend the applications of the preceding sections to the achievement of more effective behavior and personal growth in our changing world. Finally, in completing this book, we have added a new section—*Explorations in Human Experiencing*—dealing with a few of the recent and controversial ideas about "nonordinary reality."

The authors are indebted to the many scientists and writers whose work has been drawn upon in preparing this text. Our theoretical position, while eclectic, has been strongly influenced by such outstanding psychologists and scientists as Gordon Allport, Albert Bandura, Sigmund Freud, Harold Kelley, R. D. Laing, Eleanor Maccoby, A. H. Maslow, Carl Rogers, and B. F. Skinner, to mention only a few. We are grateful for the generous permission given by many authors, as well as publishers, to reprint brief selections from their writings. We are also deeply indebted to the many students and other individuals who have shared their personal life experiences with us in the interviews which are quoted throughout the text. We hope that their words will give added life to the ideas and concepts that are more formally stated in the text itself.

On a more personal level the authors are indebted to Jenny Terrell for conducting the experiential interviews, to Fay Levinson for valuable suggestions, to John Harris of Ventura College for comments and critical evaluations, and to Dr. Logan Fox of El Camino College for the many creative ideas he contributed. We would also like to express our appreciation to the senior members of the Psychology Department at UCLA, whose cooperation helped to make this project possible, and to Louise Howe, Marguerite Clark, Joanne Tinsley, Keith Gillin, Anne Gwash, and Bronwyn Moore of Scott, Foresman for their dedicated and capable assistance. The senior author, in particular, would like to express his sincere gratitude to his wife Azalea for her insightful and constructive suggestions—and for her patience, understanding, and encouragement over the long weeks and months of sustained pressure required to bring this new edition to its present form.

At the close of his journeys, Tennyson's Ulysses says, "I am a part of all that I have met." It is the profound hope of the authors that the students who read this book will feel a part of the people and ideas they have met and that what they learn will be a meaningful and useful part of their life experience.

James Coleman
Constance Hammen

The Individual in Today's World

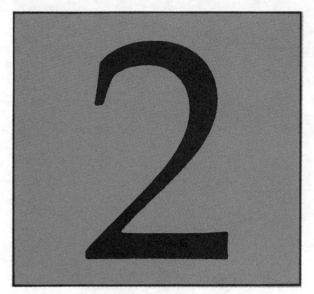

2

The Personal Context of Behavior

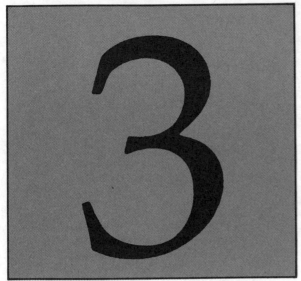

The Social Context of Behavior

4

Toward Effective Behavior and Personal Growth

"I am a human being, whatever that may be. I speak for all of us who move and think and feel and whom time consumes. I speak as an individual unique in a universe beyond my understanding, and I speak for man. I am hemmed in by limitations of sense and mind and body, of place and time and circumstances, some of which I know but most of which I do not. I am like a man journeying through a forest, aware of occasional glints of light overhead with recollections of the long trail I have already traveled, and conscious of wider spaces ahead. I want to see more clearly where I have been and where I am going, and above all I want to know why I am where I am and why I am traveling at all."

John Berrill
Man's Emerging Mind

The Individual in Today's World

1

The Human Dilemma

2

The Quest for Answers

The Human Dilemma

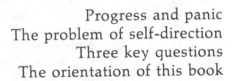

Progress and panic
The problem of self-direction
Three key questions
The orientation of this book

The tremendous and accelerating advances of modern science and technology have led to unprecedented progress and unprecedented problems. On the one hand, we can point to an increasing mastery of the secrets of nature, to an economy of abundance, to the conquest of disease, and to spectacular cultural advances; on the other, we see the dangers of a divided world, of thermonuclear warfare, of a population explosion, of ecological violations, and of grinding poverty side-by-side with affluence. These problems press for solution if the human race is to survive and advance. And the solution appears to depend less upon increased technological know-how and more upon a better understanding of ourselves and our social systems.

Progress and panic

We are living in an affluent society. The average person in the United States today is better fed, housed, clothed, and medicated than anyone else in all history. We are served by myriad slaves—powered by electricity instead of human labor—which remove much of the drudgery from everyday living and give us more time for creative pursuits. We can enjoy the finest literature, music, and art; we can experience the stimulating rewards of travel; we can participate in sports and other leisure-time activities that formerly were available only to the very rich. Through motion pictures and television, we are entertained by spectacles that would have taxed the imagination of ancient kings. Modern achievements in medicine have made us the healthiest people of all time and have greatly increased our life expectancy. We have almost unlimited opportunities for educational and creative pursuits and freedom for self-development. We live in an exciting age of scientific wonders that have seen men landing on the moon and have placed us on the threshold of still greater space conquests. In fact, men and women never before possessed such opportunity for self-determination and for enjoying life to its fullest. It might seem indeed that we have entered upon a Golden Age.

Yet it is apparent that all is not going exactly as we might hope and expect. Paradoxically, the same scientific and technological advances that have made this a Golden Age pose many problems and threats which also make it an Age of Anxiety. We have squandered the earth's resources, polluted our air and water, and made parts of our planet uninhabitable. A seething nationalism embraces half the earth; new weapons for mastery and destruction are being placed in uncertain hands; a population explosion is outstripping the world's food and other resources; there are almost universal problems of illiteracy, poverty, and disease; and there is an inevitable awareness of the "have-nots" that their lives could be improved by social change. The impact of our scientific age upon our hopes and fears for the future has been well described by the psychologist Hadley Cantril.

"As more and more people throughout the world become more and more enmeshed in a scientific age, its psychological consequences on their thought and behavior become increasingly complicated. The impact comes in a variety of ways: people begin to feel the potentialities for a more abundant life that modern technology can provide; they become aware of the inadequacies of many present political, social, and religious institutions and practices; they discern the threat which existing power and status relationships may hold to their own development; they vaguely sense the inadequacy of many of the beliefs and codes accepted by their forefathers and perhaps by themselves at an earlier age.

"The upshot is that more and more people are acquiring both a hope for a 'better life' and a feeling of frustration and anxiety that they themselves may not experience the potentially better life they feel should be available to them. They search for new anchorages, for new guidelines, for plans of action which hold a promise of making some of the dreams come true, some of their aspirations become experientially real" (1958, pp. vii–viii).

Written well over a decade ago, this statement seems equally applicable today.

Wherever we look, we see the world changing with incredible rapidity—and established customs, traditions, and values changing with it. Few are the places in the world today where the children follow, as a matter of course, the patterns of their parents. Communication problems stemming from a "generation gap" have become a matter of real concern. Indeed, one of the major problems today is the continuing adjustment individuals and social organizations must make to rapid social change. To complicate matters further, advances in communication and transportation have reduced the "size" of the world. Whether we like it or not, we have become members of an interdependent society of the world. This means learning to understand and deal with over three billion people, most of whom have different languages, different beliefs, and different-colored skins from ours. In this world context, two major ideologies—democracy and communism—are fighting a "cold war" for our minds and the shaping of our world. And there is always the possibility that this cold war may erupt into global conflict—into chemical, biological, and thermonuclear warfare that would doom modern civilization and perhaps the human race. Thus global unrest, conflict, and change form the background against

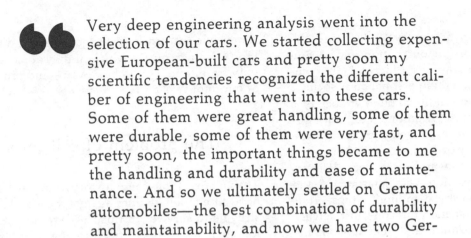

Very deep engineering analysis went into the selection of our cars. We started collecting expensive European-built cars and pretty soon my scientific tendencies recognized the different caliber of engineering that went into these cars. Some of them were great handling, some of them were durable, some of them were very fast, and pretty soon, the important things became to me the handling and durability and ease of maintenance. And so we ultimately settled on German automobiles—the best combination of durability and maintainability, and now we have two German cars.

I get $50 a week welfare and $27.50 for doing training. We're happy now because we got enough to eat. Only thing is I spend three hours every day on the bus going to training and back. What I wish is I had a car to go to training—that would help a lot—I could be home more taking care of my family. I sure could use a car.

This place reflects us—if you have disposable income, then your home, your car, whatever else you do—your hobbies—will tend to reflect your inner psyche. I've always held that money determines taste. If you have it you will develop taste.

There's seven of us sleeps over the restaurant, we got an apartment with one bedroom, we got a hot plate in the room, and a couch. We take turns with the bed. We got a toilet, but nothing else. The boys can get a shower at the Y. John leaves for school at 8:00 in the morning and gets home about midnight, sometimes for meals and goes out again during the day—he's ambitious—he delivers papers and shines shoes and hustles what he can. He sleeps on the kitchen table. He's 15.

which we function as we try to deal with the problems that confront our nation and to find our own personal way in an increasingly complex, bureaucratic, and impersonal mass society.

The strain of modern life in our own society is revealed in the incredible amounts of tranquilizing drugs, the tons of sleeping pills, and the billions of dollars worth of alcoholic beverages which Americans consume each year. It is revealed in preoccupation with marihuana and other "consciousness-expanding" drugs. It is reflected in the vast literature on "lost selves" and the dehumanization and alienation of the individual. It is revealed in the large number of young people today who lack involvement in and commitment to established social goals and standards and "drop out" of the mainstream of society. In an equally dramatic way, it is revealed in the sharp increase in suicide among our youth, in the epidemic of senseless crimes of violence, and in the high incidence of personality maladjustment and mental disorder. This is indeed an Age of Anxiety as well as a Golden Age.

In pointing to the problems of our "Golden Age of Anxiety" we are not advocating a return to the "good old days." We have come far toward realizing the dream of a great and creative society, and few would care to exchange the benefits of modern civilization for the allegedly greater stability of an earlier age. In any case, we have set out upon a path of change and there is no road back. We recognize both the necessity and the utility of change. Our hope lies not in reversing change or in trying to hold the line but in guiding change and developing new values and modes of adaptation which are appropriate to the problems and challenges of our contemporary world. In this process we must constantly guard against the danger of discarding the essential for that which is new but trivial or unsound. For change in and of itself is no guarantee of progress. As Haskins (1968) has pointed out, we must be continually aware of the danger that "in embracing new and experimental courses on myriad fronts of movement with the ardor that we must, we do not at the

same time discard long-tested values and long-tried adaptive courses which, if they are lost, will only have, one day, to be rewon—and probably at enormous cost."

The problem of self-direction

Throughout their long history, human beings have pitted their abilities against the world in the struggle to survive. In this they are not unique, for all living things strive to maintain themselves, to resist destruction, and to grow and function in accordance with their inner natures. The process by which an organism attempts to meet the demands placed upon it by its own nature and by its environment is called *adjustment*. Living things never cease to adjust. Adjustive behavior may be more or less *successful*, in terms of how well it meets external demands and satisfies the needs of the organism, but it goes on continuously. It is as basic to life as breathing—itself a form of adjustive functioning.

In the universal struggle for survival, many different adjustive patterns have emerged in the animal world. Some species manage to survive by sheer number of offspring; others rely heavily upon defensive armaments such as poisons, camouflage, or speed. Though widely different, these various patterns have one thing in common: they rely largely upon "built-in" adjustive know-how. While most animals are capable of some learning, their behavior is determined primarily by adjustive patterns that are instinctive. We might say that they come factory-equipped with adjustive know-how. As Branden has put it:

"Given the appropriate conditions, the appropriate physical environment, all living organisms—with one exception—are set by their nature to originate automatically the actions required to sustain their survival. The exception is man" (1965, p. 2).

With human beings, nature has tried out a dramatically different solution to the problem of survival. Endowed with superior mental capacities, we have few, if any, instinctive behavior patterns beyond the level of the simplest reflex. We must rely instead on our ability to learn and reason in working out the most satisfactory mode of adjustment, continually modifying our behavior to meet the demands of new situations. These superior mental gifts—and the superior adaptability that goes with them—have given us unchallenged mastery of the animal kingdom, have helped us to go far toward mastering our physical environment, and hopefully have taught us the necessity of conserving our earth's limited resources and maintaining its ecological balance.

The information problem

These unique gifts have also created unique problems, for they bring with them the responsibility of acquiring vast amounts of information about ourselves and our environment. Each person must learn about his needs, his potentials, his rational and irrational tendencies, and the many other facets of his complex nature so as to fill in a realistic self-picture. And here is where many of our basic troubles have arisen. As the Overstreets have put it:

"We have been as confused about ourselves, often—as uncertain about what our human nature is and what it requires of us—as an acorn would be if it were not sure whether its proper destiny was to be an oak or a cabbage . . ." (1956, pp. 240–241).

But if we are to direct our behavior in appropriate ways, we must clear up this confusion and gain an accurate view of the kind of creatures we truly are.

We must also learn about the world in which we live—not only the inanimate world, but the world of plants and animals and other human beings. We must learn about its potentials for meeting our needs, its pitfalls and dangers, the competencies we will need for coping, and the best means of acquiring these competencies. And as socialized human beings, we will need comparable information about the groups to which we belong and how we can contribute to their well-being and progress.

Our views of ourselves and the world, whether accurate or inaccurate, are primary determinants of our behavior. For the goals we strive for and the means we select for trying to achieve them are largely determined by what we conceive ourselves to be, by what we conceive ourselves able to become, and by the way we picture the opportunities and limitations of the world around us. Thus the problem of self-direction places a heavy demand upon us to acquire accurate information about ourselves and our world as a basis for effective coping behavior. And as scientific, technological, and cultural progress continues, acquiring the know-how for living becomes an increasingly difficult and time-consuming task.

The value problem

Coping with personal and social problems and achieving a good future for humanity is not simply a matter of acquiring information. We must also solve the problem of "know-why"— we must find a comprehensive value system to guide our choices and adjustive behavior. From among the many goals and ways of living available to us, we must identify and *choose* those we think will best meet our needs and assure our greatest well-being and progress. Thus we are engaged in a continual process of evaluating the "good" and the "bad"—in essence, of saying "This is desirable"; "That is undesirable"; "This is more desirable than that." While information is concerned with what *is* or what *could be,* values are concerned with what *ought* to be.

The problem of values inevitably involves a consideration of *meaning*—of what human existence is all about. This concern with meaning, so basic to thought and action, is unique to our species. Other animals are not concerned with their "proper" roles or with the meaning of their existence. Nor are they concerned with—or probably even aware of—their finite existence here on earth, an awareness which adds a crucial note of urgency to the human situation. As the psychoanalyst Erich Fromm (1955, pp. 23–24) has pointed out: "Man is the only animal who finds his own existence a problem which he has to solve and from which he cannot escape." Thus for the first time in the history of the animal kingdom, psychological problems centering around values and meaning enter into and complicate the adjustive process.

Eloquent testimony to the need for know-why

Yet alternative values are not always easy to find or to agree upon—particularly with the bewildering choice available among the many conflicting and changing values of our contemporary world.

Surprisingly, it is only recently that we have come to realize that our social structures are of our own making and therefore subject to change. As McCall and Simmons have pointed out: "Most people, throughout most of history, have reflected the cultures they grew up in in the important sense that they have taken the cul-

and to the difficulty of finding it in modern society is evidenced in the widely noted sense of alienation and disillusionment—especially among young people—and the often feverish search for "authenticity" and "commitment." Many are questioning the wisdom of a world that can split the atom but cannot unite humanity, or that can put men into space but cannot ensure peace on earth. Often they are repulsed by what they perceive as the superficiality, hypocrisy, materialism, and overconcern with images in the adult world or "establishment."

turally defined patterns and meanings of life for granted, even though they may have balked and quibbled about specifics" (1966, p. 254). However, the systematic study of different cultures, carried out mainly in the last hundred years, has made us aware of how many different answers human beings have worked out to the problems of existence. Today we are much more critically evaluative of our existing value patterns and social structures and also much more aware of possibilities for planned change.

The question of value judgments is crucial to

our well-being, for if we choose values which are not consonant with either the needs of our own nature or the realities of the world, they will work toward our destruction. Although we are free to act against the requirements of our nature, we are not free to escape the consequences—anxiety, misery, and destruction.

Three key questions

We have spoken of the problem of self-direction—of our need to solve the uniquely human problems of acquiring both "know-how" and "know-why." For the individual, this means trying to find the answers to three key questions: *Who am I? Where am I going? Why?* These questions deal with one's self-concept, one's life plans, and one's value patterns—in essence with the self-knowledge, goals and competencies, and value judgments involved in self-direction.

The meaningfulness of these questions varies, of course, depending upon the person's opportunities. In many parts of the world the individual's freedom for self-direction is severely curtailed by the sheer struggle for physical survival or by authoritarian forms of social organization which answer these questions for him. Even in the United States, personal limitations or stressful socioeconomic circumstances may shift the emphasis from these questions to simply "How can I cope?" Nevertheless, most young people today have a life situation which provides unprecedented opportunities for shaping their own lives.

Who am I?

By delineating the characteristics common to all men and women, we can understand much about ourselves, for we are all members of the human species. We can fill in more details by studying the patterns and values of the culture and family setting in which we have grown up. But each individual is unique and therefore has the problem of getting to know and understand *himself* or *herself.*

It is an interesting facet of our educational system that we study almost everything else before getting around to studying ourselves. Yet we must live with ourselves and work with our resources to make our lives productive and satisfying. By understanding our physical functioning, we can avoid needless damage to our bodies and ensure greater energy and vigor. On a psychological level, there are equally good reasons for adequate self-knowledge. Failure to understand the irrational forces in our make-up may play havoc with our lives, as when we blame others for our mistakes at the high price of being unable to analyze and profit from them. An inaccurate picture of our own capabilities may lead to unrealistic goals and hurtful failures. A blurred sense of self-identity may make it difficult for us to plan courses of action and make decisions that are right for us. Or we may simply be bewildered by some of the apparently irrational things we do. The latter point is made humorously by Rebecca McCann in a little poem called "Inconsistency":

"I'm sure I have a noble mind
And honesty and tact
And no one's more surprised than I
To see the way I act!"

The need for a clear-cut and realistic sense of "who we are" has become particularly crucial in modern society, where individuals often feel themselves to be puppets in the hands of a vast impersonal bureaucracy and may lose faith in their own identity or in their ability to find a place for themselves.

Where am I going?

As we acquire knowledge about ourselves and our world, we are in a better position to delineate our goals and our hopes for implementing them. For the question "Where am I going?" centers around our *life plans*—our goals, the means for achieving them, and the hazards we are likely to encounter along the way. Goals focus our energy and effort, help to determine

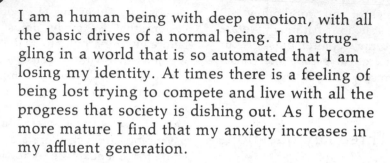

Who Am I?

I am a human being with deep emotion, with all the basic drives of a normal being. I am struggling in a world that is so automated that I am losing my identity. At times there is a feeling of being lost trying to compete and live with all the progress that society is dishing out. As I become more mature I find that my anxiety increases in my affluent generation.

I see myself as just another tiny fragment of that great pulsating body of mankind. I am only here a brief second in eternity's time, so I hope that in some small way I can make this world or its people better by my existence, through love, understanding, or sharing of our common lot.

Where Am I Going?

I am going somewhere because I want to achieve happiness. Also, my parents have ground into me ever since I was a child it was necessary to succeed in the world.

My greatest fear is not having the time in my life span to accomplish the plans I have mapped out—one of which is greater knowledge.

Why?

I'm striving towards my goals because I feel that it's important to achieve, to never allow myself to become stagnant. I must keep moving because I'm a very motivated person. My goals are to be of service and to help others in this life—I feel that other people need me as I need others.

what competencies we need to develop, and provide a basis for deciding between alternative courses of action.

The choice of long-range goals is particularly important to the individual since they dictate the subgoals that are appropriate as well as the means for achieving them. It is the long-range goals that give coherence and continuity to one's life. Some goals, of course, are more appropriate than others in relation to the individual's personal resources and opportunities, and some goals are superior to others in the satisfactions which they afford. The pursuit of unrealistically high goals leads to failure and frustration; the pursuit of goals that are too low leads to wasted opportunities and lost satisfactions; the pursuit

of "false" goals leads to disillusionment and discouragement.

Inability to formulate meaningful life plans also leads to serious difficulties. Here one is reminded of the poignant lines of Biff in Arthur Miller's *Death of a Salesman:* "I just can't take hold, Mom. I can't take hold of some kind of a life." Many individuals appear to drift through life with little or no sense of direction and usually experience a sense of dissatisfaction, aimlessness, and being "lost."

Although the specific skills required will vary with the circumstances, certain general competencies appear basic for reaching one's goals.

1. *Physical competencies:* the practice of good physical hygiene measures and the use of

medical resources to keep one's body functioning efficiently.

2. *Intellectual competencies:* the acquisition of essential information about oneself and one's world and the achievement of efficiency in learning, problem solving, and decision making.

3. *Emotional competencies:* the ability to love and be loved and to deal with fears, anxieties, anger, and other problem emotions that we all experience.

4. *Social competencies:* the ability to deal effectively with other people and to build satisfying interpersonal relationships.

Failure to develop these competencies can prevent us from "getting where we want to go," even when our goals are potentially within our reach. Despite our superior power to reason, many of us are crippled by emotional prejudices and lack of training in problem solving and decision making. Often we fail to achieve satisfying relationships with those close to us. Many marriages, for example, drag along or break up for want of the know-how that might have made them rich and happy experiences.

Besides such general competencies, we also need to equip ourselves to meet specific hazards and responsibilities that we can anticipate along the way. Although we cannot foresee all the problems we will have to face during our lifetime, there are certain adjustments—such as obtaining an education, preparing for rewarding life work, building a fulfilling marriage, bringing up children, finding a personalized philosophy of life, and growing old gracefully—which most of us will want to make. We can increase the probability of success if we know what difficulties may be involved and what information and competencies we will need in dealing with them. Such knowledge also helps us avoid inappropriate means which might defeat our plans.

Why?

"Why this life plan rather than another?" What kind of life is good or bad for human beings in general and for me as an individual? What makes this goal good and that one bad? From among whatever alternatives we see open to us, we all make choices in terms of what we see as most desirable and most likely to be satisfying to us. As Cantril (1950, p. 37) has put it, values "are the compass which give[s] man his direction both as to how he should act and what his action is for." Whether or not we have thought through our values or are even clearly aware of them, our life plans reflect our value patterns. Even if we forfeit the chance to plan for ourselves and "take life as it comes," we are making a choice and in this sense living out a value decision.

Since self-direction requires decision making and action, it is important that each of us develop an adequate system of values for guiding our behavior. The degree of trust we have in our values will determine how much we actually rely upon them in making choices; how free we are from inner conflicts; how successfully we can withstand frustration and setbacks; how much effort we will put forth in working toward our goals and living up to our commitments; and how well we find purpose in living. Lacking adequate values, we are likely to be confused and unable to find purpose and meaning in life; or we may pursue goals based on false values whose achievement is frustrating rather than satisfying and fulfilling.

Finding adequate values is not an easy task. We live in a rapidly changing world in which many old values are giving way to new ones and in which value conflicts seem to be the order of the day. And the values that prove satisfying and fulfilling to one person may not appeal to another. Nevertheless, science, religion, and the experience of the human race all offer evidence that certain values are likely to prove more realistic and fulfilling than others.

But whether or not we find adequate answers, all of us are searching—sometimes desperately—for information and values that will provide purpose and meaning in our lives. We do not easily accept the doctrine of despair so dramatically portrayed in the lines of Shakespeare that life "is a tale / Told by an idiot, full of sound and fury, / Signifying nothing."

The orientation of this book

It is apparent that psychology and allied sciences have helped us to understand many facets of human nature and human behavior, but the answers they can give to the crucial questions "Who?" "Where?" and "Why?" are far from complete. Yet we still have to deal with the myriad and increasing stresses of everyday life.

Thus it is not surprising that we see many bewildered, unhappy people around us who cannot seem to find meaningful and fulfilling lives in the face of problems that seem just too great. Although they may manage to "muddle through"—worrying along and solving their problems after a fashion—they are essentially "traveling in the dark." And tragically, they often fail to utilize the information that is available to them.

The high cost of "muddling through"

Most people would consider it sheer folly to attempt to climb a high mountain peak without studying the possible routes that might be taken, obtaining a clear understanding of the hazards to be faced, and procuring the necessary equipment. Yet many of these same people expect inadequate information, competencies, and values to carry them successfully through the journey of life—a far more difficult undertaking than the conquest of a mountain peak.

For many of us, living is a matter of muddling through. Instead of using the information and resources which modern science and human experience have put at our disposal, we go through life making many costly and needless mistakes and wasting much of our potential for self-fulfillment. Literally millions of people in our own society guide their lives by blind custom, superstition, and "common-sense" notions which science has proved to be false. They prepare for the wrong occupations, choose incompatible mates, and bring up children with the naive hope that good intentions will be sufficient. But behind the brave front of confidence they may present to the world are apt to lie deep-seated feelings of bewilderment, inadequacy, and unhappiness. The price of muddling through is ordinarily a high one. At best, it is likely to lead to a serious waste of opportunities and human resources. More commonly, it takes a high toll in unnecessary failures, missed satisfactions, and emotional wear and tear.

As the biologist Herrick has pointed out, the mistakes we make because of ignorance and immaturity have a way of catching up with us in the long run. Violation of the laws of human nature are inevitably punished.
"Transgression of these laws brings its own penalty. No prosecutor is required. If you drink whiskey to excess, your health is impaired. If you drink wood alcohol, you die. . . . The wages of sin is death, if not of the person, certainly of his richest values and satisfactions. And ignorance of the law excuses no man" (1956, p. 148).

It is a curious facet of our nature that one of the most frustrating of all experiences is awareness of lost satisfactions—of "what might have been."

A scientific and humanistic approach

Today the findings of modern science are reducing our "ignorance of the law." As people become increasingly aware of the fallibility of custom, superstition, and common sense in guiding their lives, they look increasingly to modern science—particularly to psychology—for dependable sources of information. While psychology cannot fully answer the questions of "Who?" "Where?" and "Why?" it can give us some answers and it can reduce the probability of our getting inaccurate answers.

Although still a young science, psychology has acquired a substantial body of information concerning human learning, problem solving, decision making, motivation, interpersonal relations, coping with stress, and many other aspects of behavior. Yet it has become apparent that we cannot expect science to give us all the answers; we must make the most effective use of the scientific information we do have while maintaining a clear awareness of its limitations.

In taking the view that a sound approach to human behavior should be based on scientific findings, we shall not assume that science is infallible, although it does have built-in corrective tendencies. Nor do we assume that science can solve all human problems. While science can supply the means for coping with the world population explosion, for example, the decision to use these means is a matter of values. Science can predict the outcome of using or not using birth control measures, but it cannot say which outcome is desirable and which undesirable. This is a value judgment which humanity must make for itself. So we will use scientific findings as far as we can but not expect the impossible of them. And while we will view science as a dependable source of information about human beings, we will remain free to utilize information from other sources as well.

For psychology and allied sciences have no monopoly on human behavior. In fact, there is little scientific information with respect to such vital experiences as hope, faith, concern, love, alienation, despair, and dying. Human beings alone, of all animals, can recount their experiences, describe their feelings, and compare them with one another. Often in literature, art, religion, philosophy, and autobiographical accounts we find poignant and authentic renditions of experiences meaningful to all of us. In fact, over the centuries we have accumulated a vast store of "nonscientific" information about the nature, behavior, mistakes, and grandeur of human beings. To ignore this information concerning our experiencing and existential problems would be to run the risk of dehumanizing ourselves; no description and explanation of human behavior would be complete that does not encompass the intimate experiences which characterize our existence.

So in subsequent pages we shall not hesitate to draw upon the humanities—literature, art, history, religion—and related fields for insights into human behavior. However, we shall distinguish such information from that obtained by scientific endeavor.

Belief in individual dignity and the potential for growth

The statement of the Ethical Standards of Psychologists, as formulated by the American Psychological Association, begins as follows:
"The psychologist believes in the dignity and worth of the individual human being. He is committed to increasing man's understanding of himself and others" (1963, p. 56).
Implicit in this statement is a belief in the growth potential of the individual and in his ability to direct his own life under favorable conditions. The individual human being is not seen as the helpless battleground on which heredity and environment vie for control of his behavior but as an active agent who can develop and use his abilities, his knowledge, and his environmental resources to build the kind of life he chooses.

It is not proposed, of course, that great personal growth and effectiveness can be achieved by simply reading a book. Nor does the presentation of research findings about ourselves and others ensure that we can or will utilize such findings in our own behavior. Despite medical research showing the harmful effects of smoking cigarettes, the incidence of their use in the United States has not been greatly affected. Modern psychology can provide dependable information about ourselves and our world, but the mastery and effective use of this knowledge is up to the individual. A key finding of modern psychology, however, is that most individuals, given the opportunity, do show good potential for continued intellectual, emotional, and social growth and for responsible self-direction—and hence for achieving more satisfying and fulfilling lives.

The purpose of the present book, then, is to show how the findings of contemporary psychology—in conjunction with other relevant sources of information—can help us to better understand ourselves and others, can open avenues for personal growth, and can develop our resources for effective living in today's complex and rapidly changing world.

This effort will lead us into an inquiry into the self and its significance in a world of flux, into the way we perceive ourselves and our world, into our basic needs and strivings, into the kinds of problems we face in living and how we go about trying to cope with them, and into the nature of interpersonal and individual-group relationships. Although our emphasis will be on general principles of human behavior which apply to all of us, we shall also focus on the uniqueness of each individual human being.

Summary and a look ahead

The accelerating advances of modern science and technology have led to unprecedented progress and problems. While we live in an affluent society with seemingly endless opportunities for self-determination and for enjoying life to its fullest, we are also beset by seemingly endless problems. In essence, we live in a time of progress and panic—in a "Golden Age of Anxiety."

Among the most serious of the problems which confront us is the uniquely human problem of self-direction. Unlike other animals, we have few instinctive behaviors to guide us and must rely on our ability to learn and reason in working out effective modes of adjustment and achieving meaningful and fulfilling lives. The problem of self-direction faces all of us with the tasks of achieving adequate information about ourselves and our world and working out a satisfactory value system for guiding our choices. Translated to a personal level, it confronts each of us with three key questions: "Who am I?" "Where am I going?" "Why?" Finding valid answers to these questions is of crucial importance if we are to avoid the high cost of "muddling through." In our quest for answers, we shall take a scientific and humanistic approach coupled with a firm belief in the dignity and growth potential of the individual.

Key terms and concepts:

the human dilemma (pp. 5–8)
rapid social change (6)
Age of Anxiety (6–8)
self-direction (8)
adjustment (8)
information problem (9)
value problem (9–10)
meaning (9)
alienation (10)
life plans (11)
"Who am I?" (11)
"Where am I going?" (11–14)
"Why?" (14)
physical, intellectual, emotional, social competencies (13–14)
high cost of "muddling through" (15)
scientific and humanistic approach (15–16)
growth potential of the individual (16)

2

The Quest for Answers

Conflicting views of human nature
Differing psychosocial models
A systems approach

If the crew of a spacecraft were to report finding intelligent beings on another planet, our first question would probably be "What sort of creatures are they?" Through the centuries members of the human race have asked the same question about themselves without finding a satisfactory answer.

One reason for the difficulty in getting a clear answer is that there are so many differences to be accounted for. Human beings come in many "shapes and sizes" and behave in many diverse ways. Of the more than three billion people who inhabit the earth, no two are exactly alike. The vast differences among them have made it hard to identify what they share in common as human beings. Contrast, for example, the embezzler, the civic-minded executive, the hermit, the parent who beats a child to death, the brutal dictator, the skid-row derelict, the armed robber, the rapist, the priest. It is difficult to see what "human nature" these fellow human beings have in common, and when we expand our horizons to include the people of other cultures, we find even greater differences—in values, goals, and ways of life.

Is there a hidden order beneath this diversity, comparable to the order that scientists have found in the rest of nature? Just what sort of creatures are we "down underneath"? This question is not an idle one, for on its answer hinges the type of life we should lead, the form of government best suited to us, and the kind of world we should try to construct for ourselves.

In the present chapter we will examine some of the conflicting historical views of human nature, survey the major psychosocial *models* of man, and try to get a new perspective on *human nature* by noting what we share in common with—and how we differ from—other living things.

Conflicting views of human nature

Long before modern science entered the arena, philosophers, theologians, and politicians had argued over the problem of "human nature." From a welter of conflicting views, three questions have kept recurring: whether human beings are basically *good or evil;* whether they are basically *rational or irrational;* and whether their behavior is the result of *determinism or free will.*

Good or evil

Some people have asserted that human beings are basically selfish and self-seeking. Others have denied it. Some have seen us as competi-

tive by nature, others as cooperative. Some have maintained that our "real" nature is hostile and cruel, others that it is friendly and kind. All these issues become involved in the larger one of whether human nature is basically good or evil.

Human nature as evil

The view that human beings are basically "sinful" has received substantial support from both religion and science—as well as from history and human experience. The Christian doctrine of original sin has taught that the entire human race was corrupted by the Fall and that its members are incapable of resisting temptation and living a good life without divine intervention. While contradicting the Biblical version of creation, Darwin's theory of evolution seemed to lend support to the view of humanity as selfish and cruel. In his monumental work *On the Origin of Species by Means of Natural Selection,* published in 1859, Darwin pictured the natural world as a battleground for a ruthless struggle for survival in which all species, human and nonhuman, participated. In this universal struggle, the fittest always win out at the expense of their weaker rivals. Actually Darwin himself viewed human beings as basically congenial, but the general impact of the theory of evolution was to strengthen belief in the essential selfishness, aggressiveness, and cruelty of the human race.

The theories and writings of Sigmund Freud, which have had such a pervasive impact on psychological thought, have also presented a negative view of human nature. In his *Civilization and Its Discontents,* Freud depicted the human race as essentially predatory:

". . . men are not gentle, friendly creatures wishing for love, who simply defend themselves if they are attacked, but . . . a powerful measure of desire for aggressiveness has to be reckoned as part of their instinctual endowment. The result is that their neighbor is to them not only a possible helper or sexual object, but also a temptation to them to gratify their aggressiveness . . . to seize his possessions, to humiliate him, to cause him pain, to torture and to kill him. . . .

". . . Anyone who calls to mind the atrocities of the early migrations, of the invasion of the Huns or by the so-called Mongols under Jenghiz Kahn and Tamurlane, of the sack of Jerusalem by the pious crusaders, even indeed the horrors of the last world-war, will have to bow his head humbly before the truth of this view of man" (1930, pp. 85–86).

Other social scientists as well as historians have also championed the view that humans are basically cruel and violent. In his *African Genesis,* Robert Ardrey (1961) concluded that "Man emerged and triumphed over his rival primates for this single reason—he was a killer." In fact, Ardrey has described humanity as nature's ulti-

mate version of the "armed predator." And from a historical perspective, Toynbee has emphasized the thin veneer that separates civilization from savagery: "There is a persistent vein of violence and cruelty in human nature" (1970, p. 3).

Indeed the chain of violence and cruelty evidenced by the human race reaches from the most ancient times to today's headlines, and it is not surprising that the view of human nature as basically evil has dominated much of Western thought.

Human nature as good

Despite humanity's deplorable record of pillage, rape, betrayal, torture, and destruction of our fellow human beings—often on a grandiose scale—there is another side to the picture.

Studies of different cultures have shown that there are many people in the world who as a group are friendly and kind. The Arapesh, a primitive tribe living in the mountains of New Guinea, were found by the anthropologist Margaret Mead (1939, p. xix) to be a peaceful people who thought that "all human beings . . . are naturally unaggressive, self-denying concerned with growing food to feed growing children." Even though life was difficult in the rocky terrain which they inhabited, the Arapesh were a gentle and cooperative people who seldom showed hostile aggressive behavior. Curi-

ously enough, a neighboring tribe, the Mungundumor, were highly aggressive, warlike, and cruel.

Maslow has described a similar lack of hostile aggressiveness among the Northern Blackfoot Indians. Among this group, which had a constant population of about 800, he found a record of only five fist fights in fifteen years and no other signs of overt aggression.

"These are not a weak people by any means. The Northern Blackfoot Indians are a prideful, understanding, self-evaluating group. They are simply apt to regard aggression as wrong or pitiful or crazy" (1954, p. 175).

Similarly, Winchester (1966) found violence to be extremely rare in Iceland; in fact, only three homicides had been committed in a fifty-year period. This contrasts with the FBI "crime clock" showing about one murder every 13 minutes in the United States.

Such contrasts have led many social scientists to the conclusion that human beings are highly educable creatures who are neither good nor bad by nature but have potential to develop in either direction. Whether we become selfish, cruel, and warlike or self-sacrificing, kindly, and peaceful will depend largely upon the sociocultural conditions in which we grow up. While we admittedly have the inherent capacity for selfish and cruel behavior, we clearly also have the capacity for love and goodness.

Going a step further, an increasing number of psychologists have come to view human nature as essentially good. They believe that our basic propensities are toward friendly, cooperative and loving behavior. Aggression and cruelty are

viewed as pathological behavior resulting from the distortion of our essential nature. Certainly we do tend to be both healthier and happier when we are loving and constructive in our behavior than when we are dominated by selfishness and hate. In fact, physiological processes accompanying unpleasant emotions—although potentially useful in coping with emergencies—disrupt the normal functioning of the body; and over time such negative emotions can actually lead to physical disorders.

The Judeo-Christian tradition, while emphasizing an individual's tendencies to "innate depravity" if left to his own resources, has also taught that human beings were created in the likeness of God; that there is a divine spark in each of us. Jesus said, "The kingdom of God is within you."

Belief in essential human goodness was particularly strong in the late 18th and early 19th centuries and was forcefully expressed in the writings of many Romantic poets and philosophers, who believed that if people were allowed to live "naturally" much of the evil in the world would disappear. For example, in *Émile,* a treatise on education published in 1762, the philosopher Jean Jacques Rousseau maintained that the aim of education should be self-expression rather than the suppression of natural tendencies—that the chief function of the school should be to provide the child with opportunities to develop his natural gifts, unhampered by the corrupting influence of society.

And some two decades ago, after reviewing the available evidence, the psychologist Gordon Allport concluded:

"Normal men everywhere reject, in principle and by preference, the path of war and destruction. They like to live in peace and friendship with their neighbors; they prefer to love and be loved rather than to hate and be hated. . . . While wars rage, yet our desire is for peace and while animosity prevails, the weight of mankind's approval is on the side of affiliation" (1954, p. xiv).

It is a curious reminder of history that the most "inhuman" aggressions and cruelties have been inflicted in the name of justice and moral righteousness. People do not normally follow leaders whose actions they perceive as being evil and destructive.

These diverse views of human nature as evil, neutral, or good have important social implications. All agree that human beings are highly educable creatures and that their development for good or evil can be markedly influenced or even controlled by cultural conditions. But here the agreement ends. If people are by nature selfish, predatory, and evil, society must shape them into social creatures by stringent discipline and social control. If, on the other hand, their tendencies are toward friendly, cooperative, and constructive behavior, then society can best achieve its purposes by encouraging spontaneity, naturalness, and self-direction. Techniques of restriction and control give way to techniques designed to encourage the fulfillment of inner potential.

Rational or irrational

The human race has not only been indicted for being selfish and cruel, it has also been characterized as irrational and irresponsible. In every age there have been those who scoffed at the much-touted gift of reason. Even our own Alexander Hamilton spoke with contempt of "the impudence of democracy, where the people seldom judge or determine right." The ordinary person, he insisted, is governed by emotion and is changeable and unpredictable.

Early faith in human rationality
But from earliest times reason has also had its champions. The ancient Greeks exalted reason as the highest human virtue. The Roman aristocrats emphasized human rationality and prided themselves on their pragmatic approach to social problems. Although belief in reason had its setbacks during medieval times, it emerged again as the basic fabric on which the democratic social organization of Western culture is based—the belief that given sufficient information and opportunity, human beings can direct their own affairs and those of their society with wisdom and responsibility.

Thomas Jefferson, an aristocrat by birth,

"In the history of American arms, the most revealing chapter as to the nature of the human animal does not come from any story of the battlefield but from the record of 23 white men and two Eskimos who, on August 26, 1881, set up in isolation a camp on the edge of Lady Franklin Bay to attempt a Farthest North record for the United States."

"The Expedition under command of First Lt. A. W. Greely, USA, expected to be picked up by a relief ship after 1 year, or 2 years at most. Its supply could be stretched to cover the maximum period. . . .

". . . June of the second year came and passed, and no relief ship arrived. In August, Greely decided on a retreat, intending to fall back on bases which were supposed to hold food stores. Thereafter disaster was piled upon disaster. . . . When the Greely Expedition was at last rescued at Cape Sabine on June 22, 1884 . . . seven men remained alive. Even in these, the spark of life was so feeble that their tent was down over them and they had resigned themselves to death. . . .

". . . That any survived was due to the personal force and example of Sgt. (later Brig. Gen.) David L. Brainard, who believed in discipline as did Greely, and supported his chief steadfastly, but also supplied the human warmth and helping hand which rallied other men, where Greely's strictures only made them want to fight back. Brainard was not physically the strongest man in the Expedition, nor necessarily the most self-sacrificing and courageous. But he had what counted most—mental and moral balance.

"Among the most fractious and self-centered of the individuals was the camp surgeon, highly trained and educated, and chosen because he seemed to have a way among men. Greely was several times at the point of having him shot; the surgeon's death by starvation saved Greely that necessity.

"Among the most decent, trustworthy, and helpful was Jens, the simple Eskimo, who died trying to carry out a rescue mission. He had never been to school a day in his life.

"There were soldiers in the party whom no threat of punishment, or sense of pity, could deter from taking advantage of their comrades, rifling stores, cheating on duty and even stealing arms in the hope of doing away with other survivors. . . .

"But in the greater number, the sense of pride and of honor was stronger even than the instinct for self-preservation. . . .

"Private Schneider, a youngster who loved dogs and played the violin, succumbed to starvation after penning one of the most revealing deathbed statements ever written: 'Although I stand accused of doing dishonest things here lately, I herewith, as a dying man, can say that the only dishonest thing I ever did was to eat my own sealskin boots and the part of my pants.'

"Private Fredericks, accused in the early and less-trying period of meanness and injustice to his comrades, became a rock of strength in the weeks when all of the others were in physical collapse or coma. . . .

"There is still an official report on file in the Department of the Army which describes Sergeant Rice as the 'bravest and noblest' of the Expedition. He is identified with most of its greatest heroisms. The man was apparently absolutely indomitable and incorruptible. He died from freezing on a last forlorn mission into the Arctic storm to retrieve a cache of seal meat for his friends. . . .

"Such briefly were the extremes and the middle ground in this body of human material . . ." (Department of Defense, 1950, pp. 99–102).

maintained that the average person could reason and judge rightly if given access to the facts: "Enlighten the people generally, and tyranny and oppressions of body and mind will vanish like spirits at the dawn of day." In his first inaugural address Abraham Lincoln expressed a similar faith when he asked: "Why should there not be patient confidence in the ultimate justice of the people? Is there any better or equal hope in the world?"

Deprecation of rationality in modern times
Our own age has seen this faith in innate human rationality questioned and deprecated. For despite our great scientific advances, there seems

Human nature is anything a group of people share, certain emotions and feelings. Love, hate; honesty, dishonesty; peace, war; working, loafing; all can be dubbed with the name 'human nature.' It seems funny that such opposite traits could all be common in everyone, but that's what makes us tick.

To me, human nature means just that. Being 'human,' with the ability to experience great joy, sensual pleasure, sorrow, etc. The *basic* things in life.

I feel that most people are selfish and self-centered, that they don't think of consequences, just their immediate satisfaction.

Human nature is basically good. I think people want to do generous, kind, good things, rather than bad.

I believe that the human being is basically good in nature, helpful, generous; but if he is deprived of his share by some unintentional circumstance, he may deprive others.

From my experience I would describe human nature as something that you come by naturally, like making mistakes or thinking of oneself first. You usually have to be taught not to use it wrongly.

Human nature is hard to understand.

to be no end to our difficulties in "reasoning together" and developing a more orderly, equitable and harmonious world. In addition, research in psychology and the social sciences has delineated many cultural, emotional, and motivational conditions that can distort our thinking and lead to irrational solutions to our problems.

Two of the major schools of psychological thought—psychoanalysis and behaviorism—have contributed to the downgrading of human rationality. In his *Psychopathology and Everyday Life* (1954), Freud emphasized the unconscious and irrational influences that are evident in much of our thinking and behavior. Reading of "repressed sex drives," of "unconscious hostility," and of "rationalization" and "projection," many come to the seemingly obvious conclusion that human behavior is inherently and inevitably self-deceptive and irrational.

Behaviorists, while denying the overwhelming influence of unconscious forces, have tended to undermine faith in human rationality by picturing us as passive, malleable creatures whose thinking is shaped by our environment. We may think rationally if we are trained to do so but the existence of any inherently rational force in our make-up is denied.

Unquestionably, too, rapid social change, with the uprooting of many cherished beliefs and values, has led both to confusion and to a questioning of our vaunted rationality. If men and women once believed so firmly in things which we now consider false, how much faith can we place in the rationality of newer ideas and convictions? Viewing the inequities, confusions, and conflicts which permeate our world, we can well wonder whether we have any basic propensity to be rational.

Continuing evidence of human rationality

Although faith in human rationality has been substantially weakened in recent times, it has by no means been destroyed. Many modern statesmen, philosophers, and scientists believe in natural tendencies toward common sense and reason.

Here it is of interest to note the conclusion Rogers has drawn from his extensive study of clients in psychotherapy:

"One of the most revolutionary concepts to grow out of our clinical experience is the growing recognition that the innermost core of man's nature, the deepest layers of his personality, the base of his 'animal nature,' is positive in nature—is basically socialized, forward moving, rational and realistic" (1961, pp. 90–91).

One might wonder whether rationality is not a logistic built into all animals and essential for their survival. In any event, rationality is built into computers that simulate organisms.

Of course, our tendencies toward rationality can readily be distorted by environmental influences. We can be misled by false information, all but stupefied by repetitive and blatant stimuli from mass communication media, restricted by cultural deprivation, handicapped by lack of training in learning and problem solving, and overwhelmed by the number and complexity of issues demanding our attention.

The achievements of modern science, nevertheless, indicate the human capacity and inclination for dealing with problems in rational ways. Our unremitting efforts to probe the secrets of the universe and to make sense of our world, to obtain accurate information and sound values for dealing with our problems, and to establish order in both our physical surroundings and our social relationships all seem to indicate not only a potentiality for rational behavior but a basic propensity for it.

Free or determined

In our everyday lives we operate on the assumption that we are free to make decisions and choose our course of action, at least within certain limits. We see ourselves as continually weighing alternatives and choosing among them. Yet many philosophers, theologians, and scientists have raised the question of whether this freedom of action is real or *illusory*—whether we are active and responsible agents with some measure of "free will" or puppets whose behavior is actually determined by forces beyond our control.

The assumption of determinism

Various kinds and degrees of determinism have been argued since ancient times. The great dramatic tragedies of Aeschylus and Sophocles, for example, are pervaded by the ancient Greek belief that men and women are, in the last analysis, the pawns of fate. There is an inevitability to their actions, an end from which they cannot escape. This fatalism is clearly illustrated in the well-known legend of Oedipus, who in trying to avoid fulfilling the oracle's prophecy that he would kill his father and marry his mother turned headlong into fate's trap and unwittingly did as prophesied. The Calvinist doctrine of predestination, which holds that at birth every individual has already been elected to salvation or condemned to damnation, is a later example of philosophic or religious determinism.

Another kind of determinism is the cornerstone of modern science. This is the assumption that the universe is an orderly place where all events occur in keeping with natural laws. Everything follows cause-and-effect relationships. In essence, the universe is a sort of giant machine which functions according to certain built-in principles. If we had complete information about the machine, we could understand and predict its functioning in every detail.

Applied to human behavior, the doctrine of determinism holds that human behavior is lawful—that cause must precede effect. Given a complete knowledge of the past experiences of an individual, we would be able to predict how he or she will—indeed must—act. As B. F. Skinner (1953) has so succinctly put it: "The hypothesis that man is not free is essential to the application of the scientific method to the study of human behavior." In his later writings Skinner (1971) has emphasized that he is not trying to take away our freedom, since we are not free anyway; our behavior is the result of environmentally conditioned responses.

For evidence, psychologists adhering to this "strict" determinism have pointed to the diverse customs and beliefs of people throughout the world, all shaped by cultural conditioning. They have emphasized the experimental finding that people's beliefs and values can be manipulated through punishment and reward, and that suggestion and imitation are important forces shaping a person's assumptions and behavior. Despite the "illusion" of freedom, the individual is regarded as completely at the mercy of past conditioning and present environmental conditions.

Carried to its logical extreme, strict determinism is essentially predeterminism—since all events are determined by what has happened before. "What will be will be," and we are only puppets who play our part as it is written with no chance of altering the script.

The assumption of freedom

In our own personal lives, probably none of us believes in a strict determinism. As Shibutani has expressed it:

"Each person believes that he is able to exercise some measure of control over his own destiny. He is capable of making decisions and of selecting among alternative lines of action. It is this widespread belief that provides the basis for the doctrine of 'free will' and for the concept of moral responsibility" (1964, p. 233).

Our whole way of life, with its freedom of discussion, ballot boxes, democratic institutions, and assumptions of personal responsibility, is based heavily on the assumption that we are capable of self-determination. And paradoxically enough, many of the most ardent advocates of strict determinism are among the most zealous fighters for freedom and democracy. In fact, Skinner himself has repeatedly emphasized the potential for a better world provided by modern science and technology—as if we had some freedom of choice in determining the future.

The apparently irreconcilable paradox of determinism vs. freedom has been well pointed up by Carl Rogers in relation to the therapeutic situation.

"In the therapeutic relationship some of the most compelling subjective experiences are those in which the client feels within himself the power

of naked choice. He is free—to become himself or to hide behind a facade; to move forward or to retrogress; to behave in ways which are destructive of self and others, or in ways which are enhancing; quite literally free to live or die, in both the physiological and psychological meaning of those terms. Yet as we enter this field of psychotherapy with objective research methods, we are, like any other scientist, committed to a complete determinism. From this point of view every thought, feeling, and action of the client is determined by what preceded it. There can be no such thing as freedom. The dilemma I am trying to describe is no different than that found in other fields—it is simply brought to sharper focus, and appears more insoluble" (1969, p. 294).

Although the paradox of freedom vs. determinism has by no means been resolved, many psychologists—including Rogers—have adopted a "soft" determinism that accepts the law of causation in human behavior but sees it as operating through the "self-determining" powers of the human mind. While acknowledging that human behavior is heavily influenced—and often dominated—by the individual's background of experience, scientists adhering to this viewpoint are impressed with our self-awareness, with our ability to reflect upon and to reinterpret and reorganize past experience, to be critical and evaluative of our own behavior, to formulate and weigh alternatives on the basis of both past satisfactions and probable outcomes. They are impressed by our ability to imagine new possibilities different from anything previously experienced and to make plans in the light of our dreams of the future. In short, they see us as capable of taking an active role in shaping our own destiny.

Here "freedom" is seen as an *emergent* quality in the evolutionary process which provides us with some degree of potential for planning and determining our own destiny rather than being entirely at the mercy of past learning and reinforcement. From this viewpoint, we should profit from living in a free society. In fact, an authoritarian society, which seeks to indoctrinate and rigidly prescribe the behavior of its members and hence to reduce them to autom-

atons, would be considered pathological. The fact that such efforts have never been wholly or lastingly successful seems to indicate a basic human tendency to be evaluative and active rather than simply passive and reactive.

What conclusions can we draw from our examination of these conflicting views of human nature? It seems evident that we are capable of both good and evil, of both rationality and irrationality, of being both active and reactive. These are not mutually exclusive types of behavior but poles on a continuum. Though we may operate closer to one pole at a given time, we retain the potentiality for both. None of us is always rational or irrational, selfish or altruistic, active or reactive. However, the patterns of a given society or the life style of a given individual may tend toward one extreme or the other.

In the section which follows, we shall attempt to broaden our perspective of human nature by reviewing some of the major psychosocial models of man used by psychologists and other students of human behavior.

Differing psychosocial models

A *model* is essentially an analogy which can help a scientist to see important relationships. For example, the use of the computer model of the human mind has made it commonplace in psychology to talk about input, information processing, output, and feedback. The use of any model follows a strategy of successive approximations—with each refinement making it a more adequate and accurate representation. In psychology, as in other sciences, models serve to keep investigators from being overwhelmed by masses of unwieldy factual information while at the same time avoiding the necessity of premature all-embracing theories.

Since facts owe no prior allegiance to any scientist, they can often be interpreted in several ways. This is especially true in a relatively new science such as psychology where data are far from complete. Thus we find considerable difference in the psychosocial models which have been formulated.

The psychoanalytic model

The psychoanalytic model is based on the pioneering work of Sigmund Freud which extended over a period of fifty years of observing and writing. The major principles of his model are based on the clinical study of patients undergoing psychoanalysis. This approach relies heavily on the method of free association in which the patient is asked to provide an unrestricted account of whatever comes to mind leaving nothing out.

The concepts formulated by Freud and elaborated by his followers have been deeply woven into the fabric of our thinking about human behavior. The psychoanalytic model is a complex one, but its outlines can be sketched as follows.

Id, ego, and superego

Fundamental to the psychoanalytic model is the concept that behavior results from the interaction of three key subsystems within the personality: the id, the ego, and the superego.

The *id* contains the innate, primitive, biological drives such as hunger, thirst, and aggression. These primitive drives are seen as being of two types: (1) constructive drives, primarily of a sexual nature, which provide the basic energy of life, or *libido*; and (2) destructive and aggressive urges, which are more obscure but tend toward self-destruction and death. In essence *life* instincts are opposed by *death* instincts. It may be pointed out that Freud used the term "sex" in a broad way to refer to practically anything of a pleasurable nature—from eating to bathing.

The id, according to Freud, operates in terms of the *pleasure principle* and is concerned only with immediate gratification. It is completely selfish and unconcerned with reality or moral considerations. Although the id can generate images and wishes related to need gratification (primary process), it cannot undertake direct action toward meeting its needs. Thus a second key subsystem—the *ego*—develops to mediate

between the demands of the id and the realities of the external world. Although the primary purpose of the ego is that of meeting id demands, it must do so in such a way as to ensure the individual's survival. This requires the use of reason and other intellectual resources (secondary process) in dealing with the realities of the external world as well as the exercise of control over id demands. Hence the ego is the central control or decider system of the personality and is said to operate in terms of the *reality principle.*

However, the id-ego relationship is merely one of expediency that does not make allowance for moral values. Hence Freud introduces a third key system—the *superego*—which is the outgrowth of learning the taboos and moral values of society. The superego is essentially what we refer to as *conscience* and is concerned with the good and the bad, the right and the wrong. With the development of the superego, we find an additional inner control coming into operation to cope with the uninhibited desires of the id. However, the superego, as well as the id, operates through the ego system. Thus the superego strives to compel the ego to inhibit desires which are considered immoral.

The interplay of these intrapsychic forces of id, ego, and superego is of crucial significance. Often the instinctual desires and demands of the id are in conflict with superego demands or with the demands of the external world. The adequate resolution of such conflicts by the ego is considered essential to personality adjustment. Neurotics are viewed as persons unable to resolve such inner conflicts.

Anxiety, defense mechanisms, and the unconscious

Freud distinguished three types of anxiety or "psychic pain." *Reality* anxiety stems from dangers or threats in the external world; *neurotic* anxiety arises when id impulses threaten to break through ego controls and cause behavior which will lead to punishment. *Moral* anxiety arises when the individual does something or even contemplates doing something that conflicts with his superego values and arouses feelings of guilt.

Anxiety is both a painful experience and a warning of impending danger and hence forces the individual to do something about the situation. Often the ego can cope with anxiety by rational measures; but when these do not suffice, the ego resorts to irrational protective measures—such as rationalization and repression —which are referred to as *ego-defense mechanisms.* These mechanisms will be discussed in Chapter 6.

Of key importance here is the concept of unconscious processes. Freud thought that the conscious represents a relatively small area of the mind; while the unconscious, like the submerged part of an iceberg, is much the larger portion. In the vast domain of the unconscious are the images, desires, and wishes that have been either forgotten or repressed because they arouse anxiety. The individual is unaware of many of these unconscious desires, but they actively seek expression and may be reflected in dreams and fantasies, when ego controls are temporarily lowered.

In a broad context, Freud viewed unconscious strivings—especially sexual and aggressive strivings—as reflecting an inherent conflict between the individual's instinctive animal strivings and the inhibitions and regulations imposed on the individual by society.

Essentially, then, the psychoanalytic model shows us an individual dominated by instinctual biological drives and by unconscious desires and motives. While there is the constructive libidinal side to human nature, there are also the darker forces pushing toward destruction and death. Though the ego tends toward rationality, intrapsychic conflict, defense mechanisms, and the unconscious all tend toward a high degree of irrationality. And though we are driven by inner desires and impulses, our behavior is essentially determined by social conditioning.

The behavioristic model

The general format of modern behaviorism stems from the early work of John Watson (1919). Watson insisted that if psychology were ever to become a science of behavior, it must limit itself to the study of events that could be observed objectively. Thus he rejected the introspective study of conscious states or processes as being essentially mentalistic and prescientific—because such observations were not open to verification by other investigators.

Starting with this basic assumption, Watson changed the focus of psychology from inner psychic processes to outer behavior which is objectively observable. Only through the objective observation of such behavior and the stimulus conditions which brought it about could psychologists learn to predict and control human behavior.

This viewpoint has been greatly expanded by B. F. Skinner (1953, 1971) and a host of later investigators. Largely as a result of its scientific flavor and its success in formulating and applying principles of learning, behaviorism has become a dominant theme in American psychology and has greatly influenced our thinking about human behavior.

Conditioning

Since most observable behavior is learned, behaviorists have addressed themselves primarily to the question of how learning comes about. In trying to answer this question, they have focused on conditions in the environment—stimulus conditions that could be related to the acquisition, modification, and weakening of behavior patterns.

In a now classic experiment, Watson and Rayner (1920) used a conditioning technique to demonstrate the role of learning in maladaptive behavior. Using little Albert—an eleven-month-old boy who was fond of animals—as a subject, they showed how an irrational fear or phobia could be readily learned through conditioning. Their procedure was simple. The experimenter stood behind little Albert while the boy was playing with a white rat, and whenever Albert reached for the animal, the experimenter struck a steel bar with a hammer. The sudden loud noise elicited a fear response and made Albert cry. After several repetitions of this procedure, Albert became greatly disturbed at the sight of the rat even without the loud noise being made; and his fear generalized to include other furry animals and objects as well. This dramatic demonstration of the development and generalization of an irrational fear suggested that other types of maladaptive behavior might also be the result of learning.

The experiment of Watson and Rayner involves what is called *classical* or *respondent* conditioning in which a relatively simple emotional response—crying in response to a sudden loud noise—comes to be elicited by a wide range of other stimuli. Of key significance also is the concept of *operant* conditioning. The term "operant" is used because in such responses the individual "operates" upon or modifies the environment by learning to make a response that brings about the attainment of a goal or the satisfaction of a need. For example, grades are used in school to encourage students to study. In fact, most learning is probably operant in nature in that it helps us meet our needs.

Reinforcement
Crucial to both respondent and operant conditioning is reinforcement: the strengthening of a new response by its repeated association with a specific stimulus. In the experiment of Watson and Rayner, for example, successive repetitions of the loud noise with the white rat strengthened or reinforced the conditioned fear response to the rat. Operant learning is a little more complex. Here the response may be strengthened because it is repeatedly associated with a reward, or with avoiding some aversive condition such as punishment. The specific stimuli which represent the reward or punishment—which may be anything from money to an electric shock—are referred to as *reinforcers*.

In both respondent and operant conditioning, when reinforcement is later withheld, the conditioned response eventually becomes *extinguished.* An exception to this principle, however, is found in *avoidance learning* where the subject has been conditioned to anticipate an aversive stimulus and responds in such a way as to avoid it. For example, a child who has been bitten by a vicious dog may develop a condi-tioned avoidance response in which he persistently avoids all dogs. Such avoidance behavior may continue indefinitely, since the individual's anxiety is reduced by immediate avoidance behavior at the sight of a dog; thus he is denied the opportunity to learn that dogs can be friendly.

Presumably any response which the individual is capable of making can be produced, maintained, or eliminated by the appropriate scheduling of reinforcement or lack of it, if the environment can be completely controlled. Even avoidance behavior can be eliminated by reconditioning: associating the feared object with a positive reinforcer. For example, the child's avoidance response to dogs could be modified by the gradual introduction of a friendly dog in the presence of a positive stimulus such as food.

Interestingly enough, reinforcement need not be consistent or continuous. The effectiveness of intermittent, or partial, reinforcement in the maintenance of learning has been repeatedly shown.

Generalization and discrimination
To fill in our basic sketch of the behavioristic model of man, we need to add the concepts of *generalization* and *discrimination.* Generalization is the tendency for a response which has been conditioned to one stimulus to become associated with other similar stimuli. For example, we noted in the experiment of Watson and Rayner that the infant's fear generalized from white rats to other furry animals. The greater the similarity of stimuli, the greater the generalization. Discrimination occurs when the individual learns to distinguish between similar stimuli and respond to one but not another as a consequence of differential reinforcement. According to the behavioristic model, complex processes such as perceiving, forming concepts, solving problems, and making decisions are based on an elaboration of the basic discrimination operation.

The preceding concepts represent the core of the behavioristic model. By means of these relatively few concepts, behaviorism attempts to depict the acquisition, modification, and extinguishing of all types of behavior, whether adjustive or maladjustive. Its techniques have

The differences in viewpoints of the psychoanalytic and behavioristic models are vividly underscored in the following illustration:

In 1909 Freud reported the case of little Hans to exemplify the role of sexual urges in the development of phobic reactions (irrational fears). Hans was terrified that he might be bitten by a horse. According to Freud, the basis for this phobic reaction lay in the Oedipus complex. Little Hans felt both love and hatred for his father, who represented an obstacle in the expression of his sexual feelings toward his mother. He was also afraid that his father would punish him for having incestuous impulses—a fear experienced as castration anxiety. Freud believed that this conflict had been resolved by Hans' ego through repression of his ambivalent and incestuous desires and displacement of his fear to a symbolic representation—the fear of being bitten by a horse.

The phobia dated from the time of a bus ride that Hans had taken with his mother. Hans had become very frightened when the horse pulling the bus fell down and was hurt. Freud regarded this incident as the precipitating cause of the phobia, with Hans' unconscious intrapsychic conflict as the real basis of the disorder.

Behaviorists, however, using the same descriptive data, would explain Hans' phobia as a simple conditioned fear response. In that day of horses and buggies, Hans had likely been sensitized to horses by earlier unpleasant experiences involving seeing horses beaten, being hurt while playing "horses," and being warned to avoid horses because they might bite. Thus a fear response might partially have been conditioned already, and the incident on the bus might have been the final learning trial which established it. In any case, the phobic reaction, once established by classical conditioning, was maintained by operant conditioning, because each time Hans successfully avoided a horse his anxiety was reduced; thus his avoidance behavior was strengthened and reinforced (DeNike & Tiber, 1968; Wolpe & Rachman, 1960).

been applied with increasing sophistication to complex problems in education and psychopathology as well as to basic research.

The behavioristic model makes allowance for behavior which is good or evil, rational or irrational, depending upon the individual's conditioning. But rather than attribute the causes of behavior to inferred constructs, such as an ego and a superego—which cannot be objectively observed—the behaviorists look for the causes in the reinforcement history of the individual. To the behaviorist, we are thus at the mercy of our previous conditioning and present environment; freedom of choice is only an illusion.

The humanistic model

The humanistic model is characterized more by its positive view of our basic nature and potential for self-direction and growth than by any coherent set of principles of personality development and functioning. We shall, however, attempt to fit certain underlying themes and principles into a more or less coherent picture. This picture is based on the contributions of many distinguished psychologists among whom are Allport, Maslow, and Rogers.

Although influenced by both the psychoanalytic and behavioristic models, humanistic psychologists are in disagreement with both. They view the behavioristic model, with its emphasis upon the stimulus situation and observable behavior, as an oversimplification and feel that it needs to be balanced by a consideration of the internal psychological make-up and experiencing of the individual. At the same time they do not concur with the negative and pessimistic picture painted by the psychoanalytic theorists.

The humanistic model has some roots deep in the history of psychology, but it emerged along with the existential model as a "third force" in psychology in the 1960s when middle-class America became aware of its material affluence and spiritual emptiness, and when it became apparent that psychology was not dealing with many critical aspects of human existence including love, creativity, values, meaning, and personal growth and fulfillment.

"Self" as a unifying theme

The humanistic model assumes that human behavior cannot be understood in terms of external stimulus conditions alone; internal psychological structures and processes also have a causal influence on thought, feeling, and action.

Although William James made extensive use of the self-concept in his *Principles of Psychology* (1890), the concept of self was later dropped by behaviorists and other psychologists because of its "internal" and hence unobservable nature. Eventually, however, the need for some kind of unifying principle of personality—as well as for some way of taking cognizance of the subjective experience of each individual—led to its reintroduction in the humanistic model.

The American psychologist Carl Rogers (1951, 1969) has played a major role in delineating the self-concept in the humanistic model. His views may be summarized as follows:

1. Each individual exists in a private world of experience of which he—the I, me, or myself—is the center.

2. The most basic striving of the individual is toward the maintenance, enhancement, and actualization of the self.

3. The individual reacts to situations in terms of his unique perceptions of himself and his world—he reacts to "reality" as he perceives it and in ways consistent with his self-concept.

4. Perceived threat to the self is followed by defense—including the narrowing and rigidification of perception and coping behavior and the introduction of self-defense mechanisms such as rationalization.

5. The individual's inner tendencies are toward health and wholeness, and under normal conditions he behaves in rational and constructive ways and chooses pathways toward personal growth and self-actualization or fulfillment.

Although this concept of self is similar to the psychoanalytic concept of "ego"—in that it represents an inferred subsystem concerned with decision making, planning, and coping—the humanistic model also extends the concept to include tendencies toward personal growth and self-actualization or fulfillment.

Focus on values and meaning

The humanistic psychologists place strong emphasis upon values and the process of evaluation for guiding behavior and living a meaningful life. At the same time, they consider it crucially important that the individual's values be based on personal evaluation and choice rather than upon blind acceptance of values fostered by the sociocultural environment.

In this context, great importance is given to the uniqueness of the individual. Not only is the human species unique, but each individual by virtue of his own particular learning and experience is unique. This uniqueness makes it incumbent upon him to gain a clear sense of his own identity. He must discover who he is, what sort of person he wants to become and why. For only in this way can he fully develop his potential as a self-directing human being.

At the same time, humanistic psychologists strongly emphasize the need for science to study the inherent nature of the human species and its existential problems. For only thus can we ensure that our value judgments about both individuals and society will be based on the soundest possible information.

Positive view of human potential

Humanistic psychologists emphasize the essentially positive and rational propensities of human beings and view us as having some measure of freedom for self-direction. They think the psychoanalytic and behavioristic models are unduly negative and deterministic. As Allport once succinctly stated the matter:

"Up to now the 'behavioral sciences,' including psychology, have not provided us with a picture of man capable of creating or living in a democracy. . . . They have delivered into our hands a psychology of an 'empty organism,' pushed by drives and molded by environmental circumstances. . . . But the theory of democracy requires also that man possess a measure of rationality, a portion of freedom, a generic conscience, [personal] ideals, and unique value. We cannot defend the ballot box or liberal education, nor advocate free discussion and democratic institutions unless man has the potential capacity to profit therefrom" (1955, p. 100).

Allport was not advocating, of course, that our democratic ideals should dictate our scientific findings. Rather he was concerned with what he considered the imbalance of existing models which view human beings as little more than conditioned robots. The humanistic model is an attempt—based on scientific evidence—to remedy this imbalance by focusing on the positive aspects of human nature and our potential. Thus the humanistic model attributes great importance to learning—but emphasizes reflection, reasoning, and creative imagination. Although unconscious and irrational motives occur, there is a strong propensity for overcoming irrationality—for conscious planning and rational choosing. Basic drives are recognized—but so is a concern with values, love, meaning, and personal growth. And although much of human behavior is influenced by past conditioning and experience, the view of human beings as simply reactive organisms or robots does not seem to tell the whole story. They are also self-aware, evaluative, future-oriented, and capable of resisting environmental influences.

All in all, the humanistic model—emphasizing as it does the self-concept, the uniqueness of the individual, the importance of values and meaning, and our potential for self-direction and personal growth—has had a major and increasing influence upon our contemporary thought. And although humanistic psychology has been criticized for not taking a sufficiently rigorous scientific approach to human problems, Severin has pointed out that "humanistic psychology is, in effect, all of psychology viewed through a wide-angle lens . . ." (1973, p. ix).

The existential model

Although similar in many respects to the humanistic model, the existential model had its origins in philosophy and literature rather than science. Again we do not find a close-knit school of thought but rather certain common themes and concepts stemming from the writings of such European philosophers as Heidegger, Jaspers, Kierkegaard, and Sartre. Especially influential in existential thought in the United States has been the American psychologist Rollo May.

Existentialists are very much concerned about the social predicament of the individual in the twentieth century. They emphasize the breakdown of traditional faith, the depersonalization of the individual in a standardized mass culture, and the loss of meaning in human existence. In such a situation it becomes the task of the individual to stand on his own, to shape his own identity, and to make his existence meaningful—to make his life count for something—not on the basis of philosophical or scientific abstractions but through his own experience of being.

Like the humanistic model, the existential model emphasizes the uniqueness of the individual—his quest for values and meaning, and his freedom for self-direction and self-fulfillment. However, the existential model represents a somewhat less optimistic view of human nature, with more emphasis on irrational trends and the difficulties inherent in self-fulfillment. And the existentialists place considerably less faith in modern science for dealing with our deepest problems and more faith in the inner experiencing of the individual.

Existence and essence

A basic theme in existentialism is that the individual's existence is given, but that what he makes of it—his essence—is up to him. The youth who defiantly blurts out "Well, I didn't ask to be born" is stating a profound truth. But it is irrelevant. For whether he asked to be born or not, here he is in the world and answerable for one human life—his own. What he makes of his existence is up to him. It is his responsibility to shape the kind of person he is to become and to live a meaningful life.

Finding a meaningful and fulfilling way of life, however, is not an easy task. In an age of profound cultural change and conflict, traditional beliefs and values no longer provide adequate guides for the good life or meaning for human existence. And in our bureaucratic mass society the individual tends to be depersonalized and submerged in the group. Thus he becomes alienated and estranged—a stranger to God, to himself, and to other men and women. In the social context of contemporary life he is confused and fearful that he will fail in his quest for a fulfilling life.

Yet his predicament can be viewed as a challenge to make something worthwhile of his life. In his striving for increased self-definition in *his own experience of being* lies the perilous path of self-fulfillment. "Being" is seen as a matter of commitment to increased self-awareness and self-definition, to true communication with others, to concern with values and evaluation, and to acceptance of the responsibility for making choices and directing his own destiny.

Freedom, choice, and courage

The individual's essence is created by his *choices,* for his choices reflect the values on which he bases and orders his life. As Sartre put it: "I am my choices."

In choosing what he is to become, the individual is seen as having absolute freedom; even refusing to choose represents a choice. Thus the locus of valuing is within the individual. He is inescapably the architect of his own life. Morris (1966, p. 135) has stated the situation in the form of three propositions:

1. *"I am a choosing agent, unable to avoid choosing my way through life."*
2. *"I am a free agent, absolutely free to set the goals of my own life."*
3. *"I am a responsible agent, personally accountable for my free choices as they are revealed in how I live my life."*

Despite the high value placed on this freedom, the problems of choice and responsibility often become an agonizing burden. For finding satisfying values is a lonely and highly individual matter. Each person must have the courage to break away from old patterns, to stand on his own, and to seek new and more fulfilling pathways. In a sense, his freedom to shape his own essence is "both his agony and his glory."

Often the individual lacks "the courage to be"—to follow the path to greater self-definition and actualization—and so cuts himself off from new possibilities for being. Many individuals do not want their essence to be left up to them; they want some outside authority like religion or society to advise them on how to act and what to believe. But if blind conformity and immersion in the group lead to a wasted life, the individual cannot blame anyone else or evade the consequences. To the extent that he fails to realize his potentials for being, he is a failure and feels guilty. To flee from one's freedom and obligation to life is to be unauthentic, to show bad faith, and to live in despair.

Meaning, value, and obligation

A central human characteristic is a will-to-meaning. This is primarily a matter of finding satisfying values and is a highly individual matter. For the values that give one life meaning may be quite different from those which provide meaning for another. Each person must find his own pattern of values.

This emphasis upon individual value patterns

Model	Good/Evil	Rational/Irrational	Free/Determined
Psychoanalytic	Evil	Irrational	Determined
Behavioristic	Neutral	Depends on learning	Determined
Humanistic and Existential	Good	Rational	Free

is not to be construed as moral nihilism, however. For there is a basic unity to the human race, and all people are faced with the task of learning to live constructively with themselves and others. Hence, there will be an underlying continuity in the value patterns chosen by different individuals who are trying to live authentically.

Existentialism also places strong emphasis upon the individual's *obligation* to his fellow human beings. The most important consideration is not what one can get out of life but what one can contribute to it. One's life can be fulfilling only if it involves socially constructive values and choices.

The encounter with nothingness

A final existential theme which adds an urgent and painful note to the human situation is that of *nonbeing* or *nothingness.* In ultimate form it is death, which is the inescapable fate of all human beings.

This encounter with nothingness is uniquely human; no other creature lives with the constant awareness of the possibility of nonbeing. And this awareness adds a new and crucial dimension to human existence. Thus the encounter with nothingness becomes an overpowering theme of existentialism. We can deny victory to nothingness by living a life that deserves a better fate, that counts for something, that should not be lost. If we are perishable, we can at least perish resisting—living in such a way that nothingness will be an unjust fate.

Although there are many variations on the four major models we have reviewed, the basic models remain relatively distinct and to some extent contradictory viewpoints. Although each has some "evidence" to support it, all four depend ultimately on generalizations from particular kinds of events and experiences. Like the blind men feeling different parts of the elephant and describing it as a different animal, each model makes a contribution to the part of the puzzle of human experience and behavior that it has tackled but does not seem to be adequate for some of the parts it has not tackled.

In this book we shall not limit ourselves to any one model but shall maintain an eclectic approach, utilizing concepts from differing theoretical orientations, including that of a fifth model—systems theory. This model takes cognizance in an orderly way of the continuity of all living systems and the uniqueness of the human race. It takes into account both inner experiencing and outer behaving, both actions and transactions. We will explore this model in the next section.

A systems approach to understanding human behavior

Physical and biological scientists have long been accustomed to thinking in terms of *energy systems,* and recently a number of behavioral scientists have found it helpful to study human beings in much the same way—as living systems, comparable to other living systems in many basic ways.

An energy system is an assemblage of parts held together by some form of interaction. There are nonliving systems, such as our solar system, and living systems, such as plants and animals. Living systems, in turn, can be arranged in a hierarchy extending from cells to organs, organisms, groups, societies, and supranational bodies such as the United Nations. Each higher-level system is composed of lower-level systems.

Among the scientists who have been prominent in the development of the general systems approach and its application to the behaviorial sciences have been Bertalanffy (1967, 1968), Buckley (1968), Lazlo (1972), and Miller (1965a, 1965b).

General properties of living systems

All living systems have certain characteristics in common. For example, living systems contain genetic material (DNA)—indicating the common origin of all living things. Similarly, living systems contain a central "decider" and other subsystems, integrated in such a way as to make the total system capable of self-regulation, development, and reproduction.

Depending on their level on the evolutionary scale, living systems can be simple or complex, but all have certain properties in common: *structural, integrative,* and *field* properties.

1. *Structural properties.* Each living system contains parts or subsystems which are interdependent and whose combined action enables the system to function as an integrated unit. Some of these subsystems, such as the nervous system, can be observed; others, such as the self-system, are inferred on the basis of the functioning of the system. Structural properties—and hence potentials for behavior—vary greatly from one type of living system to another. The behavior potentials of a fish are obviously not those of a human being. That is why it is important to understand the structure of a system if we are to understand its behavior.

2. *Integrative properties.* Living systems have built-in tendencies to maintain their organization and functional integrity. If a system's equilibrium is disturbed beyond a certain point, it automatically takes action necessary to restore it. This integration is achieved by means of transactions with the surrounding environment as well as by the inner organizational properties of the system itself. In both instances, these transactions involve *matter-energy processing,* as in the assimilation of food, and *information processing,* as in the recognition of danger.

3. *Field properties.* Each lower-level system is part of a higher-level system. For example, an organ is a subsystem of an individual, an individual of a group, and a group of society. The total field, of course, includes the physical as well as the sociocultural environment. Living systems are "open systems"—that is, they are not self-sufficient but can continue to exist only if they can maintain favorable transactions with their surroundings. Thus each living system is in continual transaction with its field, and this constant interaction modifies both system and field.

Special characteristics of the human system

As we go up the scale from simple to complex living systems we find that new structural and functional properties begin to appear. Often properties present in rudimentary form at lower levels of life become further refined and more influential at higher levels. The evolution of the nervous system, for example, can be traced from a very simple segmental apparatus in a worm to the highly complex human brain.

While sharing many characteristics with lower-level systems, human beings reveal many characteristics that are different and some that are unique. We shall note a few of the most significant of these.

LIVING SYSTEMS RESIST DISINTEGRATION

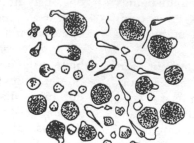

Cells just pressed out

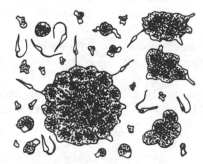

After ten minutes

Living systems tend to develop according to a pattern that is characteristic for their species and to resist disintegration or distortion. Wilson's classic study of sponges provides a remarkable demonstration of self-regulatory mechanisms. A sponge was cut up finely and forced through fine bolting cloth into a container of sea water. The minute particles sank to the bottom and promptly began to form small conglomerations and then larger ones. After eight days the new mass had formed the characteristic internal structure of the original sponge (Wilson, 1910).

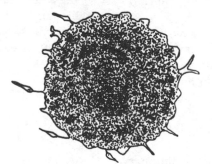

1 hour after being pressed out

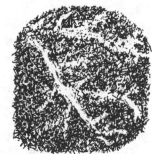

Eight days later

1. *Self-awareness.* The human race alone seems to have evolved to a high level of reflective consciousness or self-awareness; we are able not only to be aware of ourselves as unique individuals but also to reflect upon, review, and reevaluate aspects of our own experiences.

2. *Modifiability of action.* Our highly refined mental ability provides a tremendous capacity for learning, reasoning, and imagining, giving us almost unlimited flexibility for coping with new and changing situations. This flexibility is further extended by the ability to evaluate the effects of our actions and to make indicated corrections.

3. *Use of symbols.* Our unique mental endowment also enables us to deal with ideas—symbols of absent or even imaginary objects, events, and concepts. This has made possible the development of written language and of scientific procedures for understanding the order inherent in the world and making sound predictions, thus enabling us to base our behavior on

The quest for answers / 38

sound assumptions about past, present, and future conditions.

4. *Concern with information, values, and meaning.* Since human beings have the fewest "built-in" coping patterns of all living creatures, we must make our own decisions about what goals to pursue and what means are appropriate for achieving them. This requires not only that we obtain information about ourselves and the world but also that we make value judgments about what is good and bad. And, ultimately, we must come to grips with the meaning of our existence in the universe.

5. *Complexity of transactions with field.* Whereas lower animals must usually eat what they can find and rely on instinctual responses for coping with environmental hazards, human beings are not so limited. In fact, there seems almost no limit to the ways in which we can modify the environment for our own ends. As a result, our transactions with the environment are far more complex than those of other species. In fact, we are witnessing the decreasing importance of "natural selection of species" and the increasing importance of "human selection"

as a result of our fantastic ability to control and shape the world around us.

6. *Self-direction.* These various properties of human beings—reflective self-awareness, modifiability of action, use of symbols, concern with information, values, and meaning, and the complexity of transactions with the environment—make possible a high degree of self-direction. In fact, we are the only living creatures that have the resources to consciously plan and shape the future.

Changes in the system with time

Living organisms develop in accordance with their inherited potentials throughout a life cycle characteristic for each species. In humans, as in other living creatures, changes in early phases of the life cycle are toward increased size, complexity, and competence. Changes in the later phases are toward entropy—in the direction of decreasing ability, deterioration, and eventual disintegration of the system.

Not all change is genetically determined. Often change is caused by accidents, defi-

FROM NATURAL SELECTION TO HUMAN SELECTION

"In the last two decades or so, we have . . . come to the end of the era of evolution—I mean the era of evolution as Darwin interpreted it, that is, evolution by natural selection. It is rather shocking to say this about a vast period in the earth's history—a period that we now believe has lasted for about 3.6 billion years on the earth's surface. Nevertheless, it is over; and the reason it is over is not that things will not change any further (in fact, they may change more rapidly than ever!) but that we are now at the beginning of the era of evolution by human selection. It is now

our human activity, intentional or not, which determines the numbers and species of all the plants and animals on the earth's surface. . . .

"In short, the whole human race, the whole planet, is passing through a kind of watershed. It is the end of the era of innocence; it is the end of adolescence. It is a sudden incredible change. And beyond it, we will be, if we survive, a different kind of human race, and a different kind of species, on a different kind of planet. For we will be different from the past in the food we eat, in our methods of hunting and fishing

and gathering and communicating, and in our methods of living and managing the world—more different than two species of animals are from each other. . . .

"If we survive this sudden electric jump, we will move into a totally new kind of society. . . .

"This potential transformation through which we are passing today, a transformation to an integrated worldwide human organism, is what I call The Step to Man, because the new man (or woman) will look back and see us as the old, incompetent, unstable pre-men of the past" (Platt, 1972, pp. 3, 6).

ciencies, or disease. And in humans, especially, a tremendous amount of continuing change develops as we find the emergence of a fairly consistent structure of beliefs, attitudes, and habits which guide the individual's behavior and lead to a life style which is characteristic for him. And as we shall see, our psychological structure, or self-structure, becomes an increasingly important influence on further learning and change—although of course it is subject to environmental influences as well.

Thus the human system can be viewed as a "time gestalt" with an increasing "closure" of the system as the psychological configuration is filled in. For this reason, environmental conditions—except perhaps for unusual environmental change—tend to exercise their greatest influence during early development. By adulthood, the self-structure is relatively well defined, consistent, and stable. Although it may continue to change in minor ways, a radical change in a person's environment is usually required for a major change in his outlook and life style.

In summary, the general systems approach to the study of human nature covers a broad spectrum. It emphasizes both our inner experiencing and our outward behavior; our propensities for maintaining inner integration and for dealing effectively with our environment; our concern with information, values, and meaning; the ways in which we tend to change over time; and our potentialities for learning, self-direction, and personal growth. It goes beyond other models in recognizing our relationship to other living things on this planet as well as our uniqueness as human beings.

Summary and a look ahead

In viewing ourselves as living systems, we have by no means resolved the issues concerning our basic nature. However, we have tried to clarify these issues and to show the ways in which we are both like and unlike other living creatures. As humans, we have emerged as neither mechanistic, stimulus-response automatons nor mystical beings with qualities not amenable to scientific investigation. Rather we see ourselves as highly educable creatures, shaped in different ways as the result of our complex transactions with our environment. Lacking built-in mechanisms to guide most aspects of our behavior, we may become many things. But we have integrative tendencies which guide our growth and behavior in certain directions when environmental conditions permit. These tendencies seem to be in the direction of love and cooperation, rationality, and the active and purposive direction of our own behavior. Finally, in viewing ourselves as living systems, we have found a framework that encompasses both our uniqueness and our continuity with the universe of living things.

This chapter concludes our brief survey of the different ways of viewing human nature and of the major psychosocial models of man. In Part Two, we shall examine the forces that shape us, placing particular emphasis on the significance of the self, the nature of our needs and strivings, the problems we encounter in living, and the ways in which we attempt to cope with these problems.

The Personal Context of Behavior

3
The Significance of Self

The forces that shape us
Development of the self
Self-direction
The search for significant selfhood

"If a public opinion poll were to ask the question 'What is the most interesting topic on earth?' most people would probably answer, 'My own self.' No one else, even those nearest to us, can share in the same intimate way this center of centers where all life and mental activity take place. Every waking hour is filled with one's own personal thoughts and with emotions that only he can experience firsthand. They may, of course, be communicated to others or inferred from external behavior, but nonetheless they are uniquely one's own" (Severin, 1973, p. 1).

In the past, the focus has been on the role of heredity and environment in shaping our development and behavior. More recently, however, psychologists have come to realize the importance of a third determinant—the self—which emerges through the interaction of heredity and environment. As the self or self-system develops, it becomes the central point around which our experiences are organized and a crucial force in shaping our further development and behavior.

In the initial section of this chapter, we will briefly note how the interaction of heredity, environment, and self shapes us all into the recognizable mold of human beings and, paradoxically, makes each of us a

A number of recent research findings have made it apparent that there are critical periods, especially during early years, when certain types of stimulation and activity are essential for normal physiological and psychological development. Mental retardation and inability to form warm interpersonal relationships are commonly found among children who have undergone extreme emotional, social, and intellectual deprivation in infancy. In general, if needed stimulation is lacking during the critical period, then given functions: (1) may not appear, (2) may be slower in making their appearance, or (3) may be only partially adequate. And once the critical period has passed, it may be impossible to correct the physiological and/or psychological deficiencies.

little different from everyone else. Then we shall focus specifically on the development and functioning of the self-system and on our search for significant selfhood.

The forces that shape us

"How did it come about that a man born poor, losing his mother at birth and soon deserted by his father, afflicted with a painful and humiliating disease, left to wander for twelve years among alien cities and conflicting faiths, repudiated by society . . . and driven from place to place as a dangerous rebel, suspected of crime and insanity, and seeing, in his last months, the apotheosis of his greatest enemy—how did it come about that this man, after his death . . . transformed education . . . inspired the Romantic movement and the French Revolution, influenced the philosophy of Kant and Schopenhauer, the poems of Wordsworth, Byron and Shelley, the socialism of Marx, the ethics of Tolstoi, and, altogether, had more effect on posterity than any other writer or thinker of that eighteenth century in which writers were more influential than they had ever been before?"
This puzzling question is posed by Will and Ariel Durant (1967, p. 3) as an introduction to

their book *Rousseau and Revolution.* Although others might not evaluate the influence of Rousseau so highly, there is no question that it has been far-reaching. Yet the conditions of his life would have been expected to prevent the development of a person capable of making such a major impact on history. This dramatic illustration highlights the enormous complexity of the forces that shape human development and behavior. Although psychology cannot yet provide an adequate answer to the Durants' question "How did it come about . . . ?" it has become apparent that the answer lies in the interaction of three key determinants—heredity, environment, and self.

Heredity

A human life really begins at conception when the egg cell of the female is fertilized by the sperm of the male. At this time the new human being receives a genetic inheritance which provides the basic potentialities for his development and behavior. This endowment includes potentialities not only for his physical structure but also for striving, thinking, feeling, and acting, and for patterns of growth and change throughout a predictable life cycle.

Heredity influences the determination of

some traits more than others. Its influence is perhaps most noticeable in physical features such as eye color, sex, and physique. Of equal, if not greater importance, however, is the influential role our genetic inheritance plays in determining our "primary reaction tendencies"—such as activity level, sensitivity, and adaptability. Even young babies reveal differences in how they react to particular stimuli. Some cry if their face is exposed to sunlight; others are seemingly insensitive to such stimulation. Thus conditions that one baby can tolerate may be quite upsetting to another. While such primary reaction tendencies may be influenced by environmental as well as genetic factors, longitudinal studies have shown certain of them—including the three mentioned above—to be relatively stable from infancy through young adulthood.

Although much remains to be discovered about the role of such constitutional reaction tendencies in human development and behavior, it is clear that their special significance lies in their influence on the way the individual characteristically reacts to and is influenced by his environment.

Probably the most unique aspect of our genetic endowment is the human brain. It has been aptly described as the most highly organized apparatus in the universe—consisting of over 10 billion nerve cells, or neurons, with countless interconnecting pathways as well as myriad connections with other parts of the body. Even when we are asleep, more than 50 million nerve messages are being relayed between the brain and different parts of the body every second. Thus the human brain provides a fantastic communications and computing network with tremendous capabilities for learning, "storing" experience, reasoning, imagining, and for integrating the overall functioning of the human organism.

Available evidence indicates that the essential characteristics of our genetic inheritance are basically the same for all individuals, regardless of racial or ethnic background. However, the specific features of this endowment may vary considerably from one person to another. Thus, heredity not only provides common potentialities for development and behavior typical of the human species but also is an important source of individual differences.

Environment

Our physical and sociocultural environment heavily influences the way in which and the extent to which our genetic potentials are realized. Of particular importance in our present context is the sociocultural environment.

For in much the same sense that each person receives a genetic inheritance which is the end product of millions of years of biological evolution, he also receives a sociocultural inheritance which is the end product of thousands of years of social evolution. The significance of this inheritance has been well pointed up by Huxley:

"The native or genetic capacities of today's bright city child are no better than the native capacities of a bright child born into a family of Upper Paleolithic cave-dwellers. But whereas the contemporary bright baby may grow up to become almost anything—a Presbyterian engineer, for example, a piano-playing Marxist, a professor of biochemistry who is a mystical agnostic and likes to paint in water-colours—the paleolithic baby could not possibly have grown into anything except a hunter or food-gatherer, using the crudest of stone tools and thinking about his narrow world of trees and swamps in terms of some hazy system of magic. Ancient and modern, the two babies are indistinguishable. . . . But the adults into whom the babies will grow are profoundly dissimilar; and they are dissimilar because in one of them very few, and in the other a good many, of the baby's inborn potentialities have been actualized" (1965, p. 69).

Since each social group fosters its own cultural patterns by the systematic teaching of its young, all members tend to become somewhat alike—to conform to certain "basic personality types" characteristic of the group. Of course, the more uniform and thorough the education of the

DEVELOPMENTAL TASKS

At each stage of development there are fairly specific tasks—skills, attitudes, and understandings—which are appropriate to that level of maturity and which society expects the individual to master at that time. A major task of infancy, for example, is walking; during adolescence the tasks of establishing a clear sense of identity and of preparing for sexual relationships and possibly marriage and work come to the fore.

If these tasks are not mastered at the appropriate stage of development, the individual will be at a serious disadvantage in making subsequent adjustments. Young children who have not learned to talk will be at a disadvantage in nursery school; adolescents who do not date miss a key opportunity for acquiring information about themselves and members of the opposite sex that they will need later for selecting a satisfactory mate.

Specific developmental tasks vary, of course, not only with the stage of development but also with the sociocultural setting. Children in all societies learn to walk and talk, but they do not all have to master reading or the skills involved in hunting or farming. The members of each society and subgroup face somewhat different developmental tasks; and of course social change may bring new tasks for any or all stages of life.

younger members, the more alike they will become. In our own society we tend to foster a wide range of individual differences, since our children have contact with divergent beliefs and values; but even in our society there are core values that we attempt to perpetuate as essential to our way of life.

At the same time, subgroups within a society—such as family, sex, age, occupation, social class, and religious groups—also foster beliefs and values of their own, largely by means of social roles which their members are encouraged to adopt. Thus we could delineate the role behaviors expected of the child, the student, the teacher, the clergyman, the political leader, and other persons occupying specific positions in the group. The extent to which role expectations can influence development is well illustrated by Margaret Mead's (1949) study of the Tchambuli, a New Guinea tribe in which the sex roles are practically the reverse of the traditional roles in our society. Women are supposed to earn the living, handle business transactions, take the initiative in courtship, and in general head the family. Men, on the other hand, are expected to be coquettish, graceful, prone to gossip, good homemakers, and interested in dancing and theatricals. The sex roles among the Tchambuli obviously tend to channel personality development and behavior along lines considerably different from those in our own society.

Since each person belongs to different subgroups—as well as experiencing different interpersonal relationships—he participates in the sociocultural environment in a unique way. As a result of such "differential participation," no two of us grow up in quite the same world. Thus the sociocultural environment is a source of differences as well as commonalities in development and behavior.

Self

We have noted the importance of a third determinant—the self—which develops via the interaction of heredity and environment and becomes a crucial force in shaping our further development and behavior.

When psychologists refer to the self, they are not thinking of some "little person" sitting in the brain, but rather a concept necessary for explaining many aspects of our perception, feeling, thinking, and behavior. Like gravity, the self cannot be observed directly but is inferred from various behaviors that can be observed. In the present context, we shall view the self as a complex psychological process which has a developmental course, is influenced by learning, and is subject to change.

The influence of the self will depend heavily upon the extent of self-differentiation. In some

dividual in such a society may have a strong sense of self-identity, he is not likely to perceive himself as having a high degree of volition or choice, nor feel responsible for directing his own destiny. Thus his self-evaluation will probably depend less on his own actions—except possibly for adequate role behavior—than upon the overall status of the group.

In our own society, each individual is held responsible for his own behavior from an early age and is encouraged to develop and use his own capacities. Though there are many pressures toward conformity, we tend to value the individual as a unique person—in principle at least—with the right to a high degree of in-

 I have an image of myself. The physical part is that I'm slender, and my hair is long, and I wear a certain kind of clothes. That I would like to fulfill. What I want eventually is not to get so nervous as I do, just to be able to relax a little more, 'cause I'm sort of a nervous person. But sometimes I really can enjoy myself. I'm an optimistic person—sometimes I'm too optimistic. I like myself, basically, I do.

societies the individual is automatically assigned a position and role—often dependent upon the status of his family—which largely determines his self-identity and behavior. In others, he becomes "lost in the crowd" and develops very little sense of individuality or self. In still others, his self-identity appears to be collective rather than individual in nature.

In an early study of the natives of Kenya, Africa, for example, Carothers (1947) found that social roles were rigidly prescribed and that most behavior was group-determined with individual achievement strongly discouraged. While an in-

dividuality and self-determination. This deep-rooted emphasis on individuality, responsibility, and self-direction inevitably fosters self-differentiation and uniquely personal feelings of self-identity and self-evaluation.

In summary to this point, we may say that our genetic endowment provides our potentialities for both biological and psychological development, but the shaping of our potentialities—in terms of perceiving, thinking, feeling, and acting—depends heavily on our physical and socio-cultural environment as well as the self-structure which develops over time. In essence, the forces that shape us produce both likenesses and differences. The end result is that each of us is like all other persons, like some other persons, and like no other person (Allport, 1961).

Development of the self

The individual's self-concept is his picture of himself—his view of himself as distinct from other persons and things. This self-concept incorporates (1) his perception of who he is—his *self-identity;* (2) his feelings of worth and adequacy—his *self-evaluation;* and (3) his picture of the person he could and should be—his *self-ideal.*

We are not born with a sense of self. The newborn infant apparently does not know where his body leaves off and his environment begins. Only gradually does he discover the boundary lines of his body and learn to distinguish between the *me* and *not-me.* This early perception of the physical self is called the *body image* and appears to form the primitive core of his self-concept. Since others perceive and react to the individual at least partially in terms of his physical appearance, it is not surprising that body-image may continue to be an important component of his identity and self-concept throughout life.

Self-identity

Many other inner and outer forces help to shape the child's growing sense of self-identity. As he acquires language and learns labels for his mother, his father, his toys, and other objects, he also acquires a tool for forming a progressively clear-cut picture of himself. An important aid here is the child's own name. He continually hears such phrases as "Where is Johnny's nose?" "Johnny is a good boy," "Johnny, please do what I tell you." By hearing his name repeatedly in different contexts, he is helped to

see himself as a person separate from other people and things.

As the individual's experience broadens, his self-identity comes to include things outside himself with which he feels strong personal involvement. When we think of *I* or *me,* we may include the people we love, the groups we identify with, our personal possessions (often

ARE RAPID TECHNOLOGICAL AND SOCIAL CHANGE CAUSING A "MUTATION" IN OUR SELF-CONCEPT?

It has been suggested that rapid social change—including change in social norms, roles, and values—may be leading to a restructuring of the self-concept. Instead of viewing ourselves in terms of social roles, status, and related considerations—as wife, parent, citizen, teacher, affluent—we may come to view ourselves in terms of our characteristic ways of experiencing and feeling—aware, happy, lonely, anxious, alienated, concerned, authentic.

Some evidence for this basic change in the factors that determine one's self-concept may be found in certain subcultures within our society; for example, among the poor who feel they have no control over their destinies and see no hope for the future, and among those active in the human potential movement who place more emphasis on awareness, experiencing, and authenticity than on social role behavior and traditional standards of behavior (Zurcher, 1972).

including our pets), the values we believe in, and the goals we set for ourselves.

Although initially the self-concept is heavily weighted with "me" elements in which the child is an object referred to by others, parents soon place demands upon him to control himself and take responsibility for various aspects of his behavior. These demands force him to equate himself to some extent with his feelings and actions— "I want to do this" or "I must not do that" or "I have done that." This, in turn, fosters his emerging self-awareness as well as a sense of autonomy in the direction of his own behavior. Now "I" elements become increasingly incorporated in the self-concept—experiences

aspect of personality evidences considerable consistency across a wide range of situations and behaviors. It is in terms of our awareness of ourselves as unique persons that we set goals, hope, strive, fear, love, pray, and make decisions. We exist as the center of a changing world of experience, and most events in our world are perceived and dealt with in relation to the *me*. And despite changes in physical appearance, goals, values, role behaviors, and other aspects of the self, we maintain a feeling of continuity over time. Every one of us tends to think of himself as pretty much the same *me* today that he was yesterday and will be tomorrow. Our sense of continuity between past, present, and

 If someone comes to me out of the blue, that I don't know, and they know my name, that must mean I have done something or am someone that makes me worthy of recognition in their eyes— and that makes me feel good. If they are a worthwhile person (as I might come to discover) then it would take one to know one, and I might feel better still.

in which the individual perceives himself as the agent or source of action. "I can dress myself." "I can throw a ball." "I am a boy" or "I am a girl."

Other factors vital in influencing self-identity are the individual's position and role. The individual is treated in consistent ways by others in accordance with his position in the group; and role behavior considered appropriate to his position is required and reinforced by those around him. Thus his self-identity is reinforced or confirmed by recurrent and relatively consistent social interactions.

With time—despite occasional role conflicts and other problems—most of us develop a relatively coherent self-identity in which the *me*

future contributes further to the stability of our self-identity.

Self-evaluation

As a child develops a sense of self-identity, he begins to make value judgments about himself. He may evaluate himself as superior or inferior, worthy or unworthy, adequate or inadequate.

During early life, the child's self-evaluation is heavily dependent upon the way in which others view him—particularly his parents and other important people in his life. For during these early years, he has no other standards for measuring his adequacy and worth than those supplied by the people around him. If their words and behavior label him as inadequate and unworthy of love and respect, he has little choice but to accept their negative evaluations and is likely to feel inadequate and inferior. On the other hand, the child who is loved, respected as a person, and treated as adequate and capable is likely to develop a positive self-evaluation and to feel self-confident.

These early self-evaluations by the child are likely to have long-range effects on his development. Later experiences may change them but never quickly or easily. The child who grows up thinking of himself as inferior to other children is likely to behave accordingly, so that his self-evaluation becomes a self-reinforcing and self-fulfilling prophecy. For example, he is likely to interpret even small failures that are inevitable in everyone's life as adding to the already overwhelming proof of his inadequacy. On the other hand, the child who grows up feeling adequate and secure can take considerable failure in stride and realistically accept many personal shortcomings without altering his basically positive self-picture.

As we grow older, culturally defined standards of social desirability—particularly peer-group standards—increasingly provide the measure against which the individual now compares himself with respect to physical appearance, intellectual ability, athletic prowess, social status, and other characteristics. Such standards may vary considerably from one peer group to another. A middle-class adolescent may feel inferior and devaluated if he receives failing grades in high school, while an adolescent from a low socioeconomic level, whose peer group stresses athletics and tends to disapprove of academic achievement, may feel inferior and devaluated if he gets good grades. Of course, the larger society forms a background context which may influence the standards of the peer group as well as those of the individual, usually tending to foster some measure of uniformity.

A person's self-evaluation often shows considerable variance with his actual assets, liabilities, and accomplishments. A highly talented and capable person may have deep feelings of inferiority and unworthiness, while a person with mediocre or even inferior capabilities may be convinced of his superiority. Fortunately, however, there are corrective tendencies in our social interactions which tend to provide for some consistency between self-evaluation and reality. For example, the lionized high-school athlete who begins to believe his own "press notices" may be forced to an agonizing reappraisal after graduation into a world where his previous exploits no longer enable him to maintain his accustomed status. But whether fanciful or realistic, negative or positive, the individual's self-evaluation plays an important role in his subsequent development and behavior.

Self-ideal

The individual's self-concept includes not only a sense of personal identity and of worth but also of aspiration for accomplishment and growth. The individual's image of the person he would like to be and thinks he should be is called his *self-ideal.*

Depending upon whether a person's aspirations are difficult or easy to achieve in relation to his abilities and environmental opportunities, we say that he has a high or low *level of aspiration.* It is important that one's level of aspiration be realistic. If it is too high, he will suffer inevitable failure and self-devaluation no matter how well he actually performs; if it is too low, he will waste his personal resources and opportunities. Sometimes family expectations induce unrealistic aspirations. For example, a youth's parents may have their hearts set on his becoming a physician even though this goal is not in accord with his own interests and abilities. The expectations and reinforcements of the family and other social groups can work constructively as incentives for the individual to achieve his potentialities, or, by allowing too little room for individuality, can force him to accept goals that are not compatible with his own make-up. When a person accepts too easily the goals and expectations others set for him, it

It's difficult for me to describe what kind of person I am, because a part of someone is, at my stage, is made up of what they want to be. Like I could describe myself partly in terms of what I want to be.

identifications tend to be modified by later peer-group and cultural models and still later by composite models. Although the mechanism of identification can continue to work constructively in adulthood, the mature person is more likely to set his aspirations for self-growth in terms of thought-out values based upon a realistic assessment of his prior accomplishments and failures, his present assets and liabilities, and the opportunities and limitations of his environment.

In general, members of a given culture share many common standards about what is socially desirable and hence have similar conceptions of the ideal self. In a heterogeneous culture such as our own, however, conceptions of the ideal self may vary markedly with subculture as well as among the individuals in a given group.

It seems likely that some discrepancy between a person's existing self-image and self-ideal is necessary for the fostering of personal growth, but we do not know how wide a discrepancy is desirable. We do know, however, that too great a discrepancy between one's "real" and "ideal" self can lead to serious inner conflict and self-devaluation.

usually indicates that he lacks adequate self-knowledge and a clear sense of his own identity.

Typically our self-ideals are closely related to the identifications we make with various models—parents, friends, prominent personalities, national heroes, and other persons we admire. The identifications we make in childhood, especially with the parent of our own sex, are the source of many of our most basic goals for self-growth and are important in providing the early direction for our development. These early

Self-direction

The behavior systems theorist James G. Miller has pointed out that each living system contains what he describes as "a decider subsystem which receives information from all parts of the system and from the environment, makes decisions, and transmits command information which controls a significant part of the process of the units of the system" (1965a, p. 214).

After I graduated from high school, I felt all
I had to do was to find a job, stick with it
and everything will be all right. I was free!
But I wasn't as free as I thought I would be.
For one, I couldn't choose what type of work
I wanted—there were limits. I worked factory
jobs, thinking that was all I could do, since
I was such a failure at school. I had an image
I was dumb and brainless.

On a group level, an example of such a decider subsystem would be the leader, who serves as director for interpreting, coordinating, planning, and decision making for the group. On an individual level, the self functions as such a subsystem. For as the self emerges, other psychological processes—such as perceiving, learning, thinking, striving, feeling, and decision making—develop around it. The self, in essence, becomes the "operations center" of the personality and a highly selective force in shaping subsequent behavior.

Our frame of reference

In his encounters with the environment, the individual gradually builds an inner *cognitive map* or *frame of reference* which provides him with a meaningful picture of himself and his world. Key elements in the individual's frame of reference are the assumptions he makes concerning *reality, value,* and *possibility:*

1. *Assumptions concerning reality*—of how things *really are.* Included here are the individual's assumptions about himself as a person, about other people, and about the world in which he lives. Thus he may assume that he is a capable and worthy person or inadequate and worthless; that other people are for the most part honest and concerned or deceitful and selfish; that the world is a place of opportunity or a concrete jungle of dead-end streets.

2. *Assumptions concerning value*—of how things *should be*—incorporating his judgments of what is good and bad, desirable and undesirable, right and wrong. Thus he might assume that deceit and violence are acceptable ways of achieving important goals—that the ends justify the means; that homosexual acts among consenting adults are not only acceptable but desirable; that meaningful interpersonal relationships are more important than material success.

3. *Assumptions concerning possibility*—of how things *could be,* of possibilities for change and improvement. The student may assume that a college degree will enable him to get the kind of job that would not otherwise be open to him; the people of an underdeveloped country may assume that once the country is industrialized and technologically proficient, they will no longer have problems; the slum child may assume that nothing he might do could ever break the pattern of poverty his family has always known.

The goals we strive for, the things we value, and our methods for coping with the problems of living are determined largely by the pattern of assumptions we acquire. Without a coherent frame of reference an individual would be incapable of consistent and purposeful action. In evaluating new situations and choosing appropriate modes of response, he must rely upon the cognitive map which he has constructed as a basic guide. In a general sense, a person's frame of reference—together with the various competencies he develops—represents his learned

IS THE TRANSMISSION OF CULTURE REVERSING ITSELF?

Traditionally, it has been the older generation that transmits the culture of a society to the younger generation through mores, rules, rituals, and formal education. But it has recently been suggested that the direction may be changing to some extent (Farson, 1971). The younger generation may have something to teach its elders about the superficialities and incongruities in established cultural patterns, about the conduct of human relationships, about the practice of religion, about the ethics of politics and sex, and about authentic persons. Paradoxically, it is the young who seem to be the more honest generation, as they seek to discover the truth without restriction, to be more open to experience, to understand and fulfill human potentials. It is the young who appear to be most concerned about improving the world and building a good future.

know-how and know-why for coping with the world.

If this cognitive map were a simple mirror which accurately reflected the individual and the outer world, it would greatly simplify matters. But it is not. Rather each person's picture of reality, value, and possibility is built upon his own experiences—and these experiences are not only limited but often are biased by need, desire, emotion, propaganda, and other factors. Thus the individual's assumptions may be relatively accurate or inaccurate depending upon how well they correspond to "objective reality." To the extent that an individual's assumptions about either himself or his environment are inaccurate, his development and behavior are likely to be adversely affected.

Fortunately, our assumptions are subject to modification with experience—although some are much more resistant to change than others. Thus we see a built-in corrective factor in the human computer. There is no guarantee, of course, that the individual will undergo new experiences that will enable him to correct his faulty assumptions.

Perceiving and experiencing

Each new experience is perceived or interpreted in terms of its meaning and significance to the self. In essence, the process involves three alternative subprocesses (Rogers, 1969). As new experiences occur in the life of the individual, they are either: (1) categorized and organized into some relationship to the self; (2) ignored because they are not perceived as having significance for the self; or (3) perceived in a distorted way because they are incongruent with the individual's self-concept.

As a consequence, each individual experiences events and environmental conditions in a somewhat personal way. And if we are to understand an individual's reaction, we must examine the way he has perceived the situation. Often a problem which seems insignificant to one person is highly stressful to another. Not being invited to a school dance may constitute a major crisis for one girl but be brushed aside as inconsequential by another who perhaps has greater self-confidence or different values.

Although another person's response to a particular situation may seem irrational to us, we can assume that it is appropriate to the situation as he perceives it. Combs and Snygg have made this point very well:

"People do not behave according to the facts as others see them. They behave according to the facts as they see them. . . .

"When we look at other people from an external, objective point of view, their behavior may seem irrational because we do not experience things as they do. Even our own behavior may, in retrospect, seem to have been silly or ineffective. But at the instant of behaving, each person's actions seem to him to be the best and most

effective acts he can perform under the circumstances" (1959, p. 17).

In general, the activities, objects, and events that we see as potentially beneficial or threatening to the self are what command our attention and exert the most significant influence on our behavior. And since the aspects of the environment with which one person is self-involved may be quite different from those which seem important to another, we can see how the self-concept contributes to differences in development and behavior.

Planning and striving

Our experience of self and of self-direction not only involves the self as knower and perceiver but also as planner and striver. It is *I* who choose certain goals, and it is *I* who decide how much effort *I* will devote to achieving them. As we shall see, the self as striver also includes the erection of defenses to protect the self.

Miller, Galanter, and Pribram (1960) have conceptualized the striving aspect of our experience as involving the formulating and carrying out of plans. There are long-range plans, such as a plan to complete one's education or become an astronaut; there are short-range plans, such as a plan to attend a football game or concert. Some plans are executed, some are modified or held in abeyance, and some are abandoned.

The effort we devote to achieving the plans that we wish to execute or the goals we wish to achieve depends heavily upon the perceived significance of the plans or goals to *us.* If a given goal is perceived as important, we are willing to devote far more effort to attaining it than if we perceive it as desirable but not too important; and we may abandon it entirely if it appears to have lost its relevance to our needs—to the self.

An additional aspect of our striving concerns the protection of the self. Serious disorganization or devaluation of the self can disable us just as surely as a serious physical illness. We strive to maintain our existing frame of reference, for without our assumptions concerning reality, val-

ue, and possibility, we would have no basic reference point for dealing with our world. We tend to resist dissonant information and to relinquish one assumption only in favor of another that has equal or greater appeal—for example, one that enhances our feelings of adequacy and our resources for coping. In the face of failure or other threats to our feelings of adequacy and worth, we are quick to call on rationalization and other defense mechanisms to protect ourselves. We shall deal with such ego defenses in some detail in Chapter 6.

Deciding and doing

The vast quantity of information we receive from our internal and external environment is evaluated, integrated, and stored with reference to its perceived significance to the self and its usefulness to us in the pursuit of our needs and goals.

When we wish to execute a plan or when a new demand is made on us, the typical adjustive sequence appears to involve: (1) evaluating the situation by comparing it with information already on file in our "memory banks," noting how similar situations have been dealt with in the past; (2) formulating alternative courses of action for dealing with the situation; (3) making a decision—choosing the alternative which appears most suitable and taking action; (4) utilizing "feedback"—noting how well the solution is working out and making corrections if they are necessary and possible; and (5) evaluating the entire sequence and putting the conclusions back into our "memory banks" for use in similar future situations. In all these steps the individual sees himself as an active agent with conscious intent and the capacity for self-direction.

Since the ongoing activities of the individual are organized in relation to the self as the "operations center" of the personality, each of us tends to establish a relatively consistent *life style.* We develop a characteristic way of doing, thinking, feeling, and acting which tends to distinguish us from everyone else. In essence, we put our personal stamp on every role we play and on every situation we encounter.

Thus in viewing the self as the operations center of the personality—actively involved in knowing, perceiving, experiencing, striving, planning, decision making, and doing—we are focusing on the key processes involved in self-direction. We shall elaborate on these processes throughout the remainder of this book.

The search for significant selfhood

"For this is the journey that men make: to find themselves. If they fail in this, it doesn't matter much else what they find" (Michener, 1949, p. 488).

In evaluating the course or totality of his life up to the present, a person may experience a sense of fulfillment, disappointment, or even despair. Bühler noted that when persons over 50 years of age were asked to tell the story of their lives, their statements usually fell into one of three categories: "All in all it was a good life," or "There were so many disappointments," or "It all came to nothing" (1968, p. 185).

Admittedly, living a life is neither simple nor easy, and it involves far more than simply our values. Opportunities, chance factors, personal resources, and many other conditions all enter in. It is largely through our own choices and actions, however, that we shape the kind of person we will become as well as the kind of personal world that we will make for ourselves to live in.

Self in a world of flux and change

Each of us plays not just one but a variety of social roles, and sometimes we may feel as though we have several different "selves." A woman may play the roles of wife, parent, and business executive—each with different role ex-

pectations and demands. These varying roles must be integrated into a coherent "master role" of some sort, or the individual may have difficulty in working out a clear-cut and acceptable sense of self-identity.

This is often a problem during adolescence in our society when social roles are unclear and conflicting. Parents may make certain role demands, the school others, and the peer group still others on the teenager. In some instances this may lead to "identity diffusion" and to a chameleonlike pattern in which the individual adopts whatever self or social role he thinks is expected and suited to the particular setting in which he finds himself. As we have noted, however, most people eventually manage to

> The life style in which a person is raised influences greatly the outcome of his life. I feel this is an area where many college students get hung up—we have our desires and wishes, and society and family and parents often have other plans for us.

resolve such problems and achieve a relatively coherent sense of self-identity.

Unfortunately, the picture is often somewhat more complicated. For our contemporary world seems to be one of increasing flux in which rapid social change is playing havoc with traditional values, norms, and relationships. As a consequence, several social scientists have emphasized the confusion that may arise concerning "who we are" and the schism that may develop between our real selves and the false selves which we perceive as conforming to the changing expectations and demands of others. In fact, Laing has concluded that we live in a world inhabited by "bemused and crazed creatures, strangers to our true selves, to one

Drawing by Modell; © 1973
The New Yorker Magazine, Inc.

another, and to the spiritual and material world"
(1971, p. 66).

We shall pursue this point in the sections which follow. It is enough to emphasize here that both behaviorists and humanists are placing increasing emphasis upon the importance of a clear-cut sense of self-identity and of self-direction as "inner stabilizers" in our contemporary world of flux and change.

Masks

"This above all: To thine own self be true,
And it must follow, as the night the day,
Thou canst not then be false to any man."
Hamlet, Act I, Scene III

Except for the very young, most of us learn to wear "masks" to hide our true feelings and disguise our real selves—or perhaps to portray the self we wish to portray. Like ancient Greek actors who held stylized masks before their faces

to denote the character they were playing and the emotion they were portraying, we also are mask-wearers.

Some people feel that certain masks are essential to their social roles. Thus a prominent political figure may try to portray himself as a wise leader who knows the answers to our problems and does not make mistakes; or a college professor may go to great lengths to portray himself as a learned intellectual and a hard-headed scientist; or a physician may play an all-knowing and authoritarian role as he dispenses medication and instructions.

In other instances people wear masks to emphasize their expertise in certain areas and to draw attention away from their limitations—as might possibly be the case in the example of the college professor who may don the mask of an intellectual in part because he feels it essential to playing his role and in part because he feels incapable of relating to his students effectively on a more personal level. In still other instances, people may wear masks because they do not really understand or trust others and hence are fearful of dropping their façades for fear their real selves will meet with disapproval and rejection.

Does wearing a mask mean that a person is a phony? Not necessarily, for the mask he wears may portray an actual aspect of his true identity, or it may be essential for playing a constructive social role. We are all confronted with the necessity of some role playing as a means of facilitating social interactions—of behaving in ways which seem understandable, appropriate, and predictable to others.

To the extent, however, that the person seeks to pass off a limited facet of his self as his entire identity, or to the extent that he dons a mask in a deliberate attempt to disguise or conceal his real self, then he would be open to the charge of attempting to deceive others—and possibly himself as well. For one danger of habitually wearing a mask is that the individual may really begin to believe he is actually portraying his true self; he comes to believe he is the person he is trying to portray to others. And in this process he may lose the capacity to empathize with and

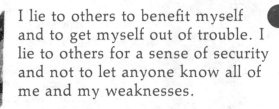

66 Many people try to show just their best sides to everyone. They don't confide in anyone, even if they are someone very close. This is probably because they don't wish to lessen themselves by showing they aren't perfect. It would be better to talk with someone close and see how they feel about it.

I lie to others to benefit myself and to get myself out of trouble. I lie to others for a sense of security and not to let anyone know all of me and my weaknesses. **99**

About the turn of the century, the noted psychologist William James (1890) stated that a person with a divided self was, in essence, "sick." Similarly, Lecky (1945) argued that the development of a clear-cut sense of self was essential for healthy and consistent behavior.

In recent years, however, some psychologists have questioned these assumptions. For example, Gergen (1972) has rejected the assumption that the development of a coherent sense of self-identity is normal and healthy. In fact, he has concluded that to the extent a person does develop a coherent sense of identity, "he may experience severe emotional distress" (p. 32). Gergen argues that a clear-cut sense of self-identity seriously limits a person's choices of how to live his life. In commitment to a particular life style, he suggests "we dash the hopes of a thousand potential selves" (p. 32). In addition, a clear-cut identity may force us to assume unrealistic, uncomfortable, and rigid social roles which lead not only to ineffective behavior but also to false assumptions about ourselves. For example, the successful lover may come to see himself as "poetic, vital, attractive, profound, intelligent, and utterly lovable" (p. 64). Ultimately, Gergen concludes, for the healthy person the self is plastic and readily molded by social circumstances and "that once donned, mask becomes reality" (p. 64).

Gergen's conclusions are based upon a series of interesting experiments with college students which demonstrated that it was easy to modify the individual's mask of identity and even his actual feelings of self-identity by the manipulation of various social expectations, conditions, and demands. Gergen's work raises some interesting questions: Does a person really ever achieve a coherent sense of self-identity? Could people stand more stress and adapt more readily to changing social demands if they did not have a coherent sense of identity but rather a chameleonlike adaptability? Or is a clear-cut sense of self-identity more necessary than ever as a guide and stabilizer for self-direction in a world of ever increasing flux and change?

understand others; in fact, he may even be taken in by the masks they wear as well. It almost takes on the eerie picture of a play in which each actor begins to believe that he is the person he is portraying and that the other actors are really the persons they are portraying.

The vicious circle that can result from wearing masks that deceive both others and ourselves is vividly depicted by Moustakas:

"Each person, not being himself to others or to himself, just as others are not themselves to themselves or to us, neither recognizes himself in the other, nor the other in himself. Hence . . . the more time he spends with others, the more lonely he becomes" (1969, p. 60).

Of course, most of us are not willing to settle for a mask which reveals only a small portion of another person, particularly if we care about him; nor are we usually comfortable with the feeling that he does not really understand us. The latter point is well brought out in excerpts from a poem by Bernice Marshall (1971, p. 29).

I say words
You say words
And I walk alone

You say words
I say words
Words words words
And I walk alone

There's a place where I go
It's a place no one knows
That's the place where I found
The me that is I
Not the me that you know

. . . .

There are clouds in the skies
Those are clouds in your eyes;
What words can I say
That will show you the way
To the place where I found
The never-here, ever-here you
And the me that is I
Not the me that you know?

Thus most of us who really care about another person usually offer him opportunities for disclosing facets of himself that are ordinarily concealed by the mask he wears; and we in turn take the risk of disclosing our true selves. This encounter of two persons is often not only an exciting adventure but a highly productive approach to the building of truly authentic interpersonal relationships.

Authenticity and becoming

"What I seek is to have meaning and to be meaningful
To love and receive love
To have meaning I must be true to myself
To be meaningful I must be responded to as I am
I want to live authentically and spontaneously
My masks are gone and I am struggling to be

I face the void with the pains of birth
And need Love to nourish me into being."
Marcantonio (1968, p. vi)

These are the goals one writer perceives as essential for achieving authenticity. They encompass meaning, dropping of masks, and love —and they acknowledge the courage and pain requisite to achieving an authentic life. While these goals would not necessarily be the ones all of us would consider essential for authenticity, it is likely that meaning, the dropping of masks, spontaneity, and love would rank high on our list.

Unfortunately, these goals are not likely to be achieved once and for all. Living authentically is a process of personal change and growth throughout life—it is a process of *becoming.* Within this framework there appear to be certain guidelines which are generally considered by psychologists to be of value. Most of these guidelines seem to fall into one or more of the following categories.

1. *Increased autonomy*—changes in the direction of increased self-reliance, self-regard, and self-direction. Implicit here is emancipation from undue social influence with increased ability to make decisions and take responsibility for and face the consequences of one's actions.

2. *More adequate assumptions*—changes in the direction of more adequate assumptions concerning reality, possibility, and value. Such changes lead to increased understanding of ourselves and our world and to greater capability for solving problems and making wise decisions.

3. *Improved competencies*—changes in the direction of increased intellectual, emotional, and social competence. Such improvements lead to greater capability in coping with problems of living as well as in carrying out one's life plans.

4. *Increased awareness and openness to experience*—changes in the direction of resolving disabling conflicts, dismantling unnecessary self-defenses, and maintaining an openness to experience, and achieving increased awareness and greater depth and scope of feeling.

All of these guidelines to becoming are in the direction of helping the individual better understand who he is and what he can realistically become, of expanding his awareness and depth of experiencing, of building warm and loving relationships with others, of gaining a greater sense of relatedness to the human enterprise, and of achieving increased confidence in himself as capable of self-direction and playing a decisive role in shaping his own destiny.

Whether or not we wish to accept these particular guidelines, each of us is confronted with the inescapable challenge of shaping a life—knowing full well that at some unknown time and place we, like all other human beings, face inevitable death. While we cannot control the length of our lives, we can play a key role in shaping our selves and our existence in the time we do have—in achieving a truly meaningful, fulfilling, and authentic way of life.

Summary and a look ahead

In this chapter we have seen that our genetic endowment provides the potentials for our development and behavior. It also influences certain primary reaction tendencies which channel our modes of interaction with our environment; and it endows us with a unique brain which provides a fantastic communications and computing network. Environment heavily influences the extent to which and the way in which our genetic potentials are realized. Each social group fosters its own cultural patterns by the systematic teaching of the young, and hence all members tend to be somewhat alike—to conform to basic personality types characteristic of the group.

Through the interaction of heredity and environment, the development of the self occurs, which is the third major force in shaping our further development and behavior. As we begin to experience ourselves as unique persons and develop a relatively consistent view of ourselves and our world—self-identity, self-evaluation, self-ideal, and assumptions about reality, value, and possibility—our view of ourselves becomes the key reference point around which our experiences and actions are integrated and provides our unique capacity for self-direction. But self-direction in our complex and changing world is not an easy task; hence the search for significant selfhood—for achieving a meaningful and fulfilling life.

In Chapter 4 we shall take up the question of motivation. What moves us to act at all, and what determines the particular goals we shall seek? What mechanisms provide the energy we use in pursuing our goals, and to what extent is our behavior determined by environmental demands?

Key terms and concepts:

heredity/environment
  (pp. 46–48)
critical periods (46)
primary reaction tendencies
  (47)
developmental tasks (48)
development of self (48–53)
body image (50)
self-concept (50)
  self-identity (50–51)
  self-evaluation (51–52)
  self-ideal (52–53)
self-direction (53–57)
frame of reference (54)
cognitive map (54)
reality, value, possibility
  assumptions (54–55)
reverse transmission of culture
  (55)
significant selfhood (57–62)
identity diffusion (57)
masks (58–61)
authenticity (61–62)

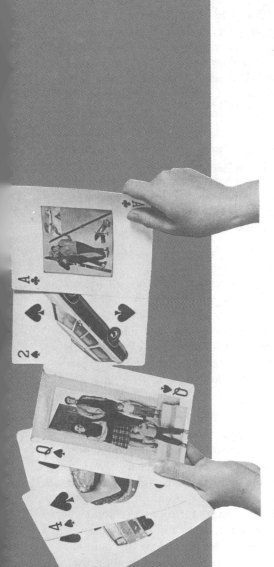

4

Motivation: Our Needs and Goals

What motivation helps to explain
Strivings toward maintenance and actualization
Motive patterns and behavior

"Kilimanjaro is a snow covered mountain 19,710 feet high, and is said to be the highest mountain in Africa. . . . Close to the western summit there is the dried and frozen carcass of a leopard. No one has explained what the leopard was seeking at that altitude."

This dramatic introduction to Ernest Hemingway's story "The Snows of Kilimanjaro" (1955, p. 52) makes two interesting assumptions: (1) that the behavior of the leopard was purposive—that he was trying to find or achieve something by climbing to the top of a snow-covered mountain—and (2) that to understand the leopard's behavior we would have to understand his purpose—what he was seeking.

Though no concept of motivation seems necessary for explaining the behavior of atoms or planets, such a concept does appear necessary for explaining the behavior of living organisms—particularly human beings.

What motivation
helps to explain

In dealing with people and attempting to understand their behavior, we give high priority to information concerning their motives. We may ponder our own motives when we contemplate marriage; the police detective may consider motives of key importance in trying to apprehend a murderer; and sociologists may be vitally interested in the intent behind delinquent behavior.

Although we are often able to infer the motives underlying a given action, our understanding of human motivation is far from complete. Research findings are spotty, and psychologists have advanced differing viewpoints which are often contradictory and confusing. However, there is an expanding body of scientific information which helps us to understand many aspects of the problem and provides us with a general perspective for thinking about human motivation.

In the present context, we shall use the term *motivation* to refer to any inner condition of the individual that initiates or directs his behavior toward a goal; and we shall use the term *motive* in a more limited sense to refer to a tendency to seek a particular goal.

Viewed in this way, motivation is a broad concept which includes the inner needs, desires, and purposes of the individual. Specifically, it helps us to understand: (1) the directionality of behavior—the goals we pursue; and (2) the activation of behavior—the effort we expend in pursuing our goals. Accounting for the direction and activation of behavior will, in turn, help us to understand both the common denominators and great diversity in human strivings.

The goals we pursue

Particularly during adolescence and young adulthood, most of us spend considerable time contemplating the goals we want to pursue. Some of us seem to resolve this problem rather easily, while others seem to experience serious difficulty in finding goals that seem likely to lead to a fulfilling life.

The following are answers given by community college students to the question "What are your life goals?"

"I am going to finish my last year here in college. Then I am going to take 'time out' and get a better idea of what the world is all about. Maybe I will join a commune of some kind for a while. Anyway, I want to live a life full of experiences and adventures. The way most adults live sure doesn't turn me on. So I will explore around until I find out what does."

"I'm not sure of what I want or what my goals are. I'm so confused right now about everything. I guess though that what I want most of all in the world is to find someone who will really love me. I don't care whether he marries me or wants to have children. But I think if he loves me enough, he will want to."

"I see life as a continual journey—always in process of becoming what the creator means for me to become. I believe there are guideposts and new possibilities all along the way and that we have free choice (or reasonably free choice) as we come to each new crossroads. I am going to try to make the most of this journey and be happy."

These replies may not be representative of those that many young people would give to the question concerning life goals. They do seem, however, to indicate that most of us are aware of the problem of life goals even though we may go about trying to solve it in quite different ways.

Many people have apparently lost confidence in the traditional view that "the future belongs to those who prepare for it." Some are deliberately planning not to plan. Others, feeling that they have no real control over their destiny anyway, consider it useless to make plans but simply "drift with the tide." Others, however, try to find the answer in living each day to its fullest while striving toward continued personal growth and long-range plans usually related to marriage, family, and career.

In any event, each of our lives is a journey which, in existential terms, we must travel alone—with all that this implies in terms of the choices we make or fail to make.

 I am just an average, ordinary person who is trying to survive in this rugged, money-making society. My whole life right now is centered around money. I go to school in the morning so that I may later get a good job and good money. I go to work to earn money. I do everything to get money. I am not money hungry, I just need it to survive.

The effort we expend in pursuing our goals

The amount of effort we are willing to expend in the pursuit of our goals depends heavily upon their perceived importance to us. We all tire quickly when our energies are directed toward goals we care little about or actually dislike—for example, when we feel compelled to work at some monotonous job because we need the money. On the other hand, we may devote tremendous effort and even sacrifice our lives in the pursuit of goals in which we really believe. Despite public ridicule and repeated failures, for example, Columbus persisted for almost 10 years in his efforts until he received the backing he needed from Queen Isabella for his expedition to the New World. But we need not resort to historical examples. We can readily point to the long hours of dedication and effort it takes to become an astronaut, an Olympic athlete, or a skilled surgeon.

In general, of course, success tends to reinforce our efforts, while failure tends to have the opposite effect. But in many cases failure may have constructive effects, leading us to intensify our efforts, to use more effective means, or to formulate more realistic goals. A student who receives failing grades in a given subject may devote more time to his studies, improve his study techniques, or perhaps change his major to one better suited to him.

Usually we gauge the strength of an individual's motivation by the amount of effort he is willing to expend in pursuing a given goal; and stronger motivation—assuming he has the necessary resources and opportunities—usually gives him a better chance of achieving his goals by leading to more energetic, persistent, and goal-focused behavior.

Similarities and differences in motive patterns

Some motives, like hunger, are powered by built-in needs; others, such as the desire for financial success, may be entirely learned. Since we can acquire almost any motive as a consequence of learning, it is inevitable that our motivational patterns should show almost infinite variety. Thus again we are confronted with the problem of finding order in the diversity of human behavior.

And at first glance human motives do appear to defy classification. Yet if we look closer, we see some common denominators. People everywhere are concerned about such matters as food, clothing, shelter, health, education, work, marriage, belonging, security, and approval. And if we look still closer, we can see that common to human activities everywhere are strivings toward *self-maintenance* or survival and toward the *actualization of potential.* In fact, all our specific strivings—toward food, shelter, security, and all the rest—are variations on these two basic themes.

Although human beings share these two basic strivings with all living creatures, there is an important difference: the strivings that satisfy maintenance often seem less important to us than do the strivings that subserve actualization. A scientist completing an exciting experiment may be much more concerned about its outcome than about eating or sleeping; a mountain climber may undergo great hardship and danger in climbing a high mountain peak; and an astronaut may risk his life on a space mission.

In fact, it is in our voluntary attempts at creative expression, at coping with great challenges, and in our quest for values and meaning that we reveal ourselves as human and distinct from other species.

Strivings toward maintenance and actualization

Although we do not fully understand the processes involved, it is apparent that digestive, circulatory, and other bodily functions operate in such a way as to maintain the physiological equilibrium of the body. Whereas we may go several hours with no food and then eat a large meal, the concentration of sugar and other chemicals in the blood must remain relatively constant; a slight increase in acidity, for example, would result in coma and death. Similarly, body temperature must remain within a very limited range even though the temperature in the environment may go above a hundred degrees or below zero. Thus living systems endeavor to maintain *steady states*—to maintain their physiological variables within a range essential for survival—an endeavor referred to as *homeostasis.*

On the psychological level, we understand even less the processes involved in maintenance. However, they appear to be an extension of the strivings we see operating on the biological level, namely focusing on an attempt to protect the self-system. Damage to the self—as through severe guilt feelings or from an overloading of the system by being forced to deal with too many problems at once—can disable a person just as surely as can the failure of homeostatic mechanisms on the biological level. Thus we also strive to maintain the steady states essential to psychological integration—for thinking, feeling, and acting in organized and coherent ways.

In attempting to understand our strivings toward maintenance, we could take up various specific motives—such as motives for social ap-

When I'm hungry I get really grumpy and sulky. I'm a bad person to be around when I'm missing a meal because of someone else. I guess that's really what makes the difference, because someone else is causing it. And I'm a bad sport about it. On the other hand, if I'm really busy and don't want to stop to eat, or if I know in advance I'm not going to be able to eat 'til two or three hours after the time when I'm used to eating, that's OK, and I just sort of put it out of my mind and that doesn't bother me too much.

proval and for achievement—and show how they relate to biological and psychological maintenance. The great diversity of human motives and motive patterns, however, argues against this approach. A second and more economical approach is to think in terms of certain basic requirements or needs that must be met for biological and psychological maintenance—to delineate a basic core of requirements that appear essential for the normal functioning of human beings.

Our first task, then, will be to review some of the generally agreed-upon requirements—biological and psychological needs—that must be met for normal functioning. Then we shall attempt to deal with the even more complex problem of actualization strivings—particularly the forms such strivings take on the psychological level as we attempt to fulfill ourselves as human beings.

Biological needs

For normal functioning the human body needs many substances, conditions, and activities ranging from food and vitamins to sleep.

In our present discussion, we shall not attempt to cover the gamut of biological needs. Rather we will briefly summarize those requirements which appear particularly relevant to an understanding of our behavior.

ACTIVATION AND BEHAVIOR

Activation refers to the energy mobilized in order to pursue our goals and meet our needs. Activation levels may vary from very low to very high—from deep sleep to intense excitement. At any given time, the individual's level of activation is influenced by a wide range of personal and situational factors. If he perceives threat, for example, his activation level is increased; similarly, it may be influenced by biological needs, emotions, drugs, fatigue, sudden loud noises, and strange and unusual stimuli.

For efficient performance, it is necessary that the individual's level of activation be appropriate to the requirements of the task. In most situations, a moderate level of activation is ideal. If the level is too low, the individual may not expend the energy necessary to attain his goals; at exceedingly high levels of activation, both physical and psychological functioning tend to be impaired.

Visceral needs

Here we are concerned with bodily needs related to food, water, sleep, and other conditions essential for normal bodily functioning and survival—and for normal growth during the early years of life.

1. *Hunger and thirst.* In our society most of us have no first-hand knowledge of the far-reaching effects that severe hunger can have on psychological as well as physiological functioning. These effects were well illustrated in an interesting study conducted during World War II by Keys and his associates (1950).

Thirty-two conscientious objectors volunteered to serve as subjects in an experimental study of the effects of semistarvation. The men existed on about 1600 calories per day, which resulted in an average weight loss of 24 percent during the six-month period of the study.

Dramatic personality changes took place during the experiment. The men became irritable, unsociable, and increasingly unable to concentrate on anything but the thought of food. By the end of the 25th week, food dominated their thoughts, conversation, and daydreams. The men even pinned up pictures of chocolate cake instead of pretty girls. In some cases, they went so far as to replan their lives in the light of their newly acquired respect for food.

In total starvation, hunger eventually disappears, but in this study, in which the men suffered prolonged semistarvation, their desire for food showed no lessening. In thirst too, the desire continues unabated. Men who have been deprived of both food and water over long periods of time have reported that feelings of hunger tended to decrease, whereas thirst remained intense and became almost maddening.

Although some people live in arid desert areas and subsist on a minimum of water, intense and prolonged thirst is probably relatively rare. Hunger, however, is a major problem in many areas of the world. Without going into the many side effects of malnutrition in stunting physical and intellectual growth, lowering resistance to disease, and producing chronic fatigue, it is apparent that hunger remains an urgent motive in our contemporary world. Where conditions

STAGES OF SLEEP AND SLEEP NEEDS

Research has shown that there are four stages of sleep, ranging from light sleep through progressively deeper stages. The normal adult spends about 20 percent of his sleeping time in Stage 1—the main stage for dreaming, as evidenced by the presence of rapid eye movements (REM)—about 60 percent in intermediary Stages 2 and 3, and about 20 percent in the deep sleep of Stage 4. Although some dreaming may occur, the latter 3 stages are referred to as non-REM or NREM sleep. Typically the individual goes through all four stages in cycles of about 90 minutes, from light through deep sleep and back again to light sleep.

Although we do not understand the precise role of REM and deep sleep in maintaining normal physiological and psychological functioning, a number of studies have pointed to the significance of normal sleep patterns for mental health. Disturbed sleep patterns are characteristic of depression, schizophrenia, and other mental disorders and are thought to play a role in the etiology and course of these disorders. As Berger (1970) has put it: "One thing is sure, regardless of what functions the REM or NREM stages may serve, we must sleep in order to stay sane" (p. 70).

are unfavorable, the struggle for subsistence may take virtually all the individual's time and effort.

2. *Sleep.* Jouvet has estimated that:

"At sixty years of age a man has spent more than 20 years in sleep. Fifteen of these years are passed in the subjective emptiness of dreamless

sleep, and about five in the imaginary and prodigiously rich life of dream activity. We thus spend more than a third of our life unconscious of the universe which surrounds us" (1967, p. 105).

From the research findings summarized on page 68 it is apparent that both the amount and the kinds of sleep one gets are important. Laboratory studies have shown that with prolonged deprivation of sleep the individual becomes uneven in his adaptive responses—he may respond accurately to stimulation at one moment but miss it completely the next. This may explain some highway crashes in which people fail to respond to signs or other visual cues; what apparently happens is described as "microsleep" when for a split second their brain waves are

body is overheating, blood vessels on the surface of the skin dilate and circulation of the blood increases, thus exposing a greater amount of the blood to the outer surfaces of the body for cooling. At the same time, activities of the sweat glands are increased, and perspiration helps to cool the surface of the body. Such homeostatic mechanisms maintain body temperature at a fairly constant 98 to 99 degrees necessary for normal functioning and survival.

The human race has shown great ingenuity in supplementing body resources for temperature control by such innovations as clothing, shelter, air conditioning, electric fans, ice water, hot drinks, and blankets. Such innovations have enabled people to survive in both very warm and

 When I'm tired I really don't do my best work. And I need a certain amount of sleep. Like, I need maybe eight hours every night, and I can manage for a while without that, but not for very long. Right now I'm really drug—I've been out the last three nights in a row, and have to get up early every morning.

those of sleep. Sleep deprivation is also associated with increased irritability and impaired judgment, as well as with a marked decline in performance on complex learning and problem-solving tasks. Prolonged and severe sleep deprivation, like severe hunger and thirst, is a painful experience; both types of deprivation have been used in extracting information and confessions from prisoners. On page 70 is a brief description of the four stages of sleep and their importance—particularly stages 1 and 4—in maintaining normal psychological functioning.

3. *Warmth and cold.* Human beings have built-in homeostatic mechanisms which enable them to adjust to variations in heat and cold up to certain limits. For example, at a signal that the

very cold geographical areas. Climate, of course, is an important factor in the popularity of some areas of our country, such as Arizona, California, Hawaii, and Florida.

Avoidance of pain and injury
Even a very young infant will withdraw from painful experiences or try to avoid objects that have brought pain or discomfort in the past. The threat or experience of pain is unpleasant and highly motivating as well as serving as a warning or indicator of bodily harm.

Pain differs from other biological drives, such as hunger and thirst, in that it is not aroused by deprivation and does not involve a cyclic pattern of occurrence and gratification but is an episodic condition of the organism that can be produced at any time by pain-inducing stimuli. Most forms of intense stimulation—such as light, sound, heat, cold, and pressure—as well as tissue inflammation and damage can produce pain. We have already noted that severe hunger, thirst, and fatigue can also be intensely painful. And certain emotions—particularly anxiety—are painful and highly motivating.

Pain-avoidance tendencies are so strong that even other needs that are necessary for survival of the individual and the species can be seriously suppressed by painful stimulation. In male dogs and cats, for example, sexual behavior can be seriously suppressed by mildly painful electric shocks; even eating can be suppressed by moderately painful shock delivered through the feet or food dish when the animal is eating (Solomon, 1964). Such suppression can be permanent, leading to fatal self-starvation.

minimal level, the individual strives to increase it; if the information input increases to the point of overloading the system, as when the individual is forced to deal with too many problems at once, he strives to decrease the input. Students who have attempted too many courses at once or who have left studying for their final exams until the last moment are well aware of the detrimental effects of information input overloading on learning and problem-solving. When such input continues over time, psychological functioning may become completely disorganized.

Similarly, lowered sensory input—in terms of a marked reduction in the quantity and variation of information input—may also have seriously detrimental effects. In a study of the psychological strains engendered when small groups are isolated from others and confined to a limited space, as in undersea stations and space capsules, Haythorn and Altman concluded:

 I could have everything I need to make me happy the majority of the time and actually get bored, go looking for excitement.

Since pain is usually produced by situations that are harmful to the organism, it is of crucial survival value in preventing bodily injury or damage. Unfortunately, even in our technologically advanced society, the basic need for avoidance of pain and injury is by no means fully met. Accidents and painful diseases, such as arthritis and cancer, affect many people. However, we can see the motivation toward ensuring safety and pain avoidance in the many safety rules and precautions that society establishes and in the search for better anesthetics, drugs, and other methods for alleviating physical pain.

Stimulation and activity

Research studies have shown that a certain level of meaningful sensory (information) input is essential for the maintenance of psychological integration. When sensory input falls below the

"People confined to dark, quiet chambers—the traditional 'solitary confinement' of the prisoner, or the sound-proof room used for training astronauts—often display bizarre stress and anxiety symptoms, including hallucinations, delusions, apathy, and the fear of losing sanity. Their performance deteriorates. In fact, recent evidence suggests that important changes may actually occur in the nervous system that will persist for some time after the isolate comes back to the normal world. Men in lonely military stations have shown similar reactions, if to a lesser degree. Men simply may not be built to adapt well to a world with too little stimulus or variety" (1967, p. 19).

Here it may be pointed out that stimulus variation as well as level of stimulation may be of crucial importance for adjustment to isolation and confinement (Weybrew, 1967). This is especially true in cases where the isolation or

When incoming stimulation is greatly reduced under experimental conditions for sustained periods of time, a person's thought processes undergo some measure of disorganization. Individuals may react differently, depending on their personality makeup, but typically there is some degree of disorientation, impairment of problem-solving ability, and other symptoms of lowered integration. In addition, individuals become more receptive to information that is "fed-in"—a tendency that suggests why "brainwashing" may be effective after long periods of solitary confinement. The individual is so eager for meaningful input that he can no longer discriminate effectively in terms of the accuracy or inaccuracy of such input.

An interesting personal account of the need for meaningful imput is told by Dr. Alain Bombard, who sailed alone across the Atlantic Ocean for 65 days on a life raft to prove that shipwrecked people could survive for longer periods of time than had formerly been supposed. He subsisted solely on the food he could get from the sea. Of this period of isolation, Dr. Bombard stated, "I wanted terribly to have someone . . . who could confirm my impressions . . . . I began to feel that . . . I would be incapable of discerning between the false and the true" (1954, pp. 106–7).

Sensory "overloading" may also lead to impaired psychological functioning and lowered integration. When information comes in too fast, efficiency drops off very rapidly and the individual becomes unable to process even the usual amount of input effectively. Gottschalk, Haer, and Bates (1972)—using high-intensity sound color movies—found serious personal disorganization, similar to that found in organic brain disturbances, to result from this type of sensory input overloading.

confinement continues over an extended period of time.

Even in the less dramatic conditions of everyday life, there appears to be an optimal level of stimulation, which varies with the individual and with time. Under some conditions—as in boredom—we may strive to increase the level of stimulation by doing something different or engaging in activities that we find "exciting." On the other hand, when we feel under excessive pressure or "overloaded," we strive to reduce the level of input. Thus we may drop a course or otherwise restrict our activities. Each individual apparently develops techniques for maintaining the level of stimulation within the limits essential for his integrated functioning.

Sex

Sexual motivation is probably second only to the hunger motive in its far-reaching implications for social living. The family is based upon a sexual union as well as on enduring emotional and other ties. And sex is a dominant theme in much of our music, art, drama, and literature.

Although the meaning and importance of sex vary greatly from one person to another, sexual tensions, fantasies, and experiences, as well as problems centering around sexual gratification, are usually important facets of most people's lives in our society. Depending on one's attitude toward his sexuality and the part he assigns it in his overall life plan, it can be an important channel for self-actualization and intimacy or a source of anxiety and self-devaluation.

Although the sex drive has a hormonal basis and stimulation of the genitals is innately pleasurable, the strength of the sex drive clearly depends upon the individual's experience. For example, the girl who is indoctrinated with the view that sex is evil and dirty may develop little sexual motivation and may even find sexual intercourse unpleasant or repugnant. As a consequence of differing cultural viewpoints and individual life experiences, there are widespread differences in the strength and perceived significance of the sex drive among adolescents and young adults. Approved patterns of sexual gratification also vary considerably from one society to another although, interestingly, incest is forbidden by all major social groups. In our own society, sexual codes seem to be becoming more liberalized. We shall deal with this trend and other aspects of sexual adjustment in a later chapter.

Now, as we turn to a consideration of psychological motives, it may be pointed out that in general our biological motives tend to foster uniformities in human behavior. Although the expression of hunger, sex, and other biological motives is influenced by differing patterns of socialization, our biological motives do not, in general, lead to the marked variations that distinguish the members of one culture from members of another.

Psychological needs

Despite the almost unlimited differences in motive patterns that we can develop, there seems to be a common core of psychological needs which must be met for normal development and func-

ing sights, sounds, tastes, and feel of objects around him. As mothers are quick to testify, as soon as the infant is mobile, he is "all over the house" and "gets into everything."

Since a child's curiosity may be positively or negatively reinforced, it is not surprising that there are wide differences among adults in the strength of this motive and the ways it is met. In general, however, human beings are inherently curious and strive to understand and to gain a coherent picture of the world. Such a picture is necessary for evaluating new situations and anticipating the outcome of our actions. Unless we can find order and predictability in our environment, we cannot respond effectively to it.

Our striving to achieve an orderly and coher-

 There is nothing that makes me feel as good as dancing. If I know I'm going out dancing tonight on a date, I get so *excited*. My body gets—like two days before, my body stores up this energy, and I can feel it, like, I can't do anything. And about five hours before the dance I start running around and saying, 'I can't wait! I can't wait!' And then when I start dancing, I could go on forever—forever!

tioning. These needs appear to represent a common psychological substratum comparable to our basic biological needs.

Although we shall deal with these psychological needs separately, they are by no means distinct from each other. Our need for love cannot be entirely separated from our needs for security, worth, and meaning. We are dealing with a complex spectrum of interrelated psychological requirements which operate together in varying combinations.

Curiosity: the need for understanding, order, predictability

An early and unmistakable characteristic of the healthy infant is his preoccupation with explor-

ent picture of our world is shown in our dislike of ambiguity, lack of structuring, chaos, or events which seem beyond our understanding and which place us at the mercy of alien forces. Even the most primitive peoples develop explanations for lightning, thunder, death, and other events which they do not understand. Accurate or not, such explanations provide order and meaning and a sense of potential prediction and control. Modern science is simply a more sophisticated attempt to meet the same need.

Our striving for understanding, order, and predictability is not only evident in our curiosity about ourselves and our world but also in our curiosity about the universe and other life which might exist in it. This striving is also apparent in

Many species of animals show a possessiveness about specific areas of land which has been called "territoriality." Early in the spring, for example, a male robin establishes an area for receiving his mate and will fight other males who try to enter this area. Lions stake out certain hunting grounds and fight off intruders. Little research has been done on territoriality in humans, but attachment to homeland has always been a strong motivating force—as has ownership of property and home. Throughout history, nations, groups, and individuals have often fought to maintain their "territorial rights." In his book *Culture Against Man,* anthropologist Jules Henry (1963) makes a strong case for territoriality as a basic motive for humans as well as many other animals.

However, Ashley Montagu (1968) has pointed out that whereas some peoples are addicted to their territories and jealously defend their boundaries, others, like the Eskimo, show no sense of territorial rights and welcome anyone who chooses to settle among them. Other tribal groups peacefully adapt themselves to those who encroach on their lands or move elsewhere. And still other groups appear to have little difficulty in giving up their homelands for other lands more favorable to their purposes. In short, some peoples are territorially minded and others are not; apparently learning rather than biological tendencies plays the key role in determining how people come to think and feel about their homeland.

 I don't ever remember being told that I wasn't a good person, or that I was worthless, or anything bad like that, or anything down that I can remember. What I do remember is that Mother did everything for us, to be sure that we didn't goof up. And as far as I know, that's the only thing I know of that was ongoing in my life that was a downer, or that made me into this downer person that I was, and that I still fight against.

our development of inner reality and ethical controls and in our tendency to maintain the stability of our frame of reference. When we experience cognitive dissonance—a discrepancy between our existing assumptions and new information—we remain uncomfortable until we somehow manage to reconcile the difference and to reestablish an orderly and coherent view of things. One can well imagine the consternation we would experience if we were to walk bareheaded in the rain and not get wet, until we were able to work out some meaningful explanation for it. Trying to get along with contradictory pictures of our world would be like trying to drive on a highway with incompatible pictures of oncoming traffic.

To say that we strive for order and meaning in our world does not mean that we always act rationally. But curiously enough, we strive to prove to ourselves and others that our actions are rational. As Fromm has pointed out: "However unreasonable or immoral an action may be, man has an insuperable urge to rationalize it—that is, to prove to himself and to others that his action is determined by reason, common sense, or at least conventional morality" (1955, p. 65). To face the fact that one's behavior may be irrational arouses anxiety, for it implies a lack of

order and dependability in oneself, comparable to what one would experience in a world lacking in order and stability.

Adequacy, competence, security

Each of us needs to feel basically capable of dealing with our problems. When we see our resources as inadequate for coping with a stressful situation, we tend to become anxious and disorganized, for we anticipate failure and painful consequences. This pattern is dramatically illustrated in the disorganization that occurs in panic reactions, but felt inadequacy in any situation can interfere with integrated, effective behavior.

Feelings of adequacy are heavily dependent upon the development of competencies for dealing with life's problems—in fact, adequacy and competence appear to be opposite sides of the same coin. White (1959) has pointed out that strivings for competence are evident even in the early playful investigatory behavior of children. Through exploration, "reality testing," and play, the child tries out different kinds of transactions with the environment and practices many basic skills. Later, these early foundations of knowledge and competence are greatly expanded by the processes of formal education. In a broad sense, it would appear that our strivings toward competence are part of our human tendency to grow toward autonomy, independence, and self-direction.

The need for security develops with and is closely related to our need for adequacy. In a general sense, security is assurance of adequacy in the future. Because we soon learn that failure to meet our needs is acutely unpleasant, we

> A lot of what I think of my achievements is based on other people's reaction. I have a feeling that I'm satisfied with what I've done, but it won't give me much personal satisfaction until I think someone else thinks it's good.

strive to establish and maintain conditions that will ensure future as well as present need gratification. Our need for security is reflected in the common preference for jobs with tenure, in social security legislation, in insurance against disability and other contingencies, and in the establishment and maintenance of law and order. A deep and pervasive sense of insecurity is likely to lead to fearfulness and apprehension and failure to participate fully in life.

The more adequate we feel, the less aware we are of our need for security. Thus the person who feels confident of his powers may value the exploration of unfamiliar paths—leaving the safe security of the known to look for richer experiences and more fulfilling ways of life. On the other hand, the more inadequate we feel, the more need we feel for security and the more we cling to the known and familiar. Undoubtedly many people continue in an uncongenial job because the challenge of starting anew is too frightening.

Love, belonging, approval

"Love alone is capable of uniting living beings in such a way as to complete and fulfill them, for it alone takes them and joins them by what is deepest in themselves" (Pierre Teilhard de Chardin, 1961, p. 265).

Both loving and being loved appear to be crucial for healthy functioning and normal personality development. Human beings appear to need and strive to achieve warm, loving relationships with others and suffer from loneliness and a sense of deficit when such relationships are lacking. The longing for intimacy with others remains with us throughout our lives, and separation from or loss of loved ones usually presents a difficult adjustment problem.

Often the need for love and affiliation is thought of simply as a need to receive love and affection from others, but our need to love is fully as great. We need to relate to and care about other people if we are to grow and function properly as human beings. Christianity and other great religions see such an outgoing love as basic to human fulfillment. Although we ordinarily meet our needs for love in marriage, family, and other intimate relationships, we are capable of "brotherly love" which goes beyond the love of family and particular individuals to a basic orientation of concern for all people. Individuals who lack such "psychological roots" often feel alienated from the mainstream of humanity—somewhat like strangers in a foreign land.

The growing infant is completely dependent on assistance from others. As we have seen, he soon learns that such assistance may be tied to approval—that socially approved behavior is rewarded, while socially disapproved behavior is punished. At first, this pattern involves only the family group, but with time it becomes necessary to be accepted and approved by others in order to meet many of his physical and psychological needs. So the individual learns to strive

> Sometimes I set up standards for myself that are really too high, but I really feel like I have to meet those. Like even if it's just cleaning this house, I feel like it has to be done a certain way, so it looks a certain way—I have an image.

for positive regard from other persons who play an important role in his life, and he strives to become and remain an approved member of the social groups with which he identifies himself.

Our need for social belonging (affiliation) and approval was well brought out many years ago by William James:

"No more fiendish punishment could be devised . . . than that one should be turned loose in society and remain absolutely unnoticed by all the members thereof. If no one turned around when we entered, answered when we spoke, or minded what we did, but if every person we met 'cut us dead,' and acted as if we were non-existing things, a kind of rage and impotent despair would ere long well up in us, from which the cruelest bodily tortures would be a relief . . ." (1890, pp. 293–294).

to place a high value on the situations and activities that bring us evidence of our own worth.

Self-esteem has its early grounding in parental affirmation of our worth and in our mastery of early developmental tasks; it receives continued nourishment from the development of new competencies and from achievement in areas that we think are important. Being a football star or earning a Phi Beta Kappa key or simply doing a competent job in our studies can contribute to our self-esteem. We also tend to depend for continuing confirmation of our worth on others' esteem for us. Most of us try to ensure such esteem by making ourselves attractive to others, conforming to their norms, and seeking acceptance in groups we respect. The esteem of the people most important to us is

 The problem of meaninglessness seems like the most important. I think most people lead shallow lives and won't admit it to themselves. There is no use to the luxuries that technology provides if people do not feel fulfilled.

Failure to gain interpersonal and group acceptance and the loneliness that results are particularly difficult and painful problems in the group-conscious society in which we live. Especially is this true for the person who depends heavily upon the regard of others as a basis for his feelings of self-identity and worth.

Self-esteem and worth

As we learn society's values and standards concerning education, physical appearance, economic status, and moral behavior, we begin to apply these standards in evaluating ourselves. We come to need not only other people's approval, but our own approval of ourselves. Only as we measure up to the standards we have accepted do we feel good about ourselves and worthy of the respect of others. If we see ourselves as falling short, we tend to feel unworthy, devaluated, and anxious. Thus we come

especially crucial. It is difficult to maintain a conviction of our own worth when those we admire look down on us.

As might be expected, our feelings of self-esteem and worth are closely linked to our feelings of adequacy and competence. It is difficult if not impossible to maintain feelings of self-esteem and worth if one feels incompetent and inadequate. Self-esteem and worth also seem to be linked to self-identity. Sargent has reported on the loss of self-identity in prison and its consequences in terms of self-esteem, worth, and adequacy.

"The prisoners increasingly depend on authority, become susceptible to suggestion, tend toward magical thinking, and become more anxious and impulsive. In some cases the symptoms reach psychotic proportions" (*Science News,* June 16, 1973, p. 390).

To guard against such loss of self-identity, Sargent—a former Federal Bureau of Prisons psy-

chiatrist—suggests a number of measures including addressing prisoners by their names and not by numbers.

Values, meaning, hope

We have emphasized the need for values as a guide to decision making and for providing meaning to human existence—for answering the crucial question "Why?" In Chapter 17 we shall deal with the quest for values and meaning in some detail. Suffice to reiterate here their central importance to our very existence. As Cantril has put it:

"In the midst of the probabilities and uncertainties that surround them, people want some anchoring points, some certainties, some faith that will serve either as a beacon light to guide them or as a balm to assuage them during the inevitable frustrations and anxieties that living engenders" (1967, p. 17).

Closely related to and guided by his values are the individual's goals and plans. For we live in the future as well as in the present and past; our plans—and our hope of fulfilling them—are the focus not only of our dreams but of much of our present behavior. Young adults in our society—particularly those in urban ghettos—who become alienated and apathetic and "drop out" often do so not because of lack of desire but because of feelings of hopelessness about achieving anything worthwhile.

In more extreme situations, reports of prisoner-of-war camps tell of cases in which prisoners who had lost hope simply pulled their blankets over their heads and waited for death to come (Nardini, 1952; *U.S. News & World Report*, April 16, 1973). Lazarus (1966) has reported that shipwreck victims who lose hope may die after a few days even though physiologically they could have survived many days longer.

Similarly, in a report published by the U.S. Department of Health, Education, and Welfare (1967), it was found that the great majority of patients hospitalized for physical illness had experienced a severe psychological disturbance shortly before they became ill; and the feelings associated with this psychological disturbance were not anxiety, fear, or anger—the emotions commonly considered to be associated with physical upset and illness—but rather feelings of helplessness and hopelessness.

Surprisingly, there has been little research on the need for goals and for hope. But like the need for love, we can infer such needs from observations of the typical results when people are "planless" or lack hope. Plans and hope appear to act as catalysts: in their presence energy is mobilized, effort is undertaken and coordinated, skills are developed and used, and satisfactions are achieved. Without them, life is meaningless and we drift; and neither we nor our society gain satisfaction from our existence.

Forms of actualization strivings

Motivation theory, as we have seen, has long been dominated by the concept of maintenance of steady states—with the emphasis on overcoming deficits, reducing tension, and returning to a state of equilibrium. But maintenance strivings do not explain the behavior of the explorer, the scientist, the artist, the composer, or the dramatist. We strive to grow, to improve, to become more capable, to express ourselves—to actualize our potentialities and fulfill ourselves as human beings. Huxley has made this point with dramatic clarity:

*"Human life is a struggle—against frustration, ignorance, suffering, evil, the maddening inertia of things in general; but it is also a struggle for something . . . . And fulfillment seems to describe better than any other single word the positive side of human development and human evolution—the realization of inherent capacities by the individual and of new possibilities by the race; the satisfaction of needs, spiritual as well as material; the emergence of new qualities of experi-*ence to be enjoyed; the building of personalities" (1953, pp. 162–163).

Our actualization strivings, like our maintenance strivings, seem to be initiated from within. They "come naturally" without having to be learned and are characteristic of human beings in widely differing cultures. Yet prevalent as this growth motivation is, growth is not universal. The person who must struggle hard for mere survival may have little time or energy left for personal growth; the neurotic is too busy defending himself to be free to grow. Because we are creatures of choice rather than instinct, we can choose stagnation instead of growth.

Our strivings toward actualization take different forms depending upon our abilities, values, and life situations. On a simple level, we see attempts at self-enhancement in the use of cosmetics and other ornamentation to make oneself attractive; on a more complex level, fulfillment strivings may take the form of learning new skills, being a good friend, spouse, or parent, or writing poetry—any activity that contributes to personal growth or that adds meaning and richness to one's life.

We have described our needs for meaning, love, and relatedness as maintenance needs, since they must be met for normal growth and functioning. However, they are also forms of actualization striving, since much of our actualization takes place as we broaden our scope of knowledge, form loving relationships with others, and expand our relatedness to our world.

Finding increased satisfactions

Our capacity to see value in our experiences results in our coming to expect a certain level of satisfaction from everything we do. When we go out to dinner, we expect the food to meet certain standards in quality and variety. When we go to a movie, we expect it to meet certain standards of plot, character portrayal, and photography. The norms that we use in evaluating new experiences as "worthwhile" or "disappointing" are based on our standards and expectations. We also use such standards in deciding which new experiences to choose and which ones to avoid. We plan a trip because we expect certain values from it. We avoid a party, a television program, or a lecture if we think it will not make a sufficient return in value received on our investment of time and participation.

But this is not all. We seem to suffer from what the poets call "divine discontent." What was perfectly satisfying yesterday seems a little flat today, and we are constantly trying to improve the quality of our experience. We wait in line to see the movie that the critics have given a top rating, watch championship football games, read interesting new novels, and attend outstanding art exhibits. The increased satisfaction that we find in any new experience becomes a part of our new standard for judging the value of subsequent experiences.

As our standards become higher, increments of satisfaction may become increasingly hard to achieve and may entail struggle and sacrifice. Yet one of our most persistent urges seems to be to build, to improve, to go beyond previous achievements and understandings, to reach just a little higher and farther than we did before.

Developing and using potentials

This may take the form of developing new competencies and improving old ones, and of expressing our capabilities in creative and constructive ways. Even though a person does not have special talents in athletics, art, writing, or other areas, he may find it highly fulfilling to develop and use the potentials he does have; where a person does have special talents, it may be very frustrating to be denied the opportunity for their development and expression.

Increasing our information and understanding about ourselves and our world are other ways in which our potentials may be fulfilled. We listen and read to find out what is going on and what has gone on and what others have thought about it. We try to broaden our viewpoint, to get a more complete picture, to expand our basic assumptions and generalizations about what is true, what is possible, and what is important—our assumptions concerning reality, possibility, and value. We may also try to improve our understanding by redefining and reorganizing the ideas and assumptions we already

have and trying to reconcile contradictory elements.

Still further, developing and using our potentials may be accomplished by enhancing our personal attractiveness, striving toward more satisfying interpersonal relationships, becoming a more authentic person, and trying out new ways of "being in the world."

Building rich linkages with the world

One of the ways we seek to grow is through the associations we form with our world, and especially with other people. We have a deep capacity for caring for others, for protecting, encouraging, and teaching others, and for helping *them* grow and find meaning and satisfaction in their lives. Unless we use this capacity we feel incomplete, unsatisfied. This is a particularly

All my life I've had a great lack of motivation. I've never known what I wanted to be, or what I wanted to do. When I was in school it worried me, but I didn't know any other way to be. I really tried to think of something—like even different specific things I might want to do for a living. But nothing, there really wasn't anything. Now, I know now that there was something that I wanted to do, but it was something I couldn't admit to myself. I wanted to paint, and that was just too great a thing for poor little me to be able to do, and it took me 'til I was an adult to be able to figure out that this thing that had been in the super back of my head since I was little was what I eventually wound up doing.

I see the greatest source of happiness in relationships with others—serving them at real points of need—discovering their 'growing edge' and mine at these points. Often this means listening—a growing point for me in a creative way.

human characteristic, and caring deeply for something outside oneself is one of the most gratifying and self-fulfilling of human experiences.

Many of the experiences we value most highly are those we have shared with others close to us. Sharing a crisis or joy or even just an hour of silence with those dear to us is an enriching thing that broadens our base of self. We treasure our family anecdotes, triumphs, and traditions. Louise Rich, in her autobiographical novel, *Happy the Land,* said:

"Of Plymouth Rock, I may tell my children: 'This is where the Pilgrims landed.' Of the rock by the side of the road, halfway up Wangan Hill, I say 'Right here is where your father found the little deer that time'" (1946, p. 19).

Throughout our lives we build landmarks of this kind which enrich our lives and add to their meaning and value by increasing our sense of relatedness to the world around us.

Self-centeredness or narrow concern with self leads to a restriction of energy and an impoverishment of meaning in one's life. By contrast, the person who can lose himself in a "cause" and feel himself part of a movement that will someday enrich life for many other people may experience exhilaration and a deep sense of fulfillment even though the gains he works for do not come to him personally or even materialize during his lifetime.

Becoming a person

Closely allied with the striving to develop one's potentials—but not quite the same thing—is the striving to become a person: to achieve a clear-cut sense of one's identity and to be one's "real self." As Rogers has put it:

"As I follow the experience of many clients in the therapeutic relationship which we endeavor to create for them, it seems to me that each one has the same problem. Below the level of the problem situation about which the individual is complaining—behind the trouble with studies, or wife, or employer, or with his own uncontrollable or bizarre behavior, or with his frightening feelings lies one central search. It seems to me that at bottom each person is asking: 'Who am I, really? How can I get in touch with this real self, underlying all my surface behavior? How can I become myself?'" (1958, pp. 9–10)

The Danish philosopher Kierkegaard described this search for self more than a century

are not. Nor are they independent of the social field in which they develop and are expressed.

In this section we will briefly examine: (1) the influence of motives on other psychological processes, (2) the extent to which we are aware of our motives, (3) the concept of a hierarchy of motives, and (4) the relation of motive patterns to life styles.

Motivational selectivity

Just as a person's various motives are related to each other, so his motivational processes are interrelated with other ongoing psychological functions. Thus his motives influence what he attends to, the way he perceives it, what he

 I'm proud of my poems, because some of them are pretty good. I'm proud of that. And I like myself when I'm writing my poetry. One thing I like when I'm doing that—first of all it sort of hits me and I'll get all this energy, and it's like a waterfall, it just comes tumbling out. When I start writing it comes out of me so *big*, and then I have to put it down in words on the paper. I like that.

ago. He pointed out that the most common despair is in being unwilling to be one's self, but that the deepest form of despair is choosing to be other than one's self.

Becoming a person seems to be bound up with a striving toward wholeness, toward integration and self-direction.

Motive patterns and behavior

We have been talking about various motives as if they were independent of each other and of other psychological processes, but indeed they

learns and remembers and what he forgets, his reasoning and related thought processes, and his fantasies and dreams.

1. *Attention and perception.* Attention and perception are active processes by means of which we select, organize, and give meaning to the information we receive from both external and internal sources. Our attention and perception may be influenced in several important ways by the motive states which predominate at the moment.

First, we are more sensitive to information related to our motives. A student scanning a bibliography to find studies on role expectations in marriage would be selectively sensitive to titles related to this subject but would tend to ignore those dealing with other topics. On a more dramatic level, a man lost in the desert and suffering from intense thirst would be searching for some indication of water and probably would not notice the beauty of the sunset. In such situations the stimuli that are relevant to the active motive tend to stand out, while irrelevant stimuli tend to fade into the background. People also pay more attention to information about themselves and to information they know they will have to act on later (de Sola Pool & Kessler, 1965). This tendency of an organism to single out what it considers most relevant to its purposes is called *selective vigilance.*

Second, we try to screen out information that would make us uncomfortable. Thus we tend to see only the aspects of a situation that are consistent with our expectations, assumptions, and wishes. Proud parents may selectively perceive the desirable traits of their children while tending not to recognize undesirable ones; or they may use the same process in evaluating themselves. This form of selectivity, in which one actively resists certain perceptions, is referred to as *perceptual defense.*

Third, we tend to perceive things as we would like them to be rather than as they are. It has been shown, for example, that many people tend to perceive their leaders as noble and strong—not so much on the basis of their actual qualities but because their own security and future depend upon having leaders with such qualities. When we encounter information that does not fit in with what we have already accepted, our need for an orderly, meaningful, predictable view of the world evidently leads us to try to change it in such a way as to produce greater consistency.

2. *Thinking and learning.* As much as we prize our ability to reason and need it for solving problems, it is all too easily subverted to a justification of what we want to do or to believe. The slogan "There are no atheists in foxholes," which became famous in World War II, is not so much a proof of God's existence as evidence of the force of the need for safety, which believing helps us to satisfy. It is notoriously difficult to think objectively about a situation when our own

needs and purposes are directly involved. A marriage counselor can be more objective about the problems of other couples than he can about his own marital problems; a mother can reason more objectively about the child-rearing problems of other mothers than she can about her own. When evidence first began to appear on the relation of smoking to lung cancer, heavy smokers, as a group, were slower to accept it and more ready to argue that a causal relation had not yet been proved.

Learning, too, subserves our motivational requirements. It is hard and uninteresting to learn things that appear unrelated to our key motives, whereas we willingly devote time and energy to learning things that we see as important and useful to us. As our effort "pays off" and we begin to experience the anticipated satisfaction from learning, our incentive for further similar learning is increased. Where learning requires changing what we have already learned rather than simply acquiring new information, motivation also plays an important role. For we tend to resist learning new information contradictory to our existing assumptions, particularly when these assumptions are perceived as central to our needs and purposes. A white-skinned individual who believes that dark-skinned peoples are genetically inferior may find it very difficult to give up his belief despite scientific evidence to the contrary, particularly if his belief helps to bolster his own feelings of adequacy and worth. Thus what we learn, how rapidly, and how much are all influenced by our motivation.

3. *Remembering and forgetting.* Psychoanalytic models of forgetting have emphasized the relationship between unpleasantness of a memory and inability to recall it. And numerous experiments have shown that pleasant memories—particularly memories favorable to the individual's self-concept—are more amenable to recall than unpleasant ones. Incidents which reflect adversely upon the adequacy and worth of the self are less likely to be remembered.

In more dramatic form, the effect of motives on recall can be seen in cases of psychogenic amnesia where the individual is unable to recall large segments of his experience which have become intolerable to him. In such cases, the material has not been forgotten but is simply inaccessible to recall; it may be readily recalled under hypnosis or such drugs as sodium pentothal. Or it may be spontaneously recalled at a later date after the traumatic effects have "cooled off."

4. *Fantasy and dreams.* The chains of thoughts and images which occur when we are not busy responding to current demands may also reflect what we are most concerned about. According to Frankl (1959), for example, fantasies of starving prisoners of war in German concentration camps in World War II most often were of things like bread, cake, cigarettes, and warm baths. Children who live in orphanages commonly dream—both in daydreams and dur-

other important motive, we are likely to react with intense negative emotions typically involving a combination of fear, anxiety, and anger. On the other hand, if the situation is perceived as enhancing our self-esteem or fostering the meeting of other key motives, it is likely to be accompanied by positive feelings and emotions.

In intimate interpersonal relationships, our motives usually play a key role in determining the feelings and emotions we experience; and our feelings and emotions, in turn, may have a marked effect on the success or failure of the relationship. Thus an awareness of our own motives as well as those of significant others is often influential in determining the course of such relationships.

Of course, thinking and other psychological

 I do daydream or fantasize, about a number of different things—about sex, about being successful, more than anything else. Maybe I'll fantasy that I'm performing on a stage somewhere. In one way it has some planning in it, and in another way it doesn't. Like when I was into acting, there was a general plan, because that was what I was doing, toward a goal I wanted to reach.

ing sleep—about being adopted into a happy family.

We have probably all experienced both fantasies and dreams concerning sexual activities, revenge, self-enhancement, and other matters in which we could readily see the influence of motivational factors. In psychotherapy, therapists often use the patient's dreams in an attempt to understand his motives and problems better.

5. *Feelings and emotions.* How we perceive a situation—its significance in terms of our motives—directly influences the feelings and emotions which may be aroused.

If the situation is perceived as a threat to our safety, self-esteem, love relationship, or any

processes are influenced by factors other than motivation, including our assumptions concerning reality, value, and possibility. In addition, our cognitive processes may lead to changes in our motives, particularly when feedback concerning the achievement of given motives turns out to be disappointing and unsatisfying. Often we must trim our motivational sails in keeping with new information.

To what extent are we aware of our motives?

Although writers and dramatists have long portrayed the influence of unconscious motives— motives of which we are unaware—on our be-

A lot of times I do things, then I ask myself why I did it, but I can't answer myself.

I am good at understanding other people, but I find it very hard to figure out my own motives.

Oftentimes others understand me better than I do myself. And that for me is one good reason for trying to learn more about my own motives.

havior, Sigmund Freud was the first to study this phenomenon systematically. He noted that unconscious motives may express themselves in several forms of behavior: (1) dreams, in which desires unknown to the dreamer may appear, (2) slips of the tongue and "forgetting" names or appointments that we do not want to remember, and (3) certain neurotic reactions, as when the individual feels compelled to wash his hands many times during the day but is unaware of why he feels this compulsion. Freud concluded that such motives were not admitted to consciousness because they were unacceptable to the individual. He saw a key goal of psychoanalysis as helping the individual to identify and learn to accept this unconscious part of himself.

Although there is still considerable controversy among psychologists concerning the nature and importance of unconscious processes in human behavior, there is abundant evidence that we are often unaware or only partially aware of the motives underlying our behavior. Sometimes we are unaware of even key motives, and others may be able to infer our motives more accurately from observing our behavior than we can from introspection. Thus it may be apparent to others—but not to us—that we continually contrive to lean on someone else, or maneuver to keep people from getting too close to us, or constantly try to build ourselves up by belittling other people. Similarly, we may show off, wear expensive clothes, even marry for

reasons which are unclear to us. Of course, we may think of good reasons to justify our behavior, but these may be only partially accurate, or they may not be the real reasons at all.

It would appear that awareness of one's motives varies considerably from one behavior pattern to another and from person to person. Most of us are probably puzzled at one time or another by some of the things we do and think, while feeling quite certain about our motives in other cases. Usually individuals who are seriously maladjusted have only a fragmentary understanding of their motivation.

Hierarchy of motives

Maslow (1971) suggested that our needs arrange themselves in a hierarchy from the basic biological needs to the need for self-fulfillment or actualization, which represents the higher development of the human personality. With slight modification for our present purposes, Maslow's hierarchy may be envisaged as involving five levels of needs:

1. *Physiological needs*—basic bodily needs including the needs for food, sleep, stimulation, and activity.

2. *Safety needs*—needs for protection from bodily harm or injury and for security from threat.

Just as social forces play an important role in shaping our overall development, so we find them shaping and channeling our motives in important ways. Social standards and rules, pressures and demands, limitations and opportunities—as well as the needs of significant others—all have an effect on our motive patterns. Social forces facilitate some motives and inhibit others. Traditional sexual mores, for example, tend to inhibit the gratification of our sexual needs. In addition, social forces prescribe the means which are considered acceptable or unacceptable for meeting given needs.

Since social conditions and standards vary markedly from one group to another, the goals that are highly valued in one group may have little or no value in another. Charms to protect the individual from witchcraft would be considered of little value in our society; the monetary goals with which most Americans are preoccupied would inspire little effort among the members of a monastic order; in some societies the members try to avoid rather than to seek leadership.

Some cultures offer rich opportunities for psychological satisfactions and the fulfillment of potentialities. Others are limiting, repressive, and rigid. Some provide fulfillment opportunities for certain groups but not others—the leaders but not the followers, the wealthy but not the poor, the men but not the women. But in any group, the goals which the individual seeks and his means for trying to achieve them depend on the opportunities, rules, and standards provided by the group.

 Survival! Right now I feel that I'm just keeping my head above water and getting along. Maybe after things straighten out a little in my life I can worry about where the joy has gone.

3. *Love and belongingness needs*—including needs for acceptance, warmth, affection, and approval.

4. *Esteem needs*—including needs for adequacy, worth, status, and self-respect.

5. *Self-actualization (fulfillment) needs*—needs for personal growth and the realization of potentialities.

Relative strength under deprivation

According to Maslow's formulation, the lowest level of unmet need is ordinarily the one that is prepotent—the one that commands the individual's attention and efforts. For example, unless the needs for food and safety are reasonably well met, behavior will be dominated by these needs. With their gratification, however, the individual is free to devote his energies to meeting his needs on higher levels. This concept of a built-in prepotency of needs is supported by observations of behavior in extreme situations. Both in the Nazi concentration camps and in the Japanese prisoner-of-war camps in World War II, it was a common pattern for prisoners subjected to prolonged deprivation and torture to lower their moral standards, take food from each other, and in other ways surrender the loyalties and values they had held under more normal conditions (Bettelheim, 1943; Nardini, 1952). Similar patterns, although involving a far lower percentage of American POWs, were observed in the Korean War; but in the war in Vietnam, these patterns occurred very rarely—apparently in part because the POWs were better educated, had been briefed in the military Code of Conduct, and had had prior training which helped to prepare the men for what to expect in the event of capture by the enemy (*U.S. News & World Report,* April 16, 1973, pp. 39–40).

While under conditions of extreme deprivation and/or torture many individuals are likely to sacrifice their higher-level actualization needs to meet their more basic needs for personal safety and survival, this pattern does not always hold—particularly in the case of people who believe in their cause. Many creative people have pursued the development and expression of their special talents despite great physical handicaps and social ridicule. Social reformers have continued their struggles despite harassment, jail sentences, and other punishment and deprivation. In all likelihood, some of the few POWs who did collaborate with the North Vietnamese did so out of sincere conviction that the United States was wrong and had the courage to back up their convictions. Every age has had its heroes and martyrs who remained faithful to their principles and beliefs despite social ostracism, physical deprivation, torture, and often certain death. Through learning and experience, our beliefs, values, and self-esteem may become more important to us than our needs for social approval and security or even our need for safety. The extent to which safety and physiological needs dominate our behavior even under extreme conditions is an individual matter.

Deficiency vs. growth motivation

Maslow has emphasized the distinction between *deficiency* and *growth* motivation. Behavior motivated primarily by maintenance needs—hunger, safety, social approval, and so on—is deficiency motivated; that is, it is motivated by the lack of something the individual needs for stability—as compared with behavior like learning to sing or developing proficiency in athletics, which is aimed at increasing one's long-term capabilities. It is the gratification of maintenance needs that releases the individual from domination by them and frees him for self-actualization.

People who remain dominated by maintenance strivings despite adequate resources or who have not found anything else worth striving for tend to be maladjusted and unhappy. Maslow (1954) has summarized it this way: "I should say simply that a healthy man is primarily motivated by his needs to develop and actualize his fullest potentialities and capacities. If a man has any other basic needs in any active, chronic sense, he is simply an unhealthy man." In a comparison of deficiency-motivated with growth-motivated people, Maslow (1954, 1971), discovered that the latter showed more efficient perception of reality and more comfortable relations with it; could tolerate uncertainty better; were more spontaneous and creative; were more accepting of themselves and others; were more problem-centered and less ego-centered; had deeper than average relationships with other people; had a philosophical, unhostile sense of humor; and felt kinship with and concern for all humanity.

Here the conclusions expressed by Helson appear particularly relevant:

"Men who have been creative, whether in science, the arts, literature, politics, or industry, have often been excited to a far greater degree by ideas than by food, sex, and sleep. The satisfaction of so-called basic needs is necessary but not sufficient for a full and truly satisfying life. . . . Let us therefore get on with [the experimental study of] those sources of motivation, which are responsible for man's unique position among all living things" (1966, p. 179).

Only as lower-level needs receive some minimum level of gratification are higher-level needs likely to become dominant; but only through efforts to meet higher-level needs can the individual actualize his potentialities as a human being.

Motive patterns and life style

As we have seen, the developing self-structure of each individual leads to a fairly consistent life style which others recognize as characteristic of him and which makes his behavior relatively predictable from one situation to another.

Key motives in our lives

Particularly important in determining an individual's life style are his *key motives*—the motives of greatest importance to him. For some persons, such key motives may focus around love and belonging; for others around social approval and security; for others around competence and actualization; and for still others around achievement and power. Since our key motives tend to be relatively enduring, they contribute to the continuity and consistency of our behavior.

Implicit in the individual's key motives is his *level of aspiration*—the difficulty of attainment of the goals which he strives for in relation to his personal resources and environmental opportunities and limitations. Well-adjusted persons generally have a reasonably accurate picture of themselves and their world and strive toward relatively realistic goals, while maladjusted persons tend to set their goals too low or too high in relation to their own personal resources and the limitations and opportunities presented by their environment. We commented on this point in Chapter 3 and need not pursue it here.

Motive change over time

Although we do tend to show a relatively consistent pattern of motives, this pattern is subject to change over time. On a simple level we can see this in the short-term changes in our physiological needs and goals, for example, our need for food. With deprivation, the need increases; with satiation, it is replaced by other needs and goals. While a periodic rhythm is not apparent on the psychological level, the achievement of given goals usually leads to their replacement by others. This is often dramatically illustrated when we achieve some long-sought goal in life, such as college graduation or a promotion at work, only to find that instead of feeling contentment we become aware of new goals which have replaced the old ones now attained.

There are also predictable changes in motive patterns as we go through life. The key motives of a child are not those of an adult. Changes in the environment and in our life situation may lead to modification of our motive pattern. For example, a college sophomore who becomes a parent may well show considerable shift in motives and behavior.

A classic example of changed motives with

DEVELOPMENT OF NEW MOTIVES

In our rapidly changing society, it seems inevitable that most of us will experience some changes in our motive patterns. The following are illustrative of the conditions which appear to foster the development of new motives (McClelland, 1965).

1. The individual has reason, in advance, to believe that he can, will, or should develop the motive.

2. The individual perceives that developing the motive is consistent with the demands of reality (and reason).

3. The individual can conceptualize the motive clearly and relate it to events in his everyday life.

4. The individual can perceive and experience the new motive as an improvement in his self-image.

5. The individual feels warmly and honestly supported and respected by others as a person capable of directing his own future behavior.

Although these generalizations are based upon motive changes in an educational setting, they would appear to be applicable to our broader life setting as well.

new environmental demands is that of young King Henry of England, as portrayed by Shakespeare in *Henry V.* Before he became king, he had been a fun-loving young man without apparent interest in anything but the next riotous party. After he became king, he developed a deep concern for the welfare of his country and disciplined himself for responsible service to it. Less dramatic but equally basic changes in motivation may occur in any one of us if we see our environment making new demands on us. Similarly we may reevaluate the worth of given goals we have been avidly pursuing if changes in our environment make more attractive ones available or lead to changes in our values.

To better understand their own motives and to make motive changes in a more systematic manner, many people participate in encounter groups and other programs directed toward personal change and growth. We shall examine some of the available psychological resources for personal change and growth in Chapter 14.

 ## Summary and a look ahead

By *motivation* we mean conditions within the organism that *activate* behavior and influence its *direction.* Despite the diversity in the specific goals we seek, our behavior can be seen as directed toward the broad goals of maintenance and actualization—on both biological and psychological levels. Among our requirements for biological maintenance are visceral needs such as food, water, and sleep; avoidance of pain and injury; stimulation and activity; and sexual expression. Among our requirements for psychological maintenance are the needs for understanding, order, and predictability; adequacy, competence, and security; love, belonging, and approval; self-esteem and worth; and values, meaning, and hope. Actualization strivings include attempts to find increased satisfactions; to develop and use our potentials; to build rich linkages with our world; and to become a person.

As individuals we each function as a unit and our attention, perception, learning, and other psychological functions are all influenced by our motives—a process known as motivational selectivity. There appears to be a hierarchy of human motives, and under conditions of deprivation, maintenance needs tend to predominate over actualization needs. However, we may choose to meet higher-level needs at the expense of lower-level ones.

Often we are unaware or only partially aware of the motives underlying our behavior. It is evident that social demands and rewards influence the goals we seek and the means we use in seeking them; they encourage the development of certain motives and discourage the development of others.

Although motives change over time, the key motives in our lives are a continuing and central part of our life style.

In this chapter we have been concerned primarily with conditions that activate us and influence the direction of our strivings. In the next chapter we shall examine what happens when our strivings are blocked or when inner or outer conditions place us under stress.

5
Problems of Adjustment (Stress)

Types and Sources of Stress
Severity of Stress
Other Key Aspects of Stress

Life would be simple indeed if our needs could always be satisfied. But as we know, there are many obstacles—both environmental and internal—which interfere with gratification of our needs and complicate our strivings toward our goals. We are all buffeted by delays, lacks, failures, losses, restrictions, obligations, illnesses, conflicts, and pressures. Such events place adjustive demands or *stress* on us. They require effort and action on our part, if we are to "stand up to the elements" and meet our needs.

Most of the stress situations we encounter in everyday life are minor and relatively easy to cope with. When we feel hungry, we may stop what we are doing and get something to eat; when we feel cold we put on a sweater or coat. Such adjustive demands require adaptive action, but they produce only minor disruption within the organism—that is, they do not lead to serious disequilibrium of physiological or psychological steady states.

From time to time, however, most of us face stress situations which are difficult to cope with and result in considerable inner disruption. A serious illness requiring major surgery, a broken engagement, marital discord or divorce, the death of a loved one, flunking out of college, being arrested, financial pressures or losses, social disapproval, severe guilt feelings, and value conflicts are examples of such stressful situations. For many people, the pressures and worries of modern living are continuing sources of severe stress, exacting a cumulative toll in wear and tear on the organism. In some cases, the stress is so severe that the coping resources of the individual are overtaxed and breakdown occurs.

Stress may involve processes on a biological and/or psychological level. Pneumonia viruses produce stress on a biological level, and the basic adjustive reaction involves defenses on the biological level. Guilt, on the other hand, is stressful chiefly on the psychological level, and self-defense mechanisms are the chief means of coping with it. We may also speak of stress on group and societal levels. Thus the loss of the father or mother constitutes a stressful situation for the family; economic inflation and wars are examples of stress situations which place adjustive demands on the society as a whole as well as on the individuals and groups within it.

In our present discussion, we shall be concerned primarily with psychological-level stress as experienced by the individual, although some consideration of both biological- and social-level stress will inevitably be entailed. We shall consider: (1) the basic types of stress we encounter and some of the particular stresses that characterize our time and place in history; (2) factors influencing the severity of stress; and (3) other key aspects of stress, including its cost to the organism. Then in the next chapter, we shall deal with our reactions to stress—with the ways in which we attempt to cope with stress situations.

Types and sources of stress

Problems of adjustment can be classified as frustrations, conflicts, and pressures. Elements of all three may of course be present in the same situation, but for simplicity we will discuss them separately.

Frustration

Frustration is the result of the thwarting of a motive—either by some obstacle that blocks or impedes our progress toward a desired goal, or by the absence of an appropriate goal object. Overly restrictive parents would be a source of frustration to an adolescent who wanted to go to a school party, while a lack of water would be a source of frustration to a man lost in the desert. Frustrations may be minor and inconsequential, or they may represent serious threats to our welfare or even survival.

Sources of frustration
There are a wide range of environmental obstacles, both physical and social, which can lead to the frustration of our needs. Floods, earthquakes, fires, accidents, and the death of loved ones are major sources of frustration. Traffic congestion when we are in a hurry, advertisements that make us want things we cannot afford, red tape that prevents us from taking a desired course in college, and long years of study before we can enter a professional field are other examples of the countless frustrations that plague us in everyday life.

Personal characteristics can also keep us from getting what we want. Physical handicaps, disease, low intelligence, inadequate competencies, and lack of self-discipline are sources of frustration that result from our own limitations. Many frustrations arise out of psychological barriers in the form of reality and ethical controls. The young adult may refrain from premarital sexual relations because of fear of pregnancy or because of moral values which make such behavior unacceptable. And if reality and ethical restraints break down, self-recrimination and guilt may follow. Of course, faulty assumptions and values may lead to unnecessary frustrations.

Common frustrations in our society
In our so-called affluent society, most of us do not suffer from malnutrition, lack of medical care, inadequate opportunities for education,

and related limitations that still are realities for over half the world's people.

More prevalent among us are frustrations stemming from delays, from discrepancies between what we have and what we would like, from the loss of someone or something precious to us, from failure, guilt, discrimination, and limitations. A complete list, of course, would be endless, but a few of those frustrations that cause us special difficulty warrant mention.

1. *Delays.* In our time-conscious culture, where we feel we must make every minute count, delays are especially galling. Yet with our concentrations of population, our specialization, and our high degree of interdependence, many delays are inevitable. We cannot all get through the intersection at the same time but must take our turn. Literally and figuratively, we are continually standing in line waiting for something we would like. We cannot marry when we are physiologically ready but must wait until we have the skills we need to earn a living. Few of us can buy the new car or the house we want the moment we decide we would like it.

Many of our delays—especially those related to material possessions—are made especially difficult by the constant barrage of advertising that keeps stimulating our desires. Necessary as this aspect of modern marketing may be for creating broader markets and greater productivity, it creates a stress for those who cannot keep pace in their purchases with the desires and standards thus created. This stress is often further intensified by our tendency to ignore what we *do* have and preoccupy ourselves with the things that are still lacking.

2. *Lack of resources.* Although most of us do not lack the basic necessities of life, probably few of us are satisfied with what we have. We would like to have more money to buy and do

the things we want—perhaps to buy a more elaborate home or a newer car, or to provide freedom to travel. Many people feel that they lack adequate opportunity for realization of their potentials. There always seem to be lacks in our material resources; and, of course, these lacks are particularly stressful for the many millions of people living on incomes below the "poverty level" established by the U.S. government.

As we have noted, personal limitations can also be highly stressful in our competitive society. For example, physical handicaps which limit our attractiveness to members of the opposite sex or place serious limitations on our activities can be highly frustrating. Similarly, lack of ability to obtain passing grades in college may be severely frustrating to an ambitious student. Cottle (1972) has vividly described the case of an undergraduate student with the highest expectations who fails at his academic work, and shows how such failure and erosion of self-confidence mark him for life.

3. *Losses.* Loss of something on which we place high value is frustrating because it deprives us of a source of gratification or a resource for meeting our needs. Loss of money or time may mean we must forego a cherished dream. Loss of friendship or love may not only deprive us of satisfactions we have come to depend on but also threaten our self-esteem. As Edna St. Vincent Millay has so poignantly expressed it, "Love has gone and left me and the days are all alike . . ." (1945). The death of one's spouse—as well as a broken love relationship—is also a severe source of frustration for most people. The losses that come with aging—loss of loved ones, loss of financial independence, loss of valued status in the group, and gradual physical deterioration—are all highly frustrating.

Losses are especially frustrating because so often they are beyond our control, and once they have occurred there is nothing we can do about them. They often seem to represent the whim of a cruel and capricious fate.

4. *Failure.* Even if we did not live in a highly competitive society, we would sometimes be bound to fail in our endeavors; the competitive setting in which we operate increases the frequency of failure and frustration. No athletic team is likely to win all of the time, nor can all who have aspirations become movie or television stars or achieve high political office. For each one who succeeds, there is an inevitable crop of failures. Even when we do well in the light of our own ability, we may feel we have failed if we have not done as well as someone else. Any failure is frustrating, even though we may learn to live with and profit from it.

A special type of failure which is often highly frustrating is *guilt.* Either doing something we feel is wrong or failing to do something we feel we should can lead to self-recrimination and guilt. Guilt is a source of frustration because it thwarts our needs for feelings of self-esteem and worth; and since we have been taught that wrongdoing leads to inevitable punishment, we may also feel insecure and fear that we will somehow be punished. As in other types of

seeking they see in the adult world; yet they see no constructive alternatives or more valid goals to substitute. Emptiness, meaninglessness, and a sense of alienation are the result. If they "drop out" or just drift, this brings frustration too and is not a satisfying long-term answer. Of course, meaninglessness and despair are by no means the sole prerogatives of young people; many older people too suffer from a frustrating sense of meaninglessness and lack of fulfillment.

In addition to the sources of frustration already mentioned, several others may be briefly noted. Feelings of inadequacy and inferiority—whether stemming from real or imagined limitations—can be debilitating frustrations. Loneliness is a serious source of frustration for many

 I cried for a whole summer once. I auditioned for a part in a play that I wanted very much. And I didn't get it. And I couldn't accept the fact. It took me three months to accept the fact that I didn't get it. Because I took it totally personally. I thought they were rejecting me as a person, instead of me as an actress.

failure, guilt may be particularly frustrating if nothing can be done to rectify the error—such as when an individual is responsible for an automobile accident in which a loved one is killed. The severe frustration which may be engendered by feelings of guilt has been well described by Gelven: "Of all the forms of mental suffering, perhaps none is as pervasive or as intense as the ache of guilt" (1973, p. 69).

5. *Meaninglessness.* A serious cause of frustration stems from an inability to find and lead a meaningful and fulfilling way of life. Apparently a somewhat new phenomenon in our generation is the inability of large numbers of young people to accept and identify with the goals and values of our culture. They are repelled by the "phoniness," hypocrisy, and materialistic status-

people. Although widely decried, racial and other minority-group prejudice and discrimination are still a serious source of frustration for many people in our society. Inflation is a source of frustration for many of us—especially older persons living on fixed incomes. Even with adequate income, many of us suffer the frustration of being stuck in jobs in which we are misfits. The frustrations that result from an unhappy marriage are especially severe since they permeate one's whole "home base" and threaten one's basic anchorages. And finally, of course, the knowledge that we are living in a world of nations armed to the teeth with weapons capable of destroying all human life is not conducive to feelings of security in our world or of faith in the future of the human race.

Conflict

Often stress comes not from a single obstacle but from a conflict of motives. You want to get married, but you feel you would have to quit college and take a job you really don't want. You are pregnant and want to have the baby, but being unmarried you are hesitant to take the responsibility and are seriously considering an abortion. We also experience value conflicts in deciding which major in college is most suitable, in finding the right person to marry, and in selecting the kind of life style that will prove most fulfilling.

Although it is convenient to make a distinction between frustration and conflict, it is the underlying threat of frustration that makes a conflict stressful. In a conflict you are threatened with frustration regardless of which course of

social, and security reasons, while at the same time fearing the responsibilities and loss of personal freedom. He has tendencies both to approach and to avoid marriage. In a similar way his desires may conflict with his moral principles or with fear of failure. Perhaps he can join a high status group only by indulging in behavior contrary to his ethical standards; or he feels intensely attracted to a beautiful and intelligent woman but recognizes that her scale of values would almost inevitably lead to the failure of their love relationship or marriage.

Approach-avoidant conflicts are sometimes referred to as "mixed blessing" conflicts, because some negative and some positive features must be accepted regardless of which course of action we select. Since many approach-avoidance conflicts involve multiple alternatives —rather than just one either-or choice—the

Being a person with a mind, body, and soul, who thinks, acts, and feels, I must cope with conflicting and confusing thoughts, actions, and feelings.

action you choose to follow. Thus it is not surprising that the person in conflict often hesitates, vacillates, and goes through agony trying to make a decision.

Types of conflict

Conflicts are usually classified in terms of the reward or punishment value the alternatives have for the individual. Thus the conflicts we all meet may be conveniently classified as approach-avoidant, double-approach, and double-avoidant conflicts.

1. *Approach-avoidant conflicts.* In an approach-avoidant conflict there are strong tendencies both to approach and to avoid the same goal. A woman may feel trapped and denied fulfillment by an unhappy marriage and yet place a high value on the security and status it gives her. A man may want to marry for sexual,

term *multiple approach-avoidance* is sometimes used here also. Thus an individual may be in conflict not only about whether to get married but also about which person would make the best spouse; or he may be in conflict about whether to major in education, law, or psychology, each of which he sees as offering both advantages and disadvantages.

2. *Double-approach conflicts.* As the name implies, double-approach conflicts involve competition between two or more desirable alternatives. On a simple level, a decision may have to be made between two courses we would like to take, between studying for an exam or going to a movie, or between two invitations for the same evening. To a large extent, such simple "plus-plus" conflicts result from the inevitable limitations in our time, space, energy, and personal resources. We cannot be in two places at once, we do not have the time and energy to do all the things we would like to do, and most of us have limited funds.

Although even simple decisions—such as whether to have steak or fish for dinner or to buy a blue or brown sweater—may be hard to make, they do not ordinarily upset us greatly because we are assured of reasonable gratification at the moment and because we are often able to obtain the other desired alternative at a later time. In more complex cases—as when a young man is torn between loyalty to his mother

dle-aged person may have a choice between a loveless marriage and a life of loneliness. An employee may have to choose between using sales techniques which he feels are unethical and giving up a lucrative job which he needs. For some young people, both conformity to the "establishment" and membership in some non-conforming group in which they do not fully believe present difficult alternatives. In wartime, an individual may have to choose between military service, with the possibility of killing others or being killed, and refusal to serve, with the

 I had a lot of feelings about moving away from my old neighborhood, where I'd lived for ten years, and the people I know there. But I wanted to upgrade myself with this modern place, and I needed the tax deductions, something to pay interest on; my old house is paid for, and if you're in the kind of income tax bracket I am, you need to pay interest, for tax deductions. And the old house is a half acre and a swimming pool, neither of which I wanted to have to take care of any longer. But I loved the old place and it was hard to leave, as attractive as the new place is. I made the decision and I made the move, but I still have some conflict about it.

and to his wife, between careers in law and medicine, between faithfulness to his absent fiancée and sexual attraction toward another girl, or between present and future satisfactions—decision making may be very difficult and stressful.

3. *Double-avoidant conflicts.* In a double-avoidant conflict we are caught "between the devil and the deep blue sea" and must try to choose the lesser of two evils. The unskilled young person may have to choose between unemployment and a disagreeable job; a mid-

possibility of social disapproval and punishment. When such "minus-minus" conflicts are severe, they can bring about serious adjustment problems because even resolution of the conflict will bring frustration rather than relief.

It can be readily seen that this classification of conflicts is somewhat arbitrary and that various combinations among these different types are the rule rather than the exception in everyday life. Thus a "plus-plus" conflict between marrying one of two desirable persons may also have its "plus-minus" aspects growing out of the

THE EXPERIENCE OF CONFLICT

Perhaps no one has better described the experience of being in conflict—of being confused and torn in different directions—than Shakespeare in Hamlet's famous soliloquy:

To be, or not to be: that is the question:
Whether 'tis nobler in the mind to suffer
The slings and arrows of outrageous fortune,
Or to take arms against a sea of troubles,
And by opposing end them? To die: to sleep;
No more; and by a sleep to say we end
The heart-ache and the thousand natural shocks
That flesh is heir to, 'tis a consummation
Devoutly to be wish'd. To die, to sleep;
To sleep: perchance to dream: ay, there's the rub;
For in that sleep of death what dreams may come
When we have shuffled off this mortal coil,
Must give us pause. . . .
For who would bear the whips and scorns of time, . . .
The oppressor's wrong, the proud man's contumely,
The pangs of despised love, the law's delay, . . .
When he himself might his quietus make
With a bare bodkin? . . .
But that the dread of something after death,
The undiscover'd country from whose bourn
No traveller returns, puzzles the will
And makes us rather bear those ills we have
Than fly to others that we know not of? . . .

Hamlet, Act III, Scene I

responsibilities and loss of personal freedom entailed in marriage.

Common conflicts in our society

Most of the conflicts in our society are *value conflicts*. They are especially common and disturbing because to a greater extent than ever before individuals must choose what they are to become, both as individuals and as participants in our society. Is it better to be manipulative or honest, to refrain from a variety of transient sexual relationships or to follow one's impulses and desires, to give of one's self to others or to play it cool, to stay in a competitive society or to "drop out," to take "mind-expanding" drugs or to follow more conventional methods of self-

exploration and growth? Each of us experiences many such value conflicts—often accompanied by considerable pressure in one direction or another from family or friends—and such conflicts are often major sources of confusion, indecision, and stress.

Although our value patterns and conflicts will be dealt with in later chapters, some of the more troubling ones will be mentioned briefly here.

1. *Self-direction vs. outer direction.* The insecurities of our anxious age and the lack of a clear pattern for young people to follow make the development of self-direction and acceptance of personal responsibility especially difficult today. Often we are torn between contradictory demands and values advocated by parents, peers, and public officials; and, of course, rapid social change, including change in traditional values, adds to the problem. Thus it is no easy task to construct a value system and chart a course of action that will meet our needs for both security and growth and for both self-esteem and social approval.

Several writers of our time have pointed to the tendency of people in our age of anxiety to surrender the risks and pains of self-direction for the security of authority. Sometimes this authority is a peer group, sometimes it is "the establishment," and sometimes it is an authoritarian religious or political group. When we are unsure of our values or lack the courage to live by them, we may find ourselves choosing value patterns, courses of action, and life styles advocated by others. But by ignoring or going counter to our own experience and values, we are likely to become strangers to our real feelings and to suffer a sense of deep frustration—for we are violating a central part of our nature.

2. *Commitment vs. noninvolvement.* The conflict between commitment and noninvolvement vividly confronts Americans each time we hear of incidents such as the stabbing of Catherine Genovese:

In March 1964, a young woman returning from work late at night to her apartment in Kew Gardens, Queens, was attacked on a well-lighted street within a hundred feet of her apartment. It was later established that her screams awakened 38 of her neighbors; and twice, as apartment lights went on, her attacker scurried away. Each time he came back; finally he stabbed her to death. Although Miss Genovese kept yelling "Please help me!" "Please help me!" not one of the 38 neighbors called the police during the 35 minutes between the first and last attack.

Although most religious and social philosophies emphasize the ideal of helping others, the impersonality and anonymity of modern urban society are not conducive to a feeling of commitment to the welfare of others. The individual in such an environment often feels part of an impersonal series of events over which he has no control. The risk of involvement and its possible repercussions seem too great a price to pay when one is dealing with "strangers." As Berkowitz (1973) has concluded from his study of this problem, a demand to help someone, whether explicit or implicit, is a bothersome threat to the individual. Unfortunately, it often seems that Seeman is more right than wrong in his statement:

"Often it seems painful but realistic to conclude that, in the last analysis, you and your family are alone, and the only ones you can really count on for help and support are yourselves. No one else cares" (1966, p. 35).

The conflict between commitment and noninvolvement is by no means confined to relationships with strangers. Even in close interpersonal relationships the individual may choose noninvolvement rather than care or love. All caring has hazards, since one who is involved is vulnerable to being hurt and a painless outcome can never be guaranteed. But noninvolvement also exacts a price in terms of lost satisfactions, feelings of estrangement and alienation, and a lack of meaning in one's existence. In a general sense, it would appear that the person who does not get involved does not really live.

Commitment also usually includes the espousal of positive values and a feeling of responsibility for working toward maintaining and improving the quality of life in the society as a whole. Every generation has had its "dropouts," who felt no responsibility for the welfare of anyone but themselves and their own families and friends; today's dropouts include also a sizable segment of idealistic young people who have taken seriously the principles of love, honesty, and open sharing and feel that to enter the adult society they see would be to surrender their integrity. Many other young people, who feel a responsibility for doing what they can to bring improvement and believe that their effort can make a difference, attempt to work for constructive change within established social structures.

3. *Avoiding vs. facing reality.* An approach-avoidant conflict familiar to all of us is the conflict between wanting to know the truth and wanting to be comfortable, especially about ourselves. Yet a central requisite of personal maturity is the ability to be objective about ourselves and the world around us and to acknowledge reality even when it is unpleasant. This is not easy because unpleasant reality makes us anxious and we defend ourselves against anxiety as automatically (and often as unconsciously) as we defend ourselves against invading germs. Most of us have experienced the ease with which our cognitive processes are subverted to the service of making us see what we want to see and believe and preventing us from seeing inconsistencies between our professed beliefs and our actions.

To face the reality that our failure in some important venture, such as a close personal relationship, has resulted from stupidity on our part would be self-devaluating, and we are likely to look for some other explanation. So perhaps we rationalize or project the blame onto the other person or onto "circumstances beyond our control." In the same way, we may underestimate or close our eyes to social injustices that might otherwise make us uncomfortable; or we may be unwilling to listen to responsible persons in public life who hold political views and values somewhat different from our own.

Facing reality not only may be uncomfortable but may confront us with the necessity for taking positive action that we fear will be hazardous and disagreeable. The unwillingness to respond to a stranger's call for help may represent an attempt to avoid possible unpleasant consequences as much as a lack of concern for others' welfare. The ways of avoiding reality are legion, and the conflict between facing and avoiding reality is not a new one, though some of the forms it takes may be novel in our time.

4. *Integrity vs. self-advantage.* We all experience times when it appears that our needs might be best served by actions that would conflict with our ethical values. We may be tempted to cheat on examinations, to be devious in business transactions, to lie or otherwise practice deceit in our attempts to get something we need, or to be silent about our beliefs because of possible social disapproval. We appear particularly prone to such behavior when we observe that others engage in it with seemingly successful results.

ples. Thus he may experience considerable conflict in adhering to his ethical standards and considerable guilt if he violates them. Throughout human history we can see examples of people wrestling with their consciences as they tried to be true to their values and to stand up for what they believed in—even though the path of personal gain lay in the other direction. It often takes great courage to follow one's convictions under such conditions. Such courage is well portrayed in the characterization of Thomas More in the play *A Man for All Seasons.*

5. *Sexual desires vs. restraints.* Present-day theorists do not consider sexual conflicts the inevitable problems that Freud judged them to be. Yet they are common enough in our society to cause considerable stress, especially among

 I find that there are major flaws in myself and my thinking. I have found myself thinking about what it would be like to have sexual relationships with girls of all ages that I see, and I fear myself for it. I really don't think I would ever have the nerve to approach any of these people with this intention, but it still exists.

Of course, individuals with very limited conscience development or with values consistent with such behavior will experience little or no conflict in such situations, nor will they have guilt feelings later if they choose expediency over principle. In fact, they may believe that the successful completion of their objective is justification for any means used in achieving it. One has only to read the daily paper to observe the frequency with which self-advantage takes priority over what most of us have been taught to consider "fair play."

The idealistic young person in our society may find it particularly disillusioning to learn that the adult world does not always abide by the standards it proclaims and that he himself is tempted to act in ways inconsistent with his own princi-

young people. The earliest sexual conflict often centers around the practice of masturbation, so long condemned as a vile, enfeebling, immoral habit. Even present-day knowledge of its physical harmlessness and of its prevalence during certain stages of development does not always prevent a sense of fear and guilt concerning it. Often, too, a child's early sexual development is complicated by an overattachment to the mother or father, accompanied by strong sexual desires and fantasies. Freudian theory has placed great emphasis on the "Oedipal conflict" as a source of stress. According to this theory, the situation is usually resolved as the little boy comes to identify with the father and the girl with her mother, and latent sexual desires give way to harmless tender affection. However, ambivalence or sexual feelings toward parents can be a source of considerable guilt and conflict while they endure.

With later adolescence and young adulthood, sexual conflicts may center around petting, premarital sexual relations, infidelity after marriage, and homosexual patterns. Adding to young people's difficulty is the confusion and disagreement they see around them concerning what is acceptable and unacceptable, right and wrong, in sexual behavior.

In general, our society appears to be moving toward a view of sexual behavior as a natural and acceptable source of enjoyment and toward decreasing restraints on permissible patterns of sexual behavior. But guidelines are not clear, and sexual values may differ markedly for different racial, socioeconomic, and religious groups. As a consequence, many young people experience intense conflict as they try to work out a code of sexual ethics which is acceptable to them.

It is apparent from our preceding discussion that many of our most difficult conflicts are those in which our basic assumptions are in conflict and we have to choose one at the sacrifice of another. For example, it is assumed that loyalty to a friend is a good thing. Does this mean that you must lend him money? Does it mean that you stand up for him when you think he is wrong? Should you be faithful to a person with whom you are romantically in love, or should sexual behavior simply be considered another source of physical pleasure which should be engaged in whenever the opportunity presents itself? Should a woman with an unwanted pregnancy have an abortion or bear the child? Should one remain with a spouse one despises in order to help bring up the children, or is divorce a valid solution to such a problem? Must one be "his brother's keeper" or is it justified to pursue one's own interest and happiness? Is it wrong to use unethical means in the pursuit of worthwhile and important goals?

In many ways conflicts are the most severe type of stress we experience, for our "peace of mind" and the type of person we become depends on the way we handle them.

Problems of adjustment come not only because our own strivings are frustrated or in conflict but also because of pressures that complicate our journey toward our goals or provide additional demands for us to meet. For example, if our parents have made sacrifices to send us to college and expect us to do well, we may feel under great pressure not to let them down. Such pressures may force us to intensify our effort and speed up our activity—often to an uncomfortable degree.

Sources of pressure

Pressures, like frustration, may stem from inner or outer sources. Inner sources typically center around our aspirations and ego-ideal. Where we have a high level of aspiration in terms of standards to be met and goals to be achieved, the pressure may be continuous and severe. Many of us drive ourselves mercilessly toward high achievement and strive to live up to unrealistically high standards of ethical behavior in order to conform to a picture of ourselves as we think we *should* be. We may feel we should get along with everyone, should show more concentration and self-control, should not feel the way we clearly do feel, and in general should do much better than we are doing. Pressures like this, stemming from unrealistic assumptions about ourselves and our world, have been referred to as the "tyranny of the *should*."

A combination of inner aspirations and outer demands often intensifies the pressure. Ambitious high-school seniors, expected to show excellence in grades, athletics, and extracurricular activities, often feel that colleges are looking for paragons rather than human beings. A young salesman anxious to distinguish himself may find himself up against quotas he thinks are unrealistically high and competition from workers who already have outstanding records of success.

Common pressures in our society

Although each of us faces a unique pattern of demands and pressures, there are several pres-

 My pressures come from both inside and outside. I sometimes feel like I'm schizophrenic, because part of me wants to do something—and it's like a mother, kind of, going 'Now this should be done this way.' And another part of me doesn't want to do that. I've always been able to see the two parts of me.

I'm in a competitive career, and I think it's the competitive part of it that makes it the most difficult for me to do it. Like, I went on this interview where I did a scene, and as long as I do that scene as well as I can, to the extent that I'm totally centered on myself, then I'm happy. I can feel how beautiful that scene is. But as soon as I start worrying about how the director thinks I am doing compared with someone else . . . I don't like competition. I'm competitive, but I just want to be better than anyone else, I don't want to have to compete.

sures that most of us share by virtue of our membership in our particular society. Prevalent among these are pressure to achieve in a competitive society; pressure to put forth sustained effort, often at an uncomfortably fast pace, and to keep adjusting to constantly changing conditions; and pressures from family and other close interpersonal relationships.

1. *The pressure to compete.* Many common pressures stem from demands for academic and occupational achievement. Although such demands are somewhat more pressing for men than for women in our society and for middle-

petition for selection for advanced training. Nor does the strain of sustained effort usually cease when the individual leaves school. At almost any occupational level a person may be under considerable pressure to advance and make the increased income often needed to support a family. In general, most of us are encouraged to be ambitious and "think big." Yet not everyone can come in first, and striving to do the impossible invites frustration and self-devaluation.

Competitive pressures have been acclaimed as leading to greater productivity, an increased

 Things change so fast, our mores—when I was brought up, a lot of them I can see were false and hypocritical. At the time I just accepted them, but now I can see that things aren't necessarily the way I was taught they were. Some things have changed too much for me to accept easily, for me to be able to accept them. For instance, sexual mores, that's really tough, and things like how you ought to live your life, I mean, you know, so what's with dropping out and what about living in communes and what about group sex? And I just don't have answers for these.

class than for lower-class individuals, they subject many of us to considerable stress.

In our highly competitive society we compete for grades, athletic honors, jobs, marital partners, and almost everything else we want. Although we endorse certain rules for playing the game and may give grudging credit for effort, it is success that gains the rewards. The losing football team does not attract crowds or gain plaudits for its performance; the company that fails to gain contracts in competition with other companies is likely to go bankrupt. It is the students with superior records who win the competition for college entrance and later the com-

sense of purpose, and higher standards of excellence. Yet inappropriate or indiscriminate competition may be harmful to the individual and divisive for the group. If it leads to a constant "overloading" of the individual's capacities, both his health and his long-term productivity may suffer. The need for mutual help and support among the members of any social group suggests that cooperation is at least as much a "law of life" as is competition.

2. *Complexity and rate of change.* All life involves change: we grow up, marry, have children, face the death of parents, undergo illnesses, and adjust to innumerable other major

In an interesting series of studies, Calhoun (1962) found that when a colony of rats was given adequate food and nesting materials but confined in an area with about twice the normal population density, many forms of maladaptive behavior appeared. For example, maternal behavior was so disrupted that few of the young survived; some rats showed extreme passivity, moving about listlessly, while others "went berserk," attacking other rats without provocation and even becoming cannibalis-tic. Even when a few of the healthier rats were moved to a "normal" environment, they produced fewer offspring than usual and none of the young survived.

A summary of a number of such studies by the National Institute of Mental Health concluded:

". . . there is abundant evidence that among animals, at least, crowded living conditions and their immediate consequence, a greatly increased level of interaction with other members of the population, impose a stress that can lead to abnormal behavior, reproductive failure, sickness, and even death" (1969, p. 20).

It is risky to generalize from these findings to human beings, but interesting parallels may be observed between the behavior of lower animals subjected to overcrowding and forms of maladaptive behavior among people living in crowded cities; for example, the increased irritability, tension, and frenetic overactivity of some individuals and the pathological alienation and withdrawal of others.

and minor changes as we go through life. Up to a point, change *per se* need not cause difficulty. In fact, we are so used to continuing change that we all expect next year's cars, TV sets, building construction, and so on to be different and generally assume that they will be better. We expect to adapt to new standards of excellence, new gadgets and innovations, and continuing new methods and concepts in our field of specialization.

The rate and pervasiveness of change today, however, are different from anything our ancestors ever experienced, and all aspects of our lives are affected—our education, our jobs, our family life, our leisure pursuits, and our beliefs and values. Constantly trying to keep up with the new adjustments demanded by these changes is a source of considerable stress.

One form of stressful change is our contemporary "information explosion." Students, for example, are expected to cover more and more material—often creating an uncomfortable situation in which they are subjected not only to the pressure of long hours of study but also to the tension created by frequent deadlines and examinations. And the information explosion not only poses a problem for students but for people working in technical and scientific fields as well. It has been estimated that one's college training is outmoded in about five years, and in many fields—such as medicine, computer technology, teaching, and psychology—it is a constant problem to keep up with new findings and new techniques.

And besides the constant and far-reaching changes within our own society, technological innovations have made the world so much smaller that many complex social problems are superimposed upon the personal problems of the individual and require his attention as a citizen. Whether we like it or not, we have to be concerned with what happens in China, Africa, and other parts of the world—for these happenings may directly affect our own security and well-being.

There is increasing evidence that chronic "overloading" from our need to make complex adaptations to accelerating social and technological change is an important factor in the increasing incidence of heart attacks and other "diseases of adaptation." In fact, Toffler (1970) has proposed the term "future shock" to describe the profound confusion and emotional upset resulting from social change that has become too rapid.

3. *Pressures from family and other relationships.* Although many of our deepest needs are satisfied through family relationships, such relationships can also place difficult pressures on us. Marriage makes many demands on an individual—demands that may be quite stressful if either partner is immature or if the external situation is not favorable. Marriage calls on the individual to adjust to an intimate relationship with another person, to help work out a mutually satisfactory approach to problems, and to resolve value conflicts. With the arrival of children there are new demands on time and patience as well as on one's ability to love. Child-rearing problems may increase marital stress. Ill or aging parents may also need our financial and emotional support and place added stress on the marriage.

Relationships with those outside our families can also be sources of pressure. We are constantly being called on by other individuals or groups to help advance their concerns. Our friends may need our help at inconvenient times. Organizations to which we belong may need long hours that we cannot easily spare. Community problems may cry out for time and effort from us as concerned citizens. All these demands add to the pressures that complicate our lives.

Many other frustrations, conflicts, and pressures could, of course, be mentioned in our discussion. Disappointments in love are probably experienced at one time or another by most of us and can be terribly hurtful. Serious accidents, major surgery, and arrest and imprisonment are highly stressful situations for those who have to face them. To one whose feelings of worth are largely dependent upon physical attractiveness, the deterioration of aging may present a particularly difficult problem. Finally, the prospect of our own inevitable death is a traumatic reality with which we must all come to terms.

Severity of stress

The *severity of stress* refers to the degree of disruption or disequilibrium that will occur if the individual fails to cope with the adjustive de-

CULTURAL CHANGE AS A SOURCE OF STRESS

Murphy and Leighton (1965), studying the effects of the rapid influx of new ideas from outside a given culture, found that stress and personality damage were most likely to occur under the following circumstances:

1. When the tempo was so rapid that major dimensions of change occurred within the life span of a single generation;

2. When a pervasive reorientation of basic assumptions was involved, especially if it involved new roles or values that did not fit into the previous system;

3. When the people were unprepared for the changes, did not see where they were leading, and were encouraged in unrealistic expectations;

4. When the new conditions created a sense of overloading by increasing the number of adjustive demands made on the members of the group rather than simply substituting new demands.

mand. The greater the potential or actual disruption, the greater the severity of stress or adjustive demand.

In mild stress there is little disturbance in equilibrium and adjustive action is usually relatively simple; in moderate and severe stress, there are proportionately greater degrees of stress imposed on the organism and adjustive action may be difficult; and in excessive stress, severe disequilibrium occurs and the adaptive capacities of the organism are overtaxed. Thus we may think of severity along a continuum from mild through moderate and severe to excessive stress.

The severity of stress is determined primarily by three factors: (1) the characteristics of the

I have been on the border line where life's realities were really too heavy to bear. A feeling of failure in anything, whether it be disappointment of someone in me or whatever, it has the tendency to irritate me to no end. I guess we all would like the security of always being on top with a few failures—very few. I know that we grow from them, but life's pressures are heavy and getting worse.

SOURCE OF THE ADJUSTIVE DEMAND

An individual's response to a stress situation is significantly affected by the specific source of the adjustive demand. If he is on a diet, for example, he may respond to hunger quite differently than if he lacks money to buy food. Sources of adjustive demands may be classified as follows:

1. *Imposed.* Civilian and military prisoners are involuntarily subjected to rigid discipline.

2. *Assigned.* Astronauts, submarine crews, and others in hazardous and confining occupations may be subjected to long periods of stress.

3. *Chosen.* An individual may knowingly subject himself to unusual stresses for personal reasons, as in the case of arctic explorers.

4. *Devised.* Individuals may be subjected to various kinds of stress in artificially devised laboratory situations designed to study human reactions.

adjustive demand; (2) the characteristics of the individual, including his stress tolerance; and (3) the external resources and supports available to him. On a biological level, for example, the severity of stress created by invading viruses depends partly on the strength and number of the invaders, partly on the organism's ability to resist and destroy them, and partly on available medical resources for implementing body defenses. On a psychological level, individual factors usually play a more crucial role. For here the severity of the adjustive demand depends not only upon the stress situation and the individual's resources—both personal and situational— but also upon the way he evaluates the situation.

Characteristics of the adjustive demand

Several characteristics of the demand affect its severity regardless of the make-up of the individual or the situational context in which it occurs.

Importance, duration, and multiplicity of demands

The severity of the stress depends first of all on the relative importance of the need being deprived or threatened with deprivation. Frustration of a central, key motive is more stressful than frustration of more peripheral desires. Thus failing one's bar exams would be more stressful than having to give up a desired vacation trip.

Ordinarily, the longer a stress situation continues, the more severe will be the strain on the organism. An individual can easily afford to miss a meal or two, but continued hunger brings severe stress. Often, too, stress appears to have a cumulative effect. An overworked employee may maintain composure through a long series of minor irritations and conflicts only to explode in the face of the final straw. The supervisor may be quite dumbfounded by the suddenness and violence of this seeming overreaction, not realizing that it represents the culmination of a long series of minor frustrations.

The number of demands made upon the individual at the same time also has a direct relationship to the degree of strain he experiences. In a high-pressure managerial job, any single problem or decision may be easily within the individual's ability to handle, but the sheer number of problems and decisions to be coped with each day may lead to severe stress. If a student loses his fiancée, flunks a course, and is robbed, all within a few days, the stress will be more severe and harder to handle than if such events are spaced further apart and he has time to cope with one before being confronted with the next.

Strength of the conflicting forces

Conflicts between weak or peripheral motives produce minimal disruption, for neither choice entails serious loss. For example, deciding between a dance and a movie does not usually create severe stress. On the other hand, conflicts between important motives—such as having to choose between self-esteem and social approval—subject the individual to much greater stress.

The comparative strength of the opposing motives is also a factor. If an individual finds guilt feelings over sexual behavior far less stressful than sexual frustration, his conflict is readily resolved. If both inner restraints and sexual desires are strong, the situation is much more stressful since either alternative will lead to serious frustration.

The picture is complicated further by the fact that the attractiveness of a given goal is not static and unchanging. The closer we get to a highly desired goal, the more we tend to want it. But if there are negative aspects, they loom larger too. Thus, if a young man is ambivalent about getting married, both his eagerness and his apprehension will become more intense as the wedding date approaches. Stress mounts accordingly.

Interestingly, the approach and avoidance trends do not increase at the same rate in such a situation. Typically, the avoidance gradient increases more sharply as the goal draws near. This helps to explain why many people experience a feeling of anxiety or near-panic on their wedding day. Suddenly, all the underlying doubts seem to well up out of proportion to the positive values, which have also increased in attractiveness but not so rapidly. Where a goal has appreciable negative as well as positive aspects, it may become essentially negative as it comes within reach.

Unfamiliarity and suddenness of the problem

Frustrations, conflicts, and pressures that we have coped with successfully before may cause little difficulty when we meet them again; for usually we can see a relatively painless way out on the basis of our past experience. But new problems which we have not anticipated, for which we have no ready-made coping pattern, and in which the requirements of the situation may not be clearly understood can put us under severe stress.

One reason major catastrophes—such as earthquakes—are so overwhelming is that all one's usual "props" have disappeared and one's knowledge and skills seem totally inadequate and irrelevant to the task at hand. Any problem we do not know how to cope with may pose a serious difficulty. By contrast, if we can anticipate and prepare for a stressful event, even a potentially catastrophic one, it loses much of its power to throw us "off base." The training of firemen, policemen, and soldiers in exactly what to expect and what to do makes it possible for them to function effectively in highly stressful situations.

The same sense of adequacy and control may be achieved when the stress has been chosen voluntarily rather than having been imposed by others or having come unexpectedly from an accident. A scientist who chooses to spend a year in the Antarctic to make observations that will test an important hypothesis is likely to find the physical rigors and loneliness less stressful than an enlisted man who is assigned to the mission against his wishes. Understanding the nature of a stressful experience, knowing it is coming, preparing for it, and knowing how long it will last all lessen the severity of the stress when it comes.

The presence of a threat

Threat is the anticipation of harm. Many stress situations do not carry any major threat to biological or psychological needs. A cold is not the threat that pneumonia is; nor is social disapproval usually the threat that would be posed by complete ostracism from the group. But stress situations which involve physical damage or threaten our survival—such as having a limb amputated or being given a diagnosis of cancer—carry a high degree of threat. Similarly, stress situations which threaten the adequacy and worth of the self—such as failing in one's chosen occupation or having desires which one considers immoral and incompatible with his self-concept—involve a strong element of threat. The individual is also likely to feel threatened in stress situations which place demands on him that he feels inadequate to meet.

In general, a situation perceived as threatening is much more stressful than one perceived as presenting a difficult but manageable problem. And, as we shall see, threat arouses anxiety, which further augments the severity of the stress.

Imminence of an anticipated stress

Anticipation of stress is itself stressful, especially as the event approaches. In a study of graduate students facing crucial examinations, Mechanic found that although the students thought about their examinations from time to time and experienced some anxiety during the three months beforehand, they were not seriously worried until near exam time.

"As the examinations approached and as student anxiety increased, various changes occurred in behavior. Joking increased, and while students still sought social support and talked a great deal about examinations, they began specifically to avoid certain people who aroused their anxiety. Stomach aches, asthma, and a general feeling of weariness became common complaints, and other psychosomatic symptoms appeared. The use of tranquilizers and sleeping pills became more frequent."

"When the examinations are nearly upon the student, anxiety is very high, even for those rated as low-anxiety persons, although students do fluctuate between confidence and anxiety. Since studying is difficult, the student questions his motivation, interest, and ability in the field" (1962, pp. 142, 144).

Probably many people undergo similar experiences as stressful situations approach.

Characteristics of the individual

Situations that one person finds very stressful may be only mildly stressful or even nonstressful for another. The individual's level of competence, his perception of the problem, his identification of the presence or absence of threat, and his level of stress tolerance all help determine the severity of the stress he experiences.

Degree of competence

Whatever the problem we face, its severity for us will depend partly on the degree to which we have the particular competence required for coping with it. The greater our competence, the less severe the stress. The well-trained debater can organize an eloquent rebuttal while his opponent is speaking, whereas one less well trained may not be able to keep track of all the points he wants to answer and may become hopelessly flustered. In most situations, the higher the individual's level of intellectual, emotional, and social development, the greater his adaptive potential.

But the individual's actual level of competence is not the whole story: the way he views his capabilities is important too. If he feels generally self-confident and expects to solve a problem successfully, he is less likely to experience severe stress even if the demand is a difficult one (Kent, 1972). By contrast, if he lacks self-confidence and is convinced he will bungle an important task, he will experience severe stress even if he actually possesses ample competencies for dealing with the situation.

Perception of the problem

Another crucial factor in determining the severity of stress is the way in which the individual perceives the problem. One person may view a broken engagement as a humiliating and self-devaluating failure, while another may view it as fortunate, in that the incompatibility became apparent before rather than after the marriage.

An individual's evaluation of a particular problem depends on his entire frame of reference. If he views the world as dangerous and hostile, he evaluates each new stress as one more element added to the burden he is already bearing. If he sees himself as generally inadequate, he interprets a failing grade as proof of his inability to do acceptable college-level work. In contrast, experience and intensive training instill in an individual the self-confidence to handle even highly stressful situations. For example, astronauts are trained to rely on both themselves and teamwork to take care of problems that may arise.

I think your frame of mind, your perception of your problems, is important. If you can maintain a sense of humor and not take things too bloody serious, if you do not perceive the daily, small, trivial crises as major critical crises, I think you get along just fine.

Even being of sound mind, I feel I could go crazy if pressured long enough. I try to be easygoing, but little things upset me. I can hardly ever do anything very good under pressure. I used to be a sales clerk at a discount house. We'd be swamped, and I'd panic. I had to quit after a month. What I always need is time enough to complete things, the right way. But I know that every person, each one, has his or her breaking point.

Such examples highlight the difficulty of predicting the stressfulness of many adjustive demands, since the severity of stress is determined not only by objective factors but also by the way the individual perceives the situation in relation to himself. Often an outsider sees no stress in a person's life situation severe enough to account for his maladjustive symptoms or perhaps even mental breakdown. Yet to that person the situation may have been intolerable.

It may also be noted that the characteristics of the individual may determine the types of stress to which the individual exposes himself. A race driver or mountain climber may expose himself to stressful situations which most of us would carefully avoid. Even being highly ambitious may expose an individual to stresses unlike those faced by less ambitious persons.

Stress tolerance

By *stress tolerance* we refer to the individual's capacity for withstanding stress or, operationally speaking, the amount of stress the individual can tolerate before his integrated functioning is seriously impaired. Tolerance for stress is fairly constant for a given individual although there are minor fluctuations with special conditions.

Both biologically and psychologically, people differ greatly in the amounts and the types of stress they can withstand. Prolonged exertion and fatigue that would be only mildly stressful to a young person may prove fatal to an older person or someone with a heart defect. Emergencies, disappointments, and other life problems that a competent, confident individual can take in stride may prove incapacitating to one who is (or believes he is) inadequate. Some people can continue to function well in very complex and difficult situations and even in the presence of strong and disturbing emotions. Others are so marginally adjusted that even minor stress can precipitate a serious disorganization of biological or psychological functioning.

Sometimes, early traumatic experiences leave the individual especially vulnerable to certain types of stress situations. The hurt felt by a little girl whose home has been broken by divorce may later make it difficult or impossible for her to accept the possibility of divorce as a solution if her own marriage is unhappy. If her marriage does fail, she may be unable to cope with the situation. Even without such early traumas, each of us has our special vulnerabilities. We may be able to cope with failure but not with social rejection; with prejudice and discrimination but not with disappointment in love. Thus the individual's tolerance for a general type of stress may play an important role in determining the severity of a particular stress situation.

External resources and supports

Usually we are not alone when we meet severe stress situations. If we have to undergo crucial surgery, we can count on the emotional support of our families and friends—and health insurance may be available to reduce the financial stress. Lack of external supports—either personal or material—makes a given stress more severe and weakens our capacity to cope with it. A divorce or the death of one's mate is more stressful if one feels alone than if one is still surrounded by people one feels close to.

Even pressures toward conformity are less stressful and more easily withstood when one has an ally than when one is alone. It is hardly surprising that studies have found a tendency for individuals exposed to highly stressful situations to turn to others for support and reassurance (Asch, 1955; Schachter, 1959).

Environmental supports are a complex matter, however, and behavior by one's family or friends which is intended to provide support may actually increase the stress. In this connection, in the study cited earlier of graduate students facing crucial examinations, Mechanic compared the effects of different types of behavior on the part of the spouses:

"In general, spouses do not provide blind support. They perceive the kinds of support the student wants and they provide it. The wife who becomes worried about examinations also may

Experiments with both lower animals and human beings reveal the existence of *circadian cycles*—24-hour rhythmic fluctuations in such metabolic processes as sleep, activity level, and body temperature. These cycles seem to function as "biological clocks" regulating normal biological functioning. Depending on their severity and the adaptability of the individual, disruptions in these cycles can bring about symptoms of serious stress. Weitzman and Luce have pointed out that technological advances such as jet travel and manned space flight, which subject individuals to abrupt time changes, may have an adverse effect on "the invisible circadian cycle that may govern our susceptibility to disease or shock, our emotions, our performance, our alertness or stupefaction" (1970, p. 279).

provide more support than the spouse who says, 'I'm not worried, you will surely pass.' Indeed, since there is a chance that the student will not pass, the person who is supportive in a meaningful sense will not give blind assurance. Rather, she will seek to find the realistic limits of the situation, the weaknesses of the spouse, and the anxieties and tensions that are being experienced; and then she will attempt to help reduce these. Often a statement to the effect, 'Do the best you can' is more supportive than, 'I'm sure you are going to do well.' The latter statement adds to the student's burden, for not only must he fear the disappointment of not passing, but also the loss of respect in the eyes of his spouse" (1962, p. 158).

Often the culture provides for specific rituals or other courses of action which support the individual in his attempts to deal with certain types of stress. For example, most religions provide rituals which help the bereaved through their ordeal; and in some religions, confession and atonement may help people to deal with the various stresses pertaining to guilt and self-recrimination.

Other key aspects of stress

In addition to type, source, and severity of stress, three additional aspects of stress are of immediate interest. First is the unique and changing nature of the stress situations we each face, however similar our life situations may appear. Second is the role of key stresses and life crises in one's life. And third is the crucial point that adaptation to stress can be expensive both physically and psychologically.

Stress patterns are unique and changing

To understand any person's behavior, it is important to understand the unique stress pattern with which he is confronted. This pattern will vary in relation to his age, sex, occupation, economic status, special interests and talents, group memberships, and other personal and cultural conditions. The stress pattern of the child is different in many respects from that of an adult; that of the patient with an incurable illness differs from that of a healthy person. The soldier in combat faces a different stress pattern from that of a civilian; the woman executive faces somewhat different occupational problems from those of a male executive. But even two people faced with the same stressful situation—for example, two middle-aged executives whose firms have gone bankrupt—may be affected quite differently, for each will perceive the situation from his own viewpoint and will have his own resources and ways of coping with it.

Changes in the individual, in his immediate life situation, and in the broader society all contribute to a continual change in the patterns of stress that he experiences. Some of these

FACTORS INFLUENCING THE SEVERITY OF STRESS

In general, stress is more severe:
1. The more important the motives being blocked and the needs deprived;
2. The longer the stress situation continues;
3. The greater the number of adjustive demands placed on the individual at once or during a short interval of time;
4. The more unfamiliar and unexpected the problem;
5. The less adequate the individual's resources, both personal and social;
6. The stronger and more equal the opposing forces in conflict situations;
7. The closer the individual gets to the goal in approach-avoidance conflict.
8. The greater and more imminent the perceived threat;
9. The less tolerance the individual has for this type and degree of stress;
10. The more the individual sees the threat as imposed on him and beyond his control.

changes bring only minor stress, as when a new business venture compels him to be away from his family from time to time; other changes, such as a divorce, the death of a child, or a technological development that makes his skills obsolete, may place him under severe stress. In any case, stress patterns, like motive patterns, change both from day to day and from one period of life to another. Your stress pattern is somewhat different today from what it was a week ago, and as a whole is quite different this year from what it will be when your oldest daughter or son is about to be married.

Furthermore, stresses, like motives, usually do not come singly or operate independently of one another. The total stress pattern at any time determines the part any one stress will play and how much difficulty we are likely to encounter in coping with it. If a student's stress pattern includes long working hours, poor grades, and new competition for the affection of his girl friend, he may deal with the situation quite differently than if he had the option of dealing with each stress independently. For example, he may disregard his fatigue and schoolwork and concentrate on winning back his girl friend—a coping pattern he would not follow if all were well with his love life.

At the same time, however, his fatigue and uneasiness about his deteriorating schoolwork may make him more irritable and less appealing to his girl friend—making his stress situation even more severe. Thus we see the continual interaction of stress patterns and coping reactions in shaping the course of our lives.

Major stresses and crises

Although we are always confronted with multiple stresses, often there is one key stress—or a limited number of key stresses—that permeates the life of an individual, particularly his adult life. Sometimes such key stresses reflect a continuing difficult life situation. For example, an individual may be stuck indefinitely in a distasteful job from which he seemingly cannot escape; or he may suffer for years in an unhappy and conflictful marriage; or he may be severely limited by a physical handicap or a chronic health problem. In other instances, the continuing stress derives from a traumatic experience from which the individual has never fully recovered. A person who fails his premedical program may always thereafter feel a sense of frustration that he was not able to become the physician that he wanted to be. The unexpected or violent death of a loved one—particularly a spouse or child—may have a lasting effect on an individual's life.

In some cases the key stresses in a person's life center around what might be called "crisis" situations. Although there is some confusion

ESSENTIAL FEATURES OF PERSONAL CRISIS

A personal crisis appears to involve four key characteristics:

1. The perception of threat to important needs and goals and the experience of feelings of inadequacy in the face of seemingly insurmountable problems;

2. The experience of fear, anxiety, and other emotions, often including feelings of helplessness, hopelessness, and depression;

3. Increasing rigidity of cognitive processes so that the individual becomes unable to reevaluate the stress situation or perceive alternative solutions—or perhaps any viable solution at all;

4. Signs of increasing decompensation.

concerning the meaning of "crisis," Lazarus has pointed out that:

"Crisis seems to imply a limited period in which an individual or group is exposed to threats and demands which are at or near the limits of their resources to cope.

"In threat the emphasis is on a particular harm, while in crisis, the focus is on a period of the person's or group's life in which major threats and frustrations that tax adaptation are prominent" (1966, pp. 407–408).

Brown (1972) has estimated that the occurrence of major crises or markedly threatening events is relatively rare in the general population—happening about once every ten years; however, this estimate may be somewhat optimistic in terms of the complex and rapidly changing stresses with which most of us are faced.

A crisis might center around a traumatic divorce, or an episode of depression in which the individual sees no hope and seriously considers suicide, or the aftermath of serious injuries or disease which force difficult readjustments in the

It is not surprising that major stressful events that bring about significant changes in an individual's life have been found to be associated with a variety of physical and mental disorders. It is now recognized, however, that a series of minor stresses may have a similar effect.

Holmes and Rahe (1967) have developed a Social Readjustment Rating Scale which provides a reliable method for assessing the stressfulness of given life events and thus the cumulative stress to which an individual has been exposed.

The SRRS is a self-rating questionnaire on which the person indicates which of 43 life change events he has been exposed to in recent months. Each of the events listed has been assigned a number designating its severity in terms of "life change units" (LCUs). These LCU ratings were determined by having large numbers of individuals rank the events in terms of severity and stressfulness. Rankings have been remarkably consistent among different segments of the U.S. population as well as in other countries (Holmes & Rahe, 1967; Ruch & Holmes, 1971; Holmes & Matsuda, 1972).

The ten stresses identified as most severe and their LCU ratings are given below:

Life event	LCUs
Death of spouse	100
Divorce	73
Marital separation	65
Jail term	63
Death of close relative	63
Major injury or illness	53
Marriage	50
Fired from job	47
Marital reconciliation	45
Retirement	45

The severity of stress during a given period can be assessed by adding up the LCUs for that period. A score of 0 to 150 indicates no significant problems; 150 to 199 indicates mild life crisis; 200 to 299, moderate life crisis; and 300 or over, major life crisis. The severity of stress indicates the probability of disorder. For example, mild life crisis carries a 33% chance of illness; moderate life crisis a 50% chance of illness; and major life crisis an 80% chance.

While most of the events listed above are aversive in nature, this is not true for less heavily weighted items on the SRRS— even Christmas carries an LCU rating of 12. It is not the type of life change that is of paramount importance, but rather the extent of the demands that are being made on the individual's coping resources.

individual's self-concept and way of life, or other events which force a mobilization of all the individual's adjustive resources. The outcome of such crises has profound significance for the individual's subsequent adjustment.

Discovering the key stresses, past and present, in a person's life—and how he has dealt and is attempting to deal with them—helps us in understanding his behavior.

Adaptation to stress can be expensive

Stress is inevitable in life, although as we have seen not all stress is imposed on us. Some is of our own deliberate choosing. We all confront situations when we can choose security or risk: Should I take on the responsibilities of marriage and family? Should I compete for a job promotion that would entail increased effort and responsibility? To say "No" to all such stresses would be to say "No" to life.

Mental health and effective adjustment result not from lack of stress but from learning how to cope with stress. All adaptation has costs, however, in energy, resources, and time. In situations of severe or long-continued stress, these costs can be great.

1. *Lowering of adaptive efficiency.* On a physiological level, severe stress may result in alterations which impair the body's ability to fight off invading viruses. On a psychological level, there is a narrowing of the perceptual field and increased rigidity of cognitive processes so that it becomes difficult or impossible for the individual to see the stress situation from a different perspective or to perceive the range of alternative coping responses available to him. This process often appears to be operative in suicidal behavior.

Our adaptive efficiency may also be impaired by the emotions that typically accompany severe stress. For example, acute stage fright may disrupt the performance of a public speaker; "examination jitters" may lead to poor performance despite adequate preparation; in a sudden catastrophe, intense fear may cause the individual to panic or freeze. In fact, high levels of fear, anger, or anxiety may lead not only to impaired performance but to actual behavior disorganization. When stress increases beyond a moderate level, the efficiency of perception, problem solving, and decision making tend to progressively decrease.

2. *Lowering of resistance to other stresses.* In using its resources to meet one severe stress, the explain how sustained psychological stress can lower biological resistance to disease, and how sustained bodily disease can lower resistance to psychological stress. Interestingly, prolonged stress may lead to either pathological over-responsiveness to stress—as illustrated by the "last straw" response—or to pathological insensitivity to stress, as in loss of hope and extreme apathy. In general, sustained stress of any kind may lead to a serious reduction in the overall adaptive capacity of the organism.

3. *Wear and tear on the system.* Probably many people believe that even after a very stressful experience, rest can completely restore them. In his pioneering studies of stress, Selye found evidence that this is a false assumption.

 I would be very frightened to go back into the hospital again. I had to go see my doctor after about a month, after the operation, and just entering that hospital I felt as if I were going back into . . . I described it as Dachau, that's what I called it. And I would start to shake and everything else. It took me a long time, it took me an awfully long time to get my nerves back, and I'd never had any problem like that—I'd just shake inside.

organism may suffer a lowering of tolerance for other stresses. The Canadian physiologist Hans Selye (1956, 1969) has found that mice exposed to extremes of cold developed increased resistance to the cold but became unusually sensitive to X rays. Similarly, soldiers who develop resistance to combat may show a lowering of tolerance to other stresses, such as bad news from home. A father who has learned to handle his difficult boss tactfully all day may find when he gets home that he has no patience left for trying to cope with his thirteen-year-old son.

It appears that the coping resources of the system are limited; if they are already mobilized to capacity against one stress, they are not available for coping with others. This helps to

"Experiments on animals have clearly shown that each exposure leaves an indelible scar, in that it uses up reserves of adaptability which cannot be replaced. It is true that immediately after some harassing experience, rest can restore us almost to the original level of fitness by eliminating acute fatigue. But the emphasis is on almost. *Since we constantly go through periods of stress and rest during life, just a little deficit of adaptation energy every day adds up—it adds up to what we call aging"* (1956, pp. 274–275).

More recent findings on the role of stress in cardiovascular and other degenerative diseases have strongly supported these earlier findings (Rahe & Lind, 1971; Parkes, Benjamin, & Fitzgerald, 1969; Thiel, Parker, & Bruce, 1973).

"Wear and tear" on the system may not only involve progressive damage to the system, but in extreme form may result in actual breakdown and disintegration of the system. We have seen that each individual has his own level of stress tolerance; when this level is exceeded he "breaks down"—physically and/or psychologically. And further exposure to the stress may lead to disintegration and death. We shall deal with reactions to excessive stress in Chapter 6.

We often assume that severe stress is inherently bad since it taxes adjustive resources, is usually accompanied by some discomfort, and may result in wear and tear on the system. But there is considerable evidence, as well, that adaptation to severe stress can have constructive rather than destructive consequences—for example, the sustained stress experienced by a medical researcher whose child dies of an incurable disease may give him the determination to eventually discover the cure for the disease. In Chapter 7, we shall examine some of the ways in which coping with stress can lead to increased personal effectiveness and growth.

Summary and a look ahead

In this chapter we have examined some of the frustrations, conflicts, and pressures that place difficult adjustive demands on us and complicate the path toward our goals. We have seen that the severity of stress depends on: (1) characteristics of the adjustive demand, such as the importance, duration, and multiplicity of demands, the strength of conflicting forces, unfamiliarity and suddenness of the stress, the presence of threat, and the imminence of the anticipated stress; (2) characteristics of the individual, such as his degree of competence, perception of the problem, and stress tolerance; and (3) the presence or absence of external resources and supports. Stress, like a motive, may be partially or wholly unconscious, although the presence of tension and anxiety may be a clue that stress is present. Each person experiences a unique and changing pattern of stress, although there are often key stresses and crises which markedly influence our lives.

Stress is inevitable, although it is sometimes chosen voluntarily. Adaptation to stress can be expensive in terms of lowered efficiency, the depletion of resources, and wear and tear on the system; excessive stress may lead to the breakdown of the system. However, adaptation to stress can be a constructive and rewarding experience in the development of more competent and mature persons.

In Chapter 6, which follows, we shall examine the general principles underlying stress reactions, the three general types of reactions that we may make to stress, and what occurs when an individual is under excessive stress.

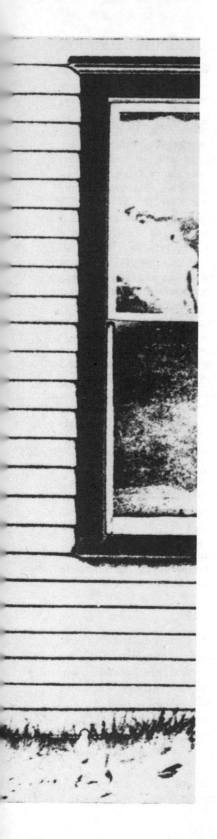

6
Reactions to Stress

Principles underlying stress reactions
Types of psychological stress reactions
Decompensation under excessive stress

All behavior—successful or unsuccessful, wise or fool-ish, rigid or flexible—is an attempt to meet the adjustive demands confronting us or which we perceive as con-fronting us. These demands may originate primarily from within (demands for food, self-esteem, social approval) or from without (demands for obedience to law, competition with others, adherence to expected role behavior).

Unfortunately, problems of adjustment do not stand in line and present themselves one at a time. They crowd in upon us, competing for our attention and coping resources. Often it seems that severe stresses never occur singly. Thus we may be trying to cope with a broken romance, financial problems, and physical illness all at once. Even though some of our problems are solved or simply disappear with time, others persist; and new problems are constantly arising. Thus coping with stress is a never ending venture for each of us.

In the present chapter, we shall focus on: (1) certain general principles underlying our stress reactions; (2) types of psychological stress reactions; and (3) decom-pensation under excessive stress. Then in Chapters 7 and 8 we shall deal with effective and ineffective ways of coping with stress.

General principles underlying stress reactions

Since stress—beyond a minimal level—endangers our well-being, it leads us to persistent attempts to cope with it; it forces us to do something about resolving it.

What we do depends upon a host of factors including our frame of reference, motives, competencies, and stress tolerance, as well as the environmental resources available to us and the demands and expectations of others. Often we meet the adjustive demand without undue difficulty; in other cases we may be only partially successful in meeting the demand; and in some cases, as we have noted, the adjustive demand may exceed our coping resources.

But whatever the outcome, there are certain general principles underlying our stress reactions. Understanding these principles will help us to gain a perspective on our coping behavior.

Reactions are holistic

The human organism functions as a whole. Just as our biological functioning is integrated in terms of a centrally controlled pattern, so our psychological functioning also follows an integrated pattern. Thus perceiving, remembering, learning, reasoning, feeling, desiring, and acting are coordinated in our efforts to meet adjustive demands. The behavior of a healthy organism is not a jumble of disconnected activities but an integrated sequence of activities directed toward achieving specific goals.

Although our adjustive resources are impressive, they are limited; and since our adjustive behavior must use the same bodily equipment—sense organs, nervous system, glands, muscles, and so on—the overall adjustive demands of the moment will determine how it is used. If there are several competing demands, the one that is most important, or is perceived as most important, commandeers our adjustive resources. Thus some functions will be *inhibited* while others are *facilitated*. This process is readily illustrated by emergency emotional

LEVELS OF ADJUSTIVE ACTION

Adjustive behavior can be viewed in terms of levels of adjustive action: biological, psychological, or social. Thus we have cellular or immunological defenses against disease; we have ego-defense mechanisms, such as rationalization, for protecting the self from devaluation; and we have police forces for maintaining law and order. Failure on any of these adjustive levels may seriously impair adjustment on other levels. Failure of our immunological defenses against disease may impair not only bodily functioning but psychological functioning as well; failure of our psychological defenses against stress may lead to various physical ailments and dysfunctions such as hypertension or coronary artery disease; and failure of the social defenses we depend on may lead to harmful consequences for the individual and the group.

The ultimate result of failure on any of these adjustive levels may be impaired overall functioning or even death. Thus again we see the integrated and holistic functioning of the human organism in its complex and continuing transactions with its environment.

responses in situations of extreme danger. Here digestive and other bodily processes not immediately essential for survival are slowed down or stopped, while resources for increased activity and effort are mobilized—with increased muscle tonus, the release of stored sugar into the bloodstream, and the secretion of adrenalin, which is a key agent in helping the body to tolerate stress.

As we have seen, the healthy organism strives to maintain its integration and "wholeness."

Under pathological conditions, however, such functioning may be interrupted, as when the function of the higher brain centers is interfered with by alcohol, drugs, or brain damage. Under normal circumstances, the organism functions as an integrated unit in coping with stress. The alternative would be disorganized behavior which would disable the individual just as surely as a football team would be disabled if each player did as he pleased instead of functioning as a member of a team.

Reactions are economical

Not only does the individual react to stress as an integrated unit, but also he reacts in a way which involves the most economical expenditure of his coping resources.

hours. This is a relatively inexpensive coping measure, at least for the moment. However, if he then fails the course and feels increasingly inadequate and anxious, he may unjustly blame his failure on an unqualified or unfair instructor. This is a more expensive stress reaction, since he cannot now profit from whatever mistakes he has made.

Of course, some of the coping patterns that people use are so self-defeating that it is hard for an outsider to see why they are not abandoned. It seems safe to assume, however, that from the individual's perspective they represent the most economical way of dealing with the stress situation. As in the case of the holistic nature of stress reactions, however, the principle of economy may break down under pathological conditions. It may also be adversely influenced by the

 Whenever things happen to me I seem to feel it in my stomach, and I feel it in my forehead. It's a tightening and it's a sinking, it's a weakening— you feel very weak. Your body, overall, feels weak, as if you probably couldn't stand up if you had to at that moment, and walk.

Since the person's resources are limited, he tends to be very thrifty in the business of living. In fact, J. G. Miller (1965b) has pointed out that the organisms that survive—whether lower or higher on the evolutionary scale—are those that tend to employ the least expensive defenses against stress first; if these are ineffective, additional and more expensive resources are brought into operation. For example, if acid is injected into a dog's veins, the first defense which appears is an adjustment in breathing; if this does not prove effective, more drastic protective mechanisms, such as biochemical changes in the blood, are brought into operation. Similarly, a student who gets an F instead of the A or B he expected on an examination may feel self-devaluated and anxious. As a consequence, he may curtail his social life and increase his study

tendency of human beings to follow established ways of perceiving, thinking, and acting—since they require less effort than learning and adopting new ones. This tendency to resist change has been referred to as "inertia" on the individual level and as "cultural lag" on the social level. It helps us to understand why established coping patterns may persist even though they are maladaptive and new, more efficient patterns have become available.

Reactions may be automatic or planned

Reactions to stress situations may be undertaken with conscious planning, with only partial awareness, or with no conscious involvement at all.

On a biological level, the repair of damaged tissue, immunological defenses against disease, and other defensive and repair processes take place automatically. Some psychological tension-reducing and repair mechanisms—such as crying, repetitive talking, and rationalization—also take place automatically. Even if the individual is aware of what he is doing, such responses are not usually planned or consciously thought out. Automatic functioning is also seen in the form of habits which we use in dealing with a wide range of adjustive demands that

tal problem, for example, is clearly reducing his chances of resolving the problem satisfactorily. In all but routine stress situations, the ability to cope effectively depends on conscious thought about the situation and the flexibility to choose an appropriate response.

Reactions involve emotions

The particular emotional states accompanying stress reactions may vary greatly. In a contest of skill or other stressful situation where the per-

once required our conscious attention, such as walking, driving, and carrying out routine work duties.

Such automatic function is of great value in helping us deal with routine adjustive demands without taking our attention from more important events which require conscious thought. It is apparent, however, that habitual behavior can also impair effective adjustive action. A person who unthinkingly employs habitual patterns of response in coping with a serious mari-

son feels he has a good chance of winning—for example, a football player going into the "big game" of the year—he may experience exhilaration. More often, however, stress elicits unpleasant emotions as in the grief experienced at the death of a loved one. For the moment, let us briefly mention three emotional patterns which are of special significance here: anger, fear, and anxiety.

1. *Frustration tends to elicit anger.* The individual's immediate reaction to frustration is typically one of anger. And anger, in turn, leads to attack or aggressive action as the individual tries to remove the obstacle to his goals. Where the frustration continues and an acceptable outlet in positive action is not possible, feelings of anger may gradually blend into hostility—characterized by feelings of wanting to hurt, damage, or destroy the person or object viewed as the source of the frustration. Where anger or hostility are intense—especially where the individual has poorly developed inner controls or where such controls are temporarily lowered by alcohol or other conditions—he may engage in impulsive behavior of a destructive nature such as assault or homicide.

2. *Specific dangers tend to elicit fear.* The perception of danger typically elicits fear; and fear, in turn, leads to withdrawal or flight. However, individuals may differ as to the direction and quality of behavior that is induced by fear. An individual who fears he may have cancer may go in immediately for a medical checkup; or he may keep postponing a visit to the doctor for fear of what might be discovered. In the face of dangers which elicit intense fear, the individual may panic or freeze and become unable to function in an organized manner. Such behavior is often observed in fires and other disasters.

Of course, both anger and fear are difficult emotions to deal with, inasmuch as civilized living permits few direct outlets. Consequently these emotions are often expressed in indirect ways, as we shall see later in this chapter.

3. *Threat tends to elicit anxiety.* Anxiety is a feeling of apprehension which tends to be elicited by situations in which the individual feels threatened. While fear is usually elicited by clearly perceived dangers, the nature of the threat eliciting anxiety may or may not be clearly perceived. Many stress situations—such as a positive diagnosis of cancer—may give rise to both fear and anxiety. Since anxiety, like physical pain, is acutely unpleasant, we are motivated to do something about it. The resulting action may range from psychological defense mechanisms such as denial to withdrawal

from the threatening situation—if this is possible.

Anger, fear, and anxiety may be aroused singly or in various combinations. Where fear or anxiety is aroused, anger often follows; for the things we fear are actual or potential sources of frustration. Of course, these so-called negative emotions may be intermeshed with more positive emotions such as love—as when an individual feels both love and hostility toward a mate who subjected him to a series of frustrations. In general, our perception of the stress situation determines the specific emotional patterns elicited.

Reactions have inner and outer determinants

As we have seen, the behavior of every living thing is determined by both its own inner properties and the nature of its environment. Sometimes inner determinants, such as a person's frame of reference, play a predominant role; at other times external factors, such as social demands, are of primary importance. But any adjustive action reflects the interplay of inner and outer determinants.

In this context, the importance of environmental resources merits reemphasis. An individual is usually most vulnerable to severe stress when he feels isolated and alone. The presence, encouragement, and emotional support of significant others make a stress situation seem less threatening and help to bolster the individual's inner resources for coping with it; and conversely, abandonment by family and friends may make a stress much more difficult to cope with.

Similarly, we cannot call a physician if there is none in the vicinity; we cannot call the police if we live in a frontier area where government has not yet been established; and we cannot go to school if there are no educational facilities in our community and we lack the means to go elsewhere. Although we live in an affluent society, few of us have all the financial and other resources we would like to have; for our poor and

The mechanism of crying provides immediate relief in a stressful situation. This marine has just learned that several of his comrades have been killed in action.

Although we are acutely aware of many of the frustrations, conflicts, and pressures that elicit coping reactions, there are others of which we may be partially or totally unaware (Lazarus, 1966). Perhaps this is not surprising, since we are so often unaware of our underlying motives and assumptions. When our unconscious attitudes toward sexual behavior, authority demands, and other life situations are in conflict with our conscious desires and ideas, the result may be vague feelings of uneasiness or apprehension that we are unable to explain. In such situations, we may lack awareness of any of the following:

1. What the adjustive demand is.

2. What fears or motives in ourselves make this demand seem threatening; what goals are being threatened.

3. The connection between the outer situation and our feeling of being threatened.

4. What resources and alternatives are available for meeting the adjustive demand.

5. The fact that we have reacted emotionally or defensively.

for many people who live in underdeveloped countries, severe limitations are placed on their adjustive behavior by lack of educational, health, occupational, and other facilities.

Although we shall sometimes discuss a bit of behavior as if it were an isolated act, it is usually impossible to pinpoint the beginning or end of an adjustive action. And ongoing, combined actions to meet a pattern of requirements may be so interrelated that they cannot be separately identified. Adjustive behavior is both complex and continuous, with evolving insights and skills, new discoveries and adaptations, and variations on recurrent themes. There is never a point when we can say we have reached adjustment—as long as we live, we are attempting to cope with and adjust to stress.

With these basic principles in mind, let us proceed to an examination of psychological reactions to stress.

Types of psychological stress reactions

Three general types of psychological reactions to stress can be delineated: (1) *"built-in"* coping and damage-repair mechanisms; (2) *learned task-oriented* reactions aimed primarily at coping directly with the stress situation; and (3) *defense-oriented* reactions aimed primarily at protecting the self from devaluation and disorganization.

It appears that there may be "built-in" mechanisms for coping with severe personal loss that follow much the same pattern regardless of the specific nature of the loss.

In a pioneering study, Cholden (1954) delineated three typical stages in the coping pattern of newly blinded persons: (1) a period of shock; (2) a period of depression or mourning involving feelings of dejection, self-pity, and hopelessness; and (3) a period of readjustment involving changes in life plans designed to salvage what the person could from the tragedy.

In a more recent study, Parkes (1972) found a similar pattern in the reactions of two groups of subjects: amputees and women suffering bereavement. The first stage was characterized by feelings of shock and numbness accompanied by a strong tendency to deny or screen out the reality of what had happened. This was followed by a second stage involving anxiety, depression, and the so-called "pangs of grief." Finally, stage three emerged in which the persons gave up hope of recovering what they had lost and began to make the necessary readjustment to life.

The above patterns appear to operate with a minimum of learning, to be characteristic of most people undergoing such personal tragedies, and to function as "damage-repair" mechanisms.

 My brother had a very serious operation, and a whole bunch of us from the family went down to the hospital to sit in their waiting room during the operation and wait for word from the doctor. So we all sat around, and we didn't joke a lot but we drank their coffee and read magazines and talked and it was the picture of complete normalcy, for about the four hours we were there. And at the end of that time the doctor appeared, still in his operating gown, sort of stained, and he said . . . he was smiling, and he said that 'it's over, he's in the recovery room, and you can see him soon,' and he told us a few details about how the operation had gone, and all of a sudden every one of us burst into tears.

An example of a "built-in" coping and damage-repair mechanism is crying in response to some distressing stress situation such as bereavement. An example of a task-oriented response would be reacting to a failing examination grade by improving one's study habits and perhaps taking other measures to ensure better preparation and performance in the future. A defense-oriented reaction to the same stress situation would be unfairly blaming the instructor for one's failure in order to protect one's feelings of adequacy and self-esteem. Many stress reactions involve components of two or even all three of these patterns, but it is usually possible to characterize an action as principally one or the other.

In the final section of this chapter we shall deal with decompensation under excessive stress. While not completely distinct from the preceding coping patterns, this reaction merits consideration in its own right.

"Built-in" coping and damage-repair mechanisms

Certain coping reactions appear to come into operation automatically rather than as a result of deliberate choice, although admittedly learning may influence them. For example, many adult males in our society would perhaps consider it a sign of weakness to cry—at least in front of other people. In any event, these built-in reactions are basically constructive in alleviating tension and anxiety, repairing psychological damage, and restoring psychological equilibrium.

Among the more common and important of these mechanisms are the following:

1. *Crying.* A built-in mechanism which is useful in relieving emotional tension and pain is crying. This reaction is commonly seen in the behavior of children who have been frustrated or hurt. And although we are often taught that "grown-ups don't cry," crying is not uncommon among adults and may serve as an important means of relieving tension and hurt and restoring inner equilibrium.

The basic purpose of "crying it out" seems to be release of emotional tension. This release is apparent in grief reactions, in which crying appears to be an essential part of the "grief work" that one must go through in the gradual regaining of emotional equilibrium. The individual may discover, however, that crying gains him sympathy, which also reduces his emotional pain. He may then develop a pattern of "crying on someone's shoulder"—of sharing his miseries with others and gaining some emotional support from their expressions of sympathy and recognition of how difficult things must be for him. This pattern is known as *sympathism.*

2. *Talking it out.* Another built-in way of relieving emotional tension is talking it out. This

THE ORIENTING REACTION

The *orienting reaction,* a built-in mechanism for paying attention to novel environmental stimuli, appears to be present in all species. As the organism turns toward the stimulus, a number of changes take place in preparation for evaluating and coping with possible threat. Among these are:

1. *Increased sensitivity,* particularly of the visual and auditory senses;

2. *Muscle changes* which serve to focus the eyes and ears and bring about a state of general alertness;

3. *Visceral changes* which prepare the body for emergency action;

4. *Brain-wave changes* which indicate increased arousal.

mechanism is so simple and so widely used that we often overlook its great reparative value.

We probably all have had friends who enjoyed telling us in gory detail about their operations or accidents or other traumatic experiences. Much of the talk teen-agers have with each other seems to be an effort to analyze and put into words feelings that are troubling them. Individuals who have survived highly traumatic experiences, such as fires or other catastrophes, often show a compulsive need to tell others of the experience. Gaining emotional relief through putting one's feelings into words is an important part of most psychotherapy; in that context the process is known as *catharsis.*

Besides relieving emotional tension, talking it out may help the individual to see his situation more clearly, new ideas and viewpoints may emerge, and there may be a constructive sharing of views. In such a case talking it out may be considered as both a task-oriented response and a defense-oriented one.

The role of built-in coping resources which we do not understand has long been illustrated by patients who manage to recover despite a terminal medical prognosis—presumably as a result of the poorly understood factor called "the will to live."

Some explanation for this tenacious hold on life may be found in the observation that many people seem determined to live until a given target date. In fact, there are reports that older persons are more likely to die after a holiday or birthday than before. Cases have even been recorded of terminally ill patients who managed to stay alive until an important event took place, such as a wedding anniversary or the birth of a grandchild.

Apparently the setting of such "target dates" for living is relatively common. Many middle-aged persons, when asked, will state that they want to live until New Year's Day of the year 2000—to see the dawning of the twenty-first century.

In somewhat similar fashion, some persons also set what amount to "target dates for death." For example, the prospect of life without the companionship of one's mate has caused many happily married older people to say they want to die when their mates do. So powerful is the loss of the will to live in some cases that the bereavement may actually precipitate the spouse's own death.

An interesting case with respect to target dates for death is that of Mark Twain (Samuel Clemens). He was born on November 30, 1835, when Halley's comet made its spectacular appearance in the sky; and he died—as he had predicted—on April 21, 1910, when Halley's comet returned. Death was attributed to angina pectoris, but the question still remains as to the underlying cause: Was it the excitement surrounding the fiery comet's return, or the conviction that the incontrovertible date for death had arrived?

3. *Laughing it off.* Trying to view one's problems with a sense of humor and laughing off setbacks and hurts is a widely used means of tension reduction. Probably we have all heard the phrase "Everything happens to me"—delivered with a shrug, indicating an attempt to see the humorous side of hurtful experiences.

In essence, this mechanism seems to be directed toward keeping things in perspective, toward an acceptance of inevitable hurts and setbacks, and toward not taking oneself too seriously. Perhaps this basic pattern can be seen in the role of the clown who laughs to cover his inner sadness and hurt. In fact, it is an interesting aspect of this mechanism that when it fails, the individual often bursts into tears.

Humor is also frequently used to reduce the tension associated with aggressive impulses and hostility toward others. Such humor tends to be hostile (Singer, 1968).

4. *Thinking it through.* After an emotional hurt, some people want to get away, as it were, to retreat to their own private mountaintop and "think things through." Often a hurtful failure leaves the individual not only damaged but somewhat confused as to what went wrong and as to the nature of his values and actions that may have contributed to the traumatic event. He may need to think about how to salvage what he can from the situation and perhaps to restructure the situation in his own mind so that he can see it more clearly and evaluate its actual significance to him more accurately.

Sometimes thinking it through is the only action available for dealing with a hurtful situation. In searching for the true meaning and significance of the situation to him, the individual becomes able to assimilate it into his cognitive structure and reduce the tension and hurt associated with it.

5. *Seeking support.* We have noted that in times of stress people often want to be with others and may seek emotional support. Thus in going through a hurtful emotional experience—such as an emotionally damaging divorce or the loss of a loved one—the individual may temporarily need to rely on others for emotional support and assistance until he can regain his equilibrium.

This pattern can be readily seen in children

I have a great sense of pride and independence, about when I get in trouble, I hold off as long as possible—I feel like I want to solve it myself, whatever it is. But occasionally when I just give in and lean on somebody else for help and support and advice—whether I take the advice or not— just the communication with somebody else makes all the difference in being able to figure out what I really ought to do about the problem.

Children often dream about situations that cause them stress. The child above is acting out his recurring nightmare of failing in school, a fear common in our competitive society.

who turn to their mothers for comfort and solace when they have been hurt. In adulthood, too, "misery loves company" and we like to be with and talk to others who care. As a habitual defensive reaction, seeking support from others may be complicated by identification, in which the individual gains strength by identifying with a strong, admired person. In some cases, however, leaning on others can be a task-oriented reaction, as when the individual is stymied in his efforts to solve a problem and turns to a professional for help.

6. *Sleep and dreams.* Although we often have difficulty sleeping when we are under stress, when sleep is possible it does appear to have a healing function. In fact, Bateson and

sleep—sometimes maintaining the medication for 24 hours or longer (Bloch, 1969). Such treatment, of course, was usually combined with reassurance, hot meals when possible, and a "duty-expectant" attitude. We shall comment briefly on combat exhaustion in Chapter 8.

Other built-in coping and damage-repair mechanisms could be mentioned—including denial and repression, which we shall deal with under the heading of learned defense-oriented reactions to stress, even though the learning in these particular defenses seems to be minimal.

However, our intent here is not to make an exhaustive list of such built-in coping and damage-repair mechanisms—which is very tentative at best in view of the scarcity of research data—

 I can express my feelings openly with my friends and family. I feel better expressing myself than climbing the walls with all of the problems and frustrations I get into sometimes. I also try to listen to others when they need help, because I know how much better you can feel by talking to someone.

Mead (1942) reported in an early study that on the island of Bali, accused prisoners often escaped from the stress of their trial by falling asleep.

People who have undergone severely traumatic experiences—such as combat experiences in wartime or civilian catastrophes such as severe earthquakes or airplane crashes—often have repeated nightmares in which they reenact their experiences and apparently are eventually desensitized to the traumatic event so that they can assimilate it into their cognitive structure without undue strain. One common treatment for soldiers evidencing combat exhaustion in the Vietnam war was medical treatment with drugs which enabled them to obtain a good night's

but rather to point up certain patterns to show how such built-in stress reactions do function in restoring and maintaining our physiological and psychological stability.

Task-oriented reactions

Task-oriented reactions, being aimed at realistically coping with the adjustive demand, tend to be based on an objective appraisal of the stress situation and on a conscious, rational, and constructive course of action.

The action itself may involve making changes in one's self or one's surroundings or both, depending upon the situation. The action may be overt—as in improving one's study habits—or covert—as in lowering one's level of aspiration or changing one's attitudes. And the action may involve attacking the problem, withdrawing from it, or finding a workable compromise.

Although we shall consider attack, withdrawal, and compromise reactions separately, a given action may embody components of all these reaction types. A student who is going to college to prepare for a career in science (basically an attack approach) may avoid courses which he feels are particularly difficult for him (basically a withdrawal or avoidance reaction), and he may be content to work less hard and make adequate rather than outstanding grades in order to take part in campus activities (basically a compromise approach). Often, too, the same action may be an attack reaction in one context and a withdrawal or compromise reaction in another. Indecision in a conflict situation might represent an attempt to avoid the further stress of making a decision, or it might be part of an attack reaction in which the individual was delaying his decision in order to study the situation further so as to ensure a wise decision.

Attack, withdrawal, and compromise reactions are not all-or-nothing patterns but rather convenient categories for ordering our discussion of stress reactions.

Attack

A hero in a western movie or television play, seeing the "bad guy" starting to draw his gun, may handle the situation by beating him to the draw. This is a simple attack response and is the prototype of much of our action. We size up the requirements of the situation and try to meet them by direct action.

Attack responses usually take somewhat different forms depending on whether the stress involves frustration, conflict, or pressure.

1. *Frustration and aggression.* Here the attack behavior takes the form of attempting to remove or surmount obstacles that block our pathway to goals. Such responses are apparently based on tendencies of living organisms toward increased activity and variation in mode of attack when obstacles to goals are encountered.

Many years ago Miller and Dollard (1941) concluded that aggression—initially viewed as attack behavior designed to damage or destroy obstacles to goals—was the logical and expected consequence of frustration. More recent evidence, however, indicates that aggression with hostile intent is usually a consequence of social learning which tends to occur in response to frustration only when it is seen as a possible way of removing the obstacle without undue cost to the individual (Bandura, 1973; Ilfeld, 1969).

If we believe, for example, that we have a good case for getting a C raised to a B in an important course but meet with a blunt refusal from our instructor, we are likely to experience anger; and in a more primitive world, the expected response might have been one of physical assault on the instructor. In our "civilized world," however, physical attack would more likely aggravate than resolve our problem. Consequently, we usually resort to more subtle and effective methods, such as going beyond the instructor to the dean or taking our grievance to a student committee.

Thus the term "aggression" has been broadened to include simply pushing toward one's goals despite opposition. When appropriate to the individual's resources and the stress situation, such coping behavior is often effective.

2. *Conflict and vacillation.* Since choices usually bring frustration, it is not surprising that people in conflict situations tend to vacillate and to be indecisive in an effort to avoid the frustration of either choice. The woman who is trying to choose between two eligible suitors—one exciting and fun to be with but sometimes irresponsible and immature and the other steady and dependable but a bit dull—may find herself deciding on first one and then the other, perhaps not even seeing the possibility that neither one would be a suitable choice.

The more equally matched the alternatives, the harder the decision. And when the conflict involves serious consequences—where the outcome is very important to us, as when we are considering marriage or an investment of our life's savings—we may try to delay a decision until we are quite sure of the consequences.

I don't very often put decisions off. I'm very much, 'Let's get it over with.'

I try not to make mistakes from making a decision too fast—I've learned to take time.

I used to believe that I never made decisions, that I was forced into whatever position I was in because there was no other choice. But of course, as I learned more, I realized that wherever you go you do make a choice.

Sometimes, of course, we may even carefully keep the alternatives open indefinitely—contriving *not* to make a decision and thus gaining some of the attractive features of both alternatives. Thus a girl may strive to maintain a relationship with two suitors and avoid making a decision as long as she can. This may represent a task-oriented reaction—keeping her options open until she is better prepared to make a sound decision.

Sooner or later, however, a choice must be made if a conflict is to be resolved by conscious intent on the part of the individual rather than by the less predictable outcome imposed by time.

3. *Pressure and resistance.* Usually the individual resists pressures on him—especially when he sees them as arbitrary and unwarranted. Children often develop highly effective techniques of resistance in coping with perfectionistic parents or teachers. Defiance and rebellion are active forms of resistance, but there are passive forms too, such as inattention, dawdling, helplessness, and deliberate underachievement. Resistance to pressure may be important in helping the individual to maintain his integrity and in protecting him from excessive demands or overloading.

Pressures on a group also tend to elicit resistance, active or passive. Workers may resist demands for a speedup by petition to the management, by union grievance committees, or by a strike, a slowdown, or excessive absenteeism. A class of fourth-graders may resist pressures toward unrealistic quietness and attention to uninteresting subject matter by apathy, by flagrant disregard of rules, or by hiding a snake in the teacher's drawer. Gandhi's India used passive resistance tellingly in its struggle against English rule.

The possible ways of attacking problems in task-oriented ways are legion and include patience, cunning, cooperation, long-range planning, increased effort, restructuring one's view of the situation, and many other patterns.

An attack reaction to stress may often be the most effective means of coordinating and using resources in constructive action. However, attack behavior may be inappropriate and self-defeating, as when the individual resists pressure to do something that would actually benefit him, makes impulsive choices in dealing with conflicts, or engages in unwarranted and destructive aggressive actions.

Withdrawal

Sometimes it is the better part of valor to avoid or withdraw from a difficult situation that is exerting demands we cannot or prefer not to meet.

1. *Escape.* Although many animals are capable of fairly well-coordinated withdrawal or flight reactions shortly after birth, the human infant has no such complex built-in patterns. He can withdraw a hand or foot from a painful stimulus, however, and he soon learns to withdraw physically from situations that are unpleasant or dangerous. He also learns to withdraw in various psychological ways, such as by admitting defeat or reducing his emotional involvement in a situation.

Although many stress situations cannot be escaped or avoided, others can be successfully dealt with in this way. A frustrating job—which is dull and for which one is not suited—may offer so little reward that we can better meet our needs by resigning and looking elsewhere. Sometimes students get halfway through teacher training or law school only to realize that this is not for them. A realistic task-oriented

woman unable to choose between two suitors may decide that she is not ready for marriage and should broaden her field of choice even if it means losing her two immediate prospects. Although she may be taking a chance in hoping to find others as eligible as those she is turning down, she manages to escape from the immediate stressful decision in a task-oriented way.

Although we cannot cope with most pressures satisfactorily by withdrawal—as in the case of pressures stemming from final examinations, being interviewed for jobs, or dealing with severe competition—there are other sources of pressure from which withdrawal is possible and may be a task-oriented reaction. If a student finds that he has registered for too many courses and his work load is excessive, he may withdraw

 I'm pretty good at getting out of bad situations. I've quit three fairly good jobs, specifically because I was unhappy and decided that was foolish. It's my policy to get out. I can do it with friendships, only that's more difficult than with jobs, but I have done it.

reaction then may involve admitting the error, writing off the lost time as perhaps not entirely lost, and switching to another field.

Of course, the situation is a little more complicated when an individual has invested a great deal of time and effort in the pursuit of a goal in which he is strongly emotionally involved—as in a love relationship or marriage. If the situation turns out to be unrewarding or perhaps impossible to maintain, a task-oriented solution may be simply to withdraw and terminate the relationship. A satisfactory resolution of many stress situations, however, depends upon knowing when to take one's losses and change one's direction.

Although most conflicts can be resolved only by a choice from among the available alternatives, some can be terminated by withdrawal from the conflict situation. Thus, for example, a

from a course to lighten his load. Similarly, a woman may withdraw from participation in various civic organizations when she finds that she has "too many things going at once."

2. *Avoidance.* As a result of learning, the individual anticipates and avoids getting into many situations that he views as potentially dangerous or threatening. Such behavior is shown by the student who avoids taking courses that he thinks will be too difficult for him or by the businessman who refuses a promotion because he feels that it would entail increased pressures that he prefers not to undertake. People of all ages often avoid emotional involvement in situations where they are afraid of being hurt.

Once again we see that the individual is not a passive recipient of stress: often he can exercise considerable control over the nature and degree of stress to which he is exposed and thus keep stress from becoming excessive.

Attack and withdrawal—fight and flight—are fundamental forms of coping with stress found in all animals: They appear to be part of the organism's built-in evolutionary heritage. Attack helps the organism to overcome obstacles and attain goals relevant to its survival; withdrawal serves to remove the organism from threatening situations which it cannot overcome. Anger is the most common emotion accompanying attack, fear the most common emotion accompanying withdrawal. In severe stress, anxiety is usually prominent also.

he would really like to date finally takes out someone else; a young woman compromises with the "dream image" husband she has always imagined and marries the young man who is actually available.

In more severe stress situations, compromises may be rather extreme in degree. A prisoner of war may collaborate with his hated captors in an effort to ensure survival and better treatment. An individual who has been subjected to prolonged semistarvation may eat insects, the bark off trees, and practically any other substitute that has nutritional value or tends to assuage his hunger. One of the men in the ill-fated Greely

 If you want to keep your psyche in good shape— anybody who exists in today's world should do this—periodically, you should go away—change your environment. How often depends on your own insides and on your particular opportunities. If you spend your life indoors, then go outdoors. If you spend your working life by a body of water, you ought to go to the mountains. If you spend your working life talking with people, go someplace where you don't talk to people and maybe be alone—completely alone.

Compromise

Most task-oriented behavior is neither entirely attack nor entirely withdrawal but a compromise. You may change what you can in yourself or the stress situation, avoid confrontation with certain aspects of it, perhaps by limiting your field of operations, and live as best you can with what cannot be changed or escaped or with what you decide is, on balance, worth the trouble. Two common compromise reactions are substitution and accommodation.

1. *Substitution.* In a situation of sustained or seemingly quite inescapable frustration, the individual often tends to reduce the stress by accepting whatever goals and satisfactions he can attain in the situation. For example, a young man who is consistently turned down by the girl

expedition to the arctic (see page 24) ate his sealskin boots. In a somewhat less dramatic way, a frustrated person may find symbolic satisfactions, such as staring at erotic pictures in lieu of sexual activity or he may gain some satisfaction from fantasies of desired goals.

Of course, the extent to which the individual will accept such substitute and symbolic goals will depend on the character and strength of the barrier and on his motivation, values, and ability to withstand stress. He is particularly likely to accept substitute goals when the barrier seems insurmountable or would require more effort and sacrifice than he thinks the original goal warrants.

2. *Accommodation.* The term *accommodation* has various meanings but here is used to refer to

CHARACTERISTICS OF TASK-ORIENTED REACTIONS TO STRESS

As we have seen, task-oriented stress reactions usually fall into one of three categories: attack, withdrawal, or compromise. Despite the diversity of reactions in each category, certain characteristics common to each type can be delineated:

ATTACK REACTIONS

Focusing coping resources

The individual musters his forces, increases his effort, and undertakes a course of action to deal with the problem.

Maintaining flexibility

The individual chooses the most promising course of action but maintains flexibility and shifts his approach if it does not seem to be working out or if a better possibility presents itself. He attempts to remain sensitive to changes in the stress situation, to avoid narrowing and rigidity of thinking, and to function rationally despite emotional arousal.

Developing new resources

The individual attempts to increase his coping resources by such means as searching out new information, developing new competencies or improving existing ones, and obtaining professional assistance if necessary.

Affiliating for group action

The individual may join with others so that the resources of the group can be added to his own in dealing with the stress situation.

WITHDRAWAL REACTIONS

Admitting defeat

The individual admits that the situation is too difficult for him or that he has chosen an inappropriate goal which he no longer wishes to pursue.

compromise behavior in which we settle for part of what we wanted. And since the resolution of so many of our problems is dependent on the action of others as well as ourselves, *mutual accommodation* is often needed, in which both parties give a little and get a little. For example, the resolution of a problem in marital adjustment usually involves mutual give and take, with some adaptation on the part of both partners.

Many problems on both interpersonal and intergroup levels are solved through negotiating, bargaining, and concessions on one or both sides—in essence, compromise behavior in which the participants accommodate their requirements and get part of what they wanted but not all. We see such patterns in labor-management disputes, student-faculty conflicts, and relationships between nations, as well as in

our relationships with friends and family members. We shall elaborate further on interpersonal accommodation in our later discussion of marriage and other social relationships. Suffice it here to note the importance of such compromise patterns in dealing with stress problems.

If the compromise reaction succeeds in meeting the essential requirements of the situation, the stress problem is satisfactorily resolved and the individual can devote his energies to other matters. Often, however, we make compromises which we cannot fully accept or live with because important needs continue to go unmet. In such instances, additional adjustive action is required.

Task-oriented reactions of all three types—attack, withdrawal, and compromise—involve the same basic steps of: (1) defining the prob-

Leaving the field	This may involve physical or psychological withdrawal from the stress situation or both—as in the case of leaving an uncongenial profession.
Establishing a new direction	Instead of drifting or indefinitely "nursing his wounds," the individual redirects his efforts toward a more appropriate goal.

COMPROMISE REACTIONS

Accepting substitute goals	When an individual realizes that he cannot attain the exact goal he is seeking, he may settle for the best substitute or approximation. This may mean reassessing his abilities and lowering his level of aspiration.
Accepting substitute means	Unable to reach his goal by one means, an individual tries another. Sometimes people lower their ethical standards to get what they want; such a reaction, though task-oriented, is maladjustive in the larger view because it meets their needs at others' expense.
Assuring minimum essentials	If an individual cannot have all he hopes for, it is important for him to know what he can and cannot do without. Sometimes people make bad compromises that they find they cannot live with, complicating rather than resolving their problems in the long run.
Taking time to deliberate	When an individual is in doubt about what decision to make and time permits a delay, he does well not to let himself be rushed into action. With a wait-and-see response he can let the situation unfold and avoid precipitous action that he might regret later. Circumstances may change, and the problem may even solve itself. In some cases, of course, the option of delay is not open or practical.

lem; (2) working out alternative solutions and deciding on an appropriate course of action; (3) taking action, and (4) evaluating the feedback. These same steps will be elaborated upon in Chapter 7.

Although a task-oriented approach usually has the best chance of resolving our problems, even a task-oriented approach can fail. If our choices are based on faulty values, we may meet the immediate demand but may lay the basis for more serious problems later. If, because of limited knowledge, we choose an unsuitable course of action, it may even compound our problem. And even when we choose well and act with skill, factors beyond our control may tip the balance in preventing our action from solving the problem. As the poet Burns put it so succinctly:

"The best-laid schemes o' mice an' men,
  Gang aft agley,
An' lea'e us nought but grief an' pain,
  For promis'd joy!"

Defense-oriented reactions

The individual who faces severe stress has two problems: (1) to meet the adjustive demand, and (2) to protect himself from psychological disorganization. In defense-oriented coping behavior, the individual is concentrating on the latter—utilizing reactions aimed primarily at alleviating tension and anxiety, lessening emotional hurt, and avoiding self-devaluation.

Here our focus will be on so-called ego-defense mechanisms. These mechanisms are in the main heavily dependent upon learning but tend to operate on habitual and unconscious levels. For the most part they lead to some measure of self-deception and reality distortion and thus are not adaptive in the sense of realistically coping with the stress situation.

Despite their drawbacks, however, all of us make some use of such defenses. They are essential for softening failure, reducing cognitive dissonance, alleviating anxiety, repairing emotional hurt, and maintaining our feelings of adequacy and worth. Thus we must consider them normal coping mechanisms unless they are used to such a degree that they impair the individual's ability to meet his life problems. Like a nation devoting its major energies to

summary chart of these and other ego-defense mechanisms appears on page 139.

Denial of reality

A primitive defense mechanism for restricting experience, observable even in young children, is to deny reality. We evade many disagreeable realities simply by ignoring or refusing to acknowledge them. Very few of us, for example, accept the full inevitability of death. Even if we act as if we were quite resigned to the idea, the full realization of our own inevitable death is usually mercifully obscured by vague feelings of omnipotence—everybody else dies but not us—or by religious convictions about life after death.

 During the Vietnam war, when I was over there fighting, I found a way to keep from losing my mind. I made the whole affair into a game and pretended that what was going on around me was an everyday occurrence. I guess for me it was. The whole time I was doing this I knew what I was doing, and yet I continued to play this game. I still don't know why.

armaments, too heavy a load of defensive activities can be self-defeating, making the individual less strong instead of more so.

Ego-defense mechanisms protect the self from external threats, such as devaluating failures, as well as internal threats, such as unacceptable desires and impulses or guilt resulting from actions we have already taken. They protect us in one or more of the following ways: (1) by denying or restricting our experience, (2) by cognitive distortion, (3) by reduction of emotional involvement, and (4) by counteraction of the threat. Often, of course, a given defense mechanism may offer more than one kind of protection.

The following ego-defense mechanisms merit special attention in our present discussion. A

Our tendency toward perceptual defense, already discussed, is part of this tendency to avoid or deny unpleasant reality. We turn away from unpleasant sights, refuse to discuss unpleasant topics, ignore or deny criticism, and refuse to face many of our real problems. Under extreme conditions, such as imprisonment, the individual may experience the feeling that "This isn't really happening to me." Here, at least temporarily, the denial appears to protect the individual from the full impact of the traumatic experience.

By ignoring or denying unpleasant reality, we do protect ourselves from a great deal of stress. But like the proverbial ostrich who buries his head in the sand when danger approaches, we may fail to take cognizance of many realities that we need to know about for effective adjustment.

SUMMARY CHART OF EGO-DEFENSE MECHANISMS

Denial of reality	Refusing to perceive or face unpleasant reality
Repression	Preventing painful or dangerous thoughts from entering consciousness
Regression	Retreating to earlier developmental level involving less mature responses and usually a lower level of aspiration
Fantasy	Gratifying frustrated desires by imaginary achievements
Rationalization	Attempting to prove that one's behavior is "rational" and justifiable and thus worthy of the approval of oneself and others
Projection	Placing blame for difficulties upon others or attributing one's own unethical desires to others
Reaction formation	Preventing the expression of dangerous desires by exaggerating the opposite attitudes and types of behavior
Identification	Increasing feelings of worth by identifying oneself with some outstanding person or institution
Introjection	Incorporating into one's own ego structure the values and standards imposed by others
Emotional insulation	Reducing ego involvement and withdrawing into passivity to protect oneself from hurt
Intellectualization	Suppressing the emotional aspect of hurtful situations or separating incompatible attitudes by logic-tight compartments
Compensation	Covering up weakness by emphasizing some desirable trait or making up for frustration in one area by overgratification in another
Displacement	Discharging pent-up feelings, usually of hostility, on objects less dangerous than those which initially aroused the emotions
Undoing	Counteracting "immoral" desires or acts by some form of atonement
Acting out	Reducing the anxiety aroused by forbidden desires by permitting their expression

Repression

This is a defense mechanism by means of which threatening or painful thoughts and desires are excluded from consciousness. This mechanism is illustrated in a dramatic way by the person who has undergone an extremely traumatic experience during a natural catastrophe—such as a tornado or earthquake—and is brought to an aid station suffering from amnesia. He does not remember the situation or his name or anything about himself. He may be nervous and depressed and show other signs of his ordeal, but the intolerable disaster situation itself is screened from his consciousness, and he is thus protected from overwhelming stress. The repressed experience is not forgotten, however, and may be brought into consciousness by means of hypnosis or Pentothal interviews. Such repressive defenses operate on a temporary basis until time and other conditions have desensitized him to the point where he can recall the event without serious psychological disorganization.

In a less dramatic situation, a boy with strong feelings of hostility toward his father may have these feelings so well repressed that he is unaware of his hatred. Similarly, sexual desires that the individual considers immoral may be blocked from his consciousness by means of repression. But repression is not always complete, and repressed memories and desires may be revealed in dreams and reveries and under the influence of alcohol or drugs. When repressive defenses are in danger of failing, the individual becomes extremely anxious, for he is again placed under threat. And if his defenses actually do fail, as when repressed homosexual desires—which he considers immoral and alien to his self-concept—enter consciousness, the individual's psychological functioning may be seriously disrupted.

Repression is an important means of helping the individual to cope with the potentially disorganizing effects of painful experiences and desires regarded as dangerous and unacceptable. In fact, in varying degrees repression enters into most other defensive patterns. However, repression may screen out stressful experiences that could better be met by realistically facing and working through the situation. We cannot solve and learn from a problem that we do not see.

Repression is an unconscious device and thus not subject to conscious evaluation and control. In this it differs from *suppression,* in which one decides not to express a feeling or not to act on a desire or even not to think about a disturbing event. Suppression is a healthy process, necessary for mature functioning in a social context; repression is a pain-softening but potentially very dangerous process.

Regression

This is a reaction involving a retreat to the use of reaction patterns which were appropriate at an earlier level of development. For example, when a new baby in the family has seemingly undermined his status, a child may revert to bedwetting, baby talk, and other infantile behavior which once brought him parental attention. But regression is a more comprehensive reaction than merely trying out older, formerly successful modes of response when new ones have failed. For in regression the individual retreats from present reality to an earlier, less demanding personal status—one which involves lowered aspirations and more readily accomplished satisfactions.

On a simple level regression is illustrated by the new bride who goes home to the protective arms of her mother at the first sign of trouble in her marriage; and by the husband who becomes "childish" and demands to be waited on when he gets the flu. A more dramatic example of regressive behavior under stress is provided by Bettelheim's description of the general "regression to infantile behavior" seen in nearly all the prisoners at the concentration camps of Dachau and Buchenwald in Nazi Germany:

"The prisoners lived, like children, only in the immediate present; . . . they became unable to plan for the future or to give up immediate pleasure satisfactions to gain greater ones in the future. . . .They were boastful, telling tales about what they had accomplished in their former lives, or how they succeeded in cheating foremen or guards, and how they sabotaged the work. Like children they felt not at all set back or ashamed when it became known that they had lied about their prowess" (1943, pp. 445–446).

Most people do not rely heavily on regression as a defense against stress. However, the emergence of developmentally lower levels of functioning is frequently seen among persons suffering severe mental disorders. Dinello (1967) has described the case of a seventeen-year-old youth who had regressed to the point of wearing a diaper. In extreme cases, such persons may become unable to dress or feed themselves or to take care of their eliminative needs. These examples of regression, of course, are clearly beyond the range of the "normal."

Fantasy

Besides screening out unpleasant aspects of reality, we also tend to use fantasy to picture things as we would like them to be. Fantasy is stimulated by frustrated desires and grows out of mental images associated with need gratification. In fantasy, the person achieves his goals and meets his needs in his imagination.

Two common varieties of wish-fulfilling fantasy are the "conquering hero" and the "suffering hero" patterns. In the first, the individual pictures himself as a great athlete, a renowned surgeon, a distinguished and courageous sol-

have treated him and give him the attention he deserves. By such fantasies, the individual avoids the admission of personal inferiority or lack of worth and to some extent also avoids the necessity of striving more strenuously toward his goals. He has actually demonstrated remarkable courage and is highly successful considering the handicaps under which he has labored. In short, he merits the sympathy and admiration of all.

Escaping temporarily from the stresses of everyday life into a more pleasant fantasy world is often helpful in adding the dash of excitement and encouragement that enables us to return to the struggle. But fantasy becomes maladjustive if we substitute the easier accomplishments of

 I must admit that sometimes the future for my mental well-being is in doubt. I tend to take off in fantasy worlds, inspired by something here in the real world and expanded upon in my own mind. I find myself seeking escape from the pressures and ugly truths of the real world. It is very easy for me to lose myself in a fantasy world—with a clever mind one can conjure up an incredibly pleasant world.

dier, a man of immense wealth, or some other remarkable figure who performs incredible feats and wins the admiration and respect of all— the basic idea being that he is respected and powerful. James Thurber used this theme in his popular "Secret Life of Walter Mitty." The conquering hero may also dissipate possible hostility safely by the fantasied destruction of all who stand in his way; such fantasies act as safety valves and provide some measure of compensatory gratification.

Another common fantasy pattern is the "suffering hero" type. Here the individual imagines that he is suffering from some horrible affliction or handicap or is an adopted and abused child; when people find out about the difficulties besetting him, they will be sorry for the way they

make-believe for real-life endeavors. This mechanism can be seen in extreme form in the case of mental patients who develop delusions of grandeur and retreat from reality into a fantasy world of their own construction.

Rationalization

This is a defense mechanism in which we justify our behavior by imputing logical and admirable or at least acceptable motivation to it. If we decide to go to a movie when we know we should study, we can usually think up various reasons to justify our decision: we only live once, everyone needs a change of pace, and the relaxation will brush away the cobwebs and make us able to think more clearly. Or we may try to justify cheating by pointing out that others cheat, that there is no virtue in being a sucker, and that in real life society doesn't ask too many questions as long as you are successful. By rationalizing, we can usually justify about everything we have done, are doing, or propose to do and hence can alleviate the devaluating effects of failure, guilt, and irrational behavior.

Rationalization is also used to soften the disappointment of thwarted desires. A common example of such rationalization is the "sour grapes" reaction—stemming from Aesop's fable of the fox who, unable to reach a cluster of delicious grapes, decided he did not want them anyway because they were probably sour. If we have little money, we may emphasize that the really important things in life—such as love and friendship—are free; if we are turned down for a date, we may decide the evening probably would have been dull anyway. The opposite of the sour grapes type of rationalization is the "sweet lemon" mechanism; not only is what we cannot have not worth having, but what we do have is remarkably satisfactory. Not only are the most important things in life free, but it is actually better to be poor because money is the root of all evil.

Rationalization is a very complex mechanism and one that is often difficult to detect because rationalizations frequently contain elements of truth. We may suspect that we are rationalizing when we: (1) hunt for reasons to justify our behavior or beliefs, (2) are unable to recognize inconsistencies that others see, and (3) become emotional when the reasons for our behavior are questioned. The questioning of our rationalizations is, of course, a threat to the defenses we have constructed against frustration and self-devaluation, and anxiety is aroused when these defenses are jeopardized or destroyed. The price of this defensive reaction, however, is self-deception, for we accept reasons for our behavior which are not the true ones. Like repression, rationalization enters in varying degree into a number of other defense mechanisms.

Projection

This is a reaction in which we blame others for our own mistakes and shortcomings or ascribe to others our own unacceptable motivations. A husband who feels guilty about his extramarital affairs may place the blame on his unsympathetic wife or on "girls who lead him on"; the boy punished for fighting protests, "He hit me first—it was his fault." The dishonest person may insist that you can't trust anybody.

Projection appears to be a common mechanism among individuals with rigid moral values and conscience development. Their rigid standards make it impossible for them to accept desires which they view as unethical as part of their own makeup. Such desires are highly threatening and self-devaluating and usually cannot be adequately handled by rationalization or other defense mechanisms. As a consequence, they are projected to someone else who now becomes the offender while the individual himself remains conveniently "pure." The individual with guilt-arousing homosexual leanings may accuse other men of trying to seduce him—while he remains unaware of his own homosexual inclinations. In extreme form, such projections are evidenced by mental patients who accuse others of "pouring filth into their minds."

Rationalization and projection probably develop from our early learning that advancing socially approved reasons for our behavior or putting the blame on others helps us to avoid disapproval and punishment. And as we learn and accept society's values, such defense reactions protect us from self-devaluation and anxiety. However, we may pay an exorbitant price for such defensive maneuvers.

Reaction formation

Here the person protects himself from dangerous desires by not only repressing them but actually developing conscious attitudes and behavior patterns directly opposed to such desires. Thus he may conceal hate with a façade of love, cruelty with kindness, or desires for sexual promiscuity with moralistic sexual attitudes and behavior. These new feelings or attitudes help the individual to keep his real but dangerous desires from entering consciousness or being carried out in action.

On a simple level, reaction formation is illustrated by the joke about the old maid who looks hopefully under her bed each night for fear that a man may be lurking there. On a more complex level, reaction formation may be manifested by people who crusade militantly against loose sexual morals or the evils of alcohol or gambling. Often such people have a background of earlier difficulties with such problems themselves, and their zealous crusading appears to be a means of

hold his own dangerous impulses in check.

Reaction formation helps to maintain socially approved behavior and protects a person from the knowledge that he has desires which he considers immoral. But the self-deception is based on an inability to accept himself as he is. Preventing an accurate self-picture, it also keeps him from realistically working through his problems and leads to rigidity and harshness in dealing with others.

safeguarding themselves against a recurrence of such behavior.

Self-appointed protectors of the public morals who devote their lives to ferreting out obscene passages in literary works or drawing attention to the inadequate attire of nightclub dancers can even gain a certain amount of vicarious satisfaction of their own repressed desires without endangering their self-concepts. In some cases, reaction formation is more subtle, as when a juror demands the most severe penalty that the law provides for an infraction that he himself has been tempted to commit. By such condemnation and punishment, he is attempting to

Identification

As we have seen in our earlier discussion, identification takes place in imitative learning—as when a boy identifies with his father and uses him as a model. Identification may also operate as a defense mechanism in enhancing feelings of worth and protecting the individual against self-devaluation.

The growing child soon realizes that other people's evaluation of him is to a large extent dependent upon his family and other group memberships. His father's occupation and the family's financial status and position in the

> I usually identify, among other things, with a company or group I'm working for, or with. So if I'm working for somebody, I'm on 'their side.' I've been in the position a lot of times of when criticisms come up about the company or criticisms about somebody I feel I represent in the company, I find myself defending like mad, and feeling personally attacked when they're attacked. It's very important to me to have the people I work for be okay, and be thought of as okay.

community are important in determining the way other people evaluate him; and his own sense of personal worth and identity may come to depend heavily upon these family characteristics. During adolescence and adulthood, the mechanism of identification is expanded to include a wide range of personal and group identifications.

Most of us identify strongly with being "an American"; some of us also identify ourselves with some region of the country and think of ourselves as Southerners, New Yorkers, or Texans. College students may bask in the reflected glory of their football or basketball teams—"We won today"; fraternity and sorority members feel personally enhanced by the social prestige of their groups. An adult's sense of identity includes the prestige accorded his occupation, the size and address of his home, his memberships in clubs or other organizations, and the accomplishments of his children. He enhances his own feelings of adequacy and worth by associating himself with respected individuals and groups either through actual activity or through name-dropping. Particularly for an individual who feels basically inferior, such identifications may have important defensive values.

Although identification may help us to feel more adequate and secure, it also has its dangers. The individual who relies too heavily on his identifications with others for his feelings of adequacy and self-worth develops an inaccurate and unrealistically favorable self-image and is highly vulnerable in stress situations in which

his identifications cannot help him or in which those with whom he identifies suffer humiliation. In the latter case, his identifications may lead to self-devaluation rather than enhancement. This is one reason why it is difficult for a coach to hold his job if his team loses consistently.

Introjection

Introjection is closely related to identification. It means acceptance of others' values and attitudes as one's own as a safety measure, even when they are contrary to one's previous values. After revolutions leading to dictatorial forms of government, for example, many people introject the new values and beliefs as a protection against behavior which might get them into trouble. By internalizing the socially prescribed values as their own, they can then trust themselves to avoid behavior that would bring social retaliation and punishment.

The use of introjection under extreme conditions was well described by Bettelheim in his report of experiences in Nazi concentration camps. Under the insidious camp experiences, previous values and identifications were broken down and new norms were introjected—Nazi norms.

"A prisoner had reached the final stage of adjustment to the camp situation when he had changed his personality so as to accept as his own the values of the Gestapo . . . old prisoners were sometimes instrumental in getting rid of the unfit,

in this way making a feature of Gestapo ideology a feature of their own behavior" (1943, pp. 447–449).

Though introjection may have defensive value in protecting the individual from hopeless frustrations and enabling him to maintain some control over his fate, it is obviously a primitive and potentially destructive defensive pattern.

Emotional insulation

Here one reduces his degree of emotional involvement in potentially hurtful situations. Since we all undergo many disappointments in life, we usually learn to keep our hopes and anticipations within bounds until a hoped-for event actually occurs. We are careful to avoid premature celebrations or to let our hopes get too high. The student who is looking forward to

individual from further hurt by a world he has found unbearably painful.

Up to a point, emotional insulation is an important mechanism for defending ourselves from both unnecessary and unavoidable hurt. But life involves calculated risks, and most of us are willing to take our chances on active participation. Although we may get badly hurt on occasion, we have the resiliency to recover and try again. Emotional insulation provides a protective shell that prevents a repetition of previous pain, but in so doing it also prevents the individual's healthy, vigorous participation in living.

Intellectualization

This mechanism is related to both emotional insulation and rationalization. Here the emo-

 I will never have a broken heart if I don't fall in love. I will never be a failure if I have no desire for status. Every year my emotional detachment from almost everything has increased. When I start to feel the symptoms of an entangling relationship cramping my style, I end that relationship. I have no goals other than to be goalless.

a date with a very attractive girl may not let himself get too emotionally involved for fear that something will go wrong or that she may not like him. Such reactions are well expressed in the common saying, "I didn't dare to hope."

In extreme conditions of long-continued frustration, as in chronic unemployment or prison confinement, many persons lose hope and become resigned and apathetic. Such "broken" individuals protect themselves from the hurt of sustained frustration by reducing their involvement—they no longer care and hence deprive the stress situation of much of its power to hurt them. In chronic schizophrenic reactions, to be examined in Chapter 8, there is often an extreme use of emotional insulation, which protects the

tional feelings that would normally accompany a hurtful event are avoided by a rational explanation which divests the event of personal significance and painful feeling. Grief over the death of one's mother may be softened by pointing out that she lived to be over 70 years of age; failures and disappointments are softened by pointing out that "it could have been worse"; cynicism may become a convenient means of preventing or reducing guilt over not living up to our ideals. Even the verbalizing of good intentions as in the glib admission that "we should be less selfish and more interested in the welfare of others" seems to cut off a good deal of guilt and relieve us of the necessity of mending our ways.

Intellectualization may be utilized under extremely stressful conditions as well as in dealing with the milder stresses of everyday life. Bluestone and McGahee (1962) found that this defense was often used by prisoners awaiting execution.

" 'So they'll kill me; and that's that'—this said with a shrug of the shoulders suggests that the affect appropriate to the thought has somehow been isolated."

Or they may feel as though it were all happening to someone else, and they are watching impersonally from a distance.

In such reactions, denial, rationalization, and other ego-defense mechanisms may play a prominent role, but it is the cutting off or insulating of the individual from his normal feelings that concerns us here. While intellectu-

Unfortunately, not all compensatory reactions are desirable or useful. The child who feels insecure may show off to try to get more attention and raise his status in the eyes of others and himself; the boy who feels inferior and unpopular may become the local bully; and the person who feels unloved and frustrated may eat too much. Some people build themselves up by bragging about their own accomplishments; others do it by criticism or innuendos in an attempt to cut other people down. In extreme cases, the individual may become markedly eccentric in an attempt to win interest and admiration from others.

In the main, compensatory reactions are ineffective because the activities engaged in are aimed not at a positive goal but at balancing a

 I developed humor so that I could get along socially. It gave me some . . . I've always felt very insecure socially, and sort of out of it. And when I found I could trade quips with people and say funny things and people would enjoy being with me, I found that was the best avenue I could find to give myself a sense of social security, so to speak.

alization may be of value in preventing unnecessary hurt, it is also apparent that it can be used in self-defeating ways to justify unethical behavior.

Compensation

In compensation the individual defends himself against feelings of inadequacy by disguising or counterbalancing a weak or undesirable trait while emphasizing or developing a desirable one. Compensatory reactions take many forms and may actually have considerable adjustive value. For example, a physically unattractive boy or girl may develop a pleasing personality and become an interesting conversationalist. As a consequence, the physical unattractiveness is no longer a major obstacle to social acceptance and success.

deficit. They tend not to be constructive—as in the case of eating too much as a reaction to frustration. Or they incur social disapproval—as in showing off—which only increases the person's sense of failure and inferiority.

Displacement

Here we shall confine the use of the term *displacement* to a redirection of hostility toward some object or person other than the one actually causing the frustration. Unable for practical reasons to express his feelings directly, the individual is able to find some relief by expressing it toward a less dangerous target. A child who has been spanked or thwarted by his mother may kick his little sister or break up his toys. A common subject for cartoons is the office clerk who has been refused a raise. Instead of expressing his hostility toward his employer—which would be dangerous to his job—he goes home and snaps irritably at his wife because dinner is a few minutes late. His frustrated wife, in turn, takes out her hostility on their son, who displaces his anger onto the dog or cat.

Displaced aggression may also take other forms. One is swearing, commonly used as a means of discharging feelings elicited by frustration. Another is to find a scapegoat[1] who can be blamed for one's problems and cannot fight back. In Hitler's Germany the Jews were blamed for the country's ills, and pent-up feelings of frustration and hostility were discharged against this group. The scapegoating mechanism is common in dictatorships, where hostility is likely to be aroused by the stern, repressive measures of the government but where any opposition or direct expression of hostility is extremely dangerous. Throughout the history of the world, racial, religious, and political prejudices have often been intertwined with displaced aggression and scapegoating.

In some instances, the individual is either afraid or unable to direct his hostility toward others and may turn it inward upon himself. In such cases, he may engage in exaggerated self-accusations and recriminations and may feel severe guilt and self-devaluation. Such intropunitive reactions may lead to depression and to suicide or threats of suicide.

Displacement may be of adjustive value, since it is a means of discharging dangerous emotional tensions without the risk of retaliation. It may also enable the person to avoid ambivalent feelings toward some powerful or loved figure. By displacing his hostility onto his spouse, an employee may maintain relatively pure feelings of respect and cordiality toward his domineering boss. Unfortunately, however, this achievement may be at the expense of harmony in his marriage; likewise, the use of minority groups as scapegoats is not likely to contribute to social

[1]*Among the ancient Israelites, the priest symbolically heaped all the sins of the people upon an unblemished goat—a* scapegoat—*which was then driven into the wilderness to die.*

progress. And turning one's hostility inward gains feelings of safety at the expense of feelings of self-respect. So displacement may enact a high price for its benefits. In most cases it is much more healthful and less painful in the long run to face and work through painful or hostility-arousing situations than to avoid them through displacement.

Undoing

This is a mechanism designed to negate or atone for some disapproved thought, impulse, or act. It is as if the individual has spelled a word wrong and then uses an eraser to clear the paper and start over. Apologizing for wrongs against others, penance, repentance, and undergoing punishment are some of the common forms that undoing may take. The opportunity for confession and the assurance of forgiveness in some religions meet a deep human need to be able to get rid of guilt feelings and make a new beginning.

Undoing, as a defense mechanism, apparently develops out of early training in which we are punished or forced to make restitution for our misdeeds. Once the restitution has taken place, our misdeed is negated and we can start with a clean slate. By returning his sister's toys with alacrity and saying he is sorry, Johnny may make sufficient restitution to avoid being punished and to reestablish parental approval and affection. Such early lessons relating wrongdoing to punishment and undoing to escape from punishment are not lost on us; in adult life the same techniques of atoning may help to alleviate the guilt we feel when we violate values that we have accepted. Thus the unfaithful husband may have a sudden impulse to bring his wife flowers; an unethical businessman may give unusually large sums of money to some charitable organization; and the rejecting mother may shower her child with material indications of her alleged care and concern.

Sometimes people feel so uncomfortable with their guilt that they confess their misdeeds in order to be punished as atonement for their sins. Not infrequently, individuals who have committed minor crimes years earlier will confess to the police in order to "pay their debt to society" and start afresh.

Since undoing promotes ethical human relations and helps us maintain our feelings of self-esteem and worth, it is one of our most valuable defense mechanisms. Again, however, we may rely on it too much—at the expense of understanding and improving our behavior. In fact, some individuals even appear to undertake unethical behavior with the expectation that they can make atonement for it later and emerge without guilt. Rationalization and projection may, of course, help make such a course seem attractive and safe. However, undoing does not always enable the individual to escape from the consequences of his actions. Even though he apologizes for lying to a friend on an important matter and attempts to atone for it, their relationship may never be the same again.

Acting out

One may reduce the tension and anxiety associated with forbidden desires by acting out—by permitting their expression. Instead of trying to deny or repress or change immoral sexual or hostile desires or hold strong aggressive impulses in check, one simply engages in the behavior. For example, an individual in conflict over his homosexual desires may go ahead and engage in an overt homosexual act; or one who has helplessly nursed a long history of grievances may finally lash out verbally or physically and may damage property associated with those he considers responsible for his frustration. Vandalism around school property often seems to be motivated by pent-up anger and frustration. Much acting out is to some degree violent and antisocial.

All of us have probably experienced times of acute conflict or stress when tension and anxiety have built up to such a level that we welcomed almost any action that would "get it over with." Soldiers, under the stress of waiting, have been known to leave their relatively safe shelter and blindly attack the enemy. Although such acting-out behavior may momentarily reduce tension and anxiety, it is obviously not well

Most of us at some time in our lives have desired to be other than we are, if only for a day. Events like Mardi Gras offer socially acceptable occasions in which we can lose ourselves and our worries for a time while acting out our wildest imaginings.

designed to deal effectively with the demand creating the anxiety.

Under most circumstances acting out is not feasible except for those who have very weak reality and ethical controls; most people are deterred not only by their own values but also by the likelihood of social disapproval or perhaps punishment. Although acting out may reduce emotional tension, it does not usually cope with the adjustive demand and often makes matters much worse.

Although the ego-defense mechanisms involved in coping with a given type of stress may vary considerably depending upon the individual and the situation, certain patterns may be considered typical:

Stress centering around	Common ego-defense mechanisms
Failure	Rationalization, projection, compensation
Guilt	Rationalization, projection, undoing
Hostility	Fantasy, displacement, repression, reaction formation
Inferiority feelings	Identification, compensation, fantasy
Disappointment in love	Insulation, rationalization, fantasy
Personal limitations	Denial of reality, fantasy, compensation
Forbidden sexual desires or behavior	Rationalization, projection, repression

In the preceding discussion we have examined the major defense mechanisms that we use in coping with the stresses of life. Although we have dealt with them singly, they are often used in combination, as when intense hostility toward an autocratic and feared father is handled by a combination of repression, reaction formation, and displacement. They may also be combined with more task-oriented behavior. Because they are essential for softening failure, alleviating tension and anxiety, and protecting one's feelings of adequacy and worth, we may consider them to be normal adjustive reactions unless they seriously interfere with the effective resolution of stress situations.

Both the positive and negative aspects of ego-defense mechanisms have been well illustrated in a study by Katz, Weiner, Gallagher, and Hellman (1970), who intensively studied the ego-defenses of 30 hospitalized women who were awaiting the outcome of breast tumor biopsy. These researchers found the defense mechanisms of denial and rationalization to be highly effective in coping with anxiety, particularly when used in combination. They also found, however, that many of the women who allayed their anxieties about having cancer by these defenses impaired their chances for survival—by not seeking medical help until the condition was well advanced.

In summary, we may emphasize that ego-defense mechanisms are in the main learned; that they are designed to deal with inner hurt, anxiety, and tension and to protect the self from threat or devaluation; that they operate on relatively habitual and unconscious levels; and that they typically involve some measure of self-deception and reality distortion.

Decompensation under excessive stress

If stress proves excessive and cannot be escaped, there is lowered integration and eventually a breakdown of the system. A model which helps to explain the course of decompensation under excessive stress has been advanced by Selye (1956, 1969) in his formulation of the *general-adaptation-syndrome.* Selye found that the body's reaction to sustained, severe stress occurs in three major phases: an *alarm reaction*, a *stage of resistance,* and a *stage of exhaustion.* Although he was concerned chiefly with physiological breakdown, psychological decompensation—as summarized below—seems to follow similar stages.

Alarm and mobilization

As in the case of biological stress, the first stage in reactions to psychological stress involves the alerting of the organism and the mobilization of resources for coping with the stress. Typically involved here are emotional arousal and increased tension, heightened sensitivity and alertness (vigilance), and determined efforts at self-control. At the same time, the individual undertakes various coping measures—which may be task-oriented or defense-oriented or a combination of the two—in his efforts to meet the emergency. In this stage, the individual may show symptoms of maladjustment, such as continuous anxiety, gastrointestinal upset or other bodily manifestations, and lowered efficiency—indications that the mobilization of adaptive resources is not proving adequate to cope with the stress.

Stage of resistance

If the stress situation continues, the individual is often able to find some way of dealing with it and thus to resist psychological disorganization. Resistance may be achieved temporarily by concerted task-oriented coping measures, such as using "kid gloves" to deal with a difficult boss or making an extra effort to stabilize a shaky marriage. At the same time, there may be an intensified use of ego-defense mechanisms. Even in the stage of resistance, however, there may be indications of inner strain—for example, psychosomatic symptoms—which Selye has referred to as the "diseases of adaptation."

During the stage of resistance the individual may be able to stabilize his defenses but at a relatively high cost in wear and tear on the system. At the same time he tends to become rigid and to cling to his present coping methods rather than trying to reevaluate the stress situation and working out more effective ways of coping.

Disorganization and exhaustion

In the face of continued severe stress, the defenses erected during the stage of resistance give way and the individual is forced to more deviant measures in his efforts to cope. Such measures may be characterized by a "break with reality" and the introduction of delusions—such as persecution—which represent attempts to salvage some measure of psychological integration and self-integrity by restructuring reality.

Such extreme defensive measures may represent a continuing attempt to cope with the stress situation as well as the severe disorganization resulting from their failure. In breaking with reality, for example, the individual may "escape" from the stress situation but at an exorbitant price, for he becomes incompetent in dealing with the everyday problems of living. Without the help of others he would not likely survive. In this sense, as Lachman has pointed out "an organism may be injured or destroyed by its own defenses" (1963, p. 247)—or, Lachman might have added, by its failure to cope with the stress situation.

If the stress continues to be excessive despite such defenses, the process of decompensation continues to the stage of exhaustion with complete psychological disintegration. At this level, decompensation may involve continuous uncontrolled violence, apathy, or stupor—and possibly death.

Occasionally, severe decompensation may be precipitated by sudden and extreme stress, but more commonly it is a gradual process involving weeks, months, or years. Typically treatment measures are instituted which may alleviate the stress situation and assist the individual in improving his coping patterns. Here the process of

The following excerpts are taken from the diary of an American soldier during a tour of duty at Guadalcanal during World War II. They provide an unusually graphic demonstration of the progressive disruption of functioning that may occur with continued exposure to very severe stress. Although this example involves a reaction to the stress of combat, a similar sequence could occur in response to continued, severe stress in civilian life.

"Aug. 7, 1942. Convoy arrived at Guadalcanal Bay at approximately 4 A.M. in the morning. Ships gave enemy a heavy shelling. At 9 A.M. we stormed the beach and formed an immediate beachhead, a very successful landing, marched all day in the hot sun, and at night took positions and rested. Enemy planes attacked convoy in bay but lost 39 out of 40 planes.

"Aug. 19, 1942. Enemy cruiser and destroyer came into bay and shelled the beach for about two hours. The cruiser left and the destroyer hung around for the entire morning. We all kept under shelter for the early afternoon a flying fortress flew over, spotting the ship and bombed it, setting it afire we all jumped and shouted with joy. That night trouble again was feared and we again slept in foxholes.

"Aug. 21, 1942. The long waited landing by the enemy was made during the night 1500 troops in all and a few prisoners were taken and the rest were killed. Bodies were laying all over beach. In afternoon planes again bombed the Island. [Here the writing begins to be shaky, and less careful than previously.]

"Aug. 28, 1942. The company left this morning in higgins Boats to the end of the Island, landed and started through thick Jungle and hills. . . . our squad was in the assault squad so we moved up the beach to take positions the enemy trapped us with machine gun and rifle fire for about two hours. The lead was really flying. Two of our men were killed, two were hit by a hand greade and my corporal received a piece of shrampnel in back,—was wounded in arm, out of the squad of eight we had five causitry. We withdrew and were taken back to the Hospital.

"Sept. 13, 1942. At on o'clock three destroyers and one cruiser shelled us contumally all night. The ships turned surch lights all up and down the beach, and stopped one my foxhole seveal time I'm feeling pritty nervese and scared, afraid I'll be a nervas reack be for long. slept in fox hole all night not much sleep. This morning a 9:00 we had a nother air raid, the raid consisted of mostly fighter planes. I believe we got several, this afternoon. we had a nother raid, and our planes went out to met them, met them someplace over Tulagi, new came in that the aircraft carrier wasp sent planes out to intersept the bombers. This eving all hell broke lose. Our marines contacted enemy to south of us and keep up constant fire all night through.

"Sept. 14, 1942. This morning firing still going on my company is scaduted to unload ships went half ways up to dock when enemyfire start on docks, were called back to our pososeion allon beach, ... Went up into hills at 4:00 P.M. found positions, at 7:00 en 8 sea planes fombed and strifed us, 151942 were strifed biy amfibious planes and bombed the concussion of one through me of balance and down a 52 foot hil. I was shaking likd a leaf. Lost my bayanut, and ran out of wathr. I nearves and very jumpy, hop I last out until morning. I hop severaly machine s guns ore oping up on our left flank there going over our heads

"Sept. 16. this moring we going in to take up new possissons we march all moring and I am very week and nerves, we marched up a hill and ran in to the affaul place y and z company lost so many men I hardly new what I was doing then I'm going nuts.

"Sept. 17. don't remember much of this day.

"Sept. 18. Today I'm on a ship leaving this awful place, called Green Hell. I'm still nearves and shakey." (Stern, 1947, pp. 583–586)

decompensation is reversed—and is known as *recompensation.* Of course, the earlier in the process of decompensation that such measures are introduced, the better. Thus emphasis is placed on early detection and treatment.

Although we shall not pursue the matter here, the concept of stages of decompensation under excessive stress appears as applicable on the group level as on biological and psychological levels.

>> Summary and a look ahead

Behavior is an attempt to meet the adjustive demands confronting us or which we perceive as confronting us. Reactions to stress are holistic, economical, and automatic or planned; they involve emotions and may have inner and outer determinants. Inner determinants include one's frame of reference, motives, competencies, and stress tolerance; outer determinants include environmental resources, social demands and expectations, and the individual's general life situation.

Psychological reactions to stress include: (1) "built-in" coping and damage-repair mechanisms, such as crying, talking it out, laughing it off, thinking it through, seeking support, and sleep and dreams; (2) task-oriented reactions, aimed at realistically meeting the adjustive demand and including attack, withdrawal, and compromise patterns; and (3) defense-oriented reactions, aimed at protecting the self from disorganization and including denial, rationalization, and other ego-defense mechanisms. Though ego-defense mechanisms are essential for alleviating tension and anxiety and protecting one's feelings of adequacy and worth, they do exact a toll in terms of self-deception, reality distortion, and often failure to deal effectively with the adjustive demand.

If stress is excessive, it leads to decompensation—a breakdown of integrated functioning. Decompensation, which can be described in terms of the general-adaptation-syndrome, typically occurs in three stages: alarm and mobilization, resistance, and exhaustion—which may lead to the death of the organism. Occasionally, severe decompensation is precipitated by sudden and extreme stress, but more commonly it is a gradual process occurring over an extended period of time. Decompensation may be reversed if the stress situation is alleviated, the individual acquires more effective coping methods, or successful corrective measures—usually involving professional assistance—are instituted.

In the next chapter we shall turn to a discussion of how to evaluate reactions to stress, the basic steps that can be used to cope effectively with stress, and ways in which stress situations can be used for personal growth.

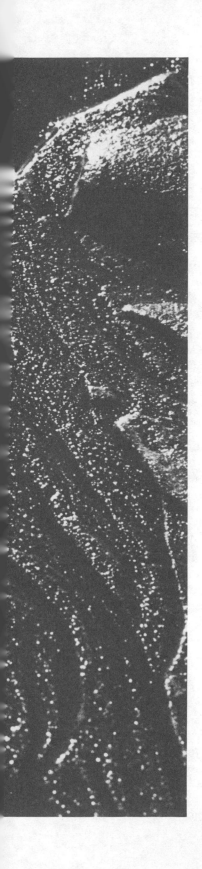

7
Effective Methods of Coping with Stress

Some basic considerations
Typical steps in coping effectively with stress
Utilizing stress situations for personal growth

While we do have useful guidelines for evaluating stress reactions and helping to ensure effective ones, the implementation of these guidelines in real life is by no means always a simple matter.

Two persons in a romantic love relationship may have various options open to them. For example, they can get married in the traditional way; they can live together on a trial basis to see if they are really compatible and wish to marry; or they can simply live together ruling out the idea of marriage—deciding as a matter of principle not to get married.

What is the most effective way of dealing with this love relationship? On the basis of what scientific evidence? Since we lack adequate scientific data to serve as a basis for sound decision making, we are entering into the realm of value judgments—of what the persons involved consider most likely to lead to satisfying results.

Thus in taking up the topic of effective methods of coping with stress, it becomes apparent that there are no simple solutions to many of life's problems which confront us. Consequently, we shall attempt to avoid the temptation to give pat answers to complex problems or to enter into unwarranted value judgments.

It does seem productive, however, (1) to review some basic considerations including possible criteria for evaluating stress reactions; (2) to examine the steps in the "processing" of stress that appear to foster effective reactions; and (3) to note certain other measures conducive to effecting coping and personal growth. Hopefully our discussion will be both thought provoking and useful.

Some basic considerations

We have seen that stress beyond a certain point endangers our well-being and leads to persistent efforts to resolve it; and that the outcome of these coping efforts determines the level of adjustment that we achieve. This results in a continuum of adjustment ranging from superior at one extreme of the continuum through average or moderate to maladjustment at the other. The majority of people manage to cope with their problems and achieve a moderate level of adjustment. A few at one extreme lead unusually effective and fulfilling lives; and a few at the other extreme are severely maladjusted.

A given individual may fall anywhere on this continuum of effective-ineffective adjustment, and his position on the continuum may change with time. Under severe and sustained stress, his level of adjustment may show a marked decline; and conversely, his level of adjustment may improve when his life situation becomes less stressful or when he learns to cope more effectively with his problems.

For the moment, let us focus on three criteria for distinguishing between effective and ineffective behavior. We shall pose these criteria in the form of questions. Then we shall briefly examine several models which have proven helpful in understanding both effective and ineffective coping behavior.

Reactions to stress may be evaluated quite differently depending upon the sociocultural and situational setting as well as the person or group doing the evaluating. Consider the following incident:

"The snowcapped Andes of South America are a cruel and unforgiving barrier. When storms are brewing, plane crashes are frequent; invariably after an aircraft goes down, mountain people remark that 'the Cordillera never gives anyone back.' Last week though, the Cordillera had been forced to give back 16 of the 45 people who had been aboard a Uruguayan air force plane that hit a mountain peak in mid-October. Incredibly, the survivors lasted for 73 days in deep snow and sub-freezing temperatures. They took extremely grim measures in order to do so—they ate the bodies of those who had died in the crash" (*Time,* Jan. 8, 1973, p. 27).

The survivors were members of a rugby team called the "Old Christians" and some of their relatives and friends. One of the group, a medical student, explained that it was acceptable to eat the dead to sustain the living just as it was acceptable to take the heart of a dead person to keep another alive. In the Vatican newspaper *L'Observatore Romano,* the Rev. Gino Concetti defended their actions concluding that "From a theological and ethical point of view, the action cannot be branded as cannibalism" (*Newsweek,* Jan. 8, 1973, p. 27). As a Chilean newspaper asked in the headlines of its account of the incident, "WHAT WOULD YOU HAVE DONE?"

Although admittedly an extreme example, this unusual episode does illustrate the difficulties that are often encountered in distinguishing between stress reactions that are effective and those that are ineffective. Despite the very real difficulties involved, however, it does seem possible to ask certain questions that apply to human behavior in most settings—from Madison Avenue to the Andes. In the following, we shall discuss these questions.

Does the action meet
the adjustive demand?

Some actions, as we have seen, do not resolve the stress situation but merely provide temporary relief. Thus the individual who uses tranquilizers as a means of alleviating tension and anxiety is not likely to be solving the adjustive demands which led to his difficulty. In some stressful situations, of course—such as the death of loved ones or disappointment in love—the wounds tend to heal with time, and temporary defensive measures may be of value.

But when defense-oriented behavior is relied upon as the major means of coping with stress, it usually only puts off the day of reckoning. Indeed, in the long run it may even increase the stress and the difficulty of meeting adjustive demands successfully. For example, the individual who escapes from an unhappy home situation by resorting to alcohol not only fails to solve his problem but usually makes his situation worse. One criterion of effective adjustment, then, is that it meets the objective requirements of the situation.

Does the action meet the
needs of the individual?

Sometimes an action seems to meet the demands of the situation but fails to meet the maintenance or actualization needs of the individual. The youth who wants to be a teacher but gives in to his father's wish for him to go into the family business may relieve the stress of parental pressures at the expense of frustrating his need for self-fulfillment. Far from being an effective adjustment, such a decision is likely to create inner conflict and cause more difficult problems of adjustment later on.

If something happens to me like I failed in a job I had worked for very hard and spent more time at it than with my family, I would be very hurt, disappointed, like I should just go out and get drunk and party all night, but I wouldn't get what I had worked for that way. So then I would stop and look at it this way: 'Well, I tried, I worked hard at it, but I failed.' Okay, then I would tell myself, 'Okay, so you failed, now you just better try something else because you're good at something, but it takes time sometimes to find out what.' So I would look at myself and say, 'Okay, you're good at this and that, but you're better at this, so try it.'

Another factor to consider in determining whether behavior is effective or ineffective is *how much it costs in relation to the satisfactions it yields.* A high-pressure executive job may offer a person rich rewards in money, prestige, and fulfillment of his potentials, but if he is constantly anxious and his long hours at work make him a stranger to his wife and children, the cost may be too great and his behavior pattern may be ineffective from the point of view of his overall adjustment.

Likewise, defenses like repression—though they may relieve anxiety—are costly because they inevitably impair the individual's ability to cope realistically with his problems. And as we saw in Chapter 5, any long-term and costly adjustment to one stress tends to lessen a person's ability to cope with other stresses.

Is the action compatible with the well-being of the group?

Ideally, effective adjustment means that the individual copes with his problems in such a way as to be in harmony with his environment and also maintain his own integrity and well-being. If he satisfies his needs at the expense of other people, his action cannot be considered truly adjustive. And if it is harmful to others, it is likely in the long run to lead to the frustration of his needs too.

The ability to maintain both inner harmony and harmonious relations with one's surroundings presupposes a "normal" environment in which the same acts *can* forward both individual and group goals. But where the group is repressive or otherwise pathological, it may be impossible for an individual to maintain his own integrity and meet his needs without running counter to group demands. Thus while freedom fighters in a dictatorship might be regarded as enemies of the state, from a broader perspective of human welfare they might be behaving in an adaptive way.

Any ultimate definition of effective and ineffective adjustment must take into consideration both the optimal development of the individual and the fostering of social conditions which are compatible with group well-being and progress.

While the preceding criteria do not completely resolve the problem of assessing stress reactions—as in the example of the behavior of the plane-crash survivors in the Andes of South America, where complex value judgments are required—they do appear to serve as useful guidelines for assessing most coping behavior. And as we learn more about human needs and behavior, we can refine the criteria accordingly.

Models for understanding coping behavior

There are a number of psychosocial models for explaining ineffective and maladaptive coping behavior. An awareness of these models can help us understand and implement effective coping behavior since avoidance or correction of the negative conditions evidenced in the models actually fosters effective coping patterns. As we shall see, each of these models has its distinctive features but also tends to share certain concepts with the other models. Thus they are by no means mutually exclusive.

1. *Anxiety-defense.* Stress situations which are perceived as threatening by the individual elicit anxiety. Anxiety in turn functions as both a warning of danger and as an acutely unpleasant condition demanding alleviation.

If the individual deals with the stress situation in a task-oriented way—for example, if he attempts to accurately appraise the nature and degree of the threat and to formulate a course of action for coping with it—he may be described as evidencing effective coping behavior. For even if he fails in his efforts, he has tried in a task-oriented way and done his best. In addition, he has left the pathway open to learning from experience. Usually, of course, task-oriented approaches are effective in dealing with stress.

On the other hand, if the individual resorts to various ego-defense mechanisms—such as denial and rationalization—as his primary method of coping, he is acting in a defense-oriented way. Such coping may be said to be ineffective, for it does not actually deal with the stress situation but only alleviates the anxiety. In addition, this process of self-defense leads to a discrepancy between the way things really are and the individual's perception and experiencing of them. If such ego defenses are used to an extreme degree—as in paranoia—they not only lead to reality distortion and self-deception but block the pathway to learning more effective behavior. In short, they exact a high cost in terms of ineffective and maladaptive coping behavior.

2. *Faulty learning.* Although learning is recognized as an important cause of effective or ineffective coping behavior in all of the psychosocial models of man (see Chapter 2), it is particularly emphasized in the behavioristic model.

This view assumes that ineffective behavior is the result of (a) the failure to learn necessary adaptive behaviors or competencies, or (b) the learning of maladaptive coping patterns. Violent delinquent behavior based on a failure to learn desirable social norms would be an example of the former, while a phobia of flying in a commercial jet would be an example of the latter. Of course, the learning of necessary competencies fosters our ability to cope effectively in our society.

The faulty learning model also places strong emphasis upon conditions that reinforce and hence maintain given behavior patterns—and these patterns may be effective as well as ineffective ones.

3. *Blocked personal growth.* As we have seen, the humanistic and existential models of man place strong emphasis upon freedom of choice and each person's obligation to shape his own life and to make it a meaningful and fulfilling one. This in turn requires the development of an adequate value pattern for guiding one's choices as well as the courage to assume responsibility for the outcome of one's actions and of one's life.

In some instances, environmental conditions may not provide the individual with the freedom for self-determination. But if environmental conditions are favorable and do provide the individual with the freedom to shape his own destiny, then if he fails to shape his potentials into the self that he feels he could and should be and to achieve a meaningful and fulfilling life, he is acting in bad faith and being unauthentic. The inevitable consequences are blocked personal growth, existential anxiety, alienation, futility, and despair.

4. *Stress-decompensation.* In dealing with reactions to stress, we described the process of decompensation under excessive stress. We noted that such decompensation may take place

in the face of sudden acute stress which is beyond the range of the individual's coping resources, as in severe earthquakes and other civilian disasters. More typically, however, this process is a gradual one that is characterized by the gradual depletion of the individual's adaptive resources and follows a predictable course from alarm and mobilization, through the stage of resistance, to eventual exhaustion and destruction of the organism.

However, we noted another point of key significance—the course of decompensation can be reversed if the stresses in the individual's life situation can be alleviated and/or he learns more effective coping patterns. Here it is important to note that the individual often plays an active role in selecting the stresses to which he chooses to expose himself—as in the case of a mountain climber or race driver, to use extreme examples.

Similarly, we strive to foster environmental conditions which are beneficial to health—physical and mental—and to provide resources for the early detection and correction of problems when things do go wrong. Unfortunately, as we are well aware, there are a wide range of pathological social conditions—such as poverty, prejudice and discrimination, and uncontrolled social change—which may block or distort personal growth and subject persons to severe or excessive stress. In fact, the extent and patterns of maladaptive behavior in a given society tend to reflect the social conditions in that society.

6. *Organic pathology.* This model emphasizes the importance of an adequate diet, rest, and other health measures which help to ensure the efficient functioning of the body and provide the needed physical resources for effective coping behavior.

 Sometimes people get sick if they are discriminated against all the time. I mean upset or mad at themselves and the world which forces them to do things like take drugs or try and kill themselves.

Thus part of effective coping often involves the reduction of stresses in one's life to manageable proportions—to a stress pattern that one is equipped to cope with—and this can often be achieved by making appropriate modifications in one's life style as well as avoiding high-risk stress situations where chance factors may well determine the outcome.

5. *Interpersonal and social pathology.* Satisfying interpersonal relationships—characterized by mutual need satisfaction, respect, integrity, and intimacy—can be important as resources for coping with stress as well as in fostering personal growth. Conversely pathological interpersonal relationships—for example, fraudulent interpersonal contracts in which one person exploits another—can be extremely destructive to the "victim." In essence, one person can make another person "sick."

Fatigue, illness, and a variety of other conditions can impair stress tolerance and hence foster ineffective coping. Also included here are a variety of factors which lead to actual brain pathology—such as drug intoxication, brain tumors, and severe nutritional deficiencies—all of which tend to impair adaptive resources and to lead to ineffective coping. In addition, it would appear that genetic and constitutional factors may predispose some persons to specific metabolic alterations under severe stress, and that these metabolic changes may in turn impair brain functioning. As we shall see, this is one viewpoint concerning the causation of severe depression, schizophrenia, and other seriously maladaptive behavior patterns.

Perhaps it bears repeating that although we have dealt with these differing models of causation in terms of their rather distinctive features, they tend to have many characteristics in common. And several or all of these models may be essential to understanding specific effective or ineffective coping patterns.

Changing concepts of causal relationships

Traditionally *cause-and-effect* relationships have involved the isolation of a given condition X (cause) which leads to condition Y (effect). Syphilitic infection of the brain (cause) has been shown to result in brain damage and mental disorder (effect) characterized by progressive personal deterioration. Where more than one causal factor leads to a given effect—which is usually the case, such as in a failing marriage—the term *causal pattern* is used. Here conditions A, B, C, and so on, lead to condition Y. In essence, the traditional concept of causation is one in which a given condition or set of conditions leads to a specific effect.

Recently with the introduction of the concept of self-regulating systems, the concept of causal relationships has become much more complex. For now *the effects of feedback on the causal agent or agents must also be taken into account.* No longer is a simple linear or straight-line relationship of cause to effect considered sufficient as a model—we are dealing with circularity in the causal relationship. For example, let us note the following marital problem:

A young couple are having serious marital difficulties. The wife accuses her husband of rejecting her and showing no affection, while the husband accuses his wife of drinking too much. From the standpoint of causation, the wife views the situation as "I drink too much because my husband does not give me the acceptance and affection which I need." The husband views the situation differently, "I don't accept my wife or wish to be affectionate with her because her excessive drinking makes her unattractive."

Over time the situation may be resolved, or, as often occurs, a vicious circle may develop. For as the husband's withdrawal continues and perhaps even increases, the wife's drinking becomes more excessive. Assuming that both contribute about equally to their marital problems, it now becomes difficult if not impossible to distinguish cause from effect.

Rather the problem now becomes one of *circularity* in which A influences B and B in turn influences A and so on as the marital situation progressively deteriorates.

In real life this circular pattern of causation seems to be typical of many interpersonal interactions. Rather than a simple A-leads-to-B relationship, we are dealing with more complex factors such as information exchange or communication, patterns of interaction and feedback, and circularity.

And this circularity can be unrewarding and destructive—and lead to personal distress and ineffective behavior; or it can foster need-fulfilling and growth-producing interpersonal relationships—and effective behavior.

Typical steps in coping effectively with stress

Despite a great deal of research, we know relatively little about how the human brain processes stress situations. At one time the brain was thought of as a "switchboard" where stimuli and responses were connected. Present-day computer-simulation studies of the brain, however, support the notion that it is more like an elaborate communication center where incoming information is continuously evaluated, alternative responses are formulated and weighed, decisions are made and implemented, and feedback is checked.

Although we can do little more than make tentative assumptions about what actually happens as the human brain processes adjustive demands, the sequence of events may be described in four basic steps: (1) evaluating the stress situation—including available resources for coping with it; (2) formulating alternatives and deciding on a course of action; (3) taking action; and (4) utilizing feedback and correcting possible error.

In this section, we shall briefly examine these steps and attempt to point up the factors involved that are intrinsic to effective coping behavior.

Evaluating the stress situation

We are continually scanning our environment—both external and internal—to see what opportunities or dangers may be present. When we become aware of a new adjustive demand,

"We begin with what seems a paradox. The world of experience of any normal man is composed of a tremendous array of discriminably different objects, events, people, impressions. There are estimated to be more than 7 million discriminable colors alone, and in the course of a week or two we come in contact with a fair proportion of these. . . .

"But were we to utilize fully our capacity for registering the differences in things and to respond to each event encountered as unique, we would soon be overwhelmed by the complexity of our environment. Consider only the linguistic task of acquiring a vocabulary fully adequate to cope with

 Most stress is from someone else, or something else, and so if you examine the source of the stress and decide, well, this is something I'm going to have to accept—I would think in the case of, well say you're raising children, I would think that you'd have to accept the stress that your children cause you, because they're your children, so there's a stress that must come to you. If you're doing a job, and there's something wrong that you or your company has done and there's some stress dropped on you, you have to accept that stress. That's part of what you're doing in life.

our first task is to define it and evaluate its degree of threat. Here it is important that we make an accurate evaluation of the problem, for an incomplete or distorted picture would place us at a disadvantage in coping with it.

Categorizing the experience

The vast volume of new information continuously being received is quickly assigned to categories on the basis of similarities to and differences from previous experiences. Our tendency to classify and categorize is so important to the way we integrate our perceptions and our experiences that it deserves a little elaboration. As Bruner, Goodnow, and Austin have stated it:

the world of color differences! The resolution of the seeming paradox—the existence of discrimination capacities which, if fully used, would make us slaves to the particular—is achieved by man's capacity to categorize. To categorize is to render discriminably different things equivalent, to group the objects and events and people around us into classes, and to respond to them in terms of their class membership rather than their uniqueness. . . . In place of a color lexicon of 7 million items, people in our society get along with a dozen or so commonly used color names . . ." (1956, p. 1).

It thus becomes apparent that our natural tendency to simplify by categorizing is a highly useful one, making our environment simple enough to evaluate. However, this tendency is also a possible source of error since our categorization of a new situation depends so heavily upon the characteristics it shares with past situations of a similar nature rather than upon its own unique characteristics. Simplification too often becomes oversimplification. This can be readily seen, for example, in overly simplified stereotypes that many people hold of Democrats and Republicans, liberals and conservatives, communists and anticommunists. All those labeled *liberals*, for example, are assumed to be unrealistic and bad, or idealistic and humanitarian, depending on the perceiver's political and social orientation. As Miller has pointed out:

"It makes the world a great deal simpler when

turn may be used in categorizing subsequent experiences.

Thus our first step in dealing with stress is to categorize and define the stress situation in terms of our coding patterns. To the extent that our coding patterns are too simplified or otherwise inaccurate, we are handicapped in dealing with stress problems. On the other hand, if they are reasonably accurate and realistic, we are aided in defining the stress situation.

Appraising the threat

An integral part of evaluating the stress situation is identifying the degree of threat which it poses. As we have seen, *threat* refers to anticipated harm, the degree of threat depending upon the

 I think, maybe somewhat optimistically, that I have learned to cope with the problems I have had. When what I consider a problem comes up, I try to focus my attention on that problem alone; something like focusing a camera on the object you want to photograph. I ask myself what caused this, what can I do about it, and more importantly, why I consider this a problem in the first place. Often I find that no problem exists.

the good guys are always smart, honest, beautiful, and brave, while the bad guys are always stupid, crooked, ugly cowards." (1962, p. 274). Although we are not usually as naïve as Miller's statement might imply, our natural tendency to simplify by categorizing and our further tendency to protect our existing frame of reference make it doubly easy for us to see things in black and white and often very difficult to see shades of gray.

Of course, when we face a stress problem for which our categories are obviously inadequate, we are forced to analyze it as a unique situation and to try to discern its key dimensions. Sometimes further information enables us to classify it in one of our established categories, but sometimes we must form a new category which in

magnitude of anticipated harm; and what is highly threatening to one person may be only mildly threatening or even nonthreatening to another.

If the individual judges the stress situation to be nonthreatening or only mildly threatening, he is likely to cope with it in terms of established patterns which require little thought or effort. On the other hand, if he interprets the adjustive demand as a serious threat, he is likely to experience anxiety and to interrupt other ongoing activities in order to focus his energies on coping with it.

Of course, the individual's appraisal may be in error. He may exaggerate or underestimate the threat; he may even see threat where none exists, or he may fail to perceive threat where it

In our society there are numerous life styles that the elderly can choose. Some may wish to leave familiar places and painful memories behind and start anew in a "retirement village," surrounded by their peers. Others may wish to remain in a long-familiar environment but at the same time find alternative occupations or pastimes and maintain contact with people of other age groups. These photos depict but two of the alternatives open to the elderly. Can you see advantages and disadvantages to both?

does exist. An inaccurate evaluation of the threat posed by the stress situation, of course, places the individual at a distinct disadvantage in coping with it. Conversely, an accurate appraisal of threat helps to further the processing of the stress situation in an effective way.

Working out an appropriate course of action

Having defined the problem and its degree of threat, the individual must next decide what he will do about it. This involves formulating alternative courses of action that might solve the problem and selecting the one most promising. Both these steps involve extremely complex processes which we can study only by inference.

Formulating the alternatives

Often in defining the problem we have already begun some formulation of possible alternatives. The categorization of the problem provides what some investigators have called a "search model" by setting the requirements that will have to be met by a suitable course of action.

In a familiar situation the whole process of definition, formulation of alternative actions, and choice of action may take place automatically with little or no conscious involvement. An example of this would be our almost instantaneous reaction to a car stopping suddenly ahead of us on a freeway. At the other extreme, a stress situation with many unfamiliar elements may not be amenable to immediate categorization, and no appropriate response pattern may be evident even when the problem has been defined. Here we may have to use reason, imagination, and other conscious processes to work out possible solutions.

The processes by which people formulate possible solutions and decide on their relative suitability vary considerably. Some of us avoid coming to grips with a difficult problem as long as we can—perhaps hoping that time will resolve the situation; some of us seek advice or help from presumably stronger or wiser persons; some of us tackle a stress situation head-

on as if we were knights of old and the problem a dragon to be slain. Most of us, of course, approach different kinds of problems in somewhat different ways. A scientist may be very objective in coping with pressures and problems in his work but irrational and emotional in dealing with a family problem.

In general, the more threatened and less confident we feel, the less rationally we tend to perceive and weigh the possibilities and the more we tend to look for safety and reduction of anxiety instead of a long-term, well-worked-out, constructive solution.

Balancing probability, desirability, and cost

Once the individual has formulated alternative solutions to the stress situation that appear feasible—having rejected those which are obviously incompatible with reality, his standards and values, or the requirements of the adjustive demand—he must assess the relative merits of these alternatives and make a choice. In so doing, he will weigh such considerations as his probabilities of success, the degree of satisfaction he will accept, and the cost he is willing to pay.

1. *Playing the probabilities.* Peterson and Beach (1967) have concluded from their research on problem solving and decision making that humans seem to be "intuitive statisticians." Other things being equal, we, as individuals, tend to select the course of action that seems to offer the greatest probability of success—as we define success. In figuring the odds, we not only examine the relevant information at our disposal but tend to assess—often unconsciously—the likelihood that chance factors will upset our calculations or that events beyond our control will interfere to prevent us from carrying out a given course of action and from reaching our goal. Although we dislike uncertainty, our world confronts us only with probabilities and we have to make the best of it and keep betting on life's contingencies.

"And man gambles well. He survives and prospers while using the fallible information to infer

the states of his uncertain environment and to predict future events" (p. 29).

Being forced by life to bet on probabilities, however, does not mean that we always calculate the odds rationally. Wishful thinking may lead a person to take untoward risks or disregard danger signs. He may even keep betting on responses which have failed consistently in the past, like the gambler who continues despite heavy losses over a period of time. If we knowingly choose to go against the odds, the element of stress is likely to be increased.

2. *Deciding on an acceptable level of satisfaction.* Though we may take bigger risks for bigger potential gains, we do not automatically choose the course which, if successful, would yield the greatest satisfaction. If the most gainful course of action also carries with it the risk of losing everything if we fail, we may settle for an alternative that is less appealing but more sure of bringing us *some* level of satisfaction. We are willing to date someone other than the most sought-after person on campus and to accept a good job rather than wait for the better one that may never come through. How high we aim— how much we demand from ourselves and our world—is an important part of our whole life style and helps make the processing of stress the individual matter that it is.

Although individuals differ in the standards of satisfaction they are accustomed to and insist on, most of us are usually content to find a course of action that we feel is "good enough" rather than try to "optimize" the outcome. In coping with the problem of selling our automobile or home, for example, we may not insist on obtaining the maximum price that could possibly be obtained but rather take the first offer which we consider "fair" and "satisfactory." In fact, we rarely have the time or inclination to ascertain every possible course of action and to ferret out and pursue the one that promises to yield maximum returns.

Of course, people differ in the extent to which they are willing to take risks for a higher possible return. They also differ in the extent to which they are willing to adapt their requirements to accept a moderately satisfactory bird-

in-hand instead of holding out for the more alluring bird they had hoped to catch. People who are content with moderate satisfactions in some areas may insist on the very best in others. The person who is content to cope with financial pressures by economizing on clothes, automobile, and home may not be willing to take the same approach when it comes to selecting a spouse. We demand a greater return on our investment and may take a higher risk when we care deeply about the results.

Although it would be self-defeating to settle consistently for too low a level of satisfaction in relation to the adjustive demand and our resources, it would also be self-defeating to consistently demand too high a level. In dealing with most adjustive demands, it would appear that effective coping usually depends upon a middle-of-the-road course which is realistic and achievable.

3. *Weighing the costs.* All behavior has its costs in effort, material resources, time, and the surrender of other possibilities. Some behavior also exacts costs in unpleasantness or pain or subsequent loss. Thus staying in school may require such long hours of study that a student must give up hobbies or social life, but dropping out of school might cost him future opportunities for more advanced occupational training.

In selecting between alternative courses of action, we balance the risks and the costs—the amount of effort, anxiety, or other costs—against the possible satisfactions. For high stakes and good odds we may be willing to work hard and undergo considerable pain and sacrifice; but if the returns look small and the risk of losing is considerable, we are usually reluctant to exert much effort. Although we often weigh the factors differently, we all look for what we regard as the best balance of probable gains and costs.

In balancing risk, satisfaction, and cost, we are also confronted with the problem of weighing the importance of a single decision. Some choices are likely to arise only once and may have a continuing influence on our lives—for example, whether we go to college or marry a particular person. Other choices may be relatively unimportant in the long run—such as

Everything that I do, in recent years, anyway, I try to weigh on an emotional level and a financial level. In time, everything boils down to that. It depends on the seriousness of the purchase. If it's a minor purchase and I have an emotional feeling about it, fine. If it's a mistake, who cares. But if it's something bigger, then I definitely look at it from those two aspects.

whether we buy a new or used car—although they may seem very important at the time.

It is also apparent that since we are dealing with probabilities and not certainties, we cannot expect to win every time. Losses must be balanced off against overall gains. As the Overstreets have pointed out:

"After all, we live by batting averages, not by perfect scores. The research scientist does not expect that every hypothesis he sets up will prove out. The teacher does not expect every day's lesson to set aflame the minds of youth. We live by making plans and by making efforts that are, so far as we can see, in line with the results we want; by improving our plans and efforts as experience dictates; and by believing that a fair batting average constitutes enough success to justify our staying on the job" (1956, p. 24).

Taking positive action

Once a decision has been made, the next step is to implement it—to put the chosen alternative into action.

In this context we are focusing primarily upon task-oriented and rational rather than defense-oriented and often irrational coping responses. However, even the implementation of task-oriented reactions is not always a simple task, particularly if we lack confidence in ourselves or in our decision. As a consequence, we may experience intense fear, anxiety, apprehension, and related feelings which can interfere with the effective implementation of our decision.

Often such emotions impair our actual performance—whether intellectual or physical—in carrying out our action. Most of us have probably had the experience of speaking or performing before a group. When the time for action arrived, we may have found that we were so fearful and anxious that our actual thought processes were partially blocked and our performance was impaired. Many trial lawyers experience excruciating stress during the first few times they address a jury. Typically, however, they have disciplined themselves to function effectively despite their inner feelings. We could cite similar instances of football players before

When things get to bothering me I find out the cause. If it's that my grades in school aren't as high as I hoped, I talk to the instructor and get help in that subject. If it's too much pressure at work, I ask my supervisor if I can have a day off and I go to a park, away from everyone, and just lie there and relax.

and during the first few minutes of play in "the big game."

Perhaps of more importance for effective coping is the delay in action that may result from such feelings. Often in dealing with serious conflicts, for example, we may vacillate, attempt to stall for time, and even get "sick"—despite the fact that we have reached a decision as to the best probable course of action. Kaufman (1973) has referred to this as "decidophobia." When time permits, such diversionary tactics may prove constructive, since they enable us to postpone the action until we may have more information, have had time to reconsider our alternatives, and feel more confident of our decision. In other instances, however, such tactics may lead to disastrous delay. For the timing of action is often of crucial importance. What might have been an effective response today may not be so tomorrow.

George, a man who had gone through a rather painful divorce some 4 years previously, decided that he was very much in love with and wanted to marry Sharon, a very attractive woman with whom he was living. Since she had told him she loved him and wanted to marry him, he felt reasonably secure about taking his time. But he did not realize that underneath, Sharon was becoming resentful and withdrawing because of his unwillingness to tell her he loved her, let alone propose marriage. In fact, he had insisted that the relationship be on his terms, which were "no strings attached."

As a consequence, she accepted a date with Bill, a man who had also been divorced some time previously. She continued to see Bill each evening and during the ensuing weekend while George was away at a convention. They had really enjoyable times together, found that they had many common interests, and before the week was over were engaging in very satisfactory sexual relations.

Sharon had told Bill about George and her relationship with him, which he understood and accepted. On Sunday, the day before George's return, Bill told Sharon that he loved her and wanted to marry her—a decision he said he had been seriously considering since their first date. Although Sharon felt that she had fallen in love

GOAL-TERMINATING MECHANISMS

A course of action undertaken to meet an adjustive demand may continue until the goal is achieved or may be terminated at some intermediate point judged "good enough." For example, a man in his thirties who is anxious to marry and have a family may start in search of an "ideal wife." His quest is likely to continue until it is terminated by one of the following:

1. *Goal achievement.* He achieves the goal he set for himself and resolves the adjustive demand: he finds someone he thinks will make an "ideal wife."

2. *Satisficing.* He ceases his search when he finds someone that he thinks is "good enough" even though not the "ideal wife" he had hoped to be able to find.

3. *Impatience.* After a certain amount of time and effort have been expended in his search without finding the ideal wife, he ceases his search, perhaps settling on the alternative that "seems best so far."

4. *Discouragement.* He stops looking because he concludes that he is getting nowhere—that his strategy and tactics have not worked out. In this case, he may work out a different strategy and launch a new effort or give up the search permanently.

with Bill, she was a little hesitant about marrying him because of the short period that she had known him. But Bill had been around enough to know what he wanted, and Sharon was it; and he convinced her. That Sunday evening they flew to Las Vegas and were married.

When George returned, Sharon went to see him to explain, but before she could say anything he told her how much he had missed her, that he did love her, and that he wanted to marry her. But his action came too late. Had he taken the same action before he left for the convention, the story might have had a different ending.

Often, of course, there is a fine line between impetuous and ineffective and effective decision making and action. Perhaps one might wonder whether Sharon had not made a somewhat impetuous decision, perhaps in part based on her resentment toward George. But she also had been divorced, was a mature person, and knew what she wanted. She decided that while both men had much to offer, Bill was the more mature, had more interests and values in common with hers, and that she really did love him.

While it is sometimes wise to delay action after making a decision—if circumstances permit and there appears to be some advantage to such a course—it is also often necessary to implement decisions without delay if they are to prove effective. For the action that might have been effective today may prove ineffective or impossible later. In George's case, he waited too long to act upon his decision.

Utilizing feedback

As the action is proceeding, we can use available feedback to gauge the wisdom of our decision and the effectiveness with which we are carrying it out. And feedback enables us to make corrections in our ongoing action where such corrections are indicated and feasible.

Here it may be noted that "feedback" also involves what Richards (1968) has called "feedforward." That is, when an individual embarks on a course of action, he has certain expectancies about what is going to happen—about the outcome of his action. There is a forward reference in his action patterns, and it is against this "expectation of outcome" that the individual evaluates feedback to see how he is doing.

The type and amount of feedback we receive and the way it is utilized in maintaining or modifying our course of action are of immediate interest.

1. *Convergent and divergent feedback.* Feedback may indicate that we either are on or off the beam. *Convergent* feedback is information telling us that we are making satisfactory progress toward our goal or that the goal has been achieved. If the adjustment problem is highly stressful and/or if we are uncertain about the course of action we have chosen, convergent feedback usually alleviates anxiety, builds self-confidence, and leads to increased effort, for it is a signal that the stress will be resolved and our needs met.

Feedback is rarely altogether favorable. When an action is not progressing as satisfactorily as we had anticipated, we get *divergent* feedback, indicating that—perhaps because of unforeseen complications or a wrong choice of action—we are not progressing toward our goal as well as we might or perhaps that our action is ineffective or even making the stress situation worse. A young person who talks too much in an effort to gain attention and approval may be informed, by the negative reactions of other people, that he is not succeeding in his efforts. Besides signaling the need for a modification of behavior, divergent feedback indicates that stress is likely to be prolonged or intensified.

In general, we interpret pain, punishment, and discomfort as cues that we are not doing well—as divergent feedback, while rewards, pleasure, and satisfying experiences are interpreted as confirmation that we are on the right track.

2. *Amount of feedback.* In some situations we receive relatively complete information concerning the progress and outcome of our actions. In other situations we may receive only partial or even zero feedback. The amount of feedback is determined not only by the information available but also by our ability to perceive it. A child may not associate a stomachache with having eaten green apples; an adult may ignore or misinterpret frowns or other signs of social disapproval.

Zero feedback usually means that the individual receives no information until his action is complete. For example, a student may not be given any grades on his lab reports until several reports have had to be submitted. In general, the delay of feedback until after the completion of an

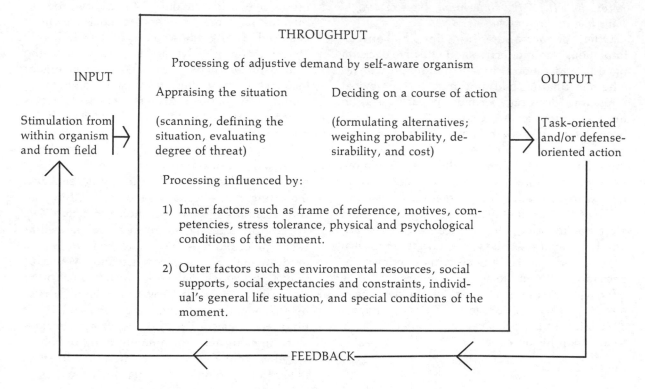

During ongoing behavior, the individual's actions and their effects are part of the input on which he bases further action and evaluation. The analogy of human adjustive behavior to information processing by a computer is useful but far from perfect. For example, the stimulation which initiates human action—unlike the input of a computer—does not have an unvarying effect: as the diagram suggests, responses to it vary with changes in the individual's frame of reference, motivational state, and other inner factors as well as with momentary and long-lasting factors in the environment. A computer, furthermore, cannot set its own goals or discover ways of processing information for which it has not previously been programed.

important action tends to foster worry and anxiety.

Often we receive prompt but only partial feedback. A student who gets a low grade on a test may have little information as to why he received such a low rating or "what he is doing wrong." Or we may notice that people seem to be avoiding or reacting negatively to us but not have any clues as to the reason. Limited feedback is often ambiguous and difficult to interpret; especially in important situations it makes us anxious and uncertain.

In some situations we receive relatively complete feedback and can modify the ongoing course of our action to make it more effective. A football player receives a great deal of feedback—both during and after a game—and can improve both immediate and later performance. Programmed instruction is based on the demonstrated principle that learning is most efficient and improvement most rapid when precise feedback is given immediately. In general, immediate and complete feedback is followed by both improved performance and increased confidence—except, of course, where it is highly divergent and the individual sees no way of improving his course of action.

3. *Using feedback to change course.* It is in

using feedback to monitor our progress toward our goal that the servomechanism analogy is most apt. Having decided on a course of action, we use divergent feedback to get us back on course, whereas convergent, congruent feedback assures us that we are on the right track and should continue as we have been going.

But the human "computer," unlike its inanimate counterpart, uses feedback not only to monitor its progress in carrying out a course of action but also to check on the validity of its goal and the wisdom of its current "program." Thus if the situation changes or if feedback tells the individual that his goal is going to be too expensive or not worth achieving, he can abandon one course of action in midstream and embark on another.

situations later. The processing of stress is thus potentially a learning experience during which we can improve both present and future performance. For this reason, people are referred to as "self-correcting energy systems."

Utilizing stress situations for personal growth

"There are no great men, there are only ordinary men forced by circumstances to face great challenges." Admiral "Bull" Halsey

Admiral Halsey was Commander of the United States Naval Forces in the Pacific during the darkest days of World War II. Faced with

 If I make a decision that I can see later wasn't good, I tuck the information away for later use. I change the situation if I can, but if I can't, I try to recognize it next time it comes around, and do it differently. I say to myself, 'Remember the problems that happened last time,' and I try not to make that mistake again.

It thus becomes apparent that once an action is begun, the feedback that becomes available is an important part of the overall situation to which we then respond. For example, if we undertake a course of action in an attempt to repair a failing marriage, the feedback we get from our marital partner's reaction to our efforts becomes an integral part of the total situation with which we are coping. In fact, such feedback may be as important as the original adjustive demand in shaping later parts of the action sequence.

When we have enough feedback and use it in such a way as to correct behavior in progress, we develop greater skill for meeting other stress

seemingly insurmountable odds, he still managed to devise a strategy which led to the defeat of the enemy in a truly crucial war for the United States. Perhaps his statement, made after the war, can serve as a source of support for those of us in civilian life who also seem to face seemingly insurmountable odds in attempting to cope with our problems. For while we have seen that stress may exact a high toll in lowering our adaptive efficiency and in wear and tear on the human system, it may also be emphasized that we often see stronger and more mature persons forged by the demands and challenges of severe stress situations.

In this section we shall try to point out some

of the ways of utilizing stress situations for personal growth. Specifically we shall focus on: (1) learning to guard against common sources of error in our coping behavior; (2) increasing our understanding of our self and our world; (3) working out more realistic goals and values; and (4) developing increased competence and stress tolerance.

Guarding against common sources of error

Present-day computer studies which simulate the functioning of the human brain in dealing with adjustive demands support the notion that the brain is an elaborate communication and control center where incoming information is continuously evaluated, alternative responses are formulated and weighed, decisions are made and implemented, and feedback is checked and used to make needed corrections.

Our self-aware "human computer" is both more efficient and less efficient at handling problems than is the electronic computer. It is more inventive and creative, but it is also slower and more subject to error. We often come up with wrong answers to stress situations not only because of a lack of accurate information or inadequate competencies but also because of time pressures, emotional involvement in the stress situation, and other conditions that are peculiarly human.

For our immediate purposes we shall simply mention some of the more common sources of error in the processing of stress situations.

1. *Inadequate information and faulty assumptions.* As Shubik has pointed out:

"Man lives in an environment about which his information is highly incomplete. Not only does he not know how to evaluate many of the alternatives facing him, he is not even aware of a considerable percentage of them. His perceptions are relatively limited; his powers of calculation and accuracy are less than those of a computer in many situations; his searching, data processing,

and memory capabilities are erratic. As the speed of transmission of stimuli and the volume of new stimuli increase, the limitations of the individual become more marked relative to society as a whole" (1967, p. 772).

And often we fail to acquire needed information about problems we are likely to encounter in life even when such information is available.

It is apparent that inadequate information in turn leads to faulty assumptions concerning reality, possibility, and value. If we assume, for example, that making a lot of money will solve all of our problems, we are likely to be sadly disillusioned. In our earlier discussion, we pointed to the crucial importance of an accurate frame of reference if we are to cope with life's problems effectively.

2. *Time pressure.* In some stress situations where conditions permit, we can take our time, get more information if we need it, weigh and balance all factors carefully, and emerge with a course of action in which we have considerable confidence. And of course problems tend to be processed more effectively when we deal with them thoughtfully and when we are not feeling intensive time pressure.

In other situations, we feel so much time pressure that we may take the first possible way out even though it promises little in positive satisfaction or even in freedom from later risk and intensified stress. When we feel we must take action but do not have time to formulate an adequate course of action, we tend to become disorganized and to act on impulse. The result, of course, is likely to be ineffective coping.

3. *Oversimplification.* We have noted the importance of accurately evaluating the stress situation, and that in this process we tend to fit it into some familiar category in terms of our coding patterns. This tends to simplify the problem and make it more understandable. This is both necessary and desirable, since many problems are not as complicated or formidable as they seem at first.

Unfortunately, however, in categorizing and defining a problem, there is the danger of oversimplification—of failing to perceive key aspects of the problem. We have all heard individuals

I've learned to evaluate things now for a longer period of time, rather than rush into it. It's still possible for me to do things that are emotionally stupid, but I can usually realize it in time to pull myself out before I cause myself any real trouble.

offering easy solutions to complex problems, such as how to establish satisfying relationships with members of the opposite sex or to achieve financial success. Although their answers are often persuasive at first glance, they are not valid because they oversimplify the problem and disregard key dimensions that must be considered if an effective reaction is to be found.

4. *Motives and emotions.* We have seen how our motives influence other psychological functions—a process we referred to as motivational selectivity. We often tend to perceive what we want to perceive and to believe what we want to believe rather than face the realities of given situations. Many people make financial investments and other important decisions based on wishful thinking rather than the cold hard facts concerning the risks and possible costs involved.

Intense emotions—such as anxiety, fear, and anger—often distort our perception and thought processes and lead to ineffective coping behavior. An action taken when we are angry and wish to "get even" with someone is likely to be an unwise one. Even positive emotions may lead to costly errors. Many people who feel that they are in love may get married when they are in fact only infatuated, and the odds against their achieving a successful marriage are overwhelmingly against them.

In many obvious as well as subtle ways, our motives and emotions may lead to errors in coping.

5. *Ego-defense mechanisms.* We have seen how our ego-defense mechanisms function to protect us against emotional hurt, anxiety-arousing stress, and self-devaluation. But this protection is gained at the cost of some measure of reality distortion and self-deception. We noted earlier that Katz and his associates (1970)

THE IMPORTANCE OF FLEXIBILITY

It is all too easy to become "weighted down" by rigid beliefs and coping styles that lack the flexibility essential for dealing with changing conditions in a changing world. The importance of flexibility has been well expressed by the famous tennis professional Pancho Gonzales, who was still competing successfully in professional circuits in his early 40s—a feat considered virtually impossible in the fast-paced world of professional tennis:

"Vary your game to the conditions. Shorten your strokes on a fast court, play more steadily on a slow court; hit harder when you are playing against the wind and softer when you are playing with it" (1972).

This advice, coming as it does from a real professional who has learned to "roll with the punches" but not at the expense of becoming nontask-oriented or inauthentic, is applicable to many areas of our daily lives.

found that women who used denial and rationalization in coping with the possibility that they might have breast cancer did alleviate their anxiety but at the cost of failing to seek early medical assistance and impairing their chances for survival.

Defending the self against hurt and devaluation may interfere with the way we appraise problems, the alternatives we find acceptable, and the particular course of action we select. This is particularly true when we are quite emotionally involved in the problem. In coping with marital difficulties, for example, a person may project the blame onto his marital partner rather than face the devaluating fact that he himself has evidenced serious deficiencies in handling the relationship.

6.   *Self-pity.* While it is often easy to detect self-pity in the behavior of others, it is often less easy to detect it in our own behavior. And when undetected and uncorrected it can be a particularly pernicious form of self-defeating behavior. For in permitting ourselves the luxury of self-pity, we are likely to alienate others as well as to neglect constructive action.

Often, of course, it is difficult to avoid self-pity. After some painful loss or setback, each of us has probably asked "Why did this have to happen to me?" or speculated about "If *only* . . . ." Both of these responses stem from a

human tendency toward self-pity and offer possible means of detecting it in ourselves and of taking possible measures to deal with it.

But the more we indulge in self-pity and permit past hurts and traumas to dominate our behavior, the more immobilized we become in taking effective action in coping with present realities. The "Serenity Prayer," attributed to Reinhold Niebuhr, summarizes it well:
*"God grant me the serenity to accept the things
   I cannot change,
Courage to change the things I can,
And wisdom to know the difference."*

Increasing our understanding of ourselves and our world

Through his experiences in a stressful situation, the individual may gain a clearer view of his needs, motives, adaptive resources, and self-

It's that old thing of, 'Nobody loves me, so I'm going to go out and eat green worms,' where I get even with somebody else by doing something to *me.* Total self-pity, martyr thing. I haven't learned not to do it, but I've learned to recognize it. I stop it a lot of times, now, before I do it.

My family and I have learned a lot the last three months. We've had to face financial problems, health problems, the possibility of death (my wife has been extremely ill but is gradually recovering now), and a change in life style (we now live for the present, just for now). Each of us now has more compassion for other people's hardships, because we can understand what it is to endure them. And now instead of 'having to do something' we look forward to 'having something to do' together.

PERSONALITY CHARACTERISTICS ASSOCIATED WITH EFFECTIVE COPING

Another approach to assessing coping and adjustment is in terms of those personality characteristics that appear to foster personal effectiveness (Jahoda, 1958).

Attitudes toward self	Emphasizing self-acceptance, adequate self-identity, realistic appraisal of one's assets and liabilities.
Perception of reality	A realistic view of oneself and the surrounding world of people and things.
Integration	Unity of personality, freedom from disabling inner conflicts, good stress tolerance.
Competencies	Development of essential physical, intellectual, emotional, and social competencies for coping with life problems.
Autonomy	Adequate self-reliance, responsibility, and self-direction—together with sufficient independence of social influences.
Growth, self-actualization	Emphasizing trends toward increasing maturity, development of potentialities, and self-fulfillment as a person.

As desirable as the above traits would appear to be, however, they do not guarantee effective coping behavior. Sometimes an individual's life situation is simply so stressful that effective coping becomes impossible.

identity. In undergoing a disappointing and hurtful divorce, for example, the individual may realize that his own wishful thinking, personal immaturity, or lack of needed competencies played a major role in the failure of the relationship. Such feedback, if viewed objectively, can be highly useful as a basis for taking corrective measures.

Similarly, a severe and possibly traumatic stress situation—whether or not we have dealt with it effectively—may help us to understand more about the nature of our world, including the experiences which other persons may undergo. Certainly a person who has never suffered a hurtful love affair is in no position to really understand the feelings of another person who is undergoing that experience.

Unless we have "been there" ourselves, it is often impossible to understand and empathize with another person's experiences or even to help him, even though we sincerely desire to do so. It is perhaps for this reason that people who

have undergone highly stressful experiences are often effective in helping others with similar problems. Thus it has been shown that members of Alcoholics Anonymous, former heroin addicts, and ex-convicts are often more effective therapists than trained mental health workers who have never undergone such experiences themselves.

In this general context, Bovet has summarized the improved understanding of self and others that may stem from our reactions to stress—even highly negative experiences—as follows: *"It is a curious fact . . . that such loss and such pain frequently enlarge a person's vision and feeling. It can lead to an enlargement of the understanding of the suffering of others . . ."* (1973, p. 6).
Similarly, Gelven has pointed out that even severe guilt, one of the most intensive forms of human stress and suffering, ". . . has the unique capacity to throw light upon what it means to be a human being" (1973, p. 20). In

essence, guilt feelings too can help the individual to better understand himself and the human situation, as well as to empathize with the agonizing guilt and self-recrimination of others. Thus, while such experiences are not without their costs, when used constructively for personal growth they have been referred to as "creative suffering."

Working out more realistic goals and values

If we fail to achieve difficult goals which are unrealistic in terms of our coping resources, we

child can walk in the hope that he will follow in his father's footsteps.

In an actual instance, a real estate salesman—who had not been very successful and was usually pressed to meet his financial obligations—had his heart set on his son's becoming either a lawyer, dentist, or physician. As a result, the son dutifully embarked on a premedical major at a large university. Unfortunately, the results were tension, failure, and feelings of having let his father down. As a consequence, he attempted suicide.

A more appropriate response to parental demands would have been to obtain professional

may utilize the feedback constructively by lowering our aspirations to a more realistic level or perhaps even substituting goals which are equally difficult but more appropriate to our resources.

Because of strong parental expectations, some students pursue educational goals which are actually inappropriate in terms of their own personal interests and resources. A physician may want his only child to become a physician; an All-American football player may start teaching his son to play football almost before the

counseling concerning his interests and capabilities prior to undertaking a college major and perhaps to have entered a technical school for training in a useful trade instead. In so doing he would have averted a highly traumatic stress situation. But even when his educational failure did occur, there still would have been ample time to have taken such constructive measures rather than attempting suicide as the only apparent way out of the dilemma.

Often, too, we find that goals we have worked

very hard to achieve are not satisfying and were certainly not worth the time and effort that went into their attainment. In such instances, we may take a hard look at the values on which our goals were based and perhaps modify our value assumptions and in turn our future goals. Interestingly, a sizeable number of professionally trained persons have decided that the competitive rat race in our contemporary society is simply not worth the cost and have adopted alternative life styles. Perhaps some people would view this as "copping out"; but many others would view it as a realistic modification of values and goals in the light of known satisfaction and cost factors.

Improving our competence and stress tolerance

In the process of dealing with life's problems, we usually learn through experience to deal more effectively with various stress situations. Unfortunately, however, hurtful failures—such as unsuccessfully trying to maintain a failing marriage—are often necessary to alert us to the need for improving our competencies in given areas.

As we have seen, severe stress may "sensitize" the individual to given types of stressful situations or it may "immunize" him and increase his feelings of self-confidence and actual coping ability. As West has pointed out:

". . . an experience may be both frightening and painful, yet its repetition may be less stressful because it is now familiar, because its limits have been perceived, because the memory and imagination of the individual enable him to equate it with other known experiences, and because defenses have been developed through fantasied re-experiences during the interval" (1958, p. 332).

He might have added that the individual may also systematically go about improving his competence if he feels he is likely to encounter the same type of stress situation in the future.

In this context, it may be noted that improving our competence and stress tolerance appears

HOW WOULD YOU EVALUATE THIS BLIND BOY'S COPING BEHAVIOR?

"Bob is 12 years old. He has been blind since birth. He is a bright boy, eagerly interested in the wonders of the world around him—a world that he has experienced in his own way, but has never seen. He is interested in science—especially electronics. He reads everything he can get under his curious fingertips. Bob has great potential. He is sensitive, intellectually gifted far beyond his years—and he desperately wants to find his place in the world."

The preceding is a description made by a mental health professional. Following are Bob's own words about some of the things he believes in and wonders about.

"There are so many things in this world, that people could all reach out and touch and keep a part of them for their very own and spread it around for everyone. Not money—because money is good for what it can do—only good if it is used to help. But people could reach out for kindness and fair play—and could spread it around for others.

"I've heard on the radio all this talk about integration in the schools. To give all children a chance to go to school together. And there seems to be such a fuss about it because some of the children are different. And I can't understand at all what this great difference is.

"They say it's their color. And what is color? I guess I am lucky that I cannot see differences in color because it seems to me that the kind of hate the people put in their minds must chase out all chance to grow in understanding" (O'Connor, 1971, pp. 153–154).

to involve two basic tasks: (1) the acquisition of essential knowledge and (2) the inner control over such knowledge (Hammond & Summers, 1972). In a study of parachutists, for example, Fenz and Epstein (1969) found that while all were anxious, the anxiety of trained parachutists peaked some time before the actual jump; while for untrained parachutists, intense anxiety continued right up to the jump and interfered with performance. A number of other investigators have made comparable findings with trained astronauts and concluded that they had learned some method for controlling anxiety during stressful situations. In essence, as an individual becomes increasingly capable of functioning in a stressful situation, any emotional distress he may experience tends to occur before or after the stress is over—thus permitting his adaptive capabilities to work best when they are most needed.

This section on utilizing stress situations for personal growth goes beyond the problem of learning to cope with simple adjustive demands to the problem of learning to cope constructively with severe, sustained, and often hurtful stress situations. This is a never ending process for most of us in which we learn to understand more about ourselves and others, to modify our goals and expectations in keeping with reality, and to increase our competence and stress tolerance. Thus while adaptation to severe stress can be expensive, it can also serve as a constructive experience in which we become wiser, stronger, and more mature persons.

» Summary and a look ahead

In this chapter we have suggested three criteria as guidelines for evaluating stress reactions: Does the action meet the adjustive demand? Does the action meet the needs of the individual? Is the action compatible with the welfare of the group? We have also noted several common models for understanding effective and ineffective coping behavior, including anxiety-defense, faulty learning, stress-decompensation, interpersonal and social pathology, and organic pathology.

The typical steps in coping effectively with stress are as follows: (1) evaluating the stress situation—usually involving categorizing the stress situation, appraising the threat, and assessing resources for coping with it; (2) working out an appropriate course of action—usually involving balancing the probability, desirability, and cost of given alternatives; (3) taking positive action—that is, implementing the decision which has been made concerning the alternative best suited for coping with the stress situation; and (4) utilizing feedback and correcting possible error if it is feasible to do so.

Although we tend to think of stress as inherently bad because of the costs which it may exact, stress situations can often be utilized for personal growth. This involves guarding against common sources of error, increasing our understanding of ourselves and our world, working out more realistic goals and values, and improving our competence and stress tolerance.

Having covered effective methods of coping with stress, in the next chapter we shall turn to a discussion of ineffective methods of coping, maladaptive behavior patterns, and finally, therapeutic resources available to an individual.

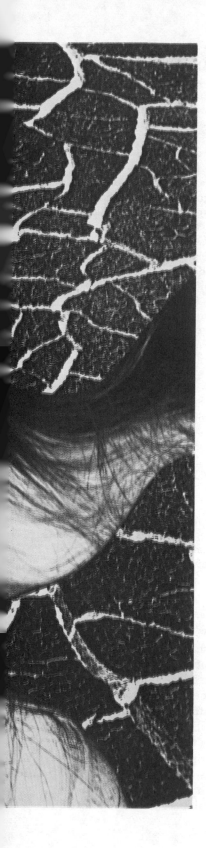

8

8
Ineffective Coping Patterns

Common self-defeating patterns
When things really go wrong
Introduction to therapeutic resources

We have seen that behavior is an attempt by the organism to adapt to inner and outer demands. This is as true of maladjustive behavior as it is of smooth, effective, successful behavior. Both represent answers to the same concerns—how best to protect one's well-being, develop one's potentials, and meet group demands. Thus the same basic principles which underlie effective behavior also underlie ineffective or maladjustive behavior.

In the present chapter, we shall attempt to: (1) describe certain common self-defeating coping patterns; (2) describe behavior that may occur when things really go wrong; and (3) undertake a brief introduction to resources for treatment and personal change.

Common self-defeating coping patterns

In applying the criteria we outlined in Chapter 7 for evaluating stress reactions—meeting the adjustive demand, the needs of the individual, and the well-being of the group—it becomes apparent that in real life we are dealing with a continuum of effective-ineffective coping behavior. Most people cluster around a central point and

181

evidence an average level of adjustment. As we approach one end of the continuum, we find a few people who lead unusually effective lives and achieve a superior level of adjustment; and as we approach the other end of the continuum, we find a minority evidencing severe maladjustment.

A given individual may fall anywhere on this continuum of effective-ineffective adjustment, and his position on the continuum may change with time. Under severe and sustained stress, the individual's level of adjustment may show a marked decline; it may improve when his life situation becomes less stressful or he learns to cope more effectively with his problems.

In this section, we shall deal with common self-defeating patterns of coping which ordinarily result in moderate degrees of maladjustment: (1) neurotic avoidance; (2) psychosomatic reactions; (3) sociopathic behavior; and (4) alienation.

Neurotic avoidance

Neurotic avoidance involves the exaggerated use of defensive patterns in coping with stress. Most contemporary investigators view these patterns as learned maladaptive responses which are maintained because they protect the individual from anxiety-arousing stress. They are considered maladaptive because they occur in response to stresses that most people could deal with effectively and without undue difficulty. In addition, they do not solve the individual's problems but instead tend to complicate them. Although such patterns may seriously interfere with the individual's effectiveness, they are not usually incapacitating. It has been estimated that over 10 million persons in the United States manifest neurotic avoidance reactions.

The principle types of neurotic avoidance reactions are briefly examined in the following section.

Anxiety reaction

An individual with this neurotic pattern typically manifests an unpleasant degree of apprehension and tension, has difficulty in sleeping, and evi-

CAUSAL RELATIONSHIPS IN MALADAPTIVE BEHAVIOR

The question of cause and effect in maladaptive behavior patterns is an extremely complex one. In general, three types of causation may be identified:

1. *Predisposing causes* are factors such as parental rejection that go before and pave the way for later maladaptive behavior.

2. *Precipitating causes* are factors—such as the loss of a job—that prove too much for the individual and trigger the onset of maladaptive behavior.

3. *Reinforcing causes* are factors in the environment—such as parental approval of a child's showing off—that tend to maintain maladaptive behavior over time.

There is, of course, no fine line between these types of causation. For example, the conditions that precipitate a schizophrenic episode may increase the individual's vulnerability and thus serve as predisposing causes for a recurrence of such episodes in the future. And as we think in terms of the concept of self-regulating systems, we must also take into account the concept of circularity and the effects of feedback on these causal factors.

dences gastrointestinal upsets and other somatic difficulties. Mild but continuous anxiety may be punctuated by acute episodes of intense anxiety which may last from a few seconds to an hour or more. During these attacks, the individual's heart pounds, he perspires profusely, and his blood pressure increases markedly. At the same time he feels acutely apprehensive—for example, that he is going insane, is about to die, or that some other calamity is about to overtake him. He is usually unable to account for the

I have sometimes experienced what they call "free-floating" anxiety—it's pretty scary. The most recent . . . about a year ago I quit a nice secure job to go into business for myself. At the same time a lot of other changes were going on in my life, really all having to do with self-actualization, growing up. After I had been on my new venture for a couple of months and could see that it was probably going to work out, and I really started having fun with it, I began to get this very anxious feeling. It was of calamity . . . an uncontrollable calamity that was just going to come out of the blue. I just had a terrible fear that some truck was going to tip over onto me, or some terrible uncontrollable thing like that. That period lasted a few weeks and then it just sort of went away. It's very frightening when it happens, and it's an unreasonable fear, an unreasonable fear of something that actually could happen but is extremely unlikely to happen.

source of his acute anxiety, which for this reason is said to be "free floating."

In general, the anxiety neurotic presents the picture of an individual anxiously attempting to cope with stresses that are too much for him. He exaggerates the severity of situations which most people take in their stride and reacts with chronic anxiety, which not only results in sub-jective distress but typically interferes with both his family life and his work. Often such persons resort to the use of drugs and alcohol to alleviate their anxiety and tension—reactions which in turn may intensify their self-defeating coping pattern.

Phobic reaction

A phobia is a persistent fear of something that actually presents no danger to the individual or in which the danger is grossly exaggerated.

Listed below are common phobias and their objects:

Acrophobia—high places
Agoraphobia—open places
Algophobia—pain
Astraphobia—storms, thunder, and lightning
Claustrophobia—closed places
Hematophobia—blood
Mysophobia—contamination or germs
Monophobia—being alone
Nyctophobia—darkness
Ocholophobia—crowds
Pathophobia—disease
Pyrophobia—fire
Syphilophobia—syphilis
Zoophobia—animals or some particular animal

Some of these phobias involve fear of situations that most of us fear to some extent, such as high places; others, such as fear of open places, involve situations that do not elicit fear in most people.

When I was in kindergarten a big dog chased me home from school. It didn't bite me or anything, it probably just wanted to play. But I was pretty scared and ran, and of course it ran after me. For a long time I was afraid of any kind of dog. Later I was only afraid of large ones. It has taken nearly 20 years to get over it, but now I'm usually not afraid of them.

I had a rather severe case of what they call obsessions and compulsions. I think it was just from whatever stresses were built up in me that I just couldn't handle. The first time I felt anything like that was when I was in the service. I had been transferred to a unit that was going where there was fighting, and I didn't know where I'd be sent or anything, and so it was a little scary. So the first indication I had was at a movie at the camp that we had one night. This was a murder mystery, about a strangler. And right at the critical moment of the movie when the strangler was about to strangle somebody, I got this compulsion to strangle this guy next to me. Then it went away. I worried about it for awhile, I sweated it for awhile, but it went away. And then it came back again later, about a month or so later. But this time it came back in the form of a suicidal compulsion. I was cleaning a .45 in my tent, and I suddenly got the urge to shoot myself. So then that became an obsession, it was first a compulsion, and then I got obsessed with that idea, that I was going to commit suicide.

Phobias are irrational or exaggerated fears that are out of proportion to any actual danger. The subject above is enacting an exaggerated version of the fear many people have of crawling things.

In neurotic phobias, the individual cannot account for his fear, experiences intense anxiety if forced to face the phobic situation, and is seriously inconvenienced by it. Marks (1970) has described the case of a young woman who, at the age of 19, developed agoraphobia (fear of open places) and left her home only twice in the next seven years. In addition, phobic reactions do not usually involve a single irrational fear but an overall pattern of fear and avoidance behavior. The pervasive influence of a phobic reaction on the life style of an individual has been referred to as "nonspecific insecurity fear" and "phobic anxiety state."

Obsessive-compulsive reaction

In obsessive-compulsive reactions, the individual is hounded by persistent irrational thoughts (obsessions) or by a compulsion to carry out irrational acts. Obsessive and compulsive reactions may occur independently of each other, but typically they go together and are considered separate aspects of a single response pattern.

Often people under heavy pressure set up strict and unvarying procedures for maintaining order and predictability, thus ensuring that nothing can go wrong that would make additional or unforeseen demands on them. Many obsessive-compulsive reactions appear to be an exaggeration of these learned and normally adaptive patterns of orderliness. Typically they take place in a personality similar to that of the anxiety neurotic. The individual is sensitized to the dangers of living and allays his chronic feelings of insecurity and inadequacy by a ritualistic exaggeration of orderliness, often involving an overconcern with some aspect of normal role behavior. Thus a housewife may be constantly cleaning, spraying the air with pesticides, emptying ashtrays, and otherwise preoccupying herself with extreme orderliness.

In other instances obsessive thoughts appear to be associated with the repression of thoughts or feelings which the individual views as highly immoral. The girl who has repressed hostility toward her unwanted baby may experience fantasies of the baby's accidental death or even of killing him. Since such thoughts cannot be banished voluntarily from consciousness, they may seem not only irrational but horrifying to the individual. Although "immoral" obsessive thoughts are common in obsessions, the individual's rigid conscience development almost inevitably prevents their being carried out in action.

Obsessive thoughts may in turn lead to compulsive actions which are symbolically designed to counteract the immoral thoughts. The young mother who has persistent thoughts of her baby dying or of killing him may feel compelled to make the sign of the cross and say "God protect my darling baby" each time such a thought enters awareness. A youth who feels terribly guilty about masturbating may have a compulsion to wash his hands every few minutes—thus symbolically "washing away" his guilt and cleansing himself.

All of us have probably experienced minor obsessive thoughts and compulsions; and during periods when we are subjected to multiple pressures we may resort to rigid ordering of our activities. The personality makeup of the obsessive-compulsive neurotic—which usually leads to feelings of inadequacy as well as rigid standards of "morality"—seems to lead to an exaggeration of such normal tendencies and to self-defeating behavior.

Neurasthenic reaction

This neurotic reaction is characterized by chronic physical and mental fatigue. The individual feels tired most of the time, has difficulty in concentrating, and lacks the vigor required to carry activities through to successful completion. Even minor tasks seem to require a herculean effort. Although he may sleep a great deal, he typically feels "just rotten," and usually suffers as well from various somatic symptoms such as dizzy spells, stomach upset, hypersensitivity to noise, and palpitation of the heart. Often he is quite concerned about his health, and he may have numerous medical examinations in an effort to determine the physical basis of his difficulties—but to no avail, since his difficulties stem from psychological rather than physical factors.

Essentially the neurasthenic reaction appears to represent the attempt of an inadequate, immature, and self-pitying person to cope with a frustrating life situation from which he sees no way out. Whereas most people could cope with such stress effectively, the neurasthenic experiences loss of hope, dejection, and chronic fatigue, which are self-defeating in that they neither resolve the stress nor meet his needs.

Hysterical (conversion) reaction

Here the individual protects himself against some anxiety-arousing situation by developing the symptoms of a disease or disability. For example, a soldier may go blind just as he is about to be sent into combat, or an individual in ordinary life, facing a threat from which he cannot escape, may become deaf or paralyzed, develop coughing or sneezing spells, lose his sensitivity to touch and pain in some body area, or even show the symptoms of some disease like malaria. No organic pathology underlies such symptoms though occasionally the picture is complicated by the fact that the symptoms are superimposed on actual organic damage, as when an individual with a history of impaired hearing suddenly becomes totally deaf.

Although the neurophysiological mechanisms involved in conversion reactions are not fully understood, three factors usually make it possible to differentiate between conversion reactions and physical illness: (1) the absence of conversion symptoms when the individual is under the influence of drugs such as sodium pentothal; (2) little concern shown by the individual over his alleged disability; and (3) sophisticated techniques of medical diagnosis. However, in conversion reactions the individual is not malingering; his symptoms are real to him and he is as baffled by them as anyone.

Conversion reactions used to be common in both military and civilian life. But in an age that no longer believes in being "struck" blind or deaf and which has the medical facilities for determining the existence of physical pathology, they have become understandably rare, for they no longer serve their defensive function. Yet they still occur in our society and are common in less "sophisticated" societies.

Hypochondriacal reaction

In this neurotic avoidance pattern the individual is preoccupied with his state of health and with various presumed physical disorders or diseases. But unlike the individual manifesting a conversion reaction, he does not usually evidence any actual physical symptoms.

These individuals usually have difficulty in describing their ailments precisely. Thus they may begin by mentioning a pain in the chest which upon questioning turns out to be not a pain but a "heavy feeling." Their general orientation keeps them constantly on the alert for new manifestations of illness; and as one might expect, they are usually avid readers of popular magazines dealing with diet and health.

Most of us, of course, are interested in our bodily functioning and state of health. In hypochondriacal reactions, however, the individual shows a morbid exaggeration of this common interest and concern—an exaggeration that enables him to avoid life stress with which he feels inadequate to cope.

Depressive reaction

In this avoidance pattern, the individual reacts to some distressing situation—such as the loss of a loved one, a severe financial reverse, or a chronic illness—with more than the usual amount of grief and dejection and fails to return to normal after a reasonable period of time.

Symptoms of neurotic depression commonly include sadness, listlessness, loss of appetite, fatigue, inability to concentrate, feelings of unworthiness, and vague tension and anxiety. Although the individual may have thoughts of committing suicide and may even do so, the danger of suicide is not usually as great as in the psychotic depressive reaction, which we will describe shortly. The depressive reaction may last for weeks or even months but eventually clears up with or without treatment.

Most of us become dejected at times and may become depressed at the death of a loved one, a disappointment in love, or some other distressing event. Neurotic depressive reactions, however, occur among persons who lack the resiliency that most people show in dealing with the inevitable hurts and setbacks of life. Since they do not resolve but rather intensify and prolong the stressful situation, they are termed self-defeating.

To summarize the factors in neurotic avoidance behavior, we seem to be dealing with a *neurotic nucleus* comprised of: (1) anxiety, resulting from basic feelings of inadequacy and the evaluation of everyday problems as threatening; (2) learned defensive maneuvers which enable the individual to avoid rather than deal with stress in task-oriented ways; and (3) inconvenience, discomfort, and distress. A second key factor is the *neurotic paradox*—the tendency to maintain such avoidance patterns even when they lead to personal distress and are self-defeating. It seems to be explained by: (1) the reinforcement of avoidance behaviors by the immediate relief they afford from anxiety-arousing stress situations; and (2) the failure of the individual to test the situation to see if his fears are realistic—for example, an individual with a conditioned fear of dogs may withdraw or take other defensive measures at the first sign of an approaching dog.

Finally, it may be emphasized that there are various mixtures and degrees of neurotic avoid-

At one time I suffered from many chest colds—I had 22 in one year! After several sessions with a therapist I came to realize that I was fighting maturity, motherhood, and marriage to a man whose occupation requires him to be away for long periods of time. I am now much more productive and much happier, and I hardly have any colds.

I get a peculiar skin reaction to stress once in awhile, sometimes after a period of sustained and intense stress like the breaking up of a long-standing relationship. After this stress is actually over and things are beginning to let up a little, I get a red patch somewhere on my stomach, on my torso. And I've noticed that that spot on my skin where it's red is warmer to the touch. It's like it's a 'hot spot,' something busting out because I didn't get the feelings out in the first place.

ance behaviors as well as personality types and stress situations represented; and such relatively clear-cut patterns as those described are the exception rather than the rule. Typically, but by no means always, neurotic avoidance reactions tend to be alleviated over time—whether or not the individual receives professional assistance. However, such assistance may facilitate matters and avoid a great deal of unnecessary distress.

"Psychosomatic" reactions

Psychosomatic reactions involve the effects of sustained emotional tension upon the structure and function of internal organs, rather than overt maladaptive behavior.

All of us, of course, experience emotional reactions involving widespread changes in circulation, respiration, and bodily processes. Normally such emotion-induced changes are short-lived, and our physiological activities return to

normal levels. Sometimes, however, emotion-arousing stress situations continue over sustained periods of time—as with a soldier in combat, a person who hates his work, or a person in an unhappy marriage. Over a period of time, such a chronic acceleration of physiological activity may lead to actual tissue damage in some bodily system—as in the case of peptic ulcers. Such pathological changes are called *psychosomatic* or *psychophysiologic* reactions or disorders. It has been estimated that there are well over 20 million adolescents and adults in the United States suffering from such psychosomatic disorders.

Psychosomatic reactions are classified according to the organ system affected, and no organ system appears to be immune. Among the more common psychosomatic reactions are the following:

   1. *Gastrointestinal reactions,* including peptic ulcers, mucous colitis, and chronic gastritis.

   2. *Respiratory reactions,* including asthma, bronchial spasms, and recurring bronchitis.

ORGAN SPECIFICITY IN PSYCHOSOMATIC REACTIONS

One question whose answer has eluded researchers in psychosomatic disorders is that of *organ specificity*—why one individual develops peptic ulcers, another high blood pressure, and still another backaches. It may be that the organ system affected is especially vulnerable as a result of prior injury, illness, or other conditions; or it may be that psychosomatic reactions, like voluntary responses, have been learned through selective reinforcement. For example, a person might learn to manifest gastrointestinal upsets when under stress if as a child he had been allowed to avoid some unpleasant task or given special attention because of stomach-aches. A third possibility is that there exist certain "personality types" prone to react to stress with specific emotions that are more likely to affect one organ system than another. For example, McQuade (1972) has delineated what he describes as a "coronary-prone" personality type who is ambitious, competitive, and aggressive. Of 287 patients who developed coronary heart disease, he found that 70 percent evidenced these personality characteristics; while a control group of subjects described as easygoing, patient, and less concerned with achievement seemed to be immune to coronary heart disease.

5. *Cardiovascular reactions,* including migraine and tension headaches, high blood pressure, and coronary heart disease.

It may be emphasized here that factors other than chronic emotion also may lead to physiological malfunction and subsequent damage or breakdown. For example, high blood pressure may be due primarily to physical disease, to chronic emotion-arousing stress, or to a combination of the two. As in the case of other faulty stress reactions, psychosomatic reactions may vary from mild to extremely severe.

We still have much to learn about the causal pattern in psychosomatic reactions—about the interacting roles of neurophysiological and psychosocial variables. In general, however, psychosomatic reactions appear to involve: (1) sustained stress which arouses emotional tension—the degree of arousal depending not only on the objective severity of the stress situation but also upon the individual's evaluation of it; (2) the failure of the individual to cope adequately with the stress—resulting in the continuation of emotional arousal on a chronic basis; and (3) organ specificity—in which the effects of chronic emotional arousal are concentrated in a specific organ system, presumably as a result of the vulnerability of the system due to such factors as prior illness or conditioning.

Psychosomatic reactions do not always seriously impair the individual's coping behavior. In fact, reactions such as tension headaches may serve as an excuse for not performing up to expected standards or bring added attention from loved ones. However, psychosomatic reactions often tend to be costly reactions to stress in terms of personal discomfort and tissue damage. In some instances, as in coronary artery disease, the tissue damage may be irreversible and can result in death.

3. *Musculoskeletal reactions,* including rheumatism, backache, and rheumatoid arthritis.
4. *Skin reactions,* including eczema and various so-called neurodermatoses.

Psychopathic behavior

Psychopathic patterns seem to differ perceptibly from neurotic avoidance and psychosomatic reactions in that psychopathic behavior does not ordinarily stem from defenses against anxiety but rather involves a pattern of "acting out" with little or no sense of personal distress.

Individuals labeled as psychopathic (antisocial) personalities are neither mentally retarded, neurotic, or psychotic. Rather, their most outstanding characteristic is a lack of ethical or moral development and an inability to follow desirable models of behavior. Basically they appear to be unsocialized and incapable of loyalty to other persons, groups, or social values. Their callous disregard for the rights of others leads to serious difficulties in interpersonal relationships and usually brings them into conflict with society.

Included in the category of psychopathic per-

of coping behavior. Of course, not all of these traits are likely to be found in a given case.

1. *Amoral, unreliable, irresponsible.* Often a marked discrepancy between intellectual level and conscience development. May deceive others by verbal endorsement of high standards, but does not understand or adhere to accepted moral values. Pathological lying, deceitfulness, and a callous disregard for the rights of others.

2. *Impulsive, hedonistic, unrealistic goals.* Prone to thrill seeking, deviant sexual patterns, and unconventional behavior. Lives in present with primary concern for immediate pleasures and no long-range goals. Shows poor judgment and often engages in impulsive acts detrimental to his own well-being as well as that of others.

 He was utterly charming, utterly delightful, until he had your confidence, and then he would see how much hell he could make out of your life. Because by that time you were very emotionally involved, he could do it. He'd do anything that would annoy you. He'd get to know you well enough to know what your weaknesses were, then he'd play upon them with great skill. He would tell lies about people to their friends, and he would have affairs with girls whose boy friends he knew so they could find out about it and be unhappy about it. Things like that.

sonality are a sizable number of unprincipled businessmen, shyster lawyers, crooked politicians, compulsive gamblers, prostitutes, drug pushers, and assorted delinquents and criminals. Despite the tendency for their behavior to lead to problems with constituted authority, the great majority of psychopaths manage to stay out of corrective institutions. The incidence of psychopathic personalities is thought to exceed 4 million adolescents and adults in our society.

The following traits are considered indicative of psychopathic personality and will help us to gain a clearer overall perspective of this pattern

Dislikes routine work and frequently changes jobs, moves from place to place, lives by his wits, or depends on others for support.

3. *Ability to impress and exploit others.* Often a charming individual with a good sense of humor and a generally optimistic outlook. Easily wins the liking and friendship of others but ruthlessly exploits the interpersonal relationships he develops. Often shows contempt for those he is able to take advantage of—the "marks." Unable to give or receive love.

4. *Lack of anxiety and guilt.* Tends to act out tensions rather than worry them out. Cynical, unsympathetic, and remorseless in his dealings with others, with little or no sense of guilt. Lack of anxiety combined with seeming sincerity often enables psychopath to lie his way out of difficulties. Undeterred by punishment.

5. *Disappointing and distressing to others.* Frequently a burden on friends and relatives. Unstable and disappointing in marital relationships. Often has history of difficulty with law enforcement agencies but not a calculating professional criminal.

The causal factors underlying psychopathic behavior are not fully understood and undoubtedly differ markedly from one case to another. There is considerable evidence that these individuals do not show normal fear or anxiety reactions or learn readily from noxious experiences, including punishment. Some investigators interpret this as due to some sort of

behavior. Still another alleged source of psychopathic behavior is direct learning from faulty models—often middle-class parents. For example, such models may emphasize the importance of appearances rather than truly ethical behavior and may encourage the development of personal charm and poise as tools for manipulating others.

Each of the preceding explanations appears to be applicable in certain cases, but in many others psychopathic behavior and its maintenance remain an enigma.

Alienation

"Which one of us has known his brother? Which of us has looked into his father's heart? Which of us has not remained forever prison-pent? Which of us is not forever a stranger and alone?
Thomas Wolfe (1929, p. 3)

 I joined this group because I thought it might have some answers—you know, make me feel different about people and things—and maybe myself, too. But so far, I feel just like I did before—completely alone and adrift in a hostile sea. I don't feel like any of you know me or really give a damn. Maybe things will change and we'll get closer to each other and I will see things differently. But I'm not betting on it.

imbalance in the central nervous system. Other investigators point to early sociocultural deprivation involving a lack of warm interpersonal relationships and other socializing experiences necessary for empathizing with others and understanding social norms and values. These investigators point to our urban ghettos as breeding grounds for psychopaths due to the climate of social disorganization, undesirable peer models, broken homes, and hostility toward established social norms and values—leading to a type of psychopath characterized by inadequate conscience development, lack of concern for others, and destructive antisocial

A great many people in our society suffer from a chronic feeling of inner emptiness, of lacking meaningful values and goals, of confusion about who or what they are, of having no control over their destiny, and of unrelatedness to others. They seem to be alienated—in varying degrees—from others, from the larger society, and even from themselves.

Some investigators have attributed this alienation to the depersonalizing and dehumanizing effect of our mass bureaucratic society; others, to the wearing of masks and the maintenance of façades, so that the individual is alienated from his true self and becomes what others expect and demand of him—much like a conditioned automaton; some investigators point to the pathogenic conditions of our urban ghettos which rob people of dignity, meaning, and hope. Still others, such as the historian Arnold Toynbee, consider the malaise to go much deeper—as resulting from a deteriorating society which he describes as "truly repulsive."

The behavioral results of alienation are varied. In an attempt to find some life style that provides a modicum of meaning, some young people join the drug subculture—often in conjunction with various types of communes; others join violent, antisocial groups with the avowed intention of destroying the establishment but with no realistic view of what they hope to replace it with; some enter into pathogenic relationships with others; some engage in brutally insensitive acts of violence; and still others commit suicide.

Some investigators have expressed concern that alienation from family and the larger society—as well as from himself—exposes a youth to becoming a captive of his peers to whom he may turn blindly for support and guidance. As Riesman has described it: "As adult authority disintegrates, the young are more and more captives of each other" (1969, p. 28).

But lest we leave the impression that alienation is restricted to the young, it may be pointed out that many so-called members of the establishment also express concern over feelings of alienation. They feel caught up in a competitive rat race from which there seems no exit; they feel that their relationships with others are inauthentic; they seem unable to find truly satisfying values; and they no longer experience themselves as being self-directing or in control of their own destiny. Rather they seem to be caught in an abyss of uncontrolled technological and social change in which established social norms and values are being abandoned before other and equally or more satisfying ones have become available. They no longer believe in themselves—if they ever did; nor do they know what to believe in. In short, they seem lost, empty, and unable to find a truly authentic,

meaningful, and fulfilling way of life. Despite their material affluence they are spiritually impoverished.

"And how am I to face the odds
Of man's bedevilment and God's?
I, a stranger and afraid
In a world I never made."

A. E. Housman (1922, p. 111)

The solution to alienation seems to be in the direction of commitment to being an authentic person, to having concern for others, and to building loving relationships with others. But this solution is not easily achieved, and it requires constructive changes in our society which reverse the trend toward depersonalization and dehumanization; in providing people with meaningful and fulfilling social roles in which they perform needed social functions; and in providing increased opportunities for their participation in building a better society and a secure future for the human race.

Problems involving sexual behavior

In referring to problems involving sexual behavior, the term *sexual deviation* is ordinarily used—referring in its broadest sense to sexual behavior that is atypical, does not follow established social norms, and is commonly subject to social sanctions. However, some serious problems have arisen in the use of the term sexual deviation. For example, socially approved and disapproved sexual patterns differ from one society to another, among subgroups within a given society, and over time. In our own society, we are witnessing a challenge to many traditional sexual mores and a marked shift in our views concerning sexual behavior.

Many people today view premarital and extramarital sexual relations as acceptable and even desirable. Mouth-genital contact—considered a "crime against nature" in many states and punishable as a criminal act—has apparently been redefined as acceptable in premarital and marital relations. Some groups are experiment-

Persons who engage in maladaptive sexual patterns for which there are legal penalties, such as exhibitionism, incest, and rape, are subjects of a number of misconceptions, including:

1. *Sexual offenders are typically homicidal sex fiends.* Homicidal acts associated with sex crimes are rare, and the offender in such cases is usually suffering from a severe mental disorder. Only about 5 percent of all convicted sex offenders inflict physical injury upon their victims. Of course, this does not preclude psychological damage.

2. *Sexual offenders are oversexed from exposure to pornography.* Most sexual deviants arrested by the police are undersexed, rather than oversexed. Typically, they have been subjected to much misinformation about sexual activities and are more prudish than nonoffenders; and usually they have been less exposed to pornography than have nonoffenders.

3. *Sexual offenders suffer from glandular imbalance.* The development of sexual patterns in human beings appears to be determined primarily by experiences and life situations rather than by hormonal secretions.

4. *Sexual offenders typically progress from minor to more serious sex crimes.* The offender may progress to major sex crimes in order to achieve satisfaction as minor deviations lose their "thrill," but this pattern is the exception. Sexual offenders usually persist in the type of behavior in which they have discovered satisfaction.

5. *Sexual offenders are usually repeaters.* Sex offenders have one of the lowest rates of repeated offenses—less than 10 percent of those convicted, as contrasted with over 60 percent of convicted criminal offenders in general. And most of the repeaters are booked for minor offenses, such as peeping or exhibitionism, rather than for serious criminal acts.

ing with "wife swapping," communal sex, and group sexual patterns. And an increasing number of people are redefining homosexual relationships among consenting adults as socially acceptable.

Thus it becomes apparent that simply labeling sexual behavior as deviant does not demonstrate that it is ineffective and maladaptive. In an attempt to put the term sexual deviation into a broader perspective, Coleman and Broen (1972) have utilized a threefold classification:

1. *"Normal" sexual deviations.* The sexual behavior in this category—though disapproved in terms of traditional social mores—is so prevalent that few persons are subjected to sanctions for engaging in it. Here we would find such patterns as masturbation, premarital sexual relations, mouth-genital relations, and extramarital coitus.

2. *"Socially organized" and related sexual deviations.* Included in this category are homosexuals—who usually prefer the term "gay"—and prostitutes. Although these patterns may have little in common, they do tend to operate in a supportive subculture which influences their social roles and conditions of operation. The sexual behavior of both of these groups is viewed with disapproval by some persons and with approval by others. While social sanctions have been applied, there appears to be an increasing tendency to treat individuals engaging in such sexual patterns as approved minority-group members rather than as socially disapproved sexual deviants.

3. *"Maladaptive" sexual deviations.* These sexual patterns may be maladaptive in varying degrees, and social sanctions may or may not be imposed depending on the pattern involved. In impotence and frigidity, for example, no social sanctions are imposed, although such patterns may seriously impair marital and related sexual adjustments. Other patterns included here—such as pedophilia, forcible rape, and incest—may be seriously maladaptive, and for this reason strong social sanctions may be imposed.

Both impotence and frigidity involve impairment in the desire for or inability to achieve sexual gratification. The most common forms of impotence are: (1) primary impotence, in which the male is unable to attain an erection long

Depending on the age of the victim, rape is defined as: (1) *statutory rape,* which involves the seduction of a minor; and (2) *forcible rape,* in which the unwilling victim is over 18 years of age. It is with the latter that we are concerned here.

Incidence

Approximately 40,000 forcible rape cases are reported each year in the United States—about one case every 90 seconds. However, actual incidence figures are considered to be about 3 times the reported figures.

Time

The incidence of forcible rape is highest from May to October, hitting a peak in August. Most forcible rapes occur between 8 p.m. and 2 a.m.

Place

Most rapists—some 80 percent or more—do not leave their own neighborhoods to seek out their victims. However, few communities of any size are free from such acts; and they may occur in parking lots, automobiles, elevators, and a wide range of other places.

Who

The most common age of an offender is 18, and almost without exception forcible rape is performed by males. About half of all rapists are married and living with their wives at the time of the offense. Usually they are unskilled workers with low income and low education. Many would be labeled as sociopathic (psychopathic) personalities.

How

Over one-third of all forcible rapes are multiple, involving more than one male. In almost half of single-offender forcible rapes, the victim is known to the offender. Threats, intimidation, brandishing a weapon are commonly used without resorting to physical violence. However, roughness, choking, and "nonbrutal" beating occur in about 30 percent of rape cases. The better known the victim is to the rapist, the more brutality is likely to be involved. Occasionally, rapists seriously injure or kill their victims. Some rapes are planned while others are impulsive acts which occur when the opportunity presents itself.

Effects on victims

The victim may not only suffer physical injury but usually experiences considerable psychological trauma. One seriously complicating factor in forcible rape is the possibility of unwanted pregnancy. In Washington, D.C. a 24-hour Rape Crisis Center has been established to provide assistance to rape victims.

Forcible rape of a homosexual as well as heterosexual type may occur; and this is a problem in some prisons. However, the preceding data refer only to forcible rape of a heterosexual nature.

enough to have successful intercourse, and (2) premature ejaculation, in which the male is unable to control ejaculation long enough to satisfy the female. The most common forms of frigidity are (1) lack of desire or interest in having sexual relations, and (2) inability to achieve an orgasm.

Impotence and frigidity may result primarily from organic factors—such as drug intoxication, disease, or damage to the genitals—but typically they are the result of psychological factors. Included in the latter are faulty learning in which the individual is rigidly indoctrinated in the view that "sex is evil," lack of emotional closeness or attraction to the particular sexual partner, and feelings of inadequacy. The latter may stem from previous difficulties in relating sexually to other persons and consequent apprehension in a new situation.

Despite the attitude of greater permissiveness toward various sexual patterns in our society as well as toward sex in general, it is interesting to note that Masters and Johnson (1970) have estimated that sexual inadequacies relating to impotence and frigidity threaten or damage half the marriages in the United States. However, therapeutic approaches developed by this research team are yielding most encouraging results.

When things really go wrong

In this section we shall deal with maladaptive behavior patterns which are highly detrimental to the individual and often to others as well. In some instances we shall be dealing with severe personality disorganization or decompensation, in others with problems of addiction, and in still others with violent self-destructive or antisocial behavior.

The specific patterns we shall cover include: (1) acute situational stress reactions; (2) schizophrenia, depression, and other psychoses; (3) alcoholism and drug dependence; (4) violent delinquent and criminal behavior; and (5) the special problem of suicide.

As in the preceding section, we shall be dealing with a wide range of persons, degrees of severity, and causal patterns. Of necessity our coverage will be limited; but we shall try to cover the key factors involved in each maladaptive pattern.

Acute situational stress reactions

Transient personality decompensation may occur when the individual continues for an extended period of time in a life situation which he finds unpleasant and stressful. A woman may feel trapped in a disappointing and unhappy marriage, but feel that she must maintain the marriage because of the children. A man may hate his work but feel obligated to keep his job because of family responsibilities or lack of training for other types of jobs. In such chronic stressful situations, persons may drink excessively, become irritable or apathetic, and show lowered effectiveness in coping with life problems.

Under conditions of overwhelming stress—as in tornadoes, earthquakes, terrifying accidents, traumatic combat experiences, and prolonged mistreatment as a prisoner-of-war—severe decompensation may occur even among previously stable persons. Usually the person shows good recovery once the stress situation is over, but in some cases there may be sustained after-effects. It is with these severe situational reactions that we are immediately concerned.

1. *Traumatic reactions to civilian catastrophes.* In civilian life people exposed to sudden terrifying experiences—such as explosions, fires, and earthquakes—may show varying degrees of personality decompensation.

Victims of such terrifying experiences often show a "disaster syndrome" involving three stages: (a) *a shock stage,* during which the victim is stunned, dazed, and apathetic, often unaware of the extent of his injuries and unable to make more than minimal efforts to help himself or others; (b) *a suggestible stage,* during which the victim tends to be passive and willing

Ineffective coping patterns / 196

to take directions from rescue workers or others less affected by the disaster; and (c) *a recovery stage,* during which the victim gradually regains his equilibrium. During stage 3 the individual tends to talk repetitively about the catastrophic event and often suffers from tension, apprehensiveness, irritability, and difficulty in concentrating and sleeping.

These three stages are well illustrated in the *Andrea Dorea* disaster.

"On July 25, 1956, at 11:05 P.M., the Swedish liner Stockholm *smashed into the starboard side of the Italian liner* Andrea Dorea *a few miles off Nantucket Island, causing one of the worst disasters in maritime history. . . . During the phase of initial shock the survivors acted as if they had been sedated . . . as though nature provided a sedation mechanism which went into operation automatically."* During the phase of suggestibility *"the survivors presented themselves for the most part as an amorphous mass of people tending to act passively and compliantly. They displayed psychomotor retardation, flattening of affect, somnolence, and in some instances, amnesia for data of personal identification. They were nonchalant and easily suggestible."* During the stage of recovery, after the initial shock had worn off and the survivors had received aid, *"they showed . . . an apparently compulsive need to tell the story again and again, with identical detail and emphasis"* (Friedman & Linn, 1957, p. 426).

In cases where loved ones have been lost in the catastrophe, the disaster syndrome may be complicated by intense grief and depression; and if the individual feels he bears some responsibility or feels he failed loved ones who perished in the disaster, the picture may be further complicated by strong guilt feelings. In a minority of cases, there may be residual effects which continue for sustained periods of time. Typical here are varying degrees of anxiety and apprehensiveness, irritability an fatigue, insomnia, impaired concentration, and social withdrawal.

2. *Traumatic reactions to combat.* In World War II, an estimated 10 percent of the men in combat developed "combat exhaustion" involving severe personality decompensation. In the Korean war, the figure was reduced to about 4 percent; and in the Vietnam war, the figure dropped to about 1.5 percent. The marked decrease in incidence during the Vietnam war can be attributed to a number of factors, including shorter duration of combat duty and improved methods for early detection and treatment.

The following are exerpts from the case of a soldier in the Vietnam war.

"The patient was an infantryman whose symptoms had developed on a day when his platoon had been caught in an ambush and then was overrun by the enemy. He was one of three who survived being pinned down by enemy fire for 12 hours. His friend told him that toward the end of that time he had developed a crazed expression and had tried to run from his hiding place. He was pulled back to safety and remained there until the helicopter arrived and flew him to the hospital . . . ."

"His hands had been tied behind him for the flight, and he had a wild, wide-eyed look as he cowered in a corner of the emergency room, glancing furtively to all sides, cringing and startling at the least noise. He was mute, although once he forced out a whispered "VC" and tried to mouth other words without success. He seemed terrified . . . . His hands were untied, after which he would hold an imaginary rifle in readiness whenever he heard a helicopter overhead or an unexpected noise. . . ." (Bloch, 1969, p. 42).

After emergency treatment which involved being kept asleep by medication for some 40 hours, he awakened dazed, subdued, and largely amnesic for the traumatic combat experience. A friend from his platoon on an adjoining ward helped him to fill in the missing details of the combat situation, and with additional treatment he made a speedy recovery and returned to duty.

Despite rapid and often dramatic recoveries from traumatic combat reactions, follow-up studies have shown long-term aftereffects to be common, for example, depression, irritability, easy fatiguability, and difficulty in concentrating (Archibald & Tuddenham, 1965). Even among combat veterans who had not evidenced traumatic reactions in the Vietnam war, evidence of residual anxiety, depression, conflicts in interpersonal relations, and the excessive use of alcohol and drugs have been reported (Goldsmith & Cretekos, 1969; Strange & Brown, 1970). Apparently combat experiences are highly traumatic for most soldiers and take their toll in adaptive resources.

3. *Traumatic reactions to extreme POW experiences.* Acute situational stress reactions are well illustrated by prisoners-of-war subjected to sustained deprivation and cruelty.

Commander Nardini—a psychiatrist, eyewitness, and fellow POW—has described the reaction of American soldiers to imprisonment by the Japanese following the fall of Bataan and Corregidor in World War II.

"Conditions of imprisonment varied from time to time in different places and with different groups. In general there was shortage, wearisome sameness, and deficiency of food; much physical misery and disease; squalid living conditions; fear and despair; horrible monotony . . . inadequate clothing and cleansing facilities; temperature extremes; and physical abuse. . . .

". . . hungry men were constantly reminded of their own nearness to death by observing the steady, relentless march to death of their comrades. . . .

". . . Men quibbled over portions of food, were suspicious of those who were in more favored positions than themselves, participated in unethical barter, took advantage of less clever or enterprising fellow prisoners, stole, rummaged in garbage, and even curried the favor of their detested captors. There was a great distortion of previous personality as manifested by increased irritability, unfriendliness, and sullen withdrawal. . . .

". . . most men experienced bouts of apathy or depression. These ranged from slight to prolonged deep depressions where there was a loss of interest in living and lack of willingness or ability to marshal the powers of will necessary to combat disease. An ever-present sign of fatal withdrawal occurred 3 to 4 days before death when the man pulled his covers up over his head and lay passive, quiet, and refusing food" (1952, pp. 242–43).

Among World War II POWs exposed to extreme conditions, there was often residual phys-

ical and psychological damage including a lowering of tolerance to stress of any kind. Wolff (1960) reported that American POWs who survived the extreme stresses of imprisonment in the Pacific area during World War II showed an excessively high mortality rate during the six years following the liberation; deaths from tuberculosis were nine times the number expected in civilian life, from gastrointestinal disease four times the number of civilians, and from suicide twice the number of civilians. In addition, the excessive use of alcohol and drugs, irritability, fatigue, and varying degrees of emotional instability were common.

Preliminary follow-up studies of POWs from the Vietnam war indicate that all of the men suffered from "stress reactions" which were considered temporary in the great majority of cases. Only 6 percent suffered serious and prolonged psychological problems as a consequence of their imprisonment (Auerbach, 1973). Researchers, who plan a minimum follow-up of these men over a five-year period, anticipate much more favorable results than were found in the case of POWs suffering imprisonment by the Japanese or North Koreans.

It may be emphasized here that one of the most stressful aspects of civilian catastrophes, combat situations, and POW experiences is the complete change from a relatively secure, friendly, and predictable world to one which is insecure, uncertain, and often extremely hostile.

Psychotic disorders

Psychotic disorders are characterized by severe personality decompensation and marked disturbances in thinking, feeling, and acting. The individual loses contact with reality, and his coping ability is seriously impaired. The term *insanity* is sometimes used in referring to psychotic disorders but this is a legal term rather than a clinical one, indicating that the individual is unable to manage his affairs or perform his social responsibilities.

Although schizophrenia and several other distinctive psychotic patterns have been delineated, most psychotic persons share the following "symptoms":

   1. *Personality disorganization*—characterized by a "break with reality" and severely impaired coping ability. In many instances the person is disoriented in regard to time, place, or person.

   2. *Delusions*—false beliefs which the individual defends despite their logical absurdity and all contrary evidence. The most common types of delusions are (1) *delusions of grandeur*, in which the individual believes he is some exalted and important being, (2) *delusions of reference,* in which the individual interprets chance happenings as being aimed directly at him, and (3) *delusions of persecution,* in which the individual feels that "enemies" are plotting against him and that he is in grave danger of attack.

   3. *Hallucinations*—perceptions of objects, odors, or other sensory phenomena without any appropriate sensory stimulation. The individual may hear "voices," taste poison in his food, smell foul odors, or feel bugs under his skin.

   4. *Emotional disturbances*—some psychotic individuals become apathetic and emotionally unresponsive. Others show extreme emotion, becoming unduly elated or depressed. In still other cases, emotions are distorted and inappropriate to the situation, as when a person laughs when informed that his spouse or child has been killed.

Many psychotics also evidence anomalies of action, such as peculiarities of movement, posture, gesture, or verbal expression.

These symptoms may vary greatly from one case to another and in the same case over time; and they may have a psychological or organic origin. For example, a delusion may result from drug intoxication or from the exaggeration of an ego-defense mechanism such as projection. Psychoses associated with demonstrable brain pathology are called *organic psychoses;* those with no known brain pathology are called *functional psychoses.* However, it is still a moot question as to whether disturbances in metabolic processes may affect brain functioning in so-called functional psychoses.

Schizophrenic reactions

The term *schizophrenia* refers to a split between thought and emotion and a loss of contact with reality. The disorder affects about one person in 100 and is the most common psychotic reaction. Although schizophrenic reactions typically occur between adolescence and the early fifties, they may occur in childhood or later life. Schizophrenic reactions occur in all societies and are most prevalent on lower socioeconomic levels.

The clinical picture may vary markedly from one person to another but is typically characterized by: (1) withdrawal from reality with a loss of interest in people and events; (2) shallow and often inappropriate emotional responses to the events that elicited them; (3) the disorganization of thought processes; (4) delusions and hallucinations—especially delusions of influence and persecution and auditory hallucinations in which the person hears voices speaking to him; and (5) the deterioration of personal habits and ethical controls. Often too, there are peculiarities of posture, movement, gesture, or speech.

Schizophrenic reactions have been classified into ten subtypes. We shall briefly describe five of these, each of which seems to involve a different strategy for coping with stress, anxiety, and self-devaluation.

   1. *Acute type.* This pattern tends to appear rather suddenly, often in a person whose behavior has previously appeared relatively normal. Brown and Birley (1968) found a marked increase in stress during the ten-week period prior to onset in cases of acute schizophrenic reactions. The clinical picture typically includes such symptoms as perplexity, confusion, emotional turmoil, excitement, delusions of reference, and fear. At the same time there seems to be a breakdown of "filtering mechanisms" so that the individual is overwhelmed by the sheer quantity of stimulation to which he is exposed, with the result that experiencing and thinking become fragmented and disorganized—much like the qualities of a nightmare. The individual tends to evidence some measure of panic at his loss of self-control and to be desperately trying to understand what is happening to him.

2. *Paranoid type.* Here the clinical picture is dominated by illogical and changeable delusions —usually of influence and persecution—and often by vivid hallucinations. In this reaction type the individual seems to be trying to maintain his feelings of adequacy and worth by blaming his difficulties on others. He may assert that his impure thoughts—for example, thoughts about committing sexual acts which he views as highly immoral and incompatible with his self-concept—are being generated by others who control his mind with electronic devices, or that his failures are due to enemies who are plotting against him. Often the individual's behavior is erratic, unpredictable, and sometimes dangerous.

3. *Catatonic type.* Here the individual typically alternates between periods of excited activity and periods of stupor. Frequently he may maintain odd postures and follow stereotyped ritualistic patterns. During the period of stupor there is a tendency to remain motionless in the same position for hours or even days. Then the clinical picture undergoes an abrupt change, with excitement coming on suddenly; the individual may shout incoherently and engage in uninhibited and sometimes dangerous behavior. The overall reaction appears to be one in which the individual is trying desperately to find a solution to his inner conflicts and problems.

4. *Hebephrenic type.* This reaction usually occurs at an early age and involves extreme personality decompensation. Emotional blunting and distortion are commonly manifested in inappropriate laughter and silliness, bizarre and often obscene behavior, and peculiar mannerisms. Here withdrawal, insulation, and disintegration seem to reach their maximum— apparently representing both giving up and at the same time "thumbing one's nose" at the world.

5. *Simple type.* Here the individual also withdraws and insulates himself from life's problems but without the extreme personality disintegration of the hebephrenic type. The simple-type schizophrenic merely gives up caring or trying to achieve anything. He tends to give the impression of being odd or stupid, curiously inaccessible, isolated, colorless, and uninteresting.

Also worthy of brief mention is the childhood type, characterized by preoccupation with fantasy, withdrawal from reality, and markedly atypical behavior prior to puberty.

Despite a great deal of research, the causal patterns in schizophrenic reactions remain largely an enigma. Much available evidence points to the role of genetic factors in predisposing some persons to schizophrenic reactions when they are under excessive stress. In fact, R. D. Laing (1967) has concluded that "the experience and behavior that are labeled schizophrenia are a special sort of strategy that a person invents in order to live in an unliveable world" (p. 56).

But this may be an oversimplification, since schizophrenia is obviously a highly complex disorder as evidenced by differences in clinical pictures, personality organization before the disorder, family backgrounds, precipitating stresses, defensive maneuvers, and duration of the disorder—which may range from 2 or 3 weeks in acute schizophrenic episodes to a lifetime in chronic cases. It may in fact be a group of disorders, with multiple and varying causes, in which biological, psychological, and sociocultural factors operate in varying combinations in different cases.

Newer methods of treatment for schizophrenia focus on short-term hospitalization—usually 20 to 60 days—with aftercare follow-up programs in the community. But while this approach is effective with acute schizophrenic episodes, it is not suitable for more severe and chronic cases, in which family and community ties have been disrupted and in which posthospitalization careers, if any, can usually be maintained only with intensive long-range aftercare treatment programs.

Paranoia

Although paranoia is rare in mental-hospital populations, many exploited inventors, fanatical reformers, self-styled prophets, crank-letter writers, and illogically suspicious husbands and wives fall into this category. Unless they become a serious nuisance, however, most individuals are able to maintain themselves in the community.

Paranoid delusions are intricate and highly systematized. Usually they center around one theme, such as financial matters, a job, or an unfaithful wife. Typically, delusions of persecution predominate—the individual feels that he is being taken advantage of, lied to, mistreated, plotted against, or otherwise persecuted. Some paranoiacs develop delusions of grandeur, fancying themselves to be someone with an important mission to perform for the benefit of mankind.

Although the "evidence" on which the paranoiac bases his delusions is extremely tenuous, he is firm in maintaining his own interpretation of the facts. He may be convinced of his wife's unfaithfulness because she has suddenly taken to buying perfume guaranteed to make her attractive to men. When he tells his friends about her unfaithfulness and they question his assumptions, he is sure they have turned against him and gone over to his wife's side—have become his enemies. Thus with time, more and more of his world comes to be integrated into his delusional system. Eventually his delusions may lead to his creation of what has been called a "pseudocommunity"—an imaginary organization of persons whose purpose is to carry out some action against him.

Many people, of course, go through life brooding about real and imagined injustices. In the case of paranoid reactions this trend is exaggerated, gradually, into a delusional system with which the individual is intensely preoccupied. Often the behavior of the paranoid involves what is called a "self-fulfilling prophecy." He behaves toward others in such a way as to elicit behavior that confirms his suspicions. For example, his paranoid accusations of infidelity against his wife may lead to a rift in their marriage and to her actually becoming interested in someone else.

Personality characteristics that commonly foreshadow paranoid reactions include a high level of aspiration, hypersensitivity to criticism, craving for praise and recognition, an overly critical and aloof attitude toward others, formal adherence to socially approved behavior, and an almost complete lack of a sense of humor. Possibly as a result of his difficulties in adjustment, the paranoid also tends to be suspicious and hostile toward others and to suffer from intense feelings of inferiority. Such characteristics are likely to lead to repeated failures in critical life situations. To defend himself against the anxiety and self-devaluation of chronic failure, he projects the blame for his difficulties to others.

Although paranoiacs are not always dangerous, there is the possibility that they may become desperate and decide to take matters into their own hands. Many people, including wives and husbands falsely accused of infidelity, have been killed by paranoiacs intent on righting the wrongs they feel have been done them.

Manic-depressive reactions

The central characteristic of manic-depressive reactions is an exaggerated elation or depression. Against this background, there are a variety of other symptoms in keeping with the prevailing mood. A person may show only the elated reaction *(manic type)*, only the depressive reaction *(depressive type)*, or an alternation between them *(circular type)* with a cycle of a few minutes to several months. Of these patterns, the depressive type is by far the most common.

In the manic reaction, the patient is elated and expresses feelings of well-being, optimism, and good humor. Initially he may give the impression of being an aggressive, witty, sociable, energetic individual who has many important projects under way. However, it soon becomes apparent that he is highly distractible, monopolizes the conversation, and does not follow through on any of his plans. As the disorder progresses, the clinical picture becomes increasingly exaggerated and the individual shows such symptoms as: (1) psychomotor overactivity—in which he is constantly talking and moving about under a "pressure of activity"; (2) flight of ideas—involving extreme distractibility and rapid shifts of thought; (3) delusions and hallucinations—usually of a transient and grandiose nature in keeping with his elated mood and excited state; (4) impaired judgment and lowered ethical restraints—which may lead to unwise financial investments, promiscuous sexual acts, and other behavior indicative of lowered inner controls. In extreme form, the manic reaction progresses to delirious ideation and disorientation, and the individual rapidly exhausts himself with his incessant activity.

In the depressive reaction the symptoms are essentially the opposite. The individual becomes discouraged and dejected, and there is a slowing

which they may carry out. In extreme form the individual may lapse into a depressive stupor with an almost complete lack of response and a dangerous reduction in heart and circulatory action.

As in schizophrenia, many investigators believe that some individuals are genetically predisposed to manic-depressive reactions when placed under severe stress; but as yet, the actual causal factors in these disorders have not been clearly delineated. However, it would appear that in general, the stress preceding manic-depressive reactions tends to build up over a

 I know this woman, she's very pleasant—young, about 22 or 23—and can carry on a conversation and you don't notice anything in particular, but I know she tries to commit suicide once in awhile. But you'd never know that if you see her in her good times—she has a career, she's not an incapacitated person. Her manic stage is, like, just a little above normal good feelings—she's kind of ebullient . . . oh, you should hear about all the wonderful things she's been doing, all the great times she's going to be having. And then—I don't know what sets it off—she jumped out of her third-story apartment window a few weeks ago. She was in the hospital for awhile, then back home and going on like nothing much had happened.

down of thought and activity. Feelings of failure, unworthiness, and guilt dominate his thinking. As the disorder progresses, delusions and hallucinations centering around his guilt may be prominent. He may be convinced that he has committed some act which he views as highly immoral—usually related to hostile or sexual behavior—which he actually has only fantasied committing. He may insist that he is suffering from some horrible disease that gives him a bad odor or complain that his brain is rotting away. Apprehensiveness and anxiety are common, and such individuals often contemplate suicide

sustained period of time—typically during the two-year period before the onset of the disorder (Brown & Birley, 1968; Brown, 1972).

Involutional reactions

An involutional reaction is a psychotic depressive reaction that develops during the "involutional" period—between about 40 and 55 years of age—without a prior history of manic-depressive reactions. Involutional reactions are more common among women than among men. In contrast to the depressed reaction of the manic-depressive, which involves a slowdown of thought and activity, the involutional reaction involves sustained agitation.

Involutional reactions usually begin with restlessness, insomnia, unprovoked spells of weeping, and excessive worry about minor matters. As the reaction becomes more acute, the individual becomes increasingly depressed and apprehensive and develops strong feelings of worthlessness and self-condemnation. He may become preoccupied with some real or imagined sin that he feels can never be forgiven. He is in utmost despair and feels there is absolutely no hope. In his agitation he may pace the floor, weep, wring his hands, pull his hair, bite his lips, and cry aloud at fate.

Hypochondriacal delusions are common: the individual may insist that his stomach is rotting away or that his brain is being destroyed by some dread disease. Yet despite his depression and anxiety, he may not be disoriented and may realize he needs help.

Involutional reactions are often complicated by the glandular changes which take place during the involutional period in both men and women. These changes are dramatically illustrated in the menopause syndrome in women, characterized by hot flashes, nervous irritability, insomnia, and mild depression. This condition is apparently due to a decrease in ovarian hormone production and can be rapidly corrected by medical treatment. However, such menopausal changes are not considered of major causal significance, and the correction of hormone deficiencies does not clear up the involutional reaction.

The primary emphasis in understanding involutional reactions has been placed upon psychological factors which predispose the individual to such reactions in the face of the severe stresses of this life period. Usually these individuals have a history of being overly conscientious, meticulous, perfectionistic, rigid, narrow in social interests, and compulsive. During the involutional period the individual comes to realize that his youth is over and that he is committed to a life pattern which he finds unsatisfactory, futile, and meaningless—and he places the blame squarely on himself. Although the painful self-recrimination may help him atone for his alleged shortcomings and misdeeds, his life situation remains so stressful that anxiety, depression, and personality decompensation remain. These reactions may have a prolonged course if not treated, but modern methods of treatment are highly effective and most reactions can be cleared up in a matter of weeks.

In concluding our discussion of the functional psychoses, it should be emphasized again that: (1) psychotics often show mixed symptoms and do not fit well into any category, (2) exact symptoms may shift markedly over short-range periods, (3) persons in any given category differ greatly in personality make-up, and (4) the causal picture is unclear, but varying combinations of biological, psychological, and sociocultural factors appear to be involved.

Disorders associated with brain pathology

There are a number of conditions—such as injuries, tumors, infectious diseases, drugs, and the deteriorative changes of old age—which interfere with the functioning of the brain and result in psychological disturbances. Such disturbances may be mild or severe depending upon both the nature and severity of the brain pathology and the personality make-up and life situation of the individual. Disorders associated with brain pathology approach the same incidence figure as that for the functional psychoses as a group.

Depending upon the reversibility of the brain pathology, such disorders are often classified as *acute* or *chronic*. An acute disorder—as in drug intoxication—is likely to be temporary and reversible. Here the individual may show such symptoms as coma and stupor or disorientation and delirium, which clear up over a period of hours or days. A chronic disorder—as in syphilis of the brain—involves permanent damage to the nervous system; here the brain pathology is not reversible or only partially so. Where the brain damage is severe, the symptoms may include a permanent impairment of intellectual functioning, emotional shallowness and instability, and

COMMON SYMPTOMS IN MENTAL DISORDERS

Symptoms reflecting thought disturbances

amnesia	total or partial loss of memory
phobia	fear which the individual recognizes as irrational but can't control
obsession	persistent idea that the individual considers irrational but cannot get out of his mind
compulsion	compelling impulse to perform some act known to be irrational
delusion	false belief held despite contrary objective evidence
hallucination	false perception unwarranted by external stimuli; most often auditory
disorientation	inability to identify time, place, or person accurately

Symptoms reflecting emotional disturbances

pathological anxiety	anxiety out of all proportion to any realistic danger or threat
euphoria	exaggerated and irrational feeling of elation and well-being
depression	irrational state of dejection, often with suicidal impulses
apathy	lack of feeling or interest in situations that normally evoke such reactions
pathological guilt	exaggerated guilt feelings out of all proportion to one's misdeeds

Symptoms reflecting disturbances in motivation and values

anomie	a feeling of not really belonging or having any place in society
impulsivity	inability to restrain impulse; action without reflection
delinquency	antisocial or illegal behavior by a minor
crime	antisocial, illegal behavior
perversion	socially condemned deviation from ordinary conduct, especially in sexual behavior
immorality	behavior that violates accepted standards of right and wrong

Symptoms reflecting disturbances in physiological processes

anesthesia	loss of sensitivity
hypesthesia	partial loss of sensitivity
hyperesthesia	excessive sensitivity
paraesthesia	unusual or inappropriate sensation
paralysis	loss or impairment of movement
tic	intermittent twitching or jerking of specific muscles
tremor	shaking or trembling
psychomotor retardation	slowing down of thought and movement
psychomotor excitement	rapidly shifting thought processes and overactivity

A variety of symptoms may, of course, be shown in a particular disorder.

a deterioration in conduct and behavior standards.

The chronic mental disorders associated with old age usually involve either (1) gradual deterioration and atrophy of the brain cells, with a lessening of mental alertness and adaptability, failing comprehension and judgment, and progressive personality deterioration; or (2) hardening of the arteries leading to the brain, with inadequate circulation, faulty nutrition of the brain cells, and in some cases, hemorrhages in the brain, with acute episodes of confusion and incoherence (Busse, 1967). The prognosis among older persons with brain disorders varies greatly. For hospitalized patients, the outcome is likely to be unfavorable unless the individual shows improvement during the first year after admission. The long-term progression of such disorders is in the direction of increasing personality deterioration, leading eventually to a vegetative existence and death.

Again however, personality and situational

My dad was an alcoholic, the kind that keeps a bottle hidden out in the garage. And the whole family knew it, and it was a terrible way to live. He went to work every day, he was a laboring man, and I suppose he felt bad about himself in many ways—in many ways he had good reason to—and my mother put him down an awful lot, and he had an accident in the car once when he'd been drinking. The thing I remember particularly was he had an accident in the car coming home from work one Valentine's Day—he arrived late, having turned the car over a couple of times, and in his hand he had this great big red heart-shaped Valentine box of candy, with one side of it all dented in, and he'd been bringing it home to us.

factors may play an important role. A number of studies have shown that individuals who are handicapped psychologically by undesirable personality traits such as rigidity, suspiciousness, and social inadequacy are much more vulnerable to the psychoses of old age. A mature and well-integrated person can usually cope with brain damage as well as other stress better than a rigid, immature, emotionally disturbed, or otherwise psychologically handicapped person. There are many cases involving relatively severe brain pathology in which behavior disturbances are relatively minor and many cases of mild brain pathology in which the individual becomes psychotic.

Similarly, a very unfavorable life situation may increase the individual's vulnerability. Unfortunately, older members of our society often face especially difficult stresses. In our youth-oriented society, we have little respect or reverence for age. Anyone who has led a busy, productive life finds it hard to be relegated to the sidelines where no one needs him or asks his advice. The death of a life partner and a narrowing circle of friends may lead to loneliness and loss of meaning. Chronic poor health may erode a previously cheerful outlook. And for most older people, an inadequate income is a reality.

During the past decade society has become increasingly aware of the problems confronting our senior citizens and has taken measures, such as Medicare, to reduce the stresses on older people. But although society can do much to improve the status of the older person, the individual can also do much to prepare himself for the problems typical of old age—to plan ahead for an active and useful life in his later years.

Alcoholism and drug dependence

Although problems of alcoholism and drug dependence are by no means new in human history, only recently has scientific attention been focused on them.

The most commonly used problem drugs are alcohol, heroin, barbiturates, amphetamines, cocaine, LSD, and marijuana. Alcohol can be purchased legally by adults; the barbiturates and amphetamines can be purchased legally under medical supervision; while cocaine, heroin, and LSD are illegal. Marijuana is also classified as an illegal drug, but whether it should be is a controversial issue.

Alcoholism

Contrary to popular belief, alcohol is not a stimulant but a depressant that numbs the higher brain centers and thus lessens their inhibiting control. Aside from this release, which may lead him to say or do things he would normally inhibit, the drinker may find that drinking gives him a sense of well-being in which unpleasant realities are minimized and his sense of adequacy is increased. When the alcohol content of the blood reaches 0.1 percent, visual-motor and thought processes are impaired and the individual is assumed to be intoxicated. When the alcoholic content reaches 0.5 percent, the neurophysiological balance is seriously disturbed and the individual "passes out."

It has been estimated that over 100 million Americans use alcoholic beverages—the preponderance of their drinking being social and generally approved. But some 9 to 12 million Americans are now labeled as alcoholics; individuals whose drinking seriously impairs their life adjustment. In the United States, alcoholism is more common among the affluent than among the less affluent; thus the popular misconception of an alcoholic as being an unkempt resident of skid row is inaccurate. In fact, less than 3 percent of the alcoholic population is represented by this group. Traditionally alcoholism has been considered more common among males than females in our society, but this distinction is gradually disappearing.

The potentially detrimental effects of alcoholism for the individual, his loved ones, and society are legion.

". . . its abuse has killed more people, sent more victims to hospitals, generated more police arrests, broken up more marriages and homes, and cost industry more money than has the abuse of heroin, amphetamines, barbiturates and marijuana combined" (Bengelsdorf, 1970, p. 7).

The life span of the average alcoholic is about 12 years shorter than that of the nonalcoholic, and alcoholism now ranks as the third leading cause of death in the United States.

Because alcoholism often progresses slowly and by subtle degrees in its potential victim, the line that separates social drinking from alcohol-

PSYCHOTIC REACTIONS ASSOCIATED WITH EXCESSIVE DRINKING

Chronic alcoholics may in time develop one of the following psychotic reactions:

1. *Pathological intoxication*—a condition in which a person with low tolerance for alcohol, perhaps because of exhaustion or emotional stress, overreacts to even a moderate amount and may become hallucinated, disoriented, and violent. In this case, the alcohol only touches off the reaction and is not the primary cause.

2. *Delirium tremens*—a reaction of disorientation, tremors, hallucinations, and intense fear. It occurs in the long-time excessive drinker largely as a result of dietary deficiency and metabolic upset and can usually be cleared up by massive doses of vitamins and a better diet.

3. *Chronic alcoholic deterioration*—an overall personality deterioration that may come with habitual excessive drinking and the disorganization of the individual's whole life pattern that this eventually involves.

ism is not always readily observable. According to the Japanese proverb, "First the man takes a drink, then the drink takes a drink, and then the drink takes the man." A general view of the stages which are commonly involved in the development may be outlined as follows:

1. *Initial phase.* The social drinker turns increasingly to alcohol for relief of tension, present or anticipated. Toward the end of this period, there are four warning signs of approaching alcoholism:

Increasing consumption—gradual or rapid. The individual may begin to worry about his drinking at this point.

Morning drinking—to reduce hangovers or get him through the day.

Extreme behavior—commission of various acts that leave the individual feeling guilty and embarrassed later.

"Blackouts"—the individual cannot remember what happened during his drinking. Not usually frequent until excessive drinking has continued for some time.

2. *Crucial phase.* The individual loses control over his drinking: One drink seems to start a chain reaction, although he can still partially control the occasions when he will or will not take the first drink. In this phase, he frequently begins to rationalize and make alibis for his drinking and often encounters reproof from family and friends.

3. *Chronic phase.* The individual's control over his drinking completely breaks down and alcohol plays an increasingly dominant role in his life. At the same time, his physiological tolerance for alcohol decreases, and he now becomes intoxicated from far less alcohol than previously. He also begins to experience tremors and other symptoms while he is sober, leading to drinking to control such symptoms. During this period, his life situation usually undergoes serious deterioration and he becomes increasingly susceptible to alcoholic psychosis.

The causal patterns in alcoholism are not fully understood, but several biological, psychological, and sociocultural factors have been emphasized. One biological possibility which is receiving increasing emphasis is that some individuals—perhaps as a result of genetic factors—develop a physiological addiction to and craving for alcohol much as others do for heroin (Bengelsdorf, 1970). Alcoholism has been viewed psychologically as stemming from excessive stress and the tendency to use alcohol as a "crutch" in trying to cope with one's problems. Eventually, the individual's drinking becomes excessive and out of control. Other studies have emphasized parental models who are alcoholic; and still others point to broader sociocultural factors. For example, alcoholism is rare among the Mormons, whose religious values prohibit the use of alcohol.

Although relatively effective methods for the treatment of alcoholism have been developed—such as aversion therapy—they are usually unsuccessful unless the alcoholic can really admit that he has a serious problem and is willing to do something about it. One practical approach which has met with considerable success is that of Alcoholics Anonymous. But even AA cannot do much until the alcoholic "hits bottom" and is willing to accept help with a problem that is bigger than he is.

Drug dependence

In recent years, increasing numbers of teenagers have been experimenting with psychoactive drugs—drugs that have marked effects on mental processes—such as amphetamines, barbiturates, and LSD. During this period, the age of the young drug experimenter has been dropping steadily, so that many schools report widespread use of drugs among children in the elementary grades. Of course, drug dependence is by no means confined to the very young; in fact, many youths are undoubtedly influenced by parental models in using drugs.

Drug dependence is an extremely complex topic. Some of the drugs which seem to pose serious problems in our society are highly dangerous, such as heroin and the barbiturates; others, such as marijuana and cocaine, fall in the controversial category since we have little information on their long-term effects. While there is evidence of the widespread use of marijuana and barbiturates—and to a lesser extent, of heroin, amphetamines, and LSD—teenagers seem to be turning increasingly to alcohol, particularly to beer and wine.

In the present section we will briefly describe four psychoactive drugs which would fall in the dangerous category—heroin, barbiturates, amphetamines, and LSD. The effects of these and other psychoactive drugs are summarized below.

1. *Heroin.* This drug is a derivative of opium and produces a feeling of euphoria and contentment together with pleasant reverie or daydreaming. It is highly addictive, and there are an

SUMMARY OF TERMS RELATING TO DRUG USE

In traditional usage, the term *dependence* has signified psychological dependence on a particular drug, while *addiction* has signified physiological dependence, as indicated by *withdrawal symptoms* if the drug is discontinued. Recently, however, the term *drug dependence* has come to include both physiological and psychological dependence on the drug. The overall term *drug abuse* refers to the excessive use of a drug whether or not the individual is dependent on it. For example, an individual may need to be hospitalized for drug abuse even though he has used a given drug, such as LSD, only once.

Tolerance refers to the need to increase the dosage of a drug to produce the effects previously produced by a smaller dose. *Psychoactive drugs* are those that have a relatively marked—and often very extensive—effect on mental processes. *Psychedelic* is a more specific term referring to drugs capable of producing hallucinations.

> I feel very strongly about not smoking dope. I stopped for awhile and I started looking at all my peers. And they just, they scare me, they are becoming so dead and like sheep—they're all sheep. I don't have respect for people like that because they're being sheep.

estimated 250,000 to 300,000 heroin addicts in the United States.

The use of heroin—as well as other opium derivatives and their synthetic counterparts—over a period of time, usually approximating 30 days, leads to physiological craving for and dependence on the drug. In addition, the users of heroin gradually build up a tolerance to the drug so that ever larger amounts are needed for the desired effect. This in turn increases the cost of the habit, and addicts often turn to criminal activities—usually of a nonviolent nature—to finance their habit. Male addicts seem prone to stealing and female addicts to prostitution.

When persons addicted to heroin do not get a dose of the drug within approximately 8 hours, they start to experience withdrawal symptoms. Contrary to popular opinion, these symptoms are not always painful or even dangerous; although in some instances, particularly where the individual is on heavy dosage and has neglected his health, withdrawal can be an agonizing and perilous experience. Withdrawal symptoms usually reach a peak in about 40 hours and are on the decline by the third or fourth day.

Since the heroin addict retains his craving for the drug long after his withdrawal symptoms are over, former treatment programs were rated as unsuccessful. Newer methadone treatment programs have proven highly promising. Although also a narcotic drug, methadone blocks the craving for heroin and is far less incapacitating. Other approaches are also being explored.

2. *Barbiturates.* These drugs are used medically to calm patients and induce sleep. They act as cortical depressants, much like alcohol.

Unfortunately, barbiturates are highly dangerous drugs, and their excessive use over a period of time leads to a building up of tolerance and to physiological dependence. Especially prone to abuse are the short-acting barbiturates, such as seconals ("red devils") and tuinals ("rainbows"); longer-acting barbiturates which do not produce quick results are less subject to abuse. There are an estimated 1 million or more barbiturate addicts in the United States.

Excessive use of barbiturates results in a number of undesirable effects, including general sluggishness, poor comprehension, impaired memory, confusion, irritability, and depression.

> I find the most together people that still smoke dope, but have a healthy attitude towards it, which is hard to get. A healthy attitude, once a month you let go, once a month you're going to see a movie that is super funny, and you're going out to dinner and you're doing all these things with someone, and you just think it would be fun to get stoned. Not that you need to. I'm talking of being healthy, of not needing it.

In fact, the barbiturates are associated with more suicides than any other drug. Heavy use of barbiturates over time can also result in brain damage.

In treatment, it is important to distinguish between barbiturate intoxication—resulting from an overdose—and the abstinence syndrome associated with withdrawal. While an overdose of barbiturates can prove lethal, the withdrawal symptoms are also very dangerous —in fact they are more severe and longer lasting than those in heroin addiction. In severe cases, an acute, delirious psychosis often develops. However, once the withdrawal symptoms have subsided, the individual does not have the physiological craving for the drug characteristic of heroin addiction, although he may still be psychologically dependent upon it.

3. *Amphetamines.* The amphetamines are "pep pills"—cortical stimulants—and are often used by truck drivers and students to stay awake and continue to function. Currently, some 8 billion amphetamine pills are manufactured each year in the United States—enough to supply every man, woman, and child with about 35 doses each.

The most potent and dangerous of the amphetamines is methedrine or "speed." Like other amphetamines, excessive use of methedrine over time leads to the building up of tolerance but not to physiological dependence. To get "high" on amphetamines, habitual users may give themselves many times the dosage that might be prescribed medically each day for losing weight. In some instances, amphetamine users go on sprees lasting for several days.

For the person who exceeds prescribed dosage, the results can be highly detrimental. In rare instances, high dosages of methedrine can be lethal. In addition, psychosis, suicide, homicide, and other acts of violence may be associated with the abuse of this drug. Since there is no physiological addiction, withdrawal from the drug is relatively painless; but psychological dependence may still have to be coped with. However, where excessive use of amphetamines has resulted in brain damage, treatment may be more complicated.

4. *LSD.* Lysergic acid diethylamide is a chemically synthesized substance first discovered in 1938. Although odorless, colorless, and tasteless, it is an extremely potent hallucinogen. In fact, LSD can produce intoxication in an amount smaller than a grain of salt.

A major effect of the ingestion of LSD is a tremendous intensification of sensory perception. Objects seem to become brighter, more colorful, and endowed with dimensions the individual has not noticed before. Thus the individual may lose himself in contemplation of a flower or some other object. Often he has the feeling of somehow being tuned in to all humankind in experiencing such universal emotions as love, loneliness, or grief.

The LSD trip, however, is not always pleasant. It can be an extremely traumatic experience in which everyday objects take on a bizarre and terrifying appearance, or the individual sees monsters which seem to be after him. It has been estimated that about 1 in 20 LSD users experience "flashbacks" or intrusive thoughts of a negative or frightening nature. It has also been estimated that about 3 percent of LSD users experience psychoses—sometimes on their first trip—which may be highly resistant to treatment. During bad trips as well as psychotic episodes, suicidal and homicidal acts are not uncommon. It should be pointed out here that such pathological behavior usually involves individuals who are in current crisis situations, who are emotionally unstable, or who have not fully recovered from some mental disorder (McWilliams & Tuttle, 1973). Finally, recent evidence indicates that LSD can lead to chromosomal breakage as well as weaken the body's ability to recover from infection or disease (Salk, 1973).

Since LSD does not result in increased tolerance or physiological dependence, treatment is usually relatively simple—except in extreme cases involving psychotic breaks or where there is strong psychological dependence on the drug.

The causal patterns in drug dependence and abuse are complex and varied. The majority of teenagers and young adults probably use drugs for thrill seeking or because of peer-group pressures or to find relief from stressful life situations. In many instances, there is a sense of excitement about getting "high" and attaining a "new sense of reality" which older "straights" and nondrug-users don't have. Some young people undoubtedly turn to the drug culture as a life style counter to that of the establishment.

Since drugs typically result in lowered anxiety and tension, their use tends to be reinforced on a psychological level; and since the body makes homeostatic adjustments to addictive drugs, their use also tends to be reinforced on a physiological level (Wikler, 1973). In addition, we live in a pill-oriented society in which we learn to believe that almost any problem can be alleviat-

since it is estimated that over half of all forcible rapes, aggravated assaults, and armed robberies are not reported to the police. Moreover, over half of those arrested for serious crimes are under 19 years of age, and about one fifth are 14 or younger.

In 1973, a Gallup Poll reported that 1 person in 3 living in the central areas of our large cities was mugged or robbed during the preceding 12 months (*Los Angeles Times,* Jan. 14, 1973). And even in our more affluent suburban areas, it is commonplace to read about older persons being robbed and then beaten or shot to death; for girls to be raped in well-lit suburban shopping malls; for shopkeepers to be murdered for $20 or

A friend of mine who drives a cab was robbed once, and he said it was the most terrible experience in his life. He said there were two guys, and one of them held the gun flat against the side of his face, and pushed him around that way, while they talked about whether or not they were going to kill him. He said he felt like, when the experience was over, he felt like he had been . . . like a rape, like he had been deeply violated. Deeply, personally violated by the experience. Weeks later it was still a vivid experience to him, and still very bad, and very personal.

ed or solved by simply taking a pill; and the young often have parental models who also act on this conviction, albeit using different types of drugs. Here we find another strong source of reinforcement on the social level.

Violence

We live in a violent society in which murder, aggravated assault, forcible rape, and armed robbery seem to be ever on the increase. From 1968 to 1973 the incidence of serious crimes almost doubled, approaching a figure of 6 million in 1973. And these statistics are misleading,

less. And in 1972 more than twice as many policemen were killed as in 1969.

Inevitably the questions arise: "Why?" "What can be done about it?" Unfortunately, we have adequate answers to neither. Violent delinquent and criminal behavior can have many different causes, ranging from severe personal pathology—as in the case of psychopaths who engage in violent crime—through alienation and rebellion, to organized crime. In some instances, unusual situational stress leads to violent acting-out behavior; and in a sizable number of others drug intoxication is involved. Many young black offenders in our penal institutions see themselves as the victims of a racist society.

Many offenders see their crime as one of "bad luck"—getting caught—rather than as one involving moral issues of right and wrong. It would also appear that our constant exposure to news of war and violence in the mass media has inured us to violence. As one district attorney put it, "The gruesome crime just isn't shocking anymore."

Unquestionably, the failure of our penal institutions has contributed its share to the overall picture. The American penal system has been variously described as "a disaster" and as "a breeding ground for crime." Inasmuch as the recidivism rate is over 60 percent nationwide—and as high as 90 percent in some areas—it would appear that our present penal procedures are not doing the job. Some see this as due to a lack of severe enough punishment for offenders, and in 1973 the President of the United States strongly urged stiffer sentencing and the death penalty. Others do not believe that keeping human beings in cages is the answer in most cases; and various innovative programs are being tried out in many states with apparently promising results. For example, prisoners may be permitted to go to high school or college during the day and then return to prison at night, or probation with follow-up in the community is emphasized rather than imprisonment for certain crimes.

Suicide

According to official statistics, over 200,000 persons attempt suicide each year in the United States, and over 25,000 succeed. This means that about every 20 minutes someone in our society attempts suicide, and that there are well over 4 million living Americans who have attempted to take their lives. Since many self-inflicted deaths are certified in official records as due to other causes "more respectable" than suicide, experts have judged that the actual number of suicides is from 2 to 5 times as high as the number officially reported. And these statistics do not begin to convey the tragedy of suicide in human terms.

Many people go through periods of severe stress in which they contemplate suicide as an answer to their problems. Most do not accept this answer, and even those who do are usually very ambivalent about taking their lives. In many instances the suicidal attempt is an accidental act, intended as a dramatic warning to some significant other that the individual is distressed and needs help. Thus an individual may take an overdose of sleeping pills and then call a friend to tell him what he has done—assuming that the friend will call the police or take other action necessary to save him. Unfortunately, matters do not always work out as intended, and the "cry for help" may be fatal.

In terms of intent, Farberow and Litman (1970) have classified suicidal behavior into three categories: (1) "To be"—the acts of persons who really do not wish to die but use a suicidal attempt as a means of trying to convey to others their intense personal distress; (2) "Not to be"—involving persons who are seemingly intent on dying, give little warning, and choose means of killing themselves in which intervention is not possible; and (3) "To be or not to be"—echoing Hamlet—involving persons who are ambivalent about dying and leave the results to chance. Usually they do not use immediately lethal means, thus allowing for the possibility of intervention but not necessarily counting on it. These investigators estimate that the "To be" group constitutes about 67 percent, the "Not to be" group about 3 to 5 percent, and the "To be or not to be" group about 30 percent of the suicidal population.

Contrary to popular opinion, most people who attempt suicide do communicate their intent to significant others by direct or indirect means —as in the letter reproduced on page 214. Based on intensive interviews with relatives of 50 successful suicides in Los Angeles and Stockholm, Rudestam (1971) concluded that at least 60 percent of the victims had made direct verbal threats of their intent; and an additional 20 percent had made indirect threats, such as stating that they "would be better off dead." Unfortunately, such communications are often ignored, perhaps largely because of the popular

INCIDENCE

Statistical

Suicide ranks seventh in causes of death in the United States. By conservative estimate, more than 4 million living Americans (approximately one percent of the total population) have made suicide attempts at some time in their lives—the incidence of such attempts having been estimated at more than 200,000 a year. In the United States, the incidence of suicide is estimated to be well over 25,000 annually, a rate in excess of 25 persons per 100,000.

Age and sex

Three times as many men as women commit suicide, but women make more suicide attempts. For both sexes, the incidence of suicide generally increases with age, with more than half of all suicides being committed by persons over 45 years old. Recently, however, the incidence of suicide among adolescents and young adults has increased.

Marital and occupational status

Suicide rates are higher among divorced persons, followed by the widowed and the single, than among married persons. Among certain professional and occupational groups, also, the rate is higher than average; e.g., it is high for physicians (particularly psychiatrists), lawyers, and dentists, and also for unskilled laborers.

LIFE STRESS

Interpersonal problems

Interpersonal difficulties are the leading type of life stress associated with suicide. These include divorce, separation, and bereavement.

Loss of hope

Persons experiencing serious or terminal illnesses show a higher than normal incidence of suicide.

Alienation

Feelings of rootlessness, confusion about one's identity, lack of authentic relationships with others including loved ones, inability to find satisfying values, and a feeling of lacking control over one's destiny seem to be related to a higher than normal incidence of suicide.

INTENT

Degree of intent

Most persons who attempt suicide either do not want to kill themselves (approximately two thirds of all who make such attempts) or are ambivalent about it (approximately one third). Only a very small minority—estimated at from 3 to 5 percent—are intent on dying.

Communication of intent

The great majority of persons who eventually attempt suicide make their distress and intentions known beforehand—either by threats or other cues. Contrary to popular belief, most persons who threaten to commit suicide actually attempt to do so.

INTERVENTION

More than 200 Suicide Prevention Centers have been established for the purpose of helping people through suicidal crises. Emotionally disturbed individuals can call such centers at any time of the day or night and get help in dealing with their problems.

October 4

This affliction .... I have to think about it.
I feel so alone, whether I should or not,
I do. I feel so stripped, nothing is left to me.
I feel as if I should fight, but I have no
weapons. I've tried to grasp my old weapons, but
I can't, they are no longer there for me.
I'm in a roundness, bare, nothing, & no corners
to hide in. I'm afraid, of myself or for myself.
I don't know which. Or, is there a difference?
There is a weight on my chest, and inside all
tightness, and in the middle of me, shaky,
no ... all over me shaky. I'm exhausted.
This terrible sadness. You say there's something
left in me, but I can't grasp that either.
There must be something awfully wrong with me
I don't feel worthy of being alive. You say
I have this left to me, but it is so difficult
to comprehend.

fallacy that "those who threaten to take their lives seldom do so." Unfortunately, also, the decision to take one's life is often made when the person is depressed, alone, and unable to evaluate his problems objectively.

Suicide prevention is an extremely difficult problem. This is in part due to the diversity of reasons for committing suicide as well as the fact that most persons contemplating suicide do not fully realize how badly they need help. However, if the person's "cry for help" can be heard in time, successful intervention is often possible. This is the goal of the over 200 professionally operated suicide-prevention centers in the United States.

Introduction to therapeutic resources

In concluding our review of ineffective coping patterns, we shall briefly outline some of the varied therapeutic resources available to the individual for personal change. Our main focus here will be on treating the seriously maladaptive patterns that we have described. However, we shall see that many of these measures also apply to more common self-defeating coping patterns.

Approaches to therapy

Therapy is directed toward modifying maladaptive behavior and fostering effective coping patterns. Within this context, however, treatment procedures may vary greatly depending upon the nature of the maladaptive behavior. In drug intoxication, for example, immediate medical measures may be indicated; in dealing with neurotic avoidance, psychotherapy may be the approach of choice; and in an acute schizophrenic episode the emphasis may be on improving disordered interpersonal relationships.

In short, therapy may involve biological, psychological, or sociocultural (sociological) approaches—or any combination of these. For this reason contemporary therapy is said to involve an *interdisciplinary approach.*

Biological therapy

Here treatment is directed toward the correction of organic pathology and/or the alleviation of mental distress and disturbed behavior. A number of different procedures may be utilized—including psychotherapeutic drugs, electroshock, brain-wave therapy, brain surgery, and the implantation of microcircuitry in the brain—depending upon the need of the particular patient. For present purposes we shall briefly mention the use of drug and electroshock therapy.

Of great importance are the use of psychotherapeutic drugs which have largely revolutionized modern treatment. These drugs typically fall into three categories: (1) antianxiety drugs, such as Librium and Valium, used to alleviate anxiety and tension; (2) antipsychotic drugs, such as Thorazine and Stelazine, used in schizophrenia and other psychoses; and (3) antidepressants, such as Nardil and Marplan, used as "mood elevators" in the treatment of depression.

Because of the effectiveness of the antidepressant drugs, the use of electroshock—which was once widely used in the treatment of depression—has been greatly reduced. However, the more rapidly acting antidepressant drugs may have undesirable side effects; thus electroshock is often the preferred method of treatment for severely depressed patients with suicidal tendencies where it is important to clear up the depression as rapidly as possible.

While drug therapy and other biological measures often lead to dramatic changes, they do not, of course, resolve inner conflicts or other life stress or modify faulty assumptions or inade-

 My daughter is hyperactive and has been a terrible strain for me to cope with. About the time I found out we could get medications for her that would help, I was at the point where I could hardly stand her, and she's my only child. Besides the medications, I have finally talked to a psychologist who also talked to my daughter. This has been a big help, especially in my attitude toward my girl. When I first had the problem, it was difficult to know what to do, because none of my friends knew about things like medications. I had to talk to people and talk to a mental health clinic, to find out what to do. Also, it was not easy to decide, because I didn't know anything about what I was getting into, but I was so desperate I went ahead and took the right course anyway. Deciding to go to the psychologist was hard too, but the first big step (medications) had helped a lot, so I went ahead and took the next step they said would help. I am very grateful that I did all this.

quate competencies. Thus psychosocial treatment measures are also usually desirable to maintain and improve upon the gains that may be achieved by means of biological treatment procedures.

Psychotherapy

During the last decade, the variety of psychological treatment procedures has multiplied dramatically; but unfortunately research with respect to their actual effectiveness—with the possible exception of behavior therapy—leaves much to be desired.

The objectives of psychotherapy and the actual procedures used depend upon the way one views the conditions that have caused and are maintaining the maladaptive behavior, which in turn is tied in with the therapist's understanding of human behavior and the model—psychoanalytic, behavioristic, humanistic, or existential—to which he or she adheres.

In general, psychotherapy may be aimed at one or more of the following objectives: (1) the rapid elimination of maladaptive behavior patterns which are impairing the individual's coping behavior; (2) improving interpersonal and other competencies essential for effective coping; (3) increasing self-understanding, modifying faulty assumptions, resolving conflicts, and opening avenues to personal growth; (4) helping the individual through an immediate crisis situation in which stress is approaching or exceeding his adjustive resources; and (5) relieving personal distress.

In Chapter 14 we shall review the major contemporary approaches to psychotherapy—psychoanalytic therapy, behavior therapy, humanistic-existential therapies, gestalt therapy, transactional analysis, and encounter groups—and examine their potential as resources for personal change and growth.

Sociocultural approaches to therapy

In *sociotherapy*, the attempt is made to modify stressful conditions in the individual's life situation which are interfering with his adjustive efforts. Often such measures are of crucial sig-

nificance in the overall treatment program. Little progress may be made with a disturbed schizophrenic patient until certain stresses in his marital or family situation can be alleviated. As a consequence, increasing attention has been directed toward the alleviation of pathogenic interpersonal and family conditions.

On a broader level, sociocultural approaches to treatment must also be concerned with alleviating poverty, group prejudice and discrimination, and other pathogenic community and social conditions. Returning a convicted offender who has "served his time" to an urban ghetto is almost a sure way of guaranteeing the recurrence of his antisocial behavior. At the same time, sociocultural measures are concerned with the establishment and maintenance of adequate community mental health services.

For purposes of clarity, we have dealt with biological, psychological, and sociocultural approaches to treatment separately. It should be reemphasized, however, that modern treatment programs are interdisciplinary and involve the integration of different procedures as determined by the needs of the patient and available treatment facilities. In severe disorders, chemotherapy is often combined with psychotherapy and sociotherapy for achieving the most effective treatment program.

New perspectives in the mental health field

We shall note here a few of the more important current trends in thinking about mental health and therapy.

Community mental health centers

Since the passage of the Community Mental Health Centers Act in 1963, the National Institute of Mental Health has made funds available for over 500 community mental health centers across the country, providing services for millions of Americans.

These centers offer at least five types of services for local residents and institutions: (1) *inpatient care* for individuals requiring short-term

In preventing maladaptive behavior we are concerned with two key tasks: (1) establishing conditions which foster effective behavior; and (2) seeking out and eradicating conditions which are conducive to maladaptive behavior. In this context, we can think in terms of primary, secondary, and tertiary preventive measures.

1. *Primary prevention* is focused on establishing conditions in the family, community, and broader society which foster healthy physical and psychological development as well as an improved society. As the National Institute of Mental Health has put it, "In the final analysis, the mental health of each citizen is affected by the maturity and health of our society—from the smallest unit to the largest" (1969, p. 120).

2. *Secondary prevention* emphasizes the early detection and prompt treatment of maladaptive behavior in the individual's family and community setting. Where such behavior involves a family or other group or even a community, essentially the same approach would be involved. Thus the intent is to detect and correct difficulties as soon as possible, before they lead to more seriously maladaptive behavior or perhaps even the breakdown of integrated behavior on the part of the individual or group.

3. *Tertiary prevention* involves prompt and intensive treatment for persons evidencing seriously maladaptive behavior, as in severe depression with suicidal tendencies, acute schizophrenia, and other severely maladaptive patterns. The intent is to correct the condition as soon as possible and return the individual to his family and community setting with a minimum of disruption of his life. Usually provisions are also made for aftercare following his return home.

In essence these preventive measures are directed toward comprehensive health care—at the goal advanced by the World Health Organization of "a sound mind, in a sound body, in a sound society."

hospitalization; (2) *partial hospitalization,* with night hospitalization for patients able to work during the day but in need of relatively intensive treatment, and day hospitalization for similar patients who are able to return home evenings; (3) *outpatient therapy* enabling patients to live at home and go about their daily activities; (4) *emergency care*—crisis intervention—with services available around the clock; and (5) *consultation and educational programs* in mental health for members and agencies of the community. These services are provided without discrimination for all who might need them—young or old, well-to-do or indigent.

The present thrust is that of shifting primary responsibility for initiating and maintaining community mental health centers and programs from federal to state and local levels of government. This also permits a greater voice on the part of community members in planning and evaluating the functioning of such community health services.

Current trends and issues in therapy
In closing our brief overview of therapeutic procedures, we shall look briefly at some of the trends and questions that exist at the "growing edge" of this field.

1. *Crisis intervention.* Crisis intervention centers provide facilities for immediate, short-term help for individuals and families confronted with highly stressful situations. An example is the "hot line" where people undergoing a crisis can call in and talk things over or make arrangements for other types of immediate assistance.

2. *The use of paraprofessionals.* There is a shortage of professionally trained mental health personnel in the United States, and increasing attention has been given to the short-term training of qualified persons who can work under professional supervision, easing the workload and improving the quality of health care.

3. *Reaction against involuntary commitment.* An individual who feels in need of such assistance can voluntarily admit himself to a mental hospital or related community mental health facility. However, there are procedures for involuntary commitment if the individual is judged to be dangerous to himself or to others. Szasz has spoken out strongly against involuntary commitment as "punishment without trial, imprisonment without time limit, and stigmatization without hope of redress"(1969, p. 57).

4. *Reaction against labeling.* Traditionally, it has been customary to assess the patient's disorder—particularly in seriously maladaptive behavior—and assign him a formal diagnostic classification, such as depression or schizophrenia. It is becoming apparent, however, that assigning a person such a "label" may have undesirable and unintended effects both on his perception of himself and on other people's perception of him. For this reason, such labels are now being used sparingly and primarily as a basis for guiding treatment programs.

 Summary and a look ahead

In this chapter we have outlined various ineffective coping patterns, including common self-defeating patterns as well as patterns that occur "when things really go wrong." Among the common self-defeating patterns are (1) neurotic avoidance, which may involve anxiety, phobic, obsessive-compulsive, neurasthenic, hysterical, hypochondriacal, and depressive reactions; (2) "psychosomatic" reactions, which are classified according to the organ system affected—and to which no bodily system seems to be immune; (3) psychopathic behavior, characterized by a lack of ethical or moral development and callous disregard for the rights and well-being of others; (4) alienation, characterized by a chronic lack of meaning in one's life, confusion about who or what one is, feelings that one has no control over his destiny, and lack of relatedness to others or to the larger society; and (5) problems involving sexual behavior, which we classified in terms of "normal," socially organized, and maladaptive sexual deviations.

In examining what happens when things go seriously wrong, we noted the nature of (1) acute situational stress reactions, including traumatic reactions to civilian catastrophes, combat, and extreme POW experiences; (2) psychotic disorders, including schizophrenia, paranoia, manic-depressive, and involutional reactions; (3) alcoholism and drug dependence; (4) violent delinquent and criminal behavior; and (5) the special problem of suicide, viewing it as frequently an attempt to communicate a "cry for help" to a significant other.

Finally we undertook a brief introduction to resources for personal change with emphasis on procedures for the treatment of seriously maladaptive behavior. Here we looked at the interdisciplinary approach to treatment, involving the integration of biological therapy, psychotherapy, and sociocultural approaches to treatment, as well as some of the current trends in the field.

Having covered the personal context of behavior in Part 2, we shall now turn in Part 3 to the social context of behavior. Chapter 9 will begin with a look at one-to-one interpersonal relationships, to be followed in later chapters by marriage and broader interpersonal interactions, including family and work relationships, and finally the individual's interactions with society.

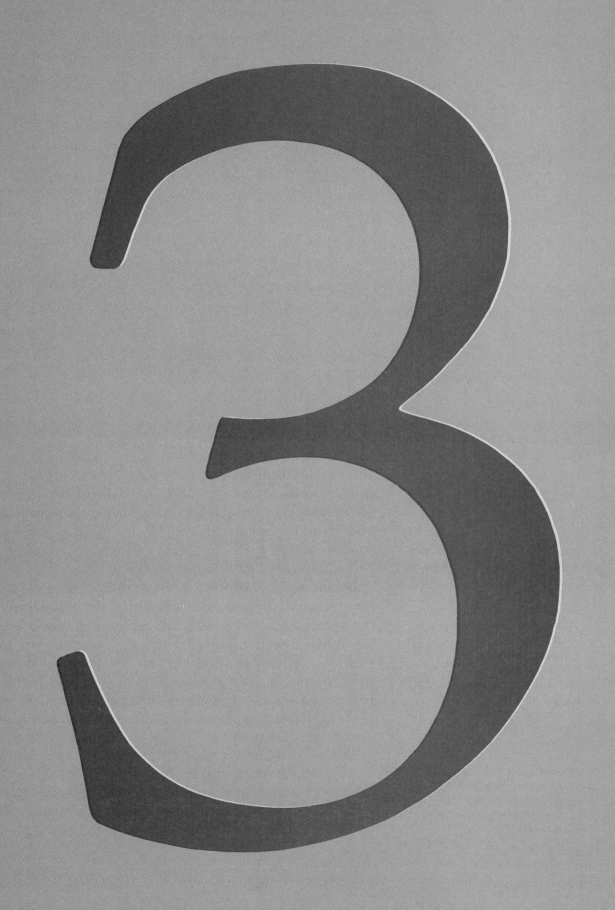

The Social Context of Behavior

9
Interpersonal Relationships

10
Marriage and Intimate Relationships

11
The Child and the Family

12
The World of Work

13
The Individual and the Group

Interpersonal Relationships

Ways of viewing interpersonal relationships
Relating to significant others
Maladaptive interpersonal patterns
Satisfying interpersonal relationships

"Selves can only exist in definite relationships to other selves" (Mead, 1934, p. 164).

Probably no aspect of our experience is more loaded with emotion or has a greater impact on our lives than our one-to-one relationships with significant others. This impact can be constructive or destructive. Our interpersonal relationships can be satisfying, growth producing, and fulfilling; and conversely, they can be frustrating, disappointing, and terribly hurtful.

Exactly what happens when one person interacts with another over time? While we can agree on the importance of interpersonal relationships in our lives, it is another matter to understand them. For each person approaches a relationship from a point central to his own being—his self. Thus his approach involves his perceptions, needs, goals, feelings, and assumptions about himself and his world. When we add another unique self to this mixture, it is apparent that the interaction which follows is likely to be a very complex one. To understand "what happens," it is necessary to understand the nature of the interactions involved, the type of relationship which develops, and the effects of the relationship on each of the persons involved. This is not an easy task.

In our approach to the understanding of interpersonal relationships, we shall focus on four topics which seem particularly important: (1) various models for viewing interpersonal relationships; (2) relating to significant others; (3) maladaptive interpersonal patterns; and (4) foundations of satisfying interpersonal relationships. While we shall deal with these topics separately, we shall see that they are closely interwoven.

Ways of viewing interpersonal relationships

It may be that at some future time a slightly frivolous historian will look back at our society in the latter half of the twentieth century and label it "The Age of Interpersonal Confusion."

Certainly many of us as individuals are examining our past and present interpersonal behavior and asking a variety of questions concerning just how satisfying or frustrating our interpersonal relationships have been and are now; we are concerned with the question of what we can realistically expect to receive from such relationships and with what satisfying interpersonal relationships require from us; and we are concerned with the change—and often confusion—in our views of interpersonal relationships and our ways of relating to others.

On a more objective and scientific level, a number of models, or ways of viewing interpersonal relationships, have recently emerged. To gain a broad perspective, we shall find it helpful to briefly review some of these different models and note their implications for our own behavior and lives. In particular we shall focus our attention on: (1) the social exchange model; (2) the role model; (3) the "games people play" model; and (4) the interactional or systems model.

Social exchange model

This model is based on the view that interpersonal relationships are formed for the purpose of satisfying our needs. Each person in the relationship wants something from the other; and the exchange which results is governed by economic principles. In essence, the relationship is viewed as a trading or bargaining one. Thibaut and Kelley, who have been influential in the development of this model, have stated the matter this way:

"The basic assumption running throughout our analysis is that every individual voluntarily enters and stays in a relationship only as long as it is adequately satisfactory in terms of his rewards and costs" (1959, p. 37).

This approach has been summarized by Swensen (1973) in terms of four basic concepts which underlie the social exchange model: (1) rewards; (2) costs; (3) outcomes and profit; and (4) comparison level.

1. *Rewards.* Any positively valued consequence which the person gains from the relationship is viewed as a reward. Thus rewards may vary from money to social approval or the validation of one's assumptions about value. And, of course, what might be highly rewarding for one person might have little or no reward value for another—or it might even be aversive. Also the value of a particular reward may change with time, depending upon a variety of factors including the individual's level of need gratification. For example, if a person has recently had sexual relations, a sexual encounter may have less immediate reward value than if he were sexually frustrated.

2. *Costs.* A cost is any negatively valued consequence incurred by a person in the relationship. Costs may take a variety of forms including time, effort, conflict, anxiety, self-devaluation, and a number of other conditions that serve either to deplete the individual's adaptive resources or have actual unpleasant and aversive consequences. Costs, like rewards, may vary over time as well as from person to person.

A person who feels inadequate and dependent may be willing to expend more effort for less reward in a friendship than he will at a time when he feels considerably more adequate and less dependent upon others. Similarly, a relationship which originally offered mutual need gratification may change over time, so that, as one client expressed it, "The relationship no longer pleasures me." The result in this case was a divorce after some 15 years of marriage.

3. *Outcomes and profit.* A key factor in the social exchange model is the outcome or profit, which is calculated as the reward minus the cost. This does not necessarily mean that the main goal in the relationship is to make the largest profit at the least cost. Rather it is a matter of mutual need satisfaction combined with an effort to keep costs down.

Presumably the individual does select alternatives and assess outcomes in terms of maximal profits to him (Komorita and Chertkoff, 1973). But this does not exclude the possibility that he the profits he has received in prior relationships of a similar type; and (2) those based on the payoffs he anticipates from other alternatives that he perceives as open to him. If his present relationship is providing a profit that is above the average he might expect, then presumably he will be satisfied with it; if the profit in the current relationship is below average—in terms of either of the above criteria—then he will be dissatisfied with the relationship. Comparison level is also influenced, as might be expected, by his observation of the payoffs which other persons seem to be obtaining in comparable relationships.

Comparison level may also change with time.

 I don't make friends easily. It's kind of a selfish thing, in a way, in that I think that a person would have to be maybe beneficial in some way, to help me in one way or another. I've been that way for a long time. When I was younger in school I'd pick out as friends people that impressed me, that I thought I'd learn things from, that seemed interesting. Also, people that might be in a position to do me a favor—even more so, now that I'm older, more worried about career connections and things like that.

expects to give equal value in return for what he receives. As Ayn Rand (1964) has pointed out, in a "just" exchange the individual does not take the undeserved. At the same time, the individual has the right to protect his own interests, and when the profit in a relationship drops to near zero or is considered insufficient to justify the cost, the person will ordinarily look for another relationship that holds the promise of more profit.

4. *Comparison level.* The comparison level represents a standard against which the person evaluates his present relationship. Essentially there are two kinds of comparisons: (1) those based on experience in which the individual evaluates his present relationship with respect to

As the person experiences satisfying relationships with a high payoff, his comparison level rises; and conversely, as he experiences frustrating and costly relationships, his comparison level drops. Comparison level may also vary depending upon the extent to which the person feels that he is self-directing and has some control over his own choices and destiny. A person who feels he has a high measure of control will presumably expect greater profits; while a person who feels he has little control is likely to have a low comparison level and to settle for a low margin of profit.

Here we have confined ourselves to sketching some basic concepts underlying the social exchange model—the exchange of anything of value between two people in an interpersonal relationship. In this context it is of interest to note that both Rand (1964) and Blau (1967) have concluded that what emerges is a compromise involving mutual concessions as well as mutual giving. In a sense it may be described as a compromise between what one might like to have (fantasy) and what one has to settle for (reality). As a consequence, each person will presumably end up with the person and relationship which he "deserves"—in terms of what he has to offer and what he is willing or forced to compromise for.

While the social exchange model may seem somewhat cynical in that it emphasizes the individual's "value" on the "open market" of interpersonal relationships as well as the relation of profits to costs, it also emphasizes the conditions which constitute an equitable exchange. In addition, it makes allowance for altruistic as well as material concerns. If a loved one is dying of cancer, for example, an individual may make great expenditures—of time, emotion, money—for that person's benefit even though he expects nothing in return.

Role model

*"All the world's a stage
And all the men and women merely players."*
                    As You Like It, Act II, Scene 7

A second way of looking at what goes on between people is the role model. The term *role* was borrowed from the theater and refers to a specified part in a play. The words and actions of the role are designated by the script and remain essentially the same regardless of who plays the role. Sophocles' *Oedipus Rex*, for example, has endured for over two thousand years and many actors have played the role of Oedipus, often adding their own interpretations up to a point. But the basic script remains the same.

Society also prescribes roles for its members which are designed to facilitate the functioning of the group; and while each individual lends his own interpretation to the role, there are usually limits to the "script" beyond which he is not expected to go. This point has been very succinctly made by Biddle and Thomas:

"In essence, the role perspective assumes, as does the theater, that performances result from the social prescriptions and behavior of others, and that variations in performance, to the extent that they do occur, are expressed within the framework created by these factors" (1966, p. 4).

Interpersonal relationships also involve role expectations and demands on the part of each person, and gross violation of these expectations and demands is likely to lead to conflict and possibly to termination of the relationship.

1. *Role expectations.* Role expectations refer to the obligations, duties, and rights that go with a given position and role in the group. Thus we can refer to the role expectations associated with being a nurse, a priest, or a general; and it can be readily seen that a general who tells people that he has a phobia of guns would not be living up to his role expectations. On a more interpersonal level, we can point to the complications likely to arise when a person fails to live up to the role expectations of his or her spouse.

2. *Role demands.* This concept refers to the social pressures that are exerted to force the individual to live up to role expectations. Where a major breach in role behavior occurs—as in the case of a priest who reveals information told him in confessional—social sanctions will be brought to bear, their severity depending upon the seriousness of the breach in role behavior as viewed by the group. In friendships and other intimate interpersonal relationships, subtle or not so subtle pressures are likely to be brought to bear as one partner attempts to elicit expected role behavior from the other.

3. *Role skills.* Some people have more of the skills required to play given social roles than do others. Often a distinction is made here between cognitive skills and action skills. Cognitive skills in this context refer to the individual's ability to perceive what other people expect of him in a given role—their role expectations. Action skills refer to his ability to enact the role in accordance with these expectations. Often the more general term *social competence* is used to

It probably doesn't occur to most people, but just because I'm a minister doesn't mean that I don't have a terribly difficult time with some of the things I have to do, like break bad news to families, or try to comfort them when somebody's died. I can't stay totally uninvolved, and I wouldn't want to, but a person can take only so much, so often, and sometimes I use my 'role' as a minister to protect my feelings. You can't hide behind the role too much, or you might lose your integrity and become hardened, but sometimes I'm grateful for that hiding place, to give me just enough relief to be able to keep going when things get too heavy.

refer to the individual's ability to perceive role expectations and to enact the role accordingly. One aspect of social competence, of course, is the individual's ability to respond to subtle feedback from others in order to make needed corrections in his role enactment.

4. *Role conflict and confusion.* As we have seen, *role conflict* occurs when the individual feels unable to reconcile contradictory role demands—for example, a young woman who tries to play the roles of wife, mother, and lawyer at the same time may feel that she is not doing justice to any of them—or when the individual feels that role expectations are incompatible with his values and self-concept. A physician whose personal moral code could not justify abortion would likely be in considerable conflict concerning his role when faced with pressures of such cases. Closely related to role conflict is the concept of *role confusion*. Here the individual is not clear about what role he is expected to play. Such role confusion is likely to occur when the individual is confronted with an unfamiliar situation in which the role expectations are not clear to him.

While the social exchange model often seems cynical, the role model often seems to carry the connotation of "phoniness," of "not being one's true self." Several psychologists have pointed

out, however, that when a person really believes in the personal and social value of his role and is committed to playing it effectively and with integrity, then he is acting sincerely—he believes in the role he is playing and is not a "phony." The fraudulent person is one who plays a role in which he does not believe and to which he is not committed, or who plays a role which arouses expectations in others that he has no intention of meeting, as in the case of a "con artist."

In any event, the role model does seem to fit a good deal of observed behavior—both sincere and insincere—and appears to be a useful model in helping us to understand various aspects of interpersonal relationships.

"Games people play"

"Oh, the games people play now
Ev'ry night and ev'ry day now,
Never meanin' what they say, now
Never sayin' what they mean now."

(South, 1968)

Another approach to the use of games in studying interpersonal interactions was originally developed to study problems in international relations. In this context, games are seen as having three basic characteristics: (1) the possible outcomes of the game in terms of "payoffs" or "losses" are specified and certain outcomes are preferred by the players; (2) the game involves some measure of risk and uncertainty—the outcome cannot be entirely assured or predicted by the players; and (3) some strategy is required for playing the game and for balancing possible payoffs against the losses or risks likely to be involved; usually this strategy may be varied on the basis of feedback obtained during the course of the game.

On a very simple level, the game of checkers illustrates all three of these characteristics: the outcomes are limited to win,

lose, or draw, and ordinarily the players would prefer to win or at least draw; there is no absolute certainty as to who will win assuming the players are fairly evenly matched; and some strategy must be devised for playing the game.

A variety of two-person games for studying interpersonal relationships have been devised. One such game is called the "Prisoner's Dilemma." In this game, the players are seen as two accomplices in a crime who have been arrested and placed in separate cells. Each is urged by the "District Attorney" to confess and testify against his partner, with the promise that he will receive only a light sentence if he does so. He is threatened with a trumped-up conviction on some minor charge if he refuses. The dilemma is this: If neither prisoner confesses, both will get off with relatively light sentences due to the lack of evidence. If one remains silent but the other

does not, the "silent" one is likely to receive the maximum sentence. If both confess, both will probably receive fairly severe sentences. If you were one of the prisoners, would you confess to avoid the maximum sentence, or remain silent and trust that your accomplice would do the same?

All of us who have played games, such as bridge, know that our method of playing reveals much about our personality. Thus the simple research tool of game playing can be used to yield rich information in terms of caution, suspicion, trust, vengefulness, and other characteristics of behavior. However, the primary concern here is not with the playing of games as such, but with applying information obtained in laboratory situations to understanding and predicting the interactions of people in interpersonal relationships outside the laboratory.

A number of models of interpersonal relationships involve some concept of "games." We shall deal here with the concept of games developed by the psychiatrist Eric Berne (1964, 1972), which is well described in his popular book *Games People Play.* This concept forms the basis of an innovative form of psychotherapy called *transactional analysis.*

To understand interpersonal transactions in terms of this model, it will be useful to review several of the underlying concepts.

Parent, Adult, Child

An individual's personality is thought of as comprising three parts or ego states—Parent, Adult, and Child (P-A-C).

1. *Parent.* This aspect of personality consists of the assumptions and behaviors we have incorporated from our parents or other parental models. Thus we automatically respond in the ways which we have learned are correct.

2. *Adult.* This part of us processes information rationally and appropriately in terms of the situation and is normally concerned with important problems which require conscious decision making.

3. *Child.* This element of personality is carried over from childhood feelings and experiences and contains the potentials for intuition, spontaneity, creativity, and enjoyment or pleasure.

Berne goes on to analyze interpersonal relationships in terms of the ego states which are actually "in use" when two people are communicating with each other. For example, married couples not infrequently find out that they have been relating to each other as mother to son or father to daughter over a period of years.

Games

Berne suggests that most people are constantly playing games in their relationships with others.

"Games are sets of ulterior transactions, repetitive in nature, with a well-defined psychological payoff. Since an ulterior transaction means that the agent pretends to be doing one thing while he is really doing something else, all games involve a con. But a con only works if there is a weakness it can hook into, a handle or 'gimmick' to get hold of in the respondent, such as fear, greed, sentimentality, or irritability. After the 'mark' is

reassurance he needs, and the respondent gets something he wants in return. In essence, the reassurance given by the friend was really a "maneuver" and not an honest interaction.

It is important to note that the games Berne is referring to are not consciously planned "con" games but rather games played unwittingly in interpersonal transactions—games of which the participants are either entirely or partially unaware. Such games are not played for fun; many of them are deadly serious and highly destructive in their effects.

Games are played because they serve two useful functions: (a) they are substitutes for true intimacy in daily life—intimacy for which there is presumably little opportunity and for which many people are unprepared; and (b) they serve as homeostatic mechanisms in maintaining interpersonal relationships. Hence games are not

 In my family, you can get more things you want if you handle it right, like if I tell my mother how nice she looks, just before I ask her for some money to go out on a date.

hooked, the player pulls some sort of switch in order to get his payoff. The switch is followed by a moment of confusion or crossup while the mark tries to figure out what has happened to him. Then both players collect their payoffs as the game ends. The payoff, which is mutual, consists of feelings (not necessarily similar) which the game arouses in both the agent and the respondent. Unless a set of transactions has these four features, it is not a game—that is, the transactions must be ulterior so that there is a con, and the con must be followed by a switch, a crossup, and a payoff" (1972, p. 23).

For example, if a person asks his friend for reassurance and the friend gives him the reassurance he needs, this transaction is not a game. But if his friend gives the reassurance and then turns it in some way to his own advantage— "now you owe me one"—it is a game. It involves a "payoff" in which the agent receives the

necessarily undesirable, and in fact, the bulk of time in most serious relationships is taken up with playing games. The question remains, however, as to whether the game being played by any individual is essentially constructive or destructive. And even at best, games are only a poor substitute for intimacy. But intimacy requires the achievement of awareness, spontaneity, and personal maturity—qualities which are not easy to come by.

Types of games

Berne (1964) has delineated and described over a hundred games that people play in their relationships with others. A few of the more common ones are described in the illustration on page 230.

The most common game played between spouses—and one which has a homeostatic function in maintaining the relationship—has been labeled by Berne "If It Weren't For You" (IWFY). For present purposes we may use it to illustrate the characteristics of games and the purposes they serve.

"Mrs. White complained that her husband severely restricted her social activities, so that she had never learned to dance. Due to changes in her attitude brought about by psychiatric treatment, her husband became less sure of himself and more indulgent. Mrs. White was then free to enlarge the scope of her activities. She signed up for dancing classes, and then discovered to her despair that she had a morbid fear of dance floors and had to abandon this project.

"This unfortunate adventure, along with similar ones, laid bare some important aspects of the structure of her marriage. Out of her many suitors she had picked a domineering man for a husband. She was then in a position to complain that she could do all sorts of things 'if it weren't for you' " (Berne, 1964, p. 53).

The "payoff" for Mrs. White in the relationship was that her husband was protecting her from doing something she was deeply afraid of and permitting her to take the stance "It's not that I'm afraid, it's that he won't let me," or even "It's not that I'm not trying, it's that he holds me back" (1964, p. 50). The payoff for the husband was presumably the enjoyment or ego boost he received from his domineering behavior.

Thus analyzing the games we play can help us to become aware of the nature of our interactions with others and their consequences in terms of our interpersonal relationships.

General systems model

A fourth conceptual view of interpersonal relationships is derived from the broader general systems model which we reviewed in Chapter 2. From a general systems viewpoint, two-person relationships can be considered as a small group or system with its own unique structural, functional, and field properties. Thus we are concerned with the characteristics of the individuals involved, the nature of the group system which

A few of the more common games delineated by Berne (1964) are the following:

TAC (Try and Collect). I go into debt to you. You try to collect and I keep putting off repaying. Finally, you take stern measures and I point out how greedy and ruthless you are.

WAHM (Why Does This Always Happen to Me?). I continually provoke people into mistreating and rejecting me; then I whine, "Why does this always happen to me?" This is the game of those who are perennially the jilted, the fired, the scorned.

NIGYSOB (Now I've Got You, You Son of a Bitch). I allow you to take advantage of me until you are quite vulnerable; then I rise in righteous indignation.

AIA (Ain't It Awful?). I constantly invite mistreatment, then complain to one person about how another is mistreating me.

SWYMD (See What You Made Me Do). I am nervous or upset and drop or break something. I turn angrily to whoever is closest and say, "See what you made me do."

YDYB (Why Don't You—Yes But). I invite you to give me advice, then find a good reason for rejecting everything you suggest—thus putting you down.

GYWP (Gee, You're Wonderful, Professor!). This is a way of getting the professor to act the way I want him to act, and, if he doesn't, I can be disappointed in him. It works especially well if he responds with YUP, "You're uncommonly perceptive."

Wooden Leg. What do you expect of a man with a "wooden leg"? Here I use any weaknesses I have to keep people from expecting things of me.

they form, and the nature of the environment or field in which the relationship occurs. Focusing on the interpersonal relationship proper, it becomes relevant to study interaction processes in terms of common goals, methods of communication, role expectations and enactments, methods of coping, and related considerations including game playing. In essence, the general systems model is capable of embracing the social exchange, role, and game models; but it is both more helpful and perhaps more accurate to depict each of the preceding models separately, since they derive from different origins and emphasize different points of view.

In the remainder of this chapter, as well as in the chapters which follow, we shall have occasion to see the importance of these four models for understanding interpersonal relationships. All are relevant to understanding marriage, family, and other intimate relationships with which we will be dealing.

grieve the other. . . . It is an ecstatic and unstable stage, bound of its own agitation to tip into the third: revulsion. One or the other makes a misjudgment; presumes; puts forth that which does not meet agreement. Sometimes there is an explosion; more often the moment is swallowed in silence, and months pass before its nature dawns. Instead of dissolving, it grows . . . forgiveness, forgetfulness, that have arrived so often, fail. Now everything jars and is distasteful. . . . Everything about the other is hateful, despicable; yet he cannot be dismissed. We have confided in him too many minutes, too many words; he has those minutes and words as hostages, and his confidences are embedded in us where they cannot be scraped away, and even rivers of time cannot erode them completely, for there are indelible stains. Now—though the friends may continue to meet, and smile, as if they had never trespassed beyond acquaintance—the death of the one would please the other" (Updike, 1962, pp. 186–87).

 In my dealings with the opposite sex, particularly at first meeting or at the beginning of a relationship, I try to determine what kind of relationship with me the individual has in mind. I do this by observing actions and listening to what is said, and analyzing this.

Relating to significant others

"I . . . experienced the pattern of friendship. There are three stages. First, acquaintance: we are new to each other, make each other laugh in surprise, and demand nothing beyond politeness. The death of one would startle the other, no more. It is a pleasant stage, a stable stage. . . . Then comes intimacy: now we laugh before two words of the joke are out of each other's mouth, because we know what he will say . . . everything we venture is right. . . . The death of one would

While some friendships would appear to follow the pattern depicted by Updike, others turn out to be more satisfying and durable. But again it becomes apparent that while the relationships we establish with significant others play a crucial role in determining the satisfactions and frustrations we experience in living, understanding the processes involved in the development of such relationships is by no means a simple matter.

Perhaps the most effective way of approaching this task is to note the typical stages as well as some of the specific problems involved in establishing interpersonal relationships. From this viewpoint, we may think in terms of: (1) the encounter; (2) interpersonal perception and at-

 I try to understand other people by relating their actions to my own experience. For example, if a stranger comes on too strong when first meeting me, I can remember my feelings of insecurity when I was in new surroundings.

traction; (3) interpersonal accommodation; and (4) the special problems of communication and self-disclosure.

The encounter

The first step in relating to others is the initial encounter with another person. Most of us find such encounters interesting or even exciting, particularly if we perceive the other person as attractive and nonthreatening. Individuals tend to avoid encounters when there are outward signs of threat or displeasure. Although there are potential risks in encounters, people gener-

ally believe that they should make themselves accessible to them.

Initiating the encounter
The encounter begins with some sort of communicative act on the part of one person inviting a response on the part of the other. Such an act may involve a smile, a gaze, or a pleasant remark. If the other person responds positively, the encounter is under way. Initially the parties usually engage in rather tentative and safe interactions until respective roles become clear.

During this initial phase of exploration, there is often a good deal of uncertainty. Lalljee and

Cook (1973), for example, found uncertainty in verbal expressions during the initial phase of the encounter; and this gradually decreased as the encounter progressed and each person received feedback from the other. In Japan social behavior is quite structured, and when two strangers meet they usually first exchange name cards so that the appropriate roles (style of language, depth of bowing, and so on) may be enacted. In the United States, most encounters are initiated on a much less formal basis and structuring

sons involved do have considerable leeway in setting their own rules, again there appear to be limitations. For example, once an encounter is begun it typically involves a sort of agreement as to the roles and interactions to be expected; and for one person to suddenly change roles or take a different stance is likely to be resented—as in the case of a woman who assumes a seductive stance and then suddenly switches to one of indignation when she finds the man is definitely interested.

 I sometimes after one date decided that I didn't like him well enough to want to go out with him again, or I might actively have disliked something about him, and I would always go along with the well, 'Yes, do give me a call,' or whatever that formula is that happens at the end of the first date. And then I would have to go through the pain of the phone call when he calls me, and I'd give him excuses enough different times when he called that he finally gets the idea that I didn't want to see him. And I'd feel bad because I know how I have felt when people I've liked haven't called me.

usually develops as the encounter progresses and each person learns more about the position, status, and relevant characteristics of the other.

Are there "rules" for encounters?

Encounters may take many different forms and involve diverse roles, interactions, and settings. A formally arranged date may involve quite different roles and interactions than would be involved with a "pick-up" in a bar; and giving a hitchhiker a ride may involve quite different roles and interactions than meeting and talking to one's instructor after class.

While there are no written rules for encounters, the setting in which the encounter takes place does tend to establish certain guidelines, and deviating markedly from these guidelines may lead to difficulties. Although the per-

Termination of the encounter

One difficult problem which may arise is the termination of an encounter—particularly if one person is dissatisfied but the other wishes to pursue the interaction with the hope of establishing a good relationship. At the end of a first date in which all seemed to go well but for some reason was not satisfactory to one of the persons involved, how can the encounter be terminated without the other person feeling rejected or devaluated? Usually this is accomplished by a sort of ritualistic role enactment in which each participant is assured that the encounter will be resumed, even though one or both parties know it has come to an end. But where one person sincerely believes that the encounter will be resumed and is looking forward to it, the later realization that it has actually been terminated may elicit feelings of disappointment and hurt.

Whether or not an initial encounter will progress or be terminated depends upon the way each person perceives the other and the attraction each feels toward the other. This brings us to the problem of interpersonal perception and attraction.

Interpersonal perception and attraction

"What attracts one person to another?" is one of the unsolved mysteries of interpersonal relationships. "What does she see in him?" or "What does he see in her?" are commonly asked about relationships that seem to work out for reasons which are unclear. Of course, we are usually ready with some "common-sense" explanation. When two people are getting along well together but are very different in background and personality make-up, we may point out that "Opposites attract each other"; or when two people who are very much alike get along well together, we may point out that "Birds of a feather flock together."

In the present section we shall have occasion to examine these two divergent viewpoints as well as other considerations that appear to influence our perception of others and whether or not we are attracted to them.

How do we perceive others?
Research findings suggest that we tend to perceive three interrelated characteristics of the other person in assessing his attractiveness to us.

1. *Physical appearance*—whether the person is male or female, young or old, physically attractive or unattractive.

2. *Beliefs and behavior*—whether we agree or disagree with the individual's beliefs, and whether he tends to be honest or dishonest, talkative or quiet, friendly or aloof.

3. *Interactional possibilities*—the ways in which the person can affect us; whether the person is a potential friend or enemy, spouse or

lover, in a position to help us meet our needs or to hurt us.

Interpersonal perception is usually a combination of all three of these factors—what the person looks like, his beliefs and acts, and what potentials we see him as having for affecting us—although one person may place much more importance on physical attractiveness or some other characteristic than another. Our purposes also influence our perceptions. A woman may view the same man quite differently depending upon whether she is looking for a spouse, a bridge partner, or an employee.

Our initial perception of another person may be subject to several sources of error. We almost invariably rely heavily upon our own experience, information, and assumptions in assessing the other person—although we may supplement our own impressions with those of a third party. But limitations or inaccuracies in our own frame of reference may lead to faulty perceptions.

A closely related source of error is the use of stereotypes. A familiar stereotype of the Irish, for example, usually includes a gift of "blarney," a fondness for alcohol, and readiness to fight at the slightest provocation. In meeting a person of Irish ancestry, we may apply a stereotype which does not fit the person in question—who may not possess any of these characteristics. Where such stereotypes are prejudicial and discriminatory—as in racial prejudice—they are likely to lead to negative interpersonal perceptions. Prejudice literally means *prejudgment*, and we may negatively assess a person belonging to some "stigmatized" minority group without ever really getting to know him.

Several additional and important sources of error in our initial perception of another person may be noted here. A person may put on a "false front," trying to project the image of himself which he thinks will be most attractive to us. Or he may disclose only certain aspects of himself, preventing us from gaining an accurate first impression. Or we, ourselves, may be misled by wishful thinking, seeing the person as we would like him to be rather than as he really is.

As we get to know the other person better—assuming that the encounter is not immediately terminated—we have an opportunity to observe many additional characteristics which were perhaps not apparent during the initial encounter. This process involves a deeper level of perception than is possible on initial encounter, enables us to see the other person in terms of his true uniqueness as a human being, and provides the opportunity for making corrections in our original perceptions and assessment.

What makes the other person attractive to us?

Personality traits regarded as socially desirable are usually associated with interpersonal attractiveness. Included here are a good sense of humor, sincerity and integrity, superior intel-

with us tends to elicit positive feelings, while one who disagrees tends to elicit negative feelings. However, it may be noted that two persons may agree on practically everything they discuss but find themselves in such bitter disagreement about a single issue that it terminates the relationship. Commonality of purpose also tends to be of crucial importance in bringing people together in striving toward agreed-upon goals and mutual need satisfaction; when the individuals' purposes are no longer congruent, such a relationship is likely to be terminated. It would appear that, in some instances, "Opposites attract each other," particularly during a short-range period of time when it seems exciting to meet and relate to someone "different"—

 When I first meet somebody, first of all I notice their outlook on what is happening right now. Like if they seem positive and they're standing there with a kind of beam in their eye, really bouncy, or even quiet. But what really turns me off is when somebody crosses their arms and looks blasé—nothing turns me off like somebody who's blasé.

ligence, and physical health and attractiveness. We also tend to be attracted to persons who are pleasant to be around; persons manifesting negative emotional traits—such as anxiety, depression, and hostility—tend to be perceived as less attractive. Social or financial status may also influence the other person's attractiveness to us.

Perhaps of even more importance is the observation made throughout history that people are attracted to those to whom they are similar in beliefs, values, purposes, and related characteristics. Similarity of beliefs and values as a source of attraction relies heavily upon conditioning and positive reinforcement. In the past, the individual presumably has associated agreement with reward and disagreement with aversive consequences. Hence a person who agrees

but it appears much more likely that over the long range, "Birds of a feather flock together."

Closely tied in with commonality of purpose is the perceived potentiality in a relationship for reciprocal reward. If a relationship is perceived as likely to be nonrewarding to one person or the other, it is likely to be terminated; whereas, if it is perceived as likely to be rewarding, the relationship is likely to continue. Thus a person may not be interested in establishing a relationship in which he feels he would be exploited and receive very little in return; conversely, a relationship which is perceived as offering mutual need gratification may lead to interpersonal attraction and continuation of the encounter or relationship.

In general, it would appear that individuals are

Nonverbal communication, by means of gestures or inflections, can impart various kinds of information that supplement whatever is being communicated on a verbal level (Mahl, 1968; Ekman & Friesen, 1968).

1. The nonverbal can express the same meaning as the verbal message. (I say I don't like you and my voice, gestures, and facial expression say so too.)

2. The nonverbal can anticipate future amplification of the concurrent verbal context. (Even before I tell the punch line, I start to laugh.)

3. The nonverbal can be contradictory to the verbal message. (I say I like you, but I'm backing away.)

4. The nonverbal can be a delayed undermining of content that has already been expressed. (I tell you something in all seriousness, then after a moment's delay I explode with laughter.)

5. The nonverbal can be related to the more global aspects of the interaction. (I call you a bad name, but I am smiling.)

6. The nonverbal can be a substitute for a word or a phrase in a verbal message. (I shrug my shoulders, meaning "Who cares!")

7. The nonverbal can fill or explain silences. (I stop talking and indicate with my eyes that the person we've been gossiping about is approaching.)

---

attracted to other persons who: (1) have socially desirable characteristics; (2) have similar purposes, values, and beliefs; and (3) can be instrumental in helping them meet their needs. It is relevant to note, however, that the qualities which attract one person to another on first acquaintance are not necessarily the ones that account for the continuation and progression of the relationship. For here we are dealing with interpersonal accommodation as well as interpersonal attraction.

Interpersonal accommodation

"Persons are decidedly the hardest things we have to deal with" (Sullivan, 1962, p. 246).

Interpersonal accommodation is the process whereby two persons evolve patterns of interaction that enable them to attain common goals, meet mutual needs, and build a satisfying relationship.

This requires that the persons involved cope with a variety of adjustive demands—both internal and external. Adjustive demands within the relationship may involve changes in role relationships, or methods of resolving conflicts; environmental demands may take such forms as inflation which depletes the resources of a re-

tired couple, or a disapproving social environment faced by a couple who have entered into an interracial marriage.

In discussing interpersonal accommodation, we shall focus on coping with the continual adjustive demands that arise within the interpersonal system itself. Since the last section of this chapter will focus on the improvement of interpersonal accommodation and the building of satisfying relationships, we shall keep our present discussion brief.

Basic processes of accommodation

Three processes appear basic to interpersonal accommodation: communication, structure, and the resolution of disagreements and conflicts.

1. *The key role of communication.* In order for an interpersonal relationship to survive and move forward toward mutual goals, it is essential that the persons communicate with each other. This communication appears to involve two kinds of information: (a) cognitive information which is concerned primarily with "facts"—facts about events, people, beliefs, and problems; and (b) affective information which is concerned primarily with the individual's feelings and emotions—with how he feels about things.

I suppose my husband makes accommodations for me—he must. But not enough. He does things his way, and nothing I can say or do changes his way. I'm not going to hurry him up when he doesn't want to be hurried up. He can more likely change the way I'm going to be than me changing him—I'm the giver-inner. I must say that he's not very demanding; actually, he doesn't try to force me into things.

There are various ways of communicating such information—spoken words, voice inflection, facial expression, gestures, body movements, and even moments of silence. Thus communication is said to take place on *nonverbal* as well as *verbal* levels. There is some evidence to indicate that verbal communication is used primarily to communicate cognitive information while nonverbal communication is used primarily to communicate information about feelings and emotions. Usually, however, verbal communication also involves nonverbal elements as well, such as facial expression or gestures; and ordinarily it is important that both the verbal and nonverbal components be perceived if the communication is to be interpreted accurately.

The actual amount of information exchange may vary greatly depending upon the particular relationship, but when the partners seem unable to express their thoughts and feelings clearly to each other or to communicate effectively about common tasks and problems, difficulties inevitably arise. Even in a relationship of some duration, misunderstandings stemming from in-adequate communication can cause serious trouble. In fact, one indication of a failing marriage is the inability of the partners to talk about their problems with any degree of objectivity or mutual understanding. Eventually such a communication breakdown may reach a point of almost total silence, signaling the failure of the relationship. Each has given up trying to "get through" to the other.

2. *Structuring the relationship.* Once an encounter is under way and channels of communication have been opened, the process of structuring begins—defining roles, responsibilities, norms, and other dimensions of the emerging relationship. For a relationship to be successful, it is important that each individual know what is expected of him and in turn make it clear what he expects of the other person. Where such expectations are not mutually satisfactory, some adjustments must be made in order to arrive at an agreed-upon structure. If such adjustment measures are not taken, the relationship will be plagued with undue misunderstanding and conflict and perhaps even be terminated.

Reviewing the available research, it would appear that the following factors play a key role in the success or failure of accommodation:

1. Whether there is commonality or conflict of purposes and goals.

2. How much incentive value the relationship has for each partner.

3. Extent of agreement between the partners on values and priorities.

4. How well the persons are able to communicate with each other.

5. Mutual commitment to whatever norms and rules have been developed to structure the relationship and make the interaction more predictable.

6. How well reciprocal actions and moves are timed—whether, for example, quarreling lovers feel like making up at the same time.

7. The strategy and tactics being used by the partners—

cooperation vs. competition, openness vs. secrecy, and so on.

8. Whether the persons involved have learned appropriate patterns of accommodation in former relationships and are able to apply them to the new situation.

9. Limitations and demands of the environmental setting.

10. Personal characteristics of the individuals involved—whether they are defense-oriented or task-oriented, rigid or flexible in their approach to problems, and similar traits.

In our discussion of the role model, we noted the emphasis placed upon role expectations, demands, and enactments in interpersonal relationships. Suppose a young couple are contemplating marriage, and the man expects that his partner will be affectionate, be an interesting companion, and earn a reasonable income. The woman may also expect that her partner will be affectionate, be an interesting companion, and earn a reasonable income. If each person is able to enact the expected role to the satisfaction of the other, the relationship is likely to be greatly facilitated.

The structuring of roles in turn tends to establish the responsibilities assigned to each person. As in the preceding example, both partners may agree to share in their financial support—as well as in other responsibilities appropriate to their agreed-upon roles. Norms soon emerge in the relationship which provide the standards for evaluating specific interactions as well as the relationship itself.

Structuring a relationship is a complex process for a number of reasons. For example, the structuring may not only occur in terms of verbally stated expectations but also in terms of

expectations of which the individual himself may not be clearly aware; for example, a husband may expect his wife to be like his mother although he does not actually realize this himself. In addition, the structuring also takes place in terms of actual behavior; that is, one partner may fail to live up to previous spoken or unspoken agreements. Here again conflicts almost inevitably arise and must be resolved if the relationship is to be a satisfactory one or even continue.

3. *Resolving disagreements and conflicts.* This process may take a variety of forms. It may involve one-sided compromise and concession, or more often an exchange of some kind. In fact, through barter, compromise, and concession, there may be a continual structuring and restructuring of the relationship as the partners attempt to deal with problems and work out agreements.

The type of interdependence in the relationship may markedly influence the pattern of accommodation that emerges. In a relationship in which one person has an authority role and the other a subordinate one, there is likely to be a disproportionate giving-in on the part of the subordinate. However, this type of social exchange in an intimate relationship may lead to serious conflict and the eventual destruction of the relationship. In relationships that continue, there is usually both barter and concession. For example, one partner gives in on some occasions, and the other at other times. In some instances a person may consider it good strategy to make many small concessions ostentatiously in order to win concessions on an issue that he considers more important.

Although barter and compromise appear to be basic methods of resolving disagreements and conflicts, other patterns may also be involved. A person who does not like his in-laws may simply have to accept them as part of the package deal;

through mediation, as when the partners seek help from a marital counselor.

Some unpredictable outcomes

In discussing interpersonal accommodation, we have focused on the adjustments likely to be necessary if a relationship is to meet the needs of the persons involved and become stable and permanent.

It may be emphasized, however, that some relationships do continue despite a lack of adequate need fulfillment and even destructive effects on the part of one or both persons involved. This point has been dramatically portrayed in the play *Who's Afraid of Virginia Woolf?* in which a highly destructive marital

 I am an athlete, and I have felt shame and anger at being defeated in intense competition—anger at the other person who has defeated and disgraced me. I have later made friends with these people, and the beginnings of very significant relationships have started with very negative emotions, turned around to positive ones.

or a woman may dislike her husband's occupation because it is hazardous or keeps him away from home a great deal, but forces herself to adjust to it. Often a difficult situation arises when a childless person marries someone with children. Here again various realities may have to be accepted—including sharing the spouse's time with the children and taking some measure of responsibility for them.

Resolving conflicts may also lead to escape patterns in which certain problems—such as those centering around sexual relations—are denied and not talked about. Sometimes one person minimizes his investment in the relationship by focusing on other life activities, as when a husband becomes absorbed in his work or a wife in her children. The resolution of disagreements and conflicts may also be achieved

relationship does endure. Apparently in such relationships there are certain basic needs which are being met; or perhaps neither partner sees the possibility of finding a more satisfying relationship with someone else, so they simply let matters drift along.

Conversely, even though a relationship may lead to mutual fulfillment and appear to be stable, there is no guarantee that it will endure. Demands on interpersonal relationships do change over time. Thus the problems faced by a young married couple are quite different from those they will face twenty years later; and while they may have accommodated to the former, they may not be able to cope with the latter, and the relationship terminates. In some instances, unforeseen circumstances—such as forced separation of a couple over a sustained period of time or long-term prison confinement—may lead to changes in the persons that make it impossible to reestablish the relationship on a successful basis at a later date.

Admittedly we still have much to learn about interpersonal accommodation—not to mention interpersonal relationships in general—but in this section we have attempted to delineate some of the key factors that appear to be involved in such accommodations.

Self-disclosure

". . . obviously, all relations which people have to one another are based on their knowing something about one another" (Simmel, 1964, p. 307).

While it is difficult to argue with this statement, it does not resolve the problem in interpersonal relationships of "What is best kept secret and what is best disclosed?" It seems apparent that the answer to this question depends in part on the type and intimacy of the relationship and the persons involved; but this simple declaration does not answer the question either. At best we can only consider certain aspects of the problem which may be helpful to the individual in making decisions about self-disclosure in his own relationships.

Nature and course of
self-disclosure

Self-disclosure may be defined as any information one person communicates about himself—usually verbally—to another. As Cozby has pointed out, the basic dimensions of the self-disclosure of information are "(a) breadth or amount of information disclosed, (b) depth or intimacy of information disclosed, and (c) duration or time spent describing each item of information" (1973, p. 75).

Levin and Gergen (1969) suggest that during the initial stage of the relationship, medium amounts of self-disclosure by one person indicate his trustfulness and desire for a closer relationship. Low self-disclosers who reveal little or nothing about themselves are likely to experience difficulty in establishing a relationship; while high self-disclosers may encounter the same problem, since they are often perceived as overly preoccupied with themselves and maladjusted.

As the relationship progresses, usually the amount and intimacy of self-disclosure gradually increases on the part of both partners. However, the eventual amount and intimacy of self-disclosure may vary greatly depending in part on the characteristics of the persons involved, the nature of the relationship, and the specific information involved. Panyard (1973) found that friends disclosed approximately the same amount of information about themselves as they had received from the other person; and there appears little reason to believe that the situation is markedly different in romantic relationships.

In this general context, it is interesting to note that Jones and Gordon (1972) found the timing of self-disclosure as well as the type of information disclosed were important considerations during the initial stage of a relationship. For example, it was found that the disclosure of positive information about oneself, such as good fortune, was not as well received during the early part of the relationship as it was later; while disclosure of a negative experience was well received early in the relationship providing that the individual was responsible for the experience—such as failure in a course due to lack of interest and unwillingness to study. Perhaps in most interpersonal relationships—regardless of the stage involved—timing of self-disclosure may play an important role in determining how it is received by the other person.

Secrets: to tell
or not to tell?

Deciding how much information about oneself to disclose often poses conflicts. Sometimes a distinction is made between "then" and "now" secrets; it has been suggested that "then" secrets of the past are often best not disclosed, whereas very few "now" secrets should be kept in intimate relationships. But this is not a simple matter. Often as a relationship progresses, one or both partners wish to know about the other's past. Then the question of whether to tell or not

I am unwilling to disclose behavior that might bring grief to a loved one. If telling something about myself is going to bring sorrow or shame to my girl friend, then I won't say it. It is a case of having nothing to gain and everything to lose.

I have a need for privacy. I need to have something about which I can say, 'Only I know about this,' or 'These things are sacred only to me.' Even if it is something I am guilty about, I can be assured that no one will ever know unless I tell them.

to tell arises. Should the person be governed by honesty and openness and reveal all; or should he consider the possible cost in damage to the relationship? Does a person owe it to a prospective spouse to reveal past sexual experiences? An abortion? A narcotics conviction? How does one realistically weigh the "risk" of self-disclosure against that of later revelation by a third party? Obviously to tell or not to tell can be far from a simple matter.

On the other hand, some investigators have pointed to powerful forces in the direction of self-disclosure, such as being open and honest with the other person and alleviating possible guilt feelings by "confessing one's sins." What is often overlooked, however, is that while these forces may be constructive for the person doing the disclosing, they may be highly upsetting to the other person. For example, confessing an extramarital affair may alleviate one's own guilt feelings but prove devastating for the unsuspecting spouse. Of course, as in all forms of self-disclosure, the persons involved are important in the equation. Whereas one person may be emotionally upset and devaluated by such information, another may be able to take it in stride.

It is interesting to note the finding of Cozby (1972) that highly intimate levels of self-disclosure tend to be rewarding at first but that the costs eventually outweigh the rewards—the most apparent cost being anxiety about upset-

ting the other person, demeaning oneself in the other person's eyes, and damaging the relationship. Perhaps if Rogers (1968) is correct in his assumption that we are moving toward more openness, trust, acceptance, and intimacy in our interpersonal relationships, the cost-reward ratio found by Cozby will eventually be reversed.

In the meantime, the fact is that we have much to learn about the consequences of unrestrained self-disclosure. In fact, Altman and Taylor (1973) have expressed concern about a "tyranny of openness" in which persons are denied privacy and perhaps even "mystery" because full self-disclosure is demanded by others in interpersonal encounters and relationships. At this point, it seems most sensible to view self-disclosure as a problem which can best be resolved by the individual in relation to his own beliefs, feelings, perception of the other person in the relationship, and the nature of the relationship itself.

Maladaptive interpersonal patterns

GEORGE: *I warned you not to go too far.*
MARTHA: *I'm just beginning.*
GEORGE: *I'm numbed enough . . . and I don't*

mean by liquor, though maybe that's been part of the process—a gradual, over-the-years going to sleep of the brain cells—I'm numbed enough now, to be able to take you when we're alone. I don't listen to you, I sift everything, I bring everything down to reflex response, so I don't really hear you, which is the only way to manage it. But you've taken a new tack, Martha, over the past couple of centuries—or however long it's been I've lived in this house with you—that makes it just too much . . . too much" (Albee, 1963, p. 155).

The preceding exerpt from the popular play *Who's Afraid of Virginia Woolf?* dramatically illustrates the point that the partners in an interpersonal relationship create their own unique patterns of interaction as well as the climate and quality of the relationship; and the outcome—as in the marriage of George and Martha—may be destructive and maladaptive for one or both partners. In essence, the partners in an intimate relationship can create their own "heaven" or "hell" or perhaps even "purgatory."

Probably all of us have been involved at one time or another in a maladaptive and hurtful interpersonal relationship. And we have probably all asked such questions as "What went wrong?" "Was it my fault?" Unfortunately, it is often difficult or impossible to ascertain exactly what did go wrong after the termination of the relationship, but in many instances we may have a good idea. In any event, it may prove helpful to examine some of the ways in which interpersonal relationships can go seriously wrong.

Here then, our focus will be on three types of maladaptive interpersonal patterns which have seriously detrimental effects on one or both partners: (1) fraudulent interpersonal contracts; (2) collusion in interpersonal contracts; and (3) discordant interpersonal patterns. In the latter, we are not concerned with minor difficulties in accommodation but rather with a consistent pattern of dissonance and conflict which is highly destructive, as that described in the interaction of George and Martha.

Fraudulent interpersonal contracts

We have noted that as a relationship progresses beyond the initial encounter, the partners enter into an arrangement—usually of a tacit or informal nature—in which the "terms" of the relationship are agreed upon, as in a type of "contract." In essence, the partners stipulate the type of relationship they hope to achieve and what each expects to contribute and to receive from the relationship. Mutual acceptance of the terms of their "contract" usually indicates that each partner believes he is receiving a fair return on his investment—that is, the interpersonal exchange is as good as he could probably effect with other persons capable of delivering the same desired "commodities." Here we are, of course, using the social exchange model because it appears particularly helpful in understanding this type of maladaptive interpersonal pattern.

In a fraudulent interpersonal contract, the terms of the contract are violated by one partner in such a way as to exploit the other. Such fraudulent patterns may take a variety of forms, but Carson (1969) has delineated a common underlying sequence which may be summarized as follows:

1. *A* implicitly offers *B* a type of relationship in which *B* has a high degree of interest because it seems to offer favorable possibilities for satisfaction.

2. *B* indicates acceptance of the contract and proceeds with activities appropriate to the terms of the contract.

3. *A* then assumes a stance which makes it seem "justified" to alter the terms of the contract.

4. *B* is forced to accept the new terms, thus enabling *A* to achieve the type of relationship which he wanted to begin with.

Such an approach is considered "fraudulent" in that *A* presumably could not have achieved his objectives by an honest and straightforward approach, but only by deceit and fraud—by "setting *B* up as a mark."

B, however, is likely to sense that he has been

Her husband played around a lot, flagrantly, and I guess he always had. And I guess that was just part of what she accepted when she married him, because she must have known it was going to be like that. She pretended that she didn't notice what he was doing, but there it was and everybody knew. The marriage hung together, but I don't know how happy she could have been, or him either, for that part, because in later years I know they were pretty distant from each other.

"had," and the new contractual terms are likely to prove highly frustrating and detrimental to him as a person as well as damaging to the quality of the relationship. In fact, over time *B* may feel so frustrated and dissatisfied that he terminates the relationship. In this case *A* is also the loser providing he really did want to make the relationship work, albeit on his own rather selfish terms. Nevertheless, it is surprising—as we have seen—to note how many fraudulent interpersonal contracts do seem to endure, in marriage as well as other interpersonal settings.

Collusion

In collusion an interpersonal relationship is established and maintained only because the partners agree that certain deviant rules and norms of their own choosing will be substituted for established social rules and norms. In effect they enter into a conspiracy or collusion.

Of course there are many permissible life styles as well as types of interpersonal relationships in our society; and many of these do not conform strictly with established social rules and norms. In the present context, however, we are referring to the use of collusion in arriving at a contract which is maladaptive and destructive— usually for both partners.

One person usually takes the initiative in laying down the "terms" of the contract which

the other must meet; and typically these terms call for the partners to jointly deny or falsify some aspects of reality. For example, a person who drinks excessively may agree to enter into an intimate relationship only if his excessive drinking is accepted as normal by the other person. While the other person may not wish to accept these specific terms, he is forced to if he wishes to consummate the contract. Of course, he may anticipate rewards from the relationship which will outweigh this particular cost.

The ensuing relationship is labeled as maladaptive, however, because the rewards do not in fact justify the costs. The excessive drinking of one partner, for example, may seriously interfere with his occupational adjustment, his sexual performance, the couple's social life, and/or other aspects of their relationship. If his excessive drinking increases and hospitalization is required for treatment, then tremendous stress may be placed on the other partner —particularly in marital relationships. In nonmarital as well as marital relationships the result is likely to be highly detrimental to the relationship as well as to the persons involved, and it may well lead to termination of the relationship.

In some instances, two persons who share the same type of maladjustment may enter into a contractual arrangement—for example, two persons may stipulate that their excessive drinking will be accepted as normal. Here the terms are mutually satisfactory to each partner; but over time such excessive drinking is likely to create serious problems for one or both partners as well as to make a satisfying relationship impossible. Collusion may also occur after a relationship has been established. To cite an extreme example, one individual may accept and actually come to believe in the paranoid-delusional system of the other—a phenomenon referred to as *folie a deux*. Here again the long-range outcome is likely to have destructive consequences for both partners.

a number of areas in the relationship; or they may center on some enduring conflict.

Nye (1973) has delineated certain common sources of conflict which include: (1) *competition*—in which one partner gains something at the expense of the other; for example, one person proving his superiority in some area in such a way that the other is made to feel put down; (2) *domination*—in which one partner attempts to control the other person and makes him feel that his rights and integrity are being violated; (3) *failure*—in which both partners

 I know when he was staying with me a few years ago, he had the most incredible ability to make me lose my temper, more than anyone else I know. I think that he is the only person in my life that I ever actually threw things at. And I did that on two occasions. But I was still under control and when I threw them I deliberately did not aim at him, I deliberately aimed past him, so that I wouldn't hurt him, and yet hopefully would make the impression on him that I was serious. And yet I think with people like that, they've gained their ego satisfaction by making you lose your temper. And the very violence of your reaction proves to them they've accomplished something.

Discordant interpersonal patterns

Some degree of friction seems inevitable in intimate interpersonal relationships, but serious and continued disagreements and conflicts are detrimental to the persons involved as well as to the quality of the relationship. Such discordant interactions may result from contractual arrangements that turn out to be unsatisfactory to one or both partners and which, for some reason, have not been dealt with adequately via processes of interpersonal accommodation. These disagreements and conflicts may involve

resort to blaming each other when things go wrong in their efforts to achieve agreed-upon goals; (4) *provocation*—in which one partner consistently does things which he knows annoy the other, often as if he received some sort of satisfaction in "keeping things stirred up"; and (5) *value differences*—which may lead to serious disagreements about a variety of topics, including the spending of money and sexual behavior.

Closely related to the preceding sources of discordance but meriting special consideration are the problems elicited by disconfirming or confusing tactics on the part of one partner toward the other. One of these tactics involves *conflicting communications* in which the sender codes a message in such a way that it has two opposite meanings. For example, a young woman may be very seductive on her first date with a young man. But when he makes physical overtures, she reacts with surprise, shock, and rejection. Such a conflict between verbal and nonverbal components of a message is likely to leave the other person baffled. It may, of course, also leave the young man feeling foolish, put down, and hostile.

A variation on the theme of conflicting communications is referred to as the *double-bind*—in which the individual is "damned if he does and damned if he doesn't." For example, a boy may complain about his girl friend never taking the initiative in matters of affection, but when she does, he finds some excuse to reject her advances. In short, she cannot win no matter what she does in such a double-bind situation; and she too may end up feeling confused, devaluated, and discouraged.

Another disconfirming and confusing tactic involves disqualifying communications, which may in turn involve two somewhat different patterns. In the first pattern, an individual makes a statement such as "I always feel adequate and confident as a person"; then he disqualifies the statement by saying "but today I feel completely inadequate and shattered." A second and much more damaging type of disqualifying communication involves one person in a relationship continually disqualifying the statements made by the other. Instead of a person disqualifying his own statement concerning his feelings of adequacy and confidence, the other person denies the validity of the statement. As Laing and Esterson (1964) have so vividly expressed it:

"The ultimate of this is . . . when no matter how [a person] feels or how he acts, no matter what meaning he gives his situation, his feelings are denuded of validity, his acts are stripped of their motives, intentions, and consequences, the situation is robbed of its meaning for him, so that he is totally mystified and alienated" (1964, pp. 135–136).

There are many other types of maladaptive interpersonal patterns—particularly of a less serious nature—but the preceding ones are among those likely to prove most destructive.

Foundations of satisfying interpersonal relationships

Several recurring themes have emerged in the present chapter, perhaps the most clear-cut of which is the extent to which each person's interpersonal relationships influence the course of his life and the frustrations and satisfactions he experiences. A person's success in making friends, in attracting a desired mate and establishing a happy marriage, in raising children, and in achieving occupational adjustment depends heavily upon the ways in which he relates to significant others.

In spite of the importance of achieving satisfying interpersonal relationships, little empirical investigation has focused on this problem. Most of the literature on the subject is in the form of popular articles and books in which the authors describe techniques that anyone can presumably use to ensure good interpersonal relationships. Actually, of course, there are no simple techniques which can be applied effectively without an understanding of the principles which appear to underlie interpersonal relationships in general. For example, the tactic of praising others, often mentioned in popular writings, may backfire if the praise is insincere or used primarily to make others more amenable to our own wishes. In this sense, popular approaches are often misleading, and many people who adopt them in order to achieve better interpersonal relationships are shocked to find that they have, instead, reaped a harvest of dislike and hostility.

We shall endeavor in this section to present available research findings in this area as well as to point out certain conclusions that appear to follow logically from the general principles we have discussed.

The most important relationship in my life right now is my boy friend. As far as I'm concerned, he is the best thing that has ever happened to me. I don't feel like I'm becoming a 'product' of him, which I often sense happens when two people are together a lot. He and I are the same type people. Not that we are exactly alike, but many of our values, standings, and levels of importance are very much alike. I always sense that he accepts me completely. He seems to love even my faults and petty wishes, along with the good side of me. He is always willing to forgive and also—something very important to me—he knows what it means to work for a relationship.

I am sort of an easy-going personality. I have set values for myself, but I'm not so rigid that I can't accept that someone else feels a different way about something. When you look at it through their shoes you can get a whole new perspective.

Recognition of mutual purposes and rights

Most of the popular literature on interpersonal relationships not only tends to oversimplify but also typically has a "sales" approach. The emphasis is on influencing and even exploiting others. Thus it seems appropriate to begin our discussion by accentuating the importance of recognizing mutual purposes, rights, and responsibilities in establishing satisfying interpersonal relationships.

Commonality of purpose

Each person tries to meet certain needs through his relationship with others—perhaps for love and affection, social approval, self-esteem and worth, adequacy, or simply feeling related to a significant other. When the relationship meets one person's needs but fails to meet those of the other person, we have noted that it is likely to be difficult or impossible to maintain. Thus even the most generous and devoted friend may become tired of a relationship in which, literally or figuratively, he is continually lending and is never repaid. In essence, "to have a friend, you must be a friend."

For a relationship to meet the needs of both persons, a commonality of purpose is required. The importance of such shared purposes can be illustrated in many ways. In wartime, for example, two soldiers in combat may become "buddies" and form a close friendship; but after the war they return to different ways of life, and the bonds which once held them together are dissolved. Or a romantic relationship may be dissolved when one person wishes to get married and the other does not. Many friendships made

Whereas objects constitute a necessary and important part of our world, we merely manipulate, control, and use them for our convenience. Our transactions with them represent what Buber (1958) called *I-It* relationships. Some people, however, regard other individuals in essentially the same way—as dehumanized objects to be manipulated or used. But another person is a "thou," a presence, a person with dignity and integrity to be respected. A meaningful encounter with another human being is an *I-Thou* relation, not an *I-It* relation.

In our fast-moving, utilitarian, time-pressured society, it is all too easy to establish *I-It* relationships with both the people and the things in our world. To do so, however, is to cut ourselves off from the chance for establishing rich, meaningful, and authentic relationships with other human beings.

earlier in our lives terminate with time as situations and purposes change. In essence, "we no longer need each other." Finally, we may note the finding by Floyd and South (1973) that youths who felt their peer group could better meet their needs tended to become alienated from rather domineering parents; while those who felt their parents could better meet their needs usually maintained close relationships with their parents—often in spite of the "pull" exerted by the peer group and the parental controls imposed on them.

It would seem then that commonality of purpose and mutual need gratification are basic essentials for establishing and maintaining lasting interpersonal relationships. Again we come face to face with the social exchange model and the relation of cost to satisfaction in enduring relationships.

Respect for the rights and autonomy of others

A basic principle in building satisfying interpersonal relationships is that of respect for the rights and autonomy of the other person.

This principle is emphasized in the biblical injunction "Whatsoever ye would that men should do to you, do ye even so to them." The respect for the rights of the other person implied by the golden rule is necessary not only from a moral standpoint but from a practical one as well. We have noted, for example, the destructive effects on intimate interpersonal relationships when one partner attempts to infringe upon the rights and autonomy of the other. Violating these rights almost inevitably destroys any common ground for mutually satisfying interaction.

In general it would appear that recognition of the rights of each person can best be achieved in the context of a democratic approach—an approach which recognizes the individuality and autonomy of each individual, providing that he does not violate the rights of others. The other person is granted "life space" in which to work out his "way of being in the world." This does not mean that we accept his beliefs and values but rather that we acknowledge his freedom to entertain his own convictions while maintaining the same freedom for ourselves.

Adequate structure and communication

In some cases, structure and communication patterns are inherent in the social context in which the relationship takes place. For example, there is general agreement about the type of structure and communication between teacher and student, employer and employee, bishop and parish priest, general and lieutenant.

But in most of our more personal relationships—such as those involving husband and wife, parent and child, or friend and friend—the structuring and communication patterns are determined by the parties involved. This places considerable responsibility on each person in the relationship, if he wishes to make it a satisfying one.

The importance of adequate structuring

All interpersonal relationships *do* become structured with time, whether or not the persons involved take it upon themselves to establish a particular type of structure. To take a simple example, we may examine the behavior of a young couple who are dating. Unless they take active measures to structure the situation in terms of permissible limits of affection, of behavior with others, of mutual effort in maintaining their relationship, of courtesy and honesty in dealing with each other, such limits will eventually become established simply by what actually takes place—whether or not these limits are satisfactory for the individuals involved. Once certain patterns have been established, it becomes increasingly difficult to change the structuring. For example, the girl who has permitted sexual intimacies will find it much more difficult to limit such behavior thereafter than if she had structured the affectional limits differently in the first place.

Unfortunately, structuring is sometimes predetermined by the existence of certain emotional limitations. A person may habitually establish competitive relationships, no matter how inappropriate they may be in some situations, as in marriage. Or he may always be cooperative, so that he is unable to say "no" even when it needs saying. When a person can see in retrospect that he has tried to carry over a type of relationship from one situation, in which it is appropriate, to

another, in which it is inappropriate, he can begin to avoid making the same mistake by evaluating new situations in advance, thereby maintaining some control over the structuring.

Many of us are rather naïve in the matter of structuring interpersonal relationships in ways that are appropriate to the situation and person. Often we unwittingly encourage others to be overly familiar or to take advantage of us—and then blame *them* for an unsatisfactory relationship that has been largely of our own making. It is always important to examine in advance the type of relationship that is desirable—whether between employer and employee, executive and secretary, husband and wife, father and daughter, or friend and friend—and to take active measures to establish and maintain the relationship in the form we consider appropriate.

Learning to communicate more effectively

It is apparent that meaningful communication does not take place automatically in interpersonal relationships. But there are a number of factors which appear to foster effective communication—ranging from awareness of one's own stimulus value to active listening. Here we shall simply mention three interrelated factors which seem to be of key importance.

1. *Being a good "sender."* As a "sender," the individual has to know what he is trying to communicate and how to code the message in such a way that the receiver can interpret it accurately. If the sender is unclear about the message he is trying to convey or if he fails to code the message so that it is meaningful to the other person, the message is not likely to be received accurately. The high incidence of failure here is evidenced by frequent complaints, such as "I didn't mean that" and "You misunderstood what I was trying to say."

One common difficulty in coding a message appropriately stems from differences in background and frame of reference. In a relationship in which the persons come from quite different ethnic backgrounds, communication problems on the part of both sender and receiver are likely

 We're all so eager to tell people what we think and what we feel about something, that we really aren't paying attention to what they're saying, we're so busy thinking up what we're going to say.

to be encountered until a better understanding of each other's viewpoints is achieved. Conversely, commonality of background, assumptions, and purposes tends to facilitate effective communication in interpersonal relationships.

2. *Being a good receiver: active listening.* If we are to be good receivers, we must "listen actively" and make a sincere effort to understand what the other person is trying to communicate to us. We have probably all had the experience of feeling that the other person was not really listening—not really tuning us in. Perhaps he was too busy to take time to listen, did not want to be interrupted or to hear what we had to say, was trying to save time by jumping to conclusions about what we were going to say, or

perhaps he was only thinking about what *he* was going to say. As one exasperated college girl said about her date: "He spent the entire evening talking about himself and ended up thinking he knew all about me."

Active listening requires the development of specific skills which help us to interpret accurately what the other person is trying to communicate. One of the most important of these skills is *being sensitive to the feelings of others;* for as we have noted earlier, there are many situations in which we are called upon to interpret feelings rather than spoken words.

Although there are no simple rules for improving one's sensitivity to the needs and feelings of others, the following techniques are

COMMON ERRORS IN INTERPERSONAL COMMUNICATION

There are a number of factors which may lead to communication problems in interpersonal relations, even though the persons involved desire to understand each other and to make their relationship work. Among the more important of these, which may work singly or in combination, are:

1. *Differences in background and experience.* Differences in educational, ethnic, and other background factors can create difficulties in communication; words may mean different things to different people, depending on their past experiences.

2. *Selective attention.* Here the receiver only processes part of the information which is communicated by the other person and ignores the remainder. As a result he receives a fragmented rather than a complete message.

3. *Motivation.* As we have noted, we tend to perceive what we want to perceive; often this means interpreting a message in terms of what we would like it to mean rather than what the sender intended it to mean.

4. *Feelings and emotions.* A wide range of feelings and emotions, including insecurity, fear, or anger elicited by the other person or by situational factors can lead to misinterpretation by the receiver.

5. *Insensitivity.* There are many situations in which the feelings behind the words are more important than the words; failure of the receiver to perceive the feelings of the sender can be a potent source of misunderstanding.

often helpful: (a) being alert to the facial expression, posture, and voice intonation of the other person may help us to detect the feeling behind his words—trying to understand what he *wants* to say rather than what he *is* saying verbally; (b) asking questions involving the word *feeling* rather than *thinking*—thus giving the person an opportunity to express his feelings and helping him to realize that his feelings do matter; and (c) mirroring or reflecting the feelings which the other person appears to be expressing—in this way helping him to bring them into the open where both persons can examine them for what they are. Through the use of these techniques, it is often possible to detect the feelings of the other person, which may or may not be at variance with what he is actually saying.

3. *Utilizing metacommunication.* One key approach to fostering better understanding in communication involves the concept of *metacommunication*—of communication about ways of communicating. In an interpersonal relationship this might entail an analysis of such factors as (a) the amount of relevant information communicated vs. "noise," (b) the typical emotional climate created by talking about problems, (c) who does most of the talking and who does most of the listening, and (d) what areas or problems seem to elicit particular difficulties in communicating and understanding. Such information can prove helpful as a basis for making needed corrections in communication patterns.

In dealing with these various aspects of communication, we are also dealing with coping behaviors and styles in interpersonal relationships. For communication is merely a means—which can be used effectively or ineffectively—for transmitting information without which such relationships could not exist.

*Awareness, caring,
and integrity*

Carl Rogers and a number of other psychologists have emphasized the importance of being more aware, more open and honest, and more caring as essential to building satisfying interpersonal relationships. At first glance this may seem like belaboring the obvious, but the processes involved are considerably more subtle than one might initially think.

Awareness

Awareness comes in many forms, but three are particularly relevant in the present context: a realistic view of self; a realistic view of the other person; and an accurate view of the relationship.

1. *A realistic view of self.* As a starting point, this involves an accurate view of a person's own "stimulus value"—of how the other person sees him. He may view himself as generous, while the other person sees him as stingy; he may view himself as flexible, while the other views him as rigid; he may view himself as cooperative

patterns on which it is based, and the type of relationships it is likely to lead to.

2. *An accurate view of the other person.* An accurate view of the other person is equally important if we are to establish a satisfying interpersonal relationship. Often our experiences with others and our basic view of human nature permeate and distort our perceptions—even of those near and dear to us. Some of us take a dim view of human nature and are generally suspicious and wary in our encounters with other persons, while some of us take an opposite approach and are too open and trusting.

A common source of error in our perception of the other person—particularly during the period of getting acquainted—is the "halo effect." For example, when we know a person to be superior in some important respect, we may tend to put a "halo" over his head and, through a process of

 I'm madly in love with my boy friend. Every time I think about him a smile comes across my face, and when I see him I get all light headed, and when he touches me I get tingly. Everything he does is perfect.

and undemanding, while the other views him as competitive and highly demanding. While the other person's view of him may be more or less inaccurate, it is well worth considering as one source of feedback concerning his actual stimulus value.

Ring, Braginsky, and Braginsky (1966) have pointed out that each of us can be characterized by a given *interpersonal style.* For example, as noted in our review of interpersonal accommodation, some of us are open and honest in our relationships, while others tend to wear a mask and to be manipulative. Although we are likely to relate to different people in somewhat different ways, it does appear useful to try to become aware of our characteristic interpersonal style, the motives, assumptions, and coping

generalization, to overrate his qualities in other areas. And as we have noted, we often tend to see the other person as we would like him to be rather than as he really is—a tendency which is readily apparent in romantic "infatuations."

3. *An accurate view of the relationship.* When one is emotionally involved in an intimate relationship, it is often difficult to perceive the situation objectively and accurately. It is not only important to understand our own needs and motives in the relationship but also those of the other person—and this is not always an easy task. It seems relevant to ask ourselves what we are paying in terms of "cost" for the satisfactions we are receiving. Are we deceiving ourselves about the value of what we are receiving from the relationship? Is the cost greater than

I have a tendency in a relationship where I get emotionally involved to do far too much fantasizing about how the other person feels and about how the other person understands the relationship to be. I frequently find that the relationship I'm having is not the relationship they're having. I am now much more aware of when I'm doing it.

If you feel for people and care about them and know that someday you might be in the same situation and think and act in the same way, and if you're human and have compassion and understanding for your fellow man and you can zero in on emotions—you'll make it, baby, in this world.

the reward? And if the relationship is a truly satisfying one, it is important that the individual be both aware and appreciative of this fact if he wishes to maintain and further it.

Furthermore, if we consider the relationship to be a satisfying one, then it is important that we be alert for possible indications of trouble, such as signs of dissatisfaction from the other person. For building a satisfying interpersonal relationship requires effort on the part of both persons and the early detection and correction of misunderstandings, communication problems, conflicting purposes, or other possible difficulties. Unfortunately, many relationships which were once satisfying are allowed to deteriorate eventually and to terminate simply because of the failure of one or both partners to realize that vigilance and effort are costs involved in ensuring the continuation of a rewarding relationship. This often tragic result is illustrated by an excerpt from Thomas Wolfe:

"'Alone,' said Eliza, with the old suspicion. 'Where are you going?'

"'Ah,' he said, 'you were not looking, were you? I've gone'" (1970, p. 456).

Caring

Caring is an elusive concept which means many things, but perhaps its central theme is concern about and commitment to the well-being of the other person. Caring may be expressed in words, as when we tell the other person "I love you"; or it may be expressed in actions ranging from simple courtesy to support in times of severe stress or crisis for the other person.

Caring may take the form of expressing sincere appreciation of the good qualities of the other person—of confirming his worth as a human being. Each of us does have good qualities which merit appreciation, but all too often these qualities are taken for granted. Instead of appreciation, we are subjected to nagging criticism for real or alleged shortcomings and mistakes. Such criticism can do great harm to an interpersonal relationship, particularly when it is vindictive, as in the response "I told you so." Even though such criticism may be intended to be constructive, it is likely to prove destructive. As the Overstreets have pointed out:

"Wherever we turn in today's world, it seems, we find human beings who look guardedly or

vengefully at one another across barriers of old mistakes: mistakes that have never been openly acknowledged and that are still, in many cases, being defended; mistakes that, even where an effort has been made to straighten things out, have never been forgiven—much less forgotten" (1956, p. 104).

While truly constructive criticism may be appropriate at times, most people find that using criticism sparingly and developing the habit of appreciating the good qualities of the other person helps to reinforce these qualities and to improve their interpersonal relationships.

Integrity

The term *integrity* essentially refers to being honest with oneself and others. But even on a simple level, being honest is not always as easy as it might sound. Suppose your friend asks you if you like her new hair style. Even though you may not think it particularly becoming, it may not be very diplomatic to say "If you really want to know, I think it looks awful." For such a statement would be far from reassuring and would be of little positive value. Perhaps a more diplomatic and supportive answer would be simply "I would like to get used to it before I render an opinion." And if your opinion remains negative, you can tell her your true feelings at a later time—perhaps suggesting an alternative hair style that you think would be more attractive. But even here, the answer is not an easy one; for the moment a person evades the truth, he tends to initiate a process of deception which may make a satisfying relationship impossible. This point is very succinctly made in the following lines by Sir Walter Scott:

"O what a tangled web we weave,
When first we practise to deceive."

Maintaining one's integrity is often far more difficult than stating a simple opinion about some matter which seems relatively unimportant. It often requires that we "take a stand" when we believe that an important issue is at stake. For to maintain our own self-respect as well as the respect of the other person requires

that we stand up for what we believe in, even though we may know that it will lead to an unwanted conflict. But truthfulness and taking a stand imply confidence in the integrity of the other person as well as one's self—trust in his willingness to approach the problem realistically and to attempt to work out a constructive and mutually satisfactory solution.

In this context it may be emphasized that building a satisfying interpersonal relationship does not require that we avoid friction at all costs, but rather that when conflicts do arise we cope with them in effective ways. While it is essential to respect, to care about, and to be sensitive to the needs and feelings of the other person, it is equally essential to maintain one's personal integrity.

Helping each other grow as persons

I love you,
Not only for what you are,
But for what I am
When I am with you.
. . . .
I love you
For the part of me
That you bring out.

(Roy Croft)

As we have seen, our intimate interpersonal relationships have a profound influence upon us—whether for better or for worse. Thus it might be equally valid to substitute the word "hate" for "love" in the above poem. In any event, our relationships with others can diminish us or they can help us to grow as persons. In our discussion of disordered interpersonal relationships, we focused on the former; in the present and final section of this chapter we shall focus on those conditions in interpersonal relationships which help us to grow as persons—to actualize our potentialities as human beings. In so doing, we shall draw upon ideas formulated by Carl Rogers, Abraham Maslow, and Clark Moustakas.

From *Hold Me!* by Jules Feiffer. Copyright © 1960, 1961, 1962 by Jules Feiffer. Reprinted by permission of Random House, Inc.

Conditions that facilitate personal growth in interpersonal relationships

In the preceding part of this section on foundations of satisfying interpersonal relationships, we have dealt with many of the conditions which appear of crucial importance in facilitating personal growth in our relationships with significant others. However, there are several additional conditions which merit consideration.

1. *Openness.* In this context, openness refers not only to the lowering of defenses and the dropping of masks by each person in the relationship but also to the willingness of each to share beliefs, hopes, feelings, defeats, achievements, and despairs with the other. As we noted in the section on "the problem of self-disclosure," this does not necessarily mean completely "baring one's soul" to the other person. But it does mean being open and willing to exchange information that will hopefully contribute to better understanding and greater security in the relationship. As Rogers has expressed it, "We shall discover that security resides not in hiding oneself but in being more fully known, and consequently in coming to know the other more fully" (1968, p. 269).

2. *Empathy.* A second condition which fosters growth is the ability of each person in the relationship to understand the private world of the other. In essence, empathy means that each knows what the other person has experienced, is experiencing, and is trying to communicate. Since each person expresses himself in terms of his own experiencing, it becomes crucially important that the other person understand.

Such a high level of understanding is not easily achieved, and there is always the danger that it will not be achieved at all. In the latter instance, the individual is forced back into his private world where significant portions of his experiencing—his beliefs, feelings, and so on—are shut off from the other. In essence, we are not dealing with one whole person communicating his experiencing to another whole person. Rather we are dealing with two people who can understand only fragments of each other. In this sense, the mutual sharing and understanding that might have fostered personal growth tends to be blocked.

3. *Unconditional acceptance.* Rogers and Stevens (1967) have suggested that "unconditional positive regard" or acceptance is essential if each person in the relationship is to feel free to share his private world with the other. Unconditional positive regard means that one person does not take a judgmental attitude toward the experiences revealed to him by the other—that he does not, for example, approve of some experiences and disapprove of others. Unconditional positive regard means listening and trying to understand the other person's experiencing without reservations or evaluations.

A judgmental attitude almost inevitably forces the other person to retreat into his own private world. This in turn has two negative results: first, it blocks further sharing—at least in certain areas—and hence mutual understanding; second, it blocks the possibility that by revealing and discussing his experiences the individual will be better able to understand his own experiencing and hence to grow as a person. Conversely, when acceptance and awareness are combined, they become powerful forces toward personal growth. Rogers has described this as the feeling that "at last someone understands how it feels and seems to be *me* without wanting to analyze me or judge me. Now I can blossom and grow and learn" (1969, pp. 111–112).

4. *Approval despite disagreement.* While we can listen and try to understand the experiencing of the other person without taking a judgmental attitude, this does not mean that we have to agree with everything he *believes in or does*. Some degree of interpersonal accommodation is essential in building a satisfying relationship, and this inevitably involves dealing with matters on which the persons involved are in disagreement.

But in disagreeing with the other person, it is important that we approve of him as a person—that we do not reject him. In a parent-child relationship, for example, it would be harmful to the child as well as to the relationship if the parent were to call the child a thief and reject him because the child had stolen something. It would be far more constructive to make it clear that the child is loved as a person, but that his behavior presents a problem that must be dealt with. This makes it unnecessary for the child to withdraw or become defensive; for by being helped to feel that he is worthy of love and respect, he is better able to look at his behavior objectively as something that he himself can benefit from changing in a particular way.

In adult interpersonal relationships too, it is of vital importance that when one person disagrees with the assumptions or actions of the other that he does not reject the other person. For to do so elicits hurt and defensiveness and makes the disagreement much more difficult to deal with in a constructive way.

Putting it all together

In our discussion of interpersonal relationships a number of recurring themes have emerged which are directly relevant to growth-producing interpersonal relationships: (1) the concept of balancing satisfaction and cost; (2) the centrality of communication; (3) the need for adequate structure; (4) the necessity of interpersonal accommodation; and (5) conditions which seem to be constructive or destructive in building satisfying interpersonal relationships. All of these themes are interrelated and form part of a total picture which provides us with needed perspective on our relationships with significant others.

Carl Rogers has attempted to extend this perspective by projecting the potential for change and enrichment in the interpersonal world by the year 2000:

"There can be more of intimacy, less of loneliness, an infusion of emotional and intellectual learning in our relationships, better ways of resolving conflicts openly, man-woman relationships which are enriching, family relationships which are real, a sense of community which enables us to face the unknown. All this is possible if as a people we choose to move into the new mode of living openly as a continually changing process" (1968, pp. 280–281).

 Summary and a look ahead

In the present chapter we have looked at the nature and impact on our lives of one-to-one relationships with significant others. We began by examining different models of interpersonal relationships, including the social exchange, role, games, and general systems models.

In the next section we dealt with the various processes involved in relating to significant others. Among these are the nature of the encounter, interpersonal perception and attraction, interpersonal accommodation, and self-disclosure. The encounter is the first step in relating to others. Once the encounter occurs, the outcome of a relationship is quite unpredictable, since there are so many factors which determine whether the relationship will continue. Similar purposes, beliefs, and values are some of the more influential characteristics that tend to make others attractive to us. In addition, the crucial importance of communication, structure, and the resolution of disagreements and conflicts are aspects of accommodation necessary for a continuing relationship.

And, as a relationship continues, self-disclosure increases, and with it all the advantages and potential dangers of revealing intimate information about oneself.

In the latter part of this chapter we discussed three common maladaptive interpersonal patterns: fraudulent interpersonal contracts, collusion, and discordant interpersonal relationships. Finally, we covered some of the foundations of satisfying interpersonal relationships, including (1) recognition of mutual purposes and rights; (2) adequate structure and communication; (3) awareness, caring, and integrity; and (4) helping each other grow as persons.

Chapter 10 will apply the principles involved in relating to others to the special setting of intimate relationships and marriage. Here we shall discuss the changing patterns and attitudes toward marriage, the factors involved in the choice of a mate, the characteristics of happy and unhappy marriages, the problems of divorce, and other forms of intimate relationships.

10
Marriage and Intimate Relationships

Changing attitudes and behaviors
Choosing a mate
"Living happily ever after"
Unhappiness and dissolution of marriage
Other forms of intimate relationships

Of all the endeavors that exert their influence on people's lives in our culture, the quest for intimate relationships must be the most sought after, longed for, dreamed about, sung about, joked about, and cursed at. Few human experiences inspire the pangs, joys, ecstasies, fears, cheers, and tears that accompany the growth and development of intimacy. Such relationships are recognized as a major source of need fulfillment, stress, and challenge in our lives.

For most individuals, the achievement of intimacy with one person of the opposite sex is a major goal of life, marking maturity and adulthood as well as personal fulfillment and achievement. Only a very small percentage of Americans will not marry at some point in their lives. The vast majority will marry at least once in the hope of experiencing the benefits, challenge, and excitement of intimacy and companionship.

Intimate relationships vary considerably from culture to culture and within cultures. In this country, both the typical form and the expected content of man-woman intimate relationships have altered significantly in recent years. The reasons for making commitments and for entering legally sanctioned relationships,

as well as the behavior of both men and women within such relationships, have changed and continue to change. This chapter will attempt to explore common experiences in today's marriages and other intimate relationships, consider changes in patterns and the reasons for them, and examine what is known about factors that affect the development and satisfactions of intimate relationships.

Changing attitudes and behaviors

Despite the amount of publicity devoted to alternatives to legally sanctioned marriage, it is still predicted that 97 percent of American men and 96 percent of American women will marry at some time in their lives (Bernard, 1973). A recent book on marriage ceremonies reports that the number of fairly traditional ceremonies is increasing rather than decreasing, while the expenditures for the caterers, chapels, flowers, gifts, and other wedding paraphernalia continue

to mount, having grossed $7 billion in 1971 (Seligson, 1973). Couples still vow to love and honor each other, although the term "obey" is increasingly deleted from the service. And most individuals who enter marriage do so with certain expectations about fidelity, security, permanence, and prescribed roles for both husband and wife.

But despite these regularities, there is considerable ferment surrounding traditional assumptions and practices, and there are many indications that the relationships men and women establish in the late 1970s and the 1980s may be different from the relationships established by their parents. Here we are concerned with pointing up some of these trends and their suspected causes.

New goals in man-woman relationships

Much has been written about the relatively new concept of marriage as primarily a companionship—a relationship to serve the individuals, and thus determined more by their particular motives and personalities than by social and economic pressures.

"With all the variations among American families, it is apparent that they are all in greater or lesser degree in a process of change toward an emerging type of family that is perhaps most aptly described as the 'companionship' form. This term emphasizes the point that the essential bonds in the family are now found more and more in the interpersonal relationships of its members, as compared with those of law, custom, public opinion, and duty in the older institutional forms of the family" (Burgess, 1964, p. 196).

Psychological need fulfillment

Young people have always seen marriage as a way of meeting their needs. But today the needs they hope to meet are different. In contempo-

affords the opportunity for change, development, inspiration, and encouragement of individuality. Carl Rogers, writing on the process of "becoming partners," expresses this emphasis as he suggests various elements which contribute to meaningful and continuing relationships:

"Perhaps I can discover and come closer to more of what I really am deep inside—feeling sometimes angry or terrified, sometimes loving and caring, occasionally beautiful and strong or wild and awful—without hiding these feelings from myself. Perhaps I can come to prize myself as the richly varied person I am. Perhaps I can openly be more of this person. If so, I can live by my own experienced values, even though I am aware of all of society's codes. Then I can let myself be all this complexity of feelings and meanings and values with my partner—be free

 I think that marriage is good after you've loved many people and done many things, and the person I would want to marry is the kind of person where we can both have whatever we're doing, and keep it going and still love each other and still need each other for certain things, but not *too* much.

rary America, most people probably do not marry primarily to meet sexual, economic, or social needs as before, but to gain psychological satisfactions. In part, this change reflects the fact of affluence in our society, in which maintenance needs are of less concern than actualization needs. Marriage is anticipated more as a means of gaining companionship, mutual emotional support, a secure "home base," and most of all an intimate relationship in which to share all aspects of one's life.

For many, even companionship is not enough. More and more, people look to an intimate relationship as a medium for personal growth and self-actualization. It is not enough to have a warm, supportive, and dependable other person with whom life is comfortable; rather, couples increasingly seek a relationship which

enough to give of love and anger and tenderness as they exist in me. Possibly then I can be a real member of a partnership, because I am on the road to being a real person. And I am hopeful that I can encourage my partner to follow his or her own road to a unique personhood, which I would love to share" (1972, p. 209).

Toward openness

Another change in the goals of intimate relationships appears to be an effort of couples to know each other fully and without façade. Many couples feel that dating and courting rituals are artificial and limited means of obtaining information necessary to make decisions about future relations. Dating often entails attempts to impress or influence the other person so that one's own needs will be met. While formal

My folks have a living-together, putting-up-with-each-other type of relationship. It was a good example of what I didn't want in a marriage, or a relationship.

 He didn't want to get married, on philosophical grounds—not believing in marriage and the strictures of marriage and all of that. So we began talking about what kind of commitment each of us would be willing to make. And when it came right down to it, I discovered I really didn't want to commit myself—sell myself into bondage, it seemed like—in some of the old traditional ways of marriage. So eventually we came to a kind of compromise agreement of what we each wanted—I wanted more than he did—and what each of us was willing to compromise on.

dating may serve some useful functions, particularly at early stages of a relationship, many couples seek to expand the range and authenticity of their mutual experience and knowledge. One outcome of this new goal is the practice of "living together" before marriage (and in some cases, instead of marriage). Premarital sexual relations may also be construed in many instances as a couple's efforts to achieve full sharing and knowledge of each other in their quest for genuineness in their relationships.

Challenges to old patterns and assumptions

Our progress upward in Maslow's need hierarchy—away from material and maintenance needs and even security needs toward personal growth and actualization—is only one factor contributing to the mounting challenges to traditional marriage. Two others are ease of divorce and the biological fact that people live longer than ever before. Instead of marrying, bearing children and raising them, and then dying, all within a 30-year period, today's couples can expect 40 or 50 years together, less than half of which may be taken up with childrearing. The mobility and density of our population are further disruptive factors, bringing us into contact with an enormous variety of persons; for most of us, the opportunity for a quiet, relatively isolated and stable existence has all but disappeared. These and other factors inevitably affect the relationships we build. Three challenges to our traditional patterns of marriage merit special discussion here.

The challenge to permanence of marriage

"Till death do us part" has been an indisputable element of marriage vows. The Western marriage has always tended to include the assumption of permanence, consistent with its recognized goal of meeting the partners' needs for security.

Few people marry today with any clear expectation that their relationship will *not* be permanent. Nevertheless, for a variety of reasons, marital permanence is difficult to attain. As Alvin Toffler notes:

". . . Even in a relatively stagnant society, the mathematical odds are heavily stacked against any couple achieving . . . the ideal of parallel growth. The odds for success positively plummet, however, when the rate of change in society accelerates, as it now is doing. In a fast-moving society, in which many things change, not once, but repeatedly, in which the husband moves up and down a variety of economic and social scales, in which the family is again and again torn loose from home and community, in which individuals move further from their parents, further from the

depend upon the law or other outside institutional props to support their marriage are likely to let the conscious, voluntary supports decay.

"Without the coercion of the formal institutional structure . . . each day the unmarried man and woman living together are more likely than married people to reaffirm their decision to be a couple and do what's needed to make the relationship stronger and happier. What they do, they do in relation to each other, not because once, long ago, they made a promise to live together the rest of their natural born lives, not because of money or social pressure" (1973, pp. 107–8).

If they can grow and change together, fine, but if not, they are free to recognize their divergence and act accordingly. There is some evidence

 The word 'permanence' in a marriage strikes me kind of funny right away. It seems like nobody ever knows if something's forever or not. I mean, you can never promise anybody that it's going to be forever, 'cause you don't know. You're getting married because you think you're two people who want to live together and make a commitment to one another. And if it lasts forever, that's fine, and if it doesn't, there's not a whole lot that you can do about it. So you just do it.

religion of origin, and further from traditional values, it is almost miraculous if two people develop at anything like comparable rates.

"If, at the same time, average life expectancy rises from, say, fifty to seventy years, thereby lengthening the term during which this acrobatic feat of matched development is supposed to be maintained, the odds against success become absolutely astronomical" (1970, p. 222).

Not only is it increasingly difficult to sustain an intimate relationship because of changes within individuals, roles, institutions, pressures, interests, and the like, but many are suggesting that a commitment to permanence should not even be made. Jessie Bernard notes that advocates of "renewable marriage" argue that couples who

from psychological research that ". . . commitment will be strongest when it is embedded in a context of continuing choice" (Rubin, 1973).

Many couples respond to the issue by either avoiding a legally binding commitment, or else establishing an agreement within a legal marriage that they will review constantly or periodically whether they wish to continue the relationship. In such a context, many report that because they keep freely choosing to stay with their partner, their caring feels more genuine and immediate.

The question of permanence poses the dilemma of freedom vs. security in relationships. Most persons appear to hope for an enduring relationship; yet individual freedom is clearly an

I have always followed him in his career, wherever he went, and been supportive of him in his career, to the extent that I had no career that *I* considered a career. In other words, to me being a mother and taking care of children is not totally fulfilling me. And housework . . . cleaning toilets still just turns me off completely.

important value and may be growing in significance for both women and men. The decision each couple makes about permanence-security-freedom will be made in a complex context of many values that each person is attempting to pursue. Renewable marriages, trial marriages, marriage contracts, and other forms that recognize the strong possibility of impermanence from the start will be appropriate only for some couples. Those who value freedom and choice may experience benefits from such an arrangement yet may pay a price in insecurity and anxiety about continuation of their relationship. Moreover, "there should be . . . no illusion that breaking up a marriage is any easier because its possibility was anticipated. There is always heartache in the breakdown of a human relationship as intense as that of marriage. . . . Divorce or nonrenewal, call it what you like, will be as painful in the future under one name as under any other" (Bernard, 1973, p. 109).

The challenge to fidelity

Along with permanence, there has always been an emphasis upon sexual fidelity in marriage in the Western world. Exclusivity is anticipated in marriage; in most marriage ceremonies couples pledge fidelity, and sexual infidelity is widely regarded as both legally and morally wrong. Nevertheless, as with permanence, the discrepancy between principle and reality is leading many to question the principle itself.

In a recent survey of attitudes of college-age subjects and their parents, Yankelovich (1969) found that while most thought that extramarital relationships were morally wrong, fewer of the younger subjects than of their parents held the view. Some psychiatrists and social scientists have argued that extramarital relations are not necessarily detrimental to marital relationships and in some cases may be beneficial.

Needless to say, the issue is an enormously complex and potentially explosive one within a given partnership. Yet, more and more often, couples reject the implied ownership of the partner which they feel complete fidelity suggests, and seek means of expressing and sharing intimacy with each other in ways that do not require sexual exclusiveness. Specific principles are yet to be formulated; there are few role models to imitate; and guidelines for decisions are absent. Meanwhile, an increasing proportion of couples will experience fidelity as something to decide about rather than simply expect.

The rejection of rigid roles

Careful examination of husbands' and wives' responses in research suggests that men and women not only regard marriage differently in general, but also experience their own marriages differently. This is true for many aspects of the marriage—sexuality, decision making, power. In one of the studies reviewed by Bernard (1973), more than 25 percent of the couples even failed to agree on who mowed the lawn. So it is misleading to speak of "marriage"; we need to specify whether it is "the husband's marriage" or "the wife's marriage" we are talking about.

1. *The husband's marriage.* Marriage often gets a bad press among men. "Men have cursed it, aimed barbed witticisms at it, denigrated it, bemoaned it—and never ceased to want and need it or to profit from it" (Bernard, 1973, p. 17). Research from a variety of sources comparing married men with men who never married is unequivocal in supporting the institution of marriage in terms of physical health, mental health, earnings, low rates of criminality, and length of life. Not only do married men show superiority on all these measures compared with unmarried men, but they are also far more likely to report themselves as "very happy" (Bradburn, 1969).

Although there are various explanations for such findings, the most potent one is that men greatly benefit from having a wife to care for their needs, physical and emotional; they thrive on the security, stability, and support of orderly, clean, well-fed, companionable lives. Although responsible for the onerous task of providing for the financial support of the family, most husbands are free to pursue the jobs and interests they wish and exercise power and authority over their families, and they can reasonably expect to be fed, sheltered, clothed, nursed, sexually fulfilled, nurtured, and humored by a wife who "knows her place."

2. *The wife's marriage.* If the above remarks seem provocative, let us consider the research findings on the wife's marriage.

"There is very considerable research literature reaching back over a generation which shows that: more wives than husbands report marital frustration and dissatisfaction; more report negative feelings; more wives than husbands report marital problems; more wives than husbands consider their marriages unhappy, have considered separation or divorce, have regretted their marriages; and fewer report positive companionship. Only about half as many wives (25%) as husbands (45%) say that there is nothing about their marriage that is not as nice as they would like. And twice as many wives (about a fourth) as husbands (about 12 percent) in a Canadian sample say that they would not remarry the same partner or have doubts about it" (Bernard, 1973, p. 28).

Not only do married women report greater marital unhappiness than married men, but they also report greater symptoms of psychological and emotional disturbance than do married men (Knupfer, Clark, & Room, 1966; National Center for Health Statistics, 1970). In addition, married women fare much worse than *single* women in terms of impaired mental health (Srole et al., 1962; Knupfer, Clark, & Room, 1966; National Center for Health Statistics, 1970). Reflecting upon such results, Bernard notes the demoralizing, nongrowth-inducing as-

 When I am working, he has dinner ready for me, or gets my breakfast and makes my lunch to take to work. But then when he's busy, I cook. We very often don't even say who's going to cook any particular meal, in advance. He enjoys cooking, and I do more so now that I know it's not expected of me—I don't 'have to' do it. There may also be nights where we're both hungry, and he doesn't get up to cook and I don't get up to cook, so we go out to eat.

pects of home management and child care with relatively few resources for personal self-development, and concludes, pithily, "in truth, being a housewife makes women sick."

Rather than maintain the traditional patterns of husband-dominance and wife-submission, husband-responsible and wife-dependent, husband-instrumental and wife-emotionally expressive, many couples have begun to question such beliefs and behaviors. The "equal partner" marriage, however, while widely accepted in theory is rarely practiced. Couples often find it extremely difficult even to modify patterns of sharing

housework, much less tackle more elusive social and emotional sex-role patterns. While both men and women acknowledge the need to modify constricting and stultifying expectations about appropriate sex-role behavior, with the goal of greater personal responsibility and individual growth for both, considerable effort is required to succeed. On the other hand, continued challenging of the traditional sex roles promises to pay off in many ways. Women can expect increased autonomy, reduced dependency, and more varied personal development, while men may hope to achieve relief from the burden of total economic responsibility and gain an opportunity to express more nurturant and intuitive traits than have been accepted in the traditional stereotype of "masculinity."

Sexual behavior and attitudes today

Changes in marriage and the new alternatives to traditional marriage are often attributed in part to changes in sexual attitudes and behavior. It seems more likely, however, that each has both caused and been caused by the other.

The "new" sexual freedom

A pressing problem for the adolescent and young adult prior to marriage is how to gratify his or her sexual needs. Although the sex drive

ment—and those who believe that the new sexual freedoms are largely a myth and that actual sexual practices have changed little, although attitudes clearly have changed. A more moderate view would be that real changes in behavior have occurred, but not necessarily in the direction of licentiousness and promiscuity. One recent study, for example, found that the most significant change in the sexual activity of college women in the past twenty years is that more of them masturbate than did previously (Simon & Gagnon, 1973). Participation in premarital sexual behavior appears to have increased, particularly for females. In a survey of the sex practices of 2200 unmarried juniors and seniors in colleges and universities in the United States, Packard (1968) found that 43 percent of the 21-year-old females and 57 percent of the 21-

 I think I'm pretty old fashioned. I have some very open views on sex, for instance—boy and girl relationships. That is up with the modern thing. Only I also feel that you go to bed when you really want to, but you don't follow every single impulse that you have.

greatly increases in strength following puberty, a young person is not usually in a position to marry until several years later. Traditional standards for sexual behavior in our society have emphasized abstinence from sexual relations prior to marriage. In the past few decades, however, the challenge to such standards has accelerated. In fact, a Gallup Poll of 1500 respondents nationwide found that in the four-year period between 1969 and 1973 the percentage believing that premarital sex was wrong dropped from 68 to 48 (*Los Angeles Times,* Aug. 12, 1973).

There is controversy between those who believe on the one hand that we have rushed into an era of promiscuity, where complete sexual expressiveness is being encouraged without regard for morals, laws, or personal commit-

year-old males reported having had sexual intercourse. This contrasts with figures of 27 and 51 percent, respectively, for college-educated subjects in the earlier Kinsey studies. A recent national survey of a cross-section of 13- to 19-year-olds revealed that 52 percent have had sexual intercourse (Sorensen & Hendin, 1973). However, these studies, and others, do suggest that despite increased sexual behavior among unmarried persons, there is no evidence of widespread indiscriminate sexual activity. Even among those who no longer consider marriage a prerequisite for sexual relations, there is a strong emphasis on some kind of loving relationship or mutual commitment before sexual involvement (Simon & Gagnon, 1973). And while many more unmarried couples live together today than they did a generation ago, it is hardly the "shacking up" for pure sexual revelry that many believe. Such couples tend to be rather traditionally monogamous. Katchadourian and Lunde (1972) suggest that their behavior resembles that of their parents, who also implicitly accepted sexual activity for engaged couples. A major difference is that today's couples may be younger than couples were in the 1930s and 1940s.

While there does not appear to be much evidence of rampaging, promiscuous sexual behavior among young people, this is not to deny that a veritable revolution has occurred in attitudes toward sexuality. There is increased acceptance of sexual expression and experimentation, and more open discussion and expectation of enjoyment among all ages. But free sexual expression does not come naturally and pain-

evidence of their sexual conquests. Such pressure violates their freedom to choose their own form of sexual expression, and for the women it adds the insults of manipulation and humiliation to the injuries of discrimination and restriction. Ingrid Bengis notes an experience common to women:

"I cannot stand to walk down the street and hear men make 'psst, psst' noises at me from the sidewalk or from the safety of their car. I cannot stand riding the subways during the rush hour. Both situations turn me into a manhater. . . . A similar kind of impersonal hatred crops up in me whenever I hitchhike and am picked up by someone who, for as long as I am with him, considers my body to be his possession. . . . Such problems occur . . . every time a woman decides to do something alone, whether it is going for a walk or

 The world has set a standard on the sexes and that is that the male should go out and sow his wild oats before he is married but the female stay a virgin till married. Unfortunately this cannot quite happen, for obvious reasons.

lessly to all. Whether or not to engage in sexual relationships remains a source of conflict for many—not only young people, but adults of all ages. Widowed and divorced women not infrequently consult their adult daughters on sexual matters as they face a challenge that was denied to women in a more restrictive day.

The double standard

It is well known that despite the traditional standards against premarital and extramarital sexual relationships for both men and women, men's "transgressions" are often met with a wink and a smile. A sexually active man may be viewed as a carefree, pleasure-loving "swinger," while a sexually active woman may be called a nymphomaniac or at least be seen as immoral. Actually, men are often under pressure to earn membership in the tribe of males by displaying

sitting in a bar or restaurant or taking a trip to the beach. Whereas there is nothing at all extraordinary about a man alone, a woman alone is often thought of as somehow incomplete, so that seeking a secluded corner of a beach means that someone will follow you . . . ; sitting at a bar, even if you just want to watch what's going on or do some thinking over a glass of something or other, means that you are waiting to be picked up, and if you walk down the street alone at night, your solitude implies to many men that you are sexually available" (1972, pp. 10, 14, 16–17).

Novelist Alix Kates Shulman, in *Memoirs of an Ex-Prom Queen* describes similar experiences of sexual depersonalization of women. The narrator, a young woman in her late teens, has taken a summer job:

"It was all very fine for Emerson to insist that 'nothing can bring you peace but the triumph of

principles'; but I could clearly see that if I wanted to keep my job I would really have to go out with Jan Pulaski.

"Two nights later right on schedule I was sitting nervously beside Jan in his two-tone blue hard-top convertible careening down a mountain toward Mirror Lake. How would I ever get out of this?

"The instant Jan had appeared behind The Zoo with his muscular neck confined in finery, a silk handkerchief protruding from his jacket pocket and his untamable curls slicked down, I saw the whole scenario.

"Though the wolf had donned sheep's clothing, he didn't fool me for an instant. He simply intended to have me as a last course instead of as a first. . . .

"I could tell by the pride in his voice that the 'little spot' was either going to be very expensive or very romantic or perhaps a place where Jan knew the head waiter. I saw the whole evening stretching before me like one of Fritz's five-course dinners, with me the pièce de résistance. First the little spot where I would be expected to drink and be impressed; then somewhere for a bite to eat; then a feeler to see if I was ready yet, and if not (and I wouldn't be!), then a nightcap at another little spot; and finally, no matter what I'd say, off to park the car at some natural wonder to admire the view and devour me. There wasn't a thing I could do to prevent it, for, having got himself up in this necktie and pomade, Jan was far too uncomfortable and ridiculous to risk not having his way. He would be spending too much and trying too hard to be willing to go away hungry" (1972, pp. 103–4).

Although research findings cited earlier indicate that women are freeing themselves somewhat from the double standard which restricts and often distorts their sexuality, the inequities have by no means vanished. Packard (1968) found that while the majority of college women said they would not be troubled by the knowledge that their marital partner had had premarital sexual experiences with one or more other persons, more than two-thirds of the college men indicated that they would be troubled to some extent at a reverse situation. On the other hand, a more recent study of adolescents' sexual attitudes found that 65 percent of the males did not agree with the statement "I wouldn't want to marry a girl who isn't a virgin at marriage" (Sorensen & Hendin, 1973).

Masters and Johnson (1970), pioneering sex researchers and therapists, report that orgasmic dysfunction and other complaints of their female patients are often related to the woman's inability to accept naturally occurring sexual arousal, due largely to social conditioning against it. Careful research (Masters and Johnson, 1966; Fisher, 1973; Sherfey, 1973) has gone a long way toward exploding myths about female sexual inferiority and myths about female responsivity and orgasm. Hopefully, these advances, along with women's growing determination to achieve full equality in all spheres of living, will contribute to mature individual choice and acceptance of responsibility sexually as in other ways. Meanwhile, as a heritage of many assumptions and attitudes about female sexuality, many women continue to experience considerable conflict and distress over sexual matters.

The emphasis on sexual performance

Growing emphasis on sexual expression in relationships offers opportunity to move away from arbitrary restriction and toward personal choice and responsibility. But there is another side to the new freedom. Many contend that we have entered a phase of overt preoccupation with sex—mass-produced, slickly marketed, dehumanizing, performance-oriented sex. Some social commentators suggest that we are "doing it more and enjoying it less," that, in fact, the new freedom causes new anxiety. Rollo May, existential psychotherapist and author, laments the "banalization of sex":

"By anesthetizing feeling in order to perform better, by employing sex as a tool to prove prowess and identity, by using sensuality to hide sensitivity, we have emasculated sex, and left it vapid and empty. The banalization of sex is well-aided and abetted by our mass communication. For the plethora of books on sex and love which flood the market have one thing in common—they oversimplify love and sex, treating the

topic like a combination of learning to play tennis and buying life insurance. In this process, we have robbed sex of its power by sidestepping eros; and we have ended by dehumanizing both" (1972, pp. 64–65).

In addition to the dehumanization of sex by overemphasis upon proficiency and performance, another problem is the lack of freedom of choice which occurs in some instances. The "embarrassed virgin" may come to feel that his or her behavior is not normal. Men and women may be drawn into sexual relations they do not wish because they imagine sex is "expected" and are unwilling to attend to their inner reluctance for fear of social disapproval.

No one can state with certainty how much effect "the pill" and other widely available contraceptives have had in increasing premarital sexual activity. Although a blessing in many ways, contraceptives have the potential for causing many conflicts. They have taken away the classic defense and forced women to make their choice on the basis of other values. Despite the pill's availability, however, the continuing high rate of unwanted pregnancies attests in part to women's difficulty in choosing to use it. Many women have remarked that they are often reluctant to use it not only because it "spoils the spontaneity of sex" but also because it signifies that they have freely, consciously decided to engage in sexual relationships.

A further difficulty is that both men and women, in an atmosphere of free sexual experimentation, expect themselves to act without inhibition and perform with great competence and variety, and make sexual excitement a high priority. As Lydon expresses it:

"Rather than being revolutionary, the present sexual situation is tragic. Appearances notwithstanding, the age-old taboos against conversation about personal sexual experience still haven't broken down. This reticence has allowed the mind-manipulators of the media to create myths of sexual supermen and superwomen. So the bed becomes a competitive arena, where men and women measure themselves against these mythical rivals, while simultaneously trying to live up to the ecstasies promised them by the marriage

manuals and the fantasies of the media. ("if the earth doesn't move for me, I must be missing something," the reasoning goes.) Our society treats sex as a sport, with its record-breakers, its judges, its rules, and its spectators" (1971, p. 66).

Obviously, all the expectations surrounding sexual behavior in our era of "sexual freedom" can be a painful burden. Perhaps more than ever before, individuals must evaluate the meaning of sexual relations for them and choose for themselves how to satisfy their sexual needs without doing violence to other needs and values. Like all freedoms, sexual freedom exacts the heavy cost of personal choice and responsibility.

Choosing a mate

Romantic myth has it that "marriages are made in heaven," that couples are "destined to marry." The fact is, however, that the origins of most partnerships are somewhat more mundane than heavenly. Although women may aspire after Paul Newman and men after Raquel Welch, they settle for people rather more like themselves. Considerable research has been conducted to determine mate selection factors. It is possible that the variables will ultimately yield a computer program capable of predicting who an individual should marry. In the present state of the science, however, as this section will show, we are probably no closer to successful computer-made marriages than to heaven-made ones.

First, however, we need to consider some of the reasons why people marry at all.

Reasons for marrying

For many, marriage is assumed to be a part of life, so that "reasons" may not be verbalized by them. Others, if asked, typically cite the following reasons for marriage.

Companionship and personal growth
As noted earlier, the search for economic security and sexual satisfactions are no longer pre-

dominant reasons for marriage for most couples. Regardless of the style of partnership they choose, most couples are after companionship, satisfaction of their psychological needs, and personal growth. Yet, the roles of love and loneliness should not be overlooked.

Romantic love

Love and marriage go together like a horse and carriage in the minds of most people. Anthropologist Ralph Linton remarked that:

"All societies recognize that there are occasional violent, emotional attachments between persons of opposite sex, but our present American culture is practically the only one which has attempted to . . . make them the basis for marriage" (1936, p. 175).

The romantic ideal which is such a preoccupation for so many has the following ingredients: the idea that love is fated and uncontrollable, strikes at first sight, transcends social bound-

"You're terribly unhappy."

"I'm morose . . . probably like it that way."

"You have suffered a great deal," she said. *"I see it in your face."*

"I've been diligent only in self-pity," he said, *"have turned away from everything difficult, and what you see is the scars of old acne shining through my beard; I could never give up chocolate and nuts."*

"You're very wise," she said.

"No, but intelligent."

They talked about love, beauty, feeling, value, love, life, work, death—and always she came back to love. They argued about everything, differed on everything, agreed on nothing, and so she fell in love with him. *"This partakes of the infinite,"* she said.

But he, being an illusionless man, was only fond of her. *"It partaketh mainly,"* he said, *"of body chemistry,"* and passed his hand over her roundest curve (1966, pp. 5–6).

 I think our relationship has changed over the couple of years we've been together. I think she's opened up more. And I think maybe the relationship is a little more down to earth than when we were first going out. It was a very romantic up-in-the-clouds type thing, and now it's more down to earth, there's more reality to it.

aries, and manifests itself in a turbulent mixture of agony and ecstasy (Rubin, 1973). The saying *"Amantes amentes"* (lovers are mad) refers to the characteristic quest for excitement, the obliviousness to developing problems, and the ignoring or denying of realistic requirements for a satisfying relationship—characteristics that may plunge a hapless couple into a short-lived, disappointing relationship.

Allen Wheelis' fantasy of "The Illusionless Man" illustrates love's "blindness":

"You are a great and good man," she said.

"I'm petty and self-absorbed," he said.

This romantic ideal derives from the "courtly love" of the middle ages, though courtly love, interestingly, was extramarital; the marital relationships of the time were companionable, pragmatic, and utilitarian. Although love is an established tradition in our times and such a major preoccupation of the dreams of young men and women, poets, writers, and singers, we have little scientific understanding of the phenomenon or of its actual importance in leading two young people to marry or in holding a marriage together. Our "folk knowledge" tells us that romantic love is an unstable base for a marriage and does not long endure without the support of a good general relationship and good communication.

One of the few researchers to focus on the scientific study of romantic love is Zick Rubin. In a recent series of studies on loving and liking (1973), he has concluded that romantic love is an important ingredient leading to marriage but only one of many, neither a necessary nor a sufficient one. Other factors to be discussed in the following section may also play key roles and even be more important in determining the outcome.

Interestingly, several studies suggest that contrary to the stereotype of young women as the ones who go about dreaming that "someday my prince will come," men are apparently more strongly imbued with the ideals of romantic love than are women. Rubin (1973) found that men scored higher on questionnaire items related to adherence to the romantic ideal. Coombs and Kenkel (1966) analyzed computer-matched dates and found that women were more stringent in their demands of what they sought in a date (except that men had higher aims for physical attractiveness of the date), and after the matched date, men were more satisfied and reported more romantic attraction and a higher likelihood of subsequent marriage. An earlier study (Burgess & Wallin, 1953) of engaged couples helped to debunk the myth that love at first sight is a common basis for marriage, and also found that 8 percent of the men and only 5 percent of the women recalled feeling "strong physical attraction" within a day or two of meeting.

According to a study by Kephart (1967), the female probably has more control over her romantic inclinations than the male. While the female experiences more romantic attachments than the male during adolescence, a kind of "matrimonial directedness" expresses itself during her young adulthood which tends to include an ability to ignore or reject some of her earlier romantic notions in the interests of achieving matrimony. Presumably the male, who is generally less matrimonially oriented, retains his no-

tions of romantic love as of central importance and makes sure that this criterion is met before seriously considering marriage.

Escape from aloneness

R. D. Laing wrote that the remark "There's nothing to be afraid of" is both the ultimate reassurance and the ultimate terror. And it is a terror that most people experience somewhat in our modern, complex, mechanized lives. Aloneness and isolation are avoided at all costs, and close relationships offer a buffer against the fear that accompanies awareness of one's separateness from everyone else. Erich Fromm wrote that mature love is our only hope for relieving the crushing weight of our aloneness. Unfortunately, however, many marriages are entered with the hope of eliminating aloneness as a major, if unspoken goal—only to discover that this, like romantic love, is usually an unsatisfactory basis for marriage.

Mate selection

Most individuals share some image of an ideal mate. Although particular men may wish to marry Miss Universe, men in general aspire after other attributes than looks. That is not to say that people hold out for the ideals to be met. Other kinds of factors than possession of ideal qualities influence mate selection.

What do people look for?

Most people have definite ideas about what they are looking for in a mate and about what categories of persons are "eligible" or "ineligible." Certain individuals tend to be excluded automatically on the basis of age, education, race, body type, and social orientation. The strength of such ideas usually leads to a screening of dating partners to a considerable degree and to the screening of potential marital partners to an even greater extent. In addition, a whole array of personal and social factors—such as special personality needs and social pres-

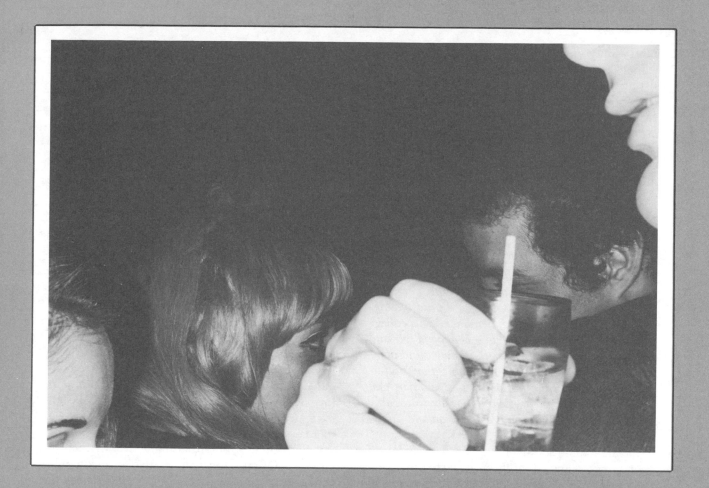

 I just always assumed I'd get married. It was just a thing that you would do. I don't know if I was especially eager or not eager, it was just one of those accepted facts of life, and by the time I got to college, and my friends were all getting married around me, there was a guy I was going with who really was in love with me, I'm sure. He asked me to marry him. And I liked him, but I wasn't in love with him. But I thought, maybe if I say 'yes,' maybe if I get engaged, then I'll feel different. Because I wanted to be like everybody else, I wanted to have those feelings that everybody else had.

sures—may enter into the selection process. A woman may consistently look for men who are strong and masterful, or socially facile, or sensitive and introvertive.

Studies of what young people are looking for in a marital partner have been generally in agreement about objective criteria like age, education, and social class, as well as on less easily measured characteristics like character, emotional stability, and a pleasant disposition. In a summary of studies extending into the early 1960s, Cavan concluded that:

"... the college man desires a wife who has an attractive and dependable personality, who is healthy, well groomed, and affectionate, whose intelligence and education preferably are not greater than his own, who is several years younger, and who is a good homemaker. The college woman prefers a husband who is dependable and mature, in love with her, well groomed and mannered, whose intelligence and education preferably are greater than her own, who is older, and whose financial prospects are good and probably will be improved through his ambition and industriousness" (1963, p. 325).

Cavan's remarks are based on data collected over a decade ago. It might be expected that new life styles would evoke different images of the ideal spouse. However, replications of a 1939 survey conducted in 1956 and 1967 produced relatively consistent findings about the choices of college students (Hudson & Henze, 1969). The only two traits which became less important over time were "chastity" and "good health," while dependable character, pleasing disposition, mutual attraction, and others continued to be important.

Such findings may be somewhat misleading, however, for when respondents are asked to formulate their own list of desired characteristics instead of ranking traits suggested to them, there is a somewhat different listing and ordering of traits (Winch, 1967; Williamson, 1965). In such lists, for example, a sense of humor is ordinarily given a high rating by both sexes, and males tend to rank physical attractiveness as more important than is indicated by the rankings in the previously cited studies.

In general, there seems to be agreement for both men and women that "physical attractiveness" and "personality" are important, with the details dependent upon both the individual's own views and the current standards of his cultural group. The physical characteristics and personality traits that "turn on" one generation may seem outmoded and irrelevant to the next.

What do people settle for?

Apart from people's stated aims, goals, and preferences in a marital partner, research studies have found considerable regularity with which certain factors are related to marriage.

1. *Propinquity—the girl next door.* Until recent decades, a girl tended to fall in love with and marry a boy with whom she had grown up and who lived within a mile or so of her (Kephart, 1967). Usually their families had known each other. Today, however, with urbanization, a high rate of family mobility, consolidated schools, and the automobile, falling in love with the boy next door appears to be an exception. Most young people today are exposed to a far wider range of acceptable dates as well as a wider range of potential mates from which to choose. Often, too, they give considerable thought to ways of improving their chances of meeting qualified potential mates.

Since social interactions take place in space and time, however, propinquity is still important—perhaps not so much residential propinquity as propinquity in one's general school or work environment. In fact, Catton and Smircich (1964) found physical proximity the most important single determinant of mate selection in a group they studied.

Early studies by Bossard (1931) and Katz and Hill (1958) report research findings in support of the proposition that the likelihood of marriage decreases steadily and markedly as the distance between the parties increases. Social psychological theory and research also support the notion that we are attracted to people who are close at hand, and mere exposure, in certain situations, increases liking.

Parents, of course, have often used these principles by encouraging a period of separation to test the endurance of an "unfortunate" love interest.

2. *Similarity.* Romantic folklore has it that "opposites attract," but numerous studies have indicated that while persons of different background and unlike outlook may have a short-term appeal, young people tend to choose persons of a similar background and orientation when it comes to marrying. This tendency for "like to marry like" is called *homogamy.* It is shown especially in relation to social background factors, such as social class, education, religion, and race. For example, 99.8 percent of whites marry whites, and 99 percent of blacks marry blacks. In recent years there has been an increase in interracial marriages, but they remain relatively uncommon. It would also appear that

attitudes and values help predict mate selection and marital satisfaction. The engaged couples studied by Burgess and Wallin (1953) shared opinions to a large extent. And later, Kerckhoff and Davis (1962) had unmarried couples rate the importance of such items as "healthy and happy children," "economic security," and other family goals. When the couples were contacted again 7 months later, the pairs who had agreed more closely were more likely to have progressed in their relationship toward permanence. On the other hand, Rubin (1973) has noted that other researchers have failed to repeat the result in similar studies.

3. *Complementarity.* The adage "opposites attract" has been modified by some behavioral scientists to the concept of *complementarity—*

 I wanted to be married, and I knew I wanted to marry him. One of the reasons was, because he was so much like me, and I figured we had an awful lot of the same things going for us, from way back in our backgrounds, and things we liked to do.

common interests and values are conducive to the formation of a serious relationship that can, in turn, lead to marriage.

Evidently, however, homogamy in mate selection applies more often to social background than to personality characteristics (Trost, 1967; Udry, 1967). Wishful thinking may lead a couple to perceive similarities rather than differences in each other, but studies fail to show marked similarities in the personality characteristics of those planning to marry. And with greater social mobility, the lowering of parental influence, and changing cultural norms, there is much greater freedom for young people to marry across color, religious, ethnic, and social-class lines—and such marriages are becoming more common.

The role of similarity of values is probably a significant one, although research has provided mixed results on the degree to which shared

attraction to one another because each would complement the other, particularly in terms of psychological and emotional needs.

Winch attempted to explain the process of selection by the hypothesis of complementary needs: ". . . within the field of eligibles, persons whose need patterns provide mutual gratification will tend to choose each other as marriage partners" (1963, pp. 606–7). For example, he believed that a person with a strong need to be protected would be likely to marry someone with a compelling need to protect and nurture others; that a person with a strong need to dominate would be gratified by and would tend to choose a marital partner with a strong need to be submissive; and that a person who lacked achievement motivation might be particularly attracted to a person with strong achievement motivation. In essence, this approach is a sophisticated way of saying that a person will tend to fall in love with and marry someone whose traits complement his own and hence meet his needs by supplying what he lacks.

Despite the plausibility of the complementary need hypothesis, research has only partially supported it, partly because of problems in assessing psychological needs, but also because many factors affect mate choice, and not just complementarity of needs.

"Living happily ever after"

Once a commitment between partners has been made, many factors come to bear upon the "success" of the relationship, some quite apart from all the influences which brought them together. What they make of their marriage depends on things that enter into their daily patterns of living—their activities, their decision-making procedures, their ways of adjusting and accommodating to each other's needs, habits, and individuality, their ability to encourage each other's growth. This section will attempt to explore factors which have been found to relate to marital "adjustment," and will consider some of the major pitfalls partnerships may face.

Marital success used to be measured largely in terms of economic maintenance and the production of a large number of healthy, well-mannered children. Standards used today are quite different.

One measure sometimes used is the duration of the marriage—whether it continues or ends in divorce. This is clearly not an adequate measure, however, since many marriages that do not end in divorce fail to provide much satisfaction to the partners, whereas many divorces occur for reasons other than deep disappointment and dissatisfaction.

If a marriage is providing an intense, intimate, and mutually satisfying experience which contributes to the personal adjustment and growth of both partners, we would tend to regard it as a "successful" relationship and likely to continue. However, researchers have had difficulty in measuring such characteristics. The general "happiness" of a marriage seems to be easier to judge, and husbands, wives, and objective observers show fairly good agreement in their evaluation of how "happy" a marriage is; in addition, happiness correlates with other indices of effective family functioning.

Predictors of marital adjustment

Why one marriage is happy and another unhappy is by no means fully understood. Factors which have some degree of correlation with marital happiness include (1) the premarital background of the marital partners; (2) the personality make-up of the marital partners; (3) sexual adjustment; (4) the degree to which the partners can accommodate to each other and function as a unit; and (5) environmental resources, limitations, and demands.

Premarital background factors

A number of premarital background factors correlate well enough with marital adjustment to be used for predictive purposes. Among the most important of these are:

1. *Family background.* A number of investigators have found that both poor marital adjustment and happiness tend to run in families (Burgess, Locke, & Thomas, 1963; Kirkpatrick, 1963). An individual's chances for marital happiness are greater if his parents were happily married than if they were unhappily married or divorced. Warm, loving relationships with one's parents and siblings also make more likely the establishment of such relationships in one's own marriage, and the young person who remembers his childhood as a happy one appears to have a greater chance for happiness in his own marriage.

2. *Social class, religion, and race.* In general, the lower the social class of a married couple the less stable and happy their marriage is likely to be—possibly reflecting in part the lack of economic and social stability in the environment on lower socioeconomic levels (Komarovsky, 1964; Renne, 1970). Cross-class marriages—which

typically involve a middle-class husband and a lower-class wife—also show a higher incidence of maladjustment and unhappiness than do middle-class marriages but may be happier than lower-class marriages. It is important to note that such studies deal with social class at the time of marriage; our society is a mobile one, and social class is not necessarily a fixed characteristic.

Interfaith marriages, although once frowned upon and considered a major source of marital conflict and unhappiness, are becoming more common and apparently more stable as well (Udry, 1966, 1971). Though findings are somewhat inconsistent, it would appear in general that Catholic-Protestant marriages are slightly less stable than Catholic marriages but not less stable than Protestant marriages. The general stability of interfaith marriages seems to result partly from the fact that individuals with strong religious convictions are not likely to enter into an interfaith marriage; those who enter such marriages are more likely to resolve later conflicts by a change of religious convictions than by a breaking up of the marriage.

A number of older studies also indicate that couples in which neither spouse has a religious affiliation are less stable than interfaith marriages, perhaps because most organized religions have discouraged divorce. With changing concepts both of religion and of marriage, it is difficult to predict the role of religious affiliation or of differing faiths in future marital adjustment.

Interracial marriages also appear to be increasing in frequency and to be meeting with less social disapproval than in the past (Udry, 1966, 1971). Although interracial marriages often pose additional problems for married couples, the stability and happiness of such marriages appear to depend on the couple involved, and studies so far have not found such marriages to be less stable or less happy than other marriages.

In general, it would appear that marriages which are "mixed"—in terms of culture, religion, social class, or race—are likely to make additional adjustive demands on the couple but

that the outcome will depend primarily upon the persons involved. Some of the earlier findings of greater hazard no longer seem to apply.

3. *Courtship.* Traditionally the courtship period has been regarded as very important in paving the way for later success in marriage, for it is during this period that the couple try to get to know each other and have an opportunity to test their ability to get along together. In an early comparison of happily married and divorced or divorce-contemplating couples, Locke (1951) found that both length of acquaintanceship and engagement and absence of conflict before marriage were positively related to later marital adjustment and happiness. Later evidence also supports the view that couples who get to know each other well during dating and courtship are more likely to make a wise decision about marrying and to achieve a happy marriage than those who marry on brief acquaintance (Landis, 1965; Udry, 1971).

4. *Age at time of marriage.* In a number of studies of early marriages—with grooms under 21 and brides under 18 years of age—more maladjustment and a higher-than-average incidence of divorce has been revealed. An interpretation of this finding is far from simple, for a high proportion of early marriages are among those of lower socioeconomic status and lower educational attainment and involve premarital pregnancy—estimates indicating that from a third to a half of teenage marriages involve a premarital pregnancy (Williamson, 1972). Thus, early marriages are especially likely to be plagued by financial as well as other problems. In addition, couples who marry later and are unhappy are less likely to get a divorce than are younger people. Thus it seems likely that the higher incidence of maladjustment and divorce among those who marry early is related to personal and social characteristics rather than to the time of marriage *per se.*

Personality factors

Studies of the role of personality factors in marital adjustment and happiness have focused on (1) identifying characteristics that appear to foster good adjustment in most marriages; (2)

delineating characteristics that appear to have a negative influence on most marriages; and (3) analyzing the patterns of husband-wife traits—the "fit" of the two personalities.

1. *Characteristics having a positive influence.* There is research support concerning the importance of some traits, such as emotional maturity, the capacity to communicate thoughts and feelings effectively, and the capacity to handle tensions constructively (Dean, 1966; Mudd, Mitchell, & Taubin, 1965; Blood, 1962). One component of emotional maturity—a clear sense of personal identity—appears of particular importance in helping the marital partners relate to each other. Wilson (1967) has also found that a generally happy person tends to be a happy

excessive drinking, has been demonstrated to be correlated with adjustment difficulties in marriage (Crago & Tharp, 1968; Hurlock, 1968). Probably this is often a circular relationship in which personal pathology leads to conflictual and unsatisfying marital relationships which, in turn, intensify the personality difficulty.

Unfortunately, negative personality traits which were not evident in the premarital relationship may show up after marriage, or traits which seemed exciting or interesting in premarital relationships may not weather well in the marital setting. It would appear, however, that the hazards of an unhappy marriage can be reduced by a thoughtful consideration during the courtship period of both the personality

 Once again, with 20/20 hindsight, we started with a very tough proposition, not counting all of our hangups. And that was, our goals were different. She wanted to be a career gal and set the business world on fire, and I wanted to get a job and have a family. I wanted the traditional thing. My model was my mother and father and the big family that they had . . . my brothers and sisters.

mate which, in turn, is likely to foster a happy marriage.

2. *Characteristics having a negative influence.* Although common sense would tell us that certain personality traits—such as selfishness, deceit, stubbornness, and irresponsibility—would lead to marital difficulties, there is actually little research data to go on. The importance of such negative traits in a marriage probably depends on the style of the marriage and the type of relationship the marital couple is trying to establish. For example, in conflict-habituated marriages, where the partners are simply coexisting, such traits may not have the same significance that they would in a more vital companionship-type marriage.

Serious personality maladjustment, including

traits that are apparent on both sides and the patterning of interests, needs, and values that is apparent in the relationship.

3. *Personality "fit" of marital partners.* We have probably all known individuals who were reasonably mature and well adjusted but whose personalities clashed when they were together very long. Not surprisingly, the patterning or "fit" of the two personalities involved is important in determining whether the marriage will be a happy one. On the other hand, research findings on personality fit are very tenuous, and Udry (1971) concluded that personality matching is probably a futile pursuit.

Several studies have pointed to similarity of values and interests as a factor in marital adjustment. Basic values and marital goals need to be

I'm proud of the fact that I'm happy in my marriage and have a warm relationship with my husband—we've had to put a lot of concern and love and caring into this marriage—love doesn't just happen or survive, it must be maintained.

in harmony if the interaction between the partners and their activities in the larger social setting are to be harmonious and satisfying to both.

Common goals and values provide a field for joint endeavors—both for emotional-social interaction and for the achievement of task goals—areas in which the partners can work together as a team and in which successes will bring satisfaction to them both. On the other hand, if they have basically different goals and values, they will find at best that they tend to operate as individuals rather than as a team—and at worst that they are working at cross-purposes, perhaps undercutting each other's efforts and each disparaging what is important to the other. It would appear that similarity of strongly held values helps to promote a marital fit (Coombs, 1966). Agreement on major values also makes many of the decisions in marriage much simpler (Price, 1968).

The role of complementary needs in marital adjustment is far from clear, but it is apparent that the ability of each partner to satisfy the needs of the other is of key importance in marital happiness. Marked differences in mo-

tives or temperament or other characteristics that lead partners to react to problems in discrepant ways are likely to be sources of conflict. If either spouse has strong needs which are unacceptable to the other, some adaptation must be made if the marriage is not to suffer (Clausen, 1966). If one partner's needs are seriously and chronically unmet, the marriage is likely to encounter difficulty; in the long run, the other partner, too, is likely to find it an unsatisfying relationship.

Pitfalls in marital adjustment

Many factors contribute to an unsatisfying relationship, leading to conflict and frustration and possibly even termination of the relationship. Although the issues on which intimate partnerships flounder are many, there are several which are quite common.

The honeymoon is over . . .
Most relationships begin with some form of courtship, in which the individuals, drawn to each other for a variety of reasons, present

  Our marriage wasn't a total disaster, or washout. She's an intelligent person, super intelligent, and when we could talk we had good talks and good rapport. But that wasn't often enough and in itself wasn't enough to do a whole thing for a marriage. Marriage really comes in many parts and pieces, and I think all of them have to kind of click. Most of them anyway. Basically, the bad parts of the marriage at the time I left far outweighed the good parts.

themselves in the most favorable light possible. With most couples, extra attention is given to behaviors and appearances that might impress or delight the other—in the hope of winning love and approval, while the "undesirable" qualities are hidden, ignored, or simply diminished in the warm glow of romance and the promise of a beautiful future. In the excitement that often accompanies the establishment of a partnership, the couple is likely to experience optimism about any possible future problems, and to expect the dramatic and tingling qualities of the relationship to continue evermore.

In some cases the process is even more insidious. Virginia Satir (1967), a noted family therapist, believes that certain individuals, especially

tion to each other's needs must develop in this "post-honeymoon" phase. Obviously, many couples either fail to make such adjustments or simply decide that their earlier expectations and hopes have been violated.

Experiencing differences and autonomy

Not only do many couples experience difficulty when each partner discovers that the other is not entirely what was expected, but relationships also face the difficult step of dealing with real differences. In the early stages of the relationship many couples assume a greater degree of similarity than exists in their values, preferences, behaviors, and wants. For the person who

 I used to wonder whether I would like being married, because I had certain preconceptions about what marriage was based on. But it turned out that I could be the way I wanted and still be married—without having to take advantage of the other person. It seemed to me that some of my friends weren't able to do that in their marriages. It seemed like they stopped being what they were, and sort of catered to the other person. I couldn't do that.

those who experience low self-esteem, are drawn to another in the hope of *getting* and not having to *give*. Enactment of certain façades characterizes the courtship, and each person anticipates that the other possesses the qualities which he himself or she herself does not possess and hopes to gain through the other.

Disappointment seems inevitable to some degree in most marriages. One partner may fail to meet the expectations of the other; or a reduction of excitement may be viewed as proof of loss of love from the partner. Couples then frequently face the challenge of reestablishing the partnership on somewhat different grounds. Mutual respect, tolerance and acceptance, "warts and all," compromise, and accommoda-

entered the partnership in the hope of bolstering his feelings of self-esteem and security, learning that the other person is an independent individual with unique needs, preferences, and expectations too can be a frightening and disruptive experience. For a husband to discover that his wife doesn't love sports as he had assumed, or for a wife to learn that her husband doesn't agree with her ideas about sharing household chores—these and similar differences may be experienced not merely as sources of disappointment and conflict, but also as a kind of invalidation of the self. Even more disconcerting for some couples is an attempt by one partner to express independence and uniqueness. The husband who wants a night out with the boys and the wife who wants a job outside the home can pose a serious threat to the spouse whose entire identity is founded on a self-contained marriage and the total sharing of experiences.

Acceptance of their differences and the fostering of their individual uniqueness and autonomy present considerable difficulties for many couples although most of them are not conscious that this is an issue. In this respect, the problem of differences is unlike the "honeymoon is over" feeling, which most people can identify and to some degree recognize as inevitable. The battleground on which the issue of differences is confronted may be quite trivial, leaving the partners to puzzle over why they are fighting over such "petty" issues. Lack of recognition of what is happening makes this pitfall all the more difficult to resolve satisfactorily.

Jealousy and possessiveness

Jealousy and possessiveness, and indeed, the issue of fidelity may be related problems; certainly they are sources of conflict in many relationships. Whatever draws the partner's attentions and energies away—whether an evening with "the boys," another woman, the children—all may arouse jealousy. The emotion may be particularly disruptive for partners who somehow feel dependent upon their relationship for their own sense of worth and competence.

Marriage does not give one partner ownership of the other. Yet, some husbands and wives make enormous demands on their spouses and try to prevent any autonomy at all. Possessiveness may increase the atmosphere of conflict and struggle in an already troubled relationship. Since jealousy and possessiveness are commonly based on feelings of insecurity in the relationship, they are often alleviated when the stability of the relationship improves.

Power and control

A related source of potential conflict concerns the distribution of "power" within the partnership. Jay Haley (1963), a psychotherapist and theorist in family relations, remarked that ". . . the major conflicts in a marriage center in the problem of who is to tell whom what to do

under what circumstances. . . ." Not all couples will face conflicts in this area. Nevertheless, when two reasonably competent, mature, assertive people enter an intimate relationship, many decisions must be made about the functions and services to be provided by each. It would be rare for one partner to assume either the role of issuing orders or that of performing like a slave. Our socially conditioned roles of husband, wife, father, or mother may provide some guidelines about who does what and who decides. Such guidelines are at best incomplete, however, and many couples engage in power struggles, sometimes overt and sometimes hidden. The couple who fights over whose turn it is to empty the trash may actually be battling about a more fundamental issue unresolved in their relationship.

Role expectations

The expectations with which couples enter marriage have to do not only with *what* should be done by each partner, but also *how* it should be done. For example, there may be agreement that the wife should prepare the meals, but disagreement as to the kind of meals that should be prepared. Difficulty arises if there is a discrepancy in the role concepts and expectations of the two partners or if either one's behavior fails to come up to the other's expectations (Dyer, 1962).

Where the marital partners come from similar backgrounds, compatible role expectations are more likely, and the problem of role accommodation may be minimal. On the other hand, couples from very different backgrounds are likely to enter a marriage with differing role expectations and to have more difficulty in accommodating to each other.

Increasingly, however, both men and women are challenging the traditional sex roles of strong, active, dominant, unemotional men, whose major task is to provide for their families, and weak, dependent, submissive, nurturant women, whose task it is to care for the home and family. The enormous costs of the restrictions such stereotypes put on both men and women are counted in terms of loss of human

Over the past months my husband and I have discussed the things we feel we have to change to bring about the kind of life we really want to live. One of the major changes we feel is necessary is that we can be free to express our own individual selves and yet remain a unit. For years, and especially when our children were growing up, we did everything together. Both of us now feel the need to find our uniqueness and to express it.

potential, as well as in the development of psychological and even physical disturbances as a result of stress and lack of fulfillment. Women in particular resent the expectation that they not only should perform all the household drudgeries, but also should *want* to perform them. And some men are beginning to ask themselves if they really want to work all day at competitive or dehumanizing jobs which rob them of energy and fulfillment.

The challenges to traditional sex roles have enormous repercussions on marriage and other partnerships. For many couples the struggle to be free of traditional roles will likely create increased conflict in their decisions about division of labor. Since accommodation is crucial in any enduring, intimate partnership, the couples who are flexible and open to change and who have high regard for one another as persons will be the ones most likely to resolve these issues satisfactorily.

Carl Rogers regards the dissolution of limiting roles as an essential element in an enduring and fulfilling relationship:
We will live by our own choices, the deepest organismic sensings of which we are capable, but we will not be shaped by the wishes, the rules, the roles which others are all too eager to thrust upon us" (1972, p. 206).

Growing apart
Rogers also stresses the importance of a relationship which provides a medium for the encouragement of personal growth, the chance "to be that self which one most truly is." More than simply tolerating differences and changes in each other, partners face the challenge of both encouraging and adapting to the growth of the other. Many relationships falter at either or both steps. Overcoming personal obstacles and growing in terms of experience of the self, of others, and of life's meaning may alter both the individual and the relationship. Confusion, animosity, defensiveness, or feelings of inadequacy are typical initial responses. Couples rarely grow and change at the same rate or in the same areas, so that the challenge of being supportive while experiencing change is a great one for the partners. Yet, to the degree that the couple has come together for mutual psychological gains, the crisis may be enormously productive.

Poor communication
Accommodation in marriage depends heavily upon effective communication—open communication lines and the ability and willingness to use them. Without good communication, information cannot be exchanged, efforts cannot be coordinated, the other person's feelings and reactions may not be understood, incipient misunderstandings can become major sources of resentment, and accommodation will not take place.

In a study of communication patterns in marriage, Navran (1967) found that happily married couples, as compared with unhappily married couples: (a) talk to each other more; (b) convey the feeling that they understand what is being said to them; (c) communicate about a wider range of subjects; (d) preserve communication channels and keep them open; (e) show more sensitivity to each other's feelings; (f) personalize their language symbols; and (g) make more use of supplementary nonverbal techniques of communication.

The feeling that it is safe to be open and honest about one's feelings, both positive and negative, is necessary if open communication is to take place between the partners.

"... in a healthy relationship, each partner feels free to express his likes, dislikes, wants, wishes, feelings, impulses, and the other person feels free to react with like honesty to these. In such a relationship, there will be tears, laughter, sensuality, irritation, anger, fear, babylike behavior, and so on.

"The range of behavior, feelings, and wishes which will be brought out into the open is not arbitrarily limited. In fact, one gauge to the health of a relationship is the breadth of topics of conversation, the range of feelings which are openly expressed, and the range of activities which are shared. In each case, the broader the range, the healthier the relationship" (Jourard, 1963, p. 343).

The content of communication between partners is important, too, and partners need to express their "persisting feelings," whether positive or negative. Many partners limit their communications to more or less polite exchanges of information, allowing their unverbalized feelings to build up and risking an explosive confrontation that can be damaging or difficult to resolve.

Rogers (1972) emphasizes the need for expressions of negative feelings to be given as statements of one's own feelings, rather than statements of blame or accusation of the partner. If, for example, the husband finds himself annoyed at his wife's appearance at breakfast, suppression of his response may lead eventually to the outburst "Why do you look like a slut in the morning?" Instead, he might express his persisting irritation by just stating his own feel-

 The only thing I had to really work on adjusting to in our marriage was that he comes from a family that's very direct, and he's very direct. And I come from a family that's more closed, and I didn't really know how to be direct. It wasn't till after we were married and being together all the time that I began to realize that this was something I had to do something about. I thought it was a good idea, to be more open and direct—but it was frightening to think about, and it was hard to accomplish. I guess I was afraid if I said something unpleasant, or that I thought he'd think was unpleasant, then he'd be angry at me. But I had underestimated him as a person, I guess, and underestimated the process of being open, and it has all worked very well. Directness is an area where we are now much more comfortable with each other—I'd say it's benefited the marriage a great deal.

ings: "You know, it bothers me when you don't comb your hair in the morning."

Risk is a part of such communications, since the individual exposes his or her inner feelings and, in some cases, puts the relationship on the line. Rogers (1972) cites the example of a wife who takes the risk of stating her persisting feeling: "I don't know the reasons, whether it's in you or me, but I find very little real satisfaction in our sex relationship." Rogers notes that she is risking the relationship for the sake of its growth.

Virginia Satir (1967) draws attention not to content but to the *form* of communication. She and colleagues Haley, Jackson, Bateson, and Weakland have formulated models of family conflict and psychopathology which derive from dysfunctional communication. Relatively mild forms of dysfunctional communication are common: overgeneralization, failure to seek feedback about communication, vagueness, failure to complete messages, or eliptical messages with idiosyncratic meaning or with essential elements omitted. A frequent source of difficulty occurs when a person sends no message at all but behaves as if he had. For example:

Wife: *We had no bread for dinner. He forgot.*
Therapist: *You mean your husband?*
Wife: *Yes.*
Therapist: *(to husband) Did you know that you were out of bread in the house?*
Husband: *No, heck no, I didn't . . .*
Therapist: *Do you remember her telling you?*
Husband: *No. No, she never told me. If I had known, I would have picked some up on the way home.*
Therapist: *Do you remember telling him that you were out of bread and asking him to pick some up?*
Wife: *Well, maybe I didn't. No, maybe I didn't. But you'd think he'd know* (p. 72).
Couples frequently miscommunicate over the definition of a word:
Husband: *She never comes up to me and kisses me. I am always the one to make the overtures.*
Therapist: *Is this the way you see yourself behaving with your husband?*
Wife: *Yes, I would say he is the demonstrative*

one. *I didn't know he wanted me to make the overtures.*
Therapist: *Have you told your wife that you would like this from her—more open demonstration of affection?*
Husband: *Well, no, you'd think she'd know.*
Wife: *No, how would I know? You always said you didn't like aggressive women.*
Husband: *I don't, I don't like dominating women.*
Wife: *Well, I thought you meant women who make the overtures. How am I to know what you want?*
Therapist: *You'd have a better idea if he had been able to tell you* (pp. 72–73).

Satir further describes the communication process as a "verbal and nonverbal process of making requests of the receiver." The requests can be direct and specific or indirect, and may occur verbally or nonverbally. Messages from different levels (e.g., verbal, facial, postural) may be congruent with each other or may contradict each other. Many couples compound other difficulties with unclear and incomplete ways of expressing themselves.

Sexual maladjustment

The change in male and female sex roles, together with the waning of Victorian views of sex as lustful and evil, has been paralleled by a corresponding change in the expectations of both marital partners. It is usually assumed today that both partners should find satisfaction in their sexual relationship, and the attitude of women in particular has changed from one of repression and inhibition of sexual desires to one of seeking and even demanding sexual satisfaction in marriage.

1. *Attitudes toward sex.* Sexual intercourse in marriage is the chief mode of sexual expression for most adults and is an important part of the marital relationship. However, the relative importance of marital intercourse varies greatly from one couple to another.

Rainwater interviewed more than 250 couples representing middle- and lower-socioeconomic class whites and blacks. He discovered that marital sexual experiences are viewed more positively and are a greater source of satisfaction for husbands than for wives, and for persons of higher social class than for those of lower.

"The major variable that seems related to this class difference concerns the quality of conjugal role relationships in the different classes. In this same study we found that middle-class couples were much more likely to emphasize patterns of jointly organized activities around the home and joint activities outside the home, while working and lower-class couples were much more likely to have patterns of role relationships in which there was greater emphasis on separate functions and separate interests by husbands and wives. . . .

that women learn to accept their own sexuality, it is likely that they will experience sexual satisfaction as fully as do men.

2. *Sexual problems.* Since sexual satisfaction is a relatively important goal for most couples, sexual problems are a source of distress, recrimination, and self-blame. In general, it can be said that problems in sexual relationships go hand in hand with marital problems, so that determination of cause and effect may often be quite difficult. Marital conflict and unresolved anger typically take their toll in the sexual area, while satisfying and mutual interpersonal relationships may both foster and be enhanced by sexual satisfaction. Fisher (1973), for example,

 Really for the first ten years of our marriage there was no mutually joyous intercourse experience, ever. In the past year there has been that, so for me it's like finally realizing that there is love that is possible through sexual contact. The change in me automatically caused him to open up. And the neat thing about it is I realized then how keyed in he really was about what was happening to me.

Close and gratifying sexual relationships (among role-segregated couples) are difficult to achieve because the husband and wife are not accustomed to relating intimately to each other" (1966, pp. 264–65).

While women in general and lower-class men in particular reported somewhat less sexual enjoyment in marriage, it seems likely that such discrepancies between men and women are diminishing. The pioneering work of Masters and Johnson (1966) helped to debunk certain myths about female sexual "inferiority," and indeed, found that given proper stimulation and setting, women could achieve more intense and longer-lasting orgasms than men and were more capable of multiple orgasms. To the degree

found that women who reported a happier marriage were more consistent in attaining orgasms in their sexual relationships.

Sexually based problems do occur, however. A fairly common potential source of sexual conflict is the incongruence between men's and women's desires for sexual relations. Kinsey, Pomeroy, & Martin (1948, 1953) had found that husbands typically wanted intercourse more often than their wives reported desiring it. In a very recent study, Fisher (1973) also noted a discrepancy between preferred intercourse frequency for wives and the preferred frequency they reported for their husbands. The work of Masters and Johnson (1966) brought to light other potential sources of difficulty: Compared with men, women typically require longer foreplay and also continuous stimulation in order to achieve orgasm.

Whereas the sexually unsatisfied male is relatively rare in our society, a large number of women, even married women, have never achieved orgasm (5–6 percent), and only 35–40 percent of married women always or almost always achieve orgasm according to one study (Fisher, 1966). Nevertheless, despite the emphasis upon expert performance and even simultaneous orgasm in our culture, Fisher's work showed that most women enjoyed sexual relations if they occurred in the context of a satisfying marriage, even if they achieved orgasm

performance-oriented. Rather, their focus is on getting couples to explore their attitudes, judgments, pleasures, and fears in the context of open, supportive discussion which helps them to perceive sexual relations as an intimate, normal, and desirable experience.

Other issues in marital adjustment

There are additional factors which affect couples' relationships. Sometimes the partners have little or no control over some of the elements affecting their marriage. Thus, personal re-

 Sex deprivation feels lousy. It wasn't only deprivation, in my marriage, it was kind of part of the battle that was going on between us, to the point where she would never admit any good feelings out of the sex that we had. She would not only not respond positively, she would respond negatively. She'd say it was terrible, not only did she not get any good feeling, she felt degraded. I felt it must be my fault somehow.

infrequently or never. Fisher's research further countered certain myths about nonorgasmic women as females who possessed particular kinds of personalities and psychopathologies. No consistent traits were characteristic, and the nonorgasmic females did not show signs of "mental illness" or neurosis.

In addition to their contributions to our limited knowledge of the human sexual response, Masters and Johnson (1970) have also pioneered in sex therapy and have successfully worked with hundreds of couples who experienced a wide range of sexual dysfunctions. Their therapy recognizes the crucial role of both partners in resolving sexual problems, and they treat couples together. Also, their approach is not

sources and the environment may present obstacles to marital happiness; and, in addition, relationships change over time.

Environmental resources, limitations, and demands
No marriage is lived in a vacuum, and the setting may either support and strengthen the marriage or undermine its stability and happiness. Like individuals, families are open systems, requiring favorable physical resources as well as chances for effective transactions with their physical and social environment. If a family's values are at odds with the values of surrounding families, its members will feel a strain. A family that never has enough to eat and must live in a tumble-

down, rat-infested, crowded building has a more difficult task in maintaining healthy interactions among its members than a family that lives in pleasant surroundings with chances for privacy. If the father cannot find work and the welfare laws provide for assistance only to families without fathers, as is true in some communities, he may leave home rather than let his family starve. Thus, the adjustment and even the continuance of a family may be determined by conditions outside the family itself. A study of several thousand married couples in a California county showed that people who face such obstacles as low income, unemployment, minority group status, and chronic physical illness reported less marital satisfaction (Renne, 1970).

Whereas in some societies an extended family, a stable social structure, and clear, consistent expectations for husbands and wives all help to bolster the stability of individual marriages, a couple in our society have few such external

supports and are largely on their own. In a shifting, rapidly changing society where contradictory values vie for acceptance, husband and wife may have a hard time finding and maintaining accord between themselves and an even harder time helping their children to develop sound values and healthy personalities. In giving up externally prescribed rituals and roles, we have also given up the comfort that external props and assurances can give.

Changes in a marriage over time
The style and content of a marriage may fluctuate markedly over the years. Such fluctuations may result from changes in attitudes and values on the part of the partners, or they may be induced by situational factors such as the advent of children.

The partners' relationship and happiness in the marriage may also change with time. Many unhappy or precarious marriages are weeded out by divorce during the first few years, but even a marriage of long duration is not immune to ending in the divorce court. Marital happiness is not something that once achieved can be counted on to continue indefinitely: rather, the couple must keep achieving it.

Unhappiness and dissolution of marriage

The divorce rate in the United States has shown a dramatic increase in the past half century. One in 7 marriages ended in divorce in 1920, compared with one in 4 in 1960 and one in 3 in 1972,

gy. Thus, many of the marriages which end in divorce have probably been as happy as or happier than some of those which endure.

Causes of divorce

Many factors undoubtedly combine to account for our high divorce rate. These factors include conditions in the social setting as well as characteristics of the two persons involved and of the pattern of interaction between them.

General social change
As we have seen, there has been a challenging and loosening of most of our traditional values and social structures in recent years. Mobility,

 I can't really tell you what all went wrong with the marriage. I think I just kept it going, through sheer need for having a marriage and not wanting to let it go, far beyond the time when it was very clear to me that it was not my kind of relationship. I kept that awareness away, I didn't really face it. I think I probably really did love her in some ways, and whether it was the need to have somebody to love, or whether it was real, I don't know.

based on U.S. Census Bureau figures. The U.S. rate of marital dissolution is considerably higher than that for other nations; and we have not included the substantial number of married couples who separate without bothering to get a divorce.

Of course, divorce and separation statistics do not tell the whole story about the incidence of unhappiness and maladjustment in marriages. Many married couples stay together, though unhappy, because of considerations other than happiness—such as religious or financial considerations, reluctance to disrupt the lives of their children, fear of not being able to do any better on a second try, or simply habit or lethar-

instability, and change appear to be both commonplace and expected—both in our society and in our own personal lives. And our high standard of living has raised our expectations for satisfactions of all kinds—including those by which we measure the acceptability of a marital relationship. It is also possible that marriages based on love and emotional need fulfillment are inherently more hazardous than those based on economic and other pragmatic considerations, where the conditions that give rise to the marriage help to maintain it.

Modern urbanization and the rise of the nuclear family have removed many of the environmental supports and the kinds of help with

SUMMARY OF BACKGROUND FACTORS RELATED TO DIVORCE

Educational level	The lower the educational level, the higher the divorce rate.
Occupational status	Divorce more common among lower socioeconomic groups than among professional groups.
Family background	Higher divorce rate among couples raised in unhappy homes and/or by divorced parents.
Racial background	Nonwhite marriages more divorce-prone than white marriages at all educational and occupational levels.
Religion	Higher divorce rates among nonchurchgoers.
Length of courtship	Divorce rates higher for those with brief courtships.
Age at time of marriage	Divorce rates very high for those marrying in their teens.
Factors not related to divorce rate	Interracial, mixed religion, sexual experience prior to marriage, age difference between spouses.

marital problems that tend to be available in the extended family living in a less hurried, less impersonal, more stable social network. At the same time, occupational opportunities for women have given dissatisfied wives an alternative to continuance that was lacking in the past: better opportunities for remarriage may also influence their decision. And with less stringent divorce laws and less stigma attached to divorced people, there is wider acceptance of divorce as a viable choice in an unsatisfactory marital situation. All these factors in our social setting make stable, satisfying marriages more difficult and separation more attractive when expectations are not being fulfilled.

Unfortunately, the rate and complexity of social change, with all its implications for mate selection and marital happiness, have not been matched by preparation of our young people in realistic expectations or in the attitudes and skills needed for a stable and satisfying marriage in this kind of society. It is often easier to obtain a marriage license than a fishing or driver's license. It would appear that a great deal of misery and many wasted years could be avoided by more adequate preparation of young people for both choosing and living with a mate.

In any case, American marriages today are undertaken against a cultural background which places an increasingly heavy burden on the marital partners for establishing stability and meeting each other's psychological needs. And as society's stake in stable family units has come to be regarded as secondary to the individuals' happiness—in marked contrast to the priorities established in many other cultural groups—the way appears to be paved for a continued high incidence of marital failure.

Reasons given for divorce

Harmsworth and Minnis (1955) surveyed the opinions of lawyers on the *actual*—as contrasted with *legal*—causes of divorce. They found adul-

289 / Unhappiness and dissolution of marriage

tery cited in 18.6 percent, financial problems in 16.8 percent, and incompatibility in 15.6 percent of the cases, with irresponsibility, cruelty, immaturity, cultural causes, in-law problems, and desertion each accounting for more than 2 percent of the remaining cases. Although these findings are interesting, they are limited by the accuracy with which lawyers can gauge their clients' reasons for seeking a divorce and by the limited grounds accepted in many states.

In a more recent and comprehensive study of the counseling records of 600 couples applying for divorce, Levinger (1966) compared the complaints of husbands and wives and of middle-class and lower-class couples. Husbands cited half as many complaints as wives; most frequently mentioned by the husbands were mental cruelty, neglect of home and children, infidelity, and sexual incompatibility. Complaints most often made by the wives were of physical and mental cruelty, financial problems, and drinking. In general, the middle-class couples were more concerned with psychological and emotional satisfactions while the lower-class couples were more concerned with financial problems and the physical actions of their partners. Again, we are reminded of Maslow's hypothesis of a hierarchy of needs in which maintenance needs must be adequately met before the individual will become concerned about and will actively seek for the satisfaction of actualization needs.

Effects of divorce

Divorce can have far-reaching effects on all members of the family. Effects of broken homes on children will be discussed in the next chapter. The effects for the couple depend upon many factors, such as the emotional involvement of the partners, the happiness and duration of the marriage prior to the divorce, the opportunities for remarriage, and the stress tolerance and other personality characteristics of all concerned.

Divorce is often interpreted as a sign of failure, and divorced persons often feel that they have failed in one of life's most important tasks. Following a divorce, many persons experience a sense of personal inadequacy, disillusionment, and depression. Often they are torn by self-recrimination and thoughts of "what might have been"—of what they might have done that would have made their marriage a success.

A divorced person is likely to face difficult adjustments brought about by the changes in his life situation: he may have to cope with loss of security, guilt and self-recrimination, the cessation or disruption of sexual satisfactions, and financial problems. Feelings of alienation and loneliness may add to the stress, and where the divorce was sought by the other partner, a sense of having been rejected usually leads to feelings of hurt and self-devaluation. Even for the partner who sought the divorce, the stress of divorce and readjustment may bring more severe problems than those from which he was trying to escape.

Bohannan (1972) has analyzed the enormously complex and overlapping experiences which divorce occasions; he terms them the "six stations of divorce":

1. *The emotional divorce.* This occurs when spouses withhold emotion from their relationship because they dislike the intensity or ambivalence of their feelings. The couple grows mutually antagonistic. The natural response to the loss of a meaningful relationship is grief. Yet, Bohannan notes, the grief has to be worked out alone.

2. *The legal divorce.* In most states, "grounds" for divorce must be determined, and the "guilty" party punished by the granting of a divorce to the "innocent" party. The process of determining grounds for divorce may be very emotional, humiliating, anxiety-provoking.

3. *The economic divorce.* This aspect of divorce involves the settling of property and the division of assets, and may involve many painful aspects including loss of wealth and support.

4. *The coparental divorce.* This aspect of divorce centers around the children—custody and visitation rights—and affects not only the children (who often feel that *they* have been divorced by one parent or the other), but also the

spouses, since the family unit changes unalterably. The loss of the relationship with the children, or the prospect of raising the children alone may, of course, be very painful experiences for the parents.

5. *The community divorce.* The spouses experience the loss of friends and, often, of community ties, in addition to all the other losses occasioned by divorce.

6. *The psychic divorce.* "Psychic divorce means the separation of self from the personality and the influence of the ex-spouse. . . ." The issue of gaining new autonomy and becoming once again whole and complete may be one of the most difficult of the six aspects, but also potentially the most personally constructive.

Remarriage

In colonial times nearly all remarriages were of widowed persons, but in recent decades there has been a gradually swelling tide of remarriages of those who have been divorced. The chance of remarriage after a divorce has greatly increased, especially for those in lower age groups; overall, about two-thirds of divorced women and three-fourths of divorced men eventually remarry. Remarriages occur, on the average, about two and a half years after the divorce.

Reasons for remarriage
Both societal pressures and individual needs steer divorced persons toward remarriage. The divorced mother may be encouraged to remarry because, she is told, the children need two parents in the home. Divorced persons often feel awkward in the company of married friends. A divorced woman may find herself incapable of handling all the responsibilities of maintaining a household for herself and her children. Factors such as these, together with the need for affection, adult companionship, and sexual intimacy lead many divorced persons to seek new marital partners.

In considering remarriage, there are often new factors to be weighed: a woman who has children from a previous marriage may be con-

cerned about how her children will accept their prospective stepfather and how he will relate to them. A man considering remarriage may have financial responsibility for children of a former marriage; if he pays alimony and child support, he may not be in a position to assume the financial responsibilities of another family. The individual may be strongly motivated by a need to overcome the emotional hurt and self-devaluation from the prior divorce. The possibility that one is "marrying on the rebound" may be a factor to be considered carefully.

How successful are remarriages?
Do second marriages have a better chance of success than first marriages? Has the divorced person's past experience taught him how to avoid the common pitfalls in marriage, or should his earlier failure be taken as a sign that he is a poor marital risk? The research evidence is both scanty and contradictory. In terms of statistics, first marriages, as a group, are the most stable, followed by remarriages in which one partner has been divorced, followed by remarriages in which both partners have had previous marriages. Marriages in which one or both of the spouses has had multiple prior marriages are probably least stable of all, though adequate statistics are not available. A study of 100 elderly couples (all over age 60) who were interviewed 5 years after a late marriage, found that only 6 marriages ended in divorce. Many persons had married for a third or fourth time and most listed companionship as the primary motive for remarriage. The investigator concluded that persons who remarry late in life have an excellent chance for making a success of their union (McKain, 1973).

About one-third of those who remarry find themselves in the divorce mill again (Packard, 1968). This figure is not surprising since obtaining a divorce in the first place signals the individual's willingness to break up an unhappy marriage by divorce. He may also have immaturities or other personality characteristics that make him divorce prone. However, divorce is usually a powerful learning experience.

Although more remarriages than first mar-

I visualize a life style characterized by freedom and independence. I feel the need to be in control of my circumstances. This means an income, derived from a satisfying job—enough money to do what I want. This means no financial burdens, no debts and monthly bills beyond those absolutely necessary. Neither marriage nor children fit into the picture. However, a meaningful male-female relationship is important to provide friendship and companionship.

riages end in divorce, remarried persons in general find that their second marriages are happier than their first. Udry has suggested several possible reasons:

"There are many factors which contribute to the satisfaction which people find in second marriages after divorce. The divorced person has probably learned something about marriage from the first failure. If age contributes anything to maturity, he should be able to make a more mature choice the second time. The significance of sex is transformed, since it can be more taken for granted in the approach to second marriage. Second marriages have the advantage of being compared with a marriage which recently ended in bitterness and conflict. The second time around, the first-time loser has probably readjusted his expectations of marriage and is simply easier to please than those without previous marital experience" (1966, p. 521).

Whether or not the divorced person has learned from his failure, and regardless of the odds against him, the potential rewards of the marital relationship appear to lead most divorced persons to try again.

Other forms of intimate relationships

The changes in attitudes toward marriage, sexual expression, and sex roles, are bringing numerous forms of experimentation in intimate re-

lationships. Research into such practices is limited, although subjective reports suggest that the various alternatives have not meant the end of more traditional pitfalls of marriage and may generate new pressures. This section will briefly mention some of the new alternatives.

Some people will never marry

As noted earlier, despite change and challenges, marriage remains a popular, nearly universal enterprise. Rubin (1973) polled 2500 college students in the Boston area; of those who replied, 97.8 percent thought that they would probably marry at some point in their lives, and 93.7 percent expected to marry within 10 years. Nevertheless, growing numbers if not proportions of individuals will elect not to marry at all. Just as there are many reasons why people marry, there are many reasons why some people do not marry. Some do not find the "right" person; others are unwilling to give up their personal freedom to share their lives with another.

It is commonly believed that the single woman must be especially deficient, having failed to perform her "basic role" as wife and mother. She is usually expected to be unhappy, unattractive, emotionally defective, or otherwise unable to attract a husband. But though the single man, as we have seen, is generally less happy, less healthy—both physically and emotionally—and less well-off financially and socially than the married man, the same does not hold for women. The single woman is typically better educated, freer of emotional dysfunctions, and happier than either married women or single men (Bernard, 1973). The future may see relatively more women seeking intimacy and fulfillment outside traditional marital relationships.

It is likely that increasing numbers of people will maintain intimate relationships which are not legally sanctioned but which have many similarities to marriage while attempting to eliminate restrictive aspects imposed by the legal bonds. And there are likely to be growing numbers of individuals who form intimate though perhaps temporary relationships, and who devote the major part of their psychological energy to their work or professions or other activities.

New forms of partnership

Observers of traditional monogamous marriage note the astonishingly high rate of divorce and infer the enormous quantity of lost human potential resulting from family instability, marital discord, or personal stultification in an unsatisfying relationship. The causes for the magnitude of this problem are unclear, but it would appear that some of them stem from the following: inexperience, personal changes over time,

aspects of the institution of marriage itself, and other reasons. Nor is there agreement on whether partnerships of the future should entail radical departures from tradition or simply alterations in our common practices and assumptions. On one point there is agreement, however: We are witnessing a time of ferment and experimentation, and the intimate partnerships of the future will differ in some important ways from those of the past. Several two-person options are currently being explored.

1. *"Trial marriage."* Margaret Mead's (1971) widely publicized two-step marriage proposes a phase of "individual marriage" which would be a licensed union of two people in which birth control is employed and which can be dissolved at will. Proponents of "trial marriage" similarly urge a time-limited formal commitment which can be renewed or dissolved at the end of a given period, according to the individuals' needs and wishes.

The apparently high incidence of premarital cohabitation has been taken as evidence of couples' experimentation with trial marriages of a sort. Macklin (1972) studied a sample of upper-division women students at Cornell University, and found that 34 percent of them had cohabited with a male student for at least three months. Problems encountered by unmarried couples living together were similar to those of married couples and others in intimate relationships, such as feelings of overinvolvement, loss of

 Our sex was always rotten, and I think that was one of the bad things about the marriage—every time we had sex it was a putdown for me, because of her nonresponse. We didn't really have intercourse before I went overseas. We did when I got back, just before we got married. But it really wasn't enough experience for me to understand the full effect of what was going to happen. I think probably if I'd just lived with her a couple of years before getting married, I think it'd have been pretty obvious.

The concept of marriage contracts is by no means a new one. In 1855 Lucy Stone and Henry B. Blackwell made the following formal commitment as a protest against conditions which still prevail in many states.

While acknowledging our mutual affection by publicly assuming the relationship of husband and wife, yet in justice to ourselves and a great principle, we deem it a duty to declare that this act on our part implies no sanction of, nor promise of voluntary obedience to such of the present laws of marriage, as refuse to recognize the wife as an independent, rational being, while they confer upon the husband an injurious and unnatural superiority, investing him with legal powers which no honorable man would exercise, and which no man should possess. We protest, especially against the laws which give to the husband:

1. the custody of the wife's person;

2. the exclusive control and guardianship of their children;

3. the sole ownership of her personal property, and use of her real estate, unless previously settled upon her, or placed in the hands of trustees, as in the case of minors, lunatics, and idiots.

4. the absolute right to the product of her industry;

5. also against laws which give to the widower so much larger and more permanent an interest in the property of his deceased wife, than give to the widow in that of the deceased husband;

6. finally, against the whole system by which "the legal existence of the wife is suspended during marriage," so that in most States, she neither has a legal part in the choice of her residence, nor can she make a will, nor sue or be sued in her own name, nor inherit property.

We believe that personal independence and equal human rights can never be forfeited, except for crime; that marriage should be an equal and permanent partnership, and so recognized by law; that until it is so recognized, married partners should provide against the radical injustice of present laws, by every means in their power. . . . (Reprinted from Bernard, 1973, pp. 97–98.)

A MARRIAGE CONTRACT: 1972

The following are excerpts from a marriage contract entered into by Harriett Mary Cody and Harvey Joseph Sadis of Seattle, Washington, in 1972, reprinted with their permission. The contract in its entirety can be found in Ms. Magazine, *June 1973.*

Recitals of intention. HARRIETT and HARVEY desire to enter into a marriage relationship, duly solemnized under the laws of the State of Washington, the rights and obligations of which relationship differ from the traditional rights and obligations of married persons in the State of Washington which would prevail in the absence of this CONTRACT. The parties have together drafted this MARRIAGE CONTRACT in order to define a marriage relationship sought by the parties which preserves and promotes their individual identities as a man and a woman contracting to live together for mutual benefit and growth. . .

Now, THEREFORE, in consideration of their affection and esteem for each other, and in consideration of the mutual promises herein expressed, the sufficiency of which is hereby acknowledged, HARRIETT and HARVEY agree as follows:

Article I. *Names.* HARRIETT and HARVEY affirm their individuality and equality in this relationship. The parties reject the concept of ownership implied in the adoption by the woman of the man's name; and they refuse to define themselves as husband and wife because of the possessory nature of these titles.

THEREFORE, THE PARTIES AGREE to retain and use the given family names of each party. . . .

Article IV. *Children.* The joy and the commitment of the parties' relationship are not dependent on raising a family. HARRIETT and HARVEY will not be unfulfilled as individuals or as partners if they choose not to have children. At this time, the parties do not share a commitment to have children.

THE PARTIES AGREE that any children will be the result of choice, not chance, and THEREFORE the decision to have children will be mutual and deliberate. . . .

Article V. *Careers; Domicile.* ... THE PARTIES AGREE that, should a career opportunity arise for one of the parties in another city at any future time, the decision to move shall be mutual. . . .

HARVEY HEREBY WAIVES whatever right he may have to solely determine the legal domicile of the parties.

Article VI. *Care and Use of Living Space.* HARRIETT and HARVEY recognize the need for autonomy and equality within the home in terms of the use of available space and allocation of household tasks. The parties reject the concept that the responsibility for housework rests with the woman in a marriage relationship while the duties of home maintenance and repair rest with the man.

THEREFORE, THE PARTIES AGREE to share equally in the performance of all household tasks, taking into consideration individual schedules and preferences. Periodic allocations of household tasks will be made, in which the time involved in the performance of each party's tasks is equal. . . .

Article VII. *Property; Debts; Living Expenses.* HARRIETT and HARVEY intend that the individual autonomy sought in the partnership shall be reflected in the ownership of existing and future-acquired property, in the characterization and control of income, and in the responsibility for living expenses.

THEREFORE, THE PARTIES AGREE that this Article of their MARRIAGE CONTRACT, in lieu of the community property laws of the State of Washington, shall govern their interests and obligations in all property acquired during their marriage, as follows:

A. Property. THE PARTIES . . . AGREE that each party shall have sole management, control, and disposition of the property which each would have owned as a single person. . . .

THE PARTIES AGREE that the wages, salary, and other income (including loans) derived by one of the parties will be the separate property of such party and subject to the independent control and/or obligation of such party. In order to avoid the commingling of the separate assets, THE PARTIES AGREE to maintain separate bank accounts. . . .

B. Debts. THE PARTIES AGREE that they shall not be obligated to the present or future-incurred debts of the other, including tuition and other educational expenses.

C. Living Expenses. THE PARTIES AGREE to share responsibility for the following expenses, which shall be called LIVING EXPENSES, in proportion to their respective incomes: (1) Mortgage payment or rent, (2) Utilities, (3) Home maintenance, (4) Food, (5) Shared entertainment, (6) Medical expenses. Other expenses shall be called PERSONAL EXPENSES and will be borne individually by the parties. . . .

THE PARTIES AGREE that extended periods of time in which one or both of the parties will be totally without income will be mutually negotiated.

HARRIETT HEREBY WAIVES whatever right she may have to rely on HARVEY to provide the sole economic support for the family unit.

Article VIII. *Evaluation of the Partnership.* HARRIETT and HARVEY recognize the importance of change in their relationship and intend that this CONTRACT shall be a living document and a focus for periodic evaluations of the partnership.

THE PARTIES AGREE that either party can initiate a review of any article of the CONTRACT at any time for amendment to reflect changes in the relationship. THE PARTIES AGREE to honor such requests for review with negotiations and discussions at a mutually convenient time.

THE PARTIES AGREE that, in any event, there shall be an annual review of the provisions of the CONTRACT . . . on or about the anniversary date of the execution of the CONTRACT.

THE PARTIES AGREE that, in the case of unresolved conflicts between them over any provisions of the CONTRACT, they will seek mediation, professional or otherwise, by a third party.

Article IX. *Termination of the Contract.* HARRIETT and HARVEY may by mutual consent terminate this CONTRACT and end the marriage relationship at any time. . . .

THEREFORE, COMES NOW, HARRIETT MARY CODY who applauds her development which allows her to enter into this partnership of trust, and SHE AGREES to go forward with this partnership in the spirit of the foregoing MARRIAGE CONTRACT.

HARRIETT MARY CODY

THEREFORE, COMES NOW, HARVEY JOSEPH SADIS who celebrates his growth and independence with the signing of this CONTRACT, and HE AGREES to accept the responsibilities of this partnership as set forth in the foregoing MARRIAGE CONTRACT.

HARVEY JOSEPH SADIS

identity, sexual difficulties, and the like. Interestingly, most of the women did not see themselves as consciously testing or even contemplating a potential marriage. The relationships tended to be viewed as pleasurable in and of themselves, and were more like the "going steady" phase of a relationship than the engagement stage. Nevertheless, the majority found the experiences rewarding and instructive, and useful in predicting the future course of their relationships.

2. *"Open marriage."* The O'Neills, husband and wife anthropologists, have introduced the term "open marriage" to describe a goal and some guidelines for marriage ". . . in which the partners are committed to their own and to each other's growth" (1972, p. 406). The closed marriage is a product of the expectation that the partner will be able to fulfill all of the other's needs—emotional, social, economic, intellectual, sexual, and so forth. Open marriage, on the other hand, stresses more realistic expectations, such as encouragement of role flexibility, deep companionship with others, open and honest communications, and similar goals. It is left to the individual couple to determine how to produce the freest, most egalitarian, and growth-producing partnership possible for them.

3. *Marriage contracts.* A form of partnership which may or may not involve legal marriage entails the use of a more or less formal contract. Such a document may explicitly state the couple's mutual expectations for the relationship, the patterns of duties, rights, and tasks to be performed by each, conditions for termination of the relationship, and other matters. Like the "open marriage" concept (of which the contract may be a part), contracts aim at enhancing the gains and minimizing some problems of marriage without a radical departure in form. Further, marriage contracts frequently have the explicit goal of ensuring equality between the sexes and breaking down stereotyped sex roles of "husband" and "wife." Other writers have similarly urged the development of "shared role" marriages or "androgynous" relationships, in which each partner freely expresses and develops all aspects of his or her potential,

without the restrictions typically imposed by traditional sex-role socialization (Osofsky & Osofsky, 1972).

4. *Serial marriage.* Serial marriage, or "progressive monogamy," in which the individual remarries one or more times following divorce or death of the previous spouse, is more a fact than an intentional experiment in alternative marital styles (Alpenfels, 1971). Since people live longer than ever before, they will have more time to become unhappy in the relationship and decide not to continue, or will simply outlive their partners and choose another. Increasingly, it appears that individuals who anticipate dissatisfactions over a long period of time are choosing not to remain married to the same person. Remaining married to one person for a lifetime may become more rare.

Communal arrangements

Rather dramatic departures from traditional one man–one woman partnerships are encountered in a growing segment of the population. Communal arrangements vary widely in purpose and form, and thus, inclusive generalizations are impossible. However, they commonly share the goal of challenging exclusivity in marriage, and attempt to enrich personal development through multiple intimate relationships.

1. *"Swinging."* It has been estimated that between two and ten million individuals have engaged in mate-swapping or "swinging." The primary purpose of this activity is sexual variety, and it is practiced not by one particular group but by a broad range of married couples. Most "swinging" occurs with both members of the couple and is entered into by mutual consent, typically in the hope of taking advantage of sexual permissiveness and for adding spice to the sexual life of the partners. Emotional intimacy between participants is not a goal, and "swinging" does not usually alter the couple's basic life style. Indeed, it is reported that a major study of mate-swapping showed that the average couple tired of the pattern after about two

years, and dropped back into a monogamous pattern (Broderick, 1973).

2. *Group marriage.* An even more relationship-oriented marriage variant involves three or more individuals. Typically, as in conventional marriage, a primary goal is companionship, with the hope and expectation that *several* people can enjoy the depth of intimacy of marriage typically practiced only by two persons at once. Normally all members participate in sexual relations, economic responsibilities, and sharing of household duties. Hence, the patterns differ from many communal arrangements in the close parallel to two-person marriage.

Group marriages are relatively rare, involving perhaps only several thousand units. Researchers find that the group marriages typically last from several months to several years, with a median length of 14 months (Constantine & Constantine, in Bremner, 1973; Ellis, 1971). Part of the cause of their relatively short duration may be pressure from the general community. However, it is generally agreed that a major problem concerns the day-to-day details of living; decision-making processes are simply more complicated—as is accommodation—with more people involved.

3. *Communes.* Individuals may join together for political, economic, social, psychological, or other goals, and attempt to share work, resources, and closeness. Such groups vary strikingly in the relations between members, freedom of sexual expression, guiding principles, and the like. Some communes may offer an alternative to marriage, while others supplement traditional marriage and family relationships in an "intimate network of families" (Stoller, 1971), or "cooperative household."

Communal groups and group marriages offer diversity in intimate relationships, among their other "advantages." However, like most structured forms of intimacy, there are sources of failure or destructiveness. Carl Rogers (1972) has noted several of these, based upon his observations:

1. Insufficient thought given to the ways in which interpersonal conflicts, hurts, and cross-purposes might be handled.

2. Failure to solve the problem of self-support.

3. Jealousy.

4. Underestimation of the need of each person for a reasonably secure, continuing, one-to-one relationship.

5. Inability to resolve problems of highly complex relationships.

6. Failure to recognize the need of the individual for privacy.

Other choices

There are numerous other departures from traditional marriage, so that it is beginning to catch up with the institutions of religion and education in variety of form and theory. Polyandry, polygyny, and tribal marriage, among others, have been practiced or proposed. Some social scientists have been concerned with the particular needs of certain groups for particular forms of marriage, such as the young or the elderly (Kassel, 1971). Other theorists have focused less on alternate forms of intimate relationships between adults than on the alternate *family* styles and variants of childrearing environments.

A discussion of alternate forms of intimate partnership would be incomplete without at least brief mention of same-sex marriage. Careful studies are not available which delineate the characteristics of stable, close relationships between homosexual pairs, and the number of such relationships is unknown. Yet, it is apparent that many gay men and women, like their heterosexual peers, desire enduring and deep relationships with one other person. And although many pressures and obstacles confront such relationships because of their visibility in an unaccepting society, many same-sex "marriages" do endure and provide gratification for the partners. While the unions are not legally sanctioned, many formal ceremonies have been performed by clergymen who believe that marriage is a sacred bond that may exist between persons committed to each other, regardless of biological gender.

The interpersonal pitfalls of such relationships do not seem to differ from those of heterosexual marriage; the problems of poor communication, unrealistic expectations, sexual difficulties, and divergence of interests, for example, may undermine any marriage.

Same-sex marriage has been claimed by some to provide more role flexibility and greater freedom of expression than many traditional heterosexual relationships (Kelly, 1972). In any event, gay marriages are now considered by a sizable segment of our population as an alternative to traditional heterosexual marriages.

 ## Summary and a look ahead

In marriage as well as other intimate relationships, people have greater opportunities than ever before to set their own goals and standards of success—with correspondingly greater opportunities for either satisfaction or failure. We are increasingly coming to view marriage as a means for meeting our psychological needs and fostering personal growth rather than as an institutional arrangement serving sexual, economic, or social needs. Our changing attitudes toward marriage also tend to emphasize greater role flexibility in marriage and the freedom to discontinue the marriage without stigma or penalty if it does not prove satisfying. Coupled with our changing views of marriage are the emergence of greater permissiveness in sexual behavior and the decline of the "double standard," as well as increased concern about sexual performance.

The great majority of people do get married at some time in their lives, and most people agree on the qualities they seek in their relationship: companionship, satisfaction of psychological needs, and personal growth. But other factors consistently enter into the actual partners they choose. Some of these are propinquity, similarity of background and interests, and complementarity of needs and purposes.

Factors related to marital success include background factors, such as family background and social class, and personality factors, such as emotional maturity and common goals. Some of the pitfalls in marital adjustment include jealousy and possessiveness, conflicts in power and control, discrepancies in role expectations, inadequate communication, sexual maladjustment, and failure of the relationship to foster personal growth.

Divorce has become more common and widely accepted in our society, and analyzing its causes and effects is a complex task. The rate of remarriage has also increased, and though more second marriages than first marriages end in separation or divorce, remarried persons, as a group, reported greater happiness in their second marriages.

In the final portion of this chapter, we noted why some people never marry, new forms of intimate relationship—such as "trial marriages," "swinging," and group marriages—and the emergence of same-sex marriage as an alternative life style to traditional heterosexual marriage.

In this chapter we have examined the factors related to adjustment and maladjustment in one important area of social living. In the next chapter we shall look at the socialization of children in the family.

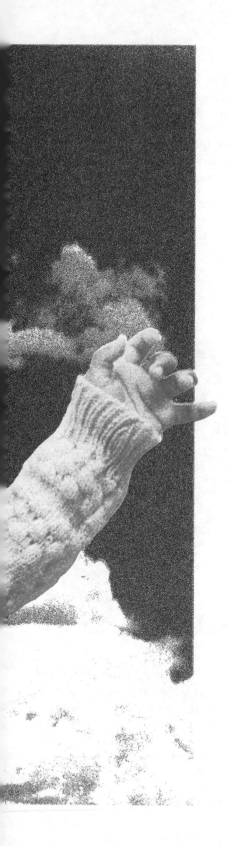

11

The Child and the Family

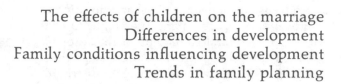

The effects of children on the marriage
Differences in development
Family conditions influencing development
Trends in family planning

It has become popular to write essays proclaiming that the family is on its way out, dying, or dead. Like Mark Twain's statement that reports about his death had been exaggerated, those of us who were raised in families and plan families of our own find such claims excessive. Nevertheless, there is no denying that deciding to have children is often a major decision; and raising them to be healthy persons can involve seemingly endless obstacles—as well as obvious satisfactions. Many people show an increasing awareness of such problems, and also an awareness of possible alternatives to the traditional manner of having and rearing children. Hence, within the last decade or so, numerous changes have occurred in attitudes and practices, and in the experience of alternatives.

The purpose of the chapter is to explore some of the psychological research and speculation on the various aspects of childrearing and family life. What are the effects for the parents of having children? What kinds of conditions appear to foster healthy development in children? What about family planning and birth control—what is new and where are we headed? Finally, what are some of the new alternatives? In addition to such changes as fewer and later children, more shared-role parenting, more working mothers, and other significant changes, what are some of the more tradition-breaking experiments in family living?

The effects of children on the marriage

There are many reasons why a couple may desire to have children. Ackerman (1958) has suggested that a woman may want to have a baby in order to counteract anxiety about sterility, to please or punish her husband, to gain the approval of her parents and friends, or to conform to the cultural stereotype of the "proper" family. Motherhood provides the stamp which validates femininity for some women (Bernard, 1973). For many women, bearing and rearing children appear to provide a sense of creativity and fulfillment; for both men and women, parenthood can be a way of achieving a measure of personal significance and meaning as one sees oneself important to others. The desire to offer life to a new human being or to bequeath a part of oneself to posterity may also be an important reason for having children.

In the past, married couples often felt obligated to have children in order to perpetuate family blood lines; with the decline of the extended family and the problem of overpopulation, this reason appears to be decreasing in importance. As with motives for getting married, reasons for having children seem to reflect increasingly the personal desires and choices of the marital partners. Whatever the reasons, they will help to determine what effect the advent of children will have on the new parents and their marriage.

The transition from couple to family necessitates major changes and adjustments. The stresses associated with the transition cannot be minimized, although most couples adjust without loss of the qualities which attracted and satisfied them as a couple. While most research attention is directed to the effects of parents on children, in this section we will consider also the significant issue of the effects of children on the parents and their relationship.

The most obvious effect of children on a marriage is the new roles they demand on the part of both husband and wife. To the role of spouse, each mate adds the role of "parent," with its attendant satisfactions and responsibilities. For both, the new role becomes a significant determinant of self-definition.

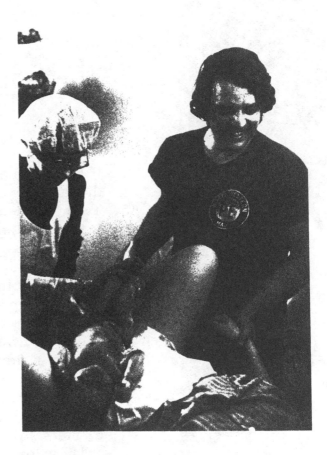

For the mother in particular, the advent of the baby is likely to lead to a drastic change in everyday activities, and she may feel that she has suddenly undertaken a new 24-hour-a-day job. If she had expected to fit the baby into an already full schedule, she may find that caring for a baby is far more time consuming than she realized and that she has little time or energy for anything else. If her husband does not help her and see that she gets "out from under" occasionally, she may feel both harassed and isolated. Eventually, of course, most women adjust to the demands so completely that, as sociologist Jessie Bernard notes, "in our country today, motherhood takes precedence over wifehood" (1973, p. 76). Lopata (1971), in a study of housewives, found that the largest proportion of them gave motherhood as a source of satisfaction (38 percent) compared with wifehood (8 percent). So significant is the woman's investment in the role of mother in many cases, that psychiatric symptoms may accompany the loss of the maternal role. For example, Bart (1972) found that women who had put the role of mother above all others were more likely to show symptoms of depression in middle age when they had to relinquish that role. Once their children left home, they felt useless and worthless.

The woman's transition from the role of "wife" to that of "mother"—which for many women signifies that they have finally achieved their "place"—has numerous implications for the marital relationship. The husband must often face the difficult adjustment of recognizing that his wife now has less time and energy to devote to meeting his needs. He must recognize that he must now share her love and attention while attempting to respond to her need for extra emotional support and physical help. Where the husband feels that he is being neglected and left out, considerable strain may be placed on the marital relationship.

How the husband and wife perceive their new roles as parents will be of key importance to their approach to childrearing as well as to their personal adjustments to parenthood. Duvall (1962), for example, has compared two types of roles that parents may take: a *traditional* role and a *developmental* one. The traditional role focuses on the physical care of the child, matters of discipline, and efforts to see that his behavior conforms to social norms and standards. A developmental role focuses on the fostering of healthy personality growth and optimal realization of the child's inherent potentials; it is concerned with the more subtle psychological aspects of parent-child relationships. Thus, a father who follows the traditional role may view himself primarily as the provider for the family and leave the details of childrearing to the mother; whereas a father who takes a more developmental role spends a good deal of time with his children to provide guidance and help and to encourage their personal growth.

Marital happiness and stability

Giving birth and raising children to be competent, well-functioning, unique persons is a notable achievement, and a source of pride and fulfillment. Most couples, when asked, report that children have added greatly to their happiness.

On the other hand, childrearing is an enormous strain on time, energy, and personal and physical resources, and both the direct and indirect effects of the presence of children may induce a variety of conflicts and frustrations in a marital relationship. In terms of marital happiness and stability, the cost of raising children may be high.

In the early months of marriage a couple is faced with many adjustive demands, and the advent of a child often appears to increase the stressfulness of such demands. Pregnancy may cause a wife to feel unwell or may bring financial worries. Whether or not they wanted the child, husband and wife usually find that they have less time to be alone together, less time for joint adult activities, and less money for their own enjoyment.

Interestingly enough, Feldman and Rogoff (1969) found that in some cases where husband and wife were especially close and dependent on each other, the advent of a baby led to a decrease in marital happiness, while in other cases, where a couple's interests were dissimilar before childbirth, the arrival of a baby strengthened their relationship. In the first situation, three appeared to be "a crowd"; in the second, the sharing of parental responsibilities brought the partners closer together.

For most couples the new responsibilities and role changes that come with the advent of children are taken in stride, though with differing degrees of enthusiasm and sophistication. In general, the better adjusted the husband and wife are to each other, the less stress they experience in adjusting to their new roles as parents and the more likely they will be to find that parenthood adds significance and satisfaction to the life they are building together. On the other hand, if the husband and wife are maladjusted in their marriage, parenthood is usually a poor solution in terms of both the success of the marriage and the happiness of the child.

It is true that the rate of divorce is higher among childless couples than in marriages where children are present. This results primarily from the legal and psychological ease of divorce when no children are present. It is

though childless husbands and fathers did not differ markedly in their perception of marital satisfaction, a much larger proportion of childless husbands reported that they were "very happy." More fathers than childless husbands felt dissatisfied with themselves and inadequate. Similar results were obtained on data collected nearly a decade later, and where race and income were held constant (Renne, 1970).

With respect to the effects of large vs. small families, the data are somewhat inconsistent, with some research suggesting no differences between large and small families, and other studies reporting bad effects of large families. (No studies confirm myths about "one big happy family.") A recent review of studies of family size draws the following conclusions:

My mother began having children one year after they were married. They didn't have much money, and children made it even harder. I don't plan to have children right away after marriage.

I just expected that all of a sudden with the child there that he would change to father and I would change to mother—and he didn't change to father. It came as a terrible shock.

literally true that children hold a marriage together, in some cases, although probably at considerable cost in terms of marital discord and family discontent.

On the other hand, there is some research evidence which suggests that marital happiness is higher among childless couples than those with children. Veroff and Feld (1970), in an analysis of data collected in the 1950s, reported that childless marriages which survive are happier than marriages with children. Mothers, compared with childless wives, are much more likely to report that they find marriage restrictive, and that there are problems in the marriage. Fewer report marital satisfaction. Al-

1. In discordant marriages, the chance for a successful outcome decreases as the number of children increases.

2. The poorest marital adjustment is found among those with unwanted children. Happiness is associated with the desire for children, whether or not couples have them at the time.

3. An inverse relationship exists between marital adjustment and family size; the more children, the less adjustment (Lieberman, 1970).

The effects children are having on the marriage depend not only on the size of the family, but also on the age of the children, and on whether it is the father's or the mother's attitudes that are assessed. Rollins and Feldman

(1970) assessed the attitudes toward various aspects of the marital relationship for a large number of wives and husbands of different ages, with children of different ages. The early years of marriage before the advent of a child are high in satisfaction, and there is a downward trend as the child grows older, with low points in the teenage and young adult years. Once the child has exited from the household and the parents have adjusted to the "empty nest," the childless retirement years show a high degree of marital satisfaction. Interestingly, wives expressed more satisfaction than husbands in the earliest and latest stages; husbands showed more satisfaction in most of the intervening periods. The "postchildren" phase is a relatively recent by-product of greater longevity and retirement laws and benefits. The postparental marriage phase will probably gain increasing attention as its prevalence increases and its potentials are recognized.

In summary, the effects of having children will depend upon a variety of factors. The reasons for having children may strongly influence the reactions of the parents to the demands of childrearing. The nature of the adjustments required by the parents, and their skills and resources for coping with such changes will be important. The changes in their patterns of relating to each other and their levels of energy and dedication to the enterprise are also among the many factors which will affect their ultimate adaptation to the enormously complex task of raising children.

Differences in development

Researchers are increasingly impressed with the uniqueness of each child they study. Though any scientific search must be for order and uniformities and predictable patterns, they keep reminding us that generalizations never fully encompass any particular individual, that the most basic fact about him is his individuality. It is always unique individuals that are being ob-

served, and it is their uniqueness that we are ultimately interested in understanding.

In studying the development of children, in all its variations, two basic questions soon arise: (1) the question of *evaluation*—what development is "healthy" and how do you get your standards of evaluation; and (2) the question of *determinants*—what factors influence and shape development to produce the infinite variations we see? In this section we will discuss the problem of evaluation and two broad classes of determinants. Then, in the following section, at greater length, we will discuss what are probably the most important determinants—the many family influences that shape development.

The problem of defining "healthy" development

Various views of healthy development have been advanced. One popular view considers development as healthy when there is no apparent physical or psychological pathology and no marked deviation from the average of the group. A second view considers development as healthy to the extent that there is an optimal realization of the individual's potentials; lack of pathology or deviation is not sufficient. A third approach to healthy development is to set up criteria—such as autonomy or a realistic frame of reference—which are commonly agreed upon as essential for psychological health. Using this approach, development is considered healthy to the extent that these characteristics are present.

"Normal" vs. "optimal" as healthy Viewing healthy development as absence of disease or pathology is a projection of the medical view that physical health is a lack of disease. Since the human system tends toward normality and health—on both biological and psychological levels—health is viewed as an almost universal phenomenon under favorable conditions, and development is considered "normal" or "healthy" when it does not deviate markedly from the norm.

Such a negative approach, however, is not very satisfactory when dealing with personality development. Take the case of an adolescent, for example, who is making passing grades in his schoolwork, getting along well with his classmates and teachers, and showing no indications of delinquency or serious maladjustment, but drifting along and using only a fraction of his superior intellectual ability. Such an adolescent is not "sick," but is he healthy?

Considerations such as this have led to a more positive view of healthy development. As defined by the World Health Organization, health is "a state of complete physical, mental, and social well-being and not merely the absence of disease or infirmity." Here, healthy development, by implication, would go beyond the average or norm in the direction of optimal development—toward self-actualization and the fulfillment of potential.

The concept of optimal development is a meaningful one, but we are a long way from agreeing on just what pattern of traits or behaviors constitutes optimal development. What people regard as desirable and optimal inevitably reflects the customs, demands, beliefs, and values of the larger society as well as the personal beliefs and values of the person making the judgment. Thus, optimal development is a general principle and not something we are yet in a position to define and measure precisely. But as a principle, it appears to be gaining adherents as modern science enables us to eliminate many conditions long assumed to be an inevitable part of the human situation and to specify and create conditions conducive to fuller development of physical and psychological potentials.

Multiple criteria approach

Neither a view of health as freedom from pathology nor a definition in terms of optimal development solves the problem of actually specifying what development is healthy. For neither approach supplies us with criteria for evaluating development in given cases.

In an attempt to supply such criteria, two major approaches have been utilized. The first derives such criteria from the conceptual framework of a particular model of human behavior. For example, psychoanalysis provides a general conceptual framework for evaluating development in terms of progression through various psychosexual stages and the development of ego and superego.

The second approach consists of arbitrarily listing qualities—for example, self-confidence and a realistic frame of reference—which appear to be components of healthy development. Such lists, of course, vary considerably depending upon the theoretical and value orientation of the investigator constructing the list. Yet, there are a number of characteristics which are common to most lists and on which most investigators would agree. One comprehensive approach of this type by Jahoda (1958) was summarized in the illustration in Chapter 7, p. 175. It listed such qualities as attitudes toward self, perception of reality, integration, competencies, autonomy, growth, and self-actualization.

Although these criteria provide useful guides for assessing development, they are limited both qualitatively and quantitatively. By *qualitative* limitations, we refer to the somewhat arbitrary nature of any list. Why these criteria rather than others? The emphasis on autonomy and self-actualization in Jahoda's list, for example, clearly reflects values of our particular culture. By *quantitative* limitations we refer to the lack of specification. Again, referring to the descriptions of the criteria in the Jahoda list, what perception is "realistic"? How much self-direction is "adequate"? How much stress tolerance is "good"? Who is to say, and on what basis? And how wide a variation is "normal"? The problem of the overall patterning of such criteria in a healthy personality is also left unspecified. And finally, in applying such criteria to a given case, it is apparent that allowances would have to be made for age, sex, social class, and other sources of variation.

The whole problem is further complicated by the fact that as we learn more about human development, we keep changing the criteria by which we make judgments. The quiet, polite little boy who never expressed anger was admired in the Victorian era but today is usually regarded as inhibited and out of touch with his real feelings. Similarly, with improved educational procedures, the intellectual development that is average or normal for a six-year-old today may be considered indicative of mental retardation in the world of the year 2000.

Although we need much more knowledge about human potentials and needs before we can establish adequate standards for evaluating an individual's psychological development, the basic dimensions and the criteria which we have examined appear to point to the variables with which we are going to have to deal as well as to certain family conditions which appear to foster healthy development.

A longitudinal study of infant development by Chess, Thomas, and Birch (1968) found that a particular type of temperament, such as that of the "difficult baby," may predispose an individual to later maladjustment. According to this study, some 7 to 10 percent of all babies are "different"—they have irregular patterns of eating, sleeping, and elimination; tend to cry a great deal and to show a predominantly negative mood; and are irritable and have difficulty in adjusting to new stimuli and change. In her efforts to deal with such a baby, the mother usually tries first one method and then another, so that she is highly inconsistent in her interactions with the infant. In addition, she does not gain the satisfaction from the infant that she

 Girls are taught nice little 'pink' girl's things and boys are taught tough 'big' boy's things. They should be taught 'human' thoughts!

Differences are apparent at birth

Characteristics present at birth are called *constitutional* characteristics because they are part of the equipment the baby arrives with. We assume that there is a large genetic component in such characteristics, but we never can be sure how much unknown prenatal influences may already have affected the development of genetic potentials. Several differences apparent at birth begin at once to influence a child's subsequent development.

Constitutional reaction tendencies
As we saw in an earlier chapter, several "primary reaction tendencies" have been observed in very young babies. Traits such as general vigor, autonomic reactivity, and sociability seem to be identifiable very early and are consistent for a given individual throughout his development, helping to determine his style of coping with life's challenges and his capacity for withstanding stress.

expected. The result is often a disturbance in the mother-infant relationship that has undesirable consequences for both of them.

Sex differences
From the moment of birth, when the infant's sex becomes known, adults' expectations and values begin to play a significant role in shaping the behavior of the child. It is extremely difficult to assess whether or not behavioral differences between boys and girls exist from birth and if so, what their consequences on subsequent development are. Preliminary studies suggest that male infants at birth are more physically active, cry and fuss more, and are less sensitive to certain kinds of tactile stimulation, while girls are quieter, less active, and have lower thresholds for tactile stimulation (Moss, 1967; Bardwick, 1971). Within a few months, girls sleep more, cry less, vocalize earlier, and, compared with males, prefer more novel and varied stimulation on the average (Moss, 1967; Goldberg & Lewis, 1972). Observations of mothers interacting with their infants in the first few months of life reveal that mothers handle boys more and

stress their musculature and movement, and handle girls less but talk to them (Moss, 1967). Young boys, of course, are expected to be stronger and more active than girls, and indeed, show more high-intensity behaviors—often labeled "aggression"—while girls are expected to be more demure and passive. While the separate effects of biological differences and social learning experiences are unclear, it is apparent that the child's sex is a direct or indirect determinant of many enduring characteristics, such as passivity and dependency for girls and aggressiveness for boys (Kagan & Moss, 1962).

Infants and parents influence each other

As a result of various dispositional characteristics and behaviors present from birth, the child may influence the parents to respond in certain ways. For example, a child who is constitutionally disposed to display assertive behaviors may provoke one or both parents to consistently angry or impatient responses. Unassertive, placid children, on the other hand, may elicit more urging and prompting behavior from their parents. The mutually influencing responses of parent and child will eventually produce unique and consistent behavior in the child, a process which helps explain how children within the same family can be quite different.

Research suggests that children and their parents can affect many of each other's behaviors. Especially provocative are indications of the mutual interaction of mother and baby in determining the amount of crying and fussing (Moss & Robson, 1968), smiling (Gewirtz, 1961), and vocalizing (Moss, 1967). The behavior of each evidently provides reinforcement for the other. Thus, if the fussing child quiets when the mother responds, a cycle of increased fussing and comforting may be perpetuated.

All of these results—the suggestions of genetic and constitutional differences which lead to different behaviors among children, and the research which suggests that the child's behavior influences the parent—indicate the need for concern with the "direction of effects." The child is more than a lump of clay to be passively molded by his or her parents; rather, he keeps eliciting responses from them and others so that the socialization process is a complex pattern of mutual interactions and influences within the family.

Sociocultural factors affect development

In addition to the constitutional disposition of the child, sex, and interaction within the family, another significant source of influence on the development of the child is the norms, attitudes, and practices of the parents as a function of their social class and cultural heritage.

Social class and racial differences in family structure

There are indications that the relationship between husband and wife is more equalitarian and the roles more flexible in middle- and upper-class marriages than in lower-class marriages. In lower-class families the lines of authority tend to be more firmly drawn, and specific tasks and functions are more sharply divided between spouses in accord with the more rigid sex typing in the lower class (Bronfenbrenner, 1961; Clausen, 1966). Besner (1967), summarizing several studies, concludes that lower-class husbands and wives are more distant from each other, feel greater emotional isolation and suspicion, and encounter more friction than middle-class couples. Their distance is reinforced by the rigid roles and relative lack of sharing; their isolation is reflected in more divergent activities and a greater clinging to premarriage ties than is true in middle-class marriages.

Another common occurrence in the very low socioeconomic groups is the single-parent, female-based family. Present welfare policy often actively encourages this pattern by refusing aid to dependent children if a man is present. Estimates of the percent of childrearing units of this type in urban slum areas are between 25 and 40 percent or even higher in particular areas (Besner, 1967). Often a grandmother or other female relative is present in the household as well. Characteristically, the mother depends heavily on the older children, particularly the older girls, to help run the household and raise the younger children.

Whether in intact or broken families, there is evidence from census data that women of the lowest classes and with the least education have the most children. Although having children is emotionally very important in the lives of many of these women, a large proportion of the children are undesired and unplanned. One indication of this is the finding of one study that women in the lowest of five socioeconomic

whites and blacks, with black mothers more often working and a much larger proportion of broken homes among blacks.

Social-class differences in childrearing

Problems in sampling, assessment technique, and terminology have hampered research on different childrearing practices among different social classes. An additional difficulty is that although class and race differences in childrearing have been documented, research has almost never examined the direct consequences of these differences on the children's behavior. Finally,

 I lived from the age of six or seven till about the age of twenty, in the same apartment house, which I know from the very top to the very bottom, and I know every brick, every loose brick. And I'm sure they're still there today and I could find them if I went back. It's a wonderful building, it had a basement where we used to skate in the wintertime, and it had a roof garden that was just wonderful. We kids had . . . there were about ten kids lived there, and we all grew up together, and we had wonderful times. It was kind of like an extended family—they all watched me grow up. Some of them loved me and some of them hated me.

groups preferred the least number of children, but had the most (Blood & Wolfe, 1960). Explanations include ignorance of and unavailability of contraceptives and abortion in the lower classes. Typical estimates are that effective contraception reaches only about 10 percent of the poor, while the vast majority would like to be able to plan their families.

Within the lower social classes, black families typically have more children, and larger family size combines with poor housing to produce greater "crowdedness" (Bloom, Whiteman, & Deutsch, 1967). In addition to family size, there are differences in the basic family patterns of

Caldwell (1964) notes that the generalizations about differences in childrearing give insufficient recognition to the "impressive interclass similarities."

It is apparent that childrearing practices have shifted over time, with the various social classes displaying different patterns from one generation to the next. Bronfenbrenner (1958) found that over a span of 25 years, parents in general, but especially middle-class parents, became more permissive of the child's spontaneous desires, more expressive of affection, and increasingly reliant on "psychological" as opposed to physical discipline. The faster rate of change in attitudes and practices by middle-class parents has often been attributed to their greater exposure to, and greater reliance upon, professional child-guidance advice.

Bronfenbrenner found a tendency for middle-class parents to be more tolerant of the child's dependency needs, and more permissive in toilet, sex, and aggression training. At the same time, middle-class parents also expected more independence and responsibility and had higher academic aspirations for their children, compared with working-class parents. The most consistent finding of his review, and one which has often been replicated, is that working-class parents more frequently used physical punishment for discipline, whereas middle-class parents more often used "love-oriented" or "psychological" techniques, such as reasoning, guilt induction, symbolic rewards and punishments, and the like. Clausen and Williams (1963) found that middle-class parents showed greater permissiveness toward the infant and young child, but working-class parents granted greater freedom from parental control and supervision to the older child and adolescent.

In terms of family organization, the lower-class family appears to be more rigid and hierarchical than the middle-class family. Consequently, parent-child as well as parent-parent relationships tend to be more egalitarian and acceptant in the middle classes, and channels of communication are more direct, with both parents more accessible to all family members than in lower classes (Bronfenbrenner, 1958; Clausen & Williams, 1963).

Poverty, discrimination, and other social pathology

When there are conditions in the community or larger society that have a pervasively detrimental effect on the development and behavior of children exposed to them, we speak of *social pathology* because a disordered society rather than a disordered organism is at the root of the trouble. Included here may be a wide range of conditions, such as poverty, racial discrimination, war, chronic violence, and social disorganization.

Even in affluent America, almost 30 million Americans are estimated to be living below the "poverty line" as defined by the Social Security Administration. Although their income is far higher in absolute terms than that of the poor in many parts of the world, it is not enough to provide a decent standard of living here. The gap between advantaged and disadvantaged has been made glaringly apparent through the mass media and represents a major problem in our society.

Adults who are trapped in low-income areas, especially in the big cities, are apt to be chronically submerged in a whole complex of difficult and often insoluble problems, thus lacking both material and psychological resources for the adequate rearing of their children. In general, studies have shown a higher rate and wider range of maladjustment problems for lower-class children, especially boys, than for middle-class children (Glidewell & Swallow, 1968).

Crucial family conditions influencing development

The family has been termed society's basic institution, the mediator between society and the individual. Psychologically, the family is the primary medium in which the functions necessary for a fulfilling and productive life are acquired—the development not only of interpersonal and emotional expression, a sense of security, worth, and belongingness, but also to a large extent, both intellectual and interpersonal competence.

In these days of chronic and pervasive social change, the family is largely cut off from the parents' own extended families. The task of socialization of young children falls almost entirely on the parents, until the children are old enough to be influenced by their peers, schools, and the mass media. Numerous aspects of child-rearing have been investigated. Our space permits only a brief summary of a few major ingredients of family life which are thought to be crucial to the quality of development.

There are numerous methodological pitfalls involved in research in child development, and findings must be interpreted with caution. It is hazardous to attempt to generalize about broad traits such as "independence" or parental "warmth," "permissiveness," and the like because such terms are typically employed somewhat differently by different investigators; moreover, since human behavior is so complex and multidetermined, many apparent inconsistencies in research outcomes make generalizations misleading. Another caution is that the topics discussed here are by no means exhaustive of what we know about family influences upon the child. For example, such features of family structure as birth order, number of siblings, family density—all enormously significant determinants of behavior—have been omitted for lack of space. Thus, the brief summaries which follow must be accepted as limited and tentative statements of the effects of several family conditions on the development of children. In many cases, the topics chosen may reflect the amount of research attention devoted to them as much as they represent crucial conditions. Finally, it should be noted that the complex interactions among the various factors have not been adequately examined by psychologists, so that much information that would be of immediate, practical use is lacking.

No parent is entirely consistent in his or her reactions to a particular child, and the two parents may differ in their treatment of and influence on the child. Nevertheless, researchers have found ways of categorizing parental reactions to a child which appear to be relatively stable over time and relatively consistent in their influence on the child's development.

Emotional warmth and acceptance

An atmosphere of love and acceptance of the child, as might be expected, has been demonstrated to be an important factor in healthy personality development. Sears, Maccoby, and Levin (1957) in one of the first comprehensive studies of childrearing practices concluded that the most crucial and pervasive of all the influences exerted in the home were the love and warmth expressed by the parents.

The positive effects of love and acceptance

A close relationship has been demonstrated between parental love and acceptance and the development of such crucial traits as self-esteem, self-reliance, independence, and self-control (Coopersmith, 1967; Peck & Havighurst, 1960; Bandura & Walters, 1963). Evidently parental warmth and acceptance determine how readily a child identifies with his parents and accepts their values and standards. If they express warmth toward the child, the child can identify with them and use their behavior as a model for expressing his own feelings toward others. Pringle (1965) found that institutionalized children who had not experienced lasting love and loyalty from any adult were unable to develop feelings of love and loyalty in their own relationships. Hurley (1965) found that intelligence was enhanced by parental acceptance and affection and diminished by parental rejection.

As with proper physical care, parental love and acceptance pay many subtle dividends in personality development. Love and acceptance help the child to develop a basic sense of trust toward his parents and the world around him, which becomes a major safeguard against fear and anxiety—thus giving him the feeling of security he needs to be able to explore his environment confidently and accept its demands; only as he does so can he master developmental tasks and develop new competencies. Furthermore, for the child who feels loved and accepted, many conditions that might otherwise seriously impair development, such as a physical handicap, poverty, or unusually strict or harsh discipline, may be to a considerable extent neutralized.

Love and acceptance usually form part of a broader pattern of positive family interrelationships. For example, love and acceptance tend to be accompanied by an interest in the child and

 I've had the great fortune to be raised in an un-
broken home, and the love of both my parents.
We have a close relationship and face problems
together. I've been brought up to cope with the
world rather than avoid it.

what he is doing, by respect for the child as a person, and by displays of warmth and affection (Coopersmith, 1967). The child is typically encouraged to interact with his world—within limits essential for his protection—and is subjected to firm but not coercive controls (Hurley, 1965). Often, too, the parents encourage the child to meet high but realistic standards. Thus, a whole cluster of attitudes and actions is usually involved in "love and acceptance." Farnsworth made this point very well in the context of the broader needs of the child:

"If a child encounters essentially friendly and accepting attitudes in the people around him during his years of helpless dependency, he has a reasonably good chance of growing up with basic attitudes of trust and a sort of optimism that enables him to make satisfying contacts with his fellows as he goes along. Every child needs affection, the feeling of belonging and being wanted, respect as an individual in his own right, a favorable setting for growth and the development of security, freedom from excessive domination, firm discipline from a respected source, and privacy enough to allow his active imagination to develop. He usually reacts more favorably to judicious praise than to indiscriminate fault finding; and he needs to feel that what he does has meaning. Most of these needs are met almost automatically when the mother and all other members of the family have a warm relationship with the child" (1966, p. 44).

 Having two children is having to be a psychologist on everyday terms. Bringing children into the world only makes you a parent. Knowing how to bring them up is something else! Each day can bring a new problem, as with each age of the child. Knowing how to handle problems and yourself can make life much easier for everyone in your home.

The negative effects of rejection

Rejection may be manifested in various ways—by physical neglect, invidious comparisons with other children, ridicule, refusing the child attention, denying him affection, not spending time with him, showing lack of respect for him and his feelings or lack of interest in him, covert or overt hostility, and coercive control techniques, such as intimidation. In a minority of cases cruel and abusive treatment is involved. Parental rejection may be partial or complete, passive or active, behavioral or verbal, and subtle or overtly cruel.

The effects of rejection vary considerably depending upon the degree of rejection, whether both parents are involved, the degree of acceptance and affection shown by the other parent or other adults, the way the parent's behav-

confident interactions with his world. Since the rejected child is not rewarded by praise and encouragement for desirable behavior, it is also more difficult for him to discriminate between approved and disapproved behavior. Nor does he have the motivation of wanting to imitate or please his parents because of admiring and identifying with them. Presumably for these reasons, rejected children have been found to be slower in conscience development than accepted children (Sears et al., 1957).

In view of their low self-esteem, it is hardly surprising that rejected children tend to need constant reassurance and often try to obtain it by attention-getting behaviors, such as showing off. The frustration created by neglect and rejection may also lead to hostile, aggressive behavior; the most overtly aggressive and poorly controlled behavior seems to result when the

 I sure wanted to please my father. When something was on television that was funny, I'd look to see if he laughed. I wanted his attention. He never paid any attention to us except to get mad at us.

ior is perceived and interpreted by the child, and other aspects of the child's total life situation. In general, however, rejected children tend to be anxious, insecure, low in self-esteem, jealous, attention seeking, aggressive, hostile, and lonely (Bandura & Walters, 1959; Siegelman, 1965; Jenkins, 1968). In later life many rejected children appear to have serious difficulty in giving and receiving love and affection.

Several of these characteristics merit further consideration. Since the child's self-concept is largely a reflection of the way significant others react to him, it is not surprising that parental rejection tends to foster a devaluated self-concept or, as Coopersmith (1967) found, "feelings of personal insignificance." If his parents do not see him as being of worth, it is difficult for the child to view himself in a positive way and to develop the feelings of self-esteem needed for

rejecting parent is both hostile and permissive toward the child (Bandura & Walters, 1959; Becker, 1964).

Baldwin (1955) found that rejected children tended to be less alert mentally and to do poorer schoolwork. Exploring this theme further, Hurley (1965) has hypothesized that the common core of discouragement and unpleasant emotional climate has a general inhibiting and suppressing effect on the child's curiosity and intellectual functioning. Whether or not we fully subscribe to Hurley's hypotheses, it is of interest to note that he found parental rejection associated with diminished intelligence during early school years, particularly for mother-daughter relationships. And we probably would agree with his conclusion that his findings tend to tie in with "many strands of evidence suggesting that punitive, coercive, and repressive interper-

sonal experiences have a brutalizing and intellectually impoverishing influence upon humans" (1965, p. 28).

Rejection is not a one-way street, and the child may reject his parents whether or not he is rejected by them. This sometimes occurs when the parents belong to a low-status minority group of which the child is ashamed. This type of rejection and its results have not been studied systematically but undoubtedly it tends to deny the child needed models, loving relationships, and other essentials for healthy development.

Perhaps paradoxically, rejection is often combined with overprotection. Maternal overprotection or "momism" involves the "smothering" of the child's growth. The mother may watch over the child constantly, prevent him from taking the slightest risk, overly clothe and medicate him, protect him from others, and make up his mind for him at every opportunity. Usually the child is protected from exposure to any kind of family illness or other emergency. Often the parent spends too much time with the child, so that he has little or no exposure to other children. In the case of mother-son relationships, there is often excessive physical contact, in which the mother sleeps with the child for years and is subtly seductive in her relationships with him. Here it is of interest to note that the early study by Levy (1943)—which first drew attention to the problem of "momism"—found that 75 percent of the abnormally protective mothers had little in common with their husbands. Apparently the mother attempted to gain satisfactions through contact with her son that should normally have been achieved in her marriage. In such cases, it is not uncommon for the mother to call her son "lover" and to encourage him in somewhat typical courting behavior.

Not surprisingly, children of overly protective mothers usually lack self-reliance and the ability to cope realistically with their problems. In a study of the family backgrounds of children referred to a child guidance clinic, Jenkins (1968) found that children characterized as "overanxious" were likely to have an infantilizing, overprotective mother. In shielding the child from every danger, the mother denies him opportunities for needed reality testing and for developing essential competencies. In addition, her overprotection tells him, in effect, that she regards him as incapable of fending for himself. It is not surprising that such children, as adolescents and young adults, often feel inadequate and threatened by a dangerous world. Although girls may also be the victims of parental overprotection, the effects seem to be more serious for boys, tending more to passivity, lack of initiative, and overdependency (Kagan & Moss, 1962).

Closely related to overprotection is restrictiveness. Here the parents exercise maximal control over the child, rigidly enforcing restrictive rules and standards and giving the child little autonomy or freedom for growing in his own way. Whether such complaints were justified or not, Douvan and Adelson (1966) found that "parental restrictions" were the most common complaint that adolescent girls made against their parents.

The effects of severe restrictiveness appear to vary considerably, depending on the nature and duration of the restrictions, the age of the child when they are introduced, the sex of the child, and the family context in which the restrictiveness occurs. The effects may not be the same where severe restrictions are introduced early and maintained throughout childhood and into adolescence as where the parents have initially been rather permissive and later "slap on restrictions" because they think the child or adolescent is misusing his freedom. In a review of available research findings, Becker (1964) concluded that while restrictiveness fosters well-controlled, socialized behavior, it also tends to foster fearful, dependent, and submissive behavior, repressed hostility, and some dulling of intellectual striving. In a study of young adult college men, Keniston (1967) has also implicated severe restrictiveness, coupled with other parental inadequacies, as a major cause of alienation.

Effective discipline

The child invariably requires help in learning appropriate behaviors. This requires both inducing and shaping desired responses and eliminating undesirable ones without also inducing unwanted side effects, such as fear of the parent, generalized inhibition, or mere temporary suppression of the behavior so that it may reappear once the parent is out of sight. This whole process, but especially the correction and shaping aspects, goes under the general term *discipline*.

Parents have been particularly baffled during recent years with respect to appropriate forms of discipline. Sometimes a misinterpretation of psychological findings and models has led to the view that all punishment and frustration should be avoided lest the child be warped in his development. In other cases parents have resorted to excessively harsh discipline for what they thought was the child's good. And in still other cases, the parents seem to have had no general guidelines, punishing the child one day and ignoring or even rewarding him the next for doing the same thing.

Research suggests that it is fruitful to consider various dimensions of discipline separately: the general degree of punitiveness or permissiveness, the form of discipline used (withdrawal of rewards, reasoning), and the consistency with which the discipline is applied.

Permissiveness-punitiveness

Some parents are unable or unwilling to interfere at all with the child's behaviors. One or both parents may cater to the child's every whim and fail to teach or reward desirable behavior.

Overly indulged children have been found to be characteristically spoiled, selfish, inconsiderate, and demanding (Becker, 1964; Watson, 1965). Sears (1961) also found high permissiveness and low punishment in the home positively correlated with antisocial, aggressive behavior, particularly during middle and later childhood. Unlike the rejected, emotionally deprived child, who may find it difficult to enter into warm human relationships, the indulged child enters

Although most parents try to protect their children from hurt, a minority are cruel and abusive. It has been estimated that some 50,000 to 70,000 infants and young children each year in the United States are severely neglected, cruelly treated, or starved and that over 300,000 children are in foster homes for such reasons (Morris, 1966). In a two-year study of this problem, Earl (1965) found that each year hundreds of the victims die and many others are paralyzed or deformed or become mentally retarded as a consequence of physical damage. The following are examples of the cases he found:

A 29-month-old boy whose mother claimed he was a behavior problem beat him with a stick and screwdriver handle, dropped him on the floor, beat his head on the wall or threw him against it, choked him to force his mouth open to eat, and burned him on the face and hands. The child eventually died after a severe beating.

A blond, blue-eyed four-year-old girl was admitted unconscious to a hospital. Examination disclosed a fractured skull, and lacerations covering her back, face, arms, and legs. Later she reportedly told the doctors, "Mama kept hitting me with a big black stick."

An indignant mother, in a fit of temper over her 2½-year-old daughter's inability to control a bowel movement, gave the child an enema with near-scalding water. A major operation was required to save the girl's life.

As one might suspect, the parents most commonly involved in such behavior appear to be emotionally unstable or mentally ill. Alcoholic fathers were found in the group, particularly in cases of rape and child beating, but disturbed mothers appeared to be the more common offenders. Some of the children were illegitimate, but the majority were not. Studies have shown that most parents who batter their children have themselves been reared with neglect and brutality and without love (Silver, Dublin, & Lourie, 1969).

A hopeful note is sounded here by the findings of Kadushin (1967) and his associates who found that the battered children they studied who had been removed from their parents by court order and placed for adoption did not appear to have been seriously damaged by their earlier experiences.

readily into such relationships but exploits them for his own purposes in much the same way that he has exploited his parents. In dealing with authority, such children are usually rebellious since they have had their own way for so long. Often they approach problems in an aggressive and demanding way and find it difficult to accept present frustrations in the interests of long-range goals. Also the overly indulged child often has little appreciation of goals or rewards because he has never had to work for them.

At the other extreme, harsh or overly severe discipline may have a variety of effects, including fear and hatred of the punishing person, little initiative or spontaneity, and a lack of friendly feelings toward others (Watson, 1965; Becker, 1964). When accompanied by rigid moral standards, overly severe discipline is likely to result in a seriously repressed child who lacks spontaneity and warmth and devotes much of his energy to controlling his own unacceptable impulses. Such children often suffer severe self-recrimination and self-punishment for real or imagined mistakes and misdeeds. Overly harsh or severe punishment, combined with general restrictiveness, may also lead to socially deviant behavior (Winder & Rau, 1962) and to rebellion as the child grows older and is subjected increasingly to outside influences which may be incompatible with the views and practices of his parents.

Any punishment conveys to the child most emphatically the message, "You've failed." For this reason, it is considered important for a parent to make it clear that in disapproving the child's behavior, he is not disapproving or rejecting the child himself. It is also important to make clear what response will be acceptable, rather than just saying in effect "No, you're wrong."

In our family we didn't have much corporal, physical punishment. What I remember is being what I consider coerced, or reasoned, into being 'good.' I knew what I was supposed to do and what I wasn't supposed to do, and I broke the rules occasionally, but we were taught to discipline ourselves from inside, from an inner knowledge of what was right and wrong. Of course, that was my mother and father's idea of what was right and wrong, but I consider that I have severely disciplined, or rather controlled, myself, and if I have done things that I considered wrong—that I've been taught were wrong—I'm punished by a feeling of guilt and a feeling of being a bad person.

Methods of discipline

Typically, most parents use a variety of discipline techniques, depending on the child and the offense: spanking, scolding, verbal threats, withdrawal of material rewards such as privileges and allowances for minor problems; also, parents depend on reasoning where feasible. Child development researchers have distinguished between physical and psychological forms of discipline.

1. *Physical punishment.* In a review of available studies, Walters and Parke concluded that "physical punishment may have diverse effects dependent on such parameters as the intensity, timing, and frequency of punishment, the strength and nature of the punished response, the relationship between the agent and recipient of punishment, and the consistency with which punishment is administered" (1967, p. 180). There are some indications that consistent use of physical punishment is associated with aggressive behavior in sons, possibly because the sons are using the aggressive, physically punitive parent as a model (Glueck & Glueck, 1950; Bandura & Walters, 1959). On the other hand, physical punishment has been shown to be effective in inhibiting undesirable behavior, particularly if the discipline is sufficiently intense

and the previous relationship with the parent satisfactory (Walters & Parke, 1967). Unwanted consequences of physical punishment, besides aggressiveness, are the possibility that the child will become fearful of the parent, that behavior in general will be inhibited, and that the child may simply learn to refrain from performing the behavior in the parent's presence.

2. *Psychological techniques.* Psychological techniques have received increasing attention from researchers. There are various forms of psychological discipline, including reasoning, demonstration of confidence and trust, and provision of opportunities for responsible behavior, with praise, recognition, and other reinforcement when it occurs. Such discipline may be based on goals, ground rules, and expectations that the child has helped to establish.

Some parents use psychological techniques only for correcting or preventing infractions; the most common techniques used for this purpose are withdrawal of love or privileges or induction of guilt. Withdrawal of privileges and rewards as a means of shaping the child's behavior seems to have inconsistent effects, evoking frustration and aggression in some children (Bandura & Walters, 1959, 1963), while successfully altering the behavior in other instances. The prior rela-

When I want to go someplace and do something and my mother doesn't want me to, she says, 'Okay, you can go,' and then starts saying a bunch of stuff that would make me feel guilty for going. So I end up not going.

tionship with the adult and, of course, the nature of the reward withdrawn are among the probable determinants of the outcome.

Expression of disapproval and withdrawal of attention are employed by many parents, and appear to be related to the successful development of certain aspects of self-control, such as resistance to temptation and nonaggressive responses in children (Becker, 1964). There is some suggestion that such techniques are related to conscience development, particularly if the child has a warm relationship with the mother (Sears, Maccoby, & Levin, 1957).

More attention has been devoted in recent years to the effects of parental use of *reasoning* as a discipline technique. Reasoning includes descriptions of the undesirable consequences of the child's misbehavior for others, provision of examples of socially acceptable behavior as an alternative to the undesirable response, explicit instructions on how to behave in certain situa-

tions, and explanations of why restraints are placed on the child's behavior (Bandura & Walters, 1963).

"Because of the forms that reasoning may take, it is clearly impossible to make a simple summary of its effects. The majority of findings nevertheless suggest that most forms of reasoning are effective means of socializing children. Unlike other forms of discipline, reasoning is commonly used when the parent anticipates a deviation; some of its effectiveness may thus arise from its occurring early in a response sequence. Probably far more important, however, is the clarity with which the nature of the anticipated deviation and its possible consequences are presented, and, for older children, the appeal then can be made to general rules. If a child has learned that an incipient activity falls in a class of previously disciplined activities, he may more readily refrain from carrying it out than if the activity is not so labeled" (Walters & Parke, 1967, p. 213).

I'm not very disciplined about school. One thing I'm really glad of is that I'm grounded at home in the evenings, because my mother and father want me to get Bs. So I'm getting straight Bs. They're putting the discipline on me that I don't have for myself.

Consistency of discipline

Consistency of discipline has many definitions: following through on threats of punishment, treating misbehaviors in the same manner each time they occur, and parental agreement concerning how and when punishment should be administered with similarity of treatment of the child by the mother and the father. Research findings from both laboratory and naturalistic settings are somewhat at variance, depending upon the form of inconsistency studied. Inconsistent discipline, as would be expected, makes it difficult for the child to establish stable values for guiding his behavior (Azrin, Holz, & Hake, 1963). Also, intermittent punishment and permissiveness for comparable behavior tends to produce highly aggressive behavior on the part of many children (Sears et al., 1957; Rosenthal, 1962). It seems highly likely that consistency of parental behavior leads to greater predictability and stability for both parent and child, whereas some forms of inconsistency may increase the difficulty of altering a child's behavior and provoke undesirable reactions in the child.

Encouragement of competence and independence

The road to mature, autonomous, self-directed functioning begins with many little steps when the child performs tasks on his own, develops persistence in his activities, and learns to rely upon his own abilities to cope with unfamiliar or frightening situations. In sharp contrast to the earlier drive-reduction theories of child behavior, which assume that the child acts in order to reduce needs for food, nurturance, and other drives, considerable attention is being directed toward hypotheses which stress the child's active tension-creating attempts at mastery through a creative interaction with the environment (White, 1959; Berlyne, 1960; Piaget, 1936). It might be predicted that to the degree that parents permit, encourage, and reward the child's own efforts at mastery, his autonomy and independence in later life would be enhanced.

Some studies have suggested that parental warmth is associated with the development of independence in the child (Moore, 1965; Clapp, 1967). It also appears that autonomy and independence may be encouraged and reinforced directly, through early training and high parental standards for excellence and independent activity (Heathers, 1953; Winterbottom, 1958; Rosen & D'Andrade, 1959). On the whole, however, research findings have been quite inconsistent, due in part to variations in the definitions of "independence" and "autonomy" and in measurement procedures.

It should be noted that, in general, parents demand earlier and more extensive independent behaviors for boys than for girls. Girls are permitted greater expression of fear, discomfort, and immature responses, and parents typically

 In general, I grew up feeling pretty confident. They did instill that in me . . . as I grew up, my parents would say to me, 'You can do anything that you want to.' That didn't mean that they would give me the wherewithal to do it, they just made me feel that anything I wanted to accomplish, I could accomplish, I had the ability. They felt that if I wanted to do something, there was nothing to hold me back.

My mother felt that if she raised me never to hear
a bad word, never to hear anything angry, never
to see anything ugly, never to experience anything that wasn't the most beautiful, that of
course I would turn out to be a beautiful person.
Of course the thing she didn't reckon with my
needing was for me to be able to encounter
anger, fight back . . . anything of that sort. So I
was completely helpless when I went out into the
real world.

I want to do a good job with my children, and
prepare all of us for the time they will no longer
need me nor I them.

give them greater support and protection (Bardwick, 1971). Indeed, dependency—variously defined but typically involving behaviors aimed at
eliciting attention and approval from others—is
generally regarded as appropriate for adult females but not males. In their extensive longitudinal study of individuals from birth until
about age 30, Kagan and Moss (1962) determined that the greatest consistencies over this
period were in characteristics related to acceptable sex roles. Thus, girls who were judged
"dependent" at early ages were more likely to
show dependent behaviors in adulthood than
were boys who showed early dependent behavior. Similarly, boys aggressive in their early
years were more likely to be aggressive at maturity than were girls who had shown early
aggressiveness.

Since the well-documented greater dependency among females cannot be attributed to initial
differences in male and female infants and small
children (Maccoby & Jacklin, 1973), it must
result from sex-role training. To the extent that
parents permit, and even encourage, dependent
behaviors in girls, however, the adult woman
may experience negative effects. Independence
and autonomy are integrally related to Maslow's
and Rogers' conceptions of the fully functioning

individual. The woman who experiences herself
as motivated primarily to please others and gain
their approval and support and who is fearful of
adventure, achievement, and autonomous functioning, may be hampered in her quest for
self-actualization. Thus, parental encouragement of independence and autonomy for girls
may require relaxation of traditional sex-role
socialization.

Appropriate role models

It is theorized that most of our learning occurs
through the observation of models, rather than
by simple trial-and-error learning or direct conditioning (Bandura, 1965). To a large extent, the
child will grow to have many of the same habits,
attitudes, feelings, and beliefs as those around
him. Because of the proximity of the parents and
their values to the child, the mother and father
will be major sources of such observational
learning for him.

The presence of a parent-model who is a
satisfactory example of appropriate, adaptive
behavior can be expected to contribute positively
to healthy development in the child. Modeling
has been shown to be an important source of
sex-role learning in which the child acquires

Achievement motivation

High: Achievement-oriented parents who have high aspirations for children, are interested in and encourage them.

Low: "Unconcerned" families, content if child keeps out of trouble; emotionally disturbed homes; socially disadvantaged homes.

Aggression (boys)

Lack of consistent standards; punitive, restrictive, cold parents; aggressive personal models; physical punishment; family disharmony; broken home.

Conscience (self-control)

Good: Parental warmth and acceptance; clear-cut standards consistently enforced; love-oriented discipline; good parental models.

Poor: Maternal coldness; rejection; unclear or shifting standards; inconsistency; overindulgence; poor parental models.

Sociability, leadership

Good: Parental warmth and involvement, democratic climate in home, love-oriented discipline; greater salience of same-sexed parent without marked dominance of either parent.

Poor: Overindulgence or parental restrictiveness; parental rejection, neglect, or absence; cold, demanding parents.

Autonomy

Parental warmth and acceptance, high parental standards strictly enforced; reinforcement of independent behavior without punishment of dependent behavior; parental guidance toward competence, parental support during special stress; chance for the child to share in formulation and enforcement of rules.

Dependency

Early severe social deprivation; rejecting, punitive parents or combination of warmth and restrictiveness; either reward or punishment for dependency.

Self-identity, self-esteem

Good: Parental love and acceptance, fostering identification and feeling of belonging; democratic home in which all members have roles and responsibilities commensurate with their maturity; stable, meaningful, supportive environment; mature, well-differentiated parental models.

Poor: Rejection; parental dominance or overprotection; power-coercive discipline; lack of close, continuing ties to desirable adult model.

many of the preferences and behaviors appropriate to his sex (Mischel, 1966). Also, observational learning is thought to be an important source of moral development in children; laboratory studies, for example, have shown that children readily imitate both self-rewarding and resistance-to-temptation behaviors of models (Mischel & Liebert, 1966, 1967).

Unfortunately, serious psychopathology or defective coping strategies can also be imitations of parental behavior. For example, recent attention devoted to childhood alcoholics notes that most of these youngsters have alcoholic parents (*Los Angeles Times*, July 1973). Seiden (1969) notes that suicidal behavior in children of suicide victims is not uncommon. Studies of delinquent youths reveal many instances in which one or both of the parents has committed criminal or antisocial acts (McCord & McCord, 1958). Even such a relatively minor maladaptive response as phobia of dogs has been shown to occur in a high percentage of parents of dog-phobic children, suggesting that the children observed and imitated their parent's fear (Bandura & Menlove, 1968).

The conditions under which a child will imitate the behaviors, attitudes, and preferences of models are somewhat unclear. Status, power, and in some cases warmth seem to enhance imitation (Bandura, Ross & Ross, 1963; Flanders, 1968).

Adequate communication

The importance of clear, complete, and honest communication in interpersonal relationships has been discussed at various points already. The family provides the context for learning not simply the language but also many additional communication skills. The child learns to observe nonverbal communication modes such as facial, postural, and vocal tone cues and to process information from various levels simultaneously. Parents who themselves use functional communications serve as models for using the language to convey and acquire information, and for correct and precise labeling of both

internal and external events. In such a family, the child also learns how to seek clarification of messages that are vague or confusing. So crucial is appropriate communication in families, that researchers have devoted much attention to various forms of faulty communication which may lead to maladaptive behaviors on the part of the child or other family members (Winter & Ferreira, 1967; Martin, 1967; Haley, 1967; Patterson & Reid, 1968).

An extreme example of dysfunctional communication is contradictory and inconsistent communications by the parent. For example, the mother who has baked her daughter a birthday cake may insist that the daughter show her appreciation by eating a large piece but later point out that boys don't like girls who are overweight and that she should be more careful. Or the mother may complain that her son does not show his love for her but testily reject his attempts to show affection with the statement that he is too grown up to be acting like a child.

This has been called a *double-bind* experience—one in which the child cannot win. No matter what he does, it is wrong. Although the double-bind phenomenon needs further study before its precise effects on development can be ascertained, it has been found to be more common in the background of emotionally disturbed adolescents and young adults than among those adequately adjusted (Bateson, 1960; Lu, 1962; Mishler & Waxler, 1965; Schuham, 1967).

Adverse family climates

There is ample evidence that particular techniques of childrearing are less important than the overall pattern of the home. In an orderly but flexible, stimulating, cooperative home in which adults show consideration for each other and all members care about each other, a child can get the warmth, the models, and the teaching he needs. In families where the adults are immature, self-centered, or at odds with each other, where there is no basic trust, order, and mutual emotional support, the child gets inadequate help in the difficult process of growing up.

I work at a boys' club where a lot of kids go. And when you watch those kids you can usually tell which ones come from the poorer families and which come from the more wealthy families and those that don't have both their parents. Those from the poorer families are usually the ones getting into trouble and destroying the games. They seem to get into most of the fights. The ones without fathers are usually the babies of the group, always crying when things don't go their way. Those with just fathers have a tendency to not care about anyone else but themselves. Those from the richer families just come in usually to play pool and the other games and not get into any kind of trouble.

I am working and raising these kids, all by myself. If I can just hang on awhile longer, get a little ahead . . . I got to get us out of this apartment, there's so much fighting between so many kids, and the neighbor kids. We got to have a bigger place. I will have to work all my life.

Faulty or dysfunctional family relationships have been implicated in every major psychopathology of both adults and children. Four patterns that are particularly pathogenic have been identified: the incomplete family, the inadequate family, the disturbed family, and the antisocial family. Unfortunately, these categories are not mutually exclusive, and the same family may, for example, be both incomplete and disturbed.

The incomplete family

The most common form of incomplete family is the broken home or father-absent family. As a result of high rates of divorce, separation, desertion, and other circumstances, a growing number of children are being reared in homes with only one parent present. Usually the remaining parent is the mother, due to the considerable social pressure and conditioning of women that their major function in life should be that of wife and/or mother. Since Freud, psychotherapists have placed high value on the continuing presence of both parents as essential to the full, healthy development of the child. Contemporary research in child development challenges the assumption of the overwhelming significance of the two-parent family, but the absence of a parent may have significant undesirable effects on the children.

The departure of the father is bound to have immediate effects for the child who is old enough to comprehend it. The child may respond with grief and mourning and perhaps feel rejected (or in some instances may experience relief from a difficult and conflict-ridden situation). Research has typically focused less on the immediate effects than on the long-term results for the child.

There are numerous methodological difficulties in father-absence research which necessitate caution in interpreting findings. Typically, the cause of the absence of the father is not specified—whether due to death, divorce, separation, or economic reasons. The cause of departure, of course, is likely to be a significant determinant of the effects for the child. Also, the child's age at the departure and the duration of the separation are often not controlled in the studies. A crucial element often neglected, too, is the quality of marriage and family life prior to the father's absence; the mother's manner of coping with the absence and her attitudes toward men are also important. The availability of father substitutes, the presence of siblings, the sex, age, race, and social class of the child may also be important determinants of the effects. These qualifications on interpretations of the data clearly imply that each situation is unique; general conclusions about father absence as a detriment to the full functioning of the child cannot be supported by the research.

1. *Effects on the social and emotional development of boys.* Some data suggest that father-absent sons show less sex-typed preferences, are more dependent on their peers, and are less assertive than father-present boys, but only if the separation occurred before about age 5 (Hetherington & Deur, 1969; Biller, 1970). For older boys, the effects of father absence are less clear, with one study reporting that older father-absent boys were more aggressive and also more dependent upon adults (McCord, McCord, & Verden, 1962). Other studies, however, have found no differences in groups of boys with fathers absent or present, especially if the separation occurred after age 5 (Biller & Bahm, 1971). On the basis of a review of the effects of father absence on sex-role development in boys, Hetherington and Deur (1969) suggest that boys with early father separation would profit from adult male figures, perhaps male nursery school teachers, whereas older boys probably gain masculine identity from their peers, siblings, teachers, and the mass media.

Several studies have related incidence of delinquency or antisocial, impulsive behavior to father absence (Monahan, 1960; Toby, 1957;

Mischel, 1961). However, absence of an adult male model for sons may be a less significant determinant of such effects than the instability and general atmosphere of some broken homes (McCord, McCord, & Thurber, 1962; Nye, 1958).

2. *Effects on the social and emotional development of girls.* Relatively few studies have explored the effects of the father's absence on their daughters—presumably since it has been assumed that the absence would have less consequence for a daughter's development. Recently, however, research has suggested that the effects for girls appear later, in adolescence (Biller & Weiss, 1970), and affect mainly relationships with males. Hetherington and Deur (1969) report that father-absent girls in adolescence often show either severe sexual anxiety or promiscuity. Such findings corroborate early studies which showed high rates of father absence among delinquent girls—whose delinquency was measured largely in terms of sexual "misconduct" (Toby, 1957; Monahan, 1960).

The research on effects of broken homes should not be construed to imply that all such families are pathogenic. An effective single parent is likely to be much more conducive to the child's well-being than parents in continuous conflict or parents who, for one reason or another, are unable to function adequately in their parental roles. In recognition of this fact, not only are many single parents justifiably proud of their success in childrearing, but also many adoption agencies are placing children with single individuals.

The inadequate family
An inadequate family is characterized by inability to cope with the ordinary problems of family living. It lacks the resources, physical or psychological, for meeting demands that most families can cope with satisfactorily. Consequently, the inadequate family relies heavily upon continued outside assistance and support in resolving its problems. Inadequacy may stem from immaturity, lack of education, mental retardation, or other shortcomings on the part of the parents. Sometimes, of course, demands are so severe

It's hard with five children. I want my children to have something better. Welfare isn't it, it just won't do it. Their father has been out of work a year. It's not that he's quit looking, there's just no jobs here. He needs a *job*.

that they overtax the adjustive resources of even highly adequate families, but we are concerned here with more typical, usually solvable family problems, such as earning a living, with which most families can deal.

A family that is floundering against odds too great for its resources, for whatever reason, cannot give its children the feeling of safety and security they need or adequately guide them in the development of essential competencies. Nor can financial or other outside assistance meet the needs of such families; for families, like individuals, need to feel they are self-directing and basically in control of their own lives.

The disturbed family

At all socioeconomic levels we find some parents who, because of personal instability or warped development, interact with other people in ways that are destructive to others and to themselves. Parents with grossly eccentric and abnormal personalities may keep the home in constant emotional turmoil. In his study of the homes of young schizophrenic patients, Lidz and his associates (1958; 1963) pointed to a type of *marital schism* in which the parents lived in a state of chronic disorder that constantly threatened the continuation of the marriage. Each parent tried to undermine the worth of the other in the eyes of the child and subjected him to irrational situations and demands. The mother in such a family, feeling unloved by her husband, might engage in seductive behavior toward her son, or

the father toward his daughter. Often the child was made to feel that by showing affection or cooperation toward one parent he was betraying the other; sometimes he was given the thankless role of mediator between the parents. Another pathological pattern identified by Lidz et al. (1958) was named *marital skew*. Here the entire family was oriented around the pathology of one or both parents. The marriage was stable but at the expense of rationality in family interactions.

Disturbed homes may involve many other pathological patterns, but such homes appear to have certain characteristics in common: (1) parents who are fighting to maintain their own equilibrium and who are unable to give the child the love and guidance that he needs; (2) exposure of the child to an irrational home environment and faulty parental models; and (3) almost inevitably, the enmeshment of the child in the emotional conflicts of the parents at the expense of his own development. In general, it would appear that maladjusted parents who are able to establish a harmonious relationship with each other are less damaging to the child than are maladjusted parents who live in disharmony (Satir, 1967).

The antisocial family

Here the family is characterized by undesirable moral values, usually leading to conflict with the wider community. In some families the parents are overtly or covertly engaged in behavior

My youngest isn't eligible for the welfare medical care, because something's wrong in the records. I used to call the social worker about once a week, but he couldn't straighten it out.

which violates the standards and interests of society and may be chronically in difficulty with the law. Such antisocial values usually handicap marital and other family relationships as well as providing undesirable guides for the development of the child.

Children in such families may be encouraged in dishonesty, deceit, and other undesirable behavior patterns; or they may simply observe and imitate the behavior of undesirable parental models. In some cases, children may develop a high degree of courage, self-discipline, and loyalty to the family group at the expense of identification with the society as a whole. More often, however, the models they see are immature and self-seeking, and the social interactions they observe and take part in are shallow and manipulative—a poor preparation for mature, responsible adulthood. Here it is of interest to note that Langner and Michael (1963), in an extensive study of mental health and mental disorder in a congested urban area, found a higher mental health risk for children who were living with both parents but saw their parents' character negatively than for those who experienced a broken home.

Trends in family planning

Many of the reasons mentioned earlier for having children have also been used to rationalize or justify large families. At earlier points in our history, Bogue (1967) notes, children often died so that "replacements" were needed: They were needed to help with the work of the household; they were an economic advantage to their families; and they also provided social security in old age. People believed that big families were happy families, and that large families promoted good marital adjustment. Children were the vehicle for continuing the family name and strengthening the clan. In terms of community and national welfare, large families were viewed as important contributions to national resources. In terms of personal needs, they served as proof of virility and fertility and, morally, it was believed that large families were God's will.

In modern times, however, many of these beliefs have been challenged, and new values now affect a couple's decision about having children. Also, the last 20 years have seen a phenomenal increase not only in the use of birth

control measures, but also in the availability of more effective and more convenient devices.

Changing attitudes toward childbearing

A majority of married couples appear to want and do have children. However, attitudes toward what was once automatic and inevitable have changed dramatically. In the past 15 years, for example, young women in the United States have sharply reduced the number of children they want—from an average of nearly 4 per family in 1957 to an average of 2 in 1972. Such a shift in attitudes will have a significant impact on the density of the population. An even more important aspect of the attitude change concerns its impact on the child and the family. We are witness to an era in which, more than ever before, each child will be the product of decision and choice, and the reduction in desired family size appears to signal to some degree couples' unwillingness to devote themselves entirely to the business of raising children.

The reduction in preferred family size over the past fifteen years reflects in part the desire of an increasing number of couples not to have children at all. According to census figures, 1 in 25 wives today expects not to have children, as compared with 1 in 100 only six years ago. Such couples may suffer censure for "selfishness," and the wife may be regarded with a mixture of pity, disapproval, and horror for "violating the sacred trust of women." Such reactions by those around them may have significant repercussions on the couple.

Not only have couples' preferences changed, but actual practice appears to have changed, too, since the national birthrate has declined considerably in recent years. Naturally, each couple is unique and the circumstances which affect the number of children born will be particular to that couple. Nevertheless, several factors have been alleged to account for changing attitudes toward childbearing, now that actual births can be regulated to a considerable extent.

Concern for self-development
Unquestionably a major source of changed attitudes and practices in childbearing arises from individuals' awareness of other alternatives to

life than raising families. Women in particular are experiencing dissatisfactions with the traditional, full-time roles of wife and mother. As Marlene Dixon expresses it:

"... the intoxicating wine of marriage and suburban life was turning sour .... For many younger women, the empty drudgery they saw in suburban life was a sobering contradiction to adolescent dreams of romantic love and the fulfilling role of women as wife and mother" (1971, p. 167).

Young women are better educated today than ever before, and many women with a college education are simply no longer content to retire with their degrees to the unpaid work of child-rearing, home management, and social entertaining. Women of all educational levels are seeking not only to escape the drudgery of housework but to pursue interesting and rewarding jobs. Census data suggest that nearly 50

find greater satisfaction than as students, workers, artists, political activists, or doctors. Many of us become pregnant because there is little else that we feel we can do well. Motherhood is the course of least resistance. Tired of looking for jobs and trying to decide who we are, we look forward to pregnancy and motherhood as a time when we can put our identity crises on the shelf and relax, secure in the 'legitimacy' of our maternal role. Yet, our essential selves don't give up. The confusion and unhappiness that many of us feel at least some of the time when faced with motherhood can be positive indications to us that our total selves, not just our mother-selves, are struggling to make themselves heard" (Boston Women's Health Book Collective, 1973; p. 154).

Clearly, the widespread availability of effective contraceptives enables women to control the number and timing of pregnancies in order to

 I feel like I'll probably want to have children, because that's part of a woman's experience of living. But I feel people should do it later in life, when they've grown a lot and they still love each other, and they still want them.

percent of young wives in their early 20s and 40 percent of those in their late 20s are now outside the home, compared with much lower proportions for older women. Among college graduates, the rates are even higher.

The quest for personal definition outside the roles of wife and mother may produce considerable conflict, however.

"We grow up in a society that leads us to believe that we will find our fulfillment as women-people by living out our reproductive function. There is a widespread idea that because women have the special biological ability to bear children, that is what all normal women should do, regardless of our individual talents ....

"Societal pressures, internalized, become psychological pressures. Because our opportunities, hence our motivations, are limited, we ourselves often begin to believe that in motherhood we will

maximize the possibilities of achieving self-esteem through other activities than childrearing if they wish.

Nor is the quest to meet other personal goals and needs limited to women. Many men also find that their career aspirations or other interests are incompatible with large families or fatherhood at a young age. They may elect to postpone starting a family or to keep their family small.

Concern about community and national welfare

There is no direct way to measure the impact of certain current social values on family planning, but it seems likely that couples have become sensitive to national concerns about overpopulation. Enormous attention has been devoted to the perils of overpopulation. Since the majority of Americans now reside in urban areas, most people come into daily contact with hundreds of others, suffer crowds at shopping areas, wait in long lines at medical, public service, and other facilities, and find roads overflowing with traffic and wilderness recreation areas teeming with people. Most people are increasingly alarmed, too, at the drain on natural resources, the depletion of natural beauty, and the accumulation of wastes and pollutants which threaten to damage the quality of life for all.

Various population control organizations have encouraged Americans to limit their family size as one step in reducing the drain on natural and community resources. So successful have such campaigns been, apparently, that it is not un-

optimal psychological and emotional climate for the child may turn to birth control procedures. The mother may wish to delay childbirth until she completes her education, or finds a satisfying job that she can combine with childraising, or simply until she feels "ready." All such decisions may be conducive to the provision of a suitable environment for the child. Similarly, the father may wish to feel secure enough or stable enough in his work, or to have completed his education, or to have experienced enough of life's adventures that he feels ready to be able to devote time and energy to being a good father.

It goes without saying that the quality and immediacy of parental care may be reduced when there are numerous and closely spaced

 If we feel like having children, then we will. At this point I'd rather not. I feel I have to get myself a little more together. Also, I just think that there are too many people, that we'd be happier if there were less people, and that if I felt like having kids, I'd just as soon adopt some as my wife have them, so we wouldn't be adding more. But then again, I might someday feel that I'd want my very own—I don't know.

common to find individuals who would feel guilty if they brought more than two children into the world "to take their parents' places." Many young couples view it as a matter of moral if not practical necessity to limit their family size so that succeeding generations may enjoy a high quality of life.

Concern for the child's welfare

Consideration for the well-being of the unborn child is an important focus for many couples who have access to birth control methods. And public concern for the child's welfare motivates the policies of various organizations and public agencies.

1. *Better care for the child.* Economic issues aside, couples who are motivated to consider the

children. For most average-income families, the possibilities of providing individual attention, supervision, and enrichment for children are reduced as their numbers increase.

2. *Better development for the child.* Several lines of research generally support the notion that being one of a large family may have undesirable consequences for the child. We know, for example, that the families which can least afford it financially are often the ones who have the most children, substantiating in part the saying, "the rich get richer and the poor get children" (Rainwater, 1965; Blood & Wolfe, 1960; Whelpton, Campbell, & Patterson, 1966). Lower socioeconomic class families do not want more children, but rather have less effective contraception. The problems for the child arising from family financial hardship need not be elaborated here.

The effects of family size on the marital relationship itself have been noted already. Research does not support the myth that big families are happier families. A number of studies suggest that achievement orientation, verbal ability, school performance, and occupational success as adults are inversely related to family size (Clausen, 1966).

Although research in the area is sketchy, "family density" may affect the child from birth. Waldrop and Bell (1966), for example, reported that, other factors controlled, infants born into high-density families were more lethargic at birth and also displayed more dependency behaviors as young children.

Many additional influencing factors, of course, also covary with family size. And there are always exceptions—like Benjamin Franklin, tenth child in a poor family.

3. *Consideration for the unwanted child.* Clinical literature is replete with cases of psychiatric disturbance attributed in part to having been unwanted as a child. Not all unplanned children are unwanted, and even unwed mothers may elect to keep their children and give them a loving home. Nevertheless, such mothers must often work to support their children or receive welfare—either of which they may see as undesirable. In many cases the child must face the stigma of illegitimacy in addition to economic disadvantage and lack of a stable home life.

The unwanted, unplanned child born to a married couple may also suffer from economic hardship and parental resentment or other negative response. Sears, Maccoby, and Levin (1957) found, for example, that mothers were less happy with a pregnancy that followed more closely a previous birth. Also, they found that mothers were rated as less warm toward the child resulting from such pregnancies, both as infants and as preschoolers.

There is some suggestion that having unplanned children is correlated with poor family and marital adjustment. Among low-income families in a public housing group, Geismar and La Sorte (1964) found that the lowest family adjustment, as measured in various ways, tended to occur in families with close spacing of births, with premarital pregnancies, and with the most children.

The effects of unwanted pregnancies are far from clear-cut, however, and research evidence is skimpy. In many cases, parents make adjustments so that an unwanted child becomes a desired and loved one as time passes (Pohlman, 1969).

Concern for the welfare of the family

As noted throughout, there are several areas of family functioning that have important consequences for decisions about conception.

1. *Protection of the mother's health.* Women appear to be increasingly aware of the high costs of full-time childbearing and childraising. Pregnancy and the raising of young children do not foster optimal energy or being well-rested, relaxed, and in robust health. Moreover, public attention has been drawn to the dangers of genetic defects in babies and in high risk of such medical problems as Down's Syndrome in children of older mothers. Many women may be motivated to limit their pregnancies with care out of a desire to protect their own health and to not run the risk of having defective children.

2. *Anticipation of economic strain.* Social class aside, raising a child is an expensive business. In 1972 the President's Commission on Population Growth and the American Future reported that to give birth to a baby and to raise and put the child through college costs an average of $40,000. Increasingly, couples are aware of the financial burdens imposed by children and are electing to regulate births according to their economic resources.

3. *Wish to continue present life style.* To the degree that the marital partners desire not to alter their roles seriously, they may be motivated not to have children or to have just one or two. Similarly, young couples appear to be more inclined than ever to enjoy leisure and entertaining; spending in these areas has grown enormously and is predicted to increase further. Thus, many couples may wish to delay as well as

limit childbearing while they seek to enjoy their leisure unhampered. Also, they may desire to pursue their sexual relationship unfettered by fear of pregnancy. They may simply be more interested in continuing their own growth and enjoyment than in nurturing new young life, with all the responsibilities and hazards this would entail.

Contraception and abortion

Nearly all couples practice some form of contraception at times, ranging from the irreversible surgical procedure of sterilization to finger-crossing (which is rarely successful). Apparently, two-thirds of wives under 30 use contraceptives. As the previous section suggested, there

tion has been a legitimate activity in the Western world. And only since the mid-1950s has a convenient, widely available, and really effective procedure been available ("the pill").

Thousands, if not millions, of women have welcomed the pill as a means of achieving control over their own bodies and avoiding unwanted pregnancies. As one index of its positive effects, Gordon (1967) found that women's rate of acceptance of their pregnancy increased from 55 percent to 72 percent after the availability of the oral contraceptive.

Overwhelmingly, it is the woman who employs the contraceptive technique and who thus assumes responsibility for birth control in fact if not by preference. Such responsibility has been related to considerable ambivalence, particularly

 I have no qualms about using the pill. What it's done, as far as I'm concerned, is liberate me from a terrible fear that I used to have of becoming pregnant. The pill has liberated me to enjoy myself sexually, and I don't mean promiscuously at all, because I'm very much a one-man woman. It's made me enjoy sex an awful lot more.

are numerous reasons why couples may be motivated to plan their families and, presumably, employ some contraceptive devices. It might be predicted that such procedures will be increasingly available and used as individuals become more aware of their options. The section which follows will focus upon some of the psychological aspects of contraception and abortion; issues of morality or public policy, while significant, are beyond the scope of this discussion.

Psychological effects of contraceptive practices

Women first employed spermicidal substances or intrauterine devices to prohibit conception several thousand years ago. However, it has only been since the last century that contracep-

with respect to the pill. Four distinct sources of resistance for both men and women for various methods of contraception have been identified:

1. Resistances based on beliefs about the positive and negative aspects of specific methods, particularly with regard to effectiveness for achieving pregnancy prevention goals and possible short-term or long-term side effects. For example, failure to use a particular method believed to interfere with sexual enjoyment, or one believed to have medical side effects.

2. Resistances anchored in social relationships, e.g., attitudes toward birth control believed to be prevalent in peer groups and reference groups, normative values concerning "natural" and "unnatural" behavior. For example, the belief that one's church views birth control devices as contrary to God's will.

3. Resistances anchored in unresolved inner conflicts, especially in connection with sex-role images and sexual relationships. For example, fear that preventing conception will reduce masculinity or femininity. A common problem with vasectomy.

4. Resistances related to cognitive or behavior styles of the individual, e.g., planful vs. impulsive, rational vs. nonrational, precise vs. vague. For example, the woman isn't methodical enough to take contraceptive pills regularly (Fawcett, 1970, p. 54).

Judith Bardwick (1971) has studied both married and unmarried women's responses to use of the pill. For unmarried women, use of the pill was not typically associated with promiscuity, contrary to dire predictions, but rather, was employed in the context of an enduring relationship with one partner. Nevertheless, she dis-

chological changes—would it take something away from it because it's so easy—any time of the day" (p. 56).

Bardwick contends that the problem occurs not only for unmarried women but for newly married women, as well, for in both cases the conscious, deliberate use of the pill negates the notion of sex as overriding spontaneous passion, or of sex for the purpose of producing children. "While on the one hand sex can now be purely romantic without fear of consequences, taking the pill means the end of sexual passivity and the conscious assumption of responsibility for contraception and therefore for sex. This conscious responsibility tends to increase anxiety and unconscious prostitution fears, with the net result that the subjects are even more fearful that men will hold them in contempt and leave them" (Bardwick, 1971, p. 57).

 I got married because I was pregnant—I can't think of any other real reason. I never used any contraceptive protection. I just assumed that I would be lucky that day . . . which leads me to believe that I wanted to be pregnant.

covered that the pill poses a psychological threat to women; it means that contraception is preplanned. ". . . The female has made a sexual decision and has difficulty in continuing to perceive her sexual participation as the result of momentary passion. Taking the pill can arouse anxiety about one's morality and this anxiety is an emotion that is strongly defended against" (Bardwick, 1971, p. 56). She notes several of her respondents' reactions:

"I feel like a hard woman because taking the pill is an admission of what I'm doing. I detest these changes! Every time I have to swallow one of these pills I dislike the relationship we have a little more" (p. 56).

"This is a big moral question for me. He was for it. Not sexually inexperienced, but before very sporadic. But now this is more serious and steady. According to my decision—I thought about psy-

A further aspect of women's reactions to the responsibility that contraceptives place on them concerns males and contraception. Most women welcome the control they have over birth control, proclaiming that they would rather trust the matter to themselves. Bardwick (1973) found that 72 percent of women preferred to have the control themselves, even if male and female "pills" were equally available. On the other hand, many women have begun to express discontent with the fact that they not only have the control, but also the side effects, the cost, and the inconvenience.

"Since men play a role equal to women's in creating pregnancy, it makes sense for them to share the burden of preventing it. It makes women angry to see so relatively little research being done on methods for males. Women suspect that male research scientists would be unwilling to offer men

a contraceptive that exposed them to as many side effects and potential risks as the pill or even the IUD does to women" (Boston Women's Health Book Collective, 1973, p. 137).

Some attempts have been made to characterize the personalities of women who employ various contraceptive methods (reported in House, 1973). However, such attempts are typically misleading and somewhat value-laden, since a variety of women employ each method, and generalizations do a great injustice to the individual differences between women.

Psychological aspects of abortion

The laws of the land are in a state of flux regarding abortion. It is clear that there is a heavy demand for it (it has been estimated that in Los Angeles alone Planned Parenthood makes 1500 abortion referrals per month). Issues of whether the decisions should be made by the individual, by her physician, or by a board of "experts," and issues regarding the medically safe and morally or psychologically significant timing of abortion are beyond the scope of this section.

Many studies have attempted to determine women's reactions to abortions, and the findings have been very inconsistent and laden with methodological deficiencies. However, it seems reasonable to conclude that abortion is commonly an upsetting experience from which the vast majority of women recover. The circumstances of the abortion are likely to influence the woman's reactions, so that climates of safe and supportive medical care would be expected to yield different outcomes than illicit and unlicensed abortions. Most women experience the abortion with relief, if not immediately then shortly, and the consequences of letting the pregnancy run to full term would be likely to produce much more serious and enduring upset. Contrary to common myth, most women who experience abortion do not suffer lasting and painful guilt reactions.

The future of family planning

Alvin Toffler in *Future Shock* (1970) presents a vision of complete family planning, including programming not only of when children come but also their sex, IQ, and other characteristics. Or perhaps parents will elect to have their babies born by professionals through embryo transplants, or in test tubes; perhaps would-be parents will even be able to purchase embryos—or babies. Such far-fetched ideas seem as implausible to us today as the pill would have to our grandmothers. Yet, it is clear that a revolution has begun in family planning which has not yet run its course.

Our culture has probably reached a stage in which family planning occurs with a moderate degree of success for many people. It is highly likely that within the next decades we will attain widespread use of contraceptive procedures that permit complete control over the timing and number of births.

The technological requirements of safe, effective, and easily available procedures are considerably less difficult to satisfy than is the need to solve ethical and moral dilemmas, educational difficulties, and psychological obstacles relating to birth control.

Alternative family styles

On the surface, the nuclear family, consisting of the conjugal pair and their children, relatively isolated from extended kin, seems fairly well suited to the demands of an industrialized society: It is highly mobile and tends to foster the characteristics of individuality, independence, and achievement which are highly compatible with technological society. The tasks of such a modern family are the socialization of children and provision of emotional fulfillment for its members. However, there appears to be inherent stress for the individual members in carrying out these functions. The relative isolation of the nuclear family places heavy burdens upon it for providing emotional support and socialization. Many tensions and conflicts, many sources of demand and frustration may accompany the family's attempts to fulfill its tasks.

As more and more persons experience this isolation and the burdens of the modern family, desirable alternatives are sought. Over the past ten to twenty years many efforts appear to have been spawned to diminish the isolation of the nuclear family and offer the experience of less restrictive forms of relating and raising children. This section will briefly consider some of the alternatives to traditional family patterns that involve children.

Single parents by choice

It is estimated that approximately 17 percent of children in the United States are now living with only one parent, usually the mother. The rates are much higher in certain social class and racial groups. Divorce and separation account for most of these instances.

not demonstrated inevitable drawbacks for the child of single parents. The child's development depends upon a good many factors and not simply whether or not the parent is married.

Communal living and cooperative families

Thousands of individuals have joined with others in experimental living ventures. It is impossible to generalize about such arrangements, since they are so heterogeneous. Communal groups range from highly organized, philosophically based groups to a few individuals who live in the same house to share resources and reduce

 It's been so different since the divorce, just the two little boys and me. I guess I relaxed, I kind of began to see the boys in a different way—more like people, not just little kids. I don't worry about how I'm supposed to be, I just kind of am their mother. It's very nice. And now with the 12-year-old away for the summer, there's just the 9-year-old at home, and he and I really talk about lots of things and I really enjoy him.

An unknown number of individuals who are not married elect to have children. Many plan, for various reasons, to give birth to children and raise them without the traditional family structure. Some single individuals adopt children. Public legal and administrative policy continue to be oriented toward the traditional nuclear family, although increasingly, unmarried women and men are being permitted to adopt, particularly in cases of "hard to place" children.

Whether single because of divorce or by other choice, single parents may face many obstacles: financial difficulties, social pressures, extra hazards in trying to provide an adequate environment for the child's healthy development. Despite these obstacles, psychological research has

personal isolation. Groups may be rural or urban, closed or open in membership, practicing celibacy, monogamy, or free sexual relationships. The groups may be democratic, anarchistic, or headed by a single charismatic leader; they may be guided by religious-spiritual principles, political or psychological principles—or no organized values. They may be oriented toward personal growth or toward economic gain. Clearly, with such a diversity of characteristics, the groups are bound to differ substantially in their childrearing goals and practices.

Almost no research exists on the effects for the child of "multiple" parents resulting from communal practices, except for a few psychoanalytically oriented studies of Israeli children raised on kibbutzim (Spiro, 1958; Bettelheim, 1969). Anecdotal information from communal experiences in this country generally emphasizes the positive aspects of shared childrearing:

"Lisa has become such a warm, open, self-sufficient girl. She doesn't cling to me as she used to. She seeks attention from other adults almost as much as from me. She has her own world with the other children here. . . . And then there's me. I have more time for myself. It's a new freedom I still have trouble getting used to although we've been here over a year. I sometimes forget that I don't have to run to meet Lisa's needs; she can and will turn to others here. My time with her has been much 'better quality' time" (Boston Women's Health Book Collective, 1973, p. 156).

The effects for the child would undoubtedly depend upon the availability of adults, consistent responses from them, congruent models to imitate, and the interpersonal atmosphere of the group. Potential advantages include availability of several models to learn from and reduction of tensions resulting from sibling rivalries, withdrawal of parental love, or other hazards of the nuclear family where so much depends on the adequacy of one man and one woman.

For the parents, many advantages may also occur: reduction in the tendency to see the child as one's "possession" and hence greater acceptance of the child as a person, freedom from the unending demands children make, sharing of special skills with the children rather than necessity to be all things to one child. Additional advantages may occur for adults to the degree that traditional sex-role stereotypes are reduced and adult males and females all share in various childrearing behaviors.

More and more "experiments" in alternative family styles are being conducted by individuals seeking novel and fulfilling ways to live. We know very little as yet about the true advantages and disadvantages for parents or children of such arrangements, but we can expect research to be focused on these interesting ventures in the next few years.

 ## Summary and a look ahead

The effects of children on a marriage are many, and the attitudes, skills, and needs of the parents are enormously important in the parents' adjustment to the birth of children. Although a profoundly gratifying experience for most parents, the raising of children has "side effects" that should be fully understood by prospective parents.

Any attempt at discussion of parental behaviors that foster healthy development must first consider what is meant by "healthy." Several models are available for this task. Also, before beneficial conditions within the family are discussed, it is necessary to adopt a perspective on child development which includes not only the effects of parents, but also the effects of the infant and the mutual interaction of parents and children. The child is born with characteristics which will affect its unique subsequent development; parental behaviors that remain the same may affect one child quite differently from another. Finally, in considering the factors which affect the development of the child, it is important to consider the social, racial, and economic milieu of the parents.

The multitude of family interactions related to the child's development cannot be covered thoroughly in a single chapter. However, several crucial conditions for healthy development were discussed: emotional warmth and acceptance, effective discipline, encouragement of competence and independence, appropriate role models, adequate communication, and family climate.

Raising children today is viewed in quite a different light than several generations ago, and even within the past decade, attitudes have altered. Birth rate has declined, and most individuals have access to relatively safe, effective, and convenient contraceptives. We discussed many of the psychological aspects of birth control, as well as factors which determine individuals' decisions to regulate family size and timing.

Finally, in view of rapidly changing attitudes and practices in childrearing, we considered some alternative family styles which contrast with the nuclear family that has been the tradition in our country. Although it is still too early to evaluate the "success" of such practices, we are eager to learn what they can reveal about optimal conditions for producing healthy children and actualizing adults.

Turning from intimate relationships and family experiences, we shall now consider another of the major life experiences of most adults: the world of work and career choice.

12
The World of Work

The meaning of work
Occupational choice and adjustment
Issues of dissatisfaction and discrimination
The future world of work

"Without work all life goes rotten. But when work is soulless, life stifles and dies."

Albert Camus

Work is one of the most basic of all human institutions. Its importance stems not only from the necessity for survival, but also from the philosophical, moral, religious, political, and psychological significance attributed to it over the centuries.

In modern America, work is an activity which takes a major portion of the energy of all but a small percentage of the available work population. In the long-term view, most people can anticipate spending at least 40 years of their lives working.

An adequate definition of work must include more than the idea of "paid employment," for this concept ignores many of its social and psychological aspects. Moreover, the housewife who spends eight or ten hours a day in cooking, cleaning, laundering, marketing, and child care does not receive a salary for her labors but "works" nonetheless. The "paid employment" definition may also implicitly equate pay with worth, which is inaccurate and misleading. Therefore, we will define work in agreement with the Special Task Force on Work in America (1972) as "an activity that produces something of value for other people."

We will consider in this chapter some psychological aspects of work and our changing views of its significance in our lives. Issues of occupational choice and adjustment will be discussed, along with a look at worker discontent, its origins and consequences. Special attention will also be focused on the particular employment problems of the young and the old, of minority workers, and of women. Finally, we will have a glimpse at the future world of work and its implications.

The economic functions of work are obvious; people work to support themselves and their families. As important as this function is, however, there are also enormously significant personal and social functions of work.

1. *Personal identity.* To a large extent, people become what they do. Asking someone, "Who are you?" almost invariably elicits occupational responses, such as "I am a lawyer," or "I work

 On my job, I felt really close to everyone. It was so hard leaving when I had to, I was so upset by it—someone else would be taking *my* job. What happened was, I turned away from school and got into the job. Getting the job meant that I had the car—those two combined, having the car and having something that made me feel important, did interfere with school. School wasn't important anymore.

I can't achieve happiness unless I am satisfied with myself and the work I do. If a person has achieved this, this is all that is important.

The meaning of work

The very word "work" conjures up odious images of toil, effort, energy-sapping activity that one *must* do. It is usually assumed that work is something few people do willingly, that everyone would prefer other activities if it weren't for financial necessity. This viewpoint, however widespread, neglects many crucial psychological aspects of work. Moreover, our views of work have changed considerably over the past decades to a point where people expect more from work than toil, effort, and sheer economic reward.

for Lockheed," or "I am a housewife." In view of the vast amounts of time and energy devoted to one's job, this is not surprising, and is certainly one of the more salient means of identifying oneself in our enormously complex, changing, fragmented society.

2. *Self-esteem.* Closely related to personal identity is the function of work for self-evaluation. Work has the capacity to assure the individual of his or her ability to master self and environment. Most work situations provide continual feedback about one's ability to perform satisfactorily. Work may also provide a sense that one is valued by society, that one is doing something which needs to be done, and that the

product, whether material or service, is valued by others. To the degree that one may take pride in the quality and significance of one's work, self-esteem may be enhanced.

3. *Social functions.* Sociologists note that one of the major determinants of status in our culture is occupation. Indeed, the entire family typically takes on the status position of the head-of-household's job.

Not only does a person's job help to identify him according to some social status position, but work also fulfills another social role. One's work is typically a source of social contacts—a place to meet people, converse, share mutual interests and concerns.

If work is an important source of personal identity, self-esteem, and social position, then

Research evidence confirms the importance of the noneconomic functions of work. One economic analysis showed that as people increase their earnings and acquire more wealth, they do not reduce the amount of time and energy they invest in work (Morgan, 1972). In another study, a cross section of workers were asked if they would continue working if they received an inheritance which would permit them to live comfortably without working. Fully 80 percent of the respondents replied that they would keep on working (Morse & Weiss, 1955). A recent Labor Department study on work orientation of welfare recipients found that "the poor of both races and sexes identify their self-esteem with work to the same extent as nonpoor persons do" (Goodwin, 1972).

 I wasn't sure what I wanted to be, and that's bad, because society in a way frowns on that—you should know you're going to be a nurse or a doctor or a fireman. I don't know why. I mean, what's important is if you end up being a productive human being. Every human being has to work—without that you're not very happy.

several important implications should be noted. For example, persons who work in low-status jobs or in boring, meaningless jobs may suffer diminished personal regard. People who have been forced to retire at an arbitrary age or persons who cannot find work are denied an important source of identity. Welfare recipients become "nobodies"—or worse, and the thousands of people who are employed in jobs they are dissatisfied with may experience temporary or chronic blows to their esteem and identity. Research has revealed many suggestive links between occupational satisfactions and mental as well as physical health, in addition to broader areas such as family stability and useful community participation. Studies in health and occupational satisfaction will be considered in a later section.

All of these studies indicate that people value the activity of work and recognize that an important aspect of their lives would be missing—finances aside—if they did not work as much as they currently do, or didn't work at all.

Changing views of work

People work not only from necessity but for a variety of other reasons as well. In recent years we have witnessed significant changes in reasons for working, and in people's expectations about what work should provide.

Decline of the Puritan work ethic
The Puritan concept of work both as necessary for survival and as a duty and virtue in and of

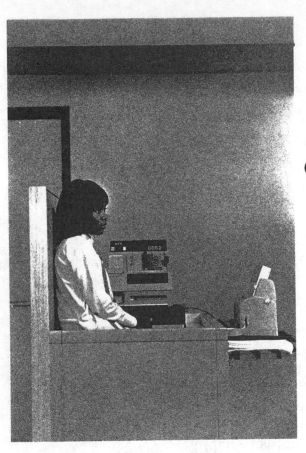

66 Money and material is not im- **99** portant—trying to make it or be somebody will only be me, naturally. I hope I never find myself working because I have to, but instead because I enjoy working.

66 It's not in my nature to stay in a really intolerable **99** job that would get me down—I'd sooner leave than let it get the best of me. I did leave one job—I began to see that a lot of the work that was going on there was pro-military—pro-war. And I was doing some of the work that was contributing to this. So I decided I couldn't stay there.

itself long dominated our culture. Work, obedience, thrift, and the delay of gratification were valued highly, and people's righteousness was often judged according to the degree of their prosperity.

These views have changed, however, at an accelerated pace. Today's worker, particularly the young worker, demands much more of himself and his job than simply "filling a slot" and earning a living. The search for a meaningful, fulfilling job has become crucial. Workers increasingly desire to have responsibility and autonomy, to have a voice, and demand not merely good physical working conditions, but also good psychological working conditions. Rigid, authoritarian work structures are increasingly rejected as the worker looks to his job as a significant source of creative self-expression.

The quest for meaningfulness

The young artisan who sells his wares on the streets of Berkeley, the middle-aged executive who seeks a new career at the pinnacle of her present occupation, the families that band together to develop a farming commune, and the college student who prolongs his or her education in the hopes of preparing not for *any* job but for a specially desired job—all have much in common. All reflect the difficult-to-measure but distinctly observable quest for occupational meaningfulness. More and more people are coming to recognize the self-defining and potentially self-fulfilling aspects of work. It is increasingly clear that wages and salary alone are not the main things people are looking for in their work. Herzberg (1968) in a series of studies of various workers at all levels, concluded: "Contrary to the prevailing belief, the studies show that basic needs of the blue-collar workers or the assembly-line worker are no different than those of the white-collar worker. The primary sources of job satisfaction for both groups are achievement and recognition."

A recent Department of Labor–sponsored survey of 1500 workers at all occupational levels showed that the aspect of work ranked first in importance was "interesting work," while "good pay" ranked fifth (Special Task Force,

1972). In a review of relevant research studies, Kahn (1972) concluded that what workers want most is to become masters of their immediate environment and to feel that they and their work are important.

It has been suggested that work environment fits into Maslow's concept of need hierarchy (see pp. 86–88). As basic needs (such as adequate wage, job security, and working safety) are met, "higher" needs emerge, including, ultimately, self-actualization needs—the quest for autonomy instead of supervision and coercion, for meaningfulness and interest instead of boredom and repetitive tasks, and for opportunity for participation and creation.

Occupational choice and adjustment

As we have noted, people seek a great deal from their jobs in terms of good psychological conditions as well as good physical working conditions. Hence, the issue of occupational choice is a critical one, which most young people take very seriously. In this section we will consider factors affecting job choice as well as factors affecting the individual's satisfaction and success in his or her chosen work.

Choosing the "right" occupation

Career choice, of course, is something relatively new. In earlier times—as well as in many other societies today—most people had their choices made for them or were at best severely limited in what they could choose. Of necessity, most males followed what their fathers had done or entered whatever apprenticeship training was available to them in their communities; women remained in the home. Most people today have an almost unlimited choice of careers, within the range of their abilities and preparations.

The choices today offer new opportunities but also new problems. Besides the enormous vari-

In choosing the "right" occupation, a person must consider a number of factors including environment, hours, scheduling, types of challenges involved, and, above all, what gives him or her satisfaction.

ety of possibilities, there are many more white-collar positions than ever before, and pay is higher than ever before. Also, there are increased opportunities for women and other minority workers. Nevertheless, in spite of these opportunities, there are still serious problems of discrimination or unsatisfying working conditions. Many occupations are oversupplied with workers; others which may be highly desirable require long years of education and preparation to keep abreast of advances in knowledge and technology. Hence, the person trying to decide about a career must be aware of both the opportunities and the obstacles associated with a particular occupational choice.

Personal characteristics

Three questions appear of particular significance from the standpoint of personal characteristics:

1. *What does the individual want to do?* The answer to this question concerns itself with interests, motives, and values. Does he like to work with people or with ideas or with things? Is he more interested in helping others or in making money? Does he thrive under pressure or does he prefer a more leisurely pace without deadlines? Relevant too are questions centering around what the individual would like to be doing ten or twenty years hence and what he would like his occupational experience to help him become.

After I'd been in college a couple of years I became very uncertain about what I wanted to do. So my folks talked to our family doctor and he recommended a psychologist that they sent me to. She gave me all kinds of tests to see what I was interested in and to see what I was suited to doing, what I might be able to do. And when it was all through, what she said to me was, 'Hitch your wagon to a star—you can do just about anything you decide to do.' Which I suppose is really great to be told, but it didn't help me one bit. Nothing came out of it as far as what I really *wanted* most of all. That, for some reason, she wasn't able to measure enough.

I don't really know what I'm going to do. I have ideas—dreams of what I'd like to become, but I can't really say yet if I can really do it.

2. *What can the individual do—or learn to do?* The answer to this question concerns his abilities and aptitudes. What is his general level of intelligence? What knowledge and skills does he have, and what is his potential for acquiring further competence in particular areas? Does he have any outstanding special abilities, such as unusual musical or athletic ability?

3. *How do the individual's abilities and resources limit the choices?* The answer to this question concerns both the individual's present qualifications and the resources available to him for further needed training. For example, some occupations, such as law and medicine, require extensive undergraduate and graduate preparation. Relevant here, too, are questions about physical limitations that might affect his potential for success in a given occupation.

Astin and Nichols (1964) found that a person's choice depends largely on the relative importance he places upon six basic factors: (1) having a good self-concept—for example, being popular and influential; (2) being personally comfortable; (3) enjoyment of artistic and creative tasks; (4) having prestige; (5) enjoyment of scientific and technical tasks; and (6) being able to help others and to become personally mature. For example, students majoring in business placed a high value on personal comfort, while students planning to enter the ministry stressed the value of helping others. These six factors, of course, cover various aspects of an individual's motives, interests, abilities, and values.

Psychologists have devised a number of assessment instruments for obtaining information about interests, abilities, values, and other personal characteristics and matching it against the requirements of given occupations. Such assessment information may be useful, but must be used with caution. A person's interests and key motives may undergo marked change with experience and learning, and occupations are undergoing many changes under the impact of technological advances.

Career choice is an important and complicated decision, and research suggests that it is a process which begins at an early age and progresses through identifiable stages. Ginzberg (1966) studied vocational choice in middle-class students, and found three general phases.

1. *Fantasy period.* For most children this period extends until about age 11, and is characterized by the child's assumption that he can become whatever he wants—police officer, doctor, teacher, or whatever.

2. *Tentative period.* From about 11 to 17 years, the young person recognizes the need to decide sometime on a future occupation, and now makes tentative choices based on whatever awareness he has of his interests, abilities, and values as well as on his environmental opportunities. At first, interests are a major consideration in career choice, but eventually, he begins to consider ability and training prerequisites, and still later, personal values become an important consideration.

3. *Realistic choice stage.* The individual tries to work out a suitable occupational plan by translating his own desires into what the external world has available. This process involves compromises between hopes and expectations, and the realities of the external world. Involved are exploration and information-gathering, narrowing of choices, and finally, commitment to a particular occupational goal.

Characteristics of the occupation

Here, too, three general questions appear to be relevant:

1. *What are the requirements and working conditions?* What training and skills are needed for admission? What general personal qualities—such as initiative, social competence, a particular temperament, or physical endurance—are required? What would the individual be doing from day to day and in what kind of setting? Equally important, how do these requirements fit what he has to offer and what he enjoys doing?

Here it may be emphasized that different positions within a broad occupational category may vary greatly in work activities and conditions. For example, a clinical psychologist working primarily with marital problems might engage in quite different daily activities and live in quite a different world from a physiological psychologist who is doing research on endocrine function in rats. Even the requisite knowledge and skills differ greatly, depending on the area of specialization and the particular job within it.

2. *What does the occupation have to offer?* What rewards and satisfactions can be expected in terms of income, social status, and opportunities for advancement and personal growth? Are the rewards and satisfactions of the kind the individual most wants? Will the individual find the work interesting and personally fulfilling? What can he expect to contribute? In the long run, he is likely to find his work more meaningful and fulfilling if he feels he is making a contribution to his chosen field.

3. *What changes are likely to occur in the field?* Since today's college students will be working beyond the year 2000 A.D., the question of future trends in one's chosen occupational area is a relevant one. With the accelerating rate of technological and social change, major shifts in many occupations are taking place even in relatively short periods of time. Thus it is important for the individual not only to gain a clear view of given occupations as they now exist but also to know about probable changes in the near and distant future which might affect his work.

Other factors influencing occupational choice

Parental expectations and examples as well as broader sociocultural factors influence both the opportunities available to the individual and the choices that are made.

1. *Family background.* Burchinal, Haller, and Taves (1962) concluded from a review of several studies that male and female students most often credit their parents with the greatest influence on their career plans. Next in influence were teachers, friends, and vocational counselors. Despite the "generation gap," parents still appear to be influential today.

Parental influences on occupational choice may be exerted directly or indirectly or both. As American society becomes more urbanized and complex and educational opportunities become

2. *Social class and ethnic factors.* Vocational choices and opportunities are also influenced by social-class and ethnic background.

Krauss (1964), studying the aspirations of high-school seniors, found that in general middle-class students had higher educational aspirations than lower-class students, as a group. However, for lower-class students whose mothers were engaged in nonmanual work, 53 percent were planning to attend college, as compared with only 29 percent for those whose mothers were performing manual work. He also found a high relationship between the educational level of the parents and the educational

 Most of the kids who come in here looking for a job have a lot of problems, not just one or two—most of them either have a language problem or they've got the wrong color skin, school dropout, no money, no work experience, sometimes a criminal record, medical and physical problems, no driver's license, no self-confidence . . . do you want me to go on?

more widely available, pressure on the son to take over a family business or succeed his father in a particular occupation seems to be on the decline. Yet in a study of over 76,000 male college freshmen, Werts (1968) found that sons tended to choose the same or similar occupations as their fathers in three areas: the social sciences, the physical sciences, and medicine. For example, teachers' sons "overchose" the occupation of college professor; scientists' sons overchose mathematician, physicist, and geologist; and the sons of physicians overchose medicine as a career. Thus Werts concluded that these broad types of occupations still appear to be passed from father to son.

and occupational plans of their children: the higher the parental educational level, the higher the aspirations of the children.

Of course, Krauss dealt with high-school seniors and hence did not adequately sample the lower extreme of the socioeconomic scale. Where children grow up in circumstances of poverty and cultural deprivation, they have much less chance of either becoming high-school graduates or attending college. Such children usually show low levels of aspiration and achievement—in keeping with their absence of opportunity. Their background of experience makes it far less likely that they will internalize the value orientation of sacrificing immediate satisfactions for long-range achievement, nor could they afford sacrificing present income for an extended period of education with the possibility of a better future job. Thus for many reasons, the social-class level of the father is a good predictor of the son's aspiration and career choice (Blau, 1965; Duncan, 1965; Werts, 1968).

Lower-class young people also tend to marry younger and so usually have the least education and the lower-level jobs that go with it. Usually they have no choice but to take the first job they can get without considering its long-range potential. They may change jobs often; rarely do they progress beyond minimal earning capacity. Yet more than a million young people—most of them from lower socioeconomic level families—drop out of high school each year and effectively limit whatever choice they might have had.

Ethnic background may also be a limiting influence on career choice. The black American has undoubtedly been subjected to the greatest discrimination in occupational opportunity and hence in career choice. However, varying degrees of discrimination have also been directed toward Americans of Mexican, Indian, and Asian ancestry; Jews and Catholics, too, have been subjected to discriminatory educational, hiring, and promotional practices.

Getting along on the job

There are two prominent areas to be considered in adjustment to the occupation of one's choice. One is the matter of facing the first job—the matter of making the transition between school and the occupation that one has prepared for. Some of the common fears and problems encountered in this area are noted. The other major area concerns general sources of satisfaction and dissatisfaction at work—what the individual wants and needs, how he or she fits with the job in terms of abilities.

Facing the first job

". . . The confrontation of the young person with the world of work is a major change in the environment. The world of work is a new world of meanings. Generally, family does not enter here, nor do peers" (Tiedeman & O'Hara, 1963, p. 49).

In making the transition from school to work, the young person now enters the "adult world of reality." Although this world differs markedly from one job setting to another, it is a world which differs in many ways from the world of high school or college. The change may not be so abrupt for the student who has had summer jobs or worked part-time while going to school, but the complete transition from school to work

 I took the job—I was delighted. But it turned out I hated it. It was my first full-time job and I really hated many things about it. Also I felt like I wasn't being a very good secretary to the president of the company. Nobody told me I was doing a bad job—I suppose I was doing all right—but after about six months I quit, and I really felt like a failure. I went out and got another job in another industry, that turned out to be a lot of fun. But it took that success to get the taste out of my mouth of the failure . . . of what I thought was the failure of that first job.

not only represents a major milestone in the person's life but often poses a difficult transition problem. We will consider two issues that most new workers face.

1. *Common fears and concerns.* In moving from the competitive but relatively protected setting of school to the more demanding and often less supportive job setting, a young person may feel that he has entered an unknown new world whose dangers and pitfalls he does not know how to anticipate. Thus it is not surprising that many young people are somewhat fearful and apprehensive concerning their ability to make the shift successfully.

One common fear is of failing—of not being able to do the work satisfactorily. Even when the individual has adequate ability, he may still fear that he will be confronted with tasks for which he has not been adequately trained. A second common fear is of not being accepted or not getting along well with one's colleagues and superiors; in the case of a young person taking a supervisory position a common fear is of not gaining the respect and cooperation of subordinates.

Other fears and concerns may focus around whether he has made the right choice and whether the new endeavor will live up to his hopes and expectations and meet his needs. If he is unsure about his own abilities and needs as well as about the demands of the job, he may feel doubly insecure in this new setting.

2. *The "first-job dilemma."* Schein has used the phrase *first-job dilemma* to refer to the problems which the college graduate commonly encounters on his first job.

"The new graduate comes from college to his first job in industry prepared to be a company president. He is ambitious, enthusiastic and ready. Then come the realities of the business world. Within a year, he is very likely to suffer a serious loss of motivation, to find himself facing the thought of quitting the job that once seemed so promising as a career opportunity, or to stop trying so hard, to ease off and lapse into a kind of apathy. What is wrong?" (1968, p. 27)

The fact that the first job often presents problems is reflected in the high incidence of job change among college graduates. In a study of the work records of graduates from the MIT business management program, Schein reported that half of the graduates of one class had already left their first job roughly 3 years later; within 5 years of graduation almost three-fourths of another group had changed jobs at least once, and some were on their third or fourth jobs. The reasons given by these graduates are summarized on page 352. Although these findings may not apply to all college graduates, it would appear that something happens early in the careers of many college graduates that causes them to change jobs.

Unfortunately, the individual's decision to leave his first job and look for another one is often a self-devaluating experience in that he feels that he has "failed" in his first venture into the world of work. However, the first job can be seen as a training experience and an opportunity to analyze oneself and one's fitness for a certain type of job. If one finds that this is not the right job, then he can make a change, knowing more about both himself and the world of work than he did before.

Factors in occupational adjustment

In describing the first-job dilemma, we have noted some of the conditions that lead to difficulties in occupational adjustment—particularly on the first job. Now let us glance briefly at some of the factors in good occupational adjustment and job satisfaction.

Although *occupational adjustment* is a meaningful and widely used concept, criteria for judging it are by no means fully agreed upon. Objective criteria can be used, such as ability to hold a job, advancement in one's occupational field, and size of remuneration or degree of prestige of one's job; or subjective criteria can be used, such as job satisfaction and happiness. Occupational adjustment generally depends upon several factors:

1. *What the job offers the individual.* The satisfactions found in work are often described as being either *intrinsic* or *extrinsic*. Intrinsic satisfactions are found in the work itself—in its ability to satisfy one's needs for self-esteem,

In analyzing the reasons for early job changes by graduates of the MIT management program, Schein (1968) pointed to several factors, including the following:

1. The graduate's views of industry and business had been shaped by what he had been taught in his classes; often this involved learning to look at problems from the perspective of a high-ranking executive. Thus he thought in terms of general concepts, rational principles, and a long-term overview rather than in terms of day-to-day operational problems.

2. While his education had taught the graduate advanced management principles, day-to-day problems required a common-sense wisdom which he unfortunately had not acquired in his formal training.

3. Most of the graduates stated that their education had prepared them very well technically but had been deficient in providing them with the psychological techniques for coping with and managing other people.

4. The graduates gave evidence of certain needs of which they were not always aware: the need for an opportunity to test themselves, to learn and grow, to retain their individuality and integrity, and to make a meaningful and worthwhile contribution. Often the new employee found that his "good ideas" were not accepted or that he received little or no feedback concerning his job performance.

5. Often unrealistic expectations had been built up by company recruiters who had made promises and painted glowing pictures of challenging work and of opportunities for personal growth and advancement that turned out to be quite remote from reality. Thus the graduate often found that his job fell far short of his expectations.

On the basis of his findings, Schein has pointed to the need for a more effective dialogue between the university, the student, and the business organization. These recommendations apply equally well when other kinds of special training are involved.

 I have found teaching under the summer parks program to be very satisfying. I find creative satisfactions, because during the summer I can direct a show, I can work with young people on creative things—I find that very exciting. And I don't have to be concerned with the commercial end of it—our show doesn't have to make money, our show doesn't have to sell tickets. So we can do the things we find exciting at the time.

relatedness, meaning, and personal growth and fulfillment. Many workers find their jobs so interesting and meaningful that they work at them longer and harder than is required. Extrinsic satisfactions are extraneous to the work itself and involve rewards such as money, fringe benefits, and working conditions.

As noted earlier, a number of studies have found that intrinsic satisfactions—which meet the higher-level psychological needs of the worker—are more important to most workers than working conditions or even monetary compensation.

Herzberg (1968), reporting on an earlier study of engineers and accountants, found that five factors stood out as strong determinants of job satisfaction: achievement, recognition for achievement, the work itself, responsibility, and advancement. All of these were considered to be factors intrinsic to the work activity. In contrast, he found that the chief causes of job dissatisfaction were company policy and administration, supervision, salary, interpersonal relations, and working conditions. All of these were considered to be extrinsic factors. Herzberg also noted that a worker can be both satisfied and dissatisfied with his job.

In general it would appear that both employers and union leaders have tended to overemphasize the importance of money and other extrinsic factors and to underestimate the importance of intrinsic factors in job satisfaction. For example, Herzberg has pointed out that:

"One example of the striking lack of success of the present money motivation system is portrayed in the case of today's computer programmers. The cause of dissatisfaction is not the pay, for these men receive high salaries and excellent fringe benefits. Rather, the problem is boredom; after the initial challenge, most companies allow their computer programming to turn into routine drudgery. This need not happen: certainly it would not be difficult to build some true motivational factors into a job with as much potential challenge as this" (1968, p. 67).

Good salary and working conditions are important, but in our affluent society these are taken pretty much for granted, at least for occupations requiring a higher education. Of course, individuals differ in their motives and values and hence in the satisfactions or dissatisfactions they find in certain types of work. In any case, a good deal of current emphasis is being placed on making jobs more meaningful and fulfilling to the worker because, as we shall see in a later section, worker discontent over psychological conditions is rather widespread.

2. *What the individual brings to the job.* As in marital adjustment, there are certain aspects of maturity that tend to foster occupational adjustment. Among these are a realistic view of oneself, tolerance for delayed gratification, and a willingness to make realistic compromises.

In an occupation, as in any other life task, a person often must endure hardships and wait for rewards which may be forthcoming only after long periods of concentrated effort. Beginning jobs, being usually low in the organizational hierarchy, are especially likely to bring frustration and dissatisfaction unless the individual realizes that they are necessary stages to go through and that promotions will come as he acquires more skill, maturity, and judgment.

Some persons are able to establish themselves in an occupation with apparent ease; although they may change jobs, they show an orderly progression of advancement in their chosen field. Other persons have a great deal of difficulty in finding a job which satisfies them and "taking hold."

It is unlikely that all the individual's needs and expectations will be satisfied in any occupation, even at more responsible levels. The young person looking for the "ideal job" may well find that it does not exist. Often it becomes necessary to compromise—that is, to lower one's expectations and desires to a realistic level. This is a relative matter, of course; making a compromise with which one cannot live comfortably may lead to more problems than it resolves. Here, as in other areas of adjustment, one needs to be able to work on what can be changed, accept what cannot, and be able to recognize the difference.

3. *The individual's life situation.* Occupational adjustment both affects and is affected by the individual's life situation. Job satisfaction or dissatisfaction can influence an individual's personal adjustment and be reflected in marital and other relationships. In fact, if the individual attaches a great deal of importance to his work, his satisfaction or dissatisfaction at work may be critical in shaping his whole personal adjustment. Particularly when he is frustrated and unhappy in his work he is likely to be irritable and depressed and to "bring his problems home."

The reverse also is true: the supports and stresses in the individual's life situation can influence his level of competence and performance on the job. If things are going well at home, he can bring zest and concentration to his work, whereas if he is emotionally upset by personal or family problems, he may find it difficult to concentrate on his work or to gain satisfaction from it. Any stressful situation outside the job may make demands on the individual which deplete his adjustive resources and leave him less flexible and resourceful in coping with the demands and pressures of his work.

The meshing of the individual and the job thus involves both his personality and his general life situation as well as the nature and demands of the job.

Issues of dissatisfaction and discrimination

Many fortunate individuals are contented with their jobs, the pay, the conditions, the nature of the work, and the like. They are successful in their career choices and in occupational adjustment. This is particularly true of upper-income and professional workers, who typically have considerable autonomy, flexibility, and opportunity to advance according to their own goals and standards. There are a substantial number of "top-level" workers who are dissatisfied with their work, however, despite such advantages, and the great majority of workers simply do not have the same level of opportunity and sources of job satisfaction. This section will attempt to explore the extent of worker discontent and some of its sources, and will also consider the worker groups in which dissatisfaction appears to be most highly concentrated.

Sources and consequences of worker discontent

If work is an important source of personal identity, self-esteem, and social position, then it could be predicted that dissatisfactions concerning employment would have many consequences for the psychological and even physical well-being of workers. It would be impossible to document all of the repercussions for the individual, the family, and the community, of some types of work situations. For example, consider the dilemma of the welfare mother who faces only the options of menial employment or remaining at home to care for her children, or the aerospace engineer who has been laid off work after many years of professional service, or the person who has been forced to retire at an arbitrary age against his or her wishes. These individuals, along with the many thousands of assembly-line workers or clerical employees whose duties are repetitive, demeaning, and offer little chance of advancement, may suffer diminished self-esteem.

Psychological and physical effects of worker dissatisfaction

Persons whose jobs make them feel like "nobodies," or who have lost their job, or who find their work stressful and unfulfilling appear to be susceptible to a variety of psychological and physical complaints, in addition to the broader and largely immeasurable difficulties of family discontent or instability and lack of useful community participation.

A survey by the Institute of Social Research of a cross section of workers has shown a variety of mental health problems related to absence of job satisfaction: psychosomatic illness, low self-esteem, anxiety, worry, tension, and impaired interpersonal relations (Sheppard & Herrick, 1972). In one of the most thorough studies of the industrial worker, Kornhauser (1965) found that in his large sample of autoworkers, approximately 40 percent had some symptoms of mental health problems, and the factor which was most strongly related was job satisfaction; education, occupational status, and other potential influences were controlled. Studies continue to suggest that relatively greater mental health problems occur in jobs that are low-status, dull, unchallenging, and repetitive, and offer little autonomy. A growing number of persons with relatively high educational achievement are in fairly low-status jobs, and a study of a sample of such workers found a high incidence of irritation, anxiety, tiredness, depression, and low self-esteem (Kasl & Cobb, 1970).

Although little quantitative research exists on the subject, many people have pointed to abuse of alcohol and drugs as ways of coping with stressful or unsatisfying occupations. The heavy-drinking executive is a familiar stereotype, but there is also anecdotal evidence of industrial workers who drink large amounts of alcohol during the lunch hour to help withstand the boredom or pressure of their jobs and of the growing numbers of people, especially the young, who use drugs on the job for similar reasons (Special Task Force, 1972).

It is rather striking that in a long-term study of aging, the strongest predictor of longevity was work satisfaction (Palmore, 1969). The second major factor was "happiness," and these factors predicted longevity better than both a rating of physical functioning by a physician and a measure of genetic inheritance of long life.

It has long been known that certain high-pressure job situations are associated with the incidence of peptic ulcer and other signs of stress. Other physical ailments are related in part to occupational characteristics. For example, symptoms such as elevated blood pressure, cholesterol, body weight, and the like, are thought to be high-risk factors in heart disease, an illness which accounts for about half of all deaths. Several job-related factors have been associated with these high-risk symptoms or directly with high mortality:

1. Job dissatisfaction, as represented by boring and repetitive work, lack of recognition, and poor working conditions (Jenkins, 1971; Sales & House, 1971).

2. Occupational stress, including work overloads, responsibility, and conflict or ambiguity in work roles.

3. Excessively rapid and continuous change in employment (Caplan, 1971).

4. Incongruity between job status and other aspects of life, such as high educational achievement but low status (Kasl & Cobb, 1970).

5. Lack of stability, security, and support in the job environment (Caplan, 1971).

Areas of worker dissatisfaction

The measurement of job satisfaction or discontent is complex; we cannot simply rely on public opinion polls for reports of attitudes toward work. Indeed, when measured in this fashion, most workers report that they are satisfied with their jobs. To be "satisfied" usually means only that the pay is acceptable and environmental conditions adequate. However, measures which are more sensitive and less susceptible to respondents' answering in the way they think they should, reveal considerable dissatisfaction at all occupational levels.

Indirect indices of worker dissatisfaction have been listed as absenteeism from the job, high turnover rates, industrial sabotage, days lost from work due to strikes, poor quality of products, and accidents on the job—all of which have been reported to be on the rise (Walton, 1972).

Discontent among workers

There are apparently no occupational groups free from some degree of dissatisfaction among workers.

1. *"Blue-collar blues."* A 1970–71 survey of white, male, blue-collar workers found that less than half claimed that they were satisfied with their jobs most of the time (Sheppard & Herrick, 1972). Kahn (1972) discovered that in response to the question "What type of work would you try to get into if you could start all over again?" only 24 percent of a cross section of blue-collar workers chose the same work they were doing.

2. *"White-collar woes" and managerial discontent.* In the public imagination only the assembly-line worker or the unskilled laborer has the work "blues." However, research suggests that discontent is not at all limited to any particular group on the basis of occupation, sex, age, color, or race. Indeed, to a large degree all occupational levels have similar aims and goals: the quest for meaningful work, achievement, individual contribution, and autonomy. The survey just cited revealed that only 43 percent of white-collar and professional workers would elect to pursue the same occupation if they could start all over again (Kahn, 1972). Studies suggest that persons in "white-collar" jobs tend to be less dissatisfied than semi-skilled or unskilled workers, yet high status is no sure guarantee of desired job qualities. Gooding (1970) reported that one of the highest levels of worker dissatis-

I'm getting awfully tired . . . I'm fed up with my job. It's a good managerial job. Anybody would look at what I do all day and say, 'That's really interesting,' and they're right, but to me . . . it's just solving the same problems over and over. I've been solving these problems for this company 17 years, and I feel like there isn't a problem left I haven't, you know, already solved twenty times, in one form or another. I guess the only problem I can't solve right now is my own.

All I've done since I've been working here is, like bust tires—all day. You know, like, taking the old tires off and putting on the new ones when somebody buys them. And I've gotta get out of . . . I'm not going to bust tires all my life. Like, there's a guy here . . . he's been busting tires two years already. Not for me—no sir. I'm going to get . . . there's got to be some better kind of . . . this job would drive you crazy—it's so damn boring—I'm not going to stay.

faction was found among young, educated persons who held low-paying clerical positions; another sign of discontent in this group was a turnover rate as high as 30 percent per year.

Further indications of top-level occupational discontent are to be found in the apparently increasing numbers of middle-aged executives and professionals seeking career changes. Workers are living longer than ever before, and many find themselves disinterested, static, or even outmoded and obsolete long before their working years end. Many experience themselves as having heavy pressures and responsibility, but little actual power. Many others report that the competition and pressure of their jobs exacts too high a toll, compared with the status, security, and salary rewards offered.

new executive who finds no channels for his innovations—all share to some degree the same goals and sources of dissatisfaction on the job.

1. *Education and rising expectations.* Increasing educational attainment is at once a source of opportunity to escape the least satisfying jobs and a potential source of dissatisfaction. For example, blue-collar workers are better educated than ever before. In 1960, 26 percent of white and 14 percent of black craftsmen and operatives had completed four years of high school. But by 1969, 41 percent of whites and 29 percent of blacks in those jobs had completed high school (Schrank & Stein, 1971). Better-educated workers are far less likely than their predecessors to be satisfied with the conditions of most monotonous forms of work.

 I didn't really have any idea right then of what I was going to do. 'Education is the panacea of everything,' I thought, so I expected something was going to emerge out of my education that would be marvelous. I think it's generally felt, isn't it, that if you get an education, then everything is going to open up for you?

Sources of satisfaction or discontent

As we have seen from research reports, workers of all levels want interesting jobs, rather than monotonous and meaningless tasks. They want autonomy instead of constant supervision, opportunity for displaying and even increasing their skills instead of dead-end work. They want greater participation in the design of work so that they can have a sense of responsibility and achievement. Repeatedly, workers whose jobs measure high on variety, autonomy, and use of skills are found to be low on measures of personal alienation. The corporate lawyer who spends all her time writing the same kinds of contracts, the factory assembler who adds the same piece to his company's product, and the

The problem is equally grave for those who have followed the dictum that higher education is the key to the future. Numerous national policies, such as the G.I. Bill and the National Defense Education Act, have offered incentives for advanced educational attainment. But as many graduates with baccalaureate and advanced degrees have discovered bitterly, the economy has not changed rapidly enough to absorb the dramatic increase in the educational level of the work force. A study by Levitan, Mangum, and Marshall (1972) showed that the expansion of professional, technical, and clerical jobs absorbed only 15 percent of the new educated workers; the remaining 85 percent accepted jobs previously performed by persons with fewer credentials. A statement by a recent college

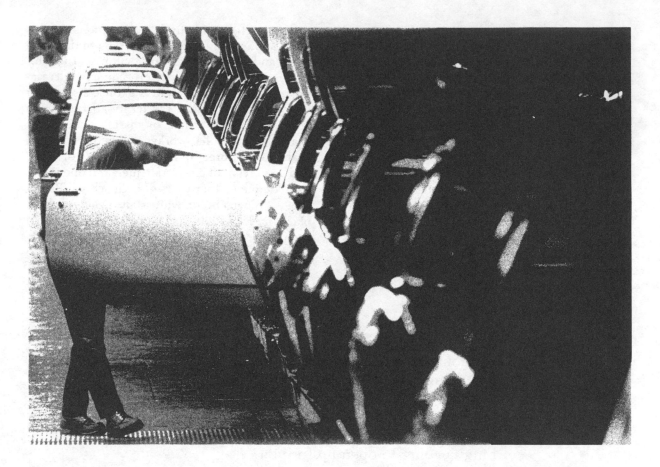

graduate illustrates the gap between education with its expectation and reality:

"I didn't go to school for four years to type. I'm bored; continuously humiliated. They sent me to Xerox school for three hours. . . . I realize that I sound cocky, but after you've been in the academic world, after you've had your own class (as a student teacher) and made your own plans, and someone tries to teach you to push a button—you get pretty mad. They even gave me a goldplated plaque to show I've learned how to use the machine" (Starr, 1972).

2. *Technology and dehumanization.* Countless words have been written about the role of technological advances in the creation of boring, repetitive, meaningless jobs which require little skill and initiative. The need for dealing with huge numbers of products or people and with complex interrelations has produced fragmentation, repetition, and monotony in many an office, factory, and service agency. Many companies and agencies are coming to recognize, however, that efficiency of operation has diminishing returns, and experiments in "job redesign" are proliferating.

In its report, the Special Task Force on Work in America (1972) presented controversial recommendations, such as extensive reforms and innovations in the workplace, aimed at reducing the apparently growing alienation and dissatisfactions of workers at all occupational levels. The report cites numerous case studies of attempts by various companies to alter significant aspects of jobs. For example, at Texas Instruments, Inc., 600 employees were given the responsibility to set their own production goals, and the results indicated both measures of increased satisfaction and increased productivity. Assembly time per unit decreased from 138 to 32 hours, and absenteeism, turnover rate, complaints, and trips to the health center decreased (Foulkes, 1969).

A variety of other major companies are experimenting with job redesign, with highly favorable results. Travelers Insurance Company was plagued with high absenteeism, low morale and productivity; projects were designed to transfer some supervisory functions to key-punch operators and broaden their jobs to include wider responsibility. Significant increases in productivity and drops in absenteeism were reported. The Medford plant of Corning Glass has work teams that set their own production schedules, vary the tasks of each worker, and make certain personnel decisions for their teams; production has increased by 20 percent and worker satisfac-

The young worker

Certain voices have been heard in the land accusing youth of abandonment of the "work ethic" in favor of welfare or hedonistic goals. While it is true that the young person espouses many values at variance with those of his elders, that is not the case in regard to work. In national attitude surveys of college students, 79 percent believe that "commitment to a meaningful career is a very important part of a person's life" (Yankelovich, 1972). Young workers at all occupational levels are better educated than ever before in American history, but they continue to seek in work a source of identity and self-esteem. However, the same survey showed that fewer students believe that "hard work will

I plan to live simply and within my means. Other people can 'keep up with the Joneses'—I'd rather not. Even if I wanted a lot of possessions, it's not worth what you have to do to yourself to get them.

I expect to try at least two different careers. I do not think that I could last an entire lifetime at the same job. I need a challenging, unroutine, satisfying career.

tion is reported high (*Newsweek,* March 26, 1973). It is reported that both congressional and private studies will continue to be directed toward the effects of job redesign on meeting some of the serious shortcomings of mass production methods.

Problems of specific groups

Although research suggests that dissatisfaction is widespread among all segments of the work force, there are particular groups for whom occupational problems seem especially prominent. These include young people, members of minority groups, and individuals approaching retirement.

always pay off" (69 percent agreement in 1968 and only 39 percent agreement in 1971). Moreover, attitudes toward authority are changing rapidly, according to the same researcher. In 1968, 56 percent of all students indicated that they did not mind the future prospect of "being bossed around" on the job; by 1971 only 36 percent indicated a willingness to submit to such authority. Another changing attitude concerns values placed on certain aspects of work. Young people have increasingly high expectations of what they hope for in a job. The American Institutes for Research (1971) reported that high-school students in 1970, when compared to a similar survey made in 1960, showed a marked shift away from valuing job security and opportunity for promotion to valuing "freedom to make my own decisions" and "work that seems important to me."

In view of the increasing education of young workers, and changes in attitudes—not away from work, but toward higher expectations of work—the mounting dissatisfactions of the young worker at all levels is not surprising. Complaints of boredom, lack of autonomy and responsibility, and overeducation for the jobs available have already been cited. There is no reason to believe that the demand of the young for fulfilling work will diminish, particularly as youth become better educated. The implications of this trend for the future of the workplace are worth pondering.

The minority worker
In spite of a growing social consciousness of the occupational needs of and obstacles to minority workers, along with significant legislation to end discriminatory employment practices, the statistics speak for themselves. One in three minority workers is employed irregularly or is unemployed or has given up looking for work. One in three minority workers is engaged mainly in jobs which pay less than living wages. The annual salary of employed minority males is far below that of the average salary of the white worker. Relatively little progress is being made to undo the damage of decades of persistent discrimination and closed-off opportunity. Even the one out of three minority workers who is employed steadily in a medium-level blue-collar, white-collar, or professional job complains of meaninglessness, routine work, and authoritarian work structures, although the major problem remains discrimination. A recent survey by Kahn (1972) found that the most dissatisfied group of all consists of young black workers in white-collar jobs. A prevalent problem among this group was the complaint of racial discrimination—an obstacle which obviously takes precedence over issues of boredom and lack of autonomy on the job. Once again we see that rising expectations not fulfilled by reality can breed bitterness and discontent, at considerable cost to the esteem and identity of the individual, as well as to the organization.

The older worker and retirement
It is predicted that by 1975 at least 20.7 million Americans will be older than 65. By the year 2000, one person in four will survive until at least 85; today only one in eight lives that long. Thus, in terms of both numbers and proportions, the older person represents a sizable and largely ignored element of the population, a fact which has several crucial implications for work.

As cited earlier, the best predictor of longevity, better even than current health status, was work satisfaction. Yet, many persons are expected to retire from work at age 62 or 65. At that point, the older person abandons the worker role, with its self-defining and esteem-building attributes, and may be forced to take on the "sick" role as he becomes less independent.

Although retirement at the arbitrary age of 62 or 65 may have many advantages and humanitarian consequences, it may also have serious implications for many workers. Occurring at a point when other role changes may take place, such as the decline of family ties and the retardation of sexual capacity, retirement may hasten mental and physical deterioration, and its accompanying financial changes may induce added stress and loss of independence.

The older worker is at a singular disadvantage in the job market. His chances for employment, if he is not already working, are slim, since

 I'm not going to quit here till they push me out the door. If they think they can replace me . . . They can give my job away to somebody . . . some younger guy . . . but they won't ever replace me.

aging *per se* is generally assumed to be associated with decline in ability to perform or acquire new skills. However, such an attitude ignores the heterogeneity of the over-60 age group, as well as the evidence which disputes the popular view of inevitable intellectual decline with aging (Geist, 1968).

A rather dramatic example of the psychological significance of work is illustrated in the following case:

"Mr. Winter single-handedly ran an operation that nobody else in his company fully understood, nor in fact cared to understand. As Mr. Winter reached his 64th birthday, a bright and talented younger man was assigned as an apprentice to learn the complex set of activities so that at the end of the year, he could take over the operation and the old master could benefit from a well-deserved retirement. Mr. Winter objected, claiming that he did not want to retire, but the company had rules. Not long after retirement a substantial change in Mr. Winter took place. He began to withdraw from people and to lose his zest for life. Within a year after his retirement this once lively and productive businessman was hospitalized, diagnosed as having a senile psychosis. Friends from work and even family soon stopped coming to visit as they could evoke no response. Mr. Winter was a vegetable. About two years after the apprentice had stepped up to his new position of responsibility he suddenly died. The company found itself in a serious predicament. The function that was vacated was essential to company operations, but which no one else in the company could effectively perform. A decision was made to approach Mr. Winter and see if he could pull himself together enough to carry on the job and train somebody to take over. Four of his closest co-workers were sent to the hospital. After hours of trying, one of the men finally broke through. The idea of going back to work brought the first sparkle in Mr. Winter's eyes in 2 years. Within a few days, this 'vegetable' was operating at full steam, interacting with people as he had years before" (Margolis & Kroes, 1972).

The issues of retirement and the aging worker are enormously complex, and clearly fall within the scope not just of company or agency policy,

but of national policy as well. And as the population statistics suggest, the problems of the aging worker will increase over time.

The special case of women and work

Family, home, and husband's occupation and status were formerly the major determinants of a woman's identity. With increasing awareness of their limited and limiting roles in life, women have begun seeking additional or alternative sources of esteem and self-fulfillment. Like most male Americans, many women turn to work for an opportunity to define themselves and make a meaningful contribution, but this path has many obstacles. Vast numbers of women find themselves limited to jobs which are damaging to their self-esteem; many find that their own socialization has poorly equipped them to better their employment status. Institutional practices, both subtle and open, make it hard to earn equal pay for equal work. And while many women cannot, because of numerous obstacles, face employment on the same terms as men, they are also frustrated and made to feel guilty and unproductive if they choose to stay at home and attend to the occupation of managing homes and raising children. This section attempts to explore the magnitude and sources of the problems of women and work.

More and more women are entering the work force with high expectations only to end up in low-status jobs with fewer fringe benefits, or jobs which are stereotypically female in character, and for which they earn less money than do men in positions of comparable status and responsibility. The scope of the problem is astounding.

Women in the work force
The Department of Labor (1971) reports that half of all women between ages 18 and 64 are in the work force, and studies suggest that 90 percent of women will work outside of the home at some time in their lives. Thus, issues such as discrimination in employment apply not to a minority of atypical females, but to millions of women workers.

Other attempts have been made to diminish the scope of the problem with the assertion that most women work for "pin money," merely to help purchase luxuries for their families, so that their occupational needs and difficulties are relatively minor. However, at least 11 percent of all families in the U.S. in the late 1960s were headed by females, most of whom were in the work force (Department of Labor, 1969). Moreover, although the income of many women is "secondary" in the sense of being less than that of their husbands, it is by no means pin money. Women work to provide their families with automobiles, houses, and college educations which could not be afforded otherwise; it is the wife's work that permits many lower-middle-class families to achieve middle-class status in cases where the husband's income alone could not have succeeded.

Salary
Women earn less money than men, at all occupational levels, even for the same work. Moreover, the gap seems to widen rather than narrow, despite legislation prohibiting occupational discriminations on the basis of sex and race. In 1955 the average female employee earned 64 percent of the wages paid to similarly employed men; by 1970 she took home only 59 percent as much (Special Task Force, 1972). Equal-pay legislation has made certain strides and has prevented certain glaring inequities, yet salary discrimination against women frequently takes the subtle form of job segregation, often with women doing the same work under a different title and earning less for it than men.

Another difficulty is that "women's jobs" pay less than "men's jobs" of comparable educational attainment. Recently, California women with four or more years of education beyond high school averaged $4151, which was only $300 more than California men who had left school at the end of the eighth grade. At the same time, California men with four or more years of college averaged $8108.

Status
Where women's occupational status is relatively high, it tends to be in "women's jobs"—teaching, nursing, and the like—in which women are paid for being nurturant, competent, taking care of others. But for the most part, the work that women do is very likely to be boring, with low prestige and low autonomy. As Bird summarizes it:
"The fascinating thing about it is that whether the measure is money, power, prestige, or achievement, and whatever the field, the proportion of

Employment barriers against women are slowly breaking down, and women are moving into positions formerly unique to men. However, the overall picture of women in the workforce remains a bleak one, with women routinely located in dead-end jobs with relatively low pay and status, and little chance to rise into supervisory jobs permitting exercise of authority and expression of creativity—characteristics which most workers desire. Many of the barriers which prevent women from taking an equal place in the world of work are due to certain myths about female workers. These myths tend to be perpetuated either subtly or overtly in the workplace. What are some of these myths?

1. *"Marriage and childbearing prevent women. . . ."* The myth has it that women's "unique" and proper role is that of wife and bearer of children. When she does work, one can expect irregularity and absenteeism due to the demands of her children and domestic duties. National statistics indicate that about 4 out of 10 working women are mothers (Schein, 1972), and of these women, only 36% have children under the age of six. A Public Health Service survey of work time lost due to illness or injury revealed very small differences between men and women, and labor turnover rates are also quite comparable for the two sexes (Department of Labor, 1971). Moreover, where an employer's figures reflect higher rates of absenteeism and turnover for women, it may reflect the tendency to employ women in the low-status jobs where satisfaction is lowest and prospects for advancement poorest.

2. *"Lady supervisors mean trouble."* Another widespread myth about women workers which "justifies" their relatively low status is that women supervisors are not as effective as males. It is charged that both women and men workers respond unfavorably to a female boss. However, an actual study by the Department of Labor which surveyed executives who had worked for females determined that at least three-fourths of the respondents had favorable views of their female supervisors (Special Task Force, 1972).

3. *"Women are suited only for 'feminine' jobs."* According to this point of view, it is best for women to limit their employment to "appropriate" work—jobs closely linked to their homemaking roles or roles as men's helpmates. These include, of course, classroom teachers, nurses, dieticians, secretaries, waitresses, cooks, receptionists, and the like. "The result of these exclusionary practices is to crowd women into a limited number of jobs where the pressures of excess supply lowers wages below the level that would otherwise prevail" (Special Task Force, 1972). Occupational structure does not reflect basic and unchanging sex differences in temperament or ability. Historically, in fact, the roles of teacher, clerk, telephone operator, and bank teller, among others, were all male domains.

4. *Stereotypes of female workers.* Related to the concentration of women in certain "female" occupations is the presence of derogatory stereotypes which are difficult to undo. For example, the secretary is often viewed as "a gum-chewing sex kitten; husband hunter, miniskirted ding-a-ling; slow-witted pencil pusher; office go-fer ('go-fer coffee,' etc.); reliable old shoe" (Klemesrud, 1972). Old maid librarian, schoolmarm, lady cabdriver, and many other stereotypes help to perpetuate the barriers to women of full participation in the employment and status structures of the work world.

5. *"Men should have higher status anyway. . . ."* This myth reflects a basic and enduring attitude of most Americans, that men rightfully should have higher status than women, that husbands need to have better jobs than their wives, and that males properly should not be supervised by females. A corollary is that men "need" to make more money in order to support their families. There are too many female heads of households to justify paying men more for the same work than women on those grounds. On the other hand, the problems of damage to male egos and threat to women when they achieve uncharacteristic power and prestige are real problems. Nevertheless, the solution to the dilemma is not to perpetuate the sources of discontent, but rather to work toward elimination of sex, class, and role stereotypes which damage the self-esteem of both men and women.

> **Cooking and sewing have mostly always been done by women, but why don't more men do them? They can, there are no physical barriers stopping them. It's just that they have always recognized them as women's jobs and therefore have no interest in them.**

women at the top is remarkably constant and low. In the mid-1960s, women were:

—*Less than 10 percent of all the professional or "knowledge" elites except classroom teachers, nurses, librarians, social workers, and journalists; 9 percent of all full professors; 8 percent of all scientists; 6 percent of all physicians; 3 percent of all lawyers; 1 percent of all engineers.*

—*Five percent of the income elite of the individuals with incomes of $10,000 or more. . . .*

—*Five percent of the prestige elite listed in* Who's Who in America *for 1967, down from 6 percent in 1930.*

—*Two percent of the power elite of business executives . . . ; less than 4 percent of all Federal civil servants in the six highest grades; 1 percent of Federal judges; 1 percent of the United States Senate"* (1971, pp. 56–57).

Nearly one-third of the entire female work force, accounting for about 9 million workers, consists of secretaries. Secretarial work not only is often enormously monotonous, involving little autonomy and offering no prestige, but also is the only kind of work available to many women. As one college graduate put it: "I have a Bachelor's degree in French literature. The smartest thing I ever did, however, was to take a typing course my junior year in high school; without it I would never be able to find a job" (Salzman-Webb, 1971). It has been estimated that women hold the majority of the worst white-collar jobs, such as keypunchers, file clerks, and other clerical workers—besides being overrepresented on the assembly lines. Bird summarizes the pattern of occupations for women: "Women are least accepted in work involving machinery, negotiation, travel, risk, profit, and substantial sums of money. But the most striking boundary of all is occupational status" (1971, p. 55).

Not only are women typically limited to low-prestige jobs, but a recent study also shows a tendency to attribute low status to jobs that women hold. Experimental subjects were led to believe that certain high-prestige occupations (such as physician, lawyer, and others) would sustain increasing proportions of female members over the next few decades. Ratings of occupational prestige and desirability decreased significantly for four of the five professions studied when subjects anticipated increased proportions of women (Touhey, 1973).

Given both the pay and status differentials between working men and women, it is not surprising that the Survey of Working Conditions found that women are nearly twice as likely as men to express negative attitudes toward their present jobs (Special Task Force, 1972).

traits of women as they differ from men have been well documented, and the role demands on women are equally clear-cut. The ascription of femaleness and its implied "basic function of women" is pervasive throughout a woman's life in ways which have strong implications for work. For example, a *New York Times* headline read, "Grandmother Wins Award," instead of "Dr. X Wins Nobel Prize," and eminent women are invariably introduced to the public as "novelist and mother of three"—a description which has no counterpart among males.

2. *The motive to avoid success.* So pervasive and far-reaching is the socialization of women toward certain qualities and tasks and away from ambition, achievement, productivity, and assertion, that researchers find evidence among many women of a motive to avoid success. Achievement in occupations typically "male," researchers speculate, produces enormous conflict in most women. The sources of the conflict are not difficult to identify: social pressure and a certain amount of negative reinforcement for intellectual achievement are apparent. For example, one university professor remarked to a female graduate student, "I know you're competent and your thesis advisor knows you're competent. The question in our minds is are you really serious about what you are doing?" And another professor remarked, "Any girl who gets this far has got to be a kook" (Women's Caucus, 1970). The achieving and ambitious female also finds her femininity challenged. Only in an atmosphere where women face strong sanctions against achievement and the abandonment of their "proper" role would a newspaper have bothered to print a news article headlined "Wife Leaves Mate, Baby for Career" (*Los Angeles Times,* May 16, 1973).

 Men have a tendency to look at the world as a place to become successful (materially). Women tend to look at the world as a place to live and raise a family.

Achievement quandaries of women

Many of the obstacles women face in taking their places as equals to men in the world of work stem from sources such as stereotypes, institutional sexism, and various overt discriminatory practices in hiring and salaries. However, women also erect barriers for themselves, based primarily upon their socialization into "proper" roles, attitudes, and behavior.

1. *Female socialization.* From the time the girl baby is wrapped in her first pink blanket, she begins to experience an enduring and pervasive lesson in being female. Her toys and her games reflect the attitude that home and family are the lot of women, and she is slowly shaped to be relatively docile, nurturant, unassertive, helpful, emotional, and the like. The personality

It has been my experience that men basically think more of their ego than women do. All the men I have known always need their egos built up—and woe to the woman who dares to harm it.

I know many girls who, even through there is a drive for women's equality with men, want the man to be dominant over them.

Research on women's motives to avoid success has been conducted by Matina Horner (1970). She asked both male and female subjects to complete various story fragments; for female subjects the fragment read, "After first-term finals, Anne finds herself at the top of her medical school class." For male subjects, the name was changed to "John." After scoring the responses for various indices of "fear of success imagery," Horner reported significant differences between male and female subjects on their fear of success. Women's stories reflected both fear of social rejection and concern about normality or femininity. For example, one woman wrote, "Anne is completely ecstatic but at the same time feels guilty. She wishes that she could stop studying so hard, but parental and personal pressures drive her. She will finally have a nervous breakdown and quit med school and marry a successful young doctor." Another woman responded, "Anne doesn't want to be number one in her class. She feels she shouldn't rank so high because of social reasons. She drops down to ninth in the class and then marries the boy who graduates number one." Other research suggests that many college women change their plans toward a less ambitious, more traditionally feminine direction— possibly in response to a fear of social rejection if they seek achievement and appear ambitious (Tangri, 1969; Schwenn, 1970). Horner's research further indicates that a significant determinant of women's conflict over achievement is the attitudes of males with whom they are involved.

Thus there appear to be internal as well as external obstacles facing women who aspire to work in positions which meet their needs for feelings of worth and meaningful contribution. The woman who is ambitious and seeks an occupation of high status and authority is likely to face a personal conflict of considerable magnitude.

Working mothers and full-time housewives

Many women attempt to resolve conflicts about their aspirations and roles by combining work and family. Such an arrangement often entails ingenuity in planning, and great reserves of energy and endurance. In addition, an added burden of guilt must be borne by many women, since it is popularly believed that women *should* stay home, at least with small children. Rossi (1972) found that half of the female college graduates sampled felt that part-time work is acceptable while children are under age five, but only 18 percent approved full-time employment while the child is a preschooler. Actual research on the effects of working mothers on the emotional and psychological development of children has been equivocal but appears to indicate that working *per se* is not detrimental, but that a variety of factors including family atmosphere, mother's attitudes, social class, age, and many other variables determine the child's response to having a working mother (Nye & Hoffman, 1963).

A dilemma women face is their inability to work on the same basis as men on the one hand,

and the guilt or devaluation that accompanies being a housewife on the other. Many men fail to regard being a homemaker as "work," and ask their wives, "What do you find to do all day?" Many people look with disapproval upon AFDC mothers who feel they have no alternative but to take welfare and stay at home with their children. And at the other extreme is that ornament of American culture, the college-educated housewife, who engages in home, family, civic, and voluntary service affairs. Such women and their sisters who work seem to face a subtle struggle in which both feel at once smug and guilty with respect to each other—an energy-draining situation which appears to have no counterpart among males.

The future world of work

Much as the Industrial Revolution amplified and largely replaced muscle power in the Western world and freed man from much of the drudgery of physical labor, the "computer revolution" is implementing our intellectual capabilities and freeing us from the bonds of routine and repetitive clerical work. In the process, new occupations are coming into being and many traditional ones are undergoing drastic change or becoming obsolete.

In concluding our discussion of the world of work, it thus seems relevant to note some of the occupational trends in our society and the relationship of these trends to education and living. Then we will risk a few brief speculations on future possibilities and horizons in the world of work.

The impact of the computer

As the computer revolution has gained momentum, we read about "the wonderful world of computers"—computers make up payrolls, check income-tax returns, handle travel reservations, keep track of insurance premiums, assist learning, operate factories, control airline traffic,

guide and monitor spacecraft, assist in problem solving and decision making, and predict the future. Computers are even used to help design better computers. In short, computers are having an increasing impact on almost every aspect of our society, including government, industry, banking, insurance, defense, agriculture, medicine, science, and education.

The impact of computers on the world of work will continue to be tremendous, for they make possible a large increase in production with fewer and fewer workers. Computer robots appear capable of reducing the average person's work week to some 10 hours or less by the year 2000, and of providing a more affluent life. It has been estimated that 1 out of every 4 families will then have an income exceeding $25,000 by today's standards—as contrasted with 1 out of 20 families in 1970. Computers will not only provide the individual with increased leisure time and a more affluent way of life, but they will also influence the types of work that will be needed and available and hence the kinds of training that will be needed for different occupations.

About a decade ago, Michael (1965) concluded—based in part on a report to the Department of Health, Education, and Welfare concerning the prospects ahead for the youth of tomorrow—that the trend is toward a three-level occupational system comprising professionals, technicians, and the unskilled. The professionals will require a long and rigorous education and will be concerned with high-level decision making and future planning; the technicians, who will constitute the great majority of the work force, will be concerned with research and with programming, monitoring, and servicing the computers and other automated equipment. The unskilled were portrayed as a disturbingly distinct group—at least in the foreseeable future—who will be relegated to relatively menial and low-paying jobs which require little in the way of education and training. This conclusion seems equally valid today, and the psychological and social problems such a situation could entail are obviously both important and complex and will require major changes if we are to ensure that all persons share in the opportunities for the better life that will hopefully be provided in our future, more affluent society.

Looking ahead: Learning, leisure, and livelihood

"Suppose instead of being about five billion years old, our planet, Earth, had come into being only 80 days ago.

"On this time scale, the first living creatures would be about 60 days old. But man would have come upon the scene about an hour ago.

"Similarly, significant numbers of modern men appeared less than a minute ago and agriculture came into being just 15 seconds ago. The use of metals would be 10 seconds old and the idea of a money-economy occurred to someone three-fourths of a second ago.

"The industrial revolution that replaced man's muscles with power-driven machines began three-tenths of a second ago, and the introduction of the electronic digital computers—machines that extend the capacity of the human mind—only about one-fifteenth of a second ago" (Bengelsdorf, 1966).

As the computer age has accelerated still further the rapid pace of social change, concern with "things to come" has become far more than a passing fad for science-fiction writers; and recently we have seen the emergence of a new group of experts—the "futurists"—who have made predicting possible and probable future change a relatively scientific enterprise (Kahn, 1972; Martino, 1973a, 1973b). If their predictions are correct, the world of the year 2000 and beyond will be different in many ways from the world of today.

Among the many changes which they predict are the continuing use of education—refresher courses, evening classes, workshops, community learning centers, and so on—throughout a person's career. Such continued education will be necessary for both the professional and the technician. As jobs change or become obsolete, retraining for new work will become commonplace, and a person may be retrained several times during his work life. A second important trend predicted by the futurists is the decreasing importance of work *per se* in the life of the individual. The great increase in time free from earning a living is expected to bring changes in our traditional ideas of leisure as "time to kill," and we will be confronted with the necessity of using leisure-time activities to meet many of the needs we now meet through work; for example, a person's status and worth will not be evaluated by his "line of work" or his material possessions but by his involvement in the drama of living.

 ## Summary and a look ahead

In the world of work, as in marriage, expectations and criteria of success have changed. We expect our work not only to provide reasonable financial rewards but to meet many of our psychological needs and to serve as an avenue for personal growth. Thus we find the decline of the Puritan work ethic and the quest for a career that will contribute to meaning and fulfillment in our lives.

The choice of a career provides both an opportunity and a challenge—particularly in a world where computers are taking over more and more routine work functions and the jobs that are left require more knowledge and longer preparation. Two factors seem to be of key importance in choosing the "right" occupation: (1) personal characteristics—involving questions about what the individual wants to do, what he can do or learn to do, and how his abilities and resources may limit the choices; and (2) characteristics of the occupation—involving the requirements or working conditions, what the occupation has to offer, and what changes appear likely to occur in the occupational area. The role of family background and socioeconomic factors also influence career choice.

Factors involved in getting along on the job include the difficulties often experienced on the first job, commonly referred to as "the first-job dilemma." Also in this general context, we noted the nature and extent of worker discontent and its far-reaching impact on physical and psychological well-being as well as interpersonal adjustment. We particularly focused on the working problems of specific groups, including the young worker, the minority worker, and the older worker, and the special difficulties—including various forms of discrimination—encountered by women in the work force and by working mothers and full-time housewives.

Finally we speculated briefly on the future world of work, again emphasizing the increasing impact of our computer age on the world of work—particularly in terms of increased leisure and the necessity for continual learning and adjustment required by the rapid pace of social change.

In the next chapter we shall turn to an even broader aspect of social behavior as we deal with the individual's interactions with society at large as demonstrated by membership in groups.

13

The Individual and the Group

Why we have groups
The group as a living system
Interaction of the individual and the group

"If it were possible for the overworked hypothetical man from Mars to take a fresh view of the people of Earth, he would probably be impressed by the amount of time they spend doing things together in groups. He would note that most people cluster into relatively small groups, with the members residing together in the same dwelling, satisfying their basic biological needs within the group, depending upon the same source for economic support, rearing children, and mutually caring for the health of one another. He would observe that the education and socialization of children tend to occur in other, usually larger, groups in churches, schools, and other social institutions. He would see that much of the work of the world is carried out by people who perform their activities in close interdependence within relatively enduring associations. He would perhaps be saddened to find groups of men engaged in warfare, gaining courage and morale from pride in their unit and a knowledge that they can depend on their buddies. He might be gladdened to see groups of people enjoying themselves in recreations and sports of various kinds. Finally he might be puzzled why so many people spend so much time in little groups talking, planning, and being 'in conference.' Surely he would conclude that if he wanted to understand much about what is happening on Earth he would have to examine rather carefully the ways

371

in which groups form, function, and dissolve" (Cartwright & Zander, 1968, p. 3).

In our discussion of interpersonal relations, marriage, and the family, we have seen the extent to which we are "group creatures." Only recently, however, have psychologists systematically studied the structure and behavior of groups and the ways in which individuals and groups mutually influence each other. Yet, simply placing the individual in his "social habitat," in terms of the groups to which he belongs and his position in these groups, takes us a long step forward in understanding his behavior. And as we probe into interactions between a group and its members, we add indispensable information to our understanding of human behavior.

take a closer look at any individual we will find that he or she is a member of a large number of groups.

Let us take a fictitious man named Mr. Smith. In describing him, or identifying him, those who know him will tell us he is a human being (species identification), he is a man (sexual identification), he is a Smith (family identification), he is a teacher (occupational identification), he is a Christian (religious identification), he is an American (national identification), he is Irish (ethnic identification), and he is a Democrat (political identification). Besides being all these, we might be told he is a veteran, a golfer, a beer drinker, a lover of popular music and impressionist art, a football fan, a regular viewer

 The groups that I belong to, I belong to for a purpose.

I'm not a joiner; I guess that's one group I'm in—nonjoiners.

I can't describe myself in terms of my affiliations and identifications—I've always felt like such an outsider that I don't feel I belong.

In this chapter, then, we shall concern ourselves with the social setting of behavior. Specifically, we shall study: (1) why we have groups, (2) the group as a living system, and (3) special problems in individual-group interaction, including conformity and nonconformity.

Why we have groups

To observe people, even casually, is to see that much of their time is spent in groups. And if we

of detective stories on television, and a user of a particular deodorant. All these adjectives indicate his membership in groups.

During the course of the day, Mr. Smith will move in and out of numerous groups, many of which will demonstrate his membership in the groups we have named. But many of the groups to which he belongs meet only infrequently, and some not at all. And at times, during the day, he will be part of groups which are so transient as to have little meaning for him: the group eating in a restaurant at one time, the group in the elevator, the group on the bus, or the group

 I'm a woman, and being a member of that group sometimes has its drawbacks. When I encounter discrimination against women, it makes me wish *not* that I wasn't a woman, but it makes me wish that things were a little more equal between those two groups—men and women.

stuck in a traffic jam. Sometimes these transient groups are suddenly transformed into much more meaningful groups, as when the elevator stalls, or there is a fire in the restaurant.

The variety of groups to which we belong

In seeking to understand the impact of groups on the behavior of individuals, we must take into account the variety of groups to which people belong, as in the hypothetical case of Mr. Smith. In looking more closely at these groups, we can see several different kinds.

1. We are involuntary members of some groups. It is difficult, if not impossible, to get out of these. Many we are born into, like our family, our race, our ethnic group (which sometimes decides our religious affiliation). Our membership in our nation and our social and economic class is also largely a matter of birth, though with difficulty we may do something to change these. Such involuntary membership, due to

birth, can be a source of pride or can be experienced as a burden; it can confer great privilege (as it does for members of high-status families) or it can saddle us with heavy difficulties (as many members of ethnic and racial minorities know).

2. We must, of necessity, belong to some *types* of groups, though we may have some choice about which particular group of this type we will belong to. For example, most of us must live in *some* community, work in *some* group, go to *some* school (usually determined by where we choose to live), associate with *some* people.

to work with others for common goals, to increase our social status, or because joining promises to be profitable in some other way. When membership in any of these groups costs more than we feel it is worth, we can usually get out without much conflict.

4. We belong to other groups not because we have joined them but because we have the trait or characteristic on the basis of which certain people have been grouped. Mr. Smith is forty years old, so he is in the forty-year-old age group. He watches TV detective stories, so he is in the group of detective-story fans, and so on.

Besides these, if we want to work at some jobs, we may have to join unions or other work-related associations; if we want to practice our religious faith, we will probably have to be part of some religious community; if we want to participate in political processes, we will have to be part of some political party or organization.

3. There are many other groups to which we choose to belong, where membership is strictly voluntary. We join these groups in order to enjoy sharing interests with others of like mind,

These groups usually have little influence on the individuals who comprise them and cause them few problems. Only if there develops some move to identify people on the basis of one of these characteristics and to do something to them would there be a problem. If a movement develops to make everyone retire at age 60, then all in this group would likely be far more conscious of their membership in this group. The same would be true if there develops a movement to outlaw the reading of *Playboy Magazine*

1. *Attraction to the members of the group.* The prospective member may find the present group members appealing. General attractiveness has been found to be strongly affected not only by physical attractiveness, but also by proximity and contact. In at least a general way, we tend to love our neighbors and form groups with them. Factors known to be related to interpersonal attraction have been shown to affect voluntary group membership.

2. *Attraction to the activities of the group.* The prospective member may be drawn to the things the group members do— skiing, playing bridge, public service, task accomplishment in business.

3. *Attraction to the goals of the group.* This category is often difficult to separate from the one above. Individuals may be drawn to the group's objectives, such as community service, recreation, pollution control, the election of a political candidate.

4. *Desire for group membership per se.* Some theorists have proposed that simply being in a group may be rewarding for many; affiliation may be especially likely to occur under conditions of stress or anxiety and, of course, loneliness. Group membership may also be valued as a way of attaining rewarding by-products, such as access to desirable people or increased social status.

or the playing of golf on Sunday or the televising of football games. Then all the people who belong to the group characterized by the interest or activity in question would be more aware of their membership in this group, and we might see this group become organized.

5. We also belong to many transient groups, which form and dissolve leaving no traces that they have ever been. We mentioned Mr. Smith's elevator companions and the group in the restaurant. While ordinarily these groups have little importance in themselves, they constitute one of the important arenas of social action. They make up what we call *the public,* and, as Goffman (1967, 1972) has pointed out, our behavior in these situations is as carefully regulated as our behavior in the most tightly controlled groups.

Thus, like it or not, we are involved in groups. What are the rewards and costs of this involvement? How do the rewards and costs balance out?

The rewards of group membership

Groups evolve and continue to exist because important needs of individuals are best met in this way. Basic here are the meeting of food and other visceral needs, security, and belongingness. But as we have seen, group membership also strongly influences our identity and opportunities for self-fulfillment.

Security and related benefits

For human beings, the protection of the group is vital, because of a long period of helplessness after birth and because of a physical make-up that leaves them defenseless against many kinds of attack. Because it is easier to see this need for group protection in primitive societies, we may be tempted to think that we are no longer so desperately dependent on the group. A little thought, however, should make us aware that life in our "advanced civilizations" is, if anything, even more group dependent. It is simply that the group's methods for protecting us generally work so well that we are not aware of them. But when the systems break down, as in inability to control violence, runaway inflation, or mob rule, we recognize how dependent we have been all along. The Preamble to the Constitution of our nation shows the concern of the founding fathers that the security-related needs of individuals be met by the group:

"We the People of the United States, in Order to form a more perfect Union, establish Justice, insure domestic Tranquility, provide for the common defence, promote the general Welfare, and secure the Blessings of Liberty to ourselves and our Posterity, do ordain and establish this Constitution for the United States of America."

But we do not belong to most groups for protection from enemies. More often it is to benefit from various kinds of mutual help. No less pressing than the need for protection are the needs for food, shelter, and companionship. While it may not be impossible for an individual adult to provide his own food and shelter and care for himself in other respects, it is not easy even in reasonably favorable circumstances. For most residents of large cities in today's America,

Not as old as our security needs, but still very old and linked to them, are our needs for identity and self-esteem. People's identity and sense of self-worth have long been provided by the group. To return to our hypothetical Mr. Smith, his sense of self-identity is strongly influenced by his membership and status in various groups—and by the roles he plays in these groups.

There is a curious paradox attached to membership in a given group. Often it is the person who has an identity apart from the group who is most valued by the group, while the person whose identity is dependent upon the group—and thus desperately needs the group—may be

 I belong to a lot of professional organizations, because they do interesting things and because I enjoy talking with other people who are involved in the same kinds of problems I am. In fact, I think I have a real need to talk about these things with others who have the same kinds of interests and goals I do—who work with the same ingredients I do all day long.

this kind of self-sufficiency would be not only difficult but impossible. As societies have become more complex, there have been greater role differentiation and specialization, with the result that today people are more interdependent than ever. And so we live and work in groups through which we cooperate for the maintenance and enrichment of our lives.

So deep is our inherited social nature and so pervasive is the social conditioning we experience that few human fears are as strong as the fear of being alone. We can learn to be alone, and some few individuals seek solitude as a way of life. But most of us panic at the thought of having to make it on our own, and the threat of ostracism is still one of the most potent of persuaders.

valued much less by the group and thus be given a less important place. Frequently, the individual who is chosen as leader of a group will be someone with a broad range of interests and activities outside the group.

Many of our finest possibilities as human beings can be fulfilled only in a group. A sense of achievement, the joys of loving and being loved, the feeling of being needed, and some of the greatest opportunities for growth are found only in a community.

Without the group there is no opportunity for leadership and there is no fellowship. Without the community there is no continuity of values that we call *heritage,* no shared vision to live and die for, no sowing of seeds that only others can harvest. Without ties to certain special others there is no enlargement of the self to include a family, a nation, a people. All of these supra-individual identities may become—and at times have become—destructive. Yet it remains true that it is through such communities that people have often fulfilled their greatest potentials.

The costs of group membership

Even as we have described the rewards of group membership we have hinted at some of the costs. There always are costs, and all of us have experienced them.

Limitations

The first cost of group membership is the experience of limitations. A word heard often by

Demands

Not only does the group set limits; it also makes demands of us, and sometimes these demands can be very heavy. There is, first of all, and perhaps most important, the demand that we be loyal to the group. "Are you with us or against us?" No words are more loaded with negative feelings than *traitor* and *renegade.* Much deviant behavior will be tolerated if there is no question about loyalty, while scrupulous conformity will be of no avail if there is a strong suspicion that one's loyalties are with "the other side."

There are also demands for conformity, especially in public. In some areas the public gesture is the important thing, while at other times (as with loyalty) it is what is in the heart that matters. The sensitive areas in which conformity may be required can be quite change-

 I don't feel any obligations to society. Society let me down when they sent me off to fight in Vietnam. Some of my friends died. Others rot away in veterans' hospitals. I struggle to survive in a society that does not care if I live or die so long as I do not interrupt their affluent lives. A piece of paper says I served honorably. It should read that I was used dishonorably.

young children is the word "No." Those who protect us and care for us have the power to restrict us. The price of dependency is to be controlled. Even as adults, we still find that membership in a group brings limitations with it. To be a member of a particular church we must limit our behavior and even our professed beliefs. Many of the commandments are "Thou shalt nots." If we are active in a political party there are boundaries that we must not cross. Even informal groups have limits. Though they may not be so clearly defined, we know when we have "gone too far."

able, depending on who has power and what is decreed to be important. The demand to conform or take the "correct" stand on issues which have been made tests of one's soundness, whether religious or political, can be one of the most onerous costs of group membership. This was the theme of the powerful story, *A Man for All Seasons.* There are times when it is precisely those with integrity and conscience (like Sir Thomas More) who are sacrificed in the name of group ideals while unethical and opportunistic persons ride high.

Then there are the demands for responsible

participation—for assuming specified roles, paying dues (taxes), voting, or backing leadership. Sometimes the demand is to fight in battles the group is involved in, and this can cost a person his life. To refuse to fight, when chosen for this role by the group, can result in imprisonment and dishonor. As we have noted, groups cannot survive and function unless certain needs of the group are met. Few groups will allow members to benefit from the rewards of group membership without sharing in the cost of group maintenance. One of the perennial questions faced by groups is how these costs should be distributed. Should each pay the same? Should each pay as he can? Or, should each pay in proportion to the benefits he receives? This is, of course, the issue involved in tax policies.

Threats to integrity

The real issue in meeting both the limitations and the demands of the group is the threat these can pose to an individual's integrity. It is, of course, the more sensitive and conscientious person who feels this threat most keenly. All group life calls for compromise. But how far can a person compromise before he loses his soul? When is silence discreet and when is it cowardly? When is dissent irresponsible and when is it courageous? There are no easy answers here, and the struggle for integrity by persons who love the group but have misgivings about the

direction it is going can be intensely painful. It is this price of group membership that makes many persons reluctant to join groups.

The balance sheet

We have noted some of the rewards and some of the costs of group membership. If we weigh one against the other, how do they balance out? Undoubtedly each individual will find a different answer. For some the costs are greater than the rewards, and for others the rewards are greater than the costs. And the balance may be different for each group to which we belong.

But once we have balanced costs against reward, what can we do? In the case of groups to which we belong voluntarily, if the costs are greater than the rewards, we can get out—but sometimes the cost of doing so is greater than the cost of staying in the unrewarding group. For this reason, many people remain in communities where they are not happy, stay on jobs they do not enjoy, or retain membership in unions with which they disagree.

For all practical purposes, we cannot withdraw or resign from the many groups in which we have involuntary membership. Thus when our life in these groups is unrewarding there may be no easy solution. Sometimes we can learn skills with which to change the group or improve our

 In college I belonged to a sorority, because I was afraid that if I didn't join as soon as I was eligible, that maybe I wouldn't get a chance to join anything, and I would be an outsider. So I joined this group of girls and went through the initiation procedures and everything, and found that I really disliked it. It seemed to me that it was silly and shallow. So I withdrew more and more from the group and went on and did my own thing. They were kind of upset, and after about a year of this, they asked me to resign. I did resign and felt much the better for it after it was all over.

position in it. We can seek as much satisfaction as possible outside the group. Or we can seek to change the image or evaluation of the group. This has been seen in recent years in the case of black Americans who have refused to accept a derogatory self-image but have found a new pride and self-identity in their assertion that "Black is beautiful."

The group as a living system

One of the most useful ways of looking at groups is to see them in terms of the general systems model outlined in Chapter 2. Groups come into being and continue because they have survival value. The individual members of systems pay a price for inclusion but are rewarded with greater probability of survival and with the opportunity for participation in a kind of life not available outside the system.

The study of groups has shown that there are many parallels between individual and group functioning—that groups must meet certain needs if they are to maintain themselves and achieve the purposes for which they were formed, and they face stresses and attempt to cope with them in ways that closely resemble the behavior of individuals. Of course, the needs and purposes of groups may often conflict with the needs and purposes of the individuals who constitute them.

For this reason, it is important that we understand how groups are structured, how they function, and how the group as a system interacts with its environment.

Structure

Every system has a structure. By this we mean that its parts are put together in such a way that they function as a system. The same parts can be put together in a way that will not form a system, as may be seen if all the parts of a watch are thrown into a box. Continuing groups, as distinguished from the transient ones mentioned earlier, are made up of individual persons held together by goals, values, and mutual needs and attractions, working together in assigned places within a communication network. They perform their roles according to rules enforced by leaders using power generated within the system from input by individual members and from the system's interaction with the environment.

Not all groups need the same kind of structure to be effective; each one needs the type of structure appropriate to its tasks. Some tasks require complex and fairly rigid organization, whereas others can be accomplished by a relatively unstructured group. Overorganization can be as detrimental to successful group functioning as can be underorganization. Yet all groups will to some degree and in some form have the following structural elements:

1. *Members.* Sometimes membership is clearly defined, sometimes not.

2. *Differentiation of parts.* There must be some differences in positions and roles which are distributed among the members. Sometimes these assignments are relatively permanent; at other times there is a fluid exchange of positions and roles.

3. *Communication.* Different members of the group must be in touch with one another to some extent. At times this can be minimal, at other times it must be continual.

4. *Rules.* There must be some regularity or dependability in the behavior of individual members if there is to be a group. Again, the amount of this regularity varies greatly from group to group.

5. *Regulation.* Regularity results from some kind of organization which involves power or influence directed by some agency. In groups leaders direct power.

In addition to these structural elements, groups may also be characterized by the degree of commonality of purpose shared by members, and by cohesiveness. The degree of cohesiveness, the "group spirit" that develops among members, appears to be an important determinant of the success and productivity of the group, and affects and is affected by the various structural features of the group.

Function

Group structure and function are so interdependent that it is difficult to separate them even for discussion. In this section, however, we are less concerned with the organization of the group and more concerned with its functioning, including its goals, the means it uses, and the results of its efforts in terms of effectiveness or ineffectiveness.

Task and maintenance goals

It is apparent that group goals may vary widely. For a football team, the winning of games may be the primary goal; in a planning group, the key objective may be to formulate strategies for dealing with a specific problem such as air pollution; in a "brainstorming" group, the goal may be the generating of new ideas; in a therapy group, the goal is the personal growth and more effective adjustment of the individual members.

The primary objectives of the group—for example, the winning of games by a football team—are referred to as *task goals.* But whatever its primary goals, the group must also take measures to maintain its organization and integration if it is to function effectively or even survive. Thus the group must also be concerned with *maintenance goals.* Usually maintenance goals center around resolving conflicts among group members and meeting their emotional-social needs; for conflict, dissension, and dissatisfaction among group members are major sources of disorganization in groups. The replacement of group members lost as a result of death or other causes is also a major maintenance goal of many groups; if such members cannot be replaced, the group may work out a new organizational equilibrium, based on different relationships and responsibilities for the members who are left.

This tendency to restore organizational equilibrium can be seen in dramatic form when a military leader is killed during an enemy attack and a new leader emerges to head the unit as it strives to regain its functional effectiveness. Similarly, the loss of the mother or father in a family may lead to changed roles and responsibilities as the family attempts to regain its organizational equilibrium.

Thus group goals and strivings are roughly analogous to those of individuals. Like individuals, too, some groups are highly task oriented, with the predominance of their effort directed toward their task goals, while other groups are more concerned with maintaining themselves as an organized entity—for example, by making the group attractive to the members or to possible new members.

Group pressures toward conformity are often decried today; yet they develop inevitably as a group tries to maintain itself and achieve its goals. In fact, no group could long function as a unit without some uniformity and discipline of its members. A football team without training rules or an established practice time would probably not win many games, and a political party would suffer if its candidates openly supported greatly differing positions. Uniformity of opinion also can increase efficiency when a group must act quickly. A group with one voice can determine its direction and reach its goal faster than a group with many voices urging different actions.

Group pressures toward uniformity thus serve basic needs of the group. If the pressure to conform is too strong, however, it can stifle individual creativity and lead to rigid, unadaptive behavior on the part of the group as a whole—for part of a group's basic resources are the initiative and enthusiasm of its individual members. The special problem of maintaining the opportunity for variation and dissent—for the society's benefit as well as the individual's—will be discussed later in this chapter.

Solving problems and making decisions

Groups process problems in much the same way that individuals do. The problem is assessed, alternative solutions are formulated, and a given alternative is chosen on the basis of such factors as probable outcome, risk, and satisfaction of needs.

In comparisons of the performance of groups and of individuals working alone on problem-solving tasks, it has been found that groups have advantages and disadvantages. Groups can often assess a problem more accurately because several perceivers are able to compare their impressions; the pooling of individual resources may lead to the formulation of a wider range of alternative choices; and the varied past experiences of group members may lead to a more accurate prediction of probable outcome, risk, and satisfaction in selecting a given alternative. In one study dealing with problems in which a high degree of inference and judgment were called for, group solutions were found to be better than the average individual solution but not better than the best individual solution (Hall, Mouton, & Blake, 1963). Thus though the less able members may reap benefits they could not earn by themselves, the more able members may be held back or inhibited by the requirement of functioning in a group.

A group's ability to solve a problem is heavily dependent upon its composition—upon the abilities and characteristics of its individual members. Where no one in the group is qualified to deal with the problems at hand, group action is not likely to have the advantages mentioned above. Sometimes, too, the members of a group are operating on the basis of different information or assumptions; in such cases, they may have serious difficulties in communicating with each other and may work at cross-purposes. Members may also have conflicting needs or belong to other groups which pull them in opposing directions.

Sometimes group members irritate each other, and emotional conflicts and tensions arise which distract attention from the task at hand and interfere with objective consideration of the problem. And, of course, as in the case of individuals, groups may become more concerned with the safety and prestige of the group than with carrying out their original goals.

Group action and feedback

As in individual action, action taken by groups may be primarily task oriented or defense ori-ented. A football team trying to perfect new plays for an important game is task oriented in its behavior; the same team trying to explain a defeat erroneously as due to "poor refereeing" would be defense oriented.

Like an individual, a defense-oriented group may rationalize, project blame, indulge in "scapegoating," or utilize other defense mechanisms. Such defensive patterns are commonly initiated by group leaders and communicated to members through established communication channels; their intent is to maintain the adequacy and worth of the group in the eyes of its members—and hence to maintain or improve group cohesiveness and morale.

As in individual behavior, task-oriented action by the group varies greatly in strength and persistence. For the big game, a football team may outdo itself, showing great effort and determination; for a less important game, the players may neither try as hard nor perform as well. In general, the amount and persistence of group effort depend heavily on the degree to which group goals are perceived as relevant to the members' needs and accepted as their own. One of the key problems faced by leaders—from football coaches to presidents of companies or countries—is that of mobilizing group effort toward key group goals.

Like individuals, groups also utilize feedback concerning the outcome of their actions as a basis for making possible changes—whether in a task-oriented or a defense-oriented way. When feedback is used in a task-oriented way, the group becomes a "self-correcting" energy system. When not, it may become so concerned with its "image" or its good name that its efforts go into defensive maneuvers instead of into more effective efforts toward its goals.

Thus group action appears to follow the same basic principles as individual coping behavior. Groups have certain potential advantages, such as the potential for specialization of function of individual members, the ability to handle multiple tasks at the same time, and the capacity to deal with problems that are beyond the range of any one individual. At the same time, groups are often at a disadvantage compared to the in-

Group members

A group's effectiveness depends heavily upon the individuals within it, since ultimately it is individuals who actually make and implement group decisions. Members with serious personality weaknesses, immaturities, or lack of essential skills may disrupt or prevent group progress, just as mature, competent, and dedicated members help to ensure group effectiveness and success. Characteristics of members—especially in terms of the possession of essential competencies and commitment to group goals—are especially important when the group is under severe stress. A group's loss of dedicated and capable members, particularly those with outstanding leadership skill or other key abilities needed by the group, can be seriously disruptive to group performance and effectiveness.

Group organization and performance

Group effectiveness is influenced by each of the major elements of group structure. Effectiveness is enhanced by a type of power and leadership structure appropriate to the group's tasks; clear-cut, realistic, and agreed-upon goals; clear and appropriate social roles compatible with the self-concepts and values of group members; sound group values and an accurate frame of reference; and efficient communication.

The group's record of past successes and failures, its level of cohesiveness and morale, the efficiency with which it uses its human and material resources, and its ability to meet the needs of group members also play key roles in group effectiveness.

Environmental (field) conditions

Group effectiveness is fostered by a reasonable correspondence between the group and its environment—between what it is trying to accomplish and the resources and possibilities provided by its setting. In many underdeveloped countries, the lack of material resources, made more acute by overpopulation, makes it well-nigh impossible for individual and group needs to be met effectively.

Intergroup relationships are also often of great importance. Where groups cooperate in the interests of common goals, their effectiveness may be enhanced. Even intense competition among groups may lead to greater group effectiveness. However, if the relations go beyond competition to hostility and conflict, the achievement of group goals may be made more difficult, and group effectiveness may be reduced.

dividual with respect to such factors as communication, decision time, and coordination of action.

Factors in group effectiveness

In recent years there has been extensive research on the variables that are related to group effectiveness—the success of the group in achieving its goals and meeting the need of its members. Three sets of factors play a role in determining how effective a group will be: (1) characteristics of the group members, (2) the group organization and manner of functioning, and (3) the setting in which the group functions. Some of the most important conditions in each of these three general categories are summarized above. These conditions contribute not only to the level of group effectiveness but also to the level of stress tolerance of the group—to the difficulty of adjustive demands with which the group can cope without undergoing serious disorganization—and hence to the quality of the group's performance under sustained stress and in crisis situations.

The group and its environment

The environment of a group includes the space-time it occupies, comprised of the physical environment, historical setting, and cultural milieu, and the other groups with which it interacts. Just as a group exists to meet the needs of its constituent members, it also comes into being and exists partly to meet the needs of other systems of which it is a part. The environment is the context in which groups function,

group can do and is likely to do. The German term *Zeitgeist* (spirit of the time) is used to denote the historical climate. Both individuals and groups find, as Shakespeare said, that "there is a tide in the affairs of men," and that actions have very different effects at different times.

The effect the larger culture has on the nature and functioning of groups within it is so obvious that we need hardly be reminded of it. The effects of the cultural setting on the development of political institutions, religion, family life, and economic enterprises are especially noteworthy.

Finally, there is the effect of other groups which make up the environment of a group. Just as individuals react to other individuals, so

 Global travel should be made more economical and instead of national service, young people should be encouraged to travel abroad for a few years, to observe other cultures and traditions— and not be coerced into conforming to our own society just through ignorance, when they could become, through exposure to other cultures, better members of our own society.

providing resources and limitations for the group and often making demands of its own.

It is difficult to investigate scientifically the way in which a physical environment shapes the behavior of people, but some relationships are obvious. Groups who live in mountainous areas like Switzerland act differently from groups who live on tropical islands like Samoa. It is not surprising that rural groups differ from city groups, that groups of fishermen differ from groups of miners, or that Eskimos differ from Tahitians. Many theorists have speculated that there is a connection between the Mediterranean climate and the Latin temperament, between the English climate and the British temperament, between German geography and Germanic culture.

The historical setting, too, determines what a

groups react to other groups. Groups may compete with one another, cooperate, seek to destroy each other, or merge. Many times the behavior of a group changes radically because of what it perceives to be the intentions of another group.

There is no more pressing problem for all national groups than to find ways of reducing conflict between themselves. The cost of war and related ills is incalculable, and with modern nuclear weapons we all know that we might not survive another world war. Yet many of us have mixed feelings about group conflict. On the one hand we love peace and hate the bitterness of strife, but on the other hand we may love the excitement and a heightened sense of self-importance that can come with conflict. This fact may be a serious barrier to peace. Someone has said, in fact, that we will have no peace until we can find a peaceful substitute for war. His point is that many of us may need the meaningful commitment, the sense of urgency, the excitement, and the simplification of life that comes when we have an enemy on whom we can blame all our troubles.

Less pressing, but surely important to us all, is the reduction of tensions generated by conflict between management groups and labor groups, between majority and minority ethnic groups, and between privileged groups and underprivileged groups. To the extent that such groups are interdependent parts of a functioning system, destructive conflict harms all concerned.

Patterning of group change

With time, group structure and functioning may undergo marked changes. Changes may take place in group goals, leadership, roles, values, membership, and other aspects of the group's structure. Similarly, the group may show improvement or deterioration in its level of performance and in its ability to achieve its goals. Such changes result from a combination of inner and outer determinants, including changes in the composition of the group.

Life-cycle changes
Many groups appear to follow a pattern of change somewhat comparable to the life cycle of the individual—with an early period of growth, a middle period of maturity, and a later period of deterioration or atrophy. The historian Toynbee (1947) has described the characteristic stages of this pattern as: (1) a formative, youthful period, during which the group is vigorous, dedicated to its aims, and highly productive; (2) a period of conservative middle age, during which initiative and dedication are reduced and the group rests on its laurels, content with the progress it has made; and (3) a period of old age and disintegration, during which internal conflicts and incon-

sistencies within the group gradually lead to its decline and fall. Rome, for example, had its period of youth and vigor, during which it conquered most of the known world and made remarkable technological and cultural advances, its period of middle age, during which it tended to maintain its gains rather than to implement them or show further creativity, and its period of old age, during which it suffered corruption, decline, and eventual fall to the barbarians some five hundred years after its founding.

But group change does not always follow this pattern. Many conditions within the group or in its environment can influence the direction and rate of change—or even keep the group from changing appreciably. Many groups remain small and ineffectual for the entire period of their existence; others have a sudden spurt in growth and effectiveness because of favorable changes in their environment. Certain types of groups also appear to follow their own characteristic patterns. For example, the family group follows a typical pattern from its inception with marriage, through the rearing of children and their eventual leaving of the family, to the dissolution of the marriage with the death of the marital partners. But here too the pattern is not always followed, as when a family is prematurely disrupted by divorce or the early death of family members.

As we have noted, rapid change in group customs, beliefs, and values may pose a threat to group integration. If old anchorages are torn away before the foundations for new ones can be laid, group members tend to become confused, uncertain of their roles, and "alienated" from the group. Thus the rate as well as the patterning and quality of social change may have far-reaching effects on individuals as well as on the survival and effectiveness of the group.

Group decompensation
Groups generally try to change in ways that will further the attainment of their goals and improve their effectiveness, but they are not always successful. In some cases, under severe

We started out as a fairly cohesive group. What we wanted was a place to practice our crafts and arts, a place where people could come to see our work, and a place where we could teach grownups and youngsters both. Eventually, it was to be a money-making venture. That is, eventually we each hoped to make a living or part-living from it. So at first we all worked very hard, and we made a little money here and there, and we enjoyed ourselves tremendously. I don't know at what point it occurred to me that the thing was going off in another direction. But it is, and that's not the kind of atmosphere, not the kind of situation I want. A couple of members have dropped out and there's a general downer feeling about the group now. My wife and I will probably drop out too.

and sustained stress, a group shows changes in the direction of disorganization or decompensation rather than increased effectiveness.

The course of group decompensation follows stages comparable to those we traced for individuals: (1) alarm and mobilization, (2) resistance, and (3) exhaustion—the end of the group as a unit. The sequence of group decompensation is vividly illustrated in the case of the Xetas, described on page 386.

Sometimes a group undergoes some measure of decompensation but manages to stabilize itself during the stage of resistance. Thus a threatened marriage may be stabilized sufficiently to continue, though without adequately meeting the needs of the marital partners or fulfilling its initial promise. On the other hand, a failing marriage may recompensate as a result of the determined efforts of the marital partners to make the necessary readjustments.

Interaction of the individual and the group

In the previous section we considered some of the structural characteristics of groups—the somewhat formal properties that help us to detect similarities among quite unlike collections of people, and which help us to predict aspects of group functioning. In this section we will look more directly at some of the effects that groups have on individual behavior. Although it is impossible to specify all of the conditions under which behavior is facilitated or inhibited in groups, we do know that on the whole groups cause people to behave differently than they would as individuals—and some of the differences are quite intriguing.

Group-individual interaction is not a one-way street, however. What about the effects of the

The Xetas were an Indian tribe discovered in southwestern Brazil in the 1950s and believed to be among the most primitive humans in existence.

*"They have no agriculture, know no metal, make no pottery. They sleep on the ground instead of in hammocks as most Brazilian primitives do. Their weapons are bows and arrows and stone axes. Their knives are sharp flakes of stone. They eat everything that they can find or kill in the jungle: fruit, insects, snakes, roots too fibrous for white men's stom-*achs." (*Time,* Jan. 5, 1959, p. 62)

The alarm and mobilization period had evidently begun for this tribe when it was driven back into rugged mountain country by stronger tribes and the white man. This pattern of resistance was successful to the extent that the Xetas managed to hide from the civilized world for several hundred years, but the weaknesses within the group and its inhospitable environment doomed it to eventual exhaus-tion. Eventually they were flushed out of hiding by starvation and the wooings of an anthropologist—who hoped the surviving members of the tribe would be given government protection in a jungle preserve.

By 1959 only about 250 remained, and for a time they lived in small bands, shifting camp every few days. Ten years later, they had left their forest retreats and the survivors had scattered, working on the farms of the area. As a tribe, they no longer exist (Crocker, 1968).

individual on the group? In particular, we will focus on the leader. What factors both within the situation and within the person are conducive to leadership behavior?

One of the most problematical effects of the group on the individual is the exertion of certain pressures toward uniformity of perception, thought, and behavior. Even the most rugged individualists among us are susceptible to various conformity pressures. In this section, we will attempt to examine the issue—the origins and extent of conformity, and its repercussions, including the effects of deviation.

will facilitate individual performance on tasks and others in which it will impede performance; we find cases in which "too many cooks spoil the broth" and others in which the product generated by a group is superior to the product of any single member; and we find situations in which individuals do things in groups that they might never do singly, perhaps taking greater risks, or even violating their principles of proper conduct. Although the effects of groups on individuals could comprise a lengthy list, in this section we will limit our discussion to several of the more widely researched topics.

How the group affects the individual

As noted earlier, collections of people become "groups" when they perceive that some common purposes will be met by their continued affiliation. A hoped-for effect of the group will be the meeting of the needs which led the individual to join the group. Beyond that, however, we find instances in which the presence of others

Social facilitation

One of the earliest topics of research in social psychology, which intrigued investigators in the early part of this century and was then temporarily abandoned, is the study of social facilitation—the study of the effects of the sheer presence of others on individual behavior. Observations and controlled studies reviewed by Zajonc (1968) indicated that in the presence of a passive "audience," humans would perform simple motor tasks more accurately, compared with performance while unobserved. And in the presence of "co-actors" performing the same behavior, chickens and rats would eat more, ants would work harder in nest-building, and cyclists would ride faster. Such effects are termed *social facilitation.* In other situations, performance appeared to be inhibited: Cockroaches were poorer in learning mazes, and human subjects made more errors on certain tasks in the presence of others. Zajonc has proposed that, for a wide variety of tasks, performance in the presence of other organisms causes greater arousal. In well-learned skills or ingrained habits, such increased activation enhances performance, but with tasks that involve new learning, the increased arousal and distractions are likely to be detrimental to performance.

members buoy each other up and exert greater effort in competitive play.

Group vs. individual task performance

Some tasks clearly require joint action, where the labor is divided, and the achievement of the final goal could not be accomplished without the group, such as playing a Beethoven string quartet, mass-producing automobiles, or providing mental-health services for a large community. In such instances, the group product clearly represents an improvement over the individual performance. On the other hand, it has long been debated whether individual or group efforts are superior in areas of intellectual or creative activity.

Obviously, the nature of the task is a major

 How it works in my profession, at our conferences each of us is a specialist—mechanical, electrical, architectural. We each present an opinion in our particular sphere, and essentially that's the governing decision. It's kind of a group decision, and not a group decision, all at the same time.

In a dramatic way, social facilitation can be seen in the mutual stimulation and "social contagion" of crowd behavior, as in a riot or in the panic reactions of individuals attempting to escape from some serious situation, such as a burning building. Apparently, especially in emotion-arousing situations, individuals respond to and, in turn, further contribute to heightened emotionality in those around them. This phenomenon of "social contagion" helps to account for both the tremendous force and the irrationality of much crowd behavior (McDavid & Harari, 1968). Social facilitation and contagion can also be observed in smaller groups, such as a football team whose high morale helps the

factor. But in general, there is research evidence which suggests that groups produce more and better solutions to problems than do individuals (Shaw, 1971). There are many factors which may account for this result: The summation or coordination of individual strengths; rejection of incorrect suggestions and the checking of errors; social stimulation and the arousal of greater interest in the task; and others. On the other hand, when time is a factor, the number of man-hours per solution is lower for the individual than for the group. Although groups may provide superior solutions in many instances, efficiency is the price that must be paid. Shaw has summarized the findings as follows:

"Groups are more effective than individuals on tasks which require a variety of information, which can be solved by adding individual contributions, and which require a number of steps that must be correctly completed in a definite order; individuals are better on tasks that call for centralized organization of parts. Groups perform better than individuals when the process is learning or problem solving, but not necessarily when the process investigated is judgment. These conclusions are based upon measures of outcome; when the measure of effectiveness is the amount of investment per man, individuals are generally shown to be more efficient" (1971, pp. 70–71).

In groups, individuals do the darndest things

Picture the usually stern, self-contained, emotionless man who finds himself weeping un-ashamedly in front of other people—something he never did until he was persuaded to attend a weekend marathon encounter group. Or imagine a conscientious, well-groomed college student, nonviolent in both ideology and demeanor, who finds herself throwing tomatoes at a politician she dislikes. Clearly, these people are engaged in behavior that they might never have expected of themselves; yet, in a group situation, such "discontinuities" seem to be quite common.

A much more dramatic and serious example is that of sadistic mob violence, such as occurred in lynch mobs in the South of the 1920s and '30s. Jones and Gerard cite an account originally reported by psychologists Dollard and Miller in the 1940s:

"The victim in the case they describe was systematically tortured for some 10 hours: castrated,

compelled to eat his own genitals, burned by hot irons plunged into his body at various points, hung several times almost to the point of death and then revived, sliced with knives, and finally killed. There is every reason to doubt that any single member of the mob could have engaged in such sustained sadism as an isolated individual. Whereas the victim was actually tortured and killed by those who were most directly involved in vengeance, the body was later delivered to a large crowd of bystanders who drove knives into the corpse, kicked it, and drove automobiles over it. Children came and drove sharpened sticks into the body. Clearly such a frenzy is not the product of some accidental collection of sadists trying to outdo each other. Many of the most prominent citizens of the community were actually involved in the planning and execution of the lynching" (1967, pp. 623–24).

One attempt to account for such behavior is the idea of "responsibility diffusion" which may occur in some groups. The individual feels submerged in the group and loses his feelings of accountability for the consequences of his own actions. A kind of deindividuation may occur among groups of strangers, or among large crowds, or among groups where individuals abdicate personal responsibility in the name of following orders or some higher principle. Not only may the individual feel anonymous and therefore not accountable, but he may not question at the time the morality of his actions. One major standard that we use for defining what is right is what everybody else seems to be doing (Jones & Gerard, 1967). Similar principles have been used to explain the "unresponsive bystander" phenomenon in which witnesses stand and watch victims being robbed or beaten to death and later justify their behavior on the grounds that they "didn't want to become involved." In simulated situations, individuals by themselves are much more likely to go to the aid of a "victim" than are individuals in groups, presumably due to "responsibility diffusion" (Darley & Latané, 1969). Principles of group contagion and social facilitation and conformity also help to account for differences between group and individual behavior.

Another interesting area of research has suggested that group participation results in individuals making higher-risk decisions than they do without group contact. Contrary to the view voiced by Whyte in *The Organization Man* (1956), who contended that the process of group discussion invariably leads to conservatism and drags the creative innovator down into mediocrity, researchers have found opposite effects (Wallach, Kogan, & Bem, 1962, 1964). In these and subsequent studies, responsibility diffusion has been supported as an explanatory principle.

  Last night we had gone out to get an ice-cream bar at that little market, and this gal had fallen . . . it looked like she could be dead or passed out . . . she was curled up in a fetal position against the wall, and the men in the store said they had called the police. And I felt like, 'Well, it's cold, why doesn't somebody put a blanket over her?' I didn't say, 'Why don't I?' So we sat down . . . they said they'd called the ambulance, and we wanted to see what was going to happen. I could have done something to help her, I suppose—or at least find out what was wrong—I guess I felt like if nobody else had done anything, why should I?

Group members appear to feel that the responsibility for failure in a high-risk situation will not be attributed to any single member. Although it has generated much activity and questions remain unanswered, the "risky-shift" phenomenon, as it is called, has been repeated frequently. It is worth contemplating possible implications of the finding; perhaps in military or high-level business situations, or other conditions which bear on the fate of many, groups will be more prone to high-risk decisions than would individuals. On the other hand, it must be noted that risky-shift experiments have typically involved homogeneous groups without leadership structure, and have employed decisions whose magnitude of importance is far less than issues of national security. These and other factors may mitigate the more harrowing possibilities of risk-taking in groups.

Leadership: The influence of the individual on the group

Groups differ greatly in their leadership structure. In informal or loosely organized groups, especially where there is unanimity of purpose, leadership may be virtually nonexistent or constantly shifting. In highly organized groups, on the other hand, leadership becomes an important characteristic of group structure. Such groups may be led by an individual or by a committee or other subgroup. Sometimes it is quite difficult to determine who is the group "leader" because the one designated by formal role may seem less influential than other members of the group. Sometimes two leaders will emerge—a task specialist who directs the group toward its primary goals, and a social specialist, who helps maintain the functional harmony of the group itself (Bales, 1958).

Leadership is a highly complex phenomenon, and is strongly influenced by other aspects of the group. It is a rather widespread but naïve view that a high level of group effectiveness will automatically follow from the provision of "good" leadership.

A further issue in leadership stems from the age-old controversy about men making history or history making men. Early concepts of leadership invariably stressed characteristics of individuals which made them unique and successful in their prominent and influential roles. A more modern viewpoint stresses the "emergence" of leaders according to situational factors operative in a given group at a given time. Many leadership situations appear to involve varying combinations of both factors.

Leadership as a personal quality

The search for qualities within the person that distinguish him as a leader from the followers has been hampered by methodological problems such as difficulty in identifying leaders (especially "good" leaders) and problems in measurement of traits. Depending upon one's biases, the results have been called "disappointing" and

the study of the needs and characteristics of the group and their effect upon the emergence of certain leaders.

Leadership as a function of the situation

As mentioned earlier, there are numerous situations which favor the development of inequities in the distribution of influence in groups, a condition we call leadership. Among them are complexity of decisions that have to be made or goals to be reached, the size of a group, and the urgency of a situation or the importance of taking decisive and effective action. Given cer-

 Some years ago, in a sensitivity group, we originally started out with a therapist as leader. Subsequently the time for separation arrived and we wanted to keep going. The therapist did leave, and said he thought we needed a leader, and that I should be the leader because I had the ability to establish relationships and also, looking at it now I should say, a certain amount of courage to follow my inclination in certain situations—to follow wherever the path went. I enjoyed leading the group. It was hard work, but pleasurable. It felt natural doing it.

support for the trait conception "not satisfactory" (Cartwright & Zander, 1968) or small but consistent (Shaw, 1971).

It has, in fact, been shown that in certain instances leaders tend to be bigger but not too much bigger, brighter but not too much brighter, show greater knowledge and skills related to the task to be accomplished, display sociability factors such as greater activity and participation, popularity, and cooperativeness, have higher initiative and persistence, and to be older than other members of the group. These findings have been disputed in many instances, and simply indicate a slight preponderance of positive instances over negative ones. A somewhat more fruitful approach to leadership comes from

tain of these elements, several factors may influence the rise to influence of particular people.

1. *Chance.* Jones and Gerard note that:
". . . *it is important to recognize the potential role of chance in the emergence of particular leaders. In the early stages of group formation it may happen that a particular person quite accidentally makes a correct suggestion or two and as a consequence finds himself thenceforth in the leadership role*" (1967, p. 670).

Chance may determine that the first person who speaks up at a meeting is assumed by the others to have leadership qualities. Or, in a group that includes one man and several women, traditional assumptions about the male role may lead to his selection as committee chairman, jury foreman, or the like. Similarly, the oldest member of a group may be thought to have greater knowledge or skill, and members may react to that person as if he or she is the group leader. In situations like these, the actual personality and skill characteristics of the individual may have little to do with his or her selection as leader.

2. *Participation rate.* Especially in the earlier stages of group formation, the rate of participation among members is likely to be related to members' evaluation of contributions to the group. A high contributor is very likely to be selected as leader. Studies have shown that high participators are frequently identified as leaders of the group. In one interesting study (Riecken, 1958), rate of participation appeared to influence members' judgments of each other more than did actual skill. Following two problem-solving discussions in four-man groups, high and low participators were identified by the researcher. For the third problem-solving task, the solution was subtle and not likely to appear freely in the discussion. For half of the groups, a hint about the solution was given to a high participator; for the other half of the groups, the hint was given to a low participator. If the solution was offered by the high participator, it was much more likely to be accepted by the group (11 of 16 acceptances) than if offered by the low participator (5 of 16 acceptances). In another study (Bavelas, Hastorf, Gross, & Kite, 1965), rate of participation in groups was induced artificially through signals from the experimenters; when subjects were asked to nominate the person making the greatest contribution to the group and to respond to questions about leadership, they uniformly chose the high participators. In both studies, rate of participation, regardless of the quality or content, is an important index of leadership in the eyes of the other members.

3. *Other factors conducive to leadership.* Communication networks have been shown to affect leadership. Studies have shown that persons central in the communication network, through whom a great deal of information is passed, are most frequently identified as leaders, even though they have not been formally speci-fied as such in the experiment (Bavelas, 1968). Certainly in real life, to maintain leadership, the leader must have access to all relevant information affecting the group.

Time, feedback, and actual competence are also important factors. Over time, and if there is feedback about the adequacy of the leader's decisions, then actual competence is likely to emerge as the key ingredient in leadership.

Types or styles of leadership

The methods used by leaders in exerting their influence and control appear to depend upon the characteristics of the leader, group, and situation. Some leaders are prone to autocratic, others to democratic, and still others to laissez-faire methods of leadership. Similarly, some groups will respond favorably to one kind of leadership and not another, often depending upon what they are used to or what the larger culture expects. For example, individuals may accept autocratic leadership in a military setting which they would not countenance in a civilian setting; or they may accept laissez-faire leadership in a neighborhood group which they would not countenance in a business organization. The general nature and effects of autocratic, democratic, and laissez-faire methods of leadership were demonstrated in the classic study by Lewin, Lippitt, and White (1939) described on page 393.

In assessing the effects of different styles of leadership on group members, it is now realized that past socialization experiences also play an important role: Individuals with different past social experience may respond differently to the same kind of leadership. In general, Americans and western Europeans are reared under conditions which lead to a preference for democratic methods of leadership—whether in the family or in a larger group setting. But in a society where leaders are expected to be autocratic, a democratic leader may be perceived as weak and inept and may elicit noncooperation instead of better member participation. Thus it is risky to predict the effects of a given method of leadership without knowing something of the experience and expectations of the particular group.

In a classic study of the effects of different kinds of leadership, clubs were formed of 10-year-old boys matched as to age, intelligence, economic background, and so on, and three different types of adult leadership were practiced in the various groups. In the *authoritarian* groups the leader set the group goals, controlled all activity with step-by-step directions, and evaluated the boys' work. In the *laissez-faire* groups the leader simply stood by and answered when spoken to: the groups were entirely on their own in planning and assigning work. In the *democratic* groups members and leader discussed and determined policies and assignments together. The factor of possible personality differences was controlled by having each leader and all the boys operate in at least two different climates.

Differences in performance and other reactions were striking. In the autocratic groups performance was fairly good, but motivation was low and the boys worked only when the leader was present to direct them. The laissez-faire groups did less work and work of a poorer quality. The boys in the democratic groups showed more interest in their work and more originality and kept on working whether the leader was present or not. There was more destruction of property and more aggressiveness and hostility in the autocratic groups, but the hostility tended to be channeled toward a scapegoat member or toward the working materials rather than toward the leader. Members of autocratic groups were also more dependent and more submissive, showed less individuality, and gave less friendly praise to each other. Morale and cohesiveness were lowest in the laissez-faire groups, highest in the democratic groups. The democratic leaders were liked best by the boys (Lewin, Lippitt, & White, 1939).

In general, it can probably be said that autocratic leadership may be efficient for meeting immediate and temporary crisis situations—as in the fighting of wars—but will tend to defeat its own purposes if maintained over a long period of time or used in situations that do not require it. For it usually reduces the initiative and creativity of individual members and subgroups, thus eventually reducing the adaptive potentiality of the group.

On the other hand, democratic leadership appears to have greater long-range survival value for a group because it elicits member involvement and places minimum restraints on their initiative and creativity, thus tending to promote the adaptability so necessary for meeting changing conditions and demands. Democratic leadership is often more difficult to achieve, however, because it demands more of the leader as well as of the group members.

The influence of leaders
The actual role of leaders in shaping human affairs is a subject of some dispute. Many social psychologists and sociologists attribute great powers to leaders and consider them key influences in shaping history. Others believe that the leaders merely symbolize what their followers want and exert influence over the group only insofar as they go in the direction that the group desires. They point out that the leader who tries to guide his followers in a direction they oppose will either lose his position of leadership, be unsuccessful, or cause the group to disintegrate.

History gives examples which seem to support both these contentions. A particular social situation must usually exist before a particular kind of leader can emerge and be accepted; a leader like Mao, for example, could come to power only during a period of great social unrest and change. Yet often a group could be led in any of several directions by a stong leader—for example, toward innovation and experiment with new ways of solving the group's problems, or toward efforts to maintain the status quo, or toward preoccupation with problems of secondary importance and denial of the reality of a major demand to be met. Also the leader can deploy

A "hierarchy of power" involving five distinct types of authority can be delineated.

1. *Force.* Authority exercised through the use of any kind of force. It is the most primitive kind of authority, seen among animals as well as man. He who is strongest has the most authority.

2. *Law.* Authority of the community. Legal codes may be based on the will of the majority or they may represent the will of the strong or influential. Compliance is compelled by force when necessary.

3. *Role.* Authority of custom and tradition. Right to act is based on playing designated role. Compliance is achieved mostly by application of pressures within the primary group.

4. *Ability.* Authority based on respect. Power is based on knowing how to do things valued by others. Once established, tends to function through prestige. Most important in leadership.

5. *Spirit.* Authority that appeals to the minds or souls of those who follow. It is the authority of truth, justice, and inspiration. This is the power of the poet, the prophet, the friend, the loving person.

It would seem to be ideal to rely most on the authority of the spirit, then ability, then role, then law, and to use a minimum of force.

 When I took on this project for the group I realized I would have to be the chairman, but I expected other members to help me out. I found that other members were not interested in helping, and they expected me to know how to organize the project and I didn't, and I felt that the whole thing was a big failure, and there was a great deal of criticism. The other members weren't living up to my expectations, really, and I certainly wasn't living up to theirs. It was disastrous.

the group's resources wisely or inefficiently; he can inspire dedication and enthusiasm or dissension and discontent; and he can raise or lower members' sights in terms of their collective goals and purposes. Different leaders can move the same group toward reasoned action, emotionalism, apathy, or violence. Thus individual leaders may have a potent influence on the group.

But what the group achieves depends on the quality of "followership" as well as on the leader. As we have seen, the motives, capabilities, attitudes, and commitment of individual members are of key importance in determining how a group functions. In fact, in an interesting study of men working in small groups during a twelve-month period of isolation in Antarctic scientific stations, several of the same personality traits were consistently found to be characteristic of both effective leaders and effective followers; these included a high degree of satisfaction with work assignments, acceptance of authority, and motivation to be part of the group and work as a team (Nelson, 1964).

Again it becomes apparent that we must have adequate knowledge of group members as well as of the leadership and of the situation in which the group is functioning—and the interaction among these three sets of factors—if we are to

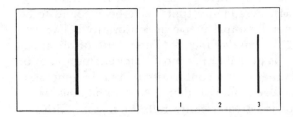

In the classic experiment by Asch (1952, 1955), groups of seven to nine college students were asked to say which of three lines on a card (right) matched the length of a standard line on a second card (left). One of the three lines they could choose from was actually the same length as the standard line; the others differed from the standard by anywhere from three fourths of an inch to an inch and three fourths. It had been determined in advance that these differences were clearly distinguishable.

In each group all but one of the "subjects" were actually stooges, previously instructed to make a *unanimous wrong* choice on most of the trials after the first two. The actual subject was always in such a position that he would not announce his own judgment until after most or all of the others had announced theirs. Thus, after hearing the false judgment given by the planted majority, the minority subject had to choose between denying the evidence of his senses and contradicting the judgment of the group.

Under such pressure, minority subjects accepted the majority's wrong selections in 36.8 percent of the trials. Some individuals, however, were able to stand up to such pressure better than others: about a fourth of the 123 naïve subjects clung consistently to their minority judgments, while a few subjects yielded to the majority decision on almost every trial.

When the test subjects were interviewed after the experiment, it was found that some had yielded out of fear of "seeming different," even though they continued to believe in the correctness of their own judgments. Others assumed that, although their own perceptions clearly *seemed* correct, the majority could not be wrong. In a few cases perception itself had apparently been distorted: the subject was apparently unaware of having yielded to group pressure.

Even subjects who consistently maintained their independent judgments tended to be considerably disturbed by their disagreement with the majority and reported that they had been seriously tempted to go along with the group in order to avoid seeming inferior or absurd. In fact, in a later study utilizing the same experimental setup, Bogdonoff et al. (1961) found that students who "called them as they saw them" suffered more anxiety, as evidenced by physiological changes. One subject who consistently disagreed with the group was dripping with perspiration by the end of the session even though his judgments were right in each instance.

understand the behavior of the group and of individuals in it.

The special problem of conformity

As we have seen, group pressures toward conformity serve a basic need of the group for self-maintenance. Thus they develop to some extent in any organized group, although the strength of such pressures—and the degree of conformity actually needed for a group's maintenance—vary greatly from one situation to another. For example, the conformity demanded and actually needed in a military organization during wartime is much greater than the conformity sought or needed in a sensitivity-training group or a college classroom. Even in the latter two cases, however, certain ground rules are established and members are under some pressure to conform to them.

We have termed conformity a special problem because of its potential for both harm and good, both for the individual and the group. Pressures toward conformity on the one hand may produce a uniformity which is stifling and unproductive, and which violates individual autonomy. On the other hand, individual behavior would be chaotic and unpredictable if it were not affected by group norms. We shall attempt to note some of the consequences, both positive and negative, of conformity.

Why do people conform?

Both in the laboratory and in natural settings, researchers and others have been intrigued with

tend to conform to majority opinion more than males (Costanzo & Shaw, 1966; Reitan & Shaw, 1964). Personality traits have been found to be generally unpredictive of conformity behaviors.

2. *Stimulus factors.* The nature of the situation is probably the most potent determinant of whether or not conformity occurs. In general, it has been shown that more ambiguous tasks produce greater conformity than tasks with unambiguous stimuli. It seems likely that when the individual has little objective evidence about reality or what is expected, he must rely upon others to provide cues or validate his opinions.

3. *Situational factors.* This includes all aspects of the group context such as size of the

 When my sister was in high school she was a member of the top elite social group. And I was a little envious, maybe, but I felt they were all hypocrites and that my sister was a hypocrite. Many years later I found out that my sister didn't particularly like the social whirl, that she didn't really like those people that much, that she was just conforming. She happened to be able to conform in that fashion, and she didn't have the personal security at all—it would have been much too painful to her—to be able to be an individual, so she just had to go along with the crowd.

the relative ease with which people can be induced to behave similarly to others. A rather dramatic example is provided in the early conformity studies by Asch, described on page 395.

Conforming behaviors have been found to result from several classes of causes.

1. *Personality factors.* Although many have attempted to link conformity to characteristics of the individual, on the whole this approach has proven of little value. There is a tendency for more intelligent persons to be less conforming than less intelligent persons (Nakamura, 1958), but correlations between intelligence and conformity are only moderately strong. Females

group, unanimity of the majority, group structure, and the like. Research evidence generally supports the idea that conformity increases with the increasing size of the majority, up to a certain point. Some studies have shown that a majority of three produced maximum conformity (Asch, 1951), while others have found increases in conformity beyond that size (Gerard, Wilhelmy, & Conolley, 1968). However, there appears to be a point beyond which increasing the size of the group majority does not make a difference in the amount of conformity behavior.

Also, as common sense suggests, a group

member is more likely to conform to group judgments when other members are in unanimous agreement than when they are not.

4. *Intragroup factors.* This term refers to the relations among the members of the group, such as amount of conformity pressure exerted, the group composition, the group's success in achieving past goals, the individual's identification with the group, and so on. All of these variables have been shown to be related to conformity. Conformity tends to be higher in cohesive groups. Also, Costanzo, Reitan, and Shaw (1968) found that persons who perceive their own competence relative to the task to be high conform less than those with low perceived competence, regardless of their perception of the majority's competence. However, an individual conforms more when the perceived

competence of the majority is high than when it is low, regardless of his own level of competence.

Techniques for inducing conformity
The techniques and pressures that groups exert to achieve conformity take many forms. Often there are role definitions that set limits to permissible behavior and thus tend to induce conformity. Group members may be subjected to a continual barrage of factual information and/or propaganda in an effort to convince them of the validity of group goals and values—and hence to elicit their cooperation and support. In small groups, the participation of members in setting goals and making decisions helps to create and maintain the involvement of group members

and some measure of conformity. In special cases, extreme measures such as "brainwashing" may be utilized in an attempt to change basic thought patterns.

Usually group pressures toward conformity rest heavily upon the manipulation of rewards and punishments. The recognition and approval of other group members, advancement to a higher position in the group, and chances for awards and honors are common incentives for inducing conformity behavior, whereas members who create difficulties for the group by their deviant behavior may suffer social disapproval, loss of position, expulsion from the group, or a wide range of other punishments.

so many personal psychological needs are normally met through close social interaction.

Not all nonconforming behavior meets with group sanctions. Sometimes nothing happens to the nonconformist—for example, if the norm he breaks is unimportant or if he is considered an important member of the group. In some cases, group leaders are allowed more latitude in behavior than are other members of the group (McDavid & Harari, 1968). The immediate situation of the group is also important. If the group is not under threat and is generally performing effectively, it is likely to permit more latitude on the part of its members than if it is struggling to establish itself or survive.

 No one should be able to say one kind of life is the only way for all 'normal' people. If a person can live in the world he chooses without being overwhelmed by it, and he can find a degree of happiness, then he has successfully reacted with his environment and is of sound mind, and has even been useful to society by taking care of himself well. I don't think that people should be considered capable of judging others. People will always condemn that which is different, even though the unfamiliar actions may, in the long run, be much more beneficial to everyone.

"Most people will give almost anything, even their lives if necessary, to retain the approval and comforting feelings of belonging to the group. It is this overwhelming need for group approval and response that makes the primary group the most powerful controlling agency known to man" (Horton & Hunt, 1968, p. 131).

In larger groups, sanctions may follow codes of law, in which norm violations and their attendant penalties are formally prescribed. In small face-to-face groups, sanctions are usually informal but may be even more influential in controlling the behavior of group members since

The group's need for nonconformists
In discussing the group as a system, we mentioned that groups have needs of their own that may differ from the needs of individual members. Paradoxically, one of these needs is for members who have integrity and enough commitment to values beyond the group to challenge the group when it makes mistakes.

Although some measure of conformity appears essential for coordinating group effort, some measure of nonconformity also appears essential for maintenance of the group's adaptability. If a group is to adapt effectively to chang-

I feel nonconformity is essential to society. Because without that there's no art, no literature, no anything of value in society. All of that comes from nonconformity—all things of any interest are created by nonconformity. I think everybody really is a nonconformist; it's just a matter of degree.

Nonconformity only means that you've got the guts to be yourself. And I don't care what you are, if you're yourself, you're happy. Not continuously, but certainly far more than other people.

ing conditions, it must be capable of making needed changes within its own structure and functioning. This means that someone in the group must recognize the new conditions, propose new approaches, and make other group members aware of the need for change.

Slavish loyalty to the group at the price of individual integrity is usually characteristic of insecure persons who are overly dependent on the group. Exploitative individuals may play the loyalty game, but they are not really loyal. And both overdependent members and the exploitative are likely to desert the group when it no longer meets their needs. Fanatically loyal members, too, can be more of a liability than an asset to a group if they are unable or unwilling to recognize weaknesses in the group that need correcting.

Groups that have no room for individuals of integrity—individuals who think for themselves and are loyal to what they value—will in time suffer from the loss of contributions that may be vital to the life of the group. This point has been well elaborated by Buckley in his concept of "requisite deviation":

"A requisite of sociocultural systems is the development and maintenance of a significant level of nonpathological deviance manifest as a pool of alternative ideas and behaviors with respect to the traditional, institutionalized ideologies and role behaviors. Rigidification of any given institutional structure must eventually lead to disruption or dissolution of the society by way of internal upheaval or ineffectiveness against external change" (1968, p. 495).

In spite of pressures toward conformity, every large group has its share of people who do not conform. Some of these deviants—like our criminals—are emotionally immature or have learned distorted values that make them unable or unwilling to conform to the norms of society—though they may be conforming to the norms of their own deviant subgroup and be reaping the usual rewards of conformity from it. But many nonconformists in man's history have been men and women of maturity and vision—individuals like Columbus, Galileo, Roger Bacon, Jane Addams, and Joan of Arc. Nonconformists like these perform lasting services to their society by initiating necessary or desirable changes in group norms, even at the cost of great personal sacrifice. Albert Einstein once said:

"I gang my own gait and have never belonged to my country, my home, my friends, or even my immediate family, with my whole heart; in the *face of all ties, I have never lost an obstinate sense of detachment, of the need for solitude—a feeling which increases with the years"* (1949, p. 3).

Unfortunately, it is often difficult for society to evaluate its nonconformists accurately. Even when there is an honest attempt to weigh historical and scientific evidence in judging new ideas, our perspective is always limited and the decision of contemporaries may be different from that of later generations. Thus it will be interesting to see how today's nonconformists are assessed 20 or 50 years from now. Sometimes history shows that nonconforming behavior has been divisive and detrimental to the group; in other instances, nonconformists who were roundly condemned in their time, like Jesus, were the prophets and founders of new ideas and movements and the instigators of needed social change.

The problem for any group is how to maintain a necessary measure of conformity, while also maintaining the degree of deviance essential for flexibility and adaptability of the group. In the long run, individual and group interests appear to be best served when conformity pressures are limited to those areas where unanimity is essential for coordinated group functioning and effectiveness. Ideally, a group concerns itself explicitly with setting up ways of fostering requisite deviation and identifying it when it occurs.

 # Summary and a look ahead

Groups are an inevitable and pervasive aspect of our lives, helping us to meet needs of various kinds, such as security, identity, and fulfillment needs. Sometimes, too, groups exert unwanted influence on us through limitations and demands they make and through threats to our integrity. But, on the whole, the rewards of group membership far outweigh the costs.

Like individual lives, groups form, grow, and try to maintain themselves through intricate patterns of structure and function. Additional factors important to the effectiveness of a group are its environment and its ability to change.

The interaction of the individual and the group is a continuing one. The group influences the individual in many ways, one of which is through social facilitation. One dramatic aspect of groups which is notable is the ability of groups to influence behavior in unexpected ways; people may often perform somewhat differently before groups than in private. Some of the discontinuities may have serious implications, as in mob violence, and we find ourselves constantly confronting—in the

Key terms and concepts:

involuntary groups (pp. 373-74)
necessary groups (374)
voluntary groups (374)
characteristic groups (374-75)
transient groups (375)
rewards of group membership (375-77)
costs of group membership (377-78)
cost/reward balance (378-79)
the group as a living system (379-85)
group structure (379)
group function (380-83)
task goals (380)
maintenance goals (380)
organizational equilibrium (380)

events of the world around us and in our own lives—issues of personal responsibility vs. susceptibility to group influence.

Individuals likewise influence groups. One of the most obvious ways in which they do so is through leadership, which is not simply a set of high moral qualities and extraordinary abilities which certain rare persons possess. Rather, leadership is a complex interaction of the group's needs, individual potentials, and other circumstances. From time to time, nearly everyone functions as a kind of leader in one situation or another. And the leader's tasks, style, and achievements affect and are also dependent upon aspects of the group and its members.

In the final section of this chapter, we discussed the special problem of conformity. The reasons that people conform are many—personality factors, stimulus factors, situational factors, and intragroup factors. Though some degree of conformity is necessary in groups, the importance of the nonconformist in a group cannot be overlooked if the group is to continue as a growing system.

Our discussion of individuals interacting in groups helps set the scene for the final section of this book in which we shall deal with effective behavior and personal growth.

Toward Effective Behavior and Personal Growth

14

Psychological Resources for Personal Change and Growth

Psychological counseling
Psychotherapy
Intensive group experience

The quest for increased understanding of ourselves and others and improved competence in our interpersonal relationships has become a pressing concern for many of us—for the achievement of these goals seems essential for achieving personal effectiveness and building a meaningful and fulfilling life in our contemporary society. Here the resources of modern psychology are proving of great assistance.

Psychological resources are essentially of three kinds: (1) counseling for educational, occupational, or marital planning, and/or help with personal problems in these and other areas; and (2) psychotherapy, which may be directed primarily toward dealing with immediate problems of adjustment or primarily toward personal change and growth; and (3) intensive group experience focusing on increasing the personal growth and effectiveness of essentially normal people.

Before taking up specific psychological resources for personal change, let us review and expand on the directions of change—previously mentioned in Chapter 3, page 61—which appear to foster personal effectiveness and growth.

1. *Increased autonomy:* changes in the direction of increased self-reliance, self-identity, and self-direction. Implicit here is emancipation from undue social influence.

2. *A more adequate frame of reference:* changes in the direction of increased and more accurate information about ourselves and our world and more satisfying values.

3. *Improved competencies:* changes in the direction of increased intellectual, emotional, and interpersonal competencies.

4. *Increased integration:* the resolution of severe inner conflicts, dismantling of unnecessary defenses, and greater openness to experience.

5. *Self-enhancement and self-actualization:* changes in the direction of creative self-expression, of the greater actualization of potentials, and of building a meaningful and fulfilling life.

to make wise educational, occupational, and marital plans. Other counselors work in rehabilitation agencies and hospitals and are primarily concerned with helping persons with physical, mental, or emotional handicaps to make vocational and other adjustments. Still another group of counselors work in industrial settings, assisting with such problems as the development of managerial talent and the placement of employees to the best advantage, and with various personal problems of employees. Finally, there are some counselors primarily concerned with premarital, marital, childrearing, and other family problems.

On an individual level, psychological counseling is directed toward one or more of the following objectives: (1) to assist the individual in gaining a more realistic picture of himself—particularly in relation to his assets and liabilities, interests, values, and methods of coping;

 I've decided I'm going to join a group. I'm trying to decide what the best way would be—to get involved in some awareness training, or just practice in being more spontaneous and open. If he doesn't want to do this with me, that's OK; I'll go ahead and do it anyway. I think whatever I do that's really good for me benefits both of us.

While there appears to be agreement among psychologists that these five directions of change do lead to increased personal effectiveness and growth, they still must be translated into specific goals and procedures appropriate to the individual if such changes are to be achieved.

Psychological counseling

Counselors help people make plans and solve personal problems. Many work in schools or colleges and are particularly concerned with helping students to gain a better view of their motives, values, interests, and capabilities so as

(2) to assist him in achieving a better understanding of some problem which is bothering him; and (3) to assist him in working out an effective solution to his problem and putting it into operation.

On an interpersonal level, the objectives of psychological counseling may include the preceding ones but also focus on ascertaining the nature of difficulties that may be or are being encountered in interpersonal relationships. In premarital counseling, for example, one key objective would be to ascertain the compatibility of the couple, possible areas of difficulty, and changes that might be indicated on the part of one or both persons in order to increase the likelihood of success if they do marry. Similarly, in marital or family counseling, the focus may be on interpersonal difficulties that are being encountered and on working out ways of coping with them. In marital and family counseling, of course, the distinction between psychological counseling and psychotherapy becomes blurred.

Psychological assessment

In a broad sense, psychological assessment represents a systematic attempt to collect, organize, and interpret relevant information about a person and his life situation. This information is then used as a starting point in planning whatever help he needs.

Types of assessment information

In Chapter 8, we noted the types of assessment data—medical, psychological, and sociological—which are ordinarily obtained about a patient in therapy. While the assessment data in counseling covers these same areas, counseling is often concerned with information which is not routinely collected in therapy, such as the client's interest in and aptitude for given educational and occupational careers.

Although the information obtained in psychological assessment may vary considerably depending upon the specific goals of counseling in a particular case, the assessment usually covers most or all of the following areas:

1. *Personal resources:* information concerning level of intelligence, special abilities, competencies, personal maturity, and related data.

2. *Frame of reference:* information concerning reality, possibility, and value assumptions, including the way the client views himself and his world.

3. *Interests, aptitudes, motives:* information which may be relevant to educational and occupational planning or to correcting difficulties in these areas.

4. *Coping patterns and adjustment:* information concerning ways of coping, including ego-defense mechanisms, and possible anxiety, depression, conflicts, and other problems of adjustment.

5. *Life situational factors:* information concerning interpersonal relationships, environmental resources and supports, group memberships, and stresses in the client's life situation.

In counseling, as in psychotherapy, it is often important to include recent medical data in the overall assessment. For example, in psychotherapy it is necessary to rule out the possibility that an organic condition—such as a brain tumor—is the primary cause of the maladjustive behavior; and in counseling, various physical factors—such as a client's heart condition—should be considered if he were interested in pursuing a career as an airline pilot.

Methods of assessment

In gathering information about the client and his life situation, psychologists may select from a wide range of assessment methods. For present purposes we may divide these various procedures into three general categories.

1. *Interviewing.* This is probably the oldest of the methods for making judgments about personality traits. For centuries men have assumed that they can "size up" another person by talking to him for a period of time.

The interview is usually defined as a face-to-face conversation between two people, conducted so that one person can obtain information from or evaluate the other. This description of the interview, however, belies the wide range and complexity of interview situations. For example, the interview may vary from the *simple interview,* in which a specific set of questions is asked, designed to gather certain information; to the *stress interview,* designed to see how a given subject will function intellectually and emotionally in a difficult situation; to the technically complex *therapeutic interview,* which may involve both assessment and therapy.

Although interview assessment is widely used and of undoubted value for obtaining certain types of information, distortions often stem from the interviewer's biases, values, motives, and limited range of experience; for example, a discrepancy of social class between interviewer and interviewee may change considerably the kind and extent of information that the interviewer obtains.

2. *Psychological tests.* There are a wide range of psychological tests designed to yield information concerning such characteristics of the individual as intelligence level, special abilities, interests, aptitudes, motive patterns, values, coping patterns, level of anxiety or depression, and his view of himself in relation to his world.

The *maximal performance test* challenges the individual to make the best response he can to certain standard tasks. For example, in an intelligence test this might include the solving of certain problems by reasoning, defining the meaning of certain words, and accurately identi-

knows him well. A rating scale item for aggressiveness, for example, might be as follows:

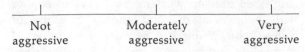

| Not aggressive | Moderately aggressive | Very aggressive |

One of the great advantages of rating scales is their simplicity, but such scales are subject to many sources of error. For example, the individual may be influenced by whether he thinks a high or low rating on a given trait is good or bad; when other people do the rating, their impression of the individual may be in error or they may be anxious to help him. However, well-designed rating scales, in the hands of trained interviewers or persons who know the

 One of the tests made me mad. It was a series of cartoon drawings showing one person taking advantage of another, or doing something to them. In the test you had to fill in what you would say if you were that second person. At the time, I was feeling anyway like the world was against me, and I wrote in some pretty hostile remarks. Later, when we were going over all my tests, this one really showed me where I was then—what my attitude was.

fying certain analogies. The primary goal of this type of test is to demonstrate the full extent of the existence of a given trait such as intelligence. Maximal performance tests are extensively used—particularly in measuring intelligence—and, on the whole, are easy to score and highly accurate. However, these tests require the subject's full cooperation if they are to provide accurate assessment data.

The *rating scale* is most often used for assessing traits that are difficult to measure by performance on set tasks. Aggressiveness, honesty, and sympathy are examples of traits that may be most easily measured by ratings made either by the subject himself or by someone who

individual well, can yield accurate and useful assessment data.

The *personality inventory* is usually made up of a series of direct questions that a subject is required to answer for himself. Inventories are widely used to measure traits relating to temperament, interests, attitudes, coping patterns, and the like. Usually the subject is required to answer "true" or "false" (or "yes" or "no") to given questions or statements, although some inventories include an intermediate category of "uncertain" or "cannot say." Examples of possible inventory items are:

I often feel as if things were
unreal.   Yes   No

The term "anti-test revolt" has been used to refer to the attitudes of suspiciousness and even hostility that have developed among many people toward psychological testing. This revolt has been fueled by three issues:

1. *The issue of confidentiality:* the possibility of an invasion of the client's privacy by the information obtained being revealed and used against the client.

2. *The issue of cultural bias:* the question of whether many commonly used psychological tests, e.g., intelligence tests, reveal valid information when administered to socially disadvantaged persons or those coming from ethnic minorities.

3. *The issue of labeling:* the use of test findings for arbitrarily labeling people—as, say, mentally retarded, sociopathic, or emotionally disturbed. Obviously such labels may have detrimental results for the persons so identified.

While psychologists have been instrumental in getting "privileged information" laws passed in some states to protect the client's right to privacy concerning information he provides, have worked diligently on developing so-called "culture-free" tests, and have tended to use psychiatric labels very sparingly, these are complex issues and have not yet been adequately resolved.

When I am disappointed, I like to talk about my hurt with someone else.   Yes No

I have engaged in deviant sexual behavior about which I feel guilty.   Yes No

Personality inventories are usually easy to score and often provide accurate data. Some inventories even have provisions for correcting intentional distortions by the subject. For example, one commonly used personality inventory has several subscales whose sole purpose is to give the examiner an indication of the test-taking attitude of the subject. If the subject is very defensive and has been distorting his answers, this tendency will show up in a high score on one of these special subscales.

The *projective test* consists of an unstructured stimulus situation to which a subject is required to give meaning. For example, he may be shown an inkblot and asked to tell what he sees in it; he may be shown a picture and asked to make up a story about it; or he may be given an incomplete sentence and asked to complete it. In performing such tasks, the subject is forced to organize and interpret the ambiguous stimuli, thereby revealing a great deal about his cognitive patterns, conflicts, self-defenses, and other aspects

of his personality make-up. Projective tests are widely used in the assessment of personality adjustment, but they have serious limitations with respect to scoring. Accurate interpretation of the subject's responses requires a high degree of training and skill, and the meaning of given responses is not always apparent to even highly trained psychologists. Their primary advantage seems to be in revealing personality characteristics of which the individual himself is not aware—which thus would not show up adequately in inventories or other assessment procedures.

3. *Direct observation in real-life situations.* For the most part, psychological tests try to identify consistent traits of the individual which are predictive of the way he behaves in real-life situations. As psychologists have become increasingly aware of the importance of situational factors in eliciting specific types of behavior, they have come to rely increasingly on observation of the client's behavior in his real-life situation. For example, an adolescent who has been evidencing emotional problems may be observed—with his knowledge and permission—at school, at home, and with his peers. Here the intent is to note the ways in which he *actually* behaves in given situations rather than to rely entirely on predictions made from psychological

tests. Often a rating scale is used by the observer to ensure that certain areas of behavior are covered and to further the degree of accuracy of the observations.

Other assessment procedures include descriptions of the client's behavior by other persons who know him well, observing his performance in simulated real-life situations, and making interpretations from such sources as handwriting, painting, or an autobiography which the client is asked to write.

Evaluation and integration of assessment data

In evaluating the significance of assessment data, psychologists are vitally concerned with the *validity, reliability,* and *standardization* of their tools. An intelligence test, for example, is *valid* if it actually measures intelligence and *reliable* if it gives consistent results at different times; if it has been *standardized,* the individual's score can be compared with the scores of a representative group of subjects and one can say whether it is a high, low, or intermediate score.

It is risky to draw conclusions from single items of information—such as a single test score or a single childhood memory. The psychologist feels more confident if he has "interlocking evidence" from independent sources. Even when the reliability of single scores is limited, as in the case of projective test scores, the probability that a conclusion is accurate is increased if several more or less independent sources of information point in the same direction. Since the overall goal of psychological assessment is to formulate a reasonably accurate "working model" of the client in relation to his life situation, it is essential that the assessment data not only be carefully evaluated but also be integrated into a coherent picture.

The counseling process

The counseling process actually begins with the first contact between client and counselor and continues with the establishment of a relationship which is suitable for the achievement of counseling goals. A key aspect of this relationship is the existence of *rapport*—feelings of trust, confidence, respect, and understanding. The client must feel free to respond honestly and completely during the assessment and later in discussions of his problem. Once rapport has been established, counseling may follow either of two general directions—directive or nondirective.

Directive counseling

In directive counseling the counselor will size up the client's problem, work out a "good" solution, and then concentrate on getting the client to accept it. The counseling sessions will center around interpreting the problem and its suggested solution to the client and considering the possible results of applying the solution offered.

This procedure is often criticized by counselors who use a nondirective approach. They insist that instead of helping the client to organize his own resources and teaching him to make his own decisions, the directive method tends to reduce his sense of responsibility and his confidence in his own adequacy for dealing with his problems; with the directive method, these critics feel, a type of parent-child relationship is established in which the counselor assumes the role of an authoritarian parent.

Such objections do not necessarily invalidate a directive approach for certain types of problems. For example, a directive approach would often appear indicated when the client's chief need is for information or reassurance, or when lack of time dictates an immediate decision and the client is too immature or emotionally upset to get over this particular hurdle on his own. In the latter case, however, once the emergency is past, the counselor may encourage the client to take more responsibility for his decisions or to obtain psychotherapy to overcome deep-seated personality problems.

Where the counselor has a strong commitment to certain values—for example, to the sanctity of certain social institutions, such as marriage—the style of counseling tends to be directive. Many persons seeking help prefer this type of counseling because it arouses less anxiety and gives them an authority to lean on for advice and guidance. Other individuals, however, resent attempts on the part of a counselor to force his own value system upon them.

Nondirective counseling

In nondirective counseling the counselor places the primary responsibility on the client for working out a solution to his own problems. The counselor largely restricts himself to supplying information the client may need—concerning job opportunities and the availability of certain kinds of training, for example, or the results of tests as to the client's own interests, values, and abilities. He then further helps the client clarify

seems most appropriate, and in putting this solution into operation and taking the responsibility for the outcome. Some clients need direction at first but later can be expected to take greater responsibility for dealing with their own problems; others have sufficient maturity and resources that the counselor can take a much more nondirective role from the start.

In general, it would appear that the most effective counselor, regardless of his general orientation, is the one who utilizes the client's resources to the fullest extent and modifies his own approach to ensure that the counseling will be a growth experience for the client, helping him to become more competent and self-reliant.

 I'm mainly nondirective in my work, but when you say 'directive' or 'nondirective,' there are areas where it gets sort of cloudy. For instance, when a patient expresses a certain wish, something he'd like to accomplish, and we talk about how he might do it, sometimes I just suggest that he go out and try a particular thing, and in that way I'm directive. But the patient still has to take the responsibility to do it.

his thinking about himself in relation to the problem—helping him to see the key dimensions of the total situation in which he finds himself. The nondirective counselor tries to avoid suggesting decisions and solutions so that the final responsibility for the outcome of the counseling rests on the client himself.

In actual practice, of course, few counselors are entirely directive or nondirective. For example, the nondirective counselor may give the client reassurance in regard to his ability to solve the problem, may supply information concerning assessment data or life problems, and so on; similarly, the directive counselor may encourage the client to utilize his own resources in thinking through the problem, in exploring various ways of coping with it, in selecting the solution which

Stages in counseling

Although there are often variations, the counseling process appears to follow a basic pattern involving three general stages.

In the first stage, as already indicated above, rapport is established, laying the foundation for mutual participation of client and counselor in the counseling process. It is important here for the client to feel that he has come to the right place for assistance, and that he will be understood, accepted, and helped. A second step at this stage is encouraging the client to express his feelings and attitudes toward other people, school, work, and other life matters that may be relevant to dealing with his problem. Here the presence of the counselor helps to reduce the anxiety that is often associated with facing one's fears, conflicts, frustrations, and concerns. This

I spent a year of my life in prison. During this time I spent many hours with a concerned counselor. We spent most of our time on my behavior patterns that led to my incarceration for selling and using drugs. We also spent much time talking about my parents and some of their problems. It was all a help—he shed some light in some areas I had never looked at.

My wife and I were having a terrible time with our young kids, particularly their behaving. We finally gave up and went to a family counselor— all of us went, my wife and I and both the kids. It saved the day. He helped us to understand what we were all doing to each other and how to start changing it.

may help the client to recognize and discuss impulses and attitudes that he would ordinarily be unwilling to face or might not be fully aware of—for example, concern over whether he is mature enough to get married, whether he is sexually adequate, or whether he has homosexual inclinations that might interfere with his marriage.

The second stage involves helping the client to understand and organize into a meaningful pattern the information he needs for making choices and decisions. This usually means providing him with (1) assessment information concerning his interests, abilities, and goals, and (2) other relevant information regarding the resources and opportunities available to him. In educational and occupational counseling, it involves the provision of information concerning various occupations and occupational opportunities and trends; in marital counseling, it may involve the provision of information concerning legal resources or the probability of finding compatibility with a particular mate. Often

the counselor does not dispense such information himself, but rather refers the client to sources where the information can be found and later answers questions and helps the client to organize and assimilate what he has learned.

The third and final stage of the counseling involves the actual making of choices and decisions. Using the information that has been gathered, client and counselor discuss various alternatives; here, with a knowledgeable person to help him see clearly, the client can try out alternatives hypothetically and gain some familiarity with their probable consequences without actually having to put them into operation in a real-life situation. This enables him to avoid premature crystallization of his thinking. Eventually, he "makes up his mind" and undertakes a course of action which seems necessary and appropriate.

At this point the counseling is terminated, at least for the time being. However, it is often helpful for the client to report to the counselor concerning the outcome of his action and to receive further assistance—if it is indicated—concerning problems that may arise.

Psychotherapy

While many of the forms of psychotherapy to be discussed in this section are often used in treating schizophrenics and other persons manifesting severely maladaptive behavior, our focus here will be on the resources of contemporary psychotherapy for: (1) modifying common self-defeating patterns of behavior, such as phobias or other neurotic avoidance reactions; and (2) opening pathways for personal growth both for individuals who are experiencing adjustment difficulties and for those who may be labeled relatively "well adjusted."

Within this framework, the specific goals of psychotherapy may vary considerably. For one client, the goals may be very limited—getting rid of a phobia, for example; for another client, the goals may involve major personality changes. Similarly, in marital or family therapy, the goals may vary greatly depending upon the problems, resources, and other considerations in the relationship. Often one key therapeutic goal is the alleviation of stressful conditions in the life situation of the client or in the environmental setting of a married couple or family that is experiencing difficulties. This may require dealing with persons other than the individuals immediately involved. For example, if a mother-in-law is creating serious problems in a marriage, it may be important to seek her understanding and cooperation if the therapy program is to succeed.

Often the psychotherapist has to work within severe limitations. He cannot suddenly cancel out the entire past history or even the present life situation of the client. In some instances the life situation of the client or clients is so unfavorable that it becomes almost impossible to utilize any procedure other than the most superficial supportive therapy. Here it may be noted that the goals of therapy often depend in large part upon the socioeconomic level of the client. The more affluent middle-class client may be concerned with marital or other immediate problems of adjustment, or he may be primarily concerned with achieving personal changes that open pathways to personal growth. On the other hand, the client coming from an urban ghetto—who usually has to cope with a highly stressful environment—is likely to be more concerned about assistance in dealing with immediate problems than about personal change and growth.

Although many people think of psychotherapy as a rather mysterious process, newer psychotherapeutic approaches are based upon the relatively straightforward application of learning concepts and other psychological principles to effecting personal change and fostering personal growth. The qualifications of various types of

 Psychotherapy has helped me so much. I think it could benefit everybody. There was a discussion of mental health and problems in one of my classes, and the ignorance displayed in some of the responses infuriated me. Someone said that a person who had had a mental breakdown shouldn't be in a position of authority because he might have a relapse. Another one said they had never known anyone who had a breakdown and they thought they might be scared of them. I wanted to stand up and ask them if they were afraid of *me!*

PERSONNEL IN PSYCHOTHERAPY

	Professional Requirements	Type of Therapy
Clinical psychologist	Ph.D. in clinical psychology plus internship training in psychological assessment and therapy	Wide range of individual and group procedures including behavior therapy
Counseling psychologist	Essentially same as for clinical psychologist but with emphasis on counseling rather than psychotherapy	Educational, occupational, marital, and family counseling
Psychiatrist	M.D. degree plus specialized training in mental hospitals or clinics	Medical therapy (drugs, shock, etc.) and/or psychotherapy
Psychoanalyst	M.D. degree plus extensive training in theory and practice of psychoanalysis	Intensive system of psychotherapy based largely upon Freudian theory
Social worker	M.A. degree in social work plus supervised experience in clinics or social service agencies	May work with spouses or other family members of clients, with groups in community, and with individuals
Occupational therapist	B.S. plus clinical internship	Therapy with children and adults suffering from physical handicaps, helping them to make the most of their resources
Speech therapist	M.A. in speech pathology plus internship training	Procedures appropriate to treatment of stuttering and other speech disorders
Paraprofessional	Limited but intensive training in clinical psychology or other areas with supervised field experience	May utilize wide range of procedures under supervision of professional in field
Interdisciplinary team	Often programs in psychotherapy include personnel from several disciplines including clinical psychologists, psychiatrists, social workers, and other professional or paraprofessional personnel as indicated. This approach is more likely to take place in a clinic setting than in private practice. Systematic research concerning the processes and outcomes of therapy is usually an essential part of such an interdisciplinary approach.	

professional persons who practice psychotherapy are summarized in the chart on page 414. It is important that the individual seeking therapy go only to a qualified psychotherapist, for psychotherapy is a complex process and requires a high degree of competence and responsibility. It may be noted, however, that there is a trend toward using paraprofessional personnel—persons with less advanced training than that of the professional clinical psychologist, for example—who work under the supervision of the professional person. This trend has arisen in large part because of the shortage of professional personnel in the mental health field.

Now as we turn to a brief review of some of the major contemporary approaches to psychotherapy, it may be noted that while there is considerable overlapping in viewpoints and procedures, these approaches do tend to conceptualize the process of psychotherapy in somewhat different ways: (1) some view psychotherapy primarily as a matter of uncovering and helping the patient to understand his unconscious memories, desires, and conflicts and to achieve better personality integration; (2) some see psychotherapy primarily as a matter of eliminating maladaptive coping patterns and/or acquiring adaptive ones; and (3) some see it primarily as cognitive restructuring—involving a change in our assumptions about reality, possibility, and value—which opens pathways to personal growth.

Psychoanalytic therapy

As developed by Sigmund Freud, psychoanalytic therapy emphasizes: (1) the important role of irrational and unconscious processes—such as repressed memories, motives, and conflicts—in self-defeating and maladaptive behavior; (2) the origin of such processes and adjustive difficulties in early childhood experiences and in the conflict between social prohibitions and basic instinctual drives such as sex and hostility; and (3) the importance of bringing these unconscious and irrational processes to consciousness so that the individual does not need to squander his

energies on repression and other ego-defense mechanisms but becomes open to experience—thus paving the way for better personality integration and more effective behavior.

As developed by Sigmund Freud, psychoanalytic therapy is a complex and long-term procedure. Perhaps the simplest way to describe it is to note the four basic techniques utilized in his approach.

1. *Free association.* This "basic rule" of psychoanalytic therapy requires that the client tell the therapist whatever comes into his mind regardless of how personal, painful, or seemingly irrelevant it may be.

2. *Dream interpretation.* Presumably when an individual is asleep his repressive defenses are lowered and forbidden desires and feelings may find an outlet in his dreams. For this reason dreams have been referred to as the "royal road to the unconscious." As the client relates his dreams, the therapist—who has undergone specialized training in this area—interprets their symbolism to the client.

3. *Analysis of resistance.* During free association or in describing his dreams, the client may be unwilling or unable to talk about certain thoughts. Since resistance prevents painful irrational material from entering consciousness, it must be dealt with if the individual is to face his inner conflicts and deal with them in a realistic way.

4. *Analysis of transference.* During the course of psychoanalysis, the client usually comes to "transfer" to the therapist his feelings toward some individual significant in the past, such as his father. An important part of therapy is helping the patient to work through this irrational transference, helping him to see his past relationships as well as his present life situation in a more realistic light.

During the early phases of psychoanalysis, the focus is on uncovering unconscious and irrational processes and helping the patient to work them through and achieve better personality integration. As the therapy approaches its termination, the emphasis shifts to helping him generalize his new insights and understandings to more effective coping in his everyday life.

Although some psychoanalysts still adhere to the standard procedures and long-term therapy program developed by Sigmund Freud, most contemporary analysts have worked out modifications in procedures designed to shorten the time and expense involved. While psychoanalytic therapy, like the psychoanalytic model on which it is based, has been criticized on a number of grounds, many persons feel that it has helped them achieve greater self-understanding, relief from anxiety-arousing conflicts, and increased personal effectiveness.

Behavior therapy

The behavioristic model views the maladjusted individual (assuming there is no brain pathology) as differing from other people in that: (1) he has failed to learn needed competencies for coping with the problems of living; and/or (2) he has learned faulty coping patterns which are being maintained by some type of reinforcement. Unlike psychoanalysis or other so-called *cognitive therapies*, behavior therapy is a planned attack on the client's maladaptive behavior patterns without much concern for their origin or self-understanding on the part of the client. Rather than exploring unconscious conflicts which presumably underlie his maladaptive coping patterns, behavior therapy attempts to modify these patterns directly by applying learning principles—particularly by manipulating environmental rewards and punishments.

Procedures used in behavior therapy include extinction via lack of reinforcement of the maladaptive behavior, desensitization to anxiety-evoking situations, aversion therapy, and positive guidance and reinforcement for learning needed competencies.

1. *Extinction.* Since learned behavior patterns tend to weaken and disappear over time if they are not reinforced, the simplest way to eliminate a maladaptive pattern is often to remove the reinforcement for it. To cite a simple illustration, a child's showing-off behavior may be reinforced if it brings him special attention from his parents or teacher. If those individuals are trained to ignore such behavior, however, it will gradually be extinguished when it no longer brings results.

2. *Desensitization.* We have previously noted the early experiment by Watson and Rayner in which they conditioned a small boy to fear a white rat by striking an iron bar to make a loud noise each time he reached for the animal. The fear then generalized to other furry objects. In a later experiment, Mary Cover Jones (1924) succeeded in eliminating similarly conditioned fear by presenting a white rabbit at a distance when the infant was reacting positively to food—an anxiety inhibitor. By bringing the animal closer and closer—but avoiding overbalancing the positive tendency by the strength of the fear tendency—the boy's fear was finally eliminated and replaced by pleasant feelings toward the white rabbit and other furry animals.

This same concept underlies the method of behavior therapy called *systematic desensitization,* which is described on page 417.

3. *Aversion therapy.* Another specific technique—essentially the opposite of desensitization—is *aversion therapy.* Perhaps the classic example of aversion therapy is the use of drugs in the treatment of alcoholism. Here the patient is repeatedly given an alcoholic drink together with a drug which causes nausea and vomiting. Eventually the mere sight of a drink will presumably evoke the conditioned response of nausea. Behavior therapists prefer to use electric shock as the aversive stimulus rather than drugs; they have utilized such aversion therapy in the treatment of a wide range of maladaptive behaviors from facial tics and persistent sneezing to maladaptive sexual patterns.

4. *Positive reinforcement.* This behavior therapy approach rests on the age-old observation that we tend to learn and maintain behaviors for which we are rewarded. In behavior therapy, it is utilized in a systematic way to deal with a wide range of maladaptive behaviors. For example, the individual may be rewarded with tokens which he can exchange for some desired object, if he observes and then imitates the behavior of a "model"—for example, a shy youth may be shown more self-assertive responses by the

Wolpe (1958, 1969) has concluded that phobias, examination jitters, and other self-defeating patterns involving anxiety are simply learned habits based on conditioning. The reaction is not subject to voluntary control and is not likely to extinguish automatically. But eliciting responses antagonistic to the anxiety in the presence of the anxiety-evoking stimuli—a process known as *systematic desensitization*—can eventually weaken and eliminate the maladaptive response.

In therapy, Wolpe formulates a list of the stimuli that elicit anxiety in the client, arranging them in order from weakest to strongest. Then, during an anxiety-inhibiting response, such as relaxation, the individual is asked to imagine a situation in which the weakest anxiety stimulus on the list is present. If relaxation is unimpaired, he is told to imagine the next item in the hierarchy. This process is continued through a series of sessions until even the strongest anxiety-evoking stimulus can be thought about without anxiety. The extinction of anxiety generalizes from the therapy situation to real-life situations, and the phobia or other maladaptive behaviors are eliminated.

Like systematic desensitization, *implosive therapy* views neurotic avoidance patterns as conditioned anxiety reactions; and the client is asked to imagine and relive aversive scenes associated with his anxiety. But rather than trying to banish anxiety through relaxation or other procedures, the therapist deliberately attempts to elicit a massive flood or "implosion" of anxiety (Stampfl & Levis, 1967).

Systematic desensitization and implosive therapy have proved effective in many cases involving a wide range of maladaptive behaviors based on conditioned anxiety responses, including phobias and final examination jitters.

This man was really suffering with his problem—he was afraid to go on elevators and escalators. Essentially, with him, we would have our meeting and I would have him stretch out on the floor and give him relaxation exercises until he was feeling calm and relaxed and no tension. And then through a process of mental pictures and suggestion that he was coming into a building—he was going to somebody's office on an upper floor, and how did he feel? Rather than any verbal response, he was to just move his little finger if he started feeling tense; then we would go back through the relaxation 'til he felt calm again. So we would go through this process of picturing going in the front door of the building, approaching the elevators—just go through the whole mental process until, through several sessions, he got so that he would see himself actually getting into the elevator and going up. And then I suggested that he have the actual experience, and he did. He was able to cope.

model and then reinforced for incorporating them into his own behavior. In *behavior shaping*, the individual is rewarded for any behavior that is in the desired direction until eventually he acquires the target response. The use of shaping in the case of a severely maladjusted patient is described on this page.

Behavior therapy has the advantage of specifying the specific maladaptive behaviors to be modified, the treatment methods to be used, and the results which are to be expected. It has proven highly effective in the elimination of phobias and a wide range of other self-defeating behaviors, as well as in the rapid acquisition of needed competencies. While behavior therapy is not aimed directly at increasing self-understanding, changing values, or fostering personal growth, the removal of maladaptive behavior patterns may alleviate deep feelings of discomfort and inadequacy and thus lead to an improvement in the individual's overall life adjustment. Whereas insight and cognitive therapies generally assume that behavior changes as a result of new thought patterns, behavior therapists have given us evidence that the reverse may also be true—that changing a person's behavior may lead to a change in his thought patterns.

Humanistic-existential therapies

There are a number of therapeutic approaches which are based upon humanistic and existential models. Here we shall confine ourselves to a few of the more prominent ones.

Client-centered therapy

Most closely associated with the name of Carl Rogers, this therapeutic approach focuses on helping the client develop the willingness and ability to be himself.

In the actual therapeutic process, as in nondirective counseling, the primary responsibility rests upon the client. The therapist plays a relatively passive role, since he assumes that the client is inherently able to solve his own problems. Approaching the client with as few pre-

In an interesting example of the use of shaping in therapy, a man who had been mute for 19 years was first given a stick of gum when he focused his eyes on it. After several sessions, the therapist began to give the gum only after the man made a small mouth movement; later, he had to make some sound. Soon he was making a croaking sound; next he had to say "gum" before receiving it. By the end of the sixth week (three sessions per week), he said "Gum, please," and began to answer questions but spoke only to the therapist.

Gradually, when the nurse and others insisted on verbalizations before complying with his wishes, he began to ask verbally. However, he still continued to use nonverbal requests whenever people would respond to them (Issacs, Thomas, & Goldiamond, 1960).

conceived notions as possible of what his problems may be or how they can be resolved, the therapist works with the material presented by the client, repeating or reflecting the client's feelings and thoughts, and helping him to clarify them but confining himself as much as possible to the client's own words and avoiding interpretation of what the client is saying or attempts to force insight on him.

As a consequence of extensive observation and research, Rogers has found that client-centered therapy follows an orderly and predictable sequence: (1) creation of the therapeutic relationship; (2) expression by the client of feelings and thoughts which had formerly been denied or distorted, including many negative feelings; (3) insight and increased self-understanding; (4) positive steps toward resolving his conflicts and more positive feelings about himself and others; and (5) termination of therapy. The last step is left to the client, who arrives at a point where he feels he no longer needs the support of the therapeutic relationship.

Rational-emotive therapy

This form of therapy stems from the work of Ellis (1957, 1973) who has pointed out that we are brought up to internalize and keep reinforcing many beliefs which inevitably lead to ineffective and self-defeating behavior. For example, Ellis has compiled an interesting list of "mistaken ideas" that he found commonly involved in neurotic patterns. These include such ideas

tration, and annoyance, with the realization that one takes a calculated risk in close relationships with others and can be hurt by them. This enables the individual to accept his losses, albeit with some hurt, but try to ascertain what happened and how he can profit from the experience in his future relationships.

The primary goal of therapy thus becomes that of helping the client to identify his inaccurate assumptions, to understand how they are causing and maintaining his self-defeating behavior, and to replace them with more accurate assumptions. This is achieved by the so-called

 The hardest thing I've ever had to learn is that I don't have to be loved by everybody all the time. It's OK to be disliked by somebody—OK to have somebody mad at me. I'm still learning it, still working on it. It scares the hell out of me to do anything that's going to make somebody else mad. But I either have to learn that or give up my whole life to trying to please other people. And I can't stand living that way any more.

as: it is necessary that we be loved and approved by everyone; one should be completely adequate and competent; it is catastrophic and unbearable when things are not as one would like them to be.

Such faulty assumptions are presumably maintained by a process of "self-talk"—a sort of internal dialogue in which the individual continually reaffirms his own faulty assumptions. For example, the individual may continually remind himself that it is essential to be approved by everyone, or that it is tragic not to be highly successful. In addition, actual stress situations may lead to aversive consequences and emotions which in turn confirm our mistaken assumptions; for example, the individual may be rejected by some significant other and feel terribly hurt, devaluated, and depressed. A more rational and appropriate reaction in such a situation would be feelings of disappointment, frus-

A-B-Cs of rational-emotive therapy. *A* stands for the *activating experience*, (e.g., rejection) which the client falsely assumes caused *C*—the emotional *consequence.* The therapist seeks to help the client see that *B*, his irrational *belief*, lies at the core of his difficulty, for rejection cannot result in such a consequence unless the client makes a particular assumption about it—otherwise everyone who was rejected would feel worthless and depressed, and this is not the case. Once the client understands the consequences of his mistaken belief, with the help of the therapist he is in a position to change his belief and find a more appropriate one.

Existential therapy

As we noted in our review of the existential model, existential psychologists are very much concerned about the predicament of the human race today. They emphasize the breakdown of

The major systematic approaches to psychotherapy can be viewed in the perspective of five key dimensions:

1. *Cognitive change vs. behavior change.* Some approaches to psychotherapy are based on the premise that changes in values and other assumptions will lead to changes in behavior; others on the premise that behavior change will in turn result in changes in assumptions.

2. *Brief vs. long-term.* The historical leader among psychotherapies—standard psychoanalysis—is a long-term process involving several sessions a week over a period of years. However, many newer forms of therapy, including modifications in psychoanalytic procedures, are designed as short-term therapies.

3. *Directive vs. nondirective.* Some therapeutic approaches and therapists place the primary responsibility for therapy upon the client; others take a highly directive role in the therapy relationship, even to the extent of making decisions for the client.

4. *Crisis intervention vs. personal growth.* Some approaches are concerned with procedures that are effective in dealing with immediate crises in the patient's present life situation; others are primarily directed toward personal change leading to avenues for personal growth.

5. *Individual vs. group.* Some approaches utilize individual or one-to-one therapy; others involve a group setting, with several patients being treated at once using the group as a therapeutic medium. Most of the major therapeutic techniques we shall discuss can be used with groups as well as individuals; some, such as transactional analysis, are used only in group settings.

traditional faith, the alienation and depersonalization of the individual in our mass society, and the loss of meaning in human existence.

Despite their predicament, however, humans are viewed as being essentially free. Unlike other living creatures, every human being has the ability to be conscious of himself as a self and to reflect on his own existence. He is aware that it is he who is in a situation and that he can do something about his problems through *his choices.* His freedom confronts him with the responsibility for *being*—for deciding what kind of person he shall be and for defining and actualizing himself.

Central to *being* is the problem of meaning. This is primarily a matter of finding satisfactory values. Frankl (1955) has distinguished three sets of values: (1) *creative values,* which relate to the achievement of tasks, (2) *experiential values,* which adhere in experiencing the good, the true, and the beautiful and in understanding and loving another human being, and (3) *attitudinal values,* which involve courage and the facing of inevitable suffering without flinching. Since some of these values can be realized regardless of the hopelessness of the objective situation, it is always possible to find some meaning in one's existence. However, each individual is unique; each must find the pattern of values capable of giving meaning to his life. As Nietzsche put it, "He who knows a Why of living surmounts almost every How." But to find values and meaning, the individual must have the courage to break away from his old defenses and escapes, face his existential anxiety, make choices, and take responsibility for his own life.

Existential therapists do not follow any prescribed procedures but believe that a flexible approach is necessary in therapy. Their primary concern is with helping the client to clarify his values and work out a meaningful way of "being-in-the-world." They stress the importance of *confrontation*—challenging the individual directly with questions concerning the meaning and purpose of his existence—and the *encounter*—the relationship which is established between two interacting human beings in the therapeutic situation. They also strongly emphasize the individual's responsibility to his fellow man and his need to relate positively to and participate with other human beings. The individual's life can be meaningful and fulfilling only if it involves socially constructive choices and values.

While existential psychotherapy is similar in many ways to client-centered psychotherapy—both approaches viewing psychotherapy as growth of the self—the existential approach places less emphasis on discovering the true self behind the facade and more emphasis on taking the responsibility for one human life—for shaping one's self into the kind of person one wants to be and living in a socially constructive and meaningful way. The Greek oracle said "Know thyself"; the poet Emerson said "Trust thyself"; and, to paraphrase Kierkegaard, the existentialists have said "Choose thyself."

The humanistic-existential therapies have been criticized for a lack of a systematized model of man on which to base their therapy, for lack of agreement on the use of various therapeutic approaches, for lack of clarity about what is supposed to happen between client and therapist, and for vagueness concerning the specific goals and outcomes of therapy. On the other hand, many humanistic-existential therapists view these alleged inadequacies as actual advantages. They point out that we do not as yet have sufficient knowledge about humans to justify basing their therapy on any systematized model and that the range of therapeutic approaches and outcomes provides the therapist with the flexibility essential for dealing with each client as a unique person. In any event, many humanistic-existential concepts—the uniqueness of the individual, his untapped potentials, his quest for values and meaning, his conflict between being and nonbeing, and his existential anxiety—have had a major impact on contemporary psychotherapy.

Gestalt therapy and transactional analysis

Two relative newcomers to the field of psychotherapy—gestalt therapy and transactional analysis—have been growing steadily in influence and are recognized today as major forces in contemporary psychotherapy.

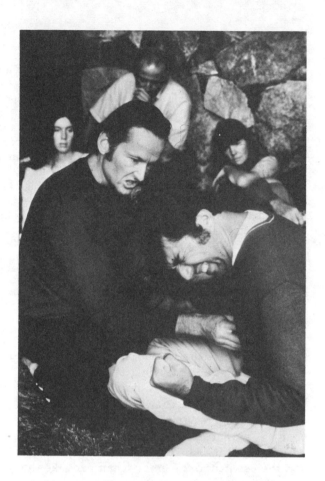

Gestalt therapy: Becoming a "whole" person

The term *gestalt* means "whole," and gestalt therapy places strong emphasis upon the integration of thought, feeling, and action.

As developed by Frederick Perls (1967, 1969) gestalt therapy is typically used in a group setting, but the emphasis is on the individual—the therapist working intensively with one client at a time, helping him to perceive those aspects of himself and his world which are "blocked out," to correct inaccuracies in his views, and to achieve greater competence in coping with the problems of living.

Gestalt therapy utilizes a number of specific techniques including "awareness training," the "hot seat," the "empty chair," and dream interpretation. Awareness training focuses on helping the individual become more perceptive and

Sports fans have long since become accustomed to closeups, split-screen images, and instant replay in viewing football games and other sports on TV. Now individuals in psychotherapy—whether in an effort to deal with some immediate problem of adjustment or to find pathways for personal growth—are learning to see themselves in a different perspective as a consequence of the use of this same technique.

In transactional analysis, for example, a husband and wife may see very clearly on instant replay how they are interacting in a Child-Parent type of relationship; an alcoholic may see tapes of his behavior when he was admitted to a community clinic for detoxification; or a person in an encounter group may see the "smug, know-it-all look" on her face and understand why the other members of the group have been giving her negative feedback about this aspect of her behavior.

In short, the use of video playback techniques in psychotherapy is opening up exciting avenues for personal change and growth.

enrich his experiencing. The "hot seat" is utilized in helping the individual perceive himself more clearly; here one person occupies the "hot seat" while the others provide feedback about their reactions to him and his behavior—with the proviso that the feedback be sincere. This may result in the individual achieving a quite different impression of himself than he had before. The "empty chair" technique involves asking the client to act out one side of his conflict—perhaps carrying on an argument with an empty chair that represents his employer—and then switch to the empty chair and take the part of the "adversary." In "dreamwork," the therapist helps the client to interpret the meaning of given dreams and to perceive their application to his real-life situations.

These various techniques are referred to as "taking care of unfinished business." According to Perls, we all go through life with blind spots and unresolved conflicts and traumas; and we carry over this unfinished business into new situations and relationships, often with detrimental results. Consequently, completing his unfinished business should help the client to achieve a more realistic awareness of himself and his world, to reduce his level of anxiety and tension, and to achieve greater effectiveness in coping with the problems of living.

Transactional analysis

As we noted in Chapter 9, Eric Berne (1964, 1972) developed an innovative technique of psychotherapy based on the notion that our personalities are composed of three "ego states": (1) Parent—the part of us we have incorporated from parents or parental models; (2) Adult—the part of us that processes information rationally and appropriately in coping with given situations; and (3) Child—the part of us carried over from childhood feelings. All three ego states are considered to be of value. The Parent makes many automatic responses simply because we have learned "That's the way it's done," thus freeing the Adult from making innumerable trivial decisions and enabling it to deal with more important matters. The Child contributes intuition, spontaneity, creativity, and pleasure.

After the client has come to understand the P-A-C concepts, he learns to analyze interpersonal relationships in terms of the ego states in which each person is communicating with and relating to the other. For example, the Parent in the wife might make some statement to her husband such as "You shouldn't eat so much." The Child in the husband might reply "I'll eat as much as I want, and don't always be shouting at me when I'm tired." As long as one person in a relationship responds to the other in the way that he is being addressed, such as a Child to a Parent, such complementary interactions may continue indefinitely on this level.

A conflict may arise, however, in the form of a "crossed transaction" which Berne concluded causes most interpersonal difficulties—whether in friendship, love, or marriage. Suppose, for example, a marital situation calls for an Adult-Adult transaction; and the Adult in the wife leads her to say "I'm concerned about the increase in your drinking." An appropriate Adult response from the husband would be something to the effect of "You know, so am I—perhaps we should talk about it." But instead the husband flares up with a Child-Parent response such as "You're always nagging me just like my mother did." In such instances the only way a complementary transaction can be resumed is if the wife becomes a Parent in response to the suddenly activated Child or if the husband's Adult is reactivated by the wife's Adult. And as Berne has pointed out, this often takes months in intimate interpersonal relationships.

Since transactional analysis takes place in a group setting, other members are encouraged to

client realizes for the first time how he is unthinkingly "playing games" which harm both himself and others. As a form of therapy, transactional analysis provides a learning situation in which we can become aware of and eliminate self-defeating ways in which we may relate to significant others; and in turn we are helped to achieve more authentic and satisfying interpersonal styles and relationships.

Berne also strongly emphasized the concept of *life script*.

"A script is an ongoing program, developed in early childhood under parental influence, which directs the individual's behavior in most important aspects of his life" (1972, p. 418).

Some persons have "bad scripts" that call for them to be repeatedly disappointed in love, to fail in their occupation, or even to become

 I'm beginning to realize that I act a lot more like I'm his daughter, sometimes, than his wife. And he must like being the daddy, because he responds to it all, and seems to enjoy the way we are.

participate in analyzing the interactions between other couples; and the way in which they participate may, in turn, invite analysis of their own relationships.

As we saw in Chapter 9, many ways of interacting in interpersonal relationships were characterized by Berne as "games" not because they are played for fun, but because they are played by rules—even though these rules are not spelled out consciously—and they involve a "gimmick" and a "payoff." Many of these games are not only deadly serious but also highly destructive to one or both persons involved.

By teaching clients to analyze the games they play, transactional analysis helps them become aware of their ways of relating to others and their consequences in terms of interpersonal relationships and life adjustment. Often the

alcoholics. Berne developed a method of *script analysis* which helps the individual understand how his script is put together and what it contains—and how to rewrite the script if it is a "bad" one. Essentially, rewriting the script involves breaking away from the dictates of the Parent and becoming an Adult—thus resulting in a new script that leads to a satisfying and fulfilling way of life.

The basic concepts and procedures in transactional analysis have been elaborated upon in a very interesting way by Harris in his popular book *I'm OK—You're OK*. In his discussion of building a strong Adult, he makes a number of suggestions including the following:

1. *"Learn to recognize your Child, its vulnerabilities, its fears, its principal methods of expressing these feelings."*

2. *"Learn to recognize your Parent, its admonitions, injunctions, fixed positions, and principal ways of expressing these admonitions, injunctions, and positions."*

3. *"Be sensitive to the Child in others, talk to that Child, stroke that Child, protect that Child, and appreciate its need for creative expression."*

4. *"Count to ten, if necessary, in order to give the Adult time to process the data coming into the computer, to sort out Parent and Child from reality."*

5. *"Work out a system of values. You can't make decisions without an ethical framework"* (1967, pp. 95–96).

In essence, it is through the integration of all three ego states into a unified person that we increase our autonomy, interpersonal competence, and capabilities for relating to others in satisfying ways and writing "good" life scripts.

Intensive group experience

"In our affluent society the individual's survival needs are satisfied. For the first time, he is freed to become aware of his isolation, aware of his alienation, aware of the fact that he is, during most of his life, a role interacting with other roles, a mask meeting other masks. And for the first time he is aware that this is not a necessary tragedy of life, that he does not have to live out his days in this fashion. So he is seeking, with great determination and inventiveness, ways of modifying this existential loneliness. The intensive group experience, perhaps the most significant social invention of this century, is an important one of these ways" (Rogers, 1968, p. 268).

In recent years we have come to realize that the average person in our contemporary society develops and uses only a small fraction of his actual potential for perceiving, thinking, feeling, creating, and experiencing. Efforts to increase this potential for personal growth and effectiveness have resulted in a general phenomenon known as the *human potential movement*. The focus of this movement is on the development of ways of helping people to lower their defenses, to remove their masks, to be more aware and open to experience, to feel more deeply, to communicate more efficiently, to be more spontaneous and creative, to become more authentic persons, to build more satisfying interpersonal relationships, and to think through and choose their own values and "way of being in the world." To these ends the human potential movement hopes to counterbalance the trend toward dehumanization and alienation in our age of impersonal mass bureaucracy.

One important tool of the human potential movement is *intensive group experience,* usually taking the form of what is commonly called the *encounter group.* While such groups vary markedly in terms of their goals and methods, all are concerned in one way or another with more valid human relationships and personal growth. A brief description of some types of groups is presented on page 425.

Encounter groups are of two distinct types, differentiated by their focus: either (1) treating maladaptive behavior—such as confrontation groups for drug-dependent patients; or (2) helping "normal" persons learn more about themselves and their interactions with others, improving interpersonal relationships, and fostering personal growth and effectiveness. It is this latter type of encounter group with which we are primarily concerned here, although much of what we shall say applies to both types of groups.

Group format and climate

Usually the encounter group consists of 6 to 12 members, including the group leader who is also a participant. The physical setting is usually relatively bare, permitting maximum freedom of movement of group members. The group leader is usually responsible for screening members for admission to the group and for scheduling group meetings. He also serves as a model by expressing his own feelings openly and honestly and accepting hostility or other negative feelings directed toward him without becoming defen-

A confusing variety of terms may be encountered in discussions of intensive group experience. A few of the more common of these are described below.

1. *Sensitivity training groups* —which initially focused on the development of human relations skills and on understanding and increasing the effectiveness of group functioning but have since become much broader in scope.

2. *Encounter groups*—which may focus either on the treatment of maladaptive behavior or on fostering the personal growth and effectiveness, including improved interpersonal relationships, of essentially normal individuals.

3. *T-groups*—this term originated as a shortened form of *sensitivity training group* but is now used in a variety of contexts.

4. *Awareness groups*—which usually focus on sensory awareness, body awareness, and body movement, utilizing awareness training, nonverbal expression, spontaneous dance, and related activities.

5. *Creativity groups or workshops*—which focus on individual spontaneity, expression, and creativity, often through painting and other artistic media.

There are also a number of other forms of intensive group experience including *team building groups,* which are widely used in industry to facilitate the attainment of production and related goals as well as providing opportunities for improved human relations and personal growth. The *Synanon group* or *"game,"* developed originally for the treatment of drug addiction, may also be considered under the general rubric of encounter groups, as may groups engaged in gestalt therapy or transactional analysis.

sive; and it is his responsibility to see that confrontations among group members are resolved in a constructive way. In general, he serves as a resource person when the group needs guidance or comes to an impasse.

The most important function of the group leader is that of establishing a climate of "psychological safety" in which each member feels free to lower his defenses, to remove his mask, to express his real feelings, and to try out new ways of interacting with others. In such a psychological climate coupled with the intensive give-and-take of group interaction, the possibilities for increased awareness, understanding, and personal growth are greatly enhanced.

Group process

As we have noted, the emphasis in encounter groups is on the removal of masks, the open and honest communication of feelings, and the constructive resolution of confrontations and other interactions that emerge within the group. This in turn requires prompt and sincere feedback from other group members. In order to foster a climate of psychological safety the group leader encourages members to give descriptive rather than evaluative feedback—for example, the descriptive response "When you said that, it made me feel uncomfortable" rather than the evaluative response "Only a real jerk would make a statement like that." In group interaction the emphasis is upon the here and now—upon present feelings and interactions—and not on the past or future.

Many therapists use nonverbal techniques as "warming up" exercises. Such techniques include the *blind mill* in which the group members walk around with their eyes closed, learning how to communicate by touch; *eyeball-to-eyeball* in which two participants may gaze into each other's eyes and maintain eye contact for 60 to 90 seconds, and *trusting exercises* in which members take turns being lifted and passed around the circle formed by the other group members. In some instances, partial or total disrobing is used and presumably tends to enhance feelings of confidence and spontaneity rather than eliciting sexual stimulation. How-

 In my group sessions, I had to practice showing
the angry, mean, demanding, vindictive side of
myself that I'd always covered up, even from myself. Sometimes I'd get jumped on by everybody,
but more often I'd get the reaction from them,
'Now you seem like a real person to me. You're
always so nice, I always felt like you were just a
cardboard phony.' Getting the good reactions for
being 'bad' was a startling experience. But even
when they jumped on me, just the experience of
letting the crud out, of expressing the stuff I usually hold back, was very exciting. It gave me a
real feeling of reality to myself, a feeling of my
own potential and worth.

To me, this body awareness and movement was
an esthetic experience as well as therapeutic; at
the time I wasn't concerned with anything therapeutic, it's just being able to move and letting
go.

Just what is it that goes on in an encounter group? On the basis of his extensive work with such groups, Rogers (1970) has delineated a pattern of events which is typical of the group process. An adaptation of his analysis is presented below.

1. *Milling around.* As the group leader makes it clear that group members have unusual freedom but also responsibility for the direction of the group, there tends to be an initial period of confusion, frustration, awkward silences, and "cocktail-party talk"—polite surface interaction intermixed with questions about who is in charge of the group and what its purpose is.

2. *Resistance to personal expression or exploration.* Initially, members tend to portray only their "public selves"; only fearfully and gradually do they begin to reveal aspects of the private self.

3. *Description of negative feelings.* Interestingly enough, the first expression of feelings concerning the here-and-now interaction in the group tends to involve negative feelings directed toward the group leader or other group members.

4. *Expression and exploration of personally meaningful material.* Despite the resistance to revealing one's private self, the voicing of critical or angry feelings, and the initial confusion, the event most likely to occur next is for some member to take the gamble of revealing some significant aspect of himself—

perhaps a seemingly hopeless problem of communication between himself and his wife. Apparently this member has come to realize that this is in effect "his" group, and he can help shape its direction; apparently also the fact that negative feelings have been expressed in the group without catastrophic results tends to foster a climate of trust.

5. *The expression of immediate interpersonal feelings in the group.* Although this may occur at any point in the group process, it involves the explicit expression of feelings, positive or negative, experienced at the moment by one member toward another. Each of these immediate expressions of feeling is usually explored in the increasing climate of trust which is developing in the group.

6. *Development of a healing capacity in the group and the beginning of change.* One fascinating aspect of the intensive group experience is the manner in which some group members evidence a spontaneous capability for responding to the pain and suffering of others in a therapeutic way—thus paving the way for change. This healing capacity may extend beyond the regular group sessions, as when a few members remain after the session is over to offer support and therapeutic assistance to a member they sense is experiencing serious difficulties.

7. *Dropping of façades, confrontations, and feedback.* As the group sessions continue, many

things are occurring simultaneously and it is difficult to organize them into any coherent pattern: the various threads and stages overlap and interweave. As time goes on, the group finds it increasingly unacceptable for any member to hide behind a mask or façade, refusing to reveal himself to the group as he really is. In a general sense, the group *demands* that each individual be himself.

This may result in a direct confrontation, often negative in tone, between two group members. In this type of *basic encounter* with other group members, individuals come into more direct, honest, and closer contact than is customary in ordinary life. This is likely to provide the individual with a good deal of totally new feedback concerning himself and his effects on others.

8. *Expression of positive feelings and behavior change.* Rogers states that "an inevitable part of the group process seems to be that when feelings are expressed and can be accepted in a relationship, then a great deal of closeness and positive feeling results. Thus as the sessions proceed, an increasing feeling of warmth and group spirit and trust is built up, not out of positive attitudes only but out of a realness which includes both positive and negative feelings" (pp. 34–35). He concludes that while there are certain risks inherent in the intensive encounter group experience, there is also great therapeutic potential.

ever, there is little evidence to support the effectiveness of this exercise.

Verbal techniques may be used to facilitate group interaction. These include the use of the "hot seat" and similar approaches which we noted briefly in our discussion of gestalt therapy. Some therapists use what is called the *marathon format* to intensify the group experience. Here the group may meet for a live-in weekend with only a brief break for sleep. Presumably the continuous contact of group members over time as well as the lowering of inhibitions that tends to accompany fatigue contribute to the "opening up" process and to reducing the time for the group to achieve

yet there is no simple solution to the reentry problem, although some group leaders utilize the final session of the group for "reflections" in which members share their feelings about the group experience and how it may carry over into their everyday lives.

Evaluation of the group experience

Although there is not yet sufficient data to accurately assess the advantages and pitfalls of encounter groups, a few comments do seem in order. That the encounter group is a potent

 A group of us graduate students one semester formed an encounter group for just that semester, which worked out a lot better than I'd expected. What happened is that we developed, within this group of people who were all potential counselors, an opportunity to try out techniques, an opportunity to try relationships. Our leader was a professor, who kind of held things together and kept us going on track, but he also was a real member of the group—entered into the encounter.

its goals. As a consequence the marathon encounter group has been called a "pressure cooker."

The actual sequence of events which typically occur in encounter groups has been well described by Rogers (1970) and is summarized on page 428. One aspect of encounter groups which is not included in Rogers' description is the *reentry problem.* This refers to the return of the group members from the climate of psychological safety and the openness of the encounter group to the everyday world where new understandings and ways of interacting may not be readily accepted. Obviously there is considerable risk in being completely open in one's interactions with family, work, or social groups—if one does not wish to endanger the relationship. As

experience is attested by the fact that in a relatively short period of time a group of strangers can learn to interact with a high degree of openness, honesty, trust, and supportiveness. And many participants in encounter groups have stated that the experience had a profound and constructive influence on their lives. Usually a good deal of warmth and affection does develop among group members, and it is not unusual for a member to comment on termination something to the effect that "I feel I know each of you better and feel closer to you than to most people I have known for years."

On the other hand, professional mental health personnel have pointed to the scarcity of research data concerning the actual effects of encounter groups on their members, to the common lack of adequate screening of individuals seeking admission to groups, and to the inadequate training of many group leaders. In addition, they cite evidence of the possibilities of short-term gains being wiped out by subsequent discouragement following reentry into the real world, of the aggravation of personal problems that do come out in the group and are not effectively resolved, and of the development of sexual involvements among group members which may jeopardize their marriages. Perhaps potential adverse effects of encounter groups can be minimized by the careful screening of partici-pants, by briefing each potential member ahead of time on possible hazards, and by adhering to the code of ethics established by the American Psychological Association for the accreditation of group leaders.

Despite possible hazards and occasional failures, it would be unfair to minimize the potential of encounter groups as a resource for personal change and growth. And once individuals do experience change in the direction of personal growth—even though it may entail some pain and difficulties—they usually consider the rewards well worth the costs.

Summary and a look ahead

Resources that modern psychology offers for helping individuals achieve increased self-understanding, more effective methods of coping, and personal growth are of three basic kinds: psychological counseling, psychotherapy, and intensive group experience.

Psychological counseling focuses on (1) helping the individual obtain a more realistic picture of himself—particularly in terms of his interests, abilities, values, and methods of coping; and (2) assisting the individual with educational, occupational, marital, or other problems with which he is concerned. In this context, the psychologist makes use of assessment data obtained from the client through interviewing, psychological tests, and direct observation of real-life situations. In addition to these data, the psychologist relies on either directive or nondirective counseling procedures, or a combination of both, when working with a client.

There are many forms of psychotherapy, but in this chapter we emphasized those aspects of the approaches that are aimed primarily at modifying common self-defeating patterns of behavior and opening pathways for personal growth. Those discussed included psychoanalytic therapy, behavior therapy, the humanistic-existential therapies, and the more recent Gestalt therapy and transactional analysis. The basic techniques used in psychoanalysis are free association, dream interpretation, analysis of resistance, and analysis of transference. Here the emphasis in therapy is on the unconscious conflicts and origins of the maladaptive behavior. The procedures used in behavior therapy are concerned with modifying the maladaptive behavior through extinction, desensitization, aversion therapy, and positive reinforcement. Among the humanistic-existential therapies, we particularly focused on client-centered therapy, rational-emotive therapy, and existential therapy.

In the final section of this chapter we briefly reviewed the nature of and the advantages and disadvantages of intensive group experiences. Here we noted the typical format, climate, and process of encounter groups. In their evaluation of group experiences, most individuals who have changed in the direction of personal growth as a result of an encounter group feel that the rewards of the experience were well worth the possible costs.

In the chapter which follows, we shall see how the development of intellectual competence helps to foster personal growth and effectiveness.

15

Toward Intellectual Competence

Foundations for effective learning
Problem solving and decision making
Creative thinking

The most unique adaptive resources that human beings possess are their intellectual capabilities—their superior capacity for learning, reasoning, and imagining. It is largely by virtue of these resources that humans have been able, as a species, to master so many facets of their environment, to establish supremacy in the struggle for survival over other members of the animal kingdom, and to gain some understanding of themselves—of what it means to be human. And it is their superior intellectual capability which now provides them with the resources for planning and shaping their own future.

On an individual level, the person who develops and learns to use his intellectual capabilities effectively has a decided advantage in adjusting to the problems of living. For such intellectual competence enhances his feelings of adequacy and worth, enriches his understanding of himself and his world, permits him to predict more accurately the probable outcome of alternative choices and courses of action, enables him to cope with a wider range of stressful situations, contributes to continued personal growth, and increases his ability to determine his own destiny.

In the present chapter we will deal with the development of our intellectual resources in terms of three categories: (1) the foundations for effective learning; (2)

problem solving and decision making; and (3) the farther reaches of intellectual competence, including creative thinking.

Foundations for effective learning

In our discussion of psychosocial models in Chapter 2 as well as in later chapters, we have emphasized the general role of learning in development, noting that practically everything a person strives for, thinks, feels, and does is influenced by his past learning. We have also noted the difference between informal learning in everyday life and more formal learning in educational and related settings; we have noted the distinction between simple conditioning and more complex operant learning involving reasoning, abstracting, and concept formation; and we have seen the contribution of such learning to personal growth and self-direction.

While our focus in the present section is on more formal and complex learning, we will try to avoid the common misconception that significant learning takes place only in school and not in everyday life. And we will attempt to show the close interrelationship between effective learning and living.

In analyzing the foundations for effective learning, it is helpful to consider the following factors: (1) the characteristics of the learner; (2) the nature of the task to be learned; (3) learning strategy, or the way the individual goes about learning; and (4) feedback.

The learner

What the individual brings to a learning situation in terms of general background, motivation, frame of reference, and personal maturity has an important influence on what he *can* learn, what he is *willing* to learn, and how *efficiently* he will learn it.

Previous learning and resources
What an individual is capable of learning is always limited by what he already knows. He cannot learn algebra without some prior mastery of arithmetic, and he cannot understand psychopathology without having learned the basic principles of normal behavior. It is in recognition of this principle that, in teaching, so much emphasis is placed on introducing new skills and concepts in systematic fashion, in order to build upon what has been learned before. Many students get into difficulty in their college studies because they ignore the suggested prerequisites for the courses they want to take.

Competence in learning also presupposes a level of intelligence adequate for mastering the task at hand. In general, the higher the individual's intelligence, the more capable he is of mastering a complex task and of doing so with a minimum of time and effort. Other resources that facilitate learning are good health and a

There are subjects that I'm interested in, and I'm a quick learner, but I'm very ignorant—what happens is, I get into a history class, and the teacher expects us to have all the basics, so he adds on and gets more intricate onto the basics, and I don't know the basics, and that really messes me up.

 I become bored in class very easily, so the more variety a class can offer me, the more I will enjoy it and will learn.

high level of energy, adequate time to devote to the task, good study skills, and special talent or interest in the area.

Motivation

The basic motivation for learning is found in the human organism's normal tendency to explore and make sense of its environment. With time, this general tendency is differentiated in terms of specific needs, interests, and goals, so that we are motivated to learn things that tie in directly with our purposes while remaining relatively uninterested in learning other things. If curiosity is disapproved or punished, as it is by some parents and by some societies, the natural incentive for learning is greatly dulled.

Learning is encouraged when it is rewarded by material or psychological satisfaction. In a school situation, where the subject matter to be learned may bear little relationship to the learner's immediate interests and purposes, motivation must sometimes be induced by the manipulation of rewards and punishments. In general, however, the successful teacher is the one who manages to relate learning tasks to the experiences and purposes of his students—to get them ego-involved in the learning situation. The mature college student can do much to improve his own learning efficiency by making his studies as meaningful as possible and relating them to both his present interests and his long-range purposes and goals.

Motivation for learning is usually increased, too, by association with people who value intellectual competence and take a positive approach to the discipline of study. The approval of intellectual achievement by those we like and admire is a powerful incentive to our own learning.

Frame of reference

As we have seen, the assumptions and attitudes that comprise an individual's frame of reference determine in large part what he sees and learns. The range of information that will be meaningful to him, the way he will interpret new material, and whether he will perceive the learning task as a challenge, a threat, or of no importance, will all depend on his picture of himself and his world. Faulty assumptions or negative attitudes in relation to a particular task will obviously hamper effective learning.

Of special importance is the relation he sees between the learning task and his needs and capabilities. Usually an individual is eager to tackle learning tasks he sees as related to his needs and purposes and within his competence to handle. On the other hand, he usually tries to avoid those tasks which appear of little value to him or with which he feels inadequate to cope. Most of us fail to realize our learning potential in many areas—perhaps in art or music, in athletics, or in math or science—because we falsely conceive ourselves to be lacking in aptitude in such fields. Thus we may insist that we cannot "draw a straight line," "sing a single note," or "add two and two." Often a vicious circle develops in which the learner, feeling inadequate, forces himself into a learning situation with anxiety and trepidation; he expects to do badly and does, and the negative feedback then reinforces his concept of himself as inadequate in that area. Thus the individual's frame of reference influences not only the way he perceives a task but also the way he attempts to deal with it and the probable outcome of his strivings.

Personal maturity and adjustment

Efficient learning is also related to personal maturity and the ability to concentrate one's efforts on a particular learning task, to look at new information and ideas objectively, and to tolerate immediate frustration in the interest of achieving long-range goals.

Immaturities that often hamper learning—in everyday life as well as in academic situations—are overdependence on others, lack of self-discipline, uncertainty about goals and values, and lack of motivation toward achievement and personal growth. Preoccupation with inner conflicts, a high level of anxiety, feelings of discouragement and depression, and other maladjustive patterns can also seriously impair one's ability to learn. Personal immaturity or maladjustment—or a combination of the two—can be fatal to educational achievement even for the individual with good intellectual capabilities and a favorable setting for learning.

 I feel like I could probably get good grades, if I could ever get off my butt and study.

The task

Four characteristics of the learning task itself influence how the learner should approach it and how easily he can master it. These are the type of task, its size and complexity, its clarity, and the conditions under which it must be learned.

The nature of the task

The nature of the task influences both how easy it will be to learn and the method of approach that will be most suitable. Whereas the learning of motor skills usually requires time and practice over a considerable period to train the muscles to function with the desired skill and coordination, a verbal task can often be mastered at a single sitting. With verbal learning, meaningful material is much easier and quicker to learn than material which must be learned by rote. For meaningful material, intensive sessions with a focus on relationships lead to the quickest learning and the best retention; for unrelated data that must simply be memorized, spaced drill is usually best.

In our rapidly changing world our learning often includes "unlearning" what we have learned before. This may be relatively easy or very difficult depending upon our frame of reference and general flexibility, how much must be unlearned, and what social conflicts or pressures may be involved.

The size and complexity of the task

In general, the smaller the amount of material to be learned, the easier the learning task. The extent to which difficulty is increased by additional material depends very largely, however, upon the kind of material to be learned. With any kind of verbatim or rote learning, an increase in the amount of material brings an increase not only in the total learning time but also in the average amount of time required for learning each unit. A list of seven nonsense syllables, for example, is within the memory span of the average individual and can be learned in a single presentation; but a list of ten syllables might require as many as eight or nine presentations. With meaningful material that does not require verbatim memorization, increased length—within reason—has a relatively small effect on rate of learning.

The complexity of material and its familiarity are other factors that influence learning difficulty. Although added complexity tends to increase the time required for study and understanding, this factor may be offset if the learner is familiar with the material in a general way and has an adequate background for organizing and understanding it. Familiarity tends to encourage learning even when motivation to learn is relatively low—a principle which teachers apply by trying to relate new concepts to what their students already know.

The clarity of the task

The clarity with which a learning task is defined seems to be an important variable in the learning process, although it has not been extensively studied. Probably every student has had the frustrating experience of listening to a teacher who failed to make clear the points he was trying to communicate or whose assignments were vague and ill-defined. In general, it would appear that the less clear the learning task, the more time and effort the learner will have to spend in mastering it—if he can master it at all.

One reason we often fail to learn what we should from our everyday experiences is that the essential elements are never pointed up clearly, either because they are too complex and interrelated or because we are too ego-involved to see them for what they are. One function of professional counselors and psychotherapists is to clarify the key dimensions of the problems the individual is trying to deal with.

The task environment

The conditions under which learning takes place represent another important variable of the learning task. If the learning is disapproved by one's associates, if conditions of study are unfavorable, if essential tools or resources are lacking, if time pressures are severe, or if other life demands are distracting, the difficulty of the learning task is increased over what it would be in a more favorable environment.

Other aspects of the task environment that may be important are its general climate (whether authoritarian or democratic), the individual's relationships to others in the learning situation, the quality of instruction available, and the social pressures and reinforcements associated with the learning task.

Learning strategy

If the student has the motivation and the intellectual and other resources necessary for mastering the learning task, then the outcome of his effort depends heavily upon his learning strategy or method of learning.

There are a wide range of learning strategies which may be adopted depending upon the task at hand. For our immediate purposes four components of learning strategy appear directly relevant.

Utilizing available facilities and resources

Although some aspects of the task environment are beyond the learner's control, others are of his own choosing. Usually a first step toward making efficient use of learning time and effort is to choose a good place to study—a spot that is well ventilated, well lighted, and as free as possible from distraction. Of course, there are wide individual differences in the conditions

better knowledge of library facilities and a greater skill in using them. Learning efficiency is sometimes impaired, too, by the failure to utilize opportunities for questions and discussion with teachers and other experts.

Building background and motivation

At the elementary and high-school level, the teacher's task is often viewed as involving a

which students find most conducive to efficient study; the important thing is to structure the situation so that the desired study behavior is most likely to occur and to eliminate stimuli that will make incompatible behavior likely.

Familiarity with available resources also facilitates the effectiveness of learning effort. Most college students could save a great deal of time and avoid much misguided effort if they had a

sequence of three steps: (1) building background and motivation, (2) guiding the learning experience, and (3) extending and enriching what has been learned. At the college level these become increasingly the responsibility of the student.

A main reason why informal, out-of-school learning usually comes so easily is that it ties in with our immediate interests and thus is highly motivated. With academic learning, such interest and motivation can be created deliberately if we build a background for the new material and try to relate it to our existing interests and to other things we are studying. It may also help to note that "interest"—in one sense—is the return we get on an investment; and one way to increase our interest in something we are studying is to put a lot into it.

Planning the learning experience

Assuming adequate background and motivation, the focus moves to planning and organizing the learning experience. This involves actively trying to gain an overall view of the learning task, organizing the task in terms of the key elements involved, and distinguishing relevant from irrelevant details. Once the task has been clearly delineated, the student then is in a position to formulate the most appropriate study program for ensuring its mastery. As already indicated, different strategies are appropriate for different kinds of tasks.

A key component in planning the learning experience is establishing a routine for study. Scheduling a place and time to study and adhering to this study pattern until it becomes habitual are of great importance in effective learning. Usually the student who formulates and follows a planned schedule makes better use of his time and hence actually has more free time than the less organized student. When a student is working to pay for his tuition and/or other expenses, the necessity of establishing an efficient study schedule becomes of crucial importance.

Another integral part of guiding the learning experience is preparing for examinations. Usually the knowledge that one will have to apply what he has learned in practical situations or be tested on it by a formal examination acts as a stimulus to effective learning and recall. The time to begin preparing for an examination, of course, is when the learning task is begun. Distributed study, periodic review, and over-learning all encourage long-range retention and give the learner real confidence in what he knows. Last-minute cramming may get a student through a particular examination, but his understanding will be so poor and his rate of

BEYOND PARKINSON'S LAW

"Parkinson's Law" states that a work operation will expand to take up whatever space or facilities are available, regardless of the actual requirement of the job to be done. This general principle has been found to apply also to studying.

In a laboratory experiment, some of the subjects were "accidentally" allowed too much time to perform a group of tasks, while others were allowed the minimum time essential. Later, when both groups were presented with a similar task and allowed to work at their own pace, those who had initially been allowed excess time required more time than the others to complete the task. Not only does a piece of work expand to fill the time available, but having once expanded, it continues to require more time (Aronson & Gerard, 1966).

forgetting so high that what he has learned will be of little use to him thereafter. Furthermore, lectures and discussion periods are often little more than a waste of time for the student who puts off all his reading until the last few days before the exam.

Adequate preparation is obviously the first defense against examination jitters, but sometimes test situations elicit anxiety on the part of even the most able students. This is to be expected, for an important examination represents a potential danger to long-range goals, to feelings of self-worth, to the relationship with one's parents or spouse, and so on. It is the student who accepts a certain amount of anxiety as natural, while resolving to function well in spite of it, whose performance shows little impairment under the stress of the test situation. In fact, up to a certain level, anxiety may even improve performance.

Learning involves change—in our assumptions, ability to discriminate, feelings, attitudes, and behavior—and it can be a rewarding or difficult and even frightening experience. In general, cognitive learning, as distinguished from simple conditioning, takes place when:

1. The information is perceived as relevant to the purposes of the learner.

2. The learner has the requisite background and ability.

3. The learner participates actively in planning and carrying out the learning experience.

4. The learning involves the "whole" person—feelings as well as intellect.

5. The learner is able to learn through doing.

6. The learner receives immediate feedback concerning the progress he is making.

7. The learning leads to positive reinforcement.

8. The learning is extended, enriched, and used over time.

Conversely, significant learning tends to be blocked or impeded when the opposite of the above conditions prevail as well as when it is perceived as threatening to the learner's self-concept, when it involves making choices that are perceived as cutting off opportunities for learning in other areas, or when it requires too rapid changes in the learner's frame of reference. (Based in part on Rogers, 1969, and Morimoto, 1973.)

Extending and enriching the learning experience

Extending the new learning through study beyond the assignment and through explicitly tying it in with other subject areas—and real life situations, where possible—can contribute both to its meaningfulness and to one's interest and motivation. Often discussing new ideas with others and questioning unclear or doubtful points can help to put the material into perspective and make it easier to understand and remember.

Important here also is promoting positive transfer. Although psychologists generally assume that all of a person's experiences affect his later behavior in one way or another, very little is actually known about how previous learning affects the ease with which we can understand and master other related tasks later. The available evidence seems to indicate that some transfer will occur if there are identical elements in the two learning situations or if they can be understood in terms of the same general principles. Transfer of ideational learning is never automatic, however, but depends upon the learner's ability to perceive the points of similarity between the old and the new. There is always a danger, too, of seeing more similarity than actually exists, in which case previous learning may actually interfere with learning something new.

Feedback

In Chapter 7 we saw how an individual continuously modifies his adjustive responses on the basis of feedback—the return information he receives concerning the progress or outcome of his behavior. With respect to the learning process, feedback not only tells the learner whether he is proceeding satisfactorily but also serves as reward or punishment.

Knowledge of results

Many studies have shown that adequate feedback facilitates both motor and ideational learning. When the learner must work in the dark, with little or no information about how much he has accomplished or whether he is learning the right things, motivation, self-confidence, and learning efficiency all suffer. Also, he is very likely to learn errors which he will later have to unlearn. For these reasons, frequent short tests are often more useful than occasional long ones. One of the great advantages of teaching machines and computer-assisted learning is that immediate feedback is provided concerning the correctness of the student's responses.

Sometimes the learner is so ego-involved with test results that it is difficult for him to perceive feedback accurately or to put the information to good use. If he receives a poorer grade than he expected, for example, he may become defensive and concentrate on trying to prove that the test was unfair or the scoring invalid rather than on trying to understand where he went wrong and why. Even good test papers should be studied for the information they provide about the desired direction of learning.

In everyday life situations, the variables are so complex that it often becomes difficult to relate

is often helpful to obtain professional assistance if we seem to be having difficulty in utilizing feedback to make needed corrections in our learning strategy and behavior.

Reward and punishment

Feedback reinforces learning when the return information is a source of satisfaction. Such rewards as good grades, praise, increased understanding, and progress toward specific goals all tend to reinforce what has been learned and to motivate further learning.

Negative or divergent feedback, on the other hand, has the effect of punishment, but its

 I don't see anything in my life now as a mistake . . . whatever I did was the best I could do at the time, the choice I made at that time. If it turns out to be something bad, then it's something I needed at the time. Over the years, you look at the choices you made that didn't turn out well, and you try to see how you can do it better next time. So with the proper perception of the situation and of yourself, the next choices you make will be ones you can live more comfortably with.

feedback accurately to the learning situation. Thus a divorced person may be confident that he has learned enough from the failure of his first marriage to ensure his ability to establish a successful marital relationship the next time around. For example, he will not make the mistake of living near his in-laws. But he may not have perceived the *real* causes of his marital failure—perhaps the choice of a partner whose purposes and values differed from his—and so make the same mistake in his second marriage. Many persons continue to make the same mistakes due to their inability to accurately interpret the feedback information available to them. Both in college and in everyday life situations, it

results may vary. Poor grades, for example, spur some students to increased effort while making others discouraged and apathetic or else so defensive that they cannot look at their failure objectively as a learning experience. The effect of divergent feedback upon the learning process depends upon the learner's goals, his attitudes toward learning, the standards of performance he sets for himself, and his general feelings of adequacy or inadequacy. Thus we see again the key role of the individual's self-structure in shaping the entire course of learning. In the next section we shall have occasion to note its equally important influence on problem solving and decision making.

Problem solving and decision making

Life presents a never ending succession of problems to be solved and decisions to be made. In fact, as we saw in Chapter 7, the entire adjustive process is essentially one of perceiving and evaluating problems and then selecting the course of action that seems most likely to meet both the demands of the situation and the overall needs of the individual.

circumstances and in ourselves. As Glucksberg has pointed out:

"When faced with a problem it would be well to remember that difficulties often stem from habitual ways of doing things. It is often our particular experiences, our particular ways of looking at things, and our ways of thinking that make problems difficult" (1966, p. 26).

This can be readily seen in the case of the mother who still sees her married daughter as her "little girl" and creates no end of problems by treating her accordingly. On a group level,

 Something that I have learned and relearned over the years is that defining a problem helps reduce anxiety. Over and over again, when I've been anxious about, say, a situation coming up . . . I sometimes have had the feeling that there's a big blob of some bad thing inherent in the situation, that I'm going to have to face. And I puzzle over what is it that's really bugging me. If I just keep working on it, I've discovered that when I finally am able to figure out what I'm actually worried about, what's actually scaring me, then it's a great burden off . . . a lot of the anxiety goes away.

Much of our problem solving is habitual and automatic. Once we have found effective ways to handle the routine problems of everyday living, we devote little or no further thought to them. There are many situations, however, which require a fresh approach. In our work, in our relationships with other people, in our role as citizens, it is often necessary to analyze carefully the problems we encounter and work out the best solutions. Indeed, even some of the problems for which we *do* have habitual solutions merit a more thoughtful approach than we give them, for our habitual ways of seeing and doing things can become outmoded with changes in

too, we can see how changes in our society and the world situation may require that we make an "agonizing reappraisal" of our habitual ways of perceiving national and international problems.

Difficulties in defining and evaluating problems

Basic to the effective solution of any new problem is an accurate assessment. It is often our failure to see the dimensions of a problem—or even to recognize that a problem exists—that accounts for our failure to respond effectively. In

discussing the methods of science, Albert Einstein and Leopold Infeld wrote: "The formulation of a problem is often more essential than its solution" (1938, p. 95).

With the sources of information available to us, we should be able to find reasonably good solutions to most of our problems, but we are often thrown off the track by our inability to see a problem for what it really is. Our failure here may stem from several sources, among which are failure to obtain needed information, faulty assumptions, a tendency to oversimplify complex problems, a rigid mental set, a defensive orientation, and stress and emotion.

Inadequate information

Often we lack needed information about a particular problem, and it may be necessary to exert considerable time and effort to learn what the facts are—to become informed. Here the ability to find relevant and accurate sources of information is often crucial. Often the information we settle for is based on the viewpoint of some alleged "expert" or on a popularized version of the problem presented in the mass media. To further complicate matters we are faced with an "information explosion" which supplies us with a wide range of information, much of which is contradictory in nature; and we are also faced with the rapid obsolescence of information, so that information that seemed accurate a few months or years ago is now superseded by new scientific findings. In short, becoming and staying informed about given life problems is far from an easy task.

Faulty assumptions and attitudes

If false information is fed into an electronic computer, there is little probability that valid answers will come out. Similarly, our reasoning powers and "common sense" fail to provide us with good solutions to problems when we start

Much cloudy thinking can be avoided if we can remain alert to the following sources of error, which underlie many of the false premises from which we reason.

1. *Overgeneralization from limited experience.* If a person fails to consider whether his own experience has been typical or whether it has been broad enough to justify *any* broad conclusion, he may make sweeping generalizations which have no support in fact.

2. *Misapplying general rules.* If he fails to translate the abstract and general into the concrete and specific, a person may apply general principles—valid in themselves—to specific situations where they do not apply.

3. *Mistaking correlation for causation.* When two things go together, people often jump to the conclusion that one has caused the other. They may be entirely overlooking the operation of some other factor which is in fact responsible for the relationship.

4. *Failure to recognize multiplicity of causes.* Closely related to mistaking correlation for causation is attributing an event or situation to a single cause, when in fact a wide variety of factors are interacting to bring it about.

5. *Dichotomous (all-or-none) thinking.* In an effort to simplify problems, we often classify individuals or situations according to the extremes of a continuum. Thus a person may be seen as absolutely good or bad, right or wrong, honest or dishonest.

6. *Thinking in terms of stereo-types.* Stereotypes represent another type of oversimplification. A certain attitude of a group or of individual members in a group is abstracted and regarded as a primary characteristic of every member. Such stereotypes usually give us a false picture of the group as a whole and are even more misleading when we apply them to individuals, who may not fit the stereotype at all.

7. *Uncritical acceptance of majority opinion.* Another source of faulty reasoning is the naïve assumption that a viewpoint or concept accepted by other people must be right. Although one cannot dismiss majority opinion offhand, it is not uncommon for the majority of a group to hold views which are later shown to be invalid.

out with false premises. If we assume that marital success can be achieved without any real effort on our part, if we permit our desires to obscure the odds against us in a business venture, or if we assume that material possessions will automatically ensure a happy life, we are likely to encounter serious difficulties in dealing with problems in these areas. Any major inaccuracy in a person's frame of reference is a potential source of error in problem solving.

We have previously emphasized our propensity for perceiving and accepting information and ideas which are compatible with our existing assumptions and attitudes and for rejecting or distorting whatever is not. Faulty assumptions and attitudes tend to be self-perpetuating, although the setbacks of failure may, of course, cause us to revise some of them with time.

Oversimplification
In our earlier discussion of the processing of problems (Chapter 7), we noted our tendency to

simplify problems to make them more easily understandable. This is both necessary and desirable, providing we simplify the problem by delineating its key dimensions. Many problems are not as complicated as they first appear once we have gotten down to the essential elements.

Unfortunately, however, in the process of defining a problem, many people tend to oversimplify it. Thus we have all heard individuals offering easy solutions to problems ranging from improving international relationships to dealing with the opposite sex. Although their answers may appear persuasive at first glance, they are not valid because they disregard key facets that must be considered if an adequate solution is to be found.

Rigid mental set
Too often, efficiency in problem solving is impaired by the tendency to think there is only one way to look at a problem and only one possible solution for it. Implicit in a flexible mental set is

a questioning and critical attitude, which Berrien described in this way:

"It is a way of thinking characterized by a kind of disrespect for the old answers, the established rules, or the accepted principles. These are not held in reverence as the inevitable and final authority, but are accepted as currently useful generalizations which may at any time be sloughed or revised if new observations fail to support the generalizations. Ideally, there is a flexibility in thinking and a breadth of observation unrestricted by preconceived notions of what one ought to experience in any given situation" (1951, p. 45).

A rigid mental set is often the result of cultural biases. We fail to see the real dimensions of many problems because our perspective is limited by the cultural setting in which we live. We learn certain approved ways of perceiving and dealing with problems and are prone to think of these as the only "right" ways; if we are aware of other approaches at all, we consider them inferior or ridiculous. There is an old story of an American who ridiculed his Chinese friend for putting food upon the graves of his loved ones —a foolish custom, he pointed out, since the dead could not eat. Whereupon the Chinese friend replied that what the American said was true but that the custom was no more foolish than the American one of putting flowers on the graves of loved ones—for neither could the dead see or smell.

Often we are unaware of how much our various group affiliations influence the way we analyze and respond to problems. However, we can readily see the differences which may stem from membership in groups such as labor or management, North or South, and ghetto or suburban communities. Sometimes, of course, cultural biases are exaggerated by group pressures to conform to group-approved views.

Established ways of dealing with problems—whether originally worked out by the individual or learned from his associates—tend to be reinforced because they add to feelings of security and predictability. Also it requires less effort to handle problems in the same old ways than it does to reexamine them.

Defensive orientation

In previous chapters we have noted that an individual who feels threatened and insecure tends to be more concerned with protecting his feelings of adequacy than with coping with a problem. In a group discussion of a problem, for example, he may be intent on proving he is right and be unwilling to examine his own viewpoint critically or to look objectively at the facts of the matter. The individual whose behavior is directed primarily toward enhancing his feelings of adequacy and worth or toward protecting an inaccurate self-concept shows considerable resistance to accepting new information or to facing unpleasant problems. His problem-solving ability is also impaired by a tendency to rationalize away his errors—which, in turn, makes it difficult for him to learn from his mistakes.

The handling of problems in which we are ego-involved is often complicated by such a defensive orientation. For example, a parent

 Sometimes I can look at a situation and predict the outcome, because I compare that situation with others I've observed before. It makes my head get big when I tell people what's going to happen before it happens. But when I'm in the situation myself, I can't see it the same, and I can't pay attention to my own warnings. This is particularly true when I have done something wrong and don't want to admit it to myself.

usually finds it hard to understand or deal effectively with a delinquent child, for his identification with the child and his need for feelings of parental adequacy are likely to prevent him from approaching the problem with any objectivity.

Emotion and stress

We are often exhorted to "put aside" our emotions in order to think clearly and rationally. This is easier said than done, for not all of our emotional processes can be consciously controlled. Whether we like it or not, we cannot banish fear or hate or joy or anticipation simply by resolving to do so. And in dealing with many situations, we may not even recognize the fact that we *are* emotionally involved. We may *think* we are being perfectly objective in our approach to a family problem, for example, not realizing that our analysis of the situation is strongly colored by our complicated emotional relationships with parents or other family members. But even if it were possible to "put aside" our emotions when dealing with problems, it would not necessarily be desirable—for it seems essential to integrate intellect and affect if we are to function as whole human beings.

It is usually under conditions of severe stress that emotions have the most dramatic effects in distorting cognitive processes—making it difficult for us to think efficiently when we most need to do so. Fear may exaggerate the severity of the problem and generate an attitude of apprehension which paralyzes action; anger may lead to impulsive and ill-considered action; and anxiety may markedly restrict our ability to see problems clearly or to formulate alternative solutions. Indeed, severe stress of any kind narrows our perceptual field and causes our behavior to become rigid and stereotyped.

Preoccupation, worry, and conflict over serious problems can even impair our ability to solve relatively simple, routine problems. We tend to make mistakes that would be unimaginable under ordinary circumstances, and later marvel at how "stupid" we have been, asking ourselves, "How could I *ever* have done that?"

Some aids in problem solving

As the foregoing discussion suggests, competence in problem solving depends first of all upon personal maturity. Each of the formal aids to problem solving is limited in its usefulness if there are personality characteristics which make it difficult for the individual to look at his problems objectively or to admit the possibility of more than one solution. The individual who is relatively free of such handicaps, on the other hand, can improve his effectiveness in solving problems by applying various intellectual "strategies" such as those we shall discuss in the following pages. Used singly or in combination, they are valuable safeguards against the all too common errors imposed upon us by "common sense."

A basic strategy for problem solving

Whatever specific techniques we may rely upon in solving everyday problems, we can often improve our effectiveness by following a strategy that James Mursell (1951) called the W-E-D approach. The name is derived from the three basic steps in problem solving: (1) obtaining a comprehensive picture of the problem as a *whole;* (2) identifying the essential *elements* of the problem and ordering them in terms of their relevance to the overall picture; and (3) gathering and ordering the necessary *details* for completing the picture and putting a plan of action into effect.

Although it may occasionally be preferable to vary the order of these three steps, and in emergencies to abandon them altogether, the W-E-D approach represents a systematic and efficient strategy for evaluating and solving most everyday problems. The following example helps to illustrate the practical application of this approach: A large business corporation took over a smaller company which was losing money and placed one of its own top executives in charge. His first step was to undertake a careful and comprehensive study of the situation. He scrutinized accounting records, examined organizational charts, interviewed key personnel, and attempted to gain an overall picture of the new company and its potential role as part of the larger corporation. He listened, observed, and took no major action even though he was eager to get on with the needed reorganization. After a few weeks, however, he had spotted faulty pricing procedures and inadequate communication between departments as critical elements in the company's failure. With further study of the details involved in these two sources of trouble, he was soon able to make a few specific recommendations that overcame the problems without undermining the morale and security of the long-time employees.

These principles of problem solving are applicable to problems as diverse as getting married and climbing Mount Everest. When used by either an individual or a group, the W-E-D approach facilitates an efficient attack on the problem as a whole, acting as a safeguard against the all too common tendency to become bogged down in relatively unimportant details or particular facets of the problem.

Logic and semantics

Over two thousand years ago Aristotle developed a technique called the *syllogism* for testing whether a given conclusion or generalization follows legitimately from the premises on which it is based. Although we tend to think of logic as an artificial exercise for the intellect, actually we use syllogistic reasoning every day, though usually not the full form. The man who says "Women drivers!" to his wife in a derogatory tone is really saying:

All women are poor drivers.

You are a woman.

Therefore you are a poor driver.

Here the conclusion, although "logically" valid, is based upon a false premise, for all women are *not* poor drivers. This illustrates the greatest limitation of syllogistic reasoning: If we begin with a false assumption, we can never depend on our conclusion. Applying the devices of formal logic can help us with our problems, however, by forcing us to state our premises fully, so

that we can examine them objectively in order to determine whether they are valid.

Important to the effective use of logic are the techniques of *semantics*, the branch of linguistic science concerned with the relationship between words and the reality they are intended to represent. Words are symbols for objects and ideas; by using words we are able to refer to things which are not physically present. But when the meaning of words becomes distorted or imprecise, our thinking becomes cloudy, and we may be led to accept a distorted picture of reality. Semantic confusion is most readily illustrated in arguments where several people, using the same words, are actually talking about quite different things.

In semantic analysis there are three trouble spots to watch out for particularly. First, symbols often change with time. The word *liberal*, for example, has quite a different meaning today than it did forty years ago. Second, the same word may have quite different meanings for different individuals, especially if it is one that commonly arouses an emotional response, such as the word *sex*. Finally, words for abstract or general concepts can be misleading when applied to a concrete or specific situation unless their meaning in the particular instance is precisely defined. In different contexts the word *gentleman* may mean any male, an aristocrat, or a man whose inherent gentleness entitles him to be named such. Our ability to manipulate linguistic symbols can either facilitate or interfere with effective thought, depending upon how accurately our symbols represent the reality with which we must ultimately deal.

Help from experts

Reliance upon the advice of a qualified expert in a given field is one of the oldest known problem-solving methods; certainly, in a complicated culture such as ours, we would find it impossible to deal with many of our problems if we did not have experts to call upon. We depend upon the specialized skills and training of the doctor, the lawyer, the political economist, the electrician, the architect, and the television re-

pairman to supplement our own areas of knowledge. Indeed, one mark of intellectual competence is the ability to recognize the limitations of one's own experience and know *when* and *where* to turn for additional information and advice.

In seeking the help of experts, the individual need not forfeit responsibility for making his own decisions. He must first check his authorities carefully to determine by what right they *are* authorities. Often he must look not just to one expert but to several, to see if there is agreement among them. And he must determine for himself when he has adequate information on which to base a decision. Frequently, the value of an expert may lie in his ability to help the individual comprehend fully the dimensions of his problem and the variety of ways in which it might be dealt with.

Most people tend to be fairly critical in choosing their authorities in such well-defined fields

as medicine and law. But the same individual who insists on having the advice of the best lawyer in the city for help with his legal problems may take his personal problems to friends and relatives who are poorly qualified to give advice. In many cases, too, we mistake experience for wisdom. The new mother who consults the experienced mother of six children will not inevitably get sound advice on childrearing; indeed, the advice may be very bad. Another danger is that of accepting information or advice as valid because it comes from someone we like personally, from someone whose prestige is great in another field, or from a large and influential group.

Group problem solving

There is ample experimental evidence to indicate that some kinds of problems can best be solved by people working as a group rather than individually. Anyone who has had the experience of participating in an effective committee has witnessed the sharing of ideas and experiences, noticed how the faulty logic of one member was checked by the thinking of others, recognized how creative thinking was sparked by the interchange of ideas, and finally seen a solution or plan of action developed which successfully embodied ideas from several different persons.

Every experience of working with a group is not necessarily a happy one, however. Against the saying that "Two heads are better than one," we must match another: "Too many cooks spoil the broth." Sometimes group problem solving is time-wasting and inefficient and frustrates the initiative of individual members. The success of many groups in solving problems which might otherwise defy solution should not obscure the fact that some types of problems can best be handled by individuals.

When group strategy is indicated, the following principles should be considered if the group is to function effectively:

1. The individuals participating should be directly concerned with the problem and prepared with enough background information to discuss it intelligently.

2. Participants should be task-oriented rather than ego-oriented—primarily concerned with solving the problem rather than promoting their own ideas or influence.

3. The entire problem should be clearly reviewed before an attempt is made to attack it.

4. The leader or leaders of the group should see that each member is given the opportunity to express his views and that the group has ample time to evaluate various suggestions before arriving at a final conclusion.

5. The group should formulate its conclusion precisely and develop a plan for putting it into operation. If a solution has not been agreed upon, the group should make specific recommendations for a further attack on the problem.

Many problems are solved in a group setting. When proper safeguards are employed against inefficiency and the stifling of individual initiative, group strategy—by pooling the creative and problem-solving resources of many individuals—can often achieve remarkable results.

Some aids in decision making

Careful and systematic analysis of a problem does not automatically indicate the action we should take. Often we must choose between two or more solutions which seem to be about equally good in terms of the risks they involve, the satisfactions they promise, and the amount of time and effort they demand. Sometimes our choice is not even between two good alternatives but between the lesser of two evils. Usually in choosing one line of action we must forego the benefits that might accrue from another. And because we cannot control all relevant variables or anticipate chance factors, we can never be entirely sure that a decision will work out as we think it will.

In spite of the difficulties inherent in making decisions, however, we must continually choose how to act—or else be acted *upon*. Recognizing that occasional failures are inevitable, we can substantially improve our odds for success by following the general principles outlined below.

Avoiding impulsive action
Acting in haste is an excuse we hear offered to explain mistakes ranging from buying inferior merchandise to quitting a job at the first sign

 When I have a problem where there's a decision to make, I'm not comfortable till it's been made. Since I tend to do this pretty fast, it's not always the best solution to the problem. But I make the decision, one way or another, right away—even if I end up having to change it.

of difficulty. Whenever snap judgments are made—especially in areas where the individual has little knowledge and experience—the likelihood of error is great. Sometimes, of course, a poor decision is of relatively little consequence, and we might rather gamble on an easy choice than waste the time and effort required for evaluating alternate possibilities. But if the decision is an important one that will have long-range effects, it is wise to examine it carefully and often to "live with it" for a time before committing oneself to action. The high percentage of failures of impulsive marriages is a matter of record.

Accepting a reasonable
level of satisfaction

Perhaps as dangerous as impulsive action on major decisions is the inability to act until an "ideal" solution can be found. The person who always insists upon maximum satisfactions often becomes the victim of vacillation and indecision. Even if a superior solution is ultimately found, it may not justify the tremendous cost in anxiety and strain.

Besides increasing the difficulty and strain of decision making, perfectionism also tends to create dissatisfaction with choices after they have been made. The man who has delayed marriage until he found a woman who seemed ideal in every respect may be upset by minor irritations in his marriage that another person would consider inconsequential.

When it comes to problems that are routine or unimportant from a long-range point of view, perfectionism has even less to recommend it. The person who debates interminably over what to wear, how to spend the evening, what restaurant to go to, or even what car to buy is wasting more time and energy than any of these decisions justifies.

Reducing the negative
aspects of choice

Most decisions involve an element of conflict. We are aware that our choices have negative as well as positive aspects, and as a result we both fear and look forward to the action we are about to undertake. The balancing of plus and minus factors is complicated, as we saw in Chapter 5, by the fact that dread increases more sharply than positive feelings as the point of no return gets closer.

The conflict is most severe when there is approximate equality of strength between approach and avoidance tendencies. We have seen, for example (page 98), that the individual who is about equally torn between the desire to marry and fear of "losing his freedom" is likely to experience severe conflict as the wedding date nears. The balance can be tilted in the direction of marriage either by building up the positive aspects of the choice or by reducing the negative ones. Strengthening the approach gradient, however, is usually a less satisfactory way to resolve conflict than is reducing the avoidance gradient. Among the techniques by which an individual can minimize the negative aspects of a choice are the following:

1. He can clarify his picture of the actual dangers involved in his decision, thus eliminating vague anxiety over the unknown.

2. He can build up the competencies that will enable him to cope with the foreseeable trouble spots. For example, adequate vocational preparation increases the probability of success in a challenging job; the development of social competencies will reduce the fear of difficult but desired new relationships.

3. He can put the decision into proper perspective. Many decisions which seem momentous at the time are actually of such small significance in terms of long-range consequences that even if they are wrong choices nothing much is lost. Recognizing this can reduce the fear involved in committing oneself to one alternative or the other.

Being prepared to
back up a decision

Although it is often foolish to maintain an obviously wrong decision, there are many times when decisions are rescinded without being put to a fair test. Usually this follows from the failure really to commit oneself to the choice made. The indecisiveness that may have preceded the decision is carried over after the decision is put into effect.

Many marriages fail because one of the partners withdraws at the first sign of difficulty. But in any human relationship difficulties may arise and new adjustments may be required. A general who commits his forces to a certain battle area may modify his plan of attack according to how circumstances develop, but while there is a reasonable chance for success he will not cut and run.

Maintaining a reserve of resources

Rarely is it advisable to venture everything on any one decision. " 'Tis the part of a wise man," said Cervantes, "to keep himself today for tomorrow, and not venture all his eggs in one basket." Conservation of resources is necessary if, in the event of failure, one is to be assured of a second chance.

Second chances sometimes are no more than the opportunity to make a first decision finally work by calling on available reserves. A man who begins his business on a small, experimental basis may not become a millionaire overnight, but neither need he become bankrupt. He is more likely to spot trouble in certain areas of operation and make changes that will put his business on a more solid foundation; or if the first venture fails, he can put other resources into a more successful attempt. Similarly, the young man or woman who does not summarily abandon his or her education when love beckons, but either postpones marriage or works out an arrangement for combining it with further schooling, is maintaining reserves that considerably reduce the risk of failure. Even the all-out emotional expenditure demanded in a relationship like marriage should be backed up with reserves in the form of developing one's interests and potentials as an individual.

Developing clear-cut values as guides

Since the solution of most problems permits considerable choice, it is obvious that the person who has a clear sense of identity, well-defined goals, and an adequate system of values will have an easier time making decisions and investing himself wholeheartedly in them than the person who is not sure who he is, where he wants to go, or what is really important to him. The alternative to being guided by one's own values is to rely upon the advice and values of others. The person who follows the latter course often finds himself making decisions which are inconsistent not only with each other but with his concept of himself. The importance of developing a personalized value system will be further discussed in Chapter 17.

Minimizing the effects of faulty decisions

A certain percentage of decisions must be expected to go wrong because of human limitations and chance factors which cannot be controlled. When failure comes, it is worth trying to analyze why, perhaps with the help of someone who can be more objective than we, so that we will not repeat the same mistake. The tendency to deny that a mistake has been made, or to rationalize mistakes by decrying unfavorable circumstances, or to project blame for them onto other people is a major stumbling block to the development of increased competence in making choices.

Often it is possible to salvage a good deal from a faulty decision. If, after three or four years of premedical training, a young man decides that his choice of a medical career was a mistake, he may still, after careful investigation and reliable vocational counseling, be able to use his education to good advantage in a profession not completely alien to medicine—perhaps as a biologist, a laboratory technician, or a veterinarian. After the failure of a marriage, professional help is often valuable in helping everyone concerned make the best of the changed situation, especially if children are involved. Most of us have far more inner strength than we realize and despite setbacks can usually rally our hopes and resources for a new assault on our goals.

Life can be viewed as a series of problem

THE ESCAPE FROM
FREEDOM AND DECISION MAKING

Becoming an autonomous person and making the major decisions that shape the course of one's life require courage—particularly when one cannot entirely predict the outcomes of given decisions but must nevertheless accept responsibility for the consequences. Many people seek escape from freedom for self-direction and the shaping of their own lives through blind conformity to the dictates of some external source of authority, such as an autocratic political philosophy, a highly systematized religion, a rigidly defined life style, or simply established customs, mores, and traditions. While they may still retain a sense of decision making and self-direction, they have in effect abandoned inner sources of direction for outer ones which determine the course of their lives.

situations and choice points—some of them of little importance, others of crucial and lasting importance. It is through learning to deal with the simpler problems and choices that we prepare ourselves for the more complex ones. Increasingly, as we go along, the choices open to us at a given time depend on how well we have solved the problems that came before and how wisely we have acted at each preceding choice point.

Creative thinking

Creative thinking—thinking which produces new methods, new concepts, new understandings, new inventions, new works of art—is at the very root of human progress. The history of civilization is the history of humans' creative

triumphs, from learning to make fire to investigating outer space. In our contemporary world, it is apparent that we need people who are capable of coming up with creative and appropriate solutions to highly complex problems—including problems centering around ecological violations, group prejudice and discrimination, economic crises, the increasing gap between the "have" and "have-not" countries, accelerating social change, and the ever present threat of thermonuclear war.

In a general sense, all problem solving is creative; each problem is unique in certain respects, and each solution requires the integration of ideas into new and meaningful patterns. On another level, creativity may manifest itself in the speculations of the philosopher and the hypotheses of the scientist; on still another, in the works of the painter, the sculptor, the composer, the novelist, and the poet. On the everyday level, there is the creative thinking that changes one's own personality. It can produce insights into some phase of oneself or one's world which one has not seen before—insights which may drastically alter one's assumptions, motives, and ways of behaving. In every case and at every level, creativity brings into existence something that is new and of some value.

The process of
creative thinking

On the basis of his comprehensive investigations of creativity, MacKinnon came to the conclusion that true creativeness, whether it takes place in a few moments or over the span of several years, must fulfill at least three conditions:

"It involves a response or an idea that is novel or at the very least statistically infrequent. But novelty or originality of thought or action, while a necessary aspect of creativity, is not sufficient. If a response is to lay claim to being a part of the creative process, it must to some extent be adaptive to, or of, reality. It must serve to solve a problem, fit a situation, or accomplish some recognizable goal. And, thirdly, true creativeness

 One of my great pleasures in teaching art is to watch the creative processes and growth of my students. We have periodic art exhibits for the student body and the community, and often individual students receive a great deal of praise, or I am complimented on their work. That's very nice, to have someone appreciate something you have worked hard on. But even more exciting, to me, is the process of doing it. That's something you can't always judge from looking just at the result.

453 / Creative thinking

In my profession, in building things—building things that have to work—you find that what's really important is simplicity. That's the most important thing, and achieving that is very creative work.

I've got lines to some poems I've never finished, that I thought I might use later. I used to get pretty uptight about not finishing everything I started, but now I know when something just isn't coming—and I really worked on it—I know to stop. When I feel like I'm dry. It's not good to keep pushing because you think you should finish—that would inhibit my thinking whenever I started something new. And sometimes you can go back and make something new out of an old line, or get other ideas from it.

involves a sustaining of the original insight, an evaluation and elaboration of it, a developing of it to the full" (1962, p. 485).

Although not all investigators would agree completely with MacKinnon's view of creativity, it serves as a useful starting point for our discussion of the process of creative thinking.

The cognitive processes involved
Guilford (1967) has distinguished three kinds of productive thinking: *deductive* thinking, in which an inference or conclusion is deduced logically from information on hand; *inductive* thinking, in which the individual goes beyond the present information, adding new elements that are not inherent in the known facts; and *evaluative* thinking, in which the individual judges the suitability or appropriateness of an idea. All three may be used in creative thinking. Deductive thinking is creative when the individual sees new relationships that he has not noticed before. Most often, however, creativity requires inductive and evaluative thinking. The individual supplies new formulations or new hypotheses and imagines the possible conse-

quences of untried solutions. Then, as he critically evaluates his work, he may make revisions and changes before it is shaped into final, usable form.

The sequence of events
Psychologists have long been intrigued with the sequence of events involved in the birth of a new idea or the solution to a problem. In dealing with new and complex problems, five steps ordinarily seem to occur:

1. *Orientation:* pointing up and delineating the dimensions of the problem.
2. *Preparation:* saturating the mind with available information that seems relevant to the problem.
3. *Incubation:* a "time-out" in which the problem is not worked on consciously, though presumably it continues to be thought about even during sleep.
4. *Illumination:* the point at which the solution occurs to the thinker, often described as an "aha!" experience.
5. *Verification:* the critical and often empirical evaluation of the solution.

These steps are not always as clear-cut as such a listing implies. In dealing with a complex problem, for example, there may be many partial illuminations, testings, further incubations, and further illuminations and verifications before the solution is complete.

Characteristics of creative thinkers

Psychologists have devoted considerable attention to the study of creative persons in an attempt to clarify the relationship between given personality traits and creative thinking.

outer stimuli, and helped to foster a wide range of interests.

3. *Independence in attitudes and social behavior.* For an individual to be himself and actualize his creative potentials he must possess sufficient autonomy from social convention and pressures. Such autonomy also seems to foster a strong sense of self-identity, acceptance, and awareness of personal goals.

While superior intelligence is helpful, this does not mean "super-intelligence"; nor does it mean that those who are above average in intelligence are necessarily creative. In a study of creativity and intelligence in children's thinking, for example, Wallach and Kogan (1967)

 I am interested in a student who can get excited about some kind of a project and carry it through —and gain something from it. It's very hard to measure that from a test. Last semester I had some students who made a film—and it was marvelous. Technically maybe it wasn't, but they were thrilled with it. Now they were not what you would call "A" students, they were probably "C" students, but something about it excited them, captured them.

In an extensive review of research studies in this area, Dellas and Gaier concluded that "despite differences in age, cultural background, area of operation or eminence, a particular consistent constellation of psychological traits emerges" (1970, p. 55). These traits were found to fall into four categories:

1. *Cognitive capacities.* Included here were an above-average level of intelligence, ideational fluency, discriminating observations, superior memory, ability to synthesize disparate ideas, cognitive flexibility, and the production of unusual but appropriate ideas.

2. *Relative lack of self-defensiveness.* This tended to make the repression of "immoral" thoughts and impulses unnecessary, accorded fuller access to conscious and unconscious experience, led to greater openness to inner and

found motivation and cognitive style to be more important determinants of creativity than intelligence.

Interestingly enough, creative thinking does not appear to correlate highly with divergent thinking, which still remains one of the most popular ways of measuring it; nor does it correlate highly with academic achievement (Dellas & Gaier, 1970; Nicholls, 1972; MacKinnon, 1964). In his study of creative architects, MacKinnon (1964) found that they earned about a B average in college, although they were capable of A performance when a course caught their interest. Roe (1953), in dealing with a number of leading artists and scientists in several different fields, found only one trait that was shared by all: the willingness to work long and hard. Of course, she assumed a basic minimum of intelligence, ability, and other traits essential to their particular area of endeavor.

It has long been popular to think of "creative genius" as being closely related to maladjustment and mental disorders. Indeed, history has recorded many highly creative persons who suffered from serious personal problems. The names of Van Gogh, Chopin, Poe, and others come readily to mind. At one time, the psychoanalytic viewpoint considered creativity to be a form of neurosis in which blocked instinctual drives are diverted into creative activities; and more recently Barron (1972), in a study of 56 professional writers, found them to have high ego strength while at the same time tending to manifest high scores on scales designed to measure psychotic-like characteristics. In general, however, it would appear that serious maladjustment is a handicap to creativity—that the individual may be creative despite his emotional difficulties but probably not as creative as he would have been were he a better integrated and more effective person.

Fostering creative thinking

How can we develop a Shakespeare, a Beethoven, or an Einstein? Equally important, how can we develop the creative potential of the average person? While we can recognize creativity and describe the characteristics of creative thinkers, it is much more difficult to specify the conditions necessary for the development of creativity. In fact, psychology does not have an answer to the first question; and we only have some promising leads to offer in answer to the second. In the present section we shall focus briefly on three of these leads which appear well worth pursuing.

Characteristics which foster creative thinking

We have noted some of the cognitive, motivational, and other characteristics evidenced by creative people. While most of these characteristics have received some attention, the greatest emphasis appears to be placed on fostering

openness to new experience. Such openness is the exact opposite of defensiveness in which new experiences which are incompatible or threatening to existing self-structure are denied admission to awareness or permitted admission only in distorted form. Openness to new experience implies a tolerance for conflict and ambiguity, a lack of rigidity in thinking, and a rejection of the notion that one has all the answers. Perhaps it is reasonably accurate to conclude that human progress has always depended most on those who have been open to new ideas, who have refused to be satisfied with habitual ways of thinking and acting, and who have had the courage to break with tradition.

In a broader context, the same conditions which appear to foster personal growth and self-actualization also appear to foster creativity. As Maslow expressed it:

"My feeling is that the concept of creativeness and the concept of the healthy, self-actualizing, fully human person seem to be coming closer and closer together, and may perhaps turn out to be the same thing" (1971a, p. 57).

In Chapter 14, we dealt with encounter groups and related methods for fostering openness to experience and other aspects of personal growth—which in turn tend to foster creativity on the part of the individual.

Specific instruction in creative thinking

In the past it was commonly assumed that creative thinking was some mysterious ability which the individual was "born with," and that some people were blessed with a high degree of creativity—or creative genius—while others evidenced little or none.

More recently, however, research studies have pointed to the potential usefulness of actual instruction in creative thinking to help the individual actualize his creative potential. Stratton and Brown (1972), for example, examined the possibility of improving creative thinking in a group of 180 college students. Their method involved formal training utilizing a problem-solving model. Essentially, the students were taught to: (a) formulate criteria for evaluating

Throughout recorded history, people have sought out "wise men" or "wise ones" for guidance. Such wise ones—whether men or women—have usually been respected and accorded high status in the group.

Today we still think of the culmination of intellectual competence as the achievement of wisdom, which we may define as the ability to make valid decisions—decisions which are most likely to have constructive consequences—when confronted with a choice of alternative goals and means. In this view, wisdom requires accurate information and the ability to perceive alternatives, to foresee the probable outcomes of given alternatives, and to weigh these outcomes in the light of an adequate value system. Often, of course, wisdom requires creative thinking and innovative solutions to problems.

Wisdom is often equated with *common sense,* which refers to the ability to make sound, practical decisions on the basis of the information at hand. Unfortunately, however, the information at hand is often inadequate; and as a consequence, the conclusions or decisions based upon it are invalid. At one time, for example, common sense dictated the conclusion that the world

was flat, and it was considered "non-sense" to conclude otherwise. Thus Columbus was subjected to years of ridicule and laughter when he said that the world was round. Similarly, people laughed in derision when the Wright brothers said that human beings could fly. Yet the decisions based upon these seemingly nonsensical conclusions have profoundly affected our lives.

In no way, however, do we intend to minimize the importance of common sense. When citizen Tom Paine wished to incite his countrymen, for example, he titled his now famous pamphlet *Common Sense;* and Oliver Wendell Holmes is reputed to have said that "science is a first-rate piece of furniture for a man's upper chamber, if he has common sense on the ground floor." Perhaps it would be fair to state that common sense is essential to wisdom but it is not sufficient. For the wise person is also the informed person. In this sense—and possibly also in the sense that wisdom is often brought to bear on far more complex problems than common sense per se—wisdom lies one important step beyond common sense.

Of course, no one can completely foresee the future or the consequences of given choices.

Yet the future is rarely so capricious as to be totally unpredictable; and even "a little wisdom" can help to ensure constructive choices, to avoid tragic mistakes, and to salvage what can be salvaged when mistakes or unforeseen disasters do occur. Thus it is not surprising that most of us place a very high value indeed on the quality of wisdom.

It is a curious fact that while our educational system has shown remarkable ingenuity in the acquisition and transmission of information, it has done very little to ensure that such information would be transmuted into the quality called wisdom. Yet there is every reason to believe that wisdom is not some gift with which we are blessed but is learned like other competencies. Thus it would seem eminently desirable to focus both research and educational attention on the problem of developing "wise persons." For wisdom is an extremely important quality for each of us if we are to apply the information we acquire in coping effectively with the problems of living and achieving a meaningful and fulfilling life; and the development of wise persons seems equally important for the maintenance and progress of our society.

possible solutions to a problem; (b) make comparisons between the information at their disposal and the criteria; and (c) evaluate completed solutions in terms of the criteria they had established. It was found that the students showed improvement in all stages of problem solving, including: limiting the use of unprofitable information, eliminating inferior solutions, and fostering innovative and appropriate solutions.

A favorable social environment

In the past, the tendency has been to concentrate on the qualities of highly creative persons and to ignore the importance of the social setting. Yet as historians have pointed out, some periods and some societies have fostered creativity while others have not. In medieval Europe, for example, freedom of thought and scientific inquiry were suppressed, while in Renaissance Italy the time was ripe for a great flourishing of the arts. In modern totalitarian countries, creativity in the sciences tends to be fostered, while that in the arts—at least in some areas, such as literature—tends to be suppressed. In the United States, we have tended to foster creativity in the sciences to a greater extent than in the arts; but we seem to be beginning to place strong emphasis upon creativity in the arts as well.

Freedom to learn and think as well as social stimulation and reinforcement are highly important environmental conditions in fostering the development of creative thinkers. In an early study, Maltzman (1960) demonstrated that if subjects were reinforced for making creative responses, they showed more creative behavior. Later studies have supported these early research findings. For example, Dutton (1972) concluded that creative people require special conditions—including special privileges—if their creative potential is to be properly utilized.

In concluding this chapter it seems relevant to look ahead to the future role of education in fostering intellectual competence, including creativity. McLuhan and Leonard have offered the following prediction:

"We are only beginning to realize what a tiny slice of human possibilities we now educate. In fragmenting all of existence, Western civilization hit upon one aspect, the literate and rational, to develop at the expense of the rest. Along with this went a lopsided development of one of the senses, the visual. Such personal and sensory specialization was useful in a mechanical age, but is fast becoming outmoded. Education will be more concerned with training the senses and perceptions than with stuffing brains. And this will be at no loss for the 'intellect.' . . .

"The student of the future will truly be an explorer . . . who ranges through the new educational world" (1967, p. 25).

 Summary and a look ahead

In this chapter we examined some of the key factors in effective learning, problem solving and decision making, and creative thinking.

Among the important factors in learning and retention are the individual's previous learning and resources, his motivation, frame of reference, and personal maturity. In addition, the characteristics of the task and the task environment are important elements in determining how to approach a learning situation. Learning and retention are aided by a learning strategy which (1) utilizes the best available facilities and resources; (2) builds background and motivation; (3) plans the learning experience; and (4) extends and enriches the learning experience. As we saw, feedback and its effective use is of crucial importance in effective learning.

Common difficulties in problem solving include lack of adequate information, faulty assumptions, oversimplification, rigidity, defensiveness, and emotional involvement. Useful aids in problem solving are logic and semantics, help from experts, group problem solving, and the W-E-D approach as a basic strategy. Successful decision making usually involves avoiding impulsive actions, accepting a reasonable level of satisfaction, reducing the negative aspects of the situation, being prepared to back up decisions, maintaining a reserve of resources, and developing clear-cut values as guides.

Creative thinking is often viewed as an innovation which is adaptive to reality and in which the original insight is worked out or elaborated. Creative thinking usually involves evaluative thinking as well as inductive and/or deductive thinking. In creative thinking, the following steps seem to occur: orientation, preparation, incubation, illumination, and verification. Assuming a basic minimum of intelligence and ability, it may be that the only personality trait creative people share in common is the willingness to work long and hard. Creativity is fostered by openness to new experience and social encouragement of innovation.

In the chapter which follows, we shall see the close relationship between intellectual competence and effective emotional experiencing.

16

Effective Emotional Experiencing

Emotional expression and full human functioning
Dealing with potentially troublesome emotions

The affective, or emotional, aspects of life are a dimension of human experiencing welcomed by many and ignored or regretted by others—an aspect capable of adding richness and meaning to life or capable of causing confusion and suffering. Successful, mature human functioning requires coming to terms with the affective side of living. Because nearly all of our human activities and relationships, our thoughts, dreams, and actions elicit feelings, it is important for the person to be able to find a balance between the richness and information imparted by feelings and the potential disruptions they may entail. Throughout our lives we must learn to be accurate and perceptive in the labeling of emotions, to live with them but not be lived *by* them, to experience and express feelings appropriate in kind and degree to the situation, and to be accessible to a range and variety of feelings. Needless to say, there are many kinds of dysfunctions in the emotional sphere of living— inaccurate labels, feelings too strong or not strong enough, feelings too transitory or too persistent, defenses that prohibit the experiencing of certain feelings or cause them to be experienced or expressed indirectly, feelings of anxiety or guilt over the experiencing of certain emotions, and many other problems. In short, the achievement of adaptive and effective emotional experiencing is a difficult and demanding task.

In this chapter we shall explore some psychological aspects of emotional life: the contribution of feelings to full human functioning, some dimensions of affective experience, and a few particular emotions which most people discover are problems from time to time.

Emotional expression and full human functioning

In order to understand more fully the realm of emotional expression and its importance to full human functioning, we shall investigate several specific aspects of emotional reactions— including various concepts of what emotions

 People who are satisfied with what they're doing, people who accept themselves for what they are, they're healthy. People who are in trouble are people with someone sitting inside them someplace saying, 'You're not doing what you ought to do.'

are, human differences in emotional patterns, how emotions relate to personal growth, and the necessary balance of expression and control of emotions.

What are emotions?

Emotions are certain affective states of consciousness, usually accompanied by physiological changes and outward manifestations. They can be measured physiologically, studied cross-culturally, observed behaviorally, and subjected to all manner of scientific exploration. Yet such information hardly does justice to the wealth of meaning and significance of emotional expression. What are some other ways of understanding emotions which are congruent with our actual human experiences?

Emotions as energizers
To have no "feelings" is to be, quite literally, unconscious or dead. Metaphorically, to be "alive" is to feel, to experience, to be responsive, to tingle, to change, and to act. To be alive is to be affected by events and to be mobilized for response. This is especially clear in anger (mobilization for attack), fear (mobilization for escape), excitement (mobilization for action), and love (mobilization to approach and enjoy).

To be unresponsive to the information of one's emotions makes one more machinelike than human. Emotions add vitality to living.

Emotions as messengers
It is no accident that the word "feeling" is used both for sensation and emotion. Through both the information of our senses and our emotions, we know where and how we are with respect to our world, both inner and outer. Emotions provide basic information which helps us to interpret our situations. For example, to an individual the experience of the emotion anger means that he is being blocked, attacked, or frustrated. Fear means that he is being threatened. Pain means that something is wrong inside him. Sadness and grief tell him that he is experiencing loss.

In this sense, there are not good emotions and bad emotions. Rather, feelings are information, and we know ourselves and understand our environment by attending to them.

Emotions as language
Emotions communicate meanings between individuals. In some cases, they are a primary medium of communication. For example, intimate relationships are maintained by the shar-

ing of feelings; if feelings are not shared, there is no true intimacy. Or if contrived or insincere feelings are shared, there is a violation of the intimacy.

Many of our emotional experiences and expressions constitute a universal language which all people understand and share. Researcher Paul Ekman (1973) and his colleagues have found, for example, that the facial expressions in response to certain emotions—such as fear, disgust, sadness, and anger—are recognized and labeled the same in many cultures.

Emotions as indicators of well-being
One major source of our knowledge of fulfillment is our emotions. We seek health, and know it when we feel well. We seek peace, and experience it in our calmness. We aspire after beauty or illumination and know by our ecstasy that we have found it. Without the information provided by our emotions, an enormously significant source of enjoyment and sense of fulfillment would be lacking.

Patterns of emotional experience

Although we often assume that other people "feel about the same way we do," there is considerable evidence that such is not the case. We seem to differ greatly in the depth and range of our feelings, in our moods, and in the proportion of our positive and negative feelings.

Intensity of feeling
Some people apparently feel great intensities of emotion; they react to the ups and downs of living with intense joy, intense disappointment, and intense concern. Others, whether from constitutional predisposition or defensive learning, are not easily stirred to either enthusiasm or distress but seem to be insulated from any strong feelings. Most of us are somewhere in between.

Effective emotional experiencing would seem to require sufficient depth of feeling to allow active, vigorous, healthy participation in living. Although wide differences in emotionalism

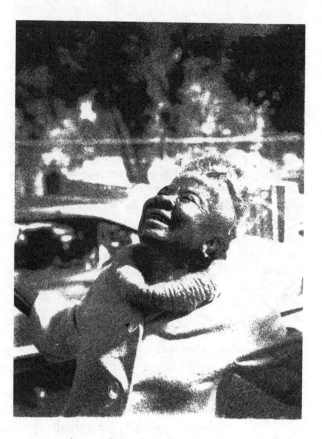

seem to be within the normal range, the extremes at either end are unadaptive. Overreaction to every minor situation squanders the individual's resources; conversely, a very shallow reaction to a major situation usually indicates a lack of normal depth, richness, and meaning in emotional experience.

In terms of intensity, emotions may be described as *mild, strong,* or *disintegrative.* Interestingly enough, different intensities of emotion are apparently related to quite different physiological processes.

With *mild* emotion there is increased alertness, a focusing of attention on meaning-producing factors in the situation, and a slight increase in tension, accompanied by feelings of being "pepped up" and of having increased vigor. Even negative emotions, such as fear and anger, may be experienced as pleasant when they occur in mild form and when the individual believes he has control over the situation and can terminate it if he wishes (Berlyne, 1967).

This is readily illustrated by the negative emotions we often experience in watching sporting events or television and movie dramas. In fact, if such events are not emotion-arousing, we are likely to find them dull.

Strong emotions present a quite different picture. In strong active emotions there is an emergency mobilization of bodily resources for immediate, more or less violent action, and the stepping up of physiological processes is both more selective and more extensive. Processes related to digestion are suspended and the mouth becomes dry, whereas heartbeat, blood pressure, respiration, and adrenaline production are all increased. The capillaries along the alimentary canal constrict, while those in the brain and the large muscles enlarge for better circulation. Red blood cells from the spleen and sugar from the liver are released into the blood. Even the factor that induces blood clotting in injuries is increased—just in case. In strong depressive

produces effects somewhat similar to hypnosis, the soldier could "relive" his combat experience and discharge some of his overwhelming fear and anxiety:

"The terror exhibited in the moments of supreme danger, such as at the imminent explosion of shells, the death of a friend before the patient's eyes, the absence of cover under a heavy dive bombing attack is electrifying to watch. The body becomes increasingly tense and rigid; the eyes widen and the pupils dilate, while the skin becomes covered with fine perspiration. The hands move about convulsively, seeking a weapon, or a friend to share the danger. The breathing becomes incredibly rapid and shallow. The intensity of the emotion sometimes becomes more than they can bear; and frequently at the height of the reaction, there is a collapse and the patient falls back in bed and remains quiet for a few minutes, usually to resume the story at a more neutral point" (Grinker & Spiegel, 1945b, p. 80).

 I think as I grow older my emotions are becoming a lot more even, but when I was younger I had a tremendously wide range of emotions. My feelings were really intense, and I had great trouble controlling them.

emotions like grief, no action is usually called for, and action potentials are restricted accordingly: pulse rate, blood pressure, and respiration are all depressed.

In addition to our mild and strong emotions, both of which may be normal and healthy, we may experience disintegrative emotions. These may be the outgrowth of normal emergency emotions too long continued, or they may be precipitated by overwhelming stress. In such circumstances, as we noted in Chapter 8, even a person normally considered stable may become mentally disturbed.

The intensity of disintegrative emotions is well illustrated by observations of soldiers who had suffered combat exhaustion in World War II and were later given sodium-pentothal interviews. Under the influence of this drug, which

Range of feeling

Human beings have the potential for experiencing a tremendous variety of emotions, from the most intense elation to the depths of depression, from the greatest happiness to the greatest sorrow, from deep and enduring love to lasting hatred.

We all tend to experience unpleasant emotions when our strivings are blocked or our values threatened and pleasant ones when we achieve our goals or anticipate doing so or when we receive confirmation of our values. Thus the events that can lead to pleasant and unpleasant emotions are as varied as our strivings and interests. And of course, the more self-involved we are in a situation or activity, the greater its emotion-arousing potential for us.

Despite their great potential, some people

seem to experience a rather limited range of emotions—often with a preponderance of negative emotions such as fear and anger or hostility—while others appear to experience a much wider range of emotions and sentiments—often with subtle nuances and fine shades of feeling. Typically, the failure to develop a full repertoire of emotions with appropriate intensity and depth seems to result from personal immaturity, faulty attitudes, or defenses against emotional involvement. Such a failure—as in the case of an individual who lacks a sense of humor or is incapable of love for someone else—may seriously limit the richness and meaningfulness of one's life.

somewhat independent of external events, though the length of the cycle and the difference between crest and trough are individual matters. For example, many women experience fairly regular mood changes related to menstrual cycle and levels of hormones (Ivey & Bardwick, 1968; Reynolds, 1969). People often find it interesting to keep a record of their moods every morning for a few weeks or months to see if they can detect a regular pattern.

Positive or negative orientation

Both positive and negative emotions are normal, healthy reactions to certain types of situations.

The only way you can be happy is if you're more positive than negative about things. Negative people have got to be the most unhappy people in the world. Of course you can be too positive, ridiculously positive, but unless you think things are always going to be better, there's no excuse for being around. Because if you think they're always going to be worse, why are you bothering?

In addition to emotional responses to particular events, we also experience *moods*—feeling states lasting hours or even days. Lorr, Daston, and Smith (1967) have delineated five mood states: vigor-activity, tension-anxiety, anger-hostility, fatigue-inertia, and depression. Such mood states color our perceptions and provide a background for whatever activity is going on. We have probably all had the experience of being in a bad mood and finding that molehills looked like mountains or of being in a good mood and sailing through a situation that normally would upset us.

The wide fluctuations of the manic-depressive are only a more extreme example of the fluctuations in mood that seem to be typical for the human species. For most of us, moods tend to fluctuate through a fairly predictable cycle that is

We all experience some of both, and the person who feels he should have only positive feelings is making unrealistic demands on himself. Yet a preponderance of negative feelings is unhealthy and maladjustive. Negative feelings indicate that the individual feels thwarted or threatened in some way, and such a perception, as we have already seen, tends to induce defense-oriented behavior. Furthermore, the person who is chronically fearful or resentful is constantly on the lookout for new dangers and thus tends to see only what confirms his worries and fears. Such a person has trouble maintaining satisfying relationships with other people, and in time his chronic emotional mobilization may even have serious effects on his physical health. Thus a preponderance of negative emotions not only blocks present effectiveness but also interferes

I'm basically pretty compassionate, I guess, although I'm also pretty selfish. When I really want to do something for someone, when I really have a good feeling about them, it's really there. Also when I hate someone it's really there, too. I've noticed that I'm pretty emotional and it's all pretty honest. I know when I'm acting, too. I can't lie to myself about my feelings, not as much as I used to. Now if I've lied about something I know that I'm doing it.

with the development of greater competence and maturity.

On the other hand, repeated studies, both clinical and experimental, have shown that "positive" feelings, such as love and sympathy, are conducive to self-esteem, adequacy, and self-actualization. Although our feelings are, of course, somewhat dependent on what life brings us, this is only part of the story; some people manage to have a predominance of positive feelings despite great adversity, whereas others are constantly fearful, angry, and resentful in what looks to us like a favorable situation. It is our attitudes and values that chiefly determine whether an experience will be gratifying or frustrating to us. Except under the most extreme stress, the emotionally competent person can usually manage to keep the balance on the side of the positive emotions.

Emotions and growth

The growth process, according to most humanistic psychotherapists, requires self-awareness and self-acceptance. However, self-knowledge is a difficult step and requires the information of the emotions. As Rollo May expresses it:
"In the achieving of consciousness of one's self, most people must start back at the beginning and rediscover their feelings. It is surprising how many people have only a general acquaintance with what they feel—they tell you they feel "fine" or "lousy," as vaguely as though they were saying

"China is in the Orient." Their connection with their feelings is as remote as if over a long-distance telephone. They do not feel directly but only give ideas about their feelings; they are not affected by their affects; their emotions give them no motion" (1953, p. 91).

The process of growth, or becoming, requires that the person become aware of all that he feels; then he is able to become what he is (Rogers, 1961). One of the requisites for the "good life" of the fully functioning person is openness to experience:
"The individual is becoming more able to listen to himself, to experience what is going on within himself. He is more open to his feelings of fear and discouragement and pain. He is also more open to his feelings of courage, and tenderness, and awe. He is free to live his feelings subjectively, as they exist in him, and also free to be aware of these feelings. He is more able fully to live the experiences of his organism rather than shutting them out of awareness" (Rogers, 1961, p. 188).

To make contact with one's feelings, however fleeting and however surprising or "unacceptable," is the source of one's self-trust and respect and the source of choices about one's existence.

Awareness of emotions
Discovery of one's emotions seems elementary, but as May remarked, many individuals have only a vague knowledge of what they feel. Considerable energy may be devoted to denying or shutting out emotional experiences. There-

fore, much of growth-oriented therapy is aimed at increasing one's *awareness* of one's organism. "The more consciousness," remarked Kierkegaard, "the more self."

Awareness of one's feelings lays the groundwork for knowing what one *wants,* in contrast to action based upon what one thinks he should want or should feel (May, 1953; Rogers, 1969). Frederick Perls, the founder of gestalt therapy, argued that awareness of one's truest, most honest emotions and reactions is inherently curative; in fact, only awareness—not therapeutic programs aimed at behavior change—can lead to growth, change, and full functioning. His procedures involved, among other things, teaching the individual to become aware of his feelings and reactions by observation of nonverbal cues, such as posture, voice, eyes, and hands. We are often scarcely in contact with our true feelings, so that mere words and descriptions of feelings are usually intellectualizations and untruths.

Expression of emotions

Along with *awareness* of feelings, emotional expression is important to full human functioning, according to the humanists. For many individuals, outward behavior is carefully measured to comply with expectations, norms, and the customs about us. We carefully monitor the actions of others so that we can know how to act—and feel. It is clear that there are enormously stringent social sanctions against display of strong feelings, especially in public; anger, tenderness, joy, and sadness are among the feelings that must be carefully modulated. However, many would argue that we pay a considerable price for emotional conformity. Grief doesn't get worked out and may remain a festering, painful shadow. Joy that isn't expressed may dissipate rapidly—more rapidly than sorrow. Anger may build until its consequences are poisonous.

"When a person is living behind a front, a facade, his unexpressed feelings pile up to some explosion point, and are then apt to be triggered off by some specific incident. But the feelings which sweep

over the person and are expressed at such a time—in a temper storm, in a deep depression, in a flood of self-pity, and the like—often have an unfortunate effect on all concerned because they are so inappropriate to the specific situation and hence seem so unreasonable. The angry flare-up over one annoyance in the relationship may actually be the pent-up or denied feelings resulting from dozens of such situations. But in the context in which it is expressed it is unreasonable and hence not understood" (Rogers, 1961, p. 318).

Thus, one goal of growth-oriented therapies is the increase in spontaneous expression of emotions, the attempt to enable the individual to perceive, accept, and express the intensity and the immediacy of his emotional experiences.

Such spontaneity of expression is not to be confused with impulsiveness, however (Rogers & Stevens, 1967). "To be aware of one's feelings and desires does not at all imply expressing them indiscriminately wherever one happens to be. Judgment and decision . . . are part of any mature consciousness of self" (May, 1953, p. 97).

Spontaneity of feeling and expression is not only a means for achieving full humanness, but may also be related to self-actualization. Maslow (1954), in his study of exceptional, self-actualizing individuals, noted that spontaneity of behavior and inner experience was a prominent characteristic of such persons.

A focus on positive emotions

Humanistic psychologists have brought to our attention the preponderant focus of traditional psychotherapy, personality theory, and philosophy on such negative human experiences as evil, guilt, suffering, pain, destructiveness, and the like. The more "positive" emotions have been given much less concern. Thus, we are encouraged to become aware of our capacities for joy, ecstasy, loving, sharing, trust, and the like (Maslow, 1954). Other kinds of experience are by no means excluded, since they are also basic human feelings. However, full functioning would include awareness and appreciation of the enjoyable, enriching feelings as well.

Expression and control of emotions

People vary not only in their patterns of emotional experience but also in their patterns of expression and control. Some are effusive and demonstrative, freely expressing their feelings in words, gestures, and other behavior. Others hide their feelings—sometimes just from other people, sometimes from themselves as well. Sometimes "admirable" emotions are expressed freely, while disapproved ones are concealed or denied. These may be culturally induced patterns, but usually they serve individual needs and purposes too.

Our culture makes rationality and self-control the key virtues in mature, adult functioning; indeed, such qualities are adaptive and are certainly conducive to flourishing industrial, technological society. Emotions are not uncommon-

ly viewed as disruptive, weak, feminine, or otherwise undesirable. To *control* emotions, not to experience them, becomes the task, according to this viewpoint. Yet the control of emotions may often result in impoverishment of the experiences which make life rich and human. On the other hand, unbridled emotional expression may also have unwanted consequences in instances where the individual overreacts to a situation or displays inappropriate emotions. Hence, the dilemma for the individual is to find a suitable balance between expression and control, seeking full functioning as a person, which includes adaptive emotional expression, and awareness and acceptance of feelings.

Clearly not every emotionally competent person will have exactly the same pattern of expression and control. As with the experience of emotion, "normal" covers a wide range. The following three characteristics, however, are as-

sociated with competence in emotional expression and control: (1) a balance of spontaneity and control; (2) a habit of acknowledging one's feelings and channeling them constructively instead of denying or suppressing them; and (3) an avoidance of distorted and disguised expression.

Spontaneity and control

Children are usually quite spontaneous in the expression of their feelings and emotions. Thus a child may shout "I hate you" at someone to express his anger even before he knows what hating someone actually means. Children, too, are initially quite uninhibited in showing affection for others. With time, however, most of us learn to inhibit the expression of certain emotions—such as crying—and to express anger and love only in socially approved ways.

Although some measure of emotional control is necessary, it can be carried too far. Thus an individual may be so inhibited in expressing anger or affection that he seems tense and rigid and lacking in warmth and spontaneity. The person who "plays it cool," avoiding involvements that might arouse strong emotions, misses the sense of emotional involvement in the human enterprise that helps make life exciting and meaningful to those who permit themselves more spontaneity of emotional experience. Although he may avoid the pain of loss or rejection, he also cuts himself off from the warmth, emotional support, and sense of continuity that can come from a deep friendship or love relationship.

With inadequate inner controls, we may overreact emotionally, flying off the handle or bursting into tears in routine situations. With too rigid controls we may be unable to "let our-

When an individual feels trapped in an anxiety-arousing situation, he may try to alleviate his anxiety through actions that are self-defeating. For example, many overweight people find that eating temporarily calms their anxieties.

> In my family, I was brought up to believe, from infancy, practically, that only 'good' boys, who never got angry or quarrelsome with people, would be loved. First it was my parents, who taught me in no uncertain manner, then I carried that over to my girl friends, then my wife. My parents still let me know I'm a 'good' boy, but I've paid for it with an ulcer and a divorce.

selves go" or to "be ourselves." Neither extreme is desirable.

Constructive channeling vs. repression

In each society, the child learns what emotions may be expressed and under what conditions. Boys in particular are often admonished not to cry and not to show fear—to act like a "man" and not a "cry baby." The expression of anger is usually discouraged: The child who expresses anger toward parents or siblings may be punished and made to feel guilty and ashamed.

When a child learns that the direct expression of his emotions brings him disapproval and punishment, or when he learns to feel ashamed and guilty for experiencing certain emotions, he may unconsciously resort to repression or emotional insulation as a means of self-protection. Thus he may repress feelings of anger toward his parents and later toward his spouse so that he consciously experiences only love and affection; or he may withdraw and insulate himself from close emotional involvement so that potentially dangerous or uncomfortable emotions will not be aroused.

Direct vs. disguised expression

Emotions that are denied direct expression often find outlets in disguised ways. Hostility, for example, may be expressed through teasing or nagging; anxiety and fear may be expressed through chronic fatigue and somatic complaints.

Often the individual is unaware of the causes of such reactions and is quite bewildered by his own behavior. Usually such outlets are not entirely adequate for reducing emotional tensions, or they may reduce the conscious tension but at the price of peptic ulcers or other psychosomatic disorders.

Effectiveness in emotional expression and control, like effectiveness in other forms of behavior, means that both inner needs and outer demands are taken into account. Emotional competence is not achieved once and for all, however. Although we can develop more realistic expectations and greater ability to acknowledge our real feelings, we can expect to have a continuing problem of finding personally satisfying and constructive ways to express negative emotions.

Dealing with potentially troublesome emotions

The mature and well-functioning individual finds that emotional experiences provide meaning and depth to living and convey important information about the self and the environment. Individuals differ, through learning and perhaps constitutional factors, in the customary kinds of reactions they may have. Everyone has to learn to accept feelings, to permit them and not judge them as bad or unacceptable, and to find appropriate and constructive ways of expressing them in a fashion which is suitable for the individual. It will be useful perhaps to discuss some of the most prevalent kinds of emotions which have the potential for presenting problems for us.

Fear, anxiety, and worry

As we have seen, the term *fear* is usually used for a response to a specific danger, and the term *anxiety* for a response to danger or threat which is less clearly perceived. Following this usage,

the frightened individual usually "knows what he is afraid of" and what he can or cannot do about it, whereas the anxious individual "senses danger" but is not clear as to its exact nature or what action to take in dealing with it. Often fear and anxiety go together—fear being elicited by clearly perceived aspects of the dangerous or stressful situation and anxiety by its unpredictable or uncertain implications. For example, a young person approaching marriage may feel fear concerning financial problems and new responsibilities and at the same time feel vaguely anxious and apprehensive about whether this is really the "right" person and whether the marriage will be a success.

Worry is a form of fear or anxiety in which the individual is emotionally involved with a troublesome situation but sees no immediate answer and feels helpless and often somewhat hopeless about the outcome. Worries usually focus around unforeseeable future events—about what may happen to the individual or his loved ones, or about other matters in which he is self-involved.

Realistic and unrealistic fears and anxieties

Since no life is free of hazard, fear and anxiety are normal and justified experiences. Yet many people consider it a form of weakness or even cowardice to feel fear and anxiety—let alone express them. It is especially difficult for men in our culture to admit their fears and anxieties because of our prevalent stereotype of the male as a strong, confident provider under whose protection his family can feel secure. Recognition of fear and anxiety as normal and permanent parts of the human condition is a first step in dealing effectively with them.

A second step in dealing with these emotions is distinguishing between realistic and unrealistic fear and anxiety. Is the fear elicited by a real danger? Is it proportional to the actual degree of danger, or is it exaggerated? Is it rational or irrational? Is it born of an actual, present stress situation, or does it reflect a pervasive feeling of inadequacy and inferiority? In this context, it is

I'm a person who worries about things. I would really like to stop, but I really can't. I worry over every little thing.

often useful to make a distinction between *situational* anxiety—anxiety which occurs under particular conditions—and *general* anxiety—in which the individual experiences a chronic, pervasive feeling of anxiety whatever the external circumstances.

Of course, it is not always easy to distinguish between realistic and unrealistic fears and anxieties or to determine whether a given individual is overly prone to fear and anxiety in dealing with the everyday problems of living. However, an awareness of this distinction and an approach to fear and anxiety as reactions to be recognized and understood rather than denied and hidden appear to be important first steps in dealing with these emotions.

As we have seen, fear and anxiety are not always negative in their effects. Fear which leads to caution or protective action is constructive; similarly, a minimal or even moderate level of anxiety may represent a necessary mechanism of arousal in getting us to undertake needed action. Mild anxiety can facilitate learning; and *existential anxiety*—anxiety centering around finding appropriate values and leading a meaningful and fulfilling life—can be a constructive force in our lives. As Levitt has said:

"Thus anxiety is a Janus-headed creature that can impel man to self-improvement, achievement, and competence, or can distort and impoverish his existence and that of his fellows" (1967, p. 200).

Knowing what to expect and what to do

Since fear and anxiety stem from a feeling of helplessness in the face of danger, the best insurance against them is actual adequacy and competence. Obviously we cannot know ahead of time all the demands we will face, but we can foresee many fairly probable ones and prepare ourselves for them. With specific preparation for marriage, vocation, parenthood, and old age, for example, we are much more likely to maintain a constructive and task-oriented approach in meeting the problems they typically bring. Knowing what to expect and what to do about it can make us feel confident instead of fearful, even in a very demanding situation.

If there are certain types of situations in which we commonly experience fear and anxiety, we can often take measures to modify our emotional responses—as in working through psychic wounds—or we can learn to carry on despite the

When I had my tonsils out, nobody told me how sick I was going to be, so it had me worried that—when it hurt so much for so long afterward—it had me worried that something had gone wrong in my throat, and I had to call the doctor to find out. After he said, 'Well, that's the way it feels afterwards,' I really got mad. If I'd known what to expect, I wouldn't have been so frightened and I would just have accepted it and endured it.

fear. As we become accustomed to functioning in fear-producing situations, we may find our fear lessening, although it may not be completely banished.

Taking action in a fear-producing situation may also be of key importance. Fear often tends to a paralysis of action—and paralysis to an intensification of the fear. Action—almost any action—can break this circle and lessen feelings of fear even when it does not lessen the actual danger. The actor usually loses his stage fright once the action begins, as does the athlete once the contest is under way.

Being a good worrier

A certain amount of anxiety and worry is probably an inevitable by-product of modern living. Most of us feel vaguely apprehensive much of the time about possible accidents, failures, setbacks, losses, or other poorly defined future possibilities.

Worrying is a form of fear and anxiety which can be realistic and constructive or unrealistic and destructive. Janis (1968) has referred to the useful "work of worrying" in preparing an individual for coping with future stress. For example, he found that patients who were unworried about impending major surgery were less able to withstand the pain and other stresses of postoperative convalescence, whereas patients who were moderately worried and apprehensive before surgery apparently tended to go through a mental rehearsal of the impending danger and were better prepared for the stressful situation when it materialized.

Chronic anxiety and worry can hamper us in three basic ways. First, as we have noted, anxiety beyond a very minimal level leads to a defensive orientation which makes us less able to face our problems objectively and work effectively toward their solution. Our perception narrows; we become more rigid and less inventive; and we develop a spiraling need to protect ourselves by denial, rationalization, and other defense mechanisms. Second, chronic anxiety keeps us physiologically mobilized for emergency action when no appropriate action is evident;

the harmful effects of such anxiety in terms of psychosomatic disorders have been mentioned. Third, chronic worrying deprives us of much of the enjoyment of living. We are continually concerned with the negative and dangerous aspects of living rather than with the positive and enriching ones. Often a chronic worrier will worry about things that never happen and then be taken unawares by the stresses that do occur.

Anger and hostility

As we have seen, anger may be viewed as a normal response to being interfered with and helps the organism to meet its needs through attack or aggressive action. Rage is anger out of control. Hostility is a more enduring condition of enmity, involving angry feelings and a tendency to inflict harm. Hate (or hatred) is roughly similar to hostility but is a more complex state centering around anger and a wish for harm or misfortune to befall the hated person, group, or object and involving a variety of action tendencies.

Although anger and hostility are normal parts of our adjustive equipment, we differ greatly, both individually and as groups, in the degree and frequency of the hostile feelings we experience. Some cultures value and encourage hostility and aggressiveness, whereas others discourage such emotions. In addition, either a repressive social setting or a constantly frustrating one, such as slum residents experience, can be expected to induce much more hostility than one that provides a favorable balance of satisfactions over frustrations. But even in a favorable social setting, immature or unrealistic expectations may lead to frequent or chronic hostilities and resentments.

Understanding and expressing anger and hostility

As with other emotions, competence in dealing with anger and hostility begins with an understanding and acceptance of our feelings rather than a denial or moral self-condemnation.

We are usually taught early in life that we should love our parents and siblings and later our spouse and children. Yet those close to us inevitably frustrate us at times and hence elicit some measure of anger and hostility. If we believe that we should feel only pure love and affection for such persons, it is often difficult for us to admit and accept hostile feelings and even more difficult to find safe and acceptable ways of expressing them. For expressing anger and hostility toward loved ones bears the risk of alienating them and eliciting rejection or retaliation and punishment, especially if they, too, believe that anger on our part means rejection and lack of love. Most children learn early that expressions of anger or hostility are likely to lead to punishment and pain for them.

When the individual views his hostile feelings as dangerous and immoral, he may resort to defense mechanisms such as denial or repression as a means of keeping his feelings out of consciousness, or he may turn his hostility inward and engage in severe self-recrimination for having such immoral and unacceptable feelings. Either approach only aggravates the problem. Chronic, unacknowledged hostility can poison the whole relationship and lead to a psychosomatic affliction; intrapunitive handling of the hostility affords some expression but undermines one's feelings of adequacy, worth, and self-esteem.

Unexpressed or indirectly expressed anger is extremely common in our culture which emphasizes polite and rational interpersonal relationships. Many of the new, growth-oriented therapies are particularly adept at facilitating the constructive expression of anger.

Constructive vs. destructive hostility

In many situations anger and hostility are normal reactions that may lead to constructive action. Anger and hostility aroused by autocratic and unjust treatment of oneself or others may be used constructively in working for social reforms. On a more personal level, expressing our anger may help another person realize that he is being inconsiderate or selfish and that his behavior is affecting people in unintended ways.

More commonly, however, anger and hostility take destructive forms. We let frustration and hostility interfere with harmonious and satisfying interpersonal relationships or become unduly upset and angered by minor delays, discourtesies, or other irritating situations that are relatively unimportant. Strong anger may lead us to ill-considered and costly action which we may later regret and for which we may receive severe punishment, including imprisonment. On a social level, demagogues often stir up and exploit feelings of bitterness and hatred to gain personal power and lead the society to calamitous action.

Thus it becomes important to distinguish between anger that is appropriate and constructive and anger that is inappropriate and destructive. Although anyone may be aroused to inappropriate anger and hostility when unduly fatigued or under the influence of alcohol, drugs, or special stress, habitual overreaction to minor frustrations or frequent extremes of anger and hostility usually indicates unrealistic expectations or underlying feelings of immaturity and inferiority.

Expecting some hostility from others

As we learn to accept and tolerate hostility in ourselves, we must also learn to accept it in others, even when it is directed against us. Perhaps the most essential aspect of dealing with overt hostility in adulthood is to be prepared for it and to give up the notion of wanting everyone to love and appreciate us at all times. Although there is a certain justice in reacting angrily to the seemingly unjustified anger of another person, this is a form of self-indulgence that seldom pays off. Two people preoccupied with defense against each other or with retaliation for past offenses only feed and perpetuate their feelings of hostility. If we can see another person's anger, especially when it is disguised, as a problem for him rather than as a threat to us, we can often make the response that will lessen his tension and thus make a better relationship possible.

 I don't think loneliness has anything to do with the amount of people that you're around. It's strictly a personal thing. Too many people make a correlation that if you live alone you're lonely. That's not true at all. For me, and I can only speak for me, living alone is an ideal way to live.

Loneliness

" 'There's nothing to be afraid of.' The ultimate reassurance, and the ultimate terror" (Laing, 1967, p. 38).

Existentialists tell us, and our lives remind us, of the pain and inevitability of our aloneness. To feel lonely—to feel cut off, apart, needy for others' attention, care, and concern, but somehow terribly unreachable—these are painful but deeply human experiences. But people dread and try to avoid loneliness. We try to help brush it away from our friends, ignore or deny it in strangers, run from it in our own lives. Clark Moustakas offers another view of loneliness which challenges us—as does the expression of many other emotions—to explore its potentials for deepening humanness.

There are many points of origin for loneliness—being separated from loved ones through emotional or physical distance or death, moments of personal creativity or achievement when the experience is so deeply personal that one senses its inability to be shared, feeling apart and unloved, among others. To experience the sense of need for others but at the same time experience the futility, the impossibility, or the brevity of the hole they can fill provokes great sadness if not terror. But to come to terms with loneliness, to experience it fully and deeply without running from the pain, says Moustakas (1961), can promote a self-awareness that we may have lacked before. The full experience of loneliness can give a person the chance to draw upon capacities and resources never before realized. Deeply lived loneliness has the potential for increasing compassion and relatedness with others. The full experience of loneliness, with its generation of insights and new approaches to loving and relating, can be a well-spring of creativity. Moustakas explores the lives and writings of various singular persons to support the claim that loneliness is not at all an emotion to be avoided or curtailed, but rather is a human experience with the potential for enrichment of life.

Guilt, depression, and grief

Humans universally experience a sense of guilt when they violate ethical or moral principles in which they believe. Guilt is characterized by a feeling of regret, lessened personal worth, and usually some measure of anxiety. And as we have seen, guilt is closely related to depression, with its characteristic discouragement, dejection, and gloomy thoughts. Both guilt and depression are commonly involved in grief that stems from the loss of loved ones.

Although these emotions are part of our adaptive resources, they may take either destructive or constructive forms and often are difficult to deal with.

Normal vs. pathological guilt
The recognition of responsibility for failure to live up to one's ethical and moral values is a necessary concomitant of self-direction. Thus guilt is potentially a normal and useful emotion

that can lead to a correction of error and reparation of damage. When guilt is out of all proportion to the magnitude of the "sin" that was committed, however, or when it focuses on self-condemnation and self-devaluation instead of future improvement or redirection of effort, it is pathological.

Normal guilt feelings can usually be dealt with through confession of guilt (to oneself or others), a sincere effort at reparation, and then a willingness to accept forgiveness and look to the future instead of dwelling on the past. This sequence usually leaves one better equipped to avoid the same mistake on subsequent occasions.

In the case of pathological guilt, however, the individual may be convinced that the slate can never really be wiped clean. He feels that he has committed a great and unpardonable sin and suffers pervasive and persistent feelings of unworthiness and self-devaluation. Often he feels dejected and depressed and finds no joy or satisfaction in anything that he does. Usually, too, he suffers from feelings of anxiety and apprehension stemming from his belief that somehow he will be "punished for his sins." Sometimes such an individual resorts to self-defense mechanisms such as projection—thus placing the blame for his misdeed on others and freeing himself from conscious feelings of guilt and self-devaluation.

Such pathological guilt feelings usually reflect immature, rigid, and unrealistic moral standards that no human being could possibly follow; with such an unrealistic but implacable conscience, the individual is foredoomed to perpetual failure and devaluation. Thus again we see the crucial importance of the individual's assumptions and values in determining the appropriateness of his response patterns.

Depression and guilt
Depression is a common response to loss and disappointment and may take the form of feelings of despair, hopelessness, low self-esteem, feeling tired, listless, and the display of certain bodily symptoms. Most individuals respond to certain situations with depression which is usu-

When I get depressed I withdraw and build up my ego again. Usually I withdraw into a book and let my imagination go. This takes my mind off of the trouble for a while. Then when I think of it again I can usually think it through better.

ally temporary. Depressive responses are very characteristic of college populations, possibly in response to the important issues of self-identity and the establishment of self-regard. Depression often perpetuates itself in the sense that the person feels too listless or preoccupied to participate in pleasurable activities which might relieve the depression and restore self-esteem. To the degree that the depressed person can be induced to engage in enjoyable enterprises and to find sources of positive reinforcement, the depressive mood may be alleviated (Lewinsohn & Libet, 1972; Glass & Hammen, 1973).

Depression may be a problem emotion for individuals to the extent that it persists or is elicited frequently. Dejection and discouragement are expected reactions to setbacks and disappointments that keep us from reaching our goals. Where the individual has an unrealistically high level of aspiration, however, he may suffer excessive feelings of dejection and depression over relatively minor setbacks that offer little threat to his long-range goals.

Severe depressive reactions may be serious, especially when there is a strong component of guilt and self-devaluation. Such guilt-tinged depression, as we saw in Chapter 8, is often part of a neurotic or psychotic reaction. This seems to be especially true in Christian and Judeo-Christian societies, with their emphasis on personal responsibility (Murphy, Wittkower, & Chance, 1967). Unrealistic aspirations, rigid conscience development, and other conditions that commonly lead to pathological guilt reactions are also commonly involved in pathological depression.

Although it may be useful to examine one's aspirations and values if one is troubled by feelings of guilt and depression, tendencies toward severe and pathological depression usually require professional assistance if they are to be alleviated. Such help is of key importance in view of the suicidal tendencies which often occur in severe depressions.

Bereavement and grief

Grief is a universal reaction to bereavement, found even among animals (Averill, 1968). It is apparently based on a close identification with the person or thing that has been lost; in a sense, the bereaved feels that a part of himself is gone. This is especially apparent with the death of a close family member, but much the same reaction may occur in public mourning over the death of a well-loved national figure.

Most grief reactions are not severe enough to be incapacitating. Typically there is a depressed mood, sleep disruption, and crying. Usually the individual "works through" the grief reaction; resorting to denial or repression in an attempt to avoid the grief reaction apparently simply prolongs the "grief work" that must be carried out for adjustment to the new situation. The psychological needs of the bereaved person usually center around freedom to express his feelings—not only of sorrow but also of guilt or hostility, if these are involved—and, a little later, emotional support as he tries to build a new life.

Of course, death is not the only source of bereavement and grief. A man's wife may leave him; his son may commit a crime and be sent to prison. The loss of an eye or limb is also a very real source of bereavement. Even the loss of a possession can bring grief if the possession has supplied important emotional supports and gratifications for the individual and, in a general sense, has been viewed as an extension of himself. Our primary concern here, however, is

with bereavement and grief stemming from the loss of loved ones.

An individual's reaction to bereavement varies depending upon the meaning of the loss to him and the strength of the ties that have been disrupted. Bereavement may involve a loss of security, friendship, companionship, emotional support, or love—or all of these. It is very common for the bereaved to experience not only grief, but also anger and hostility at the loved one for having died and deprived one. Although quite a normal reaction, such experiences typically trigger guilt responses since anger is felt to be an inappropriate reaction. Other circumstances may also arouse guilt. For example, the bereaved person may engage in self-recrimination for past neglect, for having felt hostility, or for other thoughts and acts of omission or commission for which he now feels guilty. Guilt and depression are almost inevitable when the individual has actually been involved in some way in the event that caused the death of the loved one—as in an automobile accident in which he was the driver.

Since it is now too late to make reparation for his alleged or actual misdeeds, guilt, self-recrimination, and depression may be severe. Here the process of grief work may be much more complicated and may take a much longer time, and there is a real possibility of suicide. Professional assistance during the most intense period of grief and depression is to be encouraged.

Love may be a problem

Despite its central importance in human affairs, love, as a psychological phenomenon, has received very little scientific study. In fact, many psychology books do not even have the term *love* in the index, and where the term is used, it is ordinarily in connection with sex and marriage rather than in terms of its more general place in human relationships. Yet it would probably be agreed that an ability to give and receive love is one of the most important of all emotional competencies, for all the evidence points to the necessity of loving and being loved for normal human development and functioning.

Why human beings have such a great need and desire for love has been the subject of considerable speculation. Fromm (1956) believes that love develops from a person's awareness of his separateness and his need to overcome the anxiety this separateness brings by achieving union with someone or something. But he stresses the point that the only healthy union is one in which the integrity of the individual is not threatened. We can achieve a feeling of union through dependence on another individual or through conformity to the group, but in so doing, we surrender our own individuality; likewise, we can achieve union through dominating others, but here the others suffer. Only through love, Fromm feels, can the needed sense of union be achieved without loss of individuality and integrity on either side. May has also emphasized the theme of aloneness as a basis for our need for love in his statement that:

"Every person, as a separate individual, experiences aloneness. And so we strive actively to overcome our aloneness by some form of love" (1968, p. 23).

Whatever its origin, the search for love is an extremely powerful force in human existence.

The meaning and forms of love

Many people have tried to define love. Prescott has described valid love in terms of the following components:

1. *"Love involves more or less empathy with the loved one. A person who loves actually enters into the feelings of and shares intimately the experiences of the loved one and the effects of these experiences upon the loved one.*

2. *"One who loves is deeply concerned for the welfare, happiness, and development of the beloved. This concern is so deep as to become one of the major organizing values in the personality or self-structure of the loving person. . . .*

3. *"One who loves finds pleasure in making his resources available to the loved one, to be used by the other to enhance his welfare, happiness, and development. Strength, time, money, thought, indeed all resources are proffered happily to the loved one for his use. A loving person is not merely concerned about the beloved's welfare and development, he does something about it.*

4. *"Of course the loving person seeks a maximum of participation in the activities that contribute to the welfare, happiness, and development of the beloved. But he also accepts fully the uniqueness and individuality of the beloved and . . . accords [him] full freedom to experience, to act, and to become what he desires to become. A loving person has a nonpossessive respect for the selfhood of the loved one"* (1957, p. 358).

There are also, of course, somewhat unique components in the love we feel for a parent, a child, a friend, and a mate. Fromm (1956) delineates five somewhat different love relationships, as described on p. 480.

1. *Brotherly love.* Perhaps the most basic kind of love is that for all of humanity. Fromm describes it as "the sense of responsibility, care, respect, knowledge of any other human being, the wish to further his life" (p. 47). Unlike the love of man and woman or mother and child, brotherly love is in no way exclusive. It is the orientation to all human relationships which finds expression in the Biblical injunction to "love thy neighbor as thyself."

2. *Motherly (parental) love.* Here Fromm emphasizes the parent's unconditional affirmation of his child's life and needs. Parental love involves care and responsibility for the child's well-being and growth, together with a willing acceptance of the fact that the child's life is his own. The parent assumes responsibility for a life entrusted to his care and finds his happiness in seeing that life fulfilled. True motherly love is nonpossessive.

3. *Erotic love.* Fromm describes erotic love as "the craving for a complete fusion, for union with one other person. It is by its very nature exclusive and not universal . . ." (pp. 52–53). Typically, of course, erotic love finds its culmination in the framework of marriage.

4. *Self-love.* Since love implies concern, respect, and responsibility, self-love is considered a necessity if the individual is to be capable of loving others. Self-deprecation and self-rejection interfere with all healthy love relationships.

5. *Love of God.* In discussing religious love, Fromm (p. 83) again emphasizes the human "need to overcome separateness and to achieve union"—in this case, union with ultimate reality. This point is elaborated further in Chapter 17 in connection with the quest for values.

Thus love may take several different forms and may have several different meanings. Central to all the forms of love, however, appears to be an attitude of care, concern, and responsibility for the loved one, and a desire to promote his growth, well-being, and concerns. Nor does an individual usually show only one form of love; more commonly, the ability for any of the particular forms of love is part of a broader orientation involving the valuing of other

human beings and an eagerness to form warm bonds with other people. As Fromm has put it: *"If a person loves only one other person and is indifferent to the rest of his fellow men, his love is not love but symbiotic attachment, or an enlarged egotism"* (1956, p. 46).

In the remainder of this section, we shall be concerned primarily with healthy love relationships.

Romantic love vs. infatuation

Although economic factors rather than love have often been emphasized in marriage, romantic love has played an important role in most cultures (Kurland, 1953). In our contemporary society, we are constantly exposed to portrayals of idealized romantic love in movies, television, plays, novels, and popular songs. As in the case of other forms of love, however, we know very little about romantic love in real life: Speculation about it by various alleged authorities casts little light on the subject.

Some of the many conflicting assumptions which have been held about romantic love are summarized in the chart on p. 481. Interestingly, virtually the only scientific evidence we have regarding any of these assumptions concerns the last two pairs. In his study of self-actualizing people Maslow found that these individuals were able to drop their defenses in their love relationships and be wholly themselves without fear or pretense:

"One of the deepest satisfactions coming from the healthy love relationship reported by my subjects is that such a relationship permits the greatest spontaneity, the greatest naturalness, the greatest dropping of defenses and protection against threat. In such a relationship it is not necessary to be guarded, to conceal, to try to impress, to feel tense, to watch one's words or actions, to suppress or repress. My people report that they can be themselves without feeling that there are demands or expectations upon them; they can feel psychologically (as well as physically) naked and still feel loved and wanted and secure" (1954, pp. 239–240).

Whether this finding would hold for less self-

On the basis of intuition, personal experience, and uncontrolled observation, it has been claimed:

1. That romantic love inevitably leads to disillusionment and is the principal cause of our high divorce rate—and also that romantic love mitigates the stresses of monogamous marriage, preventing its disintegration as a social institution.

2. That romantic love is blind and irrational—and also that romantic love involves a sharpening of perception so that the other person is seen realistically but loved for himself anyway.

3. That adequate sexual relationships stem from and can be found only in the context of romantic love—and also that adequate sexual relationships often pave the way for the later development of love.

4. That finding the right person is the most important ingredient in romantic love—and also that one's capacity to give and receive love is the most important determinant.

5. That each successive love relationship is a unique and distinctive experience—and also that one loves as he has loved before so that there is a continuity in his love relationships and he will keep making the same mistakes.

6. That true romantic love leads to harmony and bliss—and also that the "path of true love never does run smooth," that the intensity of feeling in romantic love will inevitably lead to conflict and anxiety.

7. That it is possible in romantic love to lower one's defenses and let one's faults be freely seen by the partner—and also that one must be lovable to be loved and hence must always keep his best foot forward in appearance and behavior.

8. That romantic love can be felt for only one love object at a time—and also that the individual may be romantically in love with more than one person simultaneously.

actualizing people in less healthy love relationships is a moot point.

In an early study of 500 American college women, Ellis (1948) reported that 58 percent admitted simultaneous infatuations and 25 percent reported being in love simultaneously with two or more men. The findings of Packard (1968) with respect to the sexual patterns of college men and women suggest that the earlier findings of Ellis may be valid for today's generation as well.

Romantic love is characterized by strong feelings of attraction toward and affection for the loved person, a desire to be with him (or her), a concern for his well-being, a willingness to make more of oneself for him, and a desire to contribute to his happiness and personal growth. Usually it also includes a desire for affection from and sexual intimacy with the loved person. Such love may endure and deepen over the years or it may wither away. In some instances there appears to be a shift from romantic love to disillusionment and hurt and sometimes even to hostility and hate.

Despite all these points of similarity any given experience of romantic love is a unique, highly personal experience that may be difficult to describe to others. In fact, writers and poets have described the experience of romantic love in quite diverse ways. It seems unlikely that a person who has never experienced romantic love can understand or imagine the quality of the experience involved.

Often the question is raised as to the distinction between romantic love and infatuation. Lacking a clear understanding of either, we can make only a general distinction. Infatuation is usually considered to be an intense romantic relationship of short duration which is a purely emotional reaction and does not take into account the "fit" of the personalities and many other rational considerations. Often infatuation involves a high degree of wishful thinking in which the lover projects a halo over the head of the loved one and sees only what he wants to see instead of what is there. Once his perceptions become more realistic, the romantic aura may suddenly be lost.

Unfortunately, as Kephart (1967) has pointed out, one usually thinks of his current romantic experience as love rather than infatuation; infatuation is usually recognized as such—at least by the person involved—only after it is over.

Although infatuation may not last, it is a powerful force while it holds sway. It provides both rose-colored spectacles and a sense of urgency to its victims, and when it leads to a hasty marriage, the individual may find himself married to someone he scarcely knows, whose weak points come to him as quite a shock.

Many other irrational elements may also make it difficult for a person to tell if he is really in love. For example, even a relatively mature individual may convince himself that he wants to get married because he is in love when actually what he wants is to have someone take care of him, or to ensure his sexual satisfaction, or to protect himself from loneliness. Often, too, the individual has been indoctrinated with the romantic notion that there is only one person in the world who is right for him; in his eagerness to believe he has found that person, it is easy for him to convince himself that he is in love.

Genuine erotic love grows out of shared experiences of many kinds. The climate of a happy marriage is not necessarily one of complete harmony at all times; but it is one in which the bonds of love are deepened by shared problems as well as by happiness, and one in which both partners can continue to grow as individuals. The latter point is particularly important, for a love which feeds on dependency is apt to destroy itself. Erotic love, like brotherly and parental love, nurtures the growth of the loved one as an individual.

The ability to love and be loved

Most investigators believe that people vary greatly in their ability to love and to maintain a durable loving interaction with another person. An individual's ability to love, like other emotional competencies, appears to depend upon a number of factors, including his early experiences with his parents, the extent to which he trusts others, his degree of personal maturity and self-acceptance, and his freedom from exaggerated self-defense.

As we have seen, the ability to give and receive love apparently begins in a healthy infant-mother relationship and then expands as we build satisfying relationships with other family members, friends, and eventually a mate and children of our own. Fromm (1956) has distinguished two components which he considers of crucial importance in such early experiences: (1) the early experience of being loved unconditionally by the mother, and (2) the later experience of having to meet certain standards to ensure love. The first experience is considered a passive one in which the infant is loved simply because he exists; while the second experience, usually largely mediated by the father, shows the child that he can work for love and achieve it—that it is potentially within his control. Later these two trends are integrated into a feeling that one is basically lovable and worthy of love but also that he can behave in ways which will increase or destroy the love that other people will feel for him.

Lacking either part of this experience, the child is handicapped later on. If he has a weak and uninterested father and an indulgent mother, for example, he is not likely to be able to love, since his orientation is a receptive one in which he expects others to love him regardless of his own behavior. Or, if the mother is cold and unresponsive and the father authoritarian, the child may later lack the ability for either giving or receiving unconditional love—always suspecting that there are strings attached to being loved.

Whether or not we agree with Fromm's formulation, it is of interest as a model for trying to understand the way in which early family patterns may influence our later approaches to love relationships. It seems a safe generalization that a minimally favorable emotional climate in childhood is usually necessary if the individual is to be able to give and receive love in later years. Yet love is a powerful force, and long-held patterns of self-doubt, cynicism, and of defensiveness may be dissipated by the experience of genuinely loving and being loved by another human being.

Summary and a look ahead

There is no denying the crucial role which emotions may play in enriching our lives or in causing confusion and suffering. Understanding the nature of emotions, including their functions as energizers, messengers, language, and facilitators of well-being is an important step in effective functioning.

The pattern of emotional experience is varied in range and intensity as well as in positive or negative orientation. The role our emotions play in our personal growth depends on the degree to which we are aware of our emotions, the ways in which we express them, and the degrees to which our emotions are spontaneous or controlled, direct or disguised. Depending on such factors, our emotions may be deep or shallow, balanced or uncontrolled, constructively channeled or suppressed, healthful or damaging. Our depth and range of feeling, characteristic balance of positive and negative feelings, and patterns of expression and control are a continuing and consistent part of our life style.

But although each of us develops a consistent emotional pattern, we need not remain the same today, tomorrow, and forever. If we find that our emotional patterns are immature and disruptive, we can take steps to improve them—not by fighting them but by understanding and accepting them, and learning to function with them and to express them constructively. In this connection, we discussed emotions that may be potentially troublesome, including fear, anxiety, worry, anger, loneliness, guilt, and depression. In addition, we examined the special challenge of love—of loving and being loved.

In the chapter which follows, we shall deal with the quest for values and show their significance for our emotions as well as all other facets of our lives.

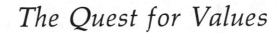

17
The Quest for Values

Assumptions about values
Values and becoming
Values and the world of the future

" 'I am not the same man,' Rusty Schweickart says, 'None of us are.' The Apollo veterans have become poets, seers, preachers, all of them evangelists for the privileged vision from space" (*Time,* Jan. 1, 1973, p. 50).

In this book we have taken a long and perhaps somewhat arduous journey into the world of the human being and his behavior. Now as we approach the end of this journey, it is fitting that we come to grips with a problem that has made its presence felt throughout the journey—the quest for values.

During the present decade, accelerating technological and social change will necessitate major changes in traditional life styles, and these changes, in turn, will modify many of our values. In essence, individuals today are searching for a coherent value system or philosophy of life which can hold its own against the impact of science and technology on society and provide meaning for their own existence in the world and for humanity's role in the universe.

We have noted that each individual gradually builds up a unique frame of reference—a set of basic assumptions concerning fact, possibility, and value—which provide him with a coherent picture of himself and his world. We have seen that these basic assumptions may be accurate or inaccurate, conscious or unconscious, and rigidly maintained or tentative and subject to disproof—but that whatever their character, they color the individual's perception of each new situation and influence his reactions to it. They constitute the cognitive map by which he tries to plot his way through his existence. And they provide the basis for his answers to the three key questions "Who am I?" "Where am I going?" and "Why?"

In our discussion so far, we have focused on the role of psychology and allied sciences in providing us with information about ourselves and our sociocultural environment—information on which accurate reality and possibility assumptions can be based. Though heavily dependent on our reality and possibility assumptions, our value assumptions go beyond them in taking

deadly thermonuclear weapons, and it will be our choice as to whether they will be used at some future date in a thermonuclear holocaust. These are choices based on value judgments.

The quest for values is not an easy one for either the individual or the group; yet on its outcome hinges the personal destiny of the individual as well as the destiny of the human species. In our present discussion, we cannot hope to solve the problem of finding valid values; rather we shall try to clarify the dimensions of the problem and point to some of the directions which a solution may take. As a starting point, we shall examine in more detail what we mean by value assumptions and some of the basic differences in people's value orientations. Then we shall look at the key sources of our

 I ponder, where do I really fit in society? After bringing four children into the world and watching them grow to be self-sufficient, I still wonder what my obligations to society are, because I don't feel I've done very much even though I've put a lot of time in on this earth. If I could find something I could do for mankind, it would be truly rewarding. Just caring is not enough. I must do something.

a position about what is *desirable* or *ought* to be. By their nature, values are not amenable to scientific verification, for they themselves are starting points—yardsticks by which we measure the meaning, merit, usefulness, worth, and validity of other ideas and activities. In short, science can provide us with information about what is good or bad for our physical, psychological, and social well-being; but it cannot make the value judgments requisite for deciding how to use this information. For example, we have ample scientific information to demonstrate that atomic bombs can be hazardous to the health—as evidenced by the results of the bombs dropped on Hiroshima and Nagasaki—but we choose to strive toward ever more powerful and

values and some tentative criteria for a sound value system. And finally, in the remainder of the chapter, we shall examine the significance of values for personal "becoming"—for personal change and fulfillment—and for determining the kind of future world for which we should strive.

Assumptions about values

"A value is a conception, explicit or implicit, distinctive of an individual or characteristic of a group, of the desirable which influences the selection from available modes, means, and ends of action" (Kluckhohn, 1954, p. 395).

Often we are told that there are no ultimate values in the sense of "good" and "evil"—that in life, values are always a compromise between realities and ideals. And indeed we often do make choices based on value judgments which we might call "shades of gray." In essence, our choices are compromises between what we think is right and what we think is realistic.

Yet in some instances—such as situations involving corruption, mindless brutality, premeditated murder, prejudice and discrimination, or genocide—it would seem that little compromise is possible. For to compromise in choices of this nature would be to destroy the very foundations upon which our society is based.

Ayn Rand has proposed an apt reply to such questions as "Surely you don't think in terms of good and bad do you?" She stated that "the proper answer (in essence, if not in form) should be: 'You're damn right I do'" (1964, p. 79).

In selecting goals, in choosing means for reaching them, in resolving conflicts, an individual is influenced at every turn by his conception of the preferable, the appropriate, the important, the good, the desirable—by what he sees as having *value*. The kind of relationship he establishes with his spouse and children, the way he transacts business matters, the degree of respect he has for others (and for himself), his political and religious activity, and the patterning of his everyday behavior—all these represent choices from among alternatives according to his hierarchy of values.

Values, of course, are subject to change over time as the individual experiences the rewarding or aversive consequences of various assumptions and actions. Nor are values the only determinants of behavior. Any act reflects a wide range of inner and outer determinants, including the individual's assumptions about reality and possibility, his immediate motivational pattern, and various situational factors. In general, however, it is his key choices that shape the type of life he builds for himself and the kind of person he becomes—and these reflect his basic values.

Value orientations

There are various ways of viewing or categorizing value orientations. We could delineate, for example, several comprehensive world views such as those advanced by Christianity or Buddhism, capitalism, or socialism. For our immediate purposes, however, the most useful way of categorizing value orientations seems to be: (1) in terms of value types and (2) in terms of conceived and operative values.

Value types
Some years ago Spranger (1928) contended that every person can be regarded as approaching—but rarely fitting perfectly within—one or more of six value types or value directions. In essence, there seem to be six main types of values which appeal to people in varying degrees and around which they build the unity of their lives. These were described by Spranger in terms of pure or "ideal" types of men.[1]

1. *The theoretical.* The primary value of the "ideal" theoretical man is the discovery of *truth.* Since this involves the use of rational, critical, and empirical processes, the theoretical man is an intellectual—often a scientist or philosopher.

2. *The economic.* The "ideal" economic man values what is *useful* and is concerned with the business world or other practical affairs involving the production, marketing, or consumption of goods. Tangible wealth and material possessions are of central interest.

3. *The esthetic.* The "ideal" esthetic man sees his highest value in *form* and *harmony.* He

---

[1] *These value types form the basis for a well-known psychological test entitled* A Study of Values, *by Allport, Vernon, and Lindzey (1960).*

Drawing by W. Miller; © 1973
The New Yorker Magazine, Inc.

 My family immigrated from the old country, from a place where material things are treasured because they have so few possessions, so much poverty. The old life style there is anchored deep in the social as well as family structure, and my parents of course brought all these ideas with them, and we, the children, brought with us our basic but not yet developed values. Such common things as throwing away perfectly good food by kids at school for no other reason than they weren't hungry, this I couldn't understand, because I had always been told that food should not be wasted. And to this day I will not throw away leftovers, which has caused me a few arguments with my husband.

To me, the thing that I'm most proud of is my ability to accept people wherever they are. I pray that I never get so secure or smug that I can't reach out to my brother.

I feel that I have compassion and real concern about people who don't have—people in our country who don't have enough to eat and who don't have any advantages to make their brains and feelings grow, like we think is normal. But in spite of all this, I don't have any motivation to get out and *do* something about it. Sending money helps take care of my conscience, and apparently that's about as far as I can go in actually giving help.

may or may not be a creative artist, but he finds his chief interest in the artistic or esthetic experiences in life. The esthetic man views the economic or theoretical man as unappreciative of and destructive of esthetic values.

4. *The social.* The "ideal" social man places great value on *affiliation* and *love.* The social man values other persons as individuals and tends to be kind and sympathetic. Often he views the theoretical and economic value orientations as cold and inhuman.

5. *The political.* The "ideal" political man places great value on *power.* His activities may not be restricted to the narrow range of politics, but his primary focus in personal relationships is on power, influence, and active competition to maintain and expand his power.

6. *The religious.* The highest value for the "ideal" religious man may be called *unity.* He is mystical and seeks to comprehend and relate himself to the cosmos and to find higher-level value experiences via his religious philosophy.

This classification of value types has been criticized on the grounds that it does not exhaust the possibilities and that it provides an overly favorable view of human values. For example, many people appear to have few if any strong values beyond those of hedonism and sensual

pleasure. Also the six "ideal" value types appear to represent nonexistent extremes and do not ordinarily exist in such perfect form in real life. Despite such limitations, however, these value orientations have the advantage of being amenable to measurement and help us to understand the general directions that our value orientations may take.

Conceived and operative values
Many people who have studied values systematically distinguish between conceived and operative values. *Conceived* values are conceptions of the ideal. For the most part, these are the values which the culture teaches and the ones most likely to be talked about in any discussion of "morality" or "ethics." But conceived values, even though held with a good deal of intellectual conviction, sometimes have little practical influence on behavior. For example, an individual who thinks he believes in human equality, nonviolence, service to humanity, and complete honesty may not be guided by these values in his actions even when circumstances would make it fairly easy for him to do so. *Operative* values, on the other hand, are the criteria or value assumptions according to which action choices are actually made.

In trying to identify a person's real values, then, we must analyze not only what he says but what he does in situations that involve an element of choice. Sometimes the discrepancy between an individual's conceived and operative values indicates an alarming schism between his "idealized" and "real" self. The business executive who professes to accept the golden rule but violates even the most basic business ethics, the parent who extols selfless love but governs his child with refined cruelty, and the politician who praises freedom but denies fellow citizens the right to vote are only very obvious examples of an all too common phenomenon.

Sometimes a person holds dual standards without realizing it, sometimes knowingly from a conviction that the ends justify the means. Unfortunately, as Emerson said, "The end pre-exists in the means," and we tend to become what we do, not what we say we want to be.

It is rarely if ever possible, of course, to bring conceived and operative values into complete harmony. The person who places a high value on nonviolence will usually fight rather than be killed, and the person who values complete honesty may lie to protect a friend. The complexities of human nature and human society make utopia an ideal against which to measure our progress rather than a goal we can realistically hope to achieve. But this does not invalidate conceptions of the ideal or strip them of their practical value. Salvador de Madariaga, a Spanish diplomat and political essayist, made this point well:

"Our eyes must be idealistic and our feet realistic. We must walk in the right direction but we must walk step by step. Our tasks are: to define what is desirable; to define what is possible at any time within the scheme of what is desirable; to carry out what is possible in the spirit of what is desirable" (Smith & Lindeman, 1951, p. 123).

Sources of values

When Neil Armstrong set his foot on the moon, declaring his first small step "one giant step for mankind," it perhaps forced most of us to realize that while we have made remarkable progress in many areas during the present century, we are barely on the threshold of understanding the physical, spiritual, mental, and moral forces in our universe. Few people today have the effrontery to claim that they have found the final answers. Where, then, can the individual find reliable values, and how can he determine their validity? How can he arrive at a system of values that is stable and at the same time flexible enough to survive change? The complexity of the problem has been well summarized by Sinnott:

"One of man's chief problems is to determine what the basis of a moral code should be, to find out what he ought to do. Is the right that which is the word of God given to man in the Ten Commandments? Is it what is revealed to us by conscience and intuition? Is it whatever will increase the sum of human happiness? Is it that which is the most reasonable thing to do? Is it whatever makes for the fullness and perfection of life? Above all, is there any absolute right, anything embedded, so to speak, in the nature of the universe, which should guide our actions? Or are right and wrong simply relative, dependent on time and place and culture pattern, and changing with environment and circumstance? What, in short, is the basis of our moral values? These questions are of vital importance in a day when intellectual power threatens to outrun moral control and thus destroy us" (1955, p. 147).

In working out his system of values, an individual can turn to four chief sources of understanding: (1) *his culture*—and other cultures with which he has contact; (2) *science*; (3) *religion*; and (4) *life experiences*—his own and those of other people.

Culture

The culture of each social group is based on certain implicit and explicit values, and although each of us has a system of values somewhat different from anyone else's, our values are usually grounded in the core values of our culture. Kluckhohn and Strodtbeck (1961) have suggested that these core values reflect the culture's orientation to five basic and universal human problems:

1. *Orientation toward human nature.* Is human nature basically good, bad, or neutral? Does the individual have intrinsic value or is he only a cog in the social system or only a bundle of atoms in the physical world? Is he essentially good or evil, rational or irrational? As we have seen, beliefs about childrearing and social controls depend on one's orientation to human nature.

2. *Orientation toward the environment.* Is a human being a helpless pawn or does he have some measure of free will? Does the culture take a fatalistic view of the natural world, view it as something to be adapted to, or see it as a resource to be used and conquered? In our own culture, we have traditionally seen our natural environment largely as a challenge to be con-

"getting things done" with what might be called a *time-pressure* orientation—a compulsion to use time efficiently for useful purposes.

5. *Interpersonal orientation.* What is the dominant or desired relationship among members of the group? Is it competitive or cooperative, friendly or hostile? Human relationships are strikingly different from one culture to another and often within subgroups in the same society. Our own culture emphasizes both a competitive orientation and one of brotherly love, although the latter is not always an operative value.

Against the background of answers generally given to these questions by those in his cultural group, the individual develops his personal system of values. And depending on his conception of what is desirable and good in human life, he selects certain goals over others and patterns his

 Today's young people—including me— are in essence searching for a coherent value system or philosophy of life that will be able to hold its own against the impacts that science may put on society.

quered in the interests of our comfort and convenience.

3. *Time orientation.* Should a person live for the present or for the future? Should old customs and traditions be preserved or should they be replaced by new standards and patterns? Our own culture has often been described as future-oriented and less concerned with maintaining old customs and traditions than with keeping up with the latest ideas and techniques for greater efficiency. There is some evidence, however, that we are becoming more present-oriented, emphasizing and glorifying the "now" for its own sake.

4. *Activity orientation.* What kind of activity is most valued? Making money? Being a good hunter? Service to other people? Contemplation? Our own society embraces several such orientations but appears to be in considerable agreement on the value of "getting going" and

behavior according to standards of what he believes to be right and worthwhile.

Science

Science has the advantage of providing information that has been checked and rechecked by objective methods. But fact is impersonal and, except as it is interpreted, does not contribute to meaning or provide a guide for action. Even the value of searching for truth—the basic premise of science—cannot be "proved" scientifically. Probably the greatest scientist of our age, Albert Einstein, acknowledged that "the scientific method can teach us nothing beyond how facts are related to, and conditioned by, each other":

"One can have the clearest knowledge of what is, and yet not be able to deduce from that what should be the goal of our human aspirations. Objective knowledge provides us with powerful instruments for the achievement of certain ends,

but the ultimate goal itself and the longing to reach it must come from another source. And it is hardly necessary to argue for the view that our existence and our activity acquire meaning only by the setting up of such a goal and of corresponding values. The knowledge of truth as such is wonderful, but it is so little capable of acting as a guide that it cannot prove even the justification and the value of the aspiration toward that very knowledge of truth. Here we face, therefore, the limits of the purely rational conception of our existence" (1950, pp. 21–22).

Science provides us with dependable information about ourselves and our world, but it helps us make value judgements only as we relate such information to value assumptions we are already making on some other basis. For example, the scientific finding that smoking is bad for our health becomes the basis for a value judgment only if we assume that what is bad for our health is undesirable. Usually, of course, we assume that life is intrinsically of value and that whatever is detrimental to life is undesirable.

Although science has thus helped greatly in identifying the paths that can take us closer to our goals, the average person often takes a somewhat defensive attitude toward new scientific information when it seems to contradict what he has believed to be true and when it seems to lessen human stature or significance in the universe. In the same way, Copernicus' discovery in the sixteenth century that the earth moved around the sun, rather than the sun around the earth, met with fierce opposition because it seemed to diminish human importance and to invalidate current human beliefs.

As we learn more about the universe, it is difficult not to see the earth and the human enterprise as an insignificant dot in the vast reaches of the cosmos. But as the astronomer Shapley has pointed out:

"The new discoveries and developments contribute to the unfolding of a magnificent universe; to be a participant is in itself a glory. With our confreres on distant planets; with our fellow animals and plants of land, air and sea . . . with all these we are associated in an existence and an evolution that inspires respect and deep reverence. We cannot escape humility. And as groping philosophers and scientists we are thankful for the mysteries that still lie beyond our grasp" (1958, p. 149).

This statement was made well over a decade before the first moon landing; yet it seems equally relevant today as we gird ourselves for exploratory trips to the planets and to farther reaches of space.

Despite the fantastic progress made each year in the physical, biological, and social sciences and the changes that result, new information is not necessarily a threat, even when it requires changes in our present frame of reference. Rather every increase in knowledge furnishes the potential for a somewhat more adequate view of reality, for better understanding the nature of the universe in which we live and conceivably our role in it, and possibly for developing a more appropriate system of values.

Religion

Both science and religion are concerned with truth. But while science remains "ethically neutral" in its pursuit of truth, religion is concerned also with values.

Religion, as we customarily think of it in its institutionalized form, is based on "revelation" believed to be from God as recorded in tradition and sacred literature. Typically religion involves a formal system of values that can be passed on from generation to generation, as well as a theology and a system of worship and prescriptions for social relationships. Many of the basic values familiar to us in Christianity are found also in other great religions of the world such as Confucianism, Judaism, Islam, and Buddhism. For example, the mandate "Do unto others as ye would have them do unto you" appears in one form or another in most religions.

Although theologians have used logic, reasoning, and historical arguments to help prove the existence of God and the validity of their beliefs, the "proof" of religious truth must rest finally on faith and judgments of probability. People who have received strength and comfort from their religion may have an unshakable

The "Golden Rule" represents one of our highest value aspirations and is found in its essential form in all of the great religions of the world.

Good people proceed while
   considering that
   what is best for others
   is best for themselves.

Hitopadesa
Hinduism

Thou shalt love
   thy neighbor
   as thyself.

Leviticus 19:18
Judaism

Therefore all things
   whatsoever ye would
   that men should do to you,
do ye even so to them.

Matthew 7:12
Christianity

Hurt not others with
   that which pains yourself.

Udanavarga 5:18
Buddhism

What you do not want done
   to yourself,
do not do to others.

Analects 15:23
Confucianism

No one of you is a believer
   until he loves for his brother
   what he loves for himself.

Traditions
Islamism

493 / Assumptions about values

 My religious beliefs are very important to me, for
I am very happy to have the freedom to believe in
God the way I choose. Since I don't go to church,
I know that he is everywhere and that I can pray
to him anywhere and any way I see fit.

belief in the reality of God, but the correctness of their belief can never, by argument alone, be made convincing to anyone who has not shared a similar experience. In the well-known words of Pascal, "The heart has its reasons which reason does not know."

In Western society organized religion has undergone a series of vicissitudes which have tended to undermine faith in many traditional religious beliefs. To some extent this has resulted from what Clark (1958) has called "stimulus-response verbalism" in religious belief. In their search for certainty in a time of change and confusion, many people have embraced formal religion without thinking through its beliefs or values or integrating them into their lives. Thus to many young people, the religious convictions espoused by their elders often seem hypocritical. As someone has put it, "They pray in church on

Sunday and they prey on their fellow man the rest of the week." People and nations have inflicted unbelievable suffering on each other in the name of religion. Finally, the frequent concern of the church as an institution with formal trappings, ritual, and ancient dogma rather than with the life problems of crucial significance to people has led many to conclude that *all* religion has lost its relevance and validity.

In part, the advances of modern science have also tended to undermine faith in traditional religious beliefs and values. For example, in discounting various traditional teachings such as the Biblical account of creation, science has cut away many of the artificial props of religion which many people had come to identify with ultimate truth. Perhaps of even greater significance in undermining traditional faith has been the realization that modern science makes it

Among wide segments of the population, "patriotism" has come to be seen as a self-righteous chauvinism, a glorying in past exploits, and a rationalization for selfish advancement of our country's interests with disregard for the interests of others. In a thought-provoking article, Ralph Nader (1971) has proposed a new kind of patriotism based on the following principles:

1. Patriotism should be rooted in the beliefs and conscience of the individual. If the "consent of the governed" is to have any meaning, it must be based upon the agreement and participation of an informed citizenry.

2. Love of country should include working to improve one's country by taking constructive action against racism, pollution, and other conditions that weaken it and prevent it from attaining its potential or living up to its ideals.

3. Acts that despoil, pollute, desecrate, or otherwise damage our country are unpatriotic. If it is unpatriotic to tear down the flag, it is also unpatriotic to engage in behavior that violates the principles for which the flag stands.

4. A patriotism equated with military exploits and wartime support of one's own country is too limited. Patriotism must also include the duty to advance our ideals toward a better community, country, and world. If patriotism is to have a "manifest destiny," it must be in building a world in which mankind is bound together by the bonds of love and peace.

Implicit in the preceding principles is the concept of patriotism as involving the duty to question and challenge current practices and to dissent from the majority if necessary in order to correct injustice and mistakes. As expressed by a loyal immigrant citizen, Carl Schurz: "Our country . . . when right, to be kept right. When wrong, to be put right." For it would appear that in this way lies our best hope of ensuring the vision so eloquently expressed by Abraham Lincoln: "We here highly resolve . . . that this nation, under God, shall have a new birth of freedom, and that government of the people, by the people, for the people, shall not perish from the earth."

possible not only for us to control our environment but to plan and create the future of our race. Thus the belief in an all-powerful God who determines each person's destiny has been called into question.

Experience

In the life of the group and of the individual, many values originate from experience. Each of us is a valuing organism, experiencing success or failure, satisfaction or dissatisfaction in different situations. We are constantly making judgments about what is good and bad, more desirable and less desirable, more meaningful and less meaningful. And as we make these judgments about our ongoing experiences, we modify our value system accordingly.

We can also draw on the experience of others. Through our libraries and our museums, we can draw upon the experience of individuals and nations throughout the world since the beginning of human history. We can trace the rise and fall of past civilizations and examine the causes which led to their downfall. We can observe the effects of dictatorships on human welfare and contrast these governments with more democratic forms of social organization in terms of their long-range contributions to human happiness and social progress. We can observe the effects of greed, selfishness, and ignorance in creating general human misery and leading to warfare. We can note the incalculable cost of humanity's incessant armed conflicts in terms of lives, property, and suffering and their futility in solving basic problems. These and many other lessons can be learned from history; although we cannot always scientifically prove such lessons to be accurate, they, too, support certain values and invalidate others.

In guiding our political and social lives, we operate on the basis of hypotheses (somewhat similar to the hypotheses of the scientist) which we continually modify and expand so that they agree more closely with the "facts" of our experience. Tack after tack has been taken through history as people have tried to determine what values they should follow—individually and collectively—to find happiness and to fulfill their destiny as human beings. Usually a society changes slowly, almost grudgingly, by a series of small modifications. At certain critical times in history, however, one human personality, or several, may lead society to accept a new set of values and to put them into action, as our own country's founders did during the period of the American Revolution. Norman Cousins has suggested how they were able to work this "magic" of winning acceptance almost overnight for a new system of political values:

"The answer is to be found in the history of ideas. An idea does not have to find its mark in the minds of large numbers of people in order to create an incentive for change. Ideas have a life of their own. They can be nourished and brought to active growth by a small number of sensitive, vital minds which somehow respond to the needs of a total organism, however diffused the parts of that organism may be. These minds sense both the need for change and the truth of ideas that define the nature of change. When the ideas are articulated and advocated, the popular response is not merely the product of logic reaping its gains but of a dormant awareness coming to life" (1958, p. 16).

Often in the history of ideas, new values, once articulated, have been readily accepted because people have *known* them to be right on the basis

of their own experience. In the long run, most of the values that actually influence our behavior are validated by the satisfaction we have experienced in pursuing them. Hence experience becomes a key factor in determining the values we follow and the ones we discard.

Criteria of a sound value system

Although values are inevitably a somewhat individual matter, worked out by each individual on the basis of what seems most valid to him, any adequate value system must probably meet the following criteria.

Integration and faith

An adequate value system is both internally consistent and integrated with the individual's total personality. It is something in which he can reasonably have a good deal of faith. An integrated value system also implies a *hierarchy* of values, which enables the individual to choose confidently between things of greater and lesser importance and to be relatively undisturbed by frustrations that interfere only with the attainment of short-range goals.

Values come alive in direct proportion to how much faith the individual has in them. Faith helps close the gap between conceived and operative values and enables the individual to achieve

When I was in college, what was important to me was survival—grades, food, love . . . in different order at different times. Now I have what money can buy. And I have a good family. Now it doesn't matter if I have to skip a meal. It matters to me that my kids grow up with their heads on straight, and they can set up their own priorities when they get out on their own—that'll be their problem. Another thing that matters to me now is how my wife and I relate, and keep on growing, hopefully together. Lots of little things may go wrong, but I keep my eye on the ones that matter most to me.

a sense of wholeness in everything he feels and says and does. His behavior reflects an intellectual and emotional surety; there is relatively little conflict between "ought" and "want." This is the kind of faith illustrated in the lives of the "self-actualizing" persons studied by Maslow (1954, 1969). "They were generally unconfused about right and wrong and made ethical decisions more quickly and more surely than average people" (1969, p. 122). It may be emphasized here, however, that the kind of faith that encourages self-actualization is quite different from the type of dogmatic faith which seems to reflect fear and uncertainty more than positive understanding and conviction.

An adequate system of values carries the conviction of truth while remaining fluid enough to allow for correction and expansion. In es-

another—to support the specious argument that *no* value can have any real validity and that the "right" values, therefore, are whichever ones seem most immediately useful. Other people seek security in the face of uncertainty by accepting ready-made the values of their various reference groups—their culture, their socioeconomic class, their religion, modern science—without thinking them through. Often a further problem is created here when the values of these different groups are inconsistent with each other, so that to live by them the individual must either divide his life into "compartments" or be in constant conflict with himself. Inconsistent faith, dogmatic faith, and lack of faith fail equally to provide the guidelines an individual needs to behave effectively in a changing world and to grow toward self-fulfillment.

 Values that form a way of life where you are at peace with yourself change constantly. I know what my values are now, but I don't know what they will be ten years from now.

sence, we need to feel that our reality, possibility, and value assumptions are valid but also to remain alert to information that may prove them false. This is essentially the attitude expressed by Mahatma Gandhi in his autobiography:

"I am far from claiming any finality or infallibility about my conclusions. One claim I do indeed make and it is this. For me they appear to be absolutely correct, and seem for the time being to be final. For if they were not, I should base no action on them" (1948, p. 5).

Such an attitude enables the individual to take forthright action based on conviction while at the same time maintaining an openness to new or fuller truth.

In a transitional age such as ours the achievement of reasoned faith is more difficult than in times of greater stability, but it has never been more needed. Some people use the concept of "cultural relativity"—the fact that value orientations may differ considerably from one culture to

Realism and flexibility

An adequate value system requires accurate assumptions concerning reality and possibility. First of all, this implies the need for the individual to be informed—to have adequate information. This relates to the Socratic belief that no person will knowingly choose falsehood over truth—as well as to the Jeffersonian concept of democracy which is based on the belief that full information leads to right action and that right action is not possible without it. Whether or not we agree with Socrates and Jefferson, it is apparent that feeling one is fully informed about a given situation makes the matter of choice or value judgment much easier and more decisive.

A realistic value system also implies the need for a certain amount of flexibility. Fundamental values may remain relatively stable, but they must be refined and their compass extended as the individual's understanding broadens. The person whose values today are exactly the same as they were ten years ago has failed to grow in one important dimension. Values must keep pace with changes in the individual himself, in his life situation, and in his physical and socio-cultural environment if they are to prove adequate.

Meaning and satisfaction

A final consideration in judging the adequacy of any value system is the amount of satisfaction that the individual derives from living by it—whether it gives meaning to his life and a sense that he is fulfilling the purposes of his existence. Dorothy Lee, an anthropologist who has made intensive studies of value in other cultures, has emphasized the experience of satisfaction as a universal criterion of value:

"... we experience value when our activity is permeated with satisfaction, when we find meaning in our life, when we feel good, when we act not out of calculating choice and not for extraneous purpose but rather because this is the only way that we, as ourselves, deeply want to act" (1959, p. 165).

In short, values are subject to the pragmatic test of their consequences both for the individual and for the group. And as the existentialists have pointed out, one's life can be meaningful and fulfilling only if it involves personally and socially constructive values and choices.

Values and becoming

Becoming refers to personal change over time. We all are in the process of becoming throughout our lives, for every experience of life leaves some change in us. We like to expect that such continuing change is in positive directions and that we are becoming more proficient, more capable, and more attractive. But sometimes change is in a negative direction, as in the case of the individual who becomes a chronic alcoholic or the individual who becomes cynical and embittered, feeling that his life has been wasted.

Admittedly, life is neither simple nor easy, and it involves far more than our values. Opportunities, chance factors, personal resources, and many other conditions all enter in. It is largely through our choices and our actions, however, that we shape the kind of person we will become as well as the kind of personal world that we will make to live in.

In this context, three aspects of becoming merit special consideration: learning to trust one's own process of valuing, becoming an authentic person, and building a favorable life world.

Trusting one's own process of valuing

As we have seen, we derive some of our values from external sources—such as science, religion, our culture, and the experience of others—and some from our own direct experiences of values. Ideally, we are selective in what we accept from external sources—enriching our insights by adding those of other people, weighing the value experiences of others for relevance to us, and choosing from all the possibilities the particular values which have validity for *us.*

When our own experiences of value contradict the value judgments of our culture or the prescriptions of science or religion, we must decide which we trust most—our experience or that of others. Rogers (1964, 1969) has found that many of those who seek therapy have, knowingly or not, chosen to follow external value judgments, ignoring or denying their own perceptions of value, with the following typical results:

1. Most of the individual's values are learned (introjected) from other individuals or groups significant to him, but he regards them as his own.

2. The locus of evaluation lies outside himself—he is essentially directed by a "program" which he has received uncritically from others.

3. Many of his accepted value assumptions are unsound and even contradictory, and they often conflict with the evidence supplied by his own experience. For example, he may calmly

In *Peer Gynt,* Henrik Ibsen portrays a man who devotes his entire life to pursuing what he believes to be his own best interests, only to discover at the end of his life that he has lost everything of real value. Ibsen is apparently concerned with selfishness as we typically think of it—which is usually egocentric, shortsighted, and unconcerned with others.

In contrast, Ayn Rand (1964) contends that our own best interests are inevitably linked with the well-being of all people, since we are social creatures, and what happens to others will ultimately affect us. As such, Rand takes the position that to be truly selfish, one has to be concerned about the needs of others and authentic in one's relationships with others. Thus, selfishness requires both honesty and integ-

rity, for being dishonest and deceitful would be self-defeating and hence not really selfish.

The apparent difference between these two views of selfishness stems from a difference of definition. Ibsen views selfishness as bad—involving self-defeating acts; Rand sees selfishness as good—comprising, of necessity, the humanitarian actions of individuals.

discuss the possibility of dropping an atomic bomb on an enemy country but feel deep sympathy when he sees the suffering of one small child.

4. Since these value assumptions have been accepted uncritically, they tend to be held in a rigid fashion and are not readily subject to critical evaluation and change; rather, discrepancies tend to be denied or rationalized.

5. The individual feels insecure and easily threatened, for he does not trust his own valuing process to resolve discrepancies and formulate a coherent, meaningful value system. So he clings to his contradictory and confusing values because he sees no reliable alternative.

The ultimate price of depending on the value judgments of others is that the individual loses contact with his own inner processes of evaluation and potential wisdom. This loss of contact appears to be a fundamental aspect of the alienation and estrangement of an individual from his self, a phenomenon so prevalent in today's world.

Thus it is of critical importance that the individual's chief locus of valuing be his own inner experience. In fact, it is in viewing humans as capable of their own value judgments that we credit them with some measure of free will and self-determination. For it is their ability to weigh the desirability of two courses of action and see one as more desirable than another that makes it

possible for them to make a choice. As Kelley has pointed out:
"Volition is high if you consciously concern yourself with which action to choose and give the choice much consideration, and if you experience uncertainty, conflict, and the potentiality of alternative responses" (1967, p. 218).

There is no guarantee that humans will always choose the good or desirable over the bad or undesirable. But the mature person, who is open to his own experiencing, is free to capitalize both on the ability he shares with other animals to utilize feedback in adapting his behavior to meet his needs and also on his uniquely human capacities for self-awareness, critical reflection, and anticipation of future events and consequences. It would appear that when the individual's locus of valuing is internal rather than dependent on what others say is valuable, and when he fully understands the consequences of the alternatives, he can usually be relied upon to choose value directions which are conducive to his self-fulfillment and the welfare of others.

As we have seen, making judgments on the basis of one's own valuing does not necessarily entail the rejection of existing social values. As Morris has pointed out:
"Revolt, rebellion, apostasy are not in themselves the mark of the existential man. Even the man who consents to convention can be the existential

> In our family there were many rules, but a strong one was, never ask questions, never talk about any unhappiness or about any problems. I worked hard at these rules—at being what was expected. Then 'fate' interfered—as a young wife, just 19, I could not deny to myself that my new son was a handicapped child, to be handicapped for the rest of his life. In a simple way I made my decision to face life head on. Sometimes I think this was a miracle, as there was so much groundwork that had been laid that could have made me run away. I was just calmly able to face each day as it came. My desire to do everything in my power to help my son was abnormally strong. Fortunately, as he has grown, we both have faced the issues and problems as they have arisen. We have been forthright at all times.

man if *he is aware of the act of consenting and hence of the necessity that he take personal responsibility for living his life in a conventional way"* (1966, p. 48).

What he does is then done intentionally, out of a conviction that this is the thing to do, regardless of whether or not it happens to follow conventional expectations. He is trusting his own process of valuing.

Becoming an authentic person

Closely related to the directions of personal growth enumerated above and to the need to trust one's own process of valuing is the concept of "becoming an authentic person." As Morris has put it:

"And who is authentic? The individual whose example is perhaps beyond the reach of most of us: the individual who is free and who knows it, who knows that every deed and word is a choice and hence an act of value creation, and, finally and perhaps decisively, who knows that he is the author of his own life and must be held personally responsible for the values on behalf of which he

has chosen to live it, and that these values can never be justified by referring to something or somebody outside himself" (1966, p. 48).

As Snyder (1967) says, the authentic person is "being a truth." He is one who has integrity, who has thought through his values and lives by them. The alternative to seeking the truth and being a truth is to be a "phony," to be unauthentic, to lead a wasted life, and to be the architect of one's own destruction.

Although the basic theme underlying authenticity is the commitment to be true to oneself—both in terms of being what one is and in terms of shaping oneself through one's own choices and actions—a second and equally important basic theme is concern for and commitment to others. In both the humanistic and the existential models of man, commitment to others follows almost automatically from commitment to oneself. For there is considered to be a basic unity to humanity, and the task of learning to live constructively automatically leads to involvement, obligation, and commitment to one's fellow human beings. As Rogers has put it:

"I believe that when the human being is inwardly free to choose whatever he deeply values, he tends

Implicit in our discussion of the role of values in personal change or becoming are the following assumptions about individuals:

1. Individual human beings have some measure of freedom for self-direction.

2. Freedom requires choices, and these choices are ultimately based on the individual's value system—his assumptions about what is valuable, desirable, preferable, and important.

3. The greater the individual's faith in his values, the greater the effort and persistence with which he will pursue goals based on them.

4. An individual may hold sound or unsound values or may be unable to find values in which he can place his faith.

5. Assuming favorable environmental conditions, each individual is ultimately responsible for his value choices and the actions based on them.

These same assumptions appear applicable to groups as they become aware of and reflect on their value orientations and alternative choices.

to value those objects, experiences, and goals which make for his own survival, growth, and development, and for the survival and development of others" (1964, p. 166).

Building a favorable life world

Positive becoming is not entirely a matter of change and growth in oneself. Of crucial importance, too, is the type of world one constructs for oneself to live in.

In choosing an occupation, in choosing a mate, in choosing whether to have children and how to bring them up, in choosing his home and its furnishings, in choosing how to spend his money, the individual builds a world for himself which may help him to meet his needs and grow or may present him with one unnecessary problem after another. Snyder has dramatically summarized the matter:

"Gradually you build up a life world which, for you, is your destiny in this world. It is the arena where you play out the struggle of life versus death for you. The rest of your life space becomes background. This life world becomes the foreground and pioneer settlement of your life" (1967, p. 19).

The structure of this life world will usually have common elements for most people, for most of us in the course of our lives build friendships, undertake specific occupations, get married, and raise families. Its quality, however, will depend in large measure on our individual value choices. For example, whether we marry, whom we marry, the type of relationships we attempt to build in marriage and other social interactions, and the ways we cope with life stresses all reflect our value choices.

Of particular importance here are our value choices in relation to material things and other people—whether we value and pursue material

 I have always been able to cope with most circumstances. Now I'm in a situation where I have to start doing something about my life and work, and make a decision about marriage. This is a period of my life that will determine the direction the whole rest of my life will take.

possessions for their own sake or largely as resources for fuller living, and whether we regard and treat other people as objects or as other valuing, experiencing beings like ourselves.

In our discussion of social competence, we compared I-It and I-Thou relationships (page 247), noting that if we view people as objects to be controlled and manipulated rather than as unique persons, we deny ourselves the possibility of establishing meaningful and authentic relationships with them. In a bureaucratic, mass society, which often seems to dehumanize and depersonalize our contacts with each other, it would seem especially important to be sure we are building a life world in which meaningful relationships with people are possible. For although we differ in the value we place upon affiliation with others, it would appear that personal growth and fulfillment, for most of us, is heavily dependent on the quality of the interpersonal relationships we establish in our life world.

In any event, the structure and quality of the life world that we construct for ourselves will be of crucial significance in determining the frustrations and stresses we will face as well as the extent to which we will meet our needs and have opportunities for continuing personal growth.

Values and the world of the future

While the "Spaceship Earth" has an efficient life support system, it is limited; yet the number of its inhabitants is increasing with frightening rapidity and overburdening its decreasing resources. At the same time we see its passengers divided into conflicting groups who often fight and kill each other; and we note that a number of these groups have developed thermonuclear weapons capable of killing every human being several times over.

It seems apparent that in the last quarter of the twentieth century, the world's peoples are faced with three herculean tasks: (1) to complete the unfinished business of eliminating poverty and discrimination and providing equal oppor-

tunity for all; (2) to cope with new problems which have become acute in the course of our technological advances—such as pollution, the population explosion, and accelerating and largely uncontrolled technological and social change; and (3) to plan and achieve a "good future" for all of us on the Spaceship Earth.

It is with the latter problem and its value implications that we shall conclude our journey into the realm of human behavior.

Exploring alternative futures

We are confronted today with the problem of survival, but even more important is the problem of *how* we shall survive—the quality of the life private foundations and organizations. They are composed of interdisciplinary teams of scientists, historians, philosophers, and other personnel from diverse fields of endeavor who devote full time to considering the range of alternatives open to us in planning a good future and the probable consequences of given alternatives.

The "futurists" point to the fact that throughout history, those organisms that have been unable to adapt to the demands of a changing environment have perished. Curiously enough the dinosaur, which was not noted for its high level of intelligence, survived for some 150 million years, while the human race is already an endangered species after some 2 million years on this planet. As Shepherd has pointed out

 A permissive society that accepts authority without question is the colossal danger past, present, and future. Another danger is a people who would hang onto 20th Century morality and standards in a 21st Century technology and population. If the world is to survive, the people must change to reflect the changing situations, or nature will make changes of her own that might not include man.

that we will be able to achieve. Saving the human race for a future world of *unsanity* or for a dehumanizing, lock-step regimentation in a world of bare subsistence is hardly sufficient. But a "good future" will not come automatically.

In recent years a growing number of organizations and scientists have become directly involved in delineating various possible futures for our own country and for the world as a whole. These groups have been set up by the federal government, by our major universities, and by

"Man may be headed for extinction, like the dinosaur," adding, however, that "unlike the dinosaur, man has options" (1971, p. 15). Thus it becomes essential that we carefully explore and evaluate the options open to us.

Perhaps the chief message of the futurists is that humans are not trapped by some absurd fate like the dinosaur but can and must choose their own future. This in turn means choosing the type of world we wish to build and the type of people that we wish to develop to live in it. We

Our society has frequently been accused of being a dehumanizing mass bureaucracy in which individuals are becoming increasingly alienated—and in which the individual feels he has little control over his own destiny, let alone that of society. In a sense, the "average citizen" has become an alienated observer rather than an active and enthusiastic participant in the American Dream.

When citizens become aware of the tremendous scope of the problems facing our society, most of them do realize that their own future as well as that of their children are directly involved. And they ask "What can I do?"

Perhaps the starting point is to become familiar with the special needs and problems of one's own community; and whatever his or her occupation—student, homemaker, teacher, lawyer, executive, trade-unionist—an interested person can find ways to contribute, such as participating in various civic organizations, serving as a part-time volunteer in a hospital or community mental health center, working for the election of given political candidates, taking an active and responsible role as a citizen. Often, over time, many persons find themselves in leadership positions where their individual influence can be more strongly exerted. In any event, if we are to survive as a society it seems essential that each person not only "does his thing" but also "does his part." As John F. Kennedy so succinctly put it, "Each man can make a difference, and each man should try."

 My worst fear is that a scientific elite may plan and exercise control over the rest of us—perhaps control our youngsters' very genetic potentials. No person has the right to control others like this, and a working value system must be accepted by us which will ensure our 'peoplehood' for the future.

are no longer limited by the "givens" in ourselves and our surroundings but are increasingly capable of directing our own destiny.

Computer technology has proven of great help in enabling us to rehearse the entire range of imaginable options open to us by simulating different "futures" and their probable advantages and disadvantages. Ultimately, however, only human beings can make the value judgments on which plans for their future will be based. For while the computer can relieve humans of much routine work and even handle many routine managerial judgments and decisions requiring a repeated analysis of information in terms of a regular set of rules, it still cannot replace humans in making value judgments concerning which goals are worthwhile and how much effort they are worth. For better or for worse, we cannot escape from the choices that will determine our destiny. The only question is whether these choices will be made by default or with imagination and the use of all the evidence now potentially at our disposal.

Many behavioral scientists—and others—are seriously worried about the possibility that some elite minority may someday plan and exercise control over the rest of us, utilizing behavioral scientists primarily as tools in achieving their

VALUES AND HUMAN SOCIETY: A TENTATIVE ORIENTATION

The following assumptions appear to be compatible with and extensions of the basic value orientation implicit in this book in relation to the planning of a "good" future for the human race.

1. The survival of humankind is desirable.

2. The life of each individual has intrinsic worth and is to be respected.

3. Social progress is both possible and desirable.

4. The pursuit of "truth," as exemplified in modern science, can be useful for achieving social progress.

5. Democracy, with its respect for the individual and its congenial atmosphere for the pursuit of truth, provides the setting most conducive to individual and group fulfillment.

6. Most of the values promulgated by Christianity and other great religions are not only compatible with a democratic society but a necessary basis for it.

7. Each individual and group has the responsibility for preserving and extending the progress made by preceding generations.

8. Humankind has some role or potential destiny in the universe; we are challenged to find out what it is and use our resources and abilities accordingly.

goals. This is the warning in such prophetic and frightening "utopias" as Huxley's *Brave New World,* Orwell's *1984,* and Skinner's *Walden Two.* More recently Skinner has argued in *Beyond Freedom and Dignity* (1971) that freedom is not only illusory but actually a dangerous goal and that scientific control of human behavior through systematic reinforcement is our best hope for a good future.

To safeguard ourselves against the possibility of science being used to restrict rather than enrich our lives, many psychologists and other investigators are becoming increasingly concerned not only with the alternative futures which science and technology are making possible but also with the value orientations on which a choice among these futures may be based.

The crucial role of values in shaping the future

As science and technology steadily increase our power not only to shape our future environment but also to control our development and behavior, most scientists consider it inevitable that such controls will be used. This has given rise to several serious questions: (1) What type of controls will be used? (2) Who will exercise these controls? (3) What values will they be based on?

Collier (1968) has suggested a basic value with which most scientists and nonscientists alike would probably agree. He defines this value as "the recognition and constructive concern for whatever capacity the individual has (for both self and others) for self-regulation and self-determination" (p. 5). This value orientation involves basic respect for the individual as always a partially self-determining system, with some potentiality for freedom and choice under favorable conditions.

The same basic ethic has been stated in other ways by many prominent Americans. For example, John Dewey wrote:

"Democracy has many meanings, but if it has a moral meaning, it is found in resolving that the supreme test of all political institutions and industrial arrangements shall be the contribution they

make to the all-round growth of every member of society" (1930, p. 221).

John W. Gardner, former Secretary of Health, Education, and Welfare, stated it this way:

"What we are suggesting is that every institution in our society should contribute to the fulfillment of the individual. Every institution, must, of course, have its own purposes and preoccupations, but over and above everything else it does, it should be prepared to answer this question posed by society: 'What is the institution doing to foster the development of the individuals within it?'" (1965, p. 814).

shaping our own future, let us hope that we will find new solutions that will change what needs to be changed while preserving essential values that are still valid. For it has taken the human race many thousands of years to achieve the imperfect level of freedom and opportunity for self-determination that we have reached; if these crucial achievements and other time-tested values are carelessly discarded, the change can bring us more loss than gain, and it may take long effort and suffering just to regain our present position. The warning that "the price of freedom is eternal vigilance" is not one

 I want to learn to relate as fully as possible to other people in meaningful ways on all levels. I am working on this. It's more than a lifetime's work, so I doubt that I'll be bored!

Implicit in this value orientation is the concept of "a participatory and anticipatory democracy in which the people are directly involved in establishing priorities and guiding social change—a society in which each individual has maximal opportunities for fulfilling his potentialities and living a meaningful and fulfilling life, a society in which human freedom and dignity are truly established" (Coleman, 1973, p. 178).

The research and writings of Maslow, Rogers, Fromm, and other humanistic psychologists, as we have seen, have all emphasized this general value orientation. The chart on page 506 summarizes the value assumptions that appear to be related to this basic value orientation.

In any event, we can, if we will, create a future society which will provide our descendants with richer lives and greater opportunities for self-direction and self-actualization than has ever been known. In fact, humans of the future may well be as different from us as we are from our Neanderthal ancestors.

As we embark upon the great adventure of

to be dismissed lightly in our age of turmoil and rapid change. And this warning applies equally to the ever present danger of global atomic war. It would seem a tragedy indeed if by some act of thermonuclear folly we were to commit mass suicide just as our exciting and challenging adventure is getting underway.

In accepting the Nobel Prize for Literature in 1950, William Faulkner made this prophetic statement, which seems equally relevant today and a fitting conclusion for our discussion:

"I decline to accept the end of man. It is easy enough to say that man is immortal simply because he will endure: that when the last ding-dong of doom has clanged and faded from the last worthless rock hanging tideless in the last red and dying evening, that even then there will still be one more sound: that of his puny inexhaustible voice, still talking. I refuse to accept this. I believe that man will not merely endure: he will prevail. He is immortal, not because he alone among creatures has an inexhaustible voice, but because he has a soul, a spirit capable of compassion and sacrifice and endurance" (1961, p. 4).

 Solving pollution, energy, political problems are
superficial goals if we can't learn to love mankind
and work for the quality of life. The greatest
danger of our future is our disregard for others,
different cultures and values. Human life is so
beautiful and so easily destroyed by aggression,
competition, hatred. And it all begins with
me . . . .

The quest for values / 508

Summary and a look ahead

In this chapter we have dealt with our never ceasing quest for values and with the necessity for finding a value orientation that can hold its own against the impact of science and technology on contemporary society.

In this context we reviewed various types of value orientations, such as the economic, social, political, and religious. We then noted the important distinction between conceived and operative values; and we pointed out the detrimental effects of glaring discrepancies between values the individual conceives as valid and ideal and those he actually uses in guiding his everyday behavior. Next we looked at the major sources of value including culture, science, religion, and experience; and we examined the criteria of a sound value system— integration and faith, realism and flexibility, and meaning and satisfaction.

We then dealt with values and becoming, particularly the importance of trusting one's own process of valuing, of becoming an authentic person, and of continuing personal growth. And finally, we emphasized the crucial role of values in building a "good future" for humanity.

As we look back over the seventeen chapters which form the basic content of this book, it is apparent that our discussion has been founded primarily on scientific findings. In the Epilogue which follows, we shall explore a different approach to human experiencing, focusing on "new" ways of perceiving reality—an approach which some psychologists view as a return to primitive magical thinking and others view as a new horizon in understanding our potential as human beings.

EXPLORATIONS IN HUMAN EXPERIENCING

There are more things in heaven and
* earth, Horatio,*
Than are dreamt of in your philosophy.

Hamlet, Act I, Scene V

Humanistic processes of discovery and scientific methodology have yielded vast areas of information about human learning, problem-solving, motives, meaning, insight, values, and other human processes. Yet, disciplined, reasoned processes of inquiry can provide only certain types of information, and there is a widespread suspicion that to rely solely on rational analysis and scientific procedure may result in missing much that is not only important but real. Moreover, we have become acutely aware that science and reason have been relatively ineffective in helping us deal with such crises as war, poverty, hatred, and ecological imbalance, and that they sometimes provide an image of human beings that feels alien to us as we know ourselves. Nor have science and reason been able to explain many phenomena that people have observed and experienced.

The purpose of this section is to broaden the perspective of the material presented in earlier chapters by providing a glimpse into other ways of knowing. There has been a recent upsurge of interest in nonrational, spiritual avenues to knowledge, leading to a study of different apprehensions of reality, altered states of consciousness, astrology and the occult, mysticism and spiritualism, and the like. It has been customary in modern Western culture to glorify the objective and rational. Hence, the new interest in other realms of knowledge is often viewed as an unhealthy regression toward superstition and an unfortunate retreat from the strenuous efforts that must be made to advance science and reason.

This section is not an attempt to glorify the mystical and intuitive sources of knowledge at the expense of other modes of knowing. It is simply a presentation of a different kind of material than we have considered previously. It might be called "far out," but it is also stimulating. We present these points of view without any effort to evaluate or judge them, since any judgment made at this time would be presumptuous. From among the enormous variety of possibilities, we have elected to present, in their own words for the most part, the experiences of Carlos Castaneda, and the views of Baba Ram Dass in his metamorphosis from Harvard professor to Yogi, and explorations of the inner self by Ronald Laing.

Carlos Castaneda and nonordinary reality

Setting out to learn about medicinal plants used by the Indians of the Southwest, anthropology graduate student Carlos Castaneda apprenticed himself to an old Yaqui Indian sorcerer he called don Juan. In a series of books, *The Teachings of Don Juan* (1968), *A Separate Reality* (1971), and *Journey to Ixtlan* (1972), he has depicted his experiences and learnings over a decade—experiences which acquaint him with a different order of reality, meaning, and value to which few of us who share the "modern scientific mind" are exposed.

The crack between the worlds

Initially, through the use of hallucinogenic substances, Castaneda encounters a world where reality as he has known it is dramatically challenged, where ". . . space does not conform to Euclidean geometry, time does not form a continuous unidirectional flow, causation does not conform to Aristotelian logic, man is not differentiated from non-man or life from death, as in our world. . . ." (*TDJ,* Foreword)

Don Juan explains to Castaneda that there is a crack between the two worlds, and that the key objective is to learn how to enter the other world:

"'There is a crack between the two worlds. . . . There is a place where the two worlds overlap. The crack is there. It opens and closes like a door in the wind. To get there a man must exercise his will. He must, I should say, develop . . . a single-minded dedication. . . . When the crack opens the man has to slide through it. It is hard to see on the other side of the boundary. It is windy, like a sandstorm. The wind whirls around. The man then must walk in any direction. It will be a short or a long journey, depending on his willpower. A strong-willed man journeys shortly. An undecided, weak man journeys long and precariously. . . .'" (*TDJ,* p. 195)

Castaneda has great difficulty learning to accept the nonordinary reality of don Juan, and his typically Western, rational approach to understanding leads to amusing and frustrating exchanges with the old man. Following his first experience with peyote—Mescalito—Castaneda and don Juan discuss the "presence" of Mescalito in Castaneda's drug state:

"'Can you tell me now, don Juan, how does peyote protect . . .'

"He did not let me finish. Vigorously he touched me on the shoulder.

"'Don't you ever name him that way. You haven't seen enough of him yet to know him.'

"'How does Mescalito protect people?'

"'He advises. He answers whatever questions you ask.'

"'Then Mescalito is real? I mean he is something you can see?'

"He seemed to be baffled by my question. He looked at me with a sort of blank expression.

"'What I meant to say, is that Mescalito . . .'

"'I heard what you said. Didn't you see him last night?'

"'I wanted to say that I saw only a dog [*during his drug trip*], but I noticed his bewildered look.

"'Then you think what I saw last night was him?'

"'He looked at me with contempt. He chuckled, shook his head as though he couldn't believe it . . . .'" (*TDJ,* pp. 35–36)

Obstacles to the "man of knowledge"

Over the years, don Juan teaches Castaneda not only to glimpse and accept a different order of reality, but also to face the fears and obstacles in the way to becoming a man of knowledge. Indeed, time and time again Castaneda experiences fear about his quest for knowledge and understanding under the old man's guidance, and don Juan constantly encourages him. Don Juan points out that such fears are natural but that "no matter how frightening learning is, it is more terrible to think of a man without . . . knowledge" (*TDJ,* p. 46).

To become a "man of knowledge" means to go as far as one can in "unraveling the secrets of power and knowledge" (*TDJ,* p. 77). But achievement of this goal can be accomplished only by defeating four natural enemies of a man of knowledge. Don Juan describes the first of these enemies:

"'When a man starts to learn, he is never clear about his objectives. His purpose is faulty; his intent is vague. He hopes for rewards that will never materialize, for he knows nothing of the hardships of learning.

"'He slowly begins to learn—bit by bit at first, then in big chunks. And his thoughts soon clash. What he learns is never what he pictured, or imagined, and so he begins to be afraid. Learning is never what one expects. Every step of learning is a new task, and the fear the man is experiencing begins to mount mercilessly, unyielding. His purpose becomes a battlefield.

"'And thus he has stumbled upon the first of his natural enemies: Fear! A terrible enemy—treacherous, and difficult to overcome. . . .'" (*TDJ,* p. 79)

To succeed, the individual must defy the fear, persevere in learning, and step by step grow more certain of himself. The person achieves freedom from fear by gaining clarity of mind, a clarity in which the person knows his desires and how to satisfy them. But clarity can be the second enemy, because the person may now be blinded by the assurance that clarity brings, and may act rashly or foolishly. To defeat this enemy, one must defy the clarity, and be patient and careful; when this patience is achieved, then one can be truly powerful. Yet, power is the third enemy, the strongest of all. If the person is not careful, power will turn him into a cruel and capricious person. To defeat this enemy, "'He has to defy it, deliberately. He has to come to realize the power he has seemingly conquered is in reality never his. He must keep himself in line at all times, handling carefully and faithfully all that he has learned. . . .'" (*TDJ*, p. 82)

By the time one has achieved self-control, many years have passed, and the final enemy is at hand—old age. The person must then struggle with the wish to rest, to "lie down and forget." "'His desire to retreat will overrule all his clarity, his power, and his knowledge'" (*TDJ*, p. 83).

"'But if the man sloughs off his tiredness, and lives his fate through, he can then be called a man of knowledge, if only for the brief moment when he succeeds in fighting off his last, invincible enemy. That moment of clarity, power, and knowledge is enough'" (*TDJ*, p. 83).

The wisdom that Castaneda learned was associated with three skills in which don Juan tried to train him: how to become a "hunter," how to become a "warrior," and how to become a "seer."

Becoming a hunter

At first don Juan was not willing to talk to Castaneda about the secrets of hallucinogenic substances, but he tried to interest him in becoming a hunter, which, he insisted, would be no small achievement. To be a hunter, Castaneda was told, he would have to erase personal history, lose self-importance, become inaccessible, and learn to disrupt the routines of life.

Erasing personal history is important in order to free ourselves from the expectations other people put on us, and to respond with alertness and an open mind to the surprises and new experiences we encounter. Don Juan scolds Castaneda: "'You take yourself too seriously. . . . You are so goddamn important that you feel justified to be annoyed with everything. You're so damn important that you can afford to leave if things don't go your way. . . .'" (*JI*, pp. 40–41)

Being inaccessible means that we are not controlled by other people or events. We decide when to be available and when not available. It means to be honest enough and humble enough to know one's limits. But to achieve this requires that we be not so dependent on our own habitual ways of perceiving, thinking, and acting.

A good hunter knows the routines of his prey, but he is able to use this knowledge in catching them because he himself has no routines. He is not, like other animals, controlled by strict routines and predictable habits; rather the hunter is free and unpredictable.

Becoming a warrior

As don Juan teaches Castaneda about the art of hunting, he begins to introduce him to a sterner life, that of the warrior. The key principles he stresses are: assuming responsibility, consulting with death, becoming accessible to power, assuming the mood of a warrior, fighting the battle of power, and taking a warrior's last stand.

A warrior takes full responsibility for his acts. Of course, he must first decide why he is taking a given action, but once this decision is made, he must proceed without doubt or remorse. A warrior makes decisions in the face of death, and this can in turn give perspective to our decisions. "'Death is our eternal companion. It is always to our left, at an arm's length. . . .The thing to do when you're impatient is to turn to your left and ask advice from your death. . . .'" (*JI*, pp. 54–55)

A warrior is a hunter who seeks power, but while he may hunt power, he can only find it if it comes to him. The final decision is not up to the hunter but lies in "'the realm of powers that guide men'" (*JI*, p. 119). Yet a warrior does not indulge in self-pity or blame others for his misfortunes.

The quest for power centers around learning to believe in the reality of one's dreams. It takes power to call forth and sustain the hidden worlds of dreams and they, in turn, give us new power. Don Juan says, "'The world is a mystery. This, what you're looking at, is not all there is to it. There is much more to the world, so much more, in fact, that it is endless. . . .'" (*JI*, p. 167)

In teaching Castaneda about a warrior's last stand, don Juan tells him that each warrior has a special place, a place where he finds power, a place where he stores his resources. Whenever he needs to he can visit this place in his dreams. Then don Juan adds:

"'*This is the place where you will die. . . . This is the site of your last stand. . . . And thus you will dance to your death here, on this hilltop, at the end of the day. And in your last dance you will tell of your struggle, of the battles you have won and of those you have lost; you will tell of your joys and bewilderments upon encountering personal power. Your dance will tell about the secrets and about the marvels you have stored. And your death will sit here and watch you'*" (*JI*, p. 187, 189).

Becoming a seer

For don Juan, it is important to be a good hunter, it is great to be a warrior, but it is best to be a *seer*. To be a seer is the goal that don Juan has set for Castaneda from the beginning, and everything else has been but preparation for this. The final lessons Castaneda had to learn were: not-doing, stopping the world, slipping between the worlds, and the journey to Ixtlan.

In order to explain *not-doing* to Castaneda, don Juan distinguishes between *looking* and *seeing*. "'The trick is in what one emphasizes . . . . Take that rock, for instance. To look at it is *doing,* but to *see* it is *not-doing*.'" (*JI*, pp. 221, 227). In order to break old habits of looking, Castaneda is urged to look at the spaces between the leaves on a tree, rather than the leaves. He is taught to look at things with eyes half shut, out

of the corners of his eyes, and in the dark. He is told to pay attention to shadows. "'Shadows are like doors, the doors of *not-doing*. A man of knowledge, for example, can tell the innermost feelings of men by watching their shadows'" (*JI*, p. 234).

The most difficult task for Castaneda is learning to stop the world. It is to aid in this that the hallucinogenic substances have been used, for, as don Juan said, "'In order to *see* one must learn to look at the world in some other fashion, and the only other fashion I know is the way of a sorcerer'" (*JI*, p. 302). Only by making it impossible to continue to look at things in the ordinary way can we learn to see what we have been missing. When Castaneda finally has the experience, after a most shattering hallucination created for him by don Juan and his fellow sorcerer, don Genaro, don Juan explains what happened. "'*What stopped inside you yesterday was what people have been telling you the world is like. You see, people tell us from the time we are born that the world is such and such and so and so, and naturally we have no choice but to see the world the way people have been telling us it is. . . . Yesterday the world became as sorcerers tell you it is. . . .'*" (*JI*, p. 299)

But stopping the world and seeing it as sorcerers do is still not *seeing*. This requires slipping between the worlds.

"'*. . . But what I want you to learn is* seeing. *Perhaps you know now that* seeing *happens only when one sneaks between the worlds, the world of ordinary people and the world of sorcerers. You are now smack in the middle point between the two. Yesterday you believed the coyote talked to you. Any sorcerer who doesn't* see *would believe the same, but one who* sees *knows that to believe that is to be pinned down in the realm of sorcerers. By the same token, not to believe that coyotes talk is to be pinned down in the realm of ordinary men'*" (*JI*, pp. 300).

The journey to Ixtlan

Castaneda has come to the end of his apprenticeship. He is now ready to *see,* but the rest is up to him. Before he leaves, don Juan and don

Genaro open their hearts to him about what lies ahead. Don Genaro tells about the time he finally met his ally (the supernatural power that made him a sorcerer). "'After my encounter with the ally nothing was real any more.'" And when he tried to return to his home in the little Mexican village of Ixtlan, he found there was no way back.

"'I will never reach Ixtlan. Yet in my feelings . . . sometimes I think I'm just one step from reaching it. Yet I never will. In my journey I don't even find the familiar landmarks I used to know. Nothing is any longer the same'" (JI, p. 311).

Don Juan tells Castaneda that this is what is in store for him.

Richard Alpert becomes Baba Ram Dass

On March 5, 1961, a promising young Harvard professor named Richard Alpert took some psilocybin (a mushroom derivative) with his colleague, Timothy Leary. This was the beginning of a series of changes that took Alpert through the psychedelic movement, a discharge from the Harvard faculty, and more experimentation with mind-altering drugs to increasing despair and finally to India where he found a guru, a new way of life, and his new name, Baba Ram Dass.

In his new identity, Baba Ram Dass is no longer concerned with taking drugs. His learning and practice of yoga and Eastern religion have led to a kind of physical asceticism, and emphasis upon states of consciousness induced by physical, mental, and spiritual purification.

How did an upper-middle-class Jewish professor become a follower of an Indian guru, and so change not only his way of life but also his very perception of "reality"?

A dead end

"By 1967 I had shot my load! I had no more job as a psychologist in a respectable establishment and I realized that we didn't know enough about psychedelics to use them profitably" (1971a, p. 14).

So, when a friend invites him to travel with him in India, Alpert goes along. For three months they travel all over the country, seeing all the sights, but this brings no satisfaction. *"We had done it all. . . . I had done everything I thought I could do, and nothing new had happened. It was turning out to be just another trip. The despair got very heavy. We didn't know enough and I couldn't figure out how to socialize this thing about the new states of consciousness. And I didn't know what to do next"* (1971a, p. 15).

Just before they are to leave for Japan, he is sitting in the Blue Tibetan restaurant in Katmandu, Nepal. A bearded young American comes in, sits at his table, and "I had the feeling I had met somebody who 'knew.'"

"I don't know how to describe this to you, except that I was deep in despair; I had gone through game after game, after game, first being a professor at Harvard, then being a psychedelic spokesman, and still people were constantly looking into my eyes, like "Do you know?" And there we were, "Do you?" "Do you?" "Maybe he . . ." "Do you . . .?" And there was always that feeling that everybody was very close and we all knew we knew, but nobody quite knew. I don't know how to describe it other than that. And I met this guy and there was no doubt in my mind. It was just like meeting a rock. It was just solid all the way through. Everywhere I pressed, there he was!" (1971a, p. 17)

On the way

Alpert decides to stay in India and follow this young man, Bhagwan Dass, as he makes a temple pilgrimage. For about three months he travels barefoot, as a holy beggar, going from temple to temple, learning from Bhagwan Dass to "be here now"; not in the past, not in the future, but here and now.

One night while in Delhi to get his visa renewed, Alpert goes outside the house where he is staying and while there, looking up at the dark sky, has a vivid experience of his mother's presence. She had died in Boston nearly a year before of a spleen illness and Alpert had been with her. During the week before her death he had become very close to her and since her death had felt a continuing closeness. There in the night, outside Delhi, he feels a great love for his mother, then goes back in the house and to bed.

Maharaji and home

The next day, Bhagwan Dass announces that he must go to his Guru. They borrow the Land Rover of a friend and drive 80 to 100 miles up into the mountains. There he meets the guru, called Maharaji.

After the greetings and a rest, they are both back with the Maharaji, and Alpert recounts the experience:

"'Come here. Sit.'" So I sat down and he looked at me and he said, 'You were out under the stars last night.'

"'Um-hum.'

"'You were thinking about your mother.'

"'Yes.' ('Wow', I thought, 'that's pretty good. I never mentioned that to anybody').

"'She died last year.'

"'Um-hum.'

"'She got very big in the stomach before she died.'

". . . Pause . . . 'Yes.'

"He leaned back and closed his eyes and said, 'Spleen. She died of spleen.'

"Well, what happened to me at that moment, I can't really put into words. He looked at me in a certain way at that moment, and two things happened—it seemed simultaneous. They do not seem like cause and effect.

"The first thing that happened was that my mind raced faster and faster and faster to try to get leverage—to get a hold on what he had just done. I went through every super CIA paranoia I've ever had: 'Who is he?' 'Who does he represent?' 'Where's the button he pushes where the

file appears?' and 'Why have they brought me here?' None of it would jell.

"It was just too impossible that this could have happened this way. The guy I was with didn't know all that stuff, and I was a tourist in a car, and the whole thing was just too far out. My mind went faster and faster and faster.

"Up until then I had two categories for 'psychic experience.'

"One was 'they happened to somebody else and they haven't happened to me, and they were terribly interesting and we certainly had to keep an open mind about it.' That was my social science approach. The other one was, 'well, man, I'm high on LSD. Who knows how it really is? After all, under the influence of a chemical, how do I know I'm not creating the whole thing?' Because, in fact, I had taken certain chemicals where I experienced the creation of total realities. . . .

"So I had had experiences where I had seen myself completely create whole environments under psychedelics, and therefore I wasn't eager to interpret these things very quickly, because I, the observer, was, at those times, under the influence of the psychedelics.

"But neither of these categories applied in this situation, and my mind went faster and faster and then I felt like what happens when a computer is fed an insoluble problem; the bell rings and the red light goes on and the machine stops. And my mind just gave up. It burned out its circuitry . . . its zeal to have an explanation. I needed something to get closure at the rational level and there wasn't anything. There just wasn't a place I could hide in my head about this.

"And at the same moment, I felt this extremely violent pain in my chest and a tremendous wrenching feeling and I started to cry. And I cried and I cried and I cried. And I wasn't happy and I wasn't sad. It was not that kind of crying. The only thing I could say was it felt like I was home. Like the journey was over. Like I had finished" (1971a, pp. 25–27).

Alpert became a follower of Maharaji, and he received instruction in various aspects of the Sikh religion and Raja Yoga, among others.

Much of his learning dealt with levels of consciousness, or *chakras*.

The transcendent states of consciousness

There are seven chakras, or focal points, and the transition from the third to the fourth state is the transition into the first transcendent state. (The first chakras deal with themes such as sexuality and power.) As Baba Ram Dass describes the fourth state:

"It's the first one into the state of compassion, that is, where one experiences the shifts over figure-ground relationship so that one sees that you and I are human beings behind not only blue-suitness or dark-suitness and white-shirtness but also behind personalities and ages and bodies, and there is a place where, although we still see each other as separate, we are experiencing a feeling of a unitive nature with one another. . . . And that compassion is the compassion that what is happening to you is happening to me, because in that place you and I are a unitive being.

"The fifth chakra is where you turn back inward, and rather than seeing the outward manifestations, you start to go deeper within or deeper up, as you might call it, and become preoccupied with higher planes of light or energy or form of it all. . . . It's sort of . . . different planes of perceptual organization of the universe. . . ." (1971b, p. 70)

The sixth chakra involves perception of the basic laws of the universe in operation everywhere, the "cosmic perspective." As Baba Ram Dass notes, "it's what we call wisdom. It's the wisdom of the ages, of these laws, these very simple laws" (1971b, p. 70). At that stage, when one is in the realm of pure ideas, the individual is no longer identified with the physical body or personality.

The seventh chakra, the highest level of consciousness, is the merging back into the "one":

"If you would look, for example, at the cyclic process of ocean mist rising off ocean, forming clouds, clouds have raindrops, raindrops fall into ocean, ocean is made up of raindrops, but it's ocean, and it's ocean in the sense of oneness. Each raindrop does not retain its individuality as a raindrop any longer. And you can see this is merely process. The seventh chakra is the ocean. It's where it all goes back into the one. It's even behind all the laws and ideas" (1971b, p. 71).

The task for Baba Ram Dass and other followers of the beliefs is to transmute their energy at the lower levels of consciousness to the higher levels, thus opening up new ways of viewing the universe and the self.

The here and now

One of the products of his new perspective is the focus on the here and now, rather than rumination over the past or anxiety about the future. His centeredness in the immediate present leads him to have quite different attitudes toward himself and others. Baba Ram Dass relates an incident in which he was giving *darshan* in New York City, and they were attended by several hundred people each night in a building next door to the fire department. At least once or twice each night they would hear the engines being called out:

"And we might in the middle of a . . . chanting a love song to God, you know, in this very intimate sound suddenly 'R-r-r—r-r,' and you'd look out into the audience and everybody was going through that pained 'O, they've loused it up and we've lost our moment.' And I looked at that and I thought, 'Wow, isn't that far out?' Here all these high beings are being brought down by a fire engine. What I do is, I see the fire engine is merely free energy the city of New York is giving us if we know how to use it, and I'm getting stoned out of my head, getting way up into these higher chakras off the fire engine. And I'm saying, instead of seeing life as full of impediments to doing what your pre-run tape says you're supposed to do, see all of it as part of the here and now moment . . . there's the fire engine and that's the way it is. You're only bugged with it if you're living a moment ago where you were busy not having the fire engine. . . ." (1971b, p. 76)

He recounts an incident of arriving home from India for a visit with his widowed father, and finding his father in a deep depression about the emptiness of his life, even though he had started Brandeis University, raised funds for the Albert Einstein Medical School, and been President of the New Haven Railroad. As his father talks of his gloom and doom in the car on the way from the airport, Dass goes through his mantra, *Om Mani Padme Hum, Om Mani Padme Hum.* At home, his father decides to make raspberry jam, which is a hobby of his. While they sterilize bottles and mash raspberries, the father continues to talk of his sadness, how he feels everyone has forgotten him.

". . . It's a very heavy story, very heavy story. I feel fantastic compassion for him because I love him very dearly and at the same moment I see the predicament his consciousness is in. I see where he's stuck. So I'm just doing my mantra and mashing raspberries and so on, and I'm saying to him things like, 'Should the bubbles all rise to the top? . . . And after awhile, since I'm giving him no reinforcement at all for this fantastic dark cloud that he's creating and holding all by himself, . . . he starts to say, 'Well, get all the bubbles up . . .' and pretty soon his conversation is shifting until it's in the here and now . . ." (1971b, pp. 53–54).

Soon the talk of the past disappears, and the father relaxes and smiles, and while they are together they find tremendous enjoyment in the present.

In another instance, Dass relates his attitudes toward his brother who had been confined for a time in a mental hospital for his "delusions":

"Now, I don't feel pity for Leonard. I just see his karma unfolding. I feel great compassion. I certainly don't want him to suffer. I realize that I can reduce his suffering by not getting caught in his suffering with him, by being with him at the highest level of consciousness we can meet at, at all times. . . . All summer long I would go to the Veterans Hospital one day a week and I would sit with him for many hours, just being as conscious as I could be. . . . And all that time he became extraordinarily right here and now, because there wasn't anybody surrounding him that said,

'You're nuts' because I don't think he's nuts. I just think he's living on another plane. . . . And he and I would sit around and we'd look at the psychiatrist and we'd say, 'Do you think he knows he's God?'" (1971b, pp. 61–62).

Baba Ram Dass continues his quest, traveling between India and the U.S. He sees himself as a "gnostic intermediary," one who "brings metaphors from one system to another," as he attempts to acquaint his audiences with glimpses of other realms of reality, wisdom, and fulfillment.

Ronald Laing: Inner experience and madness

Much of Castaneda's writings and those of others concerned with nonordinary reality are concerned with the person's relationship to the outer world; the world is perceived in unique ways, and insight and wisdom are presumably gained from the new vision. Ronald Laing has written extensively over the past fifteen years about an inner source of meaning: the inner realm.

Trained in the classical manner as a psychiatrist, Laing has rejected much of the medical model of madness, and has expounded a theory of schizophrenia which overturns our traditional notions of sanity and insanity. But fundamental to his approach to madness is a focus on the inner experience of the individual—the relationship of the self to the thoughts, fantasies, images, symbols of the inner realm which are expressive of the true self.

Alienation

Laing is a highly articulate social critic; in his *Politics of Experience* (1967a) he depicts our alienation from ourselves and from our "authentic possibilities."

"No one can begin to think, feel or act now

except from the starting point of his or her own alienation. . . .

"Humanity is estranged from its authentic possibilities. This basic vision prevents us from taking any unequivocal view of the sanity of common sense, or of the madness of the so-called madman. . . .

"At all events, we are bemused and crazed creatures, strangers to our true selves, to one another, and to the spiritual and material world—mad, even, from an ideal standpoint we can glimpse but not adopt.

"We are born into a world where alienation awaits us. We are potentially men, but are in an alienated state, and this state is not simply a natural system. Alienation as our present destiny is achieved only by outrageous violence perpetrated by human beings on human beings" (1967a, pp. 12–13).

The person, according to Laing, is but a "shriveled, desiccated fragment" of what he can be. ". . . what we think is less than what we know; what we know is less than what we love; what we love is so much less than what there is. And to that precise extent we are so much less than what we are" (p. 30).

Laing believes that much of what accounts for our "incompleteness" is the pressure for conformity. Individuality is stifled to the degree that "normality" and conformity are valued. Along with the pressure to obey conventions is the extensive conditioning we are subjected to which cuts us off from our inner experiences. ". . . we hardly know of the existence of the inner world: we barely remember our dreams, and make little sense of them when we do" (p. 26).

Fantasy, dreams, childhood memories—and many other elements of the inner realms—are frequently split off from what the person regards as his sane, rational, mature experience. We repress, deny, or otherwise destroy much of our experience. As a consequence, many individuals do not know their inner selves, their own experience—nor do they even know their bodies, other people, or the outside world as well as they might.

"When our personal worlds are rediscovered and allowed to reconstitute themselves, we first discover a shambles. Bodies half-dead; genitals dissociated from heart; heart severed from head; head dissociated from genitals. Without inner unity, with just enough sense of continuity to clutch at identity—the current idolatry. Torn—body, mind and spirit—by inner contradictions, pulled in different directions. Man cut off from his own mind, cut off equally from his own body—a half-crazed creature in a mad world" (p. 55).

Madness

Laing upends the notions of madness and sanity. What we term "normality" is, from his view-point, a "half-crazed" adjustment to a crazy world. Only in a mad world would there be such violence, destruction, misery, exploitation as we experience in our lives. What the psychiatric establishment terms "insanity" is deviation from or resistance to adjustment to such a world. But according to Laing, what we label as schizophrenic behavior in an individual is "a special strategy that a person invents in order to live in an unlivable situation" (p. 115). Whereas psychiatry typically views schizophrenia as an illness that is caused by genetic, constitutional, or psychological factors over which the patient has no control, Laing views schizophrenia as the person's effort to defy forces which threaten to obliterate his individuality.

The schizophrenic voyage

In Laing's view we have much to learn from those who are "mad" about resisting people and experiences that threaten our unique selfhood. And we learn from them the extent and depth of our alienation from our own inner experiences. To reestablish contact with fantasies, dreams, and other inner sources of knowledge can be a healing process for the alienated self and spirit. But it is also a terribly frightening step:
". . . in our present world, which is both so terrified and so unconscious of the other world (inner), it is not surprising that when 'reality,' the fabric of this world, bursts, and a person enters

the other world, he is completely lost and terrified and meets only incomprehension in others" (p. 125).

Without a "guide," such persons often confuse inner and outer realms, and typically lose their capacity to function adequately in daily situations. However, some people, especially those who may be guided by others who have had similar experiences, will embark on a "voyage of discovery" which is completed by a return to the ordinary world:

"This journey is experienced as going further 'in,' as going back through one's personal life, in and back and through and beyond into the experience of all mankind, of the primal man, of Adam, and perhaps even further into the beings of animals, vegetables and minerals" (p. 126).

Laing believes that the inner journey is healing and rejuvenating for the individual who is able to "return." Psychiatric practices such as drug treatments and shock therapy are aimed at *stopping* the "madness" and bringing the individual again to the point of compliance with norms for behavior in our society. Laing encourages the full experiencing of the "madness" so that its healing potential can be employed.

"Perhaps we will learn to accord to so-called schizophrenics who have come back to us, perhaps after years, no less respect than the often no less lost explorers of the Renaissance. If the human race survives, future men will, I suspect, look back on our enlightened epoch as a veritable Age of Darkness. They will presumably be able to savor the irony of this situation with more amusement than we can extract from it. The laugh's on us. They will see that what we call 'schizophrenia' was one of the forms in which, often through quite ordinary people, the light began to break through the cracks in our all-too-closed minds" (p. 129).

In ending this section, it is perhaps useful to again allude to so-called scientific and nonscientific ways of exploring human experiencing. Many contemporary psychologists and other scientists view the works of Castaneda, Baba Ram Dass, R. D. Laing, and other similar investigators as simply describing "believed-in imaginings." They are referred to as imaginings since presumably the events described can never be proven or disproven because they are not amenable to rigorous scientific methods of observation.

Other psychologists and scientists take a diametrically opposed point of view. For example, the physical scientist William Tiller has pointed out that "There are many other dimensions to the universe than the space-time dimension we presently percieve" (Kiester, 1973, p. 26). In his recent book, *The Natural Mind*, Weil (1972) elaborates on essentially the same theme:

"Just as we live in a universe where single realities express themselves in two opposite polarities . . . , so also we live in an infinite universe where everything is relative. At every step in the development of human consciousness, men have described limits to things only to have those limits exploded by subsequent experience of things beyond. Indeed, the history of astronomy from ancient Greece to the present is a continuing saga of an expanding universe—expanding in the conceptions of men. And try as we will with straight thinking to banish the notion of infinity, it keeps breaking in—in the heavens, in the subatomic world . . . .

". . . To defend itself. . . , the intellect often tells us that the concept of infinity is meaningless or incomprehensible. . . . [But] the more we strive to extend and maintain awareness of our flashes of stoned thinking, the more we can experience infinity positively, accept it, derive strength from it, and incorporate it consciously into our lives . . . .

". . . The only limits we encounter in the world around us are those we first create in our imagination" (p. 157–159).

We might well ask, "What is the answer?" Are we truly entering a new realm of human experiencing and expanded consciousness, or are we simply regressing to more primitive fantasies and imaginings? At this point in time and space, the answer remains to be discovered; but quite possibly the two approaches ("scientific" and "nonscientific") to understanding human behavior complement rather than conflict with each other. In any event, discovering the answer poses an exciting challenge.

Acknowledgments and References

The reference list includes not only the sources from which the authors have drawn material, but also acknowledgments of the permission granted by authors and publishers to quote directly from their works.

Ackerman, N. W. *The psychodynamics of family life.* New York: Basic Books, 1958.

Albee, E. *Who's afraid of Virginia Woolf?* New York: Pocket Books (Giant Cardinal ed.), 1963.

Allport, G. W. *The nature of prejudice.* Boston: Beacon Press, 1954.

Allport, G. W. *Becoming: Basic considerations for a psychology of personality.* New Haven, Conn.: Yale University Press, 1955.

Allport, G. W. *Pattern and growth in personality.* New York: Holt, Rinehart & Winston, 1961.

Allport, G. W., Vernon, P. E., & Lindzey, G. *A study of values.* (3rd. ed.) Boston: Houghton Mifflin, 1960.

Alpenfels, E. Progressive monogamy: An alternate pattern? In H. Otto (Ed.), *The family in search of a future.* New York: Appleton-Century-Crofts, 1971.

Alpert, R. See **Ram Dass, Baba.**

Altman, I., & Taylor, D. A. *Social penetration: The development of interpersonal relationships.* New York: Holt, Rinehart & Winston, 1973.

American Institutes for Research. *Project talent: Progress in education, a sample survey.* Washington, D.C.: Author, 1971.

American Psychological Association. *Ethical standards of psychologists.* Washington, D.C.: APA, 1963.

Archibald, H. C., & Tuddenham, R. D. Persistent stress reaction after combat. *Archives of General Psychiatry,* 1965, **12**(5), 475–81.

Ardrey, R. *African genesis.* New York: Atheneum, 1961.

Aronson, E., & Gerard, E. Beyond Parkinson's law: The effect of excess time on subsequent performance. *Journal of Personality and Social Psychology,* 1966, **3**, 336–39.

Asch, S. E. Effects of group pressure upon the modification and distortion of judgments. In H. Guetzkow (Ed.), *Groups, leaderships, and men.* Pittsburgh, Pa.: Carnegie Press, 1951.

Asch, S. E. *Social psychology.* New York: Prentice-Hall, 1952.

Asch, S. E. Opinions and social pressure. *Scientific American,* 1955, **193**(5), 31–35. Copyright © 1955 by Scientific American, Inc. All rights reserved.

Astin, A. W., & Nichols, R. C. Life goals and vocational choice. *Journal of Applied Psychology,* 1964, **48**(1), 50–58.

Auerbach, S. POWs found to be much sicker than they looked upon release. *Los Angeles Times,* June 2, 1973, Part I, 7.

Averill, J. R. Grief: Its nature and significance. *Psychological Bulletin,* 1968, **70**, 721–48.

Azrin, N. H., Holz, W. C., & Hake, D. F. Fixed ratio punishment. *Journal of the Experimental Analysis of Behavior,* 1963, **6**, 141–48.

Baldwin, A. L. *Behavior and development in childhood.* N.Y.: Holt, Rinehart & Winston, 1955.

Bales, R. F. Task roles and social roles in problem-solving groups. In E. E. Maccoby, T. M. Newcomb, & E. L. Hartley, *Readings in social psychology.* (3rd ed.) New York: Holt, Rinehart & Winston, 1958.

Bandura, A. Vicarious processes: A case of no-trial learning. In L. Berkowitz (Ed.), *Advances in experimental social psychology.* Vol. 2. New York: Academic Press, 1965.

Bandura, A. *Aggression: A social learning analysis.* New York: Prentice-Hall, 1973.

Bandura, A., & Menlove, F. Factors determining vicarious extinction of avoidance behavior through symbolic modeling. *Journal of Personality and Social Psychology,* 1968, **8**, 99–108.

Bandura, A., Ross, D., & Ross, S. A. Imitation of film-mediated aggressive models. *Journal of Abnormal and Social Psychology,* 1963, **66**, 3–11.

Bandura, A., & Walters, R. H. *Adolescent aggression.* New York: Ronald Press, 1959.

Bandura, A., & Walters, R. H. *Social learning and personality development.* New York: Holt, Rinehart & Winston, 1963.

Bardwick, J. M. *Psychology of women: A study of biocultural conflicts.* New York: Harper & Row, 1971.

Bardwick, J. M. A predictive study of psychological and psychosomatic responses to oral contraceptives. In J. T. Fawcett (Ed.), *Psychological perspectives on population.* New York: Basic Books, 1973.

Barron, F. The creative personality: Akin to madness. *Psychology Today,* 1972, **6**(2), 42–44, 84–85.

Bart, P. B. Depression in middle-aged women. In J. M. Bardwick (Ed.), *Readings on the psychology of women.* New York: Harper & Row, 1972.

Bateson, G. Minimal requirements for a theory of schizophrenia. *Archives of General Psychiatry,* 1960, **2,** 477–91.

Bateson, G., & Mead, M. *Balinese culture.* New York: Academy of Science, 1942.

Bavelas, A. Communication patterns in task-oriented groups. In D. Cartwright & A. Zander (Eds.), *Group dynamics: Research and theory.* (3rd ed.) New York: Harper & Row, 1968.

Bavelas, A., Hastorf, A., Gross, A., & Kite, W. R. Experiments on the alteration of group structure. *Journal of Experimental Social Psychology,* 1965, **1,** 55–71.

Becker, W. C. Consequences of different kinds of parental discipline. In M. L. Hoffman & L. W. Hoffman (Eds.), *Review of Child Development Research.* Vol. 1. New York: Russell Sage Foundation, 1964.

Bengelsdorf, I. S. Technology's role is vital to world peace, well-being. *Los Angeles Times,* June 4, 1966.

Bengelsdorf, I. S. Alcohol, morphine addictions believed chemically similar. *Los Angeles Times,* March 5, 1970, Part II, 7.

Bengis, I. *Combat in the erogeneous zone.* New York: Knopf, 1972. Copyright © 1972 by Ingrid Bengis. Excerpt reprinted by permission of Alfred A. Knopf, Inc. and Wildwood House Limited.

Berger, R. J. Morpheus descending. *Psychology Today,* 1970, **4**(1), 33–36.

Berkowitz, L. Reactance and the unwillingness to help others. *Psychological Bulletin,* 1973, **79**(5), 310–17.

Berlyne, D. E. *Conflict, arousal, & curiosity.* New York: McGraw-Hill, 1960.

Berlyne, D. E. Arousal and reinforcement. In D. Levine (Ed.), *Nebraska symposium on motivation—1967.* Lincoln, Nebr.: University of Nebraska Press, 1967.

Bernard, J. *The future of marriage.* New York: Bantam Books, 1973. Copyright © 1972 by Jessie Bernard. Excerpts reprinted by permission of Thomas Y. Crowell Co., Inc. and Souvenir Press Ltd.

Berne, E. *Games people play.* New York: Grove Press, Inc., 1964.

Berne, E. *What do you say after you say hello?* New York: Grove Press, 1972.

Berrien, F. K. *Comments and cases on human relations.* New York: Harper & Row, 1951.

Berrill, N. J. *Man's emerging mind.* New York: Dodd, Mead, 1955. Copyright © 1955 by N. J. Berrill. Published by Dodd, Mead, & Company, Inc., New York, and reprinted with their permission.

Besner, A. Economic deprivation and family patterns. In L. M. Irelan (Ed.), *Low-income life styles.* Washington, D.C.: Welfare Administration Publication, 1967, No. 14.

Bettelheim, B. Individual and mass behavior in extreme situations. *Journal of Abnormal and Social Psychology,* 1943, **38,** 417–52.

Bettelheim, B. *The children of the dream.* London: Macmillan, 1969.

Biddle, B. J., & Thomas, E. J. *Role theory, concepts, and research.* New York: Wiley, 1966.

Biller, H. B. Father absence and the personality development of the child. *Developmental Psychology,* 1970, **2,** 181–201.

Biller, H. B., & Bahm, R. M. Father absence, perceived maternal behavior, and masculinity of self-concept among junior high school boys. *Developmental Psychology,* 1971, **4,** 178–81.

Biller, H. B., & Weiss, S. D. The father-daughter relationship and the personality development of the female. *Journal of Genetic Psychology,* 1970, **116,** 79–93.

Bird, C. The sex map of the work world. In M. Garskof (Ed.), *Roles women play: Readings toward women's liberation.* Belmont, Calif.: Brooks/Cole, 1971.

Blau, P. M. The flow of occupational supply and recruitment. *American Sociological Review,* 1965, **30,** 475–90.

Blau, P. M. *Exchange and power in social life.* New York: Wiley, 1967.

Bloch, H. S. Army clinical psychiatry in the combat zone—1967–1968. *American Journal of Psychiatry,* 1969, **126,** 289–98.

Blood, R. O., Jr. *Marriage.* New York: The Free Press, 1962.

Blood, R. O., Jr., & Wolfe, D. M. *Husbands and wives: The dynamics of married living.* New York: The Free Press, 1960.

Bloom, R. O., Whiteman, M., & Deutsch, M. Race and social class as separate factors related to social enrichment. In M. Deutsch et al. (Eds.), *The disadvantaged child.* New York: Basic Books, 1967.

Bluestone, H., & McGahee, C. L. Reaction to extreme stress: Impending death by execution. *American Journal of Psychiatry,* 1962, **119,** 393–96.

Bogdonoff, M. D., Klein, R. F., Estis, E. H., Shaw, D. M., Jr., & Back, K. W. The modifying effect of conforming behavior upon lipid responses accompanying CNS arousal. *Clinical Research,* 1961, **9,** 135.

Bogue, D. (Ed.) *Mass communication and motivation for birth control: Proceedings of the summer workshops at the University of Chicago.* Chicago: Community and Family Study Center, University of Chicago, 1967.

Bohannan, P. The six stations of divorce. In J. Bardwick (Ed.), *Readings on the psychology of women.* New York: Harper & Row, 1972.

Bombard, A. *The voyage of the Hérétique.* New York: Simon & Schuster, 1954.

Bossard, J. H. Residential propinquity as a factor in marriage selection. *American Journal of Sociology,* 1931, **38,** 219–24.

Boston Women's Health Book Collective. *Our Bodies, our selves.* New York: Simon & Schuster, 1973.

Bovet, T. Human attitudes toward suffering. *Humanitas,* 1973, **9**(1), 5–20.

Bradburn, N. M. *The structure of psychological well-being.* Chicago: Aldine, 1969.

Branden, N. *Psychotherapy and the objectivist ethics.* New York: Nathaniel Branden Institute, 1965.

Bremner, D. Bob & Barbara & Mike & . . . ? *Los Angeles Times,* June 17, 1973.

Broderick, C. Damn those gloomy prophets—the family's here to stay. *Los Angeles Times,* June 17, 1973.

Bronfenbrenner, U. Socialization and social class through time and space. In E. Maccoby, T. Newcomb, & E. Hartley (Eds.), *Readings in Social Psychology.* New York: Holt, Rinehart & Winston, 1958.

Bronfenbrenner, U. The changing American child—a speculative analysis. *Journal of Social Issues,* 1961, **17,** 6–18.

Brown, G. W. Life-events and psychiatric illness: Some thoughts on methodology and causality. *Journal of Psychosomatic Research,* 1972, **16**(5), 311–20.

Brown, G. W., & Birley, J. Crises and life changes on the onset of schizophrenia. *Journal of Health and Social Behavior,* 1968, **9,** 203.

Bruner, J. S., Goodnow, J. J., & Austin, G. A. *A study of thinking.* New York: Wiley, 1956.

Buber, M. *I and thou.* (2nd ed.) Translated by R. G. Smith. New York: Scribner's, 1958.

Buckley, W. Society as a complex adaptive system. In W. Buckley (Ed.), *Modern systems research for the behavioral scientist.* Chicago: Aldine, 1968.

Buckley, W. (Ed.) *Modern systems research for the behavioral scientist.* Chicago: Aldine, 1968.

Bühler, C. The course of human life as a psychological problem. *Human Development,* 1968, **11**(3), 184–200.

Burchinal, L. G., Haller, A. O., & Taves, M. *Career choices of rural youth in a changing society.* Rosemount, Minn.: Agricultural Experimental Station, University of Minnesota, 1962, Bulletin 458.

Burgess, E. W. The family in a changing society. In A. Etzioni & E. Etzioni (Eds.), *Social changes: Sources, patterns, and consequences.* New York: Basic Books, 1964.

Burgess, E. W., Locke, H. J., & Thomas, M. M. *The family.* (2nd ed.) New York: American Book, 1963.

Burgess, E. W., & Wallin, P. *Engagement and marriage.* Philadelphia: Lippincott, 1953.

Burns, R. "To a mouse." In the *Poems of . . . .* New York: Heritage Press, 1965.

Busse, E. W. Geriatrics today: An overview. *American Journal of Psychiatry,* 1967, **123**(10), 1226–33.

Caldwell, B. M. The effects of infant care. In L. Hoffman & M. Hoffman (Eds.), *Review of Child Development Research.* Vol. 1. New York: Russell Sage Foundation, 1964.

Calhoun, J. B. Population density and social pathology. *Scientific American,* 1962, **206**(2), 139–50.

Cantril, H. *The "why" of man's experience.* New York: Macmillan, 1950.

Cantril, H. *The politics of despair.* New York: Basic Books, 1958.

Cantril, H. A fresh look at the human design. In J. F. T. Bugental (Ed.), *Challenges of humanistic psychology.* New York: McGraw-Hill, 1967.

Caplan, R. Organizational stress and individual strain: A social-psychological study of risk factors in coronary heart disease among administrators, engineers, and scientists. Unpublished doctoral thesis, University of Michigan, 1971.

Carothers, J. C. A study of mental derangement in Africans, and an attempt to explain its peculiarities, more especially in relation to the African attitude of life. *Journal of Mental Science,* 1947, **93,** 548–97.

Carson, R. *Interaction concepts of personality.* Chicago: Aldine, 1969.

Cartwright, D., & Zander, A. (Eds.) *Group dynamics: Research and theory.* (3rd ed.) New York: Harper & Row, 1968.

Castaneda, C. *The teachings of Don Juan: A Yaqui way of knowledge.* Berkeley, Calif.: The University of California Press, 1968. Copyright © 1968 by The Regents of the University of California. Originally published by the University of California Press; excerpts reprinted by permission of The Regents of the University of California.

Castaneda, C. *A separate reality: Further conversations with Don Juan.* New York: Simon & Schuster, 1971.

Castaneda, C. *Journey to Ixtlan.* New York: Simon & Schuster, 1972. Copyright © 1972 by Carlos Castaneda. Excerpts reprinted by courtesy of Ned Brown Associated Agency, and Simon & Schuster, Inc.

Catton, W. R., Jr., & Smircich, R. J. A comparison of mathematical models for the effect of residential propinquity on mate selection. *American Sociological Review,* 1964, **29,** 522–29.

Cavan, R. S. *The American family.* (3rd ed.) New York: Crowell, 1963.

Chess, S., Thomas, A., & Birch, H. Behavior problems revisited. In S. Chess & A. Thomas (Eds.), *Annual progress in child psychiatry and child development.* New York: Brunner/Mazel, 1968.

Cholden, L. Some psychiatric problems in the rehabilitation of the blind. *Menninger Clinic Bulletin,* 1954, **18,** 107–12.

Clapp, W. F. Dependence and competence in children: Parental treatment of four-year-old boys. *Dissertation Abstracts,* 1967, **28**(4B), 1703.

Clark, W. H. *Psychology of religion.* New York: Macmillan, 1958.

Clausen, J. A. Family structure, socialization, and personality. In L. Hoffman & M. Hoffman (Eds.), *Review of child development research.* Vol. 2. New York: Russell Sage Foundation, 1966.

Clausen, J. A., & Williams, J. R. Sociological correlates of child behavior. In H. W. Stevenson (Ed.), *Child psychology: The sixty-second yearbook of NSSE.* Chicago: The University of Chicago Press, 1963.

Cody, H. M., & Sadis, H. J. Excerpts from "The Marriage Contract of Harriett Mary Cody and Harvey Joseph Sadis" from *Ms. Magazine* (June 1973). Reprinted by permission of Harriet M. Cody and Harvey J. Sadis.

Coleman, J. C. Life stress and maladaptive behavior. *The American Journal of Occupational Therapy,* 1973, **27**(4), 169–78.

Coleman, J. C., & Broen, W. E., Jr. *Abnormal psychology and modern life.* Glenview, Ill.: Scott, Foresman, 1972.

Collier, R. M. A biologically derived basic value as an initial context for behavioral science. *Journal of Humanistic Psychology,* 1968, **8**(1), 1–15.

Combs, A. W., & Snygg, D. *Individual behavior.* (Rev. ed.) New York: Harper & Row, 1959.

Coombs, R. H. Value consensus and partner satisfaction among dating couples. *Journal of Marriage and the Family,* 1966, **28**(2), 166–73.

Coombs, R. H., & Kenkel, W. Sex differences in dating aspirations and satisfaction with computer-selected partners. *Journal of Marriage and the Family,* 1966, **28**, 62–66.

Coopersmith, S. *The antecedents of self-esteem.* San Francisco: Freeman, 1967.

Costanzo, P. R., Reitan, H. T., & Shaw, M. E. Conformity as a function of experimentally induced minority and majority competence. *Psychonomic Science,* 1968, **10**, 329–30.

Costanzo, P. R., & Shaw, M. E. Conformity as a function of age level. *Child Development,* 1966, **37**, 967–75.

Cottle, T. J. Zero man: Anatomy of an academic failure. *Change,* 1972, **4**(9), 49–55.

Cousins, N. What the founding fathers believed. *Saturday Review,* 1958, **41**(12), 15–17.

Cozby, P. C. Self-disclosure: A literature review. *Psychological Bulletin,* 1973, **79**(2), 73–91.

Crago, M., & Tharp, R. G. Psychopathology and marital role disturbance: A test of the Tharp-Otis descriptive hypothesis. *Journal of Consulting and Clinical Psychology,* 1968, **32**(3), 338–41.

Crocker, W. H. Personal communication to author, 1968.

Croft, R. From "Love" by Roy Croft. Reprinted from *The family book of best loved poems,* copyright 1952 by Doubleday & Co., Inc. by permission of Copeland & Lamm, Inc.

Darley, J., & Latané, B. When will people help in a crisis? In *Readings in Psychology Today.* Del Mar, Calif.: CRM Books, 1969.

Dean, D. G. Emotional maturity and marital adjustment. *Journal of Marriage and the Family,* 1966, **28**, 454–57.

Dellas, M., & Gaier, E. I. Identification of creativity: The individual. *Psychological Bulletin,* 1970, **73**(1), 55–73.

DeNike, L. D., & Tiber, N. Neurotic behavior. In P. London & D. Rosenhan (Eds.) *Foundations of abnormal psychology.* New York: Holt, Rinehart & Winston, 1968.

Department of Defense. *The armed forces officer.* Washington, D.C.: U.S. Government Printing Office, 1950.

Department of Health, Education, and Welfare. *Psychological factors in organic disease.* (Mental Health Program Reports, No. 1, pp. 1–23) By George L. Engel & Robert Adler. Washington, D.C.: U.S. Government Printing Office, February 1967.

Department of Labor. *Handbook on women workers.* Washington, D.C.: U.S. Government Printing Office, 1969.

Department of Labor. *Myths and reality.* Washington, D.C.: U.S. Government Printing Office, April 1971.

de Sola Pool, I., & Kessler, A. The Kaiser, the Tsar, and the computer: Information processing in a crisis. *American Behavioral Scientist,* 1965, **8**(9), 31–38.

Dewey, J. *Democracy and education.* New York: Macmillan, 1930.

Dinello, F. A. Stages of treatment in the case of a diaper-wearing seventeen-year-old male. *American Journal of Psychiatry,* 1967, **124**, 94–96.

Dixon, M. Why women's liberation. In M. Garskof (Ed.), *Roles women play: Readings toward women's liberation.* Belmont, Calif.: Brooks/Cole, 1971.

Douvan, E., & Adelson, J. *The adolescent experience.* New York: Wiley, 1966.

Duncan, O. D. The trend of occupational mobility in the United States. *American Sociological Review,* 1965, **30**, 491–98.

Durant, W., & Durant, A. *Rousseau and revolution.* New York: Simon & Schuster, 1967.

Dutton, R. E. Creative use of creative people. *Personnel Journal,* 1972, **51**(11), 818–22, 847.

Duvall, E. M. *Family development.* (2nd ed.) Philadelphia: Lippincott, 1962.

Dyer, W. G. Analyzing marital adjustment using role theory. *Marriage and Family Living,* 1962, **24**, 371–75.

Earl, H. G. 10,000 children battered and starved: Hundreds die. *Today's Health,* 1965, **43**(9), 24–31.

Einstein, A. *The world as I see it.* New York: Philosophical Library, 1949.

Einstein, A. *Out of my later years.* New York: Philosophical Library, 1950.

Einstein, A., & Infeld, L. *The evolution of physics.* New York: Simon & Schuster, 1938.

Ekman, P., & Friesen, W. V. Nonverbal behavior in psychotherapy research. In J. M. Schlien (Ed.), *Research in psychotherapy.* Washington, D.C.: American Psychological Association, 1968.

Ekman, P., Friesen, W., & Ellsworth, P. *Emotion in the human face: Guidelines for research and an integration of findings.* New York: Pergamon Press, 1973.

Ellis, A. Questionnaire versus interview methods in the study of human love relationships. II. Uncategorized responses. *American Sociological Review,* 1948, **13**, 61–65.

Ellis, A. Rational psychotherapy and individual psychology. *Journal of Individual Psychology,* 1957, **13**, 38–44.

Ellis, A. Group marriage: A possible alternative? In H. Otto (Ed.), *The family in search of a future.* New York: Appleton-Century-Crofts, 1971.

Ellis, A. The no cop-out therapy. *Psychology Today,* 1973, **7**(2), 56–60, 62.

Farberow, N. L., & Litman, R. E. A comprehensive suicide prevention program. Suicide Prevention Center of Los Angeles, 1958–1969. (Unpublished final report DHEW NIMH Grants No. MH 14946 and MH 00128) Los Angeles, 1970.

Farnsworth, D. L. Motivation for learning: Community responsibility. In E. P. Torrance & R. D. Strom (Eds.), *Mental health and achievement.* New York: Wiley, 1966.

Farson, R. E. The reverse transmission of culture. In B. Marshall, *Experiences in being.* Belmont, Calif.: Brooks/Cole, 1971.

Faulkner, W. *The Faulkner reader.* New York: The Modern Library, 1961.

Fawcett, J. *Psychology and population.* North Haven, Conn.: Van Dyke Printing Co., 1970.

Feldman, H., & Rogoff, M. Medical briefs. *Today's Health,* 1969, **47**(1), 17.

Fenz, W. D., & Epstein, S. Stress: In the air. *Psychology Today,* 1969, **3**(4), 27–28, 58–59.

Fisher, S. *The female orgasm.* New York: Basic Books, 1973.

Flanders, J. P. A review of research on imitative behavior. *Psychological Bulletin,* 1968, **69**, 316–37.

Floyd, H. H., & South, D. R. Dilemma of youth: The choice of parents or peers as a frame of reference for behavior. *Mental Health Digest,* 1973, **5**(3), 16–18.

Foulkes, F. K. *Creating more meaningful work.* New York: AMA, 1969.

Frankl, V. *The doctor and the soul.* New York: Knopf, 1955.

Frankl, V. *Man's search for meaning: An introduction to logotherapy.* Boston: Beacon Press, 1959, 1962.

Freud, S. *Civilization and its discontents.* London: Hogarth, 1930. (Republished: Westport, Conn.: Associated Booksellers, 1955.)

Freud, S. *Psychopathology of everyday life.* (2nd ed.) London: Ernest Benn, Ltd., 1954.

Friedman, P., & Linn, L. Some psychiatric notes on the Andrea Dorea disaster. *American Journal of Psychiatry,* 1957, **114**, 426–32. Copyright © 1957 the American Psychiatric Association. Reprinted by permission of Mrs. Paul Friedman and the American Psychiatric Association.

Fromm, E. *The sane society.* New York: Holt, Rinehart & Winston, 1955.

Fromm, E. *The art of loving.* New York: Harper & Row, 1956.

Gagnon, J., & Simon, W. (Eds.) *Sexual conduct: A human source of sexuality.* New York: Aldine, 1973.

Gandhi, M. *The story of my experiments with truth.* Washington, D.C.: Public Affairs Press, 1948.

Gardner, J. W. The secretary of health, education, and welfare. *American Psychologist,* 1965, **20**, 811–14.

Geismar, L. L., & La Sorte, M. A. *Understanding the multi-problem family.* New York: Association Press, 1964.

Geist, H. *The psychological aspects of the aging process.* St. Louis: Warren H. Green, 1968.

Gelven, M. Guilt and human meaning. *Humanitas,* 1973, **9**(1), 69–81.

Gerard, H. B., Wilhelmy, R. A., & Conolley, E. S. Conformity and group size. *Journal of Personality and Social Psychology,* 1968, **8**, 79–82.

Gergen, K. J. Multiple identity. The healthy, happy human being wears many masks. *Psychology Today,* 1972, **5**(12), 31–35, 64–65.

Gewirtz, J. L. A learning analysis of the effects of normal stimulation, privation & deprivation on the acquisition of social motivation and attachment. In B. M. Foss (Ed.), *Determinants of Infant Behavior.* Vol. 1. New York: Wiley, 1961.

Ginzberg, E. *The development of human resources.* New York: McGraw-Hill, 1966.

Glass, D., & Hammen, C. Increased participation and monitoring of activities in the alteration of depressed mood. Unpublished manuscript, The University of California, Los Angeles, 1973.

Glidewell, J. C., & Swallow, C. S. *The prevalence of maladjustment in elementary schools.* A report prepared for the Joint Commission on the Mental Health of Children. Chicago: The University of Chicago Press, 1968.

Glucksberg, S. *Symbolic processes.* Dubuque, Iowa: Wm. C. Brown, 1966.

Glueck, S., & Glueck, E. T. *Unraveling juvenile delinquency.* Cambridge, Mass.: Harvard University Press, 1950.

Goffman, E. *Interaction ritual: Essays on face-to-face behavior.* Garden City, N.Y.: Doubleday, 1967.

Goffman, E. *Relations in public.* New York: Harper & Row, 1972.

Goldberg, S., & Lewis, M. Play behavior in the year-old infant: Early sex differences. In J. Bardwick (Ed.), *Readings on the psychology of women.* New York: Harper & Row, 1972.

Goldsmith, W., & Cretekos, C. Unhappy odysseys: Psychiatric hospitalization among Vietnam returnees. *American Journal of Psychiatry,* 1969, **20**, 78–83.

Gonzales, P. *Tennis.* New York: Cornerstone Library, 1972.

Gooding, J. The fraying white collar. *Fortune,* December 1970, 78–81, 108.

Goodwin, L. A study of work orientations of welfare recipients. Department of Labor, 1971. Reported in Special Task Force, *Work in America.* Cambridge, Mass.: MIT Press, 1972.

Gordon, E. M. Acceptance of pregnancy before and since oral contraception, *Obstetrics and Gynecology,* 1967, **29**, 144–46.

Gottschalk, L. A., Haer, J. L., & Bates, D. E. Effect of

sensory overload on psychological state. *Archives of General Psychiatry,* 1972, **27**(4), 451–56.

Grinker, R. R., & Spiegel, J. P. *War neuroses.* Philadelphia: Blakiston, 1945.

Guilford, J. P. *The nature of human intelligence.* New York: McGraw-Hill, 1967.

Haley, J. *Strategies of psychotherapy.* New York: Grune & Stratton, 1963.

Haley, J. Speech sequences of normal and abnormal families with two children present. *Family Process,* 1967, **6,** 81–97.

Hall, E. J., Mouton, J. S., & Blake, R. R. Group problem solving effectiveness under conditions of pooling vs. interaction. *Journal of Social Psychology,* 1963, **59,** 147–57.

Hammond, K. R., & Summers, D. A. Cognitive control. *Psychological Review,* 1972, **79**(1), 58–67.

Harmsworth, H. C., & Minnis, M. S. Nonstatutory causes of divorce: The lawyer's point of view. *Marriage and Family Living,* 1955, **17,** 316–21.

Harris, R. A. *I'm OK—you're OK: A practical guide to transactional analysis.* New York: Harper & Row, 1967.

Haskins, C. P. Report of the president, 1966–1967. Washington, D.C.: Carnegie Institute of Washington, 1968.

Haythorn, W. W., & Altman, I. Together in isolation. *Trans-action,* 1967, **4**(3), 18–22.

Heathers, G. Emotional dependence and independence in a physical threat situation. *Child Development,* 1953, **24,** 169–79.

Helson, H. Some problems in motivation. In D. Levine (Ed.), *Nebraska symposium on motivation.* Lincoln, Nebr.: University of Nebraska Press, 1966.

Hemingway, E. *The short stories of . . . .* New York: Scribner's, 1955.

Henry, J. *Culture against man.* New York: Random House, 1963.

Herrick, D. J. *The evolution of human nature.* Austin: University of Texas Press, 1956.

Herzberg, F. Motivation, morale, and money. *Psychology Today,* 1968, **1,** 42–45.

Hetherington, E. M., & Deur, J. The effects of father absence on child development. Unpublished manuscript, University of Wisconsin, 1969.

Holmes, T. H., & Matsuda, M. Psychosomatic syndrome. *Psychology Today,* 1972, **5**(11), 71–72, 106.

Holmes, T. H., & Rahe, R. H. The Social Readjustment Rating Scale. *Journal of Psychosomatic Research,* 1967, **11,** 213.

Horner, M. Femininity and successful achievement: A basic inconsistency. In J. Bardwick, E. Douvan, M. Horner, & D. Gutmann (Eds.), *Feminine personality and conflict.* Belmont, Calif.: Wadsworth, 1970.

Horton, P. B., & Hunt, C. L. *Sociology.* (2nd ed.) New York: McGraw-Hill, 1968.

House, A. What contraceptive type are you? *Ms.,* March 1973, 7–14.

Housman, A. E. From "The laws of God, the laws of man." From *The collected poems of . . . .* New York: Holt, Rinehart & Winston, 1922.

Hudson, J. W., & Henze, L. F. Campus values in mate selection: A replication. *Journal of Marriage and the Family,* 1969, **31,** 772–75.

Hurley, J. R. Parental acceptance-rejection and children's intelligence. *Merrill-Palmer Quarterly,* 1965, **11**(1), 19–32.

Hurlock, E. B. *Developmental psychology.* (3rd ed.) New York: McGraw-Hill, 1968.

Huxley, A. Human potentialities. In R. E. Farson (Ed.), *Science and human affairs.* Palo Alto, Calif.: Science & Behavior Books, 1965.

Huxley, J. *Evolution in action.* New York: Harper & Row, 1953, and London: Chatto & Windus Ltd.

Ilfeld, F. W., Jr. Overview of the causes and prevention of violence. *Archives of General Psychiatry,* 1969, **20,** 675–89.

Isaacs, W., Thomas, J., & Goldiamond, I. Application of operant conditioning to reinstate verbal behavior in psychotics. *Journal of Speech and Hearing Disorders,* 1960, **25,** 8–12.

Ivey, M. E., & Bardwick, J. M. Patterns of affective fluctuation in the menstrual cycle. *Psychosomatic Medicine,* 1968, **30,** 336–45.

Jahoda, M. *Current concepts of positive mental health.* Joint Commission on Mental Illness and Health. New York: Basic Books, 1958, No. 1.

James, W. *The principles of learning.* New York: Holt, Rinehart & Winston, 1890.

Janis, I. When fear is healthy. *Psychology Today,* 1968, **1**(11), 46–49, 60–61.

Jenkins, C. Psychologic and social precursors of coronary disease. *New England Journal of Medicine,* 1971, **284,** 244–55.

Jenkins, R. L. The varieties of children's behavioral problems and family dynamics. *American Journal of Psychiatry,* 1968, **124**(10), 1440–45.

Jones, E. E., & Gerard, H. B. *Foundations of social psychology.* New York: Wiley, 1967.

Jones, E. E., & Gordon, E. M. Timing of self-disclosure and its effects on personal attraction. *Journal of Personality and Social Psychology,* 1972, **24**(3), 358–65.

Jones, M. C. A laboratory study of fear: The case of Peter. *Pedagogical Seminary,* 1924, **31,** 308–15.

Jourard, S. M. *Personal adjustment.* (2nd ed.) New York: Macmillan, 1963.

Jouvet, M. The sleeping brain. *Science Journal,* 1967, **3**(5), 105–11.

Kadushin, A. Reversibility of trauma: A follow-up study of children adopted when older. *Social Work,* 1967, **12**(4), 22–33.

Kagan, J., & Moss, H. A. *Birth to maturity: The Fels study of psychological development.* New York: Wiley, 1962.

Kahn, R. L. The meaning of work: Interpretation and proposals for measurement. In A. A. Campbell & P. E. Converse (Eds.), *Human meaning of social change.* New York: Basic Books, 1972.

Kasl, S., & Cobb, S. Blood pressure changes in men undergoing job loss: A preliminary report. *Psychosomatic Medicine,* 1970, **32,** 19–38.

Kassel, V. Polygyny after sixty. In H. Otto (Ed.), *The family in search of a future.* New York: Appleton-Century-Crofts, 1971.

Katchadourian, H. A., & Lunde, D. T. *Fundamentals of human sexuality.* New York: Holt, Rinehart & Winston, 1972.

Katz, A. M., & Hill, R. Residential propinquity and marital selection: A review of theory, method, and fact. *Marriage and Family Living,* 1958, **20,** 27–34.

Katz, J. L., Weiner, R., Gallagher, T., & Hellman, L. Stress, disease, and ego defenses. *Archives of General Psychiatry,* 1970, **23,** 131–42.

Kaufmann, W. Do you crave a life without choice? *Psychology Today,* 1973, **6**(11), 78–79.

Kelley, H. H. Attribution theory in social psychology. In D. Levine (Ed.), *Nebraska symposium on motivation—1967.* Lincoln, Nebr.: University of Nebraska Press, 1967.

Kelly, J. Sister love: An exploration of the need for homosexual experience. *The Family Coordinator,* 1972, **21,** 473–76.

Keniston, K. College students and children in developmental institutions. *Children,* 1967, **14**(1), 2–7.

Kent, H. B. Control over stress, locus of control, and response to stress. *Journal of Personality and Social Psychology,* 1972, **21**(2), 249–55.

Kephart, W. M. Some correlates of romantic love. *Journal of Marriage and the Family,* 1967, **29,** 470–74.

Kerckhoff, A. C., & Davis, K. E. Value consensus and need complementarity in mate selection. *American Sociological Review,* 1962, **27,** 295–303.

Keys, A., Brozek, J., Henschel, A., Mickelsen, O., & Taylor, H. L. *The biology of human starvation.* Minneapolis: University of Minnesota Press, 1950.

Kiester, E., Jr. Behind science's growing fascination with psychic phenomena. *Today's Health,* 1973, **51**(11), 24–27, 61–63.

Kinsey, A. C., Pomeroy, W. B., & Martin, C. E. *Sexual behavior in the human male.* Philadelphia: Saunders, 1948.

Kinsey, A. C., Pomeroy, W. B., & Martin, C. E. *Sexual behavior in the human female.* Philadelphia: Saunders, 1953.

Kirkpatrick, C. *The family as process and institution.* (2nd ed.) New York: Ronald Press, 1963.

Klemesrud, J. Secretary image: A tempest in a typewriter. *New York Times,* March 7, 1972, 34.

Kluckhohn, C. Values and value-orientations in the theory of action. In T. Parsons & E. A. Shils (Eds.), *Toward a general theory of action.* Cambridge, Mass.: Harvard University Press, 1954.

Kluckhohn, F. R., & Strodtbeck, F. L. *Variations in value orientation.* New York: Harper & Row, 1961.

Knupfer, G., Clark, W., & Room, R. The mental health of the unmarried. *The American Journal of Psychiatry,* 1966, **122**(8), 844.

Komarovsky, M. *Blue-collar marriage.* New York: Random House, 1964.

Komorita, S. S., & Chertkoff, J. M. A bargaining theory of coalition formation. *Psychological Review,* 1973, **80**(3), 149–62.

Kornhauser, A. W. *Mental health of the industrial worker: A Detroit study.* New York: Krieger, 1965.

Krauss, I. Sources of educational aspirations among working-class youth. *American Sociological Review,* 1964, **29,** 867–79.

Kurland, M. Romantic love and economic considerations: A cultural comparison. *Journal of Educational Sociology,* October 1953, **27,** 72–79.

Lachman, S. J. A behavioristic rationale for the development of psychosomatic phenomena. *Journal of Psychology,* 1963, **56,** 239–48.

Laing, R. D. *The politics of experience.* New York: Pantheon, 1967. Copyright © 1967 R. D. Laing. Excerpts reprinted by permission of Penguin Books Ltd.(a)

Laing, R. D. Schizophrenic split. *Time,* February 3, 1967, 56.(b)

Laing, R. D. Who is mad? Who is sane? *The Atlantic,* January 1971, 50–66.

Laing, R. D., & Esterson, A. *Sanity, madness, and the family.* London: Tavistock, Ltd., 1964.

Lalljee, M., & Cook, M. Uncertainty in first encounters. *Journal of Personality and Social Psychology,* 1973, **26**(1), 137–41.

Landis, P. H. *Making the most of marriage.* (3rd ed.) New York: Appleton-Century-Crofts, 1965.

Langner, T. S., & Michael, S. T. *Life stress and mental health.* Vol. 2. *The Midtown Manhattan study.* New York: The Free Press, 1963.

Lazarus, R. S. *Psychological stress and the coping process.* New York: McGraw-Hill, 1966.

Lazlo, E. *The systems view of the world.* New York: Braziller, 1972.

Lecky, P. *Self-consistency: A theory of personality.* New York: Island Press Cooperative, 1945.

Lee, D. Culture and the experience of value. In A. H. Maslow (Ed.), *New knowledge in human values.* New York: Harper & Row, 1959.

Levin, F. M., & Gergen, K. J. Revealingness, ingratiation, and the disclosure of self. *Proceedings of the 77th Annual Convention of the American Psychological Association,* 1969, **4**(Pt. 1), 447–48.

Levinger, G. Sources of marital dissatisfaction among applicants for divorce. *American Journal of Orthopsychiatry,* 1966, **36,** 803–7.

Levitan, S., Mangum, G., & Marshall, R. *Human resources and the labor market: Labor and manpower in the American economy.* New York: Harper & Row, 1972.

Levitt, E. E. *The psychology of anxiety.* Indianapolis, Ind.: Bobbs-Merrill, 1967.

Levy, D. M. *Maternal overprotection.* New York: Columbia University Press, 1943.

Lewin, K., Lippitt, R., & White, R. K. Patterns of aggressive behavior in experimentally created "social climates." *Journal of Social Psychology,* 1939, **10,** 271–99.

Lewinsohn, P. M., & Libet, J. Pleasant events, activity schedules and depression. *Journal of Abnormal Psychology,* 1972, **79,** 291–95.

Lidz, T., Cornelison, A. R., Terry, D., & Fleck, S. Irrationality as a family tradition. *Archives of Neurology and Psychiatry,* 1958, **79,** 305–16.

Lidz, T., Fleck, S., Alanen, Y. O., & Cornelison, A. R. Schizophrenic patients and their siblings. *Psychiatry,* 1963, **26,** 1–18.

Lieberman, J. E. A case for the small family. *Population Reference Bulletin,* April 1970, 2–3.

Linton, R. *The study of man.* New York: Appleton-Century-Crofts, 1936.

Locke, H. J. *Predicting adjustment in marriage: A comparison of a divorced and a happily married group.* New York: Holt, Rinehart & Winston, 1951.

Lopata, H. Z. *Occupation: Housewife.* New York: Oxford University Press, 1971.

Lorr, M., Daston, P., & Smith, I. R. An analysis of mood states. *Educational & Psychological Measurement,* 1967, **27**(1), 89–96.

Lu, Y. C. Contradictory parental expectations in schizophrenia. *Archives of General Psychiatry,* 1962, **6,** 219–34.

Lydon, S. The politics of orgasm. In M. Garskof (Ed.), *Roles women play: Readings toward women's liberation.* Belmont, Calif.: Brooks/ Cole, 1971.

Maccoby, E., & Jacklin, C. N. On the alleged passivity of women. Unpublished manuscript, Stanford University, 1973.

MacKinnon, D. W. The nature and nurture of creative talent. *American Psychologist,* 1962, **17**(7), 484–95.

MacKinnon, D. W. The creativity of architects. In C. W. Taylor (Ed.), *Widening horizons in creativity.* New York: Wiley, 1964.

Macklin, E. Heterosexual cohabitation among unmarried college students. *The Family Coordinator,* 1972, **21,** 463–72.

Mahl, G. H. Gestures and body movements in interviews. In J. M. Schlien (Ed.), *Research in psychotherapy.* Washington, D.C.: American Psychological Association, 1968.

Maltzman, I. On the training of originality. *Psychological Review,* 1960, **67,** 229–42.

Marcantonio, C. Quote from foreword. In C. Moustakas, *Individuality & encounter: A brief journey into loneliness & sensitivity groups.* Cambridge, Mass.: Howard A. Doyle, 1968. Copyright © 1968 by Clark Moustakas. Reprinted by permission of Howard A. Doyle Publishing Company.

Margolis, B., & Kroes, W. Work and the health of man. Paper commissioned by the Special Task Force, *Work in America.* Cambridge, Mass.: MIT Press, 1972.

Marks, I. M. Agoraphobic syndrome (phobic anxiety state). *Archives of General Psychiatry,* 1970, **23**(6), 538–53.

Marshall, B. "Beginning." In B. Marshall (Ed.), *Experiences in being.* Belmont, Calif.: Brooks/Cole, 1971. Copyright © 1971 by Wadsworth Publishing Company, Inc. Reprinted by permission of the publisher, Brooks/Cole Publishing Company, Monterey, California.

Martin, B. Family interaction associated with child disturbances: Assessment and modification. *Psychotherapy: Theory, Research and Practice,* 1967, **4,** 30–35.

Martino, J. P. Forecasting by professional societies. *The Futurists,* 1973, **8**(2), 79–80. (a)

Martino, J. P. *Technological forecasting for decisionmaking.* New York: American Elsevier, 1973. (b)

Maslow, A. H. *Motivation and personality.* New York: Harper & Row, 1954.

Maslow, A. H. *The farther reaches of human nature.* New York: Viking Press, 1969.

Maslow, A. H. *The farther reaches of human nature.* New York: Viking Press, 1971. (a)

Maslow, A. H. *Motivation and personality.* New York: Viking Press, 1971. (b)

Masters, W., & Johnson, V. *The human sexual response.* Boston: Little, Brown, 1966.

Masters, W., & Johnson, V. *Human sexual inadequacy.* Boston: Little, Brown, 1970.

May, R. *Man's search for himself.* New York: Norton, 1953.

May, R. The daemonic: Love and death. *Psychology Today,* 1968, **1**(9), 16–25.

May, R. *Love and will.* London: The Fontana Library, 1972.

McCall, G. J., & Simmons, J. L. *Identity & interaction.* New York: The Free Press, 1966.

McCann, R. "Inconsistency." From *Complete cheerful cherub* by Rebecca McCann. Copyright 1932 by Covici, Friede, Inc. Renewed by Crown, © 1960. Used by permission of Crown Publishers, Inc.

McClelland, D. C. Toward a theory of motive acquisition. *American Psychologist,* 1965, **20,** 321–33.

McCord, J., & McCord, W. The effects of parental role model on criminality. *Journal of Social Issues,* 1958, **14,** 66–75.

McCord, W., McCord, J., & Thurber, E. Some effects of paternal absence on male children. *Journal of Abnormal and Social Psychology,* 1962, **64,** 361–69.

McCord, W., McCord, J., & Verden, P. Familial and behavioral correlates of dependency in male children. *Child Development,* 1962, **33,** 313–26.

McDavid, J. W., & Harari, H. *Social psychology.* New York: Harper & Row, 1968.

McKain, W. C. Cited in W. Alvarez, Marriage success good among elderly. *Los Angeles Times,* April 15, 1973.

McLuhan, M., & Leonard, G. B. The future of sex. *Look,* July 25, 1967, 56–63.

McQuade, W. What stress can do to you. *Fortune,* 1972, **85**(1), 102–7, 134–37, 141.

McWilliams, S., & Tuttle, R. J. *Psychological Bulletin,* 1973, **79**(6), 341–51.

Mead, G. H. *Mind, self, and society.* Chicago: The University of Chicago Press, 1934.

Mead, M. *From the South Seas: Studies of adolescence and sex in primitive societies.* New York: Morrow, 1939.

Mead, M. *Male and female.* New York: Morrow, 1949.

Mead, M. Marriage in two steps. In H. Otto (Ed.), *The family in search of a future.* New York: Appleton-Century-Crofts, 1971.

Mechanic, D. *Students under stress.* New York: The Free Press, 1962.

Michael, D. N. *The next generation: The prospects ahead for the youth of today and tomorrow.* New York: Random House, 1965.

Michener, J. A. *The fires of spring.* New York: Random House, 1949.

Millay, E. St. Vincent From "Ashes of life." *Collected poems.* New York: Harper & Row, 1945. Copyright 1917, 1945 by Edna St. Vincent Millay. By permission of Norma Millay Ellis.

Miller, G. A. *Psychology: The science of mental life.* New York: Harper & Row, 1962.

Miller, G. A., Galanter, E., & Pribram, K. H. *Plans and the structure of behavior.* New York: Holt, Rinehart & Winston, 1960.

Miller, J. G. Living systems: Basic concepts. *Behavioral Scientist,* 1965, **10**, 193–237. (a)

Miller, J. G. Living systems: Structure and process. *Behavioral Scientist,* 1965, **10**, 337–79. (b)

Miller, N. E., & Dollard, J. *Social learning and imitation.* New Haven, Conn.: Yale University Press, 1941.

Mischel, W. Father-absence and delay of gratification: Cross-cultural comparisons. *Journal of Abnormal and Social Psychology,* 1961, **63**, 116–24.

Mischel, W. A social-learning view of sex differences. In E. E. Maccoby (Ed.), *The development of sex differences.* Stanford, Calif.: Stanford University Press, 1966, 56–81.

Mischel, W., & Liebert, R. M. Effects of discrepancies between deserved and reward criteria on their acquisition and transmission. *Journal of Personality and Social Psychology,* 1966, **3**, 45–53.

Mischel, W., & Liebert, R. M. The role of power in the adoption of self-reward patterns. *Child Development,* 1967, **38**, 673–83.

Mishler, E. G., & Waxler, N. E. Family interaction process and schizophrenia: A review of current theories. *Merrill-Palmer Quarterly,* 1965, **11**, 269–316.

Monahan, T. P. Broken homes by age of delinquent children. *Journal of Social Psychology,* 1960, **51**, 387–97.

Montagu, A. Man the warrior . . . or child of an imperfect society. *Los Angeles Times,* May 26, 1968, Section G, 1–2.

Moore, J. E. Antecedents of dependency and autonomy in young children. *Dissertation Abstracts,* 1965, **26**(3), 1766.

Morgan, J. Survey Research Center findings. Reported in Special Task Force, *Work in America.* Cambridge, Mass.: MIT Press, 1972.

Morimoto, K. Context for learning. *Harvard Educational Review,* 1973, **43**(2), 245–57.

Morris, M. G. Psychological miscarriage: An end to mother love. *Trans-action,* 1966, **3**(2), 8–13.

Morris, V. C. *Existentialism in education.* New York: Harper & Row, 1966.

Morse, R., & Weiss, N. The function and meaning of work and the job. *American Sociological Review,* 1955, **20**, 191–98.

Moss, H. A. Sex, age, and state as determinants of mother-infant interaction. *Merrill-Palmer Quarterly,* 1967, **13**, 19–36.

Moss, H. A., & Robson, K. S. The role of protest behavior in the development of the mother-infant attachment. Paper presented at the meeting of the American Psychological Association, San Francisco, 1968.

Moustakas, C. E. *Loneliness.* New York: Prentice-Hall, 1961.

Moustakas, C. E. *Personal growth: The struggle for identity and human values.* Cambridge, Mass.: Howard A. Doyle, 1969.

Mudd, E., Mitchell, H., & Taubin, S. *Success in family living.* New York: Association Press, 1965.

Murphy, H. B., Wittkower, E. D., & Chance, N. A. Cross-cultural inquiry into the symptomatology of depression: A preliminary report. *International Journal of Psychiatry,* 1967, **3**(1), 6–22.

Murphy, J. M., & Leighton, A. H. *Approaches to cross-cultural psychiatry.* New York: Cornell University Press, 1965.

Mursell, J. L. *Using your mind effectively.* New York: McGraw-Hill, 1951.

Nader, R. We need a new kind of patriotism. *Life,* 1971, **71**(2), 4.

Nakamura, C. Y. Conformity and problem solving. *Journal of Abnormal and Social Psychology,* 1958, **56**, 315–20.

Nardini, J. E. Survival factors in American prisoners of war of the Japanese. *American Journal of Psychiatry,* 1952, **109**, 242–43. Copyright 1952, the American Psychiatric Association. Reprinted by permission of the author and the American Psychiatric Association.

National Center for Health Statistics. *Selected symptoms of psychological distress.* U.S. Department of Health, Education, and Welfare, 1970.

National Institute of Mental Health. *The mental health of*

urban America. Washington, D.C.: U.S. Government Printing Office, 1969.

Navran, L. Communication and adjustment in marriage. *Family Process,* 1967, **6**(2), 173–84.

Nelson, P. D. Similarities and differences among leaders and followers. *Journal of Social Psychology,* 1964, **63,** 161–67.

Nicholls, J. G. Creativity in the person who will never produce anything original and useful: The concept of creativity as a normally distributed trait. *American Psychologist,* 1972, **27**(8), 717–27.

Nye, F. I. *Family relationships and delinquent behavior.* New York: Wiley, 1958.

Nye, F. I., & Hoffman, L. *The employed mother in America.* Chicago: Rand-McNally, 1963.

Nye, R. D. *Conflict among humans.* New York: Springer Publishing Co., 1973.

O'Connor, E. *Our many selves.* New York: Harper & Row, 1971.

O'Neill, N., & O'Neill, G. Open marriage: A synergic model. *The Family Coordinator,* 1972, **21,** 403–10.

Osofsky, J., & Osofsky, H. Androgyny as a life style. *The Family Coordinator,* 1972, **21,** 411–18.

Overstreet, H., & Overstreet, B. *The mind goes forth.* New York: Norton, 1956.

Packard, V. *The sexual wilderness.* New York: David McKay, 1968.

Palmore, E. Predicting longevity: A follow-up controlling for age. *Gerontologist,* 1969, **9,** 247–50.

Panyard, C. Self-disclosure between friends: A validity study. *Journal of Consulting Psychology,* 1973, **20** (1), 66–68.

Parkes, C. M. Components of the reaction to loss of limb, spouse, or home. *Journal of Psychosomatic Research,* 1972, **16**(5), 343–49.

Parkes, C. M., Benjamin, B., & Fitzgerald, R. G. Broken hearts: A statistical study of increased mortality rates among widowers. *British Medical Journal,* 1969, **1,** 740.

Patterson, G. R., & Reid, J. B. Reciprocity and coercion: Two facets of social systems. Mimeographed manuscript, Oregon Research Institute, 1968.

Peck, R. F., & Havighurst, R. J. *The psychology of character development.* New York: Wiley, 1960.

Perls, F. S. Group vs. individual therapy. ETC, 1967, **34,** 306–12.

Perls, F. S. *Gestalt therapy verbatim.* Lafayette, Calif.: Real People Press, 1969.

Peterson, C. R., & Beach, L. R. Man as an intuitive statistician. *Psychological Bulletin,* 1967, **68**(1), 29–46.

Piaget, J. *The origins of intelligence in children.* New York: International University, 1936.

Platt, J. A fearful and wonderful world for living. In College of Home Economics, *Families of the future.* Ames, Iowa: The Iowa State University Press, 1972. Excerpt reprinted by permission, © 1972 by the Iowa State University Press, Ames, Iowa.

Pohlman, E. *The psychology of birth planning.* Cambridge, Mass.: Schenkman Publishing Co., 1969.

Prescott, D. A. *The child in the educative process.* New York: McGraw-Hill, 1957.

Price, D. A technique for analyzing the economic value system. *Journal of Marriage and the Family,* 1968, **30**(3), 467–72.

Pringle, M. L. K. *Deprivation and education.* New York: Humanities Press, 1965.

Rahe, R. H., & Lind, E. Psychosocial factors and sudden cardiac death: A pilot study. *Journal of Psychosomatic Research,* 1971, **15**(1), 19–24.

Rainwater, L. *Family design.* Chicago: Aldine, 1965.

Rainwater, L. Some aspects of lower class sexual behavior. In J. Bardwick (Ed.), *Readings on the psychology of women.* New York: Harper & Row, 1972. Reprinted from *Journal of Social Issues,* 1966, **22,** 96–108.

Ram Dass, Baba (Richard Alpert) *Be here now.* San Cristobal, N.M.: Lama Foundation, 1971. © Lama Foundation 1971. Excerpts reprinted by permission of the Lama Foundation and the author.(a)

Ram Dass, Baba (Richard Alpert) Excerpts from "Ram Dass Lecture at the Menninger Foundation: Part II" by Baba Ram Dass. *The Journal of Transpersonal Psychology,* 1971, **3**(1), 47–84. Copyright © 1971 by the Journal of Transpersonal Psychology. Reprinted by permission.(b)

Rand, A. *The virtue of selfishness.* New York: The New American Library, 1964.

Reitan, H. T., & Shaw, M. E. Group membership, sex-composition of the group, and conformity behavior. *Journal of Social Psychology,* 1964, **64,** 45–51.

Renne, K. S. Correlates of dissatisfaction in marriage. *Journal of Marriage and the Family,* 1970, **32,** 54–67.

Reynolds, E. Variations of mood and recall in the menstrual cycle. *Journal of Psychosomatic Research,* 1969, **13,** 163–66.

Rich, L. D. *Happy the land.* Philadelphia: Lippincott, 1946.

Richards, I. A. The secret of feedforward. *Saturday Review,* 1968, **51**(5), 14–17.

Riecken, H. W. The effect of talkativeness on ability to influence group solution of problems. *Sociometry,* 1958, **21,** 309–21.

Riesman, D. The young are captives of each other. *Psychology Today,* 1969, **3**(5), 28–31.

Ring, K., Braginsky, D., & Braginsky, B. Performance styles in interpersonal relations: A typology. *Psychological Reports,* 1966, **18,** 203–20.

Roe, A. *The making of a scientist.* New York: Dodd, Mead, 1953.

Rogers, C. R. *Client-centered therapy.* Boston: Houghton Mifflin, 1951.

Rogers, C. R. *Becoming a person.* Austin: University of Texas, 1958.

Rogers, C. R. *On becoming a person: A therapist's view of psychotherapy.* Boston: Houghton Mifflin, 1961. Copyright © 1961 by Carl R. Rogers. Excerpts reprinted by permission of Houghton Mifflin Company.

Rogers, C. R. Toward a modern approach to values: The valuing process in the mature person. *Journal of Abnormal and Social Psychology,* 1964, **68**(2), 160–67.

Rogers, C. R. Interpersonal relationships: U.S.A. 2000. *Journal of Applied Behavioral Science,* 1968, **4**(3), 265–80.

Rogers, C. R. *Freedom to learn: A view of what education might become.* Columbus, Ohio: Charles E. Merrill, 1969.

Rogers, C. R. *Carl Rogers on encounter groups.* New York: Harper & Row, 1970.

Rogers, C. R. *Becoming partners: Marriage and its alternatives.* New York: Delacorte Press, 1972.

Rogers, C. R., & Stevens, B. *Person to person: The problem of being human.* Lafayette, Calif.: Real People Press, 1967.

Rollins, B. C., & Feldman, H. Marital satisfaction over the family cycle. *Journal of Marriage and the Family,* 1970, **32**, 20–28.

Rosen, B. C., & D'Andrade, R. G. The psychological origins of achievement motivation. *Sociometry,* 1959, **22**, 188–218.

Rosenthal, M. J. The syndrome of the inconsistent mother. *American Journal of Orthopsychiatry,* 1962, **32**, 637–44.

Rossi, A. Barriers to the career choice of engineering, medicine, or science among American women. In J. Bardwick (Ed.), *Readings on the psychology of women.* New York: Harper & Row, 1972.

Rubin, Z. *Liking and loving.* New York: Holt, Rinehart & Winston, 1973.

Ruch, L. O., & Holmes, T. H. Scaling of life change: Comparison of direct and indirect methods. *Journal of Psychosomatic Research,* 1971, **15**(2), 221–28.

Rudestam, K. E. Stockholm and Los Angeles: A cross-cultural study of the communication of suicidal intent. *Journal of Consulting and Clinical Psychology,* 1971, **36**(1), 82–90.

Sales, S., & House, J. Job dissatisfaction as a possible risk factor in coronary heart disease. *Journal of Chronic Diseases,* 1971, **23**, 861–73.

Salk, L. Which decisions parents should allow children to make. *Today's Health,* June 1973, 39–41.

Salzman-Webb, M. Woman as secretary, sexpot, spender, sow, civic actor, sickie. In M. Garskof (Ed.), *Roles women play: Readings toward women's liberation.* Belmont, Calif.: Brooks/Cole, 1971.

Satir, V. *Conjoint family therapy.* Palo Alto, Calif.: Science & Behavior Books, 1967.

Schachter, S. *The psychology of affiliation: Experimental studies of the sources of gregariousness.* Stanford, Calif.: Stanford University Press, 1959.

Schein, E. H. The first job dilemma. *Psychology Today,* 1968, **1**(10), 26–37.

Schein, V. Implications and obstacles to full participation of the woman worker. *Best's Review,* April 1972.

Schrank, R., & Stein, S. Yearning, learning and status. In S. A. Levitan (Ed.), *Blue collar workers: A symposium on middle America.* New York: McGraw-Hill, 1971.

Schuham, A. I. The double-bind hypothesis a decade later. *Psychological Bulletin,* 1967, **68**, 409–16.

Schwenn, M. Arousal of the motive to avoid success. Unpublished Junior Honors Paper, Harvard University, 1970.

Sears, R. R. Relation of early socialization experiences to aggression in middle childhood. *Journal of Abnormal and Social Psychology,* 1961, **63**, 466–92.

Sears, R. R., Maccoby, E. E., & Levin, H. *Patterns of child rearing.* New York: Harper & Row, 1957.

Seeman, M. Antidote for alienation: Learning to belong. *Trans-action,* 1966, **3**(4), 35–39.

Seiden, R. Suicide among youth: A review of the literature, 1900–1967. Supplement to the *Bulletin of Suicidology.* Washington, D.C.: National Clearinghouse for Mental Health Information, December 1969.

Seligson, M. *The eternal bliss machine.* New York: Morrow, 1973.

Selye, H. *The stress of life.* New York: McGraw-Hill, 1956.

Selye, H. Stress. *Psychology Today,* 1969, **3**(4), 24–26.

Severin, F. T. *Discovering man in psychology: A humanistic approach.* New York: McGraw-Hill, 1973.

Shapley, H. *Of stars and men: The human response to an expanding universe.* Boston: Beacon Press, 1958.

Shaw, M. E. *Group Dynamics.* New York: McGraw-Hill, 1971.

Shepherd, J. Rebirth. *Look,* 1971, **35**(1), 15.

Sheppard, H., & Herrick, N. *Where have all the robots gone?* New York: The Free Press, 1972.

Sherfey, M. J. *The nature and evolution of female sexuality.* New York: Vintage Books, 1973.

Shibutani, T. The structure of personal identity. In E. E. Sampson (Ed.), *Approaches, contexts, and problems of social psychology.* Englewood Cliffs, N. J.: Prentice-Hall, 1964.

Shubik, M. Information, rationality, and free choice in a future democratic society. *Daedalus,* 1967, **96**, 771–78.

Shulman, A. K. *Memoirs of an ex-prom queen.* New York: Bantam Books, 1972. Copyright © 1969, 1971, 1972 by Alix Kates Shulman. Excerpt reprinted by permission of Alfred A. Knopf, Inc. and Curtis Brown, Ltd.

Siegelman, M. College student personality correlates of early parent-child relationships. *Journal of Consulting Psychology,* 1965, **29**, 558–64.

Silver, L. B., Dublin, C. C., & Lourie, R. S. Does violence breed violence? Contributions from a study of the child abuse syndrome. *American Journal of Psychiatry,* 1969, **126,** 404–7.

Simmel, G. The secret and the secret society. In K. Wolff (Ed.), *The sociology of Georg Simmel.* New York: The Free Press, 1964.

Singer, D. L. Aggression, arousal, hostile humor, and catharsis. *Journal of Personality and Social Psychology,* 1968, **8**(1, Pt. 2).

Sinnott, E. W. *The biology of the spirit.* New York: Viking Press, 1955.

Skinner, B. F. *Science and human behavior.* New York: Macmillan, 1953.

Skinner, B. F. *Beyond freedom and dignity.* New York: Knopf, 1971.

Smith, T. V., & Lindeman, E. C. *The democratic way of life.* New York: New American Library, 1951.

Snyder, R. *On becoming human.* New York: Abingdon Press, 1967.

Solomon, R. L. Punishment. *American Psychologist,* 1964, **19,** 239–53.

Sorensen, R. C., & Hendin, D. A "Kinsey Report" on sex and today's teenager. *Los Angeles Times,* February 18, 1973.

South, J. "Games people play." Atlanta: Lowery Music Co., 1968.

Special Task Force, to the Secretary of Health, Education, and Welfare. *Work in America.* Cambridge, Mass.: MIT Press, 1972.

Spiro, M. E. *Children of the Kibbutz.* Cambridge: Harvard University Press, 1958.

Spranger, E. *Lebensforman.* (3rd ed.) Halle: Niemeyer, 1923. (Translated: P. Pigors. *Types of men.* New York: Steckert, 1928.)

Srole, L., Langner, T., Michael, S., Opler, M., & Rennie, T. *Mental health in the metropolis: The midtown Manhattan study.* New York: McGraw-Hill, 1962.

Stampfl, T. G., & Levis, D. J. Essentials of implosive therapy: A learning-theory-based psychodynamic behavioral therapy. *Journal of Abnormal Psychology,* 1967, **72,** 496–503.

Starr, J. Adaptation to working conditions. Paper commissioned by the Special Task Force, *Work in America.* Cambridge, Mass.: MIT Press, 1972.

Stern, R. L. Diary of a war neurosis. *Journal of Nervous and Mental Disease,* 1947, **106,** 583–86. Reprinted by permission of The Smith Ely Jelliffe Trust.

Stoller, F. The intimate network of families as a new structure. In H. Otto (Ed.), *The family in search of a future.* New York: Appleton-Century-Crofts, 1971.

Strange, R. E., & Brown, D. E., Jr. Home from the wars. *American Journal of Psychiatry,* 1970, **127**(4), 488–92.

Stratton, R. P., & Brown, R. Improving creative thinking by training in the production and/or judgment of solutions. *Journal of Educational Psychology,* 1972, **63**(4), 390–97.

Sullivan, H. S. *Schizophrenia as a human process.* New York: Norton, 1962.

Swensen, C., Jr. *Introduction to interpersonal relations.* Glenview, Ill.: Scott, Foresman, 1973.

Szasz, T. S. The crime of commitment. *Psychology Today,* 1969, **2**(10), 55–57.

Tangri, S. Role innovation in occupational choice. Unpublished doctoral thesis, University of Michigan, 1969.

Teilhard de Chardin, P. *The phenomenon of man.* New York: Harper & Row, 1961.

Thibaut, J. W., & Kelley, H. H. *The social psychology of groups.* New York: Wiley, 1959.

Thiel, H., Parker, D., & Bruce, T. Stress factors and the risk of myocardial infarction. *Journal of Psychosomatic Research,* 1973, **17**(1), 43–58.

Tiedeman, D. V., & O'Hara, R. P. *Career development: Choice and adjustment.* New York: College Entrance Examination Board, 1963.

Toby, J. The differential impact of family disorganization. *American Sociological Review,* 1957, **22,** 505–12.

Toffler, A. *Future shock.* New York: Random House, 1970.

Touhey, J. C. Effects of additional women professionals on ratings of occupational prestige and desirability. Paper presented at the meeting of the Western Psychological Association, Anaheim, California, April 1973.

Toynbee, A. *A study of history.* Vol. 1. New York: Oxford University Press, 1947.

Toynbee, A. Human savagery cracks thin veneer. *Los Angeles Times,* September 6, 1970, Section C, 3.

Toynbee, A. Our present society is truly repulsive. *Los Angeles Times,* June 24, 1973, Part VII, 1.

Trost, J. Some data on mate-selection: Homogamy and perceived homogamy. *Journal of Marriage and the Family,* 1967, **29,** 739–55.

Udry, J. R. *The social context of marriage.* Philadelphia: Lippincott, 1966.

Udry, J. R. Personality match and interpersonal perception as predictors of marriage. *Journal of Marriage and the Family,* 1967, **29,** 722–25.

Udry, J. R. *The social context of marriage.* (2nd ed.) Philadelphia: Lippincott, 1971.

Updike, J. From "The dogwood tree." In M. Levin (Ed.), *Five boyhoods.* Garden City, N.Y.: Doubleday, 1962. Published by Doubleday & Co. Copyright © 1962 by Martin Levin. Reprinted by permission.

Veroff, J., & Feld, S. *Marriage and work in America.* New York: Van Nostrand Reinhold, 1970.

Von Bertalanffy, L. The world of science and the world of value. In J. F. T. Bugental (Ed.), *Challenges of humanistic psychology.* New York: McGraw-Hill, 1967.

Von Bertalanffy, L. General systems theory. In W. Buckley (Ed.), *Modern systems research for the behavioral scientist.* Chicago: Aldine, 1968.

Waldrop, M. F., & Bell, R. Q. Effects of family size and density on newborn characteristics. *American Journal of Orthopsychiatry,* 1966, **36**, 544–50.

Wallach, M. A., & Kogan, N. Creativity and intelligence in children's thinking. *Trans-action,* 1967, **4**(3), 38–43.

Wallach, M. A., Kogan, N., & Bem, D. J. Group influence on individual risk taking. *Journal of Abnormal and Social Psychology,* 1962, **65**, 75–87.

Wallach, M. A., Kogan, N., & Bem, D. J. Diffusion of responsibility to level of risk takings in groups. *Journal of Abnormal and Social Psychology,* 1964, **68**, 263–74.

Walters, R., & Parke, R. The influence of punishment and related disciplinary techniques on the social behavior of children: Theory and empirical findings. In B. Maher (Ed.), *Progress in experimental personality research.* Vol. 4. New York: Academic Press, 1967.

Walton, R. Work place alienation and the need for major innovation. Paper commissioned by the Special Task Force, *Work in America.* Cambridge, Mass.: MIT Press, 1972.

Watson, J. B. *Psychology from the standpoint of a behaviorist.* Philadelphia: Lippincott, 1919.

Watson, J. B., & Rayner, R. Conditioned emotional reactions. *Journal of Experimental Psychology,* 1920, **3**, 1–14.

Watson, R. *Psychology of the child.* (2nd ed.) New York: Wiley, 1965.

Weil, A. *Natural mind: A new way of looking at drugs and the higher consciousness.* Boston: Houghton Mifflin, 1972.

Weitzman, E. D., & Luce, G. Biological rhythms: Indices of pain, adrenal hormones, sleep, and sleep reversal. In NIMH, *Behavioral sciences and mental health.* Washington, D.C.: U.S. Government Printing Office, 1970.

Werts, C. E. Paternal influence on career choice. *Journal of Counseling Psychology,* 1968, **15**(1), 48–52.

West, L. J. Psychiatric aspects of training for honorable survival as a prisoner of war. *American Journal of Psychiatry,* 1958, **115**, 329–36.

Weybrew, B. B. Patterns of psychophysiological response to military stress. In M. H. Appley & R. Trumbull (Eds.), *Psychological stress.* New York: Appleton-Century-Crofts, 1967.

Wheelis, A. *The illusionless man.* New York: Harper Colophon, 1966.

Whelpton, P. K., Campbell, A., & Patterson, J. *Fertility and family planning in the United States.* Princeton, N.J.: Princeton University Press, 1966.

White, R. W. Motivation reconsidered: The concept of competence. *Psychological Review,* 1959, **66**, 297–333.

Whyte, W. H. *Organization man.* New York: Simon & Schuster, 1956.

Wikler, A. Dynamics of drug dependence. *Archives of General Psychiatry,* 1973, **28**(5), 611–16.

Williamson, R. C. Dating, courtship, and the "ideal mate": Some relevant subcultural variables. *Family Life Coordinator,* 1965, **14**(3), 137–43.

Williamson, R. C. *Marriage and family relations.* (2nd ed.) New York: Wiley, 1972.

Wilson, H. V. Development of sponges from dissociated tissue cells. *Bulletin of the Bureau of Fisheries,* 1910, **30**, 1–30. Reprinted by the courtesy of the Department of Commerce, NOAA.

Wilson, W. Correlates of avowed happiness. *Psychological Bulletin,* 1967, **67**, 294–306.

Winch, R. F. *The modern family.* (Rev. ed.) New York: Holt, Rinehart & Winston, 1963.

Winch, R. F. Another look at the theory of complementary needs in mate-selection. *Journal of Marriage and the Family,* 1967, **29**(4), 756–62.

Winchester, J. H. Iceland: A nation hurrying toward tomorrow. *Reader's Digest,* June 1966, **88**, 197–200.

Winder, C. L., & Rau, L. Parental attitudes associated with social deviance in preadolescent boys. *Journal of Abnormal and Social Psychology,* 1962, **64**, 418–24.

Winter, W. D., & Ferreira, A. J. Interaction process analysis of family decision-making. *Family Process,* 1967, **6**, 155–72.

Winterbottom, M. The relation of need for achievement to learning experiences in independence and mastery. In J. Atkinson (Ed.), *Motives in fantasy, action, and society.* New York: Van Nostrand, 1958.

Wolfe, T. *Look homeward angel.* New York: Scribner's, 1929, 1970.

Wolff, H. G. Stressors as a cause of disease in man. In J. M. Tanner (Ed.), *Stress and psychiatric disorder.* London: Oxford, 1960.

Wolpe, J. *Psychotherapy by reciprocal inhibition.* Stanford, Calif.: Stanford University Press, 1958.

Wolpe, J. *The practice of behavior therapy.* New York: Pergamon Press, 1969.

Wolpe, J., & Rachman, S. Psychoanalytic "evidence": A critique based on Freud's case of little Hans. *Journal of Nervous and Mental Diseases,* 1960, **131**, 135–38.

Women's Caucus, Political Science Department, University of Chicago. The halls of academe. In R. Morgan (Ed.), *Sisterhood is powerful.* New York: Random House, 1970.

Yankelovich, D. *Generations apart.* A study of the generation gap conducted for CBS News, Columbia Broadcasting System, Inc., 1969.

Yankelovich, D. *The changing values on campus: Political and personal attitudes on campus.* New York: Washington Square Press, 1972.

Zajonc, R. Social facilitation. In D. Cartwright & A. Zander (Eds.), *Group dynamics: Research and theory.* (3rd ed.) New York: Harper & Row, 1968.

Zurcher, L. A. The mutable self. *The Futurist,* October 1972, 181–85.

Picture Credits

The photographers whose work appears in this book are cited below. To all, the authors and publisher wish to express their appreciation.

10 David Powers/Jeroboam
13 Arthur Tress
20–22 Michael Vollan
46 "Identity"/Photograph © by Alfred Gescheidt
53 Harvey Stein
59 Harvey Stein
60 Harvey Stein
67 Geoffrey Gove
76 "Baby on Pool Table" 1970, Ronald Mesaros
79 Danny Lyon/Magnum
81 Charles Gatewood
95 Heinrich Riebesehl, Hannover, West Germany
96 "Sorrow at Parting"/Mary Ellen Mark
104 "Liz at Bailey's Mistake"/Christian Sunde
110 Geoffrey Gove
124 Paul Sequeira
126 Larry Burrows/Time-Life Picture Agency © 1972, Time Inc.
130 Arthur Tress
143 Elliot Erwitt/Magnum
148 George Gardner
157 Charles Gatewood
164 Joyce R. Wilson/D.P.I. (top); Al Lieberman (bottom)
176 Robert Altman/BBM Associates
185 Arthur Tress
196 Dan Budnik/Woodfin Camp & Associates
208 Bob Combs/Rapho Guillumette Pictures
232 George Gardner
237 David J. Kern
249 Marion Bernstein
260 Roger Lubin/Jeroboam
266 Bill Owens/BBM Associates
273 Lee Friedlander
287 Laurence Fink
297 Paul Conklin
302 Michael Vollan

311 Henry Monroe/D.P.I.
313 Martin Weaver/Woodfin Camp & Associates
314 Leonard Freed/Magnum
316 Eileen Christelow
328–329 From the Collection of Chester S. Burgette
330 Roger Lubin/Jeroboam
344 Peter Goodman/BBM Associates
346 Jay King
356 Ken Graves/Jeroboam
358 Michael Mauney
361 Paul Sequeira
364 Philip Bailey/Stock, Boston
373 Jean-Claude Lejeune
374 Laurence Fink
388 George Gardner
390 Jeffrey Blankfort/BBM Associates
397 Mitchell Payne/Jeroboam
421 Arthur Schatz/Time-Life Picture Agency © 1972, Time Inc.
426 Ian Berry/Magnum
427 Paul Fusco/Magnum
435 Jean-Claude Lejeune
438 Rae Russel
443 Cornell Capa/Magnum
448 Susan Ylvisaker
453 Suzanne Szasz
463 Frank Briggs
468 Sepp Seitz/Magnum
469 Sepp Seitz/Magnum
470 Ronald Partridge/BBM Associates
475 Jay King
478 George Gardner
484–485 NASA
494 George Gardner
502 Edward Kaufman (top); Bruce Davidson/Magnum (bottom)
503 Terry L. Husebye/Magnum (top); Charles Harbutt/ Magnum (bottom)
508 Denny Witz

Cover and chapter-opening photographs by J. W. Moore

Abnormal behavior. Maladaptive action detrimental to the individual and/or the group.

Abortion. Premature termination of a pregnancy.

Achievement motivation. Desire to excel or perform well according to some standard of excellence.

Achilles' heel. Special vulnerability to a specific type of stress.

Acting out. Ego-defense mechanism in which the individual reduces anxiety, hostility, or other unpleasant emotions by permitting their expression in overt behavior.

Activation. General energizing of behavior.

Actualization strivings. Strivings toward growth and fulfillment.

Acute type. Type of schizophrenic reaction.

Adaptability. Flexibility in meeting changed circumstances and adjustive demands.

Adjustment. Outcome of the individual's efforts to deal with stress and meet his needs.

Affective dimension. Emotional dimension of living; the feeling aspects of life.

Alarm and mobilization. First stage of the general-adaptation-syndrome, characterized by the mobilization of defenses to cope with a stressful situation.

Alcoholic intoxication. State reached when alcohol content of the blood is 0.1 percent or above.

Alcoholics Anonymous. Organization composed of alcoholics for treatment of alcoholism and maintaining abstinence via personal, religious, and social reinforcement.

Alcoholism. Excessive use of and dependence on alcohol to the extent that occupational, marital, or other important life adjustments are seriously impaired.

Alienation. Lack or loss of relationships to others; often confusion about one's identity.

Ambivalence. Simultaneous existence of contradictory emotional attitudes toward the same person, e.g., love and hate.

Antisocial family. Family which engages in and teaches child antisocial and often illegal types of behavior.

Anxiety. Generalized feelings of fear and apprehension.

Anxiety-defense model. Causal model of psychopathology emphasizing excessive use of ego-defense mechanisms in the face of anxiety-arousing stress.

Anxiety reaction. Type of neurotic reaction characterized by chronic anxiety and apprehension, often with occasional acute episodes of anxiety.

Approach-avoidant conflict. Type of stress situation involving both positive and negative features and requiring choice.

Assertion training. Behavior-therapy technique for helping individuals become more self-assertive in interpersonal relations.

Atrophy. Wasting away or shrinking of a bodily organ.

Authenticity. The human quality of being spontaneous and genuine, of being one's true self without a "false front" or facade.

Autocratic leadership. Form of leadership in which leader sets the goals and controls the activity of the group.

Automatic responses. Habits and other "automatic" responses which do not require conscious attention or decision making.

Aversion therapy. Behavior-therapy technique in which punishment or aversive stimuli are used to eliminate undesired response.

"Bad trip." An unpleasant or traumatic experience suffered by an individual while under the influence of a hallucinogenic drug, such as LSD.

"Basic personality type." The characteristic personality type or types fostered by a particular group.

"Becoming." Refers to personal growth (as used in the present text).

Behavior control. Shaping and manipulation of behavior by persuasion, drugs, propaganda, therapy, and other techniques.

Behavior therapy. Form of psychotherapy based primarily on application of learning principles to modification of maladaptive behavior.

Biological therapy. Electroshock, chemotherapy, and other medical measures for treating mental disorders.

Brainwashing. Intensive form of propaganda conducted under highly stressful conditions, as in a prisoner-of-war camp.

"Built-in" coping mechanisms. Crying, repetitive talking, and other patterns (in which learning seems to play a minimal role) that an individual uses in reacting to a stress situation.

Catatonic reaction. Type of schizophrenic reaction.

Charismatic leadership. Form of leadership in which the influence of the leader depends heavily upon his personal mystique.

Chemotherapy. Use of drugs in treatment of mental disorders.

Circularity. Spiraling result of cause and effect in which feedback from the effect influences the causal agent, and so on.

Classical (respondent) conditioning. Basic form of learning in which a previously neutral stimulus is paired with a stimulus that elicits the desired response.

Client-centered therapy. A nondirective approach to psychotherapy developed chiefly by Carl Rogers.

Collusion (in interpersonal relationships). Agreement of partners in an interpersonal relationship to substitute deviant rules and norms of their own choosing for established norms when creating and maintaining the relationship.

Commonality of purpose. The possession of mutual purposes or goals.

Communal living. An alternative family style characterized by individuals living together in a group and sharing to some degree common goals, tasks, activities, and properties.

Communication. The receiving or sending of information.

Communication net. Stable lines and patterns of communication within a group or organization.

Compensation. Ego-defense mechanism by means of which an undesirable trait is covered up by exaggerating a desirable one.

Competence. Being adequate in a given area; having a high level of ability in a given area.

Complementarity. Principle that attraction among couples occurs because each person supplements the other and helps the other to meet psychological and emotional needs.

Compulsion. An irrational and repetitive impulse to perform some act.

Computer assessment. Use of computers in diagnosis.

Conceived values. Values which an individual feels are valid and ideal, but not necessarily the values he actually lives by.

Concept. Abstract idea derived from the grouping of objects or ideas in terms of some common property.

Conditioning. See **Classical conditioning** and **Operant conditioning.**

Confidentiality. Commitment on the part of a professional person to keep private information he obtains from a client.

Conflict. Simultaneous arousal of two or more incompatible motives.

Conformity. Acceptance of and abidance by established social norms and rules of a group.

Confrontation. Situation in an encounter group where one or several members of the group confront another member with their feelings concerning his behavior.

Contraception. Voluntary prevention of conception.

Convergent feedback. Information concerning the outcome of behavior, indicating that it is appropriate.

Cost. Energy, time, tension, or other conditions exacted by a given course of action.

Creative thinking. Innovative thinking which is applied to dealing with some aspect of reality.

Crisis. Stress situation which approaches or exceeds the adaptive capacities of the individual or group.

Critical period. Period of development during which the organism most needs certain inputs or is most ready for the acquisition of a given response.

Culture. The sum total of ways of living built up by a given group, including the artifacts produced—e.g., technological innovations.

Cybernetics. Study of complex electronic devices and their similarity to the human brain.

Decider subsystem. Subsystem that exercises control over entire system (general systems model).

Decompensation. Self or personality disorganization under excessive stress.

Defense mechanism. See **Ego-defense mechanism.**

Defense-oriented reaction. Reaction designed to protect one's feelings of adequacy and worth and/or alleviate anxiety rather than deal realistically with the stress situation.

Deficiency motivation. Domination of behavior by maintenance needs and strivings.

Democratic leadership. Form of leadership in which leader and members of group jointly discuss and determine policies and activities.

Denial of reality. Ego-defense mechanism by means of which the individual protects himself from unpleasant aspects of reality by refusing to perceive it.

Depression. Emotional state of dejection, gloomy rumination, feelings of worthlessness, often accompanied by guilt and apprehension.

Deprivation. Lack of need gratification.

Desensitization. Behavior-therapy technique whereby reactions to traumatic experiences are reduced in intensity by repeatedly exposing the individual to them in mild form, either in reality or in fantasy.

Determinism. View that cause must precede effect and that individual is of causal influence only to extent that his prior conditioning enters into determination of final outcome of given event; no freedom for self-determination. (**"Soft" determinism.** View that human beings have some measure of freedom for self-direction.)

Developmental task. A competency that is considered essential to master during a particular stage of development, e.g., learning to talk during infancy.

"Differential participation." Referring to differing ways in which individuals participate in the culture depending on position, status, and related factors.

Directive counseling. Type of counseling in which counselor supplies direct answers to problems and takes much of the responsibility for the progression and outcome of the counseling process. (**Directive therapy.** Comparable meaning with respect to role of therapist.)

Discipline style. Method typically used by parent in enforcing limits of behavior on child.

Discordant interpersonal contracts. Relationships involving serious and continued disagreements and conflicts detrimental to quality of the relationship.

Discrimination learning. Learning to interpret and

respond differently to two or more similar stimuli.

Disintegrative emotions. Extremely intense emotions causing maladaptive functioning and possible mental disorder.

Displacement. Transfer of an emotional attitude or symbolic meaning from one object or concept to another. Also an ego-defense mechanism for redirection of emotions to less dangerous objects; e.g., hostility aroused by one's boss may be taken out on one's spouse.

Disqualifying communication. Communication in which sender or receiver disqualifies content of communication.

Disturbed family. Family in which one or both parents are suffering from serious psychopathology which is reflected in family interactions.

Divergent feedback. Information concerning outcome of behavior indicating that it is inappropriate or ineffective and that some correction is needed.

Double-approach conflict. Type of stress situation in which individual is confronted with choosing between two or more desirable alternatives.

Double-avoidant conflict. Type of stress situation in which individual is confronted with choosing between two or more aversive alternatives.

Double bind. Situation in which an individual will be disapproved for performing a certain act and disapproved if he does *not* perform it.

Double-bind communication. Conveying of conflicting messages simultaneously, e.g., one message verbally and another nonverbally at the same time.

Double standard. Presence of different norms and expectations for males and females, usually pertaining to sexual behavior.

Dream interpretation. Use of dream analysis in the process of psychotherapy.

Drug abuse. Use of drugs to extent that it interferes with health and/or life adjustment.

Drug dependence. Physiological and/or psychological dependence on a drug.

Dyad. Two-person group.

Ecology. Study of mutual relations between organisms and their physical environment.

Economy (principle of). View that the individual meets stress in the simplest way possible, with the least expenditure of resources.

Ego. The rational subsystem of the personality which mediates between the demands of the superego, the id, and reality (psychoanalytic model).

Egocentric. Preoccupied with one's own concerns and relatively insensitive to needs of others.

Ego-defense mechanism. Type of reaction designed to maintain individual's feelings of adequacy and worth and alleviate anxiety rather than to cope directly with the stress situation.

Electroshock. Form of treatment commonly used in depressive reactions.

Emotion. Complex state of feeling involving conscious experience, internal and overt responses, and power to motivate the organism to action.

Emotional disturbance. Psychological upset or imbalance, often used in referring to psychopathology or mental disorders, especially those involving children.

Emotional divorce. Marital or other intimate relationship which continues despite emotional withdrawal of the partners from each other.

Emotional insulation. Ego-defense mechanism in which the individual reduces the tensions of need and anxiety by withdrawing into a shell of passivity.

Emotionally disturbed. See **Emotional disturbance**.

Encounter. An interaction between two persons; also, an interaction between therapist and client in existential therapy.

Encounter group. Small group designed to provide an intensive interpersonal experience focusing on feelings and group interactions; used in therapy and/or to promote personal growth.

Encounter with nothingness. Realization of the inevitability of one's own death (existentialism).

Euphoria. Exaggerated feeling of well-being and contentment.

Existential anxiety. Concern about finding a meaningful and fulfilling way of life (existentialism).

Existential model. A psychosocial model of man that emphasizes being, values, meaning, and shaping a meaningful and fulfilling life.

Existential therapy. Therapy based on existential model, emphasizing the development of values, self-direction, and meaning in one's existence.

Experiencing. Personally encountering or undergoing an event.

Extended family. Relatives other than parents and their children who maintain contact with each other.

Extinction. Gradual disappearance of conditioned response when no longer reinforced.

Extrovert. Personality type characterized by interests directed toward the external environment of people and things rather than toward inner experiences and oneself; outgoing, sociable.

Family planning. Process of deliberate concern and use of procedures to control timing and number of children.

Family therapy. Form of therapy focusing on relationships within the family.

Fantasy. Daydream; also an ego-defense mechanism by means of which the individual escapes from the world of reality and gratifies his desires in fantasy achievements.

Feedback. Knowledge of results of one's behavior; used in judging appropriateness of one's responses and making corrections where indicated and feasible.

"First-job dilemma." Situation of a new worker approaching his first job with enthusiasm and ambition only to find it necessary to adjust to realities and demands which he did not expect and does not like.

Flashback. The recurrence of a drug experience without further ingestion of the drug, usually of a negative nature.

Frame of reference. Assumptions concerning reality,

value, and possibility which form an individual's "cognitive map" for interpreting and coping with his world.

Fraudulent interpersonal contracts. Violation of rules or norms governing satisfying interpersonal relationships through use of deceit or other "fraudulent" means.

Free association. Psychoanalytic procedure for probing the unconscious in which individual gives a running account of his every thought and feeling.

Freedom. View that humans have some measure of control over their own behavior and destiny—some degree of freedom for self-determination—under favorable conditions.

Frustration. Thwarting of a need or desire.

Future shock. Condition brought about when social change proceeds so rapidly that the individual cannot cope with it adequately.

Games model. View of interpersonal relationships as based on game theory.

"Games people play." View of interpersonal relationships as controlled by or heavily influenced by various "games" the persons involved play without realizing it.

Gay. Referring to homosexuals.

Gay marriage. Marriage of homosexual partners.

Generalization. Tendency of a response that has been conditioned to one stimulus to become associated with other similar stimuli.

Gestalt therapy. Type of psychotherapy emphasizing the wholeness of the patient and the integration of thought, feeling, and action.

Goal. Object or condition for which an individual strives.

Group decompensation. Disorganization of group under excessive stress.

Group marriage. An intimate relationship between three or more people, not legally sanctioned, but similar in other ways to traditional marriage.

Group process. Nature and sequence of interaction in encounter or related groups.

Growth motivation. Domination of behavior by actualization needs and strivings.

Guilt. Feelings arising from behavior or desires contrary to one's ethical principles, usually involving both self-devaluation and apprehension growing out of fear of punishment.

Hallucination. Sense perception for which there is no appropriate external stimulus.

Hebephrenic type. Type of schizophrenic reaction.

Hierarchy of needs. The concept that needs arrange themselves in a hierarchy in terms of importance or "prepotence," from the most basic biological needs to psychological needs concerned with self-actualization.

Holistic approach. A scientific approach to science involving the study of the whole person; the view of the individual as an integrated psychobiological organism.

Homeostasis. Tendency of organisms to maintain conditions making possible a constant level of physiological functioning.

Hope. Expectation of achieving some desired goal.

Hostility. Emotional reaction directed toward the destruction or damage of a person or object interpreted as a source of frustration; may or may not lead to overt behavior.

Human nature. The basic make-up of human beings.

Hypnosis. Trance-like mental state induced in a cooperative subject by suggestion.

Hypochondriacal reaction. Neurotic reaction characterized by preoccupation with bodily processes and fear of presumed diseases.

Hysterical (conversion) reaction. Neurotic reaction characterized by involuntary loss of motor or sensory function without corresponding organic pathology.

Id. The primitive part of the unconscious composed of instinctual cravings and characterized by unrestrained pleasure seeking (psychoanalytic model).

Identification. Ego-defense mechanism in which the individual identifies himself with some person or institution, usually of an illustrious nature.

Inadequate family. Family which lacks the resources for adequately raising a child.

Incomplete family. Family lacking mother or father.

Infatuation. An intense romantic relationship, usually brief and characterized by disregard of realistic considerations which affect the quality and longevity of the relationship.

Inferiority complex. Strong feelings of inadequacy and insecurity which affect an individual's entire adjustive efforts.

Information. Knowledge or facts received or communicated.

Inhibition. Conscious restraint of a desire or impulse.

Integration. Organization of parts to make a functional whole.

Integrity. Quality of being unified and honest with self and others.

Intellectualization. Ego-defense mechanism by which the individual achieves some measure of insulation from emotional hurt by cutting off or distorting the emotional charge which normally accompanies hurtful situations.

Intelligence. Complex mental ability involving both verbal and nonverbal components.

Intensive group experience. Participation in an encounter or other group in which the members remove their "masks" and interact with each other openly and honestly.

Interpersonal accommodation. Process of adjusting to problems that arise in interpersonal relationships.

Interpersonal attraction. Extent to which another person attracts or repels us.

Interpersonal perception. Way in which we perceive another person.

Interpersonal relationship. Relationship established between two or more people.

Introjection. Incorporation of qualities or values of another person or group into one's own self-structure with a tendency to identify with them and to be affected by what happens to them.

Intropunitive. Responding to failure and frustration by placing blame on oneself.

Introvert. Personality type characterized by the direction of interest toward one's inner world of experiencing.

Involutional melancholia. Depressive psychotic reaction characterized by depression, agitation, and apprehension.

Jealousy. Envious resentment toward a successful rival, related to feelings of insecurity and apprehension in an intimate relationship—often involving suspicion.

Key motives. Important and continuing motives which exert a profound influence on a person's life.

Laissez-faire leadership. Leadership in which leader exerts no influence and group members determine policies and activities.

Learning strategy. Combination of methods used by individual to facilitate learning.

Life cycle. The typical sequence of stages in life of a given species from birth to death.

Life style. The general pattern of assumptions, motives, cognitive styles, and coping techniques that characterize the behavior of a given individual and give it consistency.

Loneliness. Emotional state of feeling alone, solitary, without perceived concern or care of others.

Love. Loosely defined as a strong or passionate affection for another person.

Maintenance strivings. Strivings directed toward maintenance of biological and/or psychological equilibrium and integration.

Manic-depressive psychoses. Group of psychotic reactions characterized by prolonged periods of excitement and overactivity (mania) or by periods of dejection and underactivity (depression) or by alternation of the two.

Marriage contract. Implicit or explicit agreement between partners in goals, activities, rights, obligations, and limitations of each within the marriage.

Meditation. Serious and sustained contemplation or reflection in which individual may strive toward increased understanding or the integration of feelings, intuitions, and objective reality.

Metacommunication. Communication about the way in which two persons typically communicate.

Model. Essentially an analogy which helps a scientist to see important relationships among his data; e.g., the computer model of human thinking.

Modeling. Form of learning in which individual learns by watching someone else (the model) perform the desired response.

Motivation. Inner needs and strivings which direct organism toward given goals.

Motivational selectivity. Effect of our motives on perception and other psychological processes.

Motive. Internal condition which directs or impels organism toward some goal.

Multiple criteria approach. Use of several different criteria for defining a given condition, e.g., mental health.

Mutation. Change in the composition of a gene.

Need. Biological or psychological condition whose gratification is necessary for the maintenance of homeostasis actualization.

Neurasthenic reaction. Neurotic behavior characterized by complaints of chronic fatigue, weakness, and lack of enthusiasm.

Neurosis. Mental disorder characterized by exaggerated use of avoidance behavior and defenses against anxiety.

Neurotic avoidance. Avoidance behavior which simplifies stress-provoking concepts or situations to the point where they are no longer accurately depicted, thus blocking the development of more effective coping patterns.

Nonbeing. Lack of authenticity, death (existentialism).

Nondirective counseling. Type of counseling in which therapist refrains from direct interpretations or advice and places primary responsibility for outcome of counseling process on client. **Nondirective therapy.** Comparable meaning with respect to role of therapist.

Nonordinary reality. "Reality" as viewed from other than a rational, objective, scientific viewpoint; e.g., via altered states of consciousness.

Nuclear family. Parents and their children.

Obsession. Persistent idea or thought which the individual recognizes as irrational but cannot get rid of.

Obsessive-compulsive reaction. Neurotic reaction characterized by persistent intrusion of unwanted desires, thoughts, or impulses.

"Open marriage." Marriage dedicated to individual growth by encouragement of role flexibility, open communication, and pursuit of activities and relationships in addition to the marriage.

Operant conditioning. Form of learning in which the correct response is reinforced and becomes more likely to occur.

Operative values. Values which actually guide the behavior of the individual, as opposed to the values he may profess to believe in.

Orgasmic dysfunction. Condition whereby orgasms are achieved infrequently or never; failure to achieve satisfaction in sexual relations due to one's own attitudes or other characteristics.

Oversimplification. Interpretation of concepts or situations to point where they are no longer accurately depicted because key factors or dimensions are left out.

Pain. Bodily or mental suffering or distress.

Panic. Severe personality disorganization involving intense anxiety and usually either paralyzed immobility or blind flight.

Paradigm. An accepted "model." See also **Model.**

Paranoia. Psychosis characterized by a systematized delusional system.

Pathogenic family. Family pattern having a detrimental effect on development of children; also may have detrimental effect on one or both parents.

Pathology. Diseased or abnormal physical or mental condition.

Payoff. Reward value of a given outcome.

Pecking order. Dominance hierarchy or pattern of power relationships that frequently evolves in groups of animals and humans.

Perceptual defense. Selective perception; the unconscious screening out of unpleasant or threatening perceptions.

Personal maturity. Behaving in ways appropriate to one's age and resources; usually implies effective behavior.

Phobia. Irrational fear; the individual often realizes the irrationality of the fear but is unable to do anything about it.

Phobic reaction. Neurotic reaction characterized by intense fear of an object or situation which the individual consciously realizes poses no real danger to him.

"Pill, the." Oral medication for prevention of pregnancy.

Placebo. Inactive substance administered in such a way that the subject believes he is receiving an active drug.

Possibility assumptions. Assumptions or beliefs about the way things could be.

Precipitating cause. The particular stress which precipitates, or causes, a disorder.

Predisposing cause. Condition which lowers the individual's stress tolerance and paves the way for the later appearance of a disorder.

Prejudice. Prejudgment based on biased information.

Prematurity. Birth of baby before the end of normal period of pregnancy.

Pressure. Demand made on an organism, or the response resulting from the demand.

Primary reaction tendencies. Constitutional tendencies apparent in infancy, such as activity level and sensitivity, which influence the ways in which the infant interacts with his environment.

Projection. Ego-defense mechanism in which the individual attributes his own unacceptable desires and impulses to others.

Projective tests. Psychological assessment technique utilizing relatively unstructured stimuli which reveal the subject's conflicts and other characteristics.

Propinquity. Nearness in place; principle that people located near each other are more likely to develop attraction to each other.

Pseudomutuality. Relationship among family members that appears to be mutual, understanding, and open, but in fact is not.

Psychedelic drugs. Drugs, such as LSD and mescaline, which lead to vivid imagery, hallucinations, and often disorganization of thought processes.

Psychogenic. Of psychological origin.

Psychological assessment. Use of psychological tests and other methods for the diagnosis of maladaptive behavior.

Psychological counseling. Professional service performed by psychologist in helping another person solve certain adjustment problems, usually pertaining to education, marriage, or occupation.

Psychological testing. Standardized procedure designed to measure subject's performance on a specified task.

Psychopathic personality. Disorder characterized by lack of moral development and inability to show loyalty to other persons or groups.

Psychopathology. Mental disorder; maladaptive behavior.

"Psychosomatic" reactions. Physical symptoms, which may involve actual tissue damage, resulting from continued emotional mobilization under stress; usually involves single-organ system.

Psychotherapy. Use of psychological methods in treatment of mental disorders.

Punishment. Application of aversive stimulation in response to behavior considered undesirable.

Puritan work ethic. Historically, a Christian concept of work as a duty and a virtue in itself. Hard work valued as a sign of righteousness.

Q-sort test. Personality inventory in which subject, or someone evaluating him, sorts a number of statements into piles according to their applicability to the subject.

Rating scale. Psychological assessment technique for evaluating oneself or someone else on a specified trait.

Rational-emotive therapy. Form of psychotherapy which encourages patient to substitute rational for irrational assumptions in his inner dialogue with himself.

Rationalization. Ego-defense mechanism in which the individual thinks up "good" reasons to justify what he has done, is doing, or intends to do.

Reaction formation. Ego-defense mechanism in which individual's conscious attitudes and overt behavior are opposite to his repressed unconscious wishes.

Reactive depression. Neurotic depression in face of loss or environmental setback.

Reality assumptions. Assumptions or beliefs about the ways things "really" are.

Recidivism. A shift back to one's original behavior (often delinquent or criminal) after a period of treatment or rehabilitation.

Regression. Ego-defense mechanism in which the individual retreats to the use of less mature responses in attempting to cope with stress and maintain self-integration.

Reinforcement. In classical conditioning, the process of following the conditioned stimulus with the unconditioned stimulus; in operant conditioning, the rewarding of desired responses.

Rejection. Lack of acceptance of another person, usually referring to such treatment of a child by his parents.

Reliability. Degree to which a test or measuring device produces the same result each time it is used to measure the same thing.

REM sleep. Stage of sleep involving rapid eye movements and associated with dreaming.

Renewable marriage. Proposed time-limiting marriage, which may be continued only by mutual consent of spouses.

Repression. Ego-defense mechanism by means of which anxiety-arousing desires or intolerable memories are kept out of consciousness.

Resistance. Tendency to resist uncovering of repressed material in therapy; also tendency to maintain maladaptive behavior or symptoms and resist treatment.

Respondent conditioning. Classical conditioning in which a previously neutral stimulus is paired with a stimulus that elicits the desired response.

"Responsibility diffusion." Hypothesized tendency of people in groups to take less personal responsibility for their actions because they experience others in the group as sharing the responsibility for the events in which the group takes part.

Rigid mental set. Tendency to follow established coping patterns with failure to see alternatives; extreme difficulty in changing one's established patterns of perceiving and coping.

Risky shift. Phenomenon of groups in which the members make riskier decisions following group discussion than the individuals would singly.

Role. See **Social role.**

Role conflict. Condition arising when roles individual feels obligated to play are incompatible.

Role demands. Role expectations.

Role enactment. Way in which social role is enacted or performed.

Role model. A person who manifests desired behavior and is used as a guide and model for another person to copy or emulate; usually refers to parental models in relation to child.

Schizophrenia. Psychosis characterized by the breakdown of integrated functioning, withdrawal from reality, emotional blunting and distortion, and disturbances of thought and behavior.

Self. The central reference point in the personality around which experience and actions are organized.

Self-acceptance. Satisfaction with one's attributes and qualities while remaining aware of one's limitations; does not negate striving toward self-improvement and personal growth.

Self-concept. The individual's sense of his own identity, worth, capabilities, and limitations.

Self-direction. The basing of one's behavior on inner assumptions rather than on external contingencies.

Self-disclosure. Disclosure of information about oneself to another person.

Self-esteem. Feeling of personal worth.

Self-evaluation. Way in which the individual views himself in terms of worth and adequacy.

Self-ideal. The self the individual thinks he could and should be or become.

Self-identity. The individual's perception of "who he is."

Sensory deprivation. Lack of stimulus input needed for maintaining homeostasis.

Sensory "overload." Excessive stimulus input leading to impaired functioning.

Sentence-completion test. Form of psychological assessment utilizing incomplete sentences which the subject is to complete.

Serial marriage. Two or more marriages for an individual; one marriage follows the termination of the preceding one, through death or divorce.

Sexual deviation. Nonconforming sexual behavior, markedly different from the usual.

Shaping. Form of instrumental conditioning in which all responses resembling, or in the direction of, the desired one are reinforced, then only the closest approximations, until finally the desired response is attained.

Significant other. Referring to person who is very important to the individual.

Significant selfhood. Self-concept which provides the individual with a feeling of worth and meaning.

Simple type. Type of schizophrenic reaction.

Social exchange model. View that interpersonal relationships are governed by exchanges which meet the needs of the persons involved; relationship viewed as a trading or bargaining one.

Social facilitation. Effects of presence or observation of others upon behavior of individual; also pertains to lowering of inner controls of individual in group setting who may then engage in behavior he would not engage in on his own.

Social norms. Group standards concerning behaviors viewed as acceptable or unacceptable by the group.

Social pathology. Conditions in society, such as poverty and racial discrimination, which foster maladaptive behavior and psychopathology.

Social role. Behavior expected of individual occupying a given position in a group.

Sociometric structure. Patterns of personal attraction within a group.

Sociotherapy. Use of sociocultural measures and modification of an individual's life situation in treatment of mental disorders.

Somatic. Pertaining to the body.

Spontaneity Natural and unrestrained behavior, usually referring to desirable behavior.

Stage of exhaustion. Third and final stage in the general-adaptation-syndrome in which the organism is no longer able to resist continuing stress; may result in death.

Stage of resistance. Second stage of general-adaptation-syndrome.

Statutory rape. Sexual intercourse with a minor.

"Steady state." Physiological equilibrium.

Stereotype. A generalization of how people of a given sex, religion, or other group appear, think, feel, and act.

Stimulus. A physical event which, if strong enough, will excite a receptor or sense organ.

Stress. Any adjustive demand that requires coping behavior on the part of the individual or group.

Stress-decompensation. Causal model of psychopathology emphasizing decompensation in the face of excessive stress.

Stress interview. Interview of a subject under simulated or real stress.

Stress tolerance. Nature, degree, and duration of stress which an individual can tolerate without undergoing serious personality disorganization or decompensation.

Structuring a relationship. Setting limits in interpersonal relationships in terms of permissible behavior.

Substitution. Acceptance of substitute goals or satisfactions in place of those originally sought after or desired.

Suicide. Taking one's own life, or the attempt to do so.

Superego. Ethical or moral dimension; conscience of psyche.

Supernatural. Beyond or transcending the laws of nature or ordinary human experiencing.

"Swinging." Participation in group sex; especially, when both marital partners engage in sexual activities with other couples.

Symbol. Image, object, or activity used to represent something.

System. An assemblage of interdependent parts, living or nonliving.

"Talking it out." Form of coping technique utilized to relieve tension.

Task-oriented reaction. Realistic rather than ego-defensive approach to stress.

Tension. Condition arising out of the mobilization of psychobiological resources to meet a threat; involves an increase in muscle tension and is characterized by feelings of uneasiness or anxiety.

Theory. Systematic view which accounts for all of the data that is pertinent to it and is logically consistent; should explain phenomena observed and suggest new areas for research.

Therapy. Treatment; application of various treatment procedures.

Threat. Real or imagined danger to individual or group.

"Time gestalt." Gradual "filling in" or "closure" of personality characteristics over time, making change more difficult (general systems model).

Tolerance (drug). Physiological condition in which increased dosage of an addictive drug is needed to obtain effects previously produced by smaller doses.

Trait. Characteristic of individual which can be observed or measured.

Transactional analysis. Form of interpersonal therapy based on interaction of "Child," "Parent," and "Adult" ego states.

Transference. Process whereby patient projects attitudes and emotions applicable to another significant person onto the therapist; emphasized in psychoanalysis.

Trauma. Severe psychological or physiological stress resulting from injury or wound.

"Trial marriage." Proposed arrangement similar to legally sanctioned marriage which may be terminated by mutual consent; a testing phase prior to possible marriage.

Unconscious. Lacking awareness.

Undoing. Ego-defense mechanism by means of which the individual performs activities designed to atone for his misdeeds, thereby in a sense "undoing" them.

Validity. Extent to which a measuring instrument actually measures what it is designed to measure.

Values. Assumptions or beliefs concerning good and bad, desirable and undesirable.

Vicious circle. Chain reaction in which the individual resorts to a defensive reaction in trying to cope with a problem which only serves to complicate the problem and make it more difficult to cope with.

Visceral needs. Pertaining to the needs of the internal organs or body.

Wisdom. Good judgment, common sense, ability to foresee outcomes of given alternatives in dealing with problem situations.

Withdrawal symptoms. Wide range of symptoms evidenced by addicts when the drug on which they are physiologically dependent is not available.

Name Index

de Madariaga, S., 490
DeNike, L. D., 32
de Sola Pool, I., 84
Deur, J., 326
Deutsch, M., 309
Dewey, J., 506–7
Dinello, F. A., 140
Dixon, M., 331
Dollard, J., 132, 388–89
Douvan, E., 317
Dublin, C. C., 318
Duncan, O. D., 350
Durant, A., 46–47
Durant, W., 46–47
Dutton, R. E., 458
Duvall, E. M., 303
Dyer, W. G., 281

Earl, H. G., 318
Einstein, A., 399–400, 443, 491–92
Ekman, P., 236, 463
Ellis, A., 297, 419, 481
Emerson, R. W., 421, 490
Epstein, S., 178
Esterson, A., 245
Estis, E. H., 395

Farberow, N. L., 212
Farnsworth, D. L., 314
Farson, R. E., 55
Faulkner, W., 507
Fawcett, J., 335
Feld, S., 304
Feldman, H., 303, 304, 305
Fenz, W. D., 178
Ferreira, A. J., 324
Fisher, S., 269, 285, 286
Fitzgerald, R. G., 117
Flanders, J. P., 324
Fleck, S., 327
Floyd, H. H., 247
Foulkes, F. K., 358–59
Frankl, V., 85, 420
Freud, S., 21, 26, 30–32, 34, 86, 102,
    325, 415, 416
Friedman, P., 197
Friesen, W. V., 236
Fromm, E., 10, 75, 272, 479, 480,
    482, 507

Gagnon, J., 267
Gaier, E. I., 455
Galanter, E., 56
Gallagher, T., 149, 173

Gandhi, M., 497
Gardner, J. W., 507
Geismar, L. L., 333
Geist, H., 361
Gelven, M., 97, 175
Gerard, E., 439
Gerard, H. B., 388–89, 391, 396
Gergen, K. J., 60, 240
Gewirtz, J. L., 308
Ginzberg, E., 348
Glass, D., 477
Glidewell, J. C., 310
Glucksberg, S., 442
Glueck, E. T., 319
Glueck, S., 319
Goffman, E., 375
Goldberg, S., 307
Goldiamond, I., 418
Goldsmith, W., 198
Gonzales, P., 173
Gooding, J., 355
Goodnow, J. J., 162
Goodwin, L., 343
Gordon, E. M., 240, 334
Gottschalk, L. A., 73
Grinker, R. R., 464
Gross, A., 392
Guilford, J. P., 454

Haer, J. L., 73
Hake, D. F., 321
Haley, J., 281, 284, 324
Hall, E. J., 381
Haller, A. O., 349
Halsey, Admiral, 171
Hamilton, A., 23
Hammen, C., 477
Hammond, K. R., 178
Harari, H., 387, 398
Harmsworth, H. C., 289–90
Harris, R. A., 423–24
Haskins, C. P., 8
Hastorf, A., 392
Havighurst, R. J., 312
Haythorn, W. W., 73
Heathers, G., 321
Heidegger, M., 34
Hellman, L., 149, 173
Helson, H., 88
Hemingway, E., 65
Hendin, D., 267, 269
Henry, J., 76
Henschel, A., 70
Henze, L. F., 274
Herrick, D. J., 15
Herrick, N., 354, 355

Herzberg, F., 345, 352–53
Hetherington, E. M., 326
Hill, R., 274
Hoffman, L., 366
Holmes, O. W., 457
Holmes, T. H., 116
Holz, W. C., 321
Horner, M., 366
Horton, P. B., 398
House, A., 336
House, J., 355
Housman, A. E., 192
Hudson, J., W., 274
Hunt, C. L., 398
Hurley, J. R., 312, 314, 315–16
Hurlock, E. B., 278
Huxley, A., 47, 506
Huxley, J., 80

Ibsen, H., 499
Ilfeld, F. W., Jr., 132
Infeld, L., 443
Isaacs, W., 418
Ivey, M. E., 465

Jacklin, C. N., 322
Jackson, D., 284
Jahoda, M., 175, 306
James, W., 33, 60, 78
Janis, I., 473
Jaspers, K., 34
Jefferson, T., 23, 497
Jenkins, C., 355
Jenkins, R. L., 315, 317
Jesus, 22, 400
Johnson, V. E., 195, 269, 285–86
Jones, E. E., 240, 388–89, 391
Jones, M. C., 416
Jourard, S. M., 283
Jouvet, M., 70–71

Kadushin, A., 318
Kagan, J., 308, 317, 322
Kahn, R. L., 355, 360, 368
Kasl, S., 354, 355
Kassel, V., 298
Katchadourian, H. A., 268
Katz, A. M., 274
Katz, J. L., 149, 173
Kaufmann, W., 168
Kelley, H. H., 224, 499
Kelly, J., 298
Keniston, K., 317
Kenkel, W., 272

Werts, C. E., 349, 350
West, L. J., 177
Weybrew, B. B., 72
Wheelis, A., 271
Whelpton, P. K., 332
White, R. K., 392, 393
White, R. W., 76, 321
Whiteman, M., 309
Whyte, W. H., 389
Wikler, A., 211
Wilhelmy, R. A., 396

Williams, J. R., 310
Williamson, R. C., 274, 277
Wilson, H. V., 38
Wilson, W., 278
Winch, R. F., 274, 275
Winchester, J. H., 22
Winder, C. L., 318
Winter, W. D., 324
Winterbottom, M., 321
Wittkower, E. D., 477
Wolfe, D. M., 309, 332

Wolfe, T., 191, 252
Wolff, H. G., 198
Wolpe, J., 32, 417

Yankelovich, D., 264, 359

Zajonc, R., 386–87
Zander, A., 371–72, 391
Zurcher, L. A., 50

of, 51–52, 53, 305–10, 482; and divorce, 290–91; effect of, on marriage, 294, 302–5, 384; and family planning, 332–33; and faulty family conditions, 310–28, 415; and interpersonal relations, 228, 245, 255; and maladjustment, 199, 200, 310–28; and stress, 107, 114, 128, 131, 133, 138, 140

Choices, 14, 32, 34, 35, 50, 60, 66, 159, 420, 421, 433; and adjustive behavior, 165–67; and childbearing, 328–34; and conflict, 132–33; and the future, 502–7; and learning, 440, 449, 452, 457; and marriage and intimate relationships, 263–64, 269–70, 282; occupational, 342, 345–50; and values 34, 35, 498–507

Circadian cycles, 113

Civilian catastrophe reactions, 195–97

Classical conditioning. *See* Respondent conditioning

Claustrophobia, 183

Client-centered therapy, 418–19, 420, 421, 430

Clinical psychologist, 414

Cocaine, 205, 207

Cognitive dissonance, 75, 138

Cognitive map. *See* Frame of reference

Cognitive therapies, 416, 418, 420

Cohesiveness, of a group, 379, 381, 382, 393

Collusion in interpersonal contracts, 243–44, 257

Combat exhaustion, 131, 195, 197–98, 219, 464

Commitment, 8, 10, 134, 382, 384, 398, 500–501; and marriage, 263, 267; vs. noninvolvement, 100–101, 192; voluntary/involuntary, 217–18

Communal sex, 193, 296–97

Communes, 192, 297, 337–38

Communication, 161, 425, 462; difficulties in, 249, 284; within the family, 310, 324, 339; within groups, 379, 381, 382, 392; interpersonal, 231, 232, 236–37, 238, 240, 245, 247–50, 255, 257; in marriage, 278, 282–84, 296, 298, 299; nonverbal, 236, 237, 283, 284, 324

Community: concern for, 252, 331–32; role of, in mental health, 200, 216, 217

Companionship, 261, 265, 270, 271, 278, 291, 296, 299, 376

Comparison level in social exchange theory, 224, 225

Compensation, 139, 146–47, 149

Competence and competencies, 13–14, 15, 54–55, 61, 215–16, 281, 306, 406, 407, 450; and adjustive behavior, 159, 170, 172, 174, 175, 177–78, 179; emotional, 461–83; intellectual, 433–59; interpersonal 223–57, 391, 392, 397, 382; need for, 76, 78, 81, 89, 90, 94, 416; and parent-child relations, 301, 312, 316, 321–322, 323, 327, 339; and stress, 111, 119, 122, 136, 152; and work, 347, 353

Competition, 189, 191, 357, 382; and interpersonal relations, 238, 244, 248; and stress, 96, 100, 104, 105, 121

Complementarity, and marriage, 275–76, 279, 299

Complexity: of modern life, 5–8, 14, 17, 35, 60, 106, 107; of transactions, 39

Compromise, 353, 378, 487; in interpersonal relations, 226, 238, 280; and stress, 132, 135–36, 137, 152

Compulsions, 86, 185, 197, 204

Computer: analogy of, and adjustive behavior, 170–71, 174; and technology revolution, 367, 369, 505

Concentration, difficulty with, 186, 187, 197

Concern for others, 81–82, 90, 252–53, 257, 479–80, 506

Concept formation, 31, 38, 434

Conditioning, 27, 30–32, 34, 416–18, 420, 434

Confidence, 111, 165, 167, 170, 245, 253, 319, 425. *See also* Self-confidence

Conflict, 14, 26, 29, 30, 35, 61, 126, 407, 431; and adjustment, 94, 98–103, 114, 119, 157, 175, 416; approach-avoidance, 98–99, 109; avoiding vs. facing reality, 101; commitment vs. noninvolvement, 100–101; double-approach, 99; double-avoidance, 99; between group and individual, 378–79, 380, 381, 382, 383–84; integrity vs. self-advantage, 102; in interpersonal relations, 226, 238, 244–45, 253, 256, 257; and learning, 437, 446, 450, 456; and marriage, 277, 279, 281, 285, 299, 326; occupational, 345, 355, 365, 366; in parent-child relations, 326, 327; self-direction vs. outer direction, 100; severity of, 109; sexual, 102–3; 268, 269, 270, 335, 415; and therapy, 215, 407, 415, 418; and values, 100–103; and vacillation, 132–33

Conformity, 35, 48, 49, 52, 62, 79, 445, 452, 467; problem of, 372, 377, 380, 390, 395–400, 401; and stress, 99, 104, 113

Confrontation: in encounter groups, 424, 425, 428; in therapy, 420

Conscience, 29, 102, 140, 142–43; development of, 186, 190, 191, 315, 320, 323, 477; and group membership, 377–78

Consciousness, 142, 186, 415, 446, 474

Consistency, parental, 307, 317, 319, 321, 338

Constitutional characteristics and development, 307–8, 339

Constitutional predisposition, 160, 200

Continuity, sense of, 51–52

Continuum of adjustment, 156, 181–82

Contraceptives, 270, 331, 334–36, 339. *See also* Family planning

Contracts: fraudulent interpersonal, 242–43, 257; marriage, 264, 294–95

Conversion reactions. *See* Hysterical reaction

Cooperation, 22, 23, 41, 105, 133, 238, 248, 351, 391, 397

Coping, 54–55, 56, 61, 75, 123, 128, 149, 254; "built-in," 126–31, 152; effective, 155–79; improving, 407, 408, 415, 416, 430; ineffective, 181–219; on the job, 351–54; and severity of stress, 94, 107–14, 116, 151

Costs: of adaptation, 114–16; of demands, 15, 158, 165, 170, 173, 177, 179; of encounter groups, 430, 431; of group membership, 375, 377–79, 400; of interpersonal relations, 224–25, 226, 241, 243, 247, 251, 255

Counseling, 405, 406–13, 414, 430; directive, 410–11, 420, 430; nondirective, 410, 411, 418, 420, 430; stages in, 411–13

Counseling psychologist, 414

Courage to be, 35

Courtship, 261, 277, 278, 279–80, 289

"Creative suffering," 176

Creativity, 33, 68, 81, 88, 228, 302, 347, 363, 380, 387, 389, 393, 422, 424, 425, 452–58, 476; group's, 425; in thinking, 449, 452–58, 459

Crime, 195, 204, 209, 211–12, 219, 399

Crisis, 114, 115–16, 119, 210, 216, 252
Crisis intervention, 213, 214, 217, 420
Critical periods, 46
Criticism: hypersensitivity to, 201; and interpersonal relations, 252–53
Crossed transactions, 422
Crowding, 286–87, 310
Crying, 124, 128, 129, 152, 203, 477
Cultural bias, of tests, 409
Cultural groups (examples): Arapesh, 21–22; Blackfoot Indians, 22; Eskimos, 75; Ituri tribesmen, 22; Kenya tribesmen, 48; Mungundumor, 22; Tchambuli, 48; Xetas, 385, 386
Cultural lag, 123
Cultural models, 52–53, 62
Culture, 74, 107, 113–14, 343, 383–84; and cultural relativity, 497; and development, 48, 50, 53, 55, 62, 306, 308–10; and marriage, 259, 289; reverse transmission of, 53; and values, 490–91, 497, 498, 509

Damage repair mechanisms, 124, 126–31, 152; crying, 124, 128, 129; laughing it off, 129; seeking support, 129, 131; sleep and dreams, 131; talking it out, 128; thinking it through, 129
Dating, 48, 261, 277
Death, 16, 74, 79, 206; and human nature, 29, 36; of loved one (*See* Bereavement); reactions to, 124, 126, 129, 138, 145; and stress, 96, 107, 115, 116, 118, 151, 157; target dates for, 129
Decision making, 14, 16, 26, 27, 31, 33, 360, 367, 424, 433, 442–52, 458, 459; aids in, 449–52; and adjustive behavior, 155, 161, 165–67, 168, 169, 172, 173, 179; and development, 54, 56–57, 61; faulty, 451–52; by groups, 380–81, 389–90; and marriage, 264, 276, 297; and stress, 98–99, 117, 132, 137
Decompensation: of group, 384–86; in psychosis, 195, 198, 203; and stress, 115, 127, 149–51, 153, 159–60, 195; transient, 195–98
Deduction, 454, 459
Defense-oriented reactions, 29–30, 33, 56, 94, 122, 126, 127, 137–49, 150, 152, 199, 407, 415, 443; acting out, 139, 148–49, 190; in adjustive behavior, 157, 159, 167, 170, 173–74; chart of, 139; compensation, 139, 146–47, 149; denial of reality, 125, 127, 131, 139, 146, 149; displacement, 139, 146–47, 149; emotional insulation, 139, 145, 149; escapism, 133–35; fantasy, 135, 139, 141, 149; in a group, 381; identification, 131, 139, 143–44, 149; intellectualization, 139, 145–46; introjection, 139, 144–45, 498; and learning, 445–46, 459; and problem emotions, 463, 465, 473, 476; rationalism, 139, 141–42, 145, 146, 148, 149, 153; reaction formation, 139, 142–43, 149; regression, 139, 140–41; repression, 139, 142, 143, 148, 149; undoing, 139, 147–48, 149
Deficiency motivation, 88
Definition of problem, 442–46
Dehumanization, 8, 16, 35, 191, 192, 247, 424, 502, 504, 505; of sex, 269; and work, 358–59

Dejection, 127, 186, 204, 477
Delinquency, 190, 195, 204, 211, 219, 324, 326
Delirium tremens, 206
Delusions: and deprivation, 72; of grandeur, 199, 201, 202; of guilt, 202; of influence, 199, 200; of persecution, 199, 200, 201; of pseudocommunity, 201; and psychosis, 199, 200, 201, 202, 203, 204; in reactions to stress, 141, 150; of reference, 199
Democracy, 34, 323, 506–7
Democratic leadership, 392–93
Denial of reality, 125, 127, 131, 139, 146, 149, 152, 159, 173, 473, 474, 477
Deprivation, 26, 108, 191, 349; of biological needs, 70–71, 87–88, 90; sensory, 72–73
Desensitization, 140, 416, 417, 431
Determinants: of development, 305, 307–10; of reactions, 125–26, 152
Determinism, 20, 26–28, 34, 36
Development: critical periods in, 46; determinants of, 307–10, 337; differences in, 305–10; faulty, 310–28; "healthy," 305–7, 339; heredity and environmental roles in, 46–48; moral, 318, 324; multiple criteria approach to, 306–7; of self, 48–53; sociocultural factors in, 308–10
Developmental tasks, 48, 312
Dichotomous thinking, 444
Disapproval, 93, 99, 102, 110, 146, 148, 169, 467; and marriage, 277; and nonconformity, 398; parental, 318, 320
Disaster syndrome, 195
Discipline styles, 108, 303, 309–10, 312, 314, 317–21, 323, 339; permissiveness vs. punitiveness, 309, 310, 317–18, 323; psychological, 309, 310, 319–20
Discontinuities, group, 388–90
Discordant interpersonal patterns, 244–45, 257
Discrimination, 31, 160, 216, 234, 268, 310, 452, 502; and jobs, 346, 350, 354, 359–67, 369; and stress, 95, 97, 113
Disease, stress-related, 94, 106, 113, 115, 117, 122
"Diseases of adaptation," 150
Disintegration, 38, 118
Disorganization: of group, 380, 383, 385; and psychosis, 199; and stress, 73, 76, 112, 117, 137, 150–52, 152, 195
Disorientation, and psychosis, 73, 199, 202, 203, 204, 206
Displacement, 139, 146–47, 149
Disturbed family, 325, 327
Divorce, 174, 262, 264, 265, 268, 276, 277, 288–92, 293, 299, 384, 441, 481; children and, 304, 325–26, 337; as a source of stress, 93, 104, 113, 115, 116, 129, 213
DNA, 37
Domination in interpersonal relations, 230, 244, 247, 275, 323
Double-approach conflict, 98–99
Double-avoidance conflict, 99
Double-bind, 245, 324
Double standard, 268–69, 299
Down's Syndrome, 333
Dreams, 30, 415; interpretation of, 415, 431; and motive state, 70–71, 85, 86; and stress, 131, 140, 153
"Dreamwork," 421–22

Drives. *See* Motivation

Drugs, 8, 67; and brain pathology, 160; dependency and abuse, 183, 195, 199, 203, 207–11, 219, 474; terminology of, 208; treatment of addiction, 209, 214, 424, 425; use of, under stress, 100, 111, 123, 140, 198; use of, in therapy, 85, 215, 414, 416

Education: and counseling, 406, 407, 412, 414, 431; for creativity, 457, 458; and parent-child relations, 326, 331; and work, 346, 349–50, 353, 355, 357–58, 359, 360, 367, 368, 369

Effectiveness, and groups, 151, 387–88, 401

Ego, 29, 30, 33, 306

Ego-defense mechanisms. *See* Defense-oriented reactions

Ego states, 228–29, 422–24

Electroshock therapy, 215, 414, 416

Emotion, 14, 58, 61, 69, 80, 85, 193, 249, 322, 440, 461–83; blunting of, 200; distortion of, in psychosis, 199, 200, 203–04; expression vs. control, 468–71, 483; and groups, 387, 424–25, 428; and growth, 466–67, 483; and interpersonal relations, 223, 236, 249–50, 253, 254; and learning, 445–46, 459; and marriage, 283–84; positive and negative, 465–66, 467, 483; and problem solving, 443, 446, 459; and reactions to stress, 124–25, 135, 152, 167, 172, 173

Emotional competence, 14, 406, 461–83; and full human functioning, 462–71; and problem emotions, 471–82

Emotional insulation, 139, 145, 149, 463, 470

Empathy, 174, 175, 191, 254, 479

"Empty chair," 421–22

Encounter, 231, 232–34, 235, 242, 256–57, 420

Encounter groups, 216, 388, 422, 424–30; evaluation of, 429–30; format and climate of, 424–25; marathon, 429; process in, 425–29; reentry problem of, 429

Environment, 16, 24, 34, 40, 41; and effective adjustment, 158, 159, 160; and group effectiveness, 379, 382, 383–84, 401; and interpersonal adjustment, 231, 236; and learning, 437, 458; and maladjustment, 182, 286–87, 324–28; and marital adjustment, 276, 286–87; and self-development, 45, 46, 47–48, 49–50, 53, 56, 62; and values, 491, 498

Equilibrium, 80, 128, 380. *See also* Steady states

Escape, 133–35, 151

"Establishment," 192, 211

Esteem needs. *See* Self-esteem

Ethical values: development of, 54, 75, 489, 497; lack of, 190, 191; loss of, 199, 202; as source of stress, 75, 94, 98, 102, 104, 137

Evaluation: of group experience, 429–30; of "healthy" development, 305–7; of interpersonal relations, 248; of problems, 442–46; of stress situation, 156–58, 161, 162–65, 172, 189; of value assumptions, 498–500

Evaluative thinking, 454, 459

Evil, human nature as, 20–21, 23, 36, 487

Exhaustion, stage of, 151–52, 153, 160, 385

Exhibitionism, 193

Existential anxiety, 35, 421, 472

Existential model and existentialism, 34–36, 159, 216, 475, 500–501

Existential therapy, 419–21, 431

Expectations, 152, 319; occupational, 348–49, 353, 358, 360; unrealistic, 288–89, 292, 298, 352

Experience: and behavior, 28, 34, 100, 249; as a source of values, 490, 495–96, 498, 509

Experiencing, 55–56

Extended family, 287, 289, 302

Extinction, 31, 416, 417, 431

Extramarital sexual relations, 192, 193, 264, 268, 271

Facilitation: of adjustive functions, 122; social, 386–87, 389, 401

Failure, 67, 76, 318, 451; and defense mechanisms, 123, 127, 129, 138, 142, 146, 149; and development, 52, 53, 56, 318; divorce as, 290, 298; in interpersonal relations, 244; in job, 351; and maladjustment, 202; and stress, 95, 96–97, 98, 101, 110, 113, 176

Faith, in values, 497–97, 509

Familiarity: and learning, 437, 438; of problem, 109, 114, 119

Family: climate of, 324–28, 339; and communication, 284, 324; counseling and therapy for, 216, 217, 406, 407, 413, 414; and development, 52–53, 310–28, 482; and divorce, 289, 290; and interpersonal relations, 231, 256, 372; and maladjustment, 192, 216, 217; and marital adjustment, 276, 286–87, 289, 333; nuclear, 288, 336, 337, 338, 339; occupational choice, 349–50, 369; pathogenic, 324–28; size of, 304, 328, 329–34, 339; sociocultural factors and, 286–87, 308–10; as source of stress, 100, 101, 105, 107, 125, 136, 143–44; style of, 336–38, 339; and working mother, 366

Family planning, 293, 301, 328–38, 339

Fantasy, 30, 85, 348; as a defense reaction, 135, 139, 141, 149; and maladjustment, 186, 200, 202

Father, 32, 94, 102, 140, 287; absence of, 325–26; and child's development, 304, 305, 318, 322, 325–26, 327, 482; identification with, 143–44; and occupational choice, 350

Fatigue, 112, 117, 160, 186, 187, 197, 198, 465, 470, 474

Faulty assumptions, 94, 172, 215, 216, 443–44, 447, 459

Faulty learning, 159, 179, 195

Fear, 14, 32, 58, 77, 85, 249; dealing effectively with, 167, 173, 462, 463, 464, 465, 466, 470, 471–73, 483; and maladjustment, 183–85, 191, 204, 206, 416; and occupational adjustment, 351, 365–66; and parent-child relations, 312, 318, 319, 321; in phobias, 32, 183–85, 416; and reactions to stress, 102, 115, 117, 125, 126, 135

Feedback: divergent, 169, 441; within a group, 381, 392; importance in learning, 434, 436, 440–41, 444, 459; in therapy, 422, 425, 428; utilizing for adjustment, 161, 162, 169–72, 174, 176, 179, 499

Feedforward, 169

Fidelity, marital, 260, 264, 281

Field properties, 37

Financial problems: and aging, 360; and divorce, 290; and

marital maladjustment, 287; and parent-child relations, 303, 332, 333, 337; and stress, 93, 187

"First-job dilemma," 351, 369

"Flashbacks," and drugs, 210

Flexibility, 38, 41, 124, 136, 173, 238, 296, 299, 354, 400, 420; and learning, 437, 444–45, 455; and values, 497–98, 509

Folie à deux, 244

Frame of reference, 75, 234, 248, 382, 407, 486; and adjustment, 163, 170, 172; and assumptions, 54–55, 56, 172, 406, 485, 492; and development, 305, 306; and learning, 434, 436, 437, 440, 444; and stress, 111, 122, 125, 152

Fraudulent interpersonal contracts, 242–43, 257

Free association, 415, 431

Freedom, 26, 27, 28, 32, 33, 34, 35, 159, 247, 359, 420, 428, 507; in marriage and intimate relationships, 263–64, 268, 269–70, 293, 298; in parent-child relations, 316, 338; sexual, 267–68, 269–70; and stress, 98, 100, 172

"Free floating" anxiety, 182–83

Free will, 20, 26, 27–28, 36

Friends, 125, 128, 136, 246–47, 291. *See also* Peer groups

Frustration, 14, 419; in interpersonal relations, 243, 474; in marriage, 265, 279; occupational, 353; in parent-child relations, 319, 362; reactions to, 124–25, 132, 135, 142, 145, 146, 148; in our society, 94–97, 473; as cause of stress, 94–97, 98, 99, 100, 104, 105, 108, 109, 115, 119, 126

Fulfillment, 14, 16, 18, 33, 34, 35, 62, 400, 405, 406; and adjustment, 156, 159, 192; and the future, 506, 507; and interpersonal relations, 223, 239; and marriage or intimate relationship, 259, 282, 293; and motivation, 66, 80, 82, 86, 87, 97; in parent-child relations, 302, 303, 331, 336; and values, 502, 506, 507; from work, 345, 348, 352, 353, 360, 361, 368

Functional psychoses, 199

Future: and values, 487, 491, 502–7, 509; and work, 336, 348, 367–68

"Future shock," 106

Games, 224, 228–30, 231, 256, 423

Gastrointestinal reactions to stress, 151, 182, 186, 188, 198

General-adaptation-syndrome, 149, 153

Generalization, 31, 252, 444

General systems model. *See* Living systems

Genetics: and constitutional characteristics, 307, 308; development, 37, 39–40, 45–47, 48, 49, 62; and predisposing factors, 160, 200, 207

Gestalt therapy, 216, 421–24, 425, 431, 467

Ghettos: and maladjustment, 191, 192, 216, 308–9, 413, 473

Goals: and adjustment, 168, 170, 172, 176–77, 179; and authenticity, 61; and groups, 374, 375, 380, 381, 382, 384, 391, 393, 397; in interpersonal relations, 223, 231, 236, 238, 244; in learning, 435, 436, 439, 451, 455, 457; and level of aspiration, 52–53; for life, 11, 13, 66, 127, 487; marital, 278–79, 299; as motivators, 62, 66–69, 79–80, 87, 89, 90; of psychopath, 190; and standards, 8, 9–11, 19, 318, 412, 487; and self-concept, 11, 50, 51, 56;

and stress, 93, 94, 96, 104, 109, 114, 115, 126, 132, 135, 141; and values, 487, 491, 505; withdrawal from, 136

Goal-terminating mechanisms, 168

Good vs. evil, and human nature, 20, 21–23, 36, 487

Grief, 124, 128, 145, 197, 290; dealing with, 462, 464, 467, 476–79; and grief work, 477, 479

Group discontinuities, 388–90

Group effectiveness, 382–83, 388, 400, 401

Group function, 380–83, 400

Group marriage, 297, 299

Group sexual patterns, 193

Group stress, 94, 152

Groups, 158, 371–401, 445, 501; and change, 384–85; and conformity, 395–400, 401; and costs and rewards of membership, 375–79, 401; effectiveness of, 387–88, 401; and encounter groups, 405, 420, 424–30; and the individual, 385–400, 401; involuntary, 373–74, 378–79; leadership of, 391–95, 401; as living systems, 379–85, 398; necessary, 374; and problem solving, 380–81, 448–49, 459; and social facilitation, 386–87, 389, 401; structure of, 379, 385, 390, 396, 400–401; transient, 372–73, 375, 379; voluntary, 374, 378

Growth, blocked, 159

Growth potential: and actualization strivings, 80–83, 87, 88, 90, 96; and development, 46, 47, 49, 52, 62, 305, 306, 307; and encounter groups, 424; through group membership, 376–77, 401; and intellectual competencies, 451, 455; and interpersonal competencies, 253–56; and social competencies, 347, 376–77, 401

Guilt, 207, 241, 290; and growth, 175–76; induction of, 310, 319; lack of, 190–91; pathological, 186, 202, 204, 476; as a problem emotion, 467, 470, 476–79, 483; and sex, 102–3, 109, 186; and stress, 93–94, 95, 97, 102, 109, 114, 138, 142, 145, 147, 149; and working women, 362, 366–67

Habits, 199, 322, 442; reactions as, 124, 138, 149, 417

Hallucinations, 72; drug-induced, 199, 208, 210; and psychosis, 199, 200, 201–2, 204, 206

"Halo effect," 251–52, 481

Hans, phobia of, 32

Happiness: in marriage, 276–79, 299, 303–5; and work, 355. *See also* Satisfaction

"Healthy" development, 305–7, 338

Heart disease, and stress, 106, 117, 122, 189, 355

Hebephrenic schizophrenia, 200

Help: demand for, 101, 105; for problem solving, 447–48, 459

Helplessness, feelings of, 80, 115, 471, 472

Hematophobia, 183

Heredity, 16. *See also* Genetics

Heritage, sense of, 376–77

Heroin, 205, 206, 207–9, 210

Hierarchy: of needs, 86–88, 91, 262, 290, 345; of power, 394; of values, 487, 496

Holistic reactions, 122–23, 152

Homeostasis, 68

Homogamy in mate selection, 275

Interpersonal style, 251
Interview in personality assessment, 407–8, 430
Intimate relationships, 77, 160, 229, 231, 239, 240, 241, 259, 291, 292–98, 462, 481
Introjection, 139, 144–45, 498
Intuition, 228, 422
Involutional reactions, 202–3, 218
Involvement, 134, 135, 172, 389, 393. *See also* Commitment
Irrationality: and emotions, 55–56, 481–82; and human nature, 20, 23, 24, 28, 30, 34, 36, 75, 387; and maladjustment, 185, 186, 204, 327, 415
Irritability, 71, 354; and addiction, 210; and maladjustment, 195, 197, 198, 203; and overcrowding, 106
Isolation, 72–73, 78, 125, 272, 303, 308, 336–37, 394, 424

Jealousy, 281, 297, 299, 315
Job: changes, 351, 352; dissatisfactions, 350, 353, 354–59; satisfactions, 342, 351–54. *Seealso* Work
Judgment, 71, 255, 306, 388, 395, 467; lack of, 190, 202, 204

Key motives, 88–89, 91
Key stresses, 114, 115–16

Labeling, revolt against, 218, 409
Laissez-faire leadership style, 392–93
Leaders and leadership, 505; in encounter groups, 425, 428, 429, 430; in groups, 84, 323, 376, 379, 380, 381, 382, 384, 386, 390, 391–95, 401, 449
Learning, 16, 34, 40, 75, 90, 322, 413, 433–59; creative thinking, 452–58, 459; and development, 54, 308, 324; effective, 434–46, 458; and emotions, 470, 471; faulty, 159, 179, 195, 416–18; and groups, 387, 388; and the learner, 434–36; and motivation, 68, 76, 84, 88, 90; problem solving and decision making, 442–53, 459; strategy for, 437–40, 458–59; and stress, 122, 123
Leisure time, 367, 368, 369
Level of aspiration. *See* Aspiration
Libido, 29, 30
Life change units (LCUs), 116
Life crisis or stress, 114, 116, 213
Life cycle changes, 384
Life pattern or style, 40, 56, 60, 243, 452, 485, 487; and adjustment, 166, 177; and family planning, 333–34; and maladjustment, 185, 192, 203, 206, 211; and motives, 88–89, 91; and stress, 98, 100, 160
Life plans. *See* Goals
Life script, 423–24
Life situation, 152, 353–54, 407, 413
"Life space," 247, 501
Life span: of alcoholics, 206; of former POWs, 198; and marriage, 262, 265, 296
Life world, building a, 498, 501–2
Limitations: personal, 89, 94, 95, 96, 97, 149, 248, 276, 286–87, 347, 447–48

Living systems: groups as, 379–85, 398; and interpersonal relations, 224, 230–31, 256; man as, 36–41, 53–57
Logic and semantics, 447, 449, 459
Loneliness, 60, 77, 78, 97, 99, 205, 256, 315, 375, 376; and marriage, 271, 272, 290, 482; as a problem emotion, 475–76, 482, 483
Longevity, and work satisfaction, 355, 360
Losses, as cause of stress, 96, 187
Love, 14, 16, 23, 33, 34, 41, 462, 466, 474, 479–82; ability to, 482; child's need for, 52, 61, 77–78, 303, 309, 312–14, 318, 319, 321, 339; human needs for, 77–78, 80, 87, 89, 90, 246, 376; inability to, 190, 465; and infatuation, 480–82; and marriage, 271–72, 280–88; reactions to loss of, 149, 157, 174, 187; romantic, 371–72, 480–82; and stress, 96, 101, 103, 107, 113, 125, 134; types of, 480
Lower class: and divorce, 290; and parent-child relations, 308–10, 333; pressures of, 105; and sexual adjustments, 284–85; and work, 349–50, 362
LSD, 205, 207, 208, 210

Maintenance strivings, 68–80, 86, 87–88, 90, 261, 262, 290; biological, 69–74, 90; of groups, 380, 395; psychological, 74–80, 90
Maladjustment, 151, 156, 159–61, 181–219, 413; acute situational stress, 195–98; alienation and self-pity in, 182, 191–92; causal relationships in, 161, 182, 189, 191, 200, 202–3, 207; and creativity, 456; after divorce, 290–91; effect of, on marriage, 191, 201; and faulty parent-child relations, 310, 314–18, 324–28; in interpersonal relations, 224, 241–45, 257; neurotic avoidance, 182–88; psychosomatic reactions, 182, 188–89; psychotic disorders, 198–205, 210; sexual, 192–95, 284–86, 299; sociopathic behavior, 182, 189–91; suicide, 212–14; treatment and prevention of, 200, 203, 214–18, 219; use of alcohol, 205–7; use of drugs, 207–11
Malnutrition, 70, 94, 160
Man-woman relationships, 260–70. *See also* Intimate relationships and Marriage
Manic-depressive reaction, 201–2, 203, 218, 465
Marathon encounter groups, 429
Marijuana, 205, 206, 207
Marital fidelity, 260, 264, 281
Marital schism, 327
Marital skew, 327
Marriage, 14, 48, 66, 77, 259–99, 350, 441; adjustment in, 276–86, 328, 384, 385; and changing attitudes and behaviors, 260–70, 293, 298; circularity in, 161; contracts in, 264, 294–95; and counseling, 406–7, 412, 413, 414, 430; effect of children on, 302–5, 333, 338; group, 297, 299; happiness in, 276–79, 299, 303–5, 333, 482; and interpersonal relations, 230, 231, 237, 239, 245, 248, 372; and maladjustment, 191, 193, 195, 230, 316, 327–28; and mate selection, 48, 270–76, 289, 299; and new forms of partnerships, 293–98, 299; open, 296; permanence in, 260, 262–64; and separation, 93, 116, 213, 288, 325, 326, 337; serial, 296; trial, 293, 296, 299. *See also* Divorce and Family

Masks, and self-identity, 58–61, 191, 251, 254, 424, 425, 428

Master role, 57

Masturbation, 102, 186, 193, 267

Mate selection, 48, 272–76, 289, 299

Mate-swapping, 296–97

Maturity, 101, 175, 229, 259, 278, 299, 353, 407, 411, 434, 436, 482

Maximal performance test, 408

Meaning and meaninglessness, 9–10, 14, 18, 33, 34, 35–36, 39, 62, 97, 159, 203, 205, 247, 302, 405, 406, 420; as a need, 79–80, 90, 97, 101, 191, 192; and values, 498, 502, 509; and work, 345, 348, 352, 353, 355, 357, 358, 360, 366, 368

Men: and addiction, 206, 209; and conformity, 396; and divorce, 290, 291; and family planning, 331, 335–36; and marriage, 264–65, 284–86, 291; in parent-child relations, 304, 305, 322, 325–26; and pressure, 105; and psychosis, 202; and sexual attitudes, 267, 268, 269, 284–85; single, 265; and suicide, 213

Mental retardation, 46, 318, 326

Mental set, 443, 444–45

Metacommunication, 250

Methadone treatment, 209

Methedrine, 210

Middle-class: and divorce, 290; and parent-child relations, 308–10; pressures of, 105; and sexual adjustment, 284–85; and work, 348, 349, 362

Minority groups, 234, 287, 316, 374, 384, 409; and work, 346, 350, 359, 360, 369

"Mixed blessing" conflicts, 98

Mob violence, 375, 388–89, 401

Mobility, 263, 274, 275, 288–89, 336

Models: faulty, 191, 207, 319, 323, 327, 328; of healthy development, 305–8, 339; and identification, 143–44, 416; for interpersonal relations, 224–31, 256; of man, 28–36, 216, 421; parental, 143–44, 191, 207, 211, 312, 316, 319, 322–24, 326, 339; for understanding coping behavior, 159–60

"Momism," 316

Money: and family planning, 332, 333, 337; and job satisfaction, 341, 345, 348, 350, 352, 353, 357, 368; lack of, as a source of stress, 158, 166, 177, 205, 224, 487

Monophobia, 183

Moods, 465

Morale, group, 381, 382, 387, 393

Moral values, 29, 92, 212, 318, 335, 336, 389, 486; development of, 218, 318, 324, 327–28; lack of, 190, 327–28; and projection, 142, 476

Mother, 32, 94, 102; and ability to love, 480, 482; and child's development, 302–3, 304, 305, 307, 308–9, 315, 316, 318, 320, 322, 323, 325, 326, 327, 337, 480, 482; employment of, 349, 366

Motivation, 16, 62, 65–91, 249, 315, 351, 393, 394; and activation, 69, 90; actualization strivings as, 68, 80–83, 86, 90; biological maintenance strivings as, 69–74, 90; deficiency vs. growth, 88; and learning, 434, 435, 436,

437, 438–39, 440, 455, 459; money as, 352–53; psychological maintenance strivings as, 74–80, 90

Motivational selectivity, 83–85, 91, 173

Motive patterns, 68, 83–90, 407

Motives, 68–69, 85–91, 251; and adjustment, 170, 173, 174; changes in, 89–90, 452; conscious and unconscious, 85–86, 91, 415; hierarchy of, 86–88, 91; inhibition and facilitation of, 87; key, 88–89, 91; and life style, 88–89; and stress, 94, 122, 126, 152; territoriality as, 76; and work, 346, 347

Multiple approach-avoidance conflict, 98

Multiple criteria approach to development, 306–7

Mutual purposes, recognition of, 246–47, 257

Mysophobia, 183

Natural selection, 39

Need fulfillment, 259, 261, 265, 288, 296

Needs, 55, 66, 90; biological, 69–74, 90, 424; complementary, 275–76, 279, 299; deprivation of, 70–71, 87–88, 108; and groups, 375, 379, 380, 381, 382, 383, 400, 401; hierarchy of, 86–88, 91, 262, 290, 354; and interpersonal relations, 223, 224, 235, 236, 239, 246, 247; and learning, 435, 436; and marriage and intimate relationships, 259, 261, 265, 271, 274, 275–76, 279, 280, 290, 296, 298, 299; in parent-child relations, 303, 307, 331; psychological, 74–80, 90, 271; sexual, 87, 90; and work, 351, 352

Neurasthenia, 186, 218

Neurotic anxiety, 29

Neurotic avoidance, 86, 182–88, 214, 218, 413, 417; anxiety reaction, 182–83; depressive reaction, 187; hypochondria, 187; hysteria, 186–87; neurasthenia, 186; obsession-compulsion, 185–86; phobia, 30, 32, 159, 183, 185, 204, 324, 413, 417

Neurotic nucleus, 187

Neurotic paradox, 187

Nonbeing, 36, 421

Nonconformity, need for, 372, 398–400, 401

Noninvolvement, 100–101, 139

"Normal" vs. "optimal" development, 305–6

NREM sleep, 70

Nuclear family, 288, 336, 337, 338, 339

Nyctophobia, 183

Observations, and counseling, 409–10, 430

Obsessive-compulsive reaction, 185–86, 204, 218

Occupational adjustment, 342, 351–54

Occupational choice, 342, 345–50, 369

Occupational counseling, 406, 407, 412–14, 430

Occupational therapist, 414

Ocholophobia, 183

Oedipus complex, 32, 102

Open marriage, 296

Openness, 61, 238, 253–54, 406, 429, 456; and creativity, 456, 459; in interpersonal relations, 238, 241, 250, 251, 253–54

Operant conditioning, 30, 31, 32, 434
Opportunities, access to, 94, 96, 498, 502
Order: and maladjustment, 185–86; need for, 74–76, 84, 90, 324
Organic pathology, 160, 179, 186, 189, 218, 407
Organic psychoses, 199, 203–5, 218
Organizational equilibrium, 380
Orgasm, 195, 285, 286
Orientation: toward emotions, 465–66; and thinking, 454–55, 459; values and cultural, 490–91
Orienting reaction, to stimuli, 128
Outcomes and profits in interpersonal relations, 224–25, 380–81
Overcrowding, 106
Overgeneralization, 444
Overload, 68, 72, 73, 105, 106, 107, 133, 355
Overorganization, 379
Overpopulation, 6, 331–32, 504
Overprotection, 316–17, 323
Oversimplification, 172–73, 443, 444, 459

Pain avoidance, 71–72, 90
Paraesthesia, 204
Paranoia, 159, 200–201, 218, 244
Paranoid schizophrenia, 200
Paraprofessionals, use of, 217, 414, 415
Parent/Adult/Child (PAC), 228, 422–24
Parent: and child's development, 51–52, 78, 310–28, 338, 482; and discipline style, 317–21, 339; and maladjustment of child, 182, 255, 314–17, 324–28, 339; and marital adjustment, 276; as model, 143–44, 191, 207, 211, 228, 276, 312, 319, 322–24, 327, 328, 338, 339; and occupational choice, 348–49; and parental love, 480, 482; and pathogenic family, 324–28; role change as, 302–3; single, 308–9, 337; state in transactional analysis, 228, 422–24; as cause of stress, 94, 100, 102, 107, 133, 157, 176, 470
Parkinson's law, 439
Participation, and leadership, 392
Passivity, 195, 197, 308, 317
Pathogenic families, 324–28; antisocial, 327–28; disturbed, 327; inadequate, 326–27; incomplete, 325–26
Pathophobia, 183
Patriotism, a new kind of, 495
Payoffs in interpersonal relations, 225, 229, 230, 423
Peer groups, 100, 247, 334; and development, 52, 53, 57, 310; and maladjustment, 192, 210, 326
Perception, 31, 33, 67, 91, 204, 210, 395, 445, 465; and adjustive behavior, 159, 172, 173, 175; and frame of reference, 54–55, 234, 306, 436, 485; and interpersonal relations, 223, 231–32, 234–36, 251, 256; and motive state, 83–85, 91, 173, 249, 481; and stress, 111–12, 116, 117, 119, 122, 123, 125, 473
Perceptual defense, 84
Perfectionism, 133, 203, 450
Permissiveness: in discipline, 309–10, 312, 316, 317–18, 321; sexual, 267–68, 299

Personal crisis, 115, 116
Personal growth: aiding others toward, 253; blocked, 159, 160, 254–55; and child rearing, 303, 306, 337; dealing with emotion, 462, 466–67, 472, 473, 475, 482, 483; and human nature, 23, 33, 34, 40; and intellectual competencies, 433, 434, 436, 456; in interpersonal relations, 223, 253–56, 257, 376; and love, 481, 482; in marriage and intimate relationships, 261–62, 266, 270–71, 276, 282, 294, 296, 298, 299; resources for, 405–6, 413, 415, 418, 420–21, 422, 424, 430, 431; through self-actualization, 80–83, 87, 88, 90, 96, 406, 421, 451, 455, 507; and therapy, 216, 380; utilizing stress for, 171–78, 179; and values, 498–502, 509; through work, 348, 351, 368
Personal limitations, and stress, 89, 94, 95, 96, 97, 149
Personality: assessment of, 408–9; and conformity, 396, 401; and creativity, 452, 455–56; effect of environment on, 34, 40, 41; family influence on, 306–28, 365; genetic factors in, 37, 39–40; and job adjustment, 353–54, 369; and leadership, 391, 392, 393, 401; and mate selection and marital adjustment, 272, 274, 276, 277–79; psychopathic, 190–91; self as determiner of, 45–62, 172, 174–76
Personality "fit," 278–79, 481
Personality inventories, 408–9
Perversion, sexual, 192–95
Phobias, 30, 32, 159, 183–85, 204, 218, 324, 413, 417, 418
Physical discipline, 310, 319
Physical handicaps, 94, 312, 414
Physiological needs. See Biological needs.
Physiological reactions: and emotion, 462, 463–64; and maladjustment, 186, 188–89, 218; and stress, 111, 123, 150, 471, 473
Pill, the effects of, 270, 334, 335, 336
Pleasure principle, 29
Pollution, 6, 495, 504
Possessiveness, 75, 281, 299
Possibility assumptions, 172, 406, 415, 485, 486, 487, 497; and development, 54–55, 56, 61, 62; and motive state, 81, 85
Potential. See Growth potential
Power: in groups, 379, 382, 390–95; and job, 357, 363; in marital relationships, 281, 299
Predestination, 27
Predictability, 74–75, 90, 185, 321, 445
Predisposition, to maladjustment, 160, 182, 200, 202, 203
Pregnancy, unwanted, 194, 331, 333, 334, 336
Prejudice, 97, 113, 160, 216, 234, 452
Premarital sexual relations, 94, 103, 192, 193, 262, 267–69, 270
Preparation, and thinking, 454–55, 459
Pressure: and group membership, 380, 385, 395, 399, 400, 445; reactions to, 126, 133, 134; resistance to, 133; in our society, 105–7, 268, 331; and stress, 93, 94, 100, 104–7, 109, 119; time-, 172; work-related, 349, 355, 357, 365–66
Primary reaction tendencies, 47, 62, 307
Prison, effect of, 79, 116, 145, 211–12
Prisoner-of-war experiences, 80, 85, 87, 135, 195, 198, 219
Probability, in decision making, 165, 170, 179

and becoming, 500, 501; in counseling, 410, 411, 418, 425, 428; diffusion of, 389; economic, 265, 266, 267, 291, 294, 297; and family planning, 334, 335; and group membership, 377–78, 380, 389, 401; in interpersonal relations, 237, 238, 246, 248, 266; and job, 343, 352, 355, 357, 358, 360, 362, 365; in marriage and intimate relationships, 265, 266, 267, 269, 270, 291, 297; in parent-child relations, 302, 303, 310, 323

Restrictiveness, parental, 317, 323

Retirement, 116, 305, 343, 354, 360–61

Rewards, 27, 31, 98, 105, 169, 318; in discipline, 310, 317, 318, 323; of group membership, 375–77, 378–79, 398, 400; in interpersonal relations, 224–25, 228, 235, 241, 243, 252, 416, 430, 431; and job satisfaction, 351–53, 368; and learning, 416, 435, 440, 441

Rights of others: disregard for, 190, 191; recognition of, 246–47

Rigidity, 238, 399, 463; as hindrance to learning, 444–45, 446, 459; in maladjustment, 186, 203, 205; rejection of, in sex roles, 264–67; in response to stress, 115, 116, 136, 143, 151

Risk taking, 166, 172, 428; by groups, 380–81, 389–90; and interpersonal relations, 228, 232; in marriage, 284

"Risky-shift" phenomenon, 389–90

Role: conflict and confusion over, 227; and development, 48, 51, 57, 58, 60, 193; expectations and demands of, 226, 230, 231, 238, 281–82, 299, 365; and groups, 376, 379, 382, 384, 394, 397; learning of, in parent-child relations, 308, 322, 324, 326, 339; in marriage, 260, 264–68, 281–82, 296, 298; model for interpersonal relations, 224, 226–27, 231, 256; rejection of rigid sex, 48, 264–67, 281–82, 296, 298; shift in, after children, 302–3; skills, 226–27

Romantic love, 271–72, 331, 480–82

Safety needs, 86, 87, 88, 345

Salary, 341, 345, 346, 348, 350, 352, 353, 355, 357, 362, 363, 368

Same-sex marriage, 298, 299

Satisfaction, 80–81, 90, 101, 380–81; and adjustment, 158, 165, 166, 169, 172, 177; and children, 302, 304, 305, 307; and interpersonal relations, 223, 242, 245–56; and learning, 435, 441, 450, 459; in marriage, 261, 271, 276–79, 284–85, 292, 298; and values, 498, 509; and work, 343, 350, 351–54, 360, 363

Satisficing, 168

Scanning, 162, 170

Scapegoat, 147, 381, 393

Schizophrenia, 70, 145, 160, 182, 199–200, 218, 413; and faulty parent-child relations, 195, 198, 199–200, 202, 217; treatment of, 200, 214, 216; types of, 199–200

Science: and the future, 505–6; as a source of values, 15–16, 490, 491–92, 497, 498, 506, 509

Script analysis, 423–24

Security, 52, 146, 445; child's need for, 310, 312, 314, 315, 327; in group membership, 375–76, 400; and interpersonal relations, 249, 254; in job, 351, 355, 357, 359; and

maladjustment, 185–86; in marriage, 261, 262, 264, 281, 290, 363–64, 265, 270, 280; as a need, 68, 76–77, 84, 86, 88, 89, 90, 355; threat to, and stress, 97, 98, 100, 106, 116

Selective attention, 249

Selective vigilance, 84

Self, 45–62, 223, 251; and alienation, 191–92; and change, 57–58, 420, 428; and dealing with emotions, 466–71, 479; development of, 45, 48–53, 62, 306; increasing understanding of, 172, 174–76; and learning, 434–36, 441; in marriage, 280–81, 282; operations of, 53–57; search for, 57–62, 82–83

Self-acceptance, 175, 466, 482

Self-actualization, 33, 35, 406, 456, 466, 467; and development, 306, 322; as a need, 68, 73, 80–83, 87, 88; through love and marriage, 261, 262, 480; through work, 345; and values, 497, 507

Self-advantage vs. integrity, 102

Self-awareness, 38, 39, 50, 51, 61–62, 455, 466, 476, 499

Self-concept, 11–15, 33, 50, 227, 382, 440; and development, 50–53, 55–56, 315; and motivation, 84; "mutation" in, 50; and reactions, 143, 200; and stress, 110, 116; and work, 347

Self-confidence, 55, 96, 111, 169, 177, 306, 440

Self-control, 151, 312, 320, 323, 468

Self-deception, 149, 152, 159

Self-determination, 6, 506, 507

Self-devaluation: in interpersonal relations, 224, 241, 290, 291; and job, 351, 367; and maladjustment, 199, 201; causing stress, 101, 105, 111, 123, 137, 142, 143, 144, 147, 149, 173

Self-development, 329–31

Self-differentiation, 49, 50

Self-direction, 76, 406, 501, 507; and adjustment, 175, 192, 476; in development, 53–57, 58, 61–62, 83, 321, 327; in interpersonal relations, 225; and learning, 434, 452; vs. outer direction, 100; problem of, 8–11, 14, 16; and views of man, 23, 33, 34, 39, 40, 41

Self-disclosure, 232, 240–41, 254, 256, 257

Self-esteem, 246, 331, 466; from groups, 376; in marriage, 280; need for, 78, 85, 87, 88, 90; and parent-child relations, 312, 315, 323, 331; and stress, 96, 97, 100, 109, 121; and stress reactions, 127, 147, 474, 476, 477; and work, 342–43, 351–52, 354, 359, 360, 361, 363

Self-evaluation, 50, 51–52, 62, 342

Self-fulfilling prophecy, 52, 201

Self-fulfillment, 34–35, 62, 157, 175, 375, 499

Self-ideal, 50, 52–53, 57, 62

Self-identity, 11, 33, 49, 50–51, 57–58, 62, 78, 82–83, 174, 175, 323, 376, 379, 406, 477

Self-image, 89, 379

Self-pity, 127, 174, 182, 186

Self-reliance, 175, 312, 316, 406, 411

Self-system, 37, 40, 45–46, 48–62

Self-understanding, 216, 416, 418, 425, 430; increased, and stress, 172, 174–76, 179; need for, 74–75, 90, 254, 255, 433

4 5 6 7 8 9 10 -RM- 80 79 78 77 76